THE NEW ROLE OF INTELLECTUAL PROPERTY IN COMMERCIAL TRANSACTIONS

SUBSCRIPTION NOTICE

The New Role of Intellectual Property in Commercial Transactions
Recent Trends in the Valuation, Exploitation and Protection of Intellectual Property

General Editors

Melvin Simensky, Esq.

Hall, Dickler, Kent, Friedman & Wood
New York, New York
Adjunct Professor of Law
New York University School of Law

Lanning G. Bryer, Esq.

Ladas & Parry
New York, New York

JOHN WILEY & SONS, INC.

New York   •   Chichester   •   Brisbane   •   Toronto   •   Singapore

This text is printed on acid-free paper

Copyright © 1994 by Melvin Simensky and Lanning G. Bryer.
Published by John Wiley & Sons, Inc.
All rights reserved. Published simultaneously in Canada.

This publication is designed to provide accurate and authoritative
information in regard to the subject matter covered. It is sold with the
understanding that the publisher is not engaged in rendering legal,
accounting, or other professional services. If legal advice or other expert
assistance is required, the services of a competent professional person
should be sought.

Library of Congress Cataloging in Publication Data:
The New role of intellectual property in commercial transactions /
   edited by Melvin Simensky and Lanning G. Bryer.
       p.   cm.
     Includes index.
     ISBN 0-471-59575-6 (cloth: acid-free paper)
     1. Intellectual property—United States.   2. Commercial law—
   United States.   3. Intellectual property (International law)
   4. Competition, International.   I. Simensky, Melvin.   II. Bryer,
   Lanning G.
   KF2979.N49   1994
   346.7304'8—dc20   93-47637
   [347.30648]   CIP

Printed in the United States of America

10 9 8 7 6 5 4 3 2 1

DEDICATION

For my smart and beautiful daughter Joanna.

Melvin Simensky

For my mother and father, Rella and Mort, who showed me the way, and for my wife, Laura, and son, Ben, for sharing the journey.

Lanning G. Bryer

ABOUT THE EDITORS

MELVIN SIMENSKY

Melvin Simensky is a Partner and Coordinator of the Intellectual Property Group at Hall, Dickler, Kent, Friedman & Wood in New York. His practice includes the counseling and litigation of trademark, copyright, advertising and entertainment law matters. He specializes in the intellectual property aspects of commercial transactions involving both mergers and acquisitions, and financings. Mr. Simensky is Adjunct Professor of Law at New York University School of Law, where he teaches a graduate school seminar on the intellectual property aspects of the entertainment business. He is formerly a columnist on entertainment and intellectual property law issues for the *New York Law Journal*. Mr. Simensky is on the Board of Editors of *The Trademark Reporter* and *Copyright World*, and has been an expert witness on U.S. intellectual property law in numerous domestic and foreign court proceedings. Mr. Simensky is co-author of both a four volume treatise entitled *Entertainment Law*, as well as a case book of the same name. Mr. Simensky has published many articles and lectured at numerous conferences on intellectual property and entertainment law. He is a graduate of Yale University, and New York University School of Law.

LANNING G. BRYER

Lanning G. Bryer is a Partner in the New York office of Ladas & Parry and is Director of the firm's Mergers, Acquisitions and Licensing Group. Mr. Bryer is an active committee member of several intellectual property organizations, including the Committee on Law and Government of Licensing Executives Society (U.S.A. and Canada) and the Editorial Board of *The Trademark Reporter*. He recently served on the International Editorial Board of The International Trademark Association (formerly The United States Trademark Association). Mr. Bryer has written and lectured extensively on foreign trademark practice and commercial transactions involving the acquisition, financing and licensing of intellectual property. Mr. Bryer is co-author and co-editor of a treatise entitled "Worldwide Trademark Transfers," and is a frequent columnist in the entertainment section of the *New York Law Journal*. He is a graduate of Johns Hopkins University and Hofstra University School of Law.

CONTRIBUTORS

Carol Anne Been is a Partner in the Chicago firm of Sonnenschein Nath & Rosenthal, practicing in the areas of intellectual property, computer law and media/entertainment law.

Gabriel Bentata is a Partner in the Venezuelan firm of Bentata Hoet & Asociados and a member of several Chambers of Commerce in Venezuela. He is the author of several publications on Procedural and Commercial Law.

David Bressman is Vice President–General Counsel at the Donna Karan Company. He was formerly a partner at Phillips, Nizer, Benjamin, Krim & Ballon in New York.

Soon Yung Cha was Commisioner of the Korean Patent Office from 1952 to 1954. He is a member of the Korean Patent Attorneys Association.

Yoon Kun Cha has practiced patent law since 1975. He is a member of the Korean Patent Attorneys Association.

C.T. Chang is a senior attorney with the Taiwanese firm of Lee & Li, where he specializes in banking, security and financial service matters.

Al J. Daniel, Jr. is an attorney with the New York firm of Frankel & Abrams. He is involved in a broad range of litigation issues involving intellectual property and contractual rights in the music and entertainment fields, among others. In addition, he is the author of several articles on intellectual property.

Domenico de Simone is a patent attorney with the Italian firm of Ing. Barzano & Zanardo.

Michael A. Diamond served as Dean of the School of Accounting at the University of Southern California and director of the school's SEC and Financial Reporting Institute. He is currently on sabbatical and is serving a faculty internship at Ernst & Young from July 1994 through June 1995.

Luiz Henrique Do Amaral is a lawyer at the Brazilian firm of Dannemann, Siemsen, Bigler & Ipanema Moreira. He is Legal Director of the Brazilian Franchising Association and Chairman of the Franchising Committee of the Brazilian Association of Industrial Property.

Leslie Dunlop is a lawyer with the Quaker Oats Company. She was formerly with the intellectual property group at the Ontario firm of Fasken Campbell Godfrey.

Andreas Ebert-Weidenfeller is an attorney-at-law in the German firm of Boehmert & Boehmert, Nordemann & Partner. His work emphasizes all aspects of intellectual property law, including litigation.

Samuel Fifer is a Partner in the Chicago firm of Sonnenschein Nath & Rosenthal, practicing in the areas of intellectual property, computer law and media/entertainment law.

Raymond F. Gehan is a Partner in the Litigation Consulting Group of Deloitte & Touche in New York. He has over 25 years of experience in the valuation field, specializing in the appraisals of closely held securities and intangible assets. In addition, he is author of numerous articles and lectures on valuation and amortization of intangible assets.

Steven Michael Getzoff is Director of American Express' Intellectual Property Unit in New York. He has been responsible for managing the company's worldwide intellectual property portfolio since 1980. He is the author of several books and articles on intellectual property issues.

Andrew Kelly Gill is a member of the Canadian firm of Gowling, Strathy & Henderson, which specializes in intellectual property transactions, registration and enforcement.

William M. Goldman is a Partner in the New York firm of Brown & Wood, where he is the head of the firm's corporate Reorganization and Bankruptcy Group.

Howard A. Gootkin is Assistant General Counsel for Sanus Corporation Health Systems in New York, where he supervises litigation.

Giovanni Guglielmetti is a trial attorney specializing in intellectual property in the Italian firm of Ing. Barzano & Zanardo.

Paul F. Herrera is a Tax Partner in the International Tax Group of Deloitte & Touche in New York. His areas of expertise include international tax issues relating to mergers and acquisitions, taxation of financial products and foreign currency transactions, foreign tax credit planning, and international reorganizations.

Nancy Hirsch is an associate with the firm of Phillips, Nizer, Benjamin, Krim & Ballon in New York.

Julia Ho is an Associate in the Taiwanese firm of Lee & Li, where she specializes in trademark law.

Thomas W. Hoens is a Senior Vice President for Fitch Investors Service, Inc. in New York. He is responsible for credit ratings of companies in the beverage and tobacco industries.

R. Scott Jolliffe is a member of the Canadian firm of Gowling, Strathy & Henderson, which specializes in intellectual property transactions, registration and enforcement.

Kate Johnson is a solicitor of the Supreme Courts of New South Wales and England and a principal in the Australian firm of Williams Niblett, specializing in intellectual property.

Ian Jay Kaufman is a Partner in the international firm of Ladas & Parry, specializing in international protection of trademarks, copyrights, patents, and licensing. He is the author of numerous international articles on intellectual property.

Charles G. Klink is an associate in the New York office of Brown & Wood. He received his JD from the University of California at Los Angeles School of Law.

Eiichiro Kubota is in charge of intellectual property cases (including litigation) in the Japanese firm of Nakamura & Partners.

Mark Lewis is a partner in the Corporate Finance Group at the London firm of Bird & Bird. He has extensive experience in corporate finance and mergers and acquisition work.

Kwan-Tao Li is a Senior Consultant of the Taiwanese firm of Lee & Li, where he concentrates his practice in intellectual property, commercial transactions and general corporate matters. He is the author of several articles on intellectual property.

Morag Macdonald is a partner in the London firm of Bird & Bird in the Intellectual Property Department. She has a broad range of experience in all aspects of contentious and non-contentious intellectual property law.

Theodore Max is a partner at Phillips, Nizer, Benjamin, Krim & Ballon in New York. He is currently the International Articles Editor for *The Trademark Reporter* and specializes in intellectual property law.

Donald T. Nicolaisen is a partner and National Director of Accounting and SEC Services for Price Waterhouse in New York. He is a member of the Emerging Issues Task Force of the FASB and a member of the AICPA, as well as various other civil and social organizations.

Russell L. Parr is Vice President of the Valuation Services Group of AUS Consultants of New Jersey. He is an expert at assessing the value of intellectual property and intangible assets. In addition, he is the author of four books on intellectual property published by John Wiley & Sons, Inc.

Horacio Rangel-Ortiz is a partner in the Mexico City firm of Uthoff, Gomez Vega & Uthoff. He serves as president of the Mexican Association for the Protection of Industrial Property and as Chairman of the Intellectual Property Committee of the Mexican Bar.

John Richards is a partner in the international firm of Ladas & Parry. He has written and spoken frequently on international intellectual property issues, especially in the fields of patents and copyrights.

Peter Dirk Siemsen is a lawyer and patent attorney for the Brazilian firm of Dannemann, Siemsen, Bigler & Ipanema Moreira. He is President of Honor of both the Brazilian and the Inter American Associations of Intellectual Property.

Gordon V. Smith is President of AUS Consultants of New Jersey. He has lectured widely on valuation subjects in the U.S. and internationally, and is the author of three books published by John Wiley & Sons, Inc.

Wilhelm J.H. Stahlberg is a partner in the German firm of Boehmert & Boehmert, Nordemann & Partner. He specializes in matters relating to intellectual property law, including litigation.

Dr. Eva Szigeti is head of the Trademark Division of the Hungarian firm of Danubia Patent & Trademark Attorneys. She is the author of several articles involving trademark practice.

C.W. Ting is a Senior Associate in the Taiwanese firm of Lee & Li, where she concentrates her practice in copyright and trademark matters.

Daisy Wang is an attorney at the Taiwanese firm of Lee & Li, where she specializes in patent issues (prosecution, enforcement, and licensing) as well as other intellectual property matters.

Gervas W. Wall is a partner in the Canadian firm of Deeth Williams Wall. He has practiced in the intellectual property field, and has a special interest in commercial transactions involving intellectual property.

Neil J. Wilkof practices intellectual property law at the Tel-Aviv firm of Friedman and Wilkof. He serves as an adjunct professor of intellectual property law and computer law at the Bar-Ilan University. He is the author of *Trademark Licensing*, to be published in fall 1994 in London.

Simon D. Williams is a solicitor of the Supreme Court of New South Wales and a principal in the Australian firm of Williams Niblett. He practices in intellectual property, including licensing and litigation.

Colleen Spring Zimmerman is a Partner in the Ontario firms of Fasken Campbell Godfrey and Fasken Martineau where she serves as director of the Intellectual Property Group. She is certified by the Law Society of Upper Canada as a Specialist in Intellectual Property (Patent, Trademark, and Copyright) Law.

SPECIAL ACKNOWLEDGMENT

The Editors wish to express their sincere appreciation to Stuart Williams, President of Strategic Research Institute in New York, for his aid and cooperation in the preparation of this book, and without whose urging this book would not have been written.

ACKNOWLEDGMENTS

The Editors of this book owe significant debts of gratitude to many people without whose time and effort this work would not have been possible.

First, we wish to thank our spouses and children who patiently endured the lost evenings and weekends during the birth, development and publication of this work.

We are indebted to our law partners for their understanding and forbearance, and for believing in the value of this project. We are specifically grateful to Allan S. Pilson, Esq. and Frederick Reichwald, Esq. who painstakingly read portions of the manuscript relating to foreign security interests.

We also wish to express our sincerest appreciation to our two energetic law students and research assistants, Laura Land Siegel and Ethan Stein, who persevered for long hours and no compensation, to assist us in the research, writing and creation of this work.

We are also grateful to Georgia N. Gounaris, Esq. and Concettina Sacheli, Esq., two of our colleagues, who helped organize this unwieldy project and spent endless hours proof-reading.

The Editors would be seriously remiss if they did not, at every opportunity, extend their deep appreciation to the many contributors who submitted chapters, and sections of chapters, to make this work what it is. We owe a special debt to Russell Parr who introduced us to our Publisher, and who convinced us that this book would make a contribution, and offered continual moral support and inspiration throughout its preparation.

Finally, we thank the splendid professional and trade editor of John Wiley and Sons, Marla J. Bobowick, for her encouragement and assistance in making this book a reality.

PREFACE

We live in extraordinary times, politically, economically and socially. The Cold War has ended, but what will replace it? Bastions built for adversarial purposes, such as NATO (North American Treaty Organization), which was long thought necessary for the preservation of Western society, are now viewed differently, and their future roles are a daily question. The world is becoming smaller, and the reasons for geopolitical conflicts between East and West are disappearing. Over the past year we have witnessed the increasing development of market economies in Eastern Europe, the first bilateral peace agreement between Palestinians and Israelis, and the continuing desire to gain membership in the European Community. Unfortunately, conflict has accompanied these changes, as in Bosnia and the Middle East.

The role of intellectual property in the global marketplace is also changing as part of this process, and the advances affecting intellectual property are just as extraordinary. Indeed, at the time of this writing, the world has recently witnessed the U.S. Congress' passage of NAFTA (North American Free Trade Agreement), and the decision by the United States and Europe to put aside major trade disputes to clear the way for a world trade accord covering more industries and more countries under GATT (General Agreement on Tariffs and Trade) than any other trade agreement in history.

The GATT requires that all countries, including developing ones, protect patents, copyrights, trade secrets and trademarks. For years, pirated computer programs, record albums, videocassettes and prescription drugs have been available in developing countries without the benefit of intellectual property protection. The failure to protect intellectual property rights is costing the global business economy billions of dollars a year in lost revenues. GATT will help attack this problem. It is estimated by the turn of the century that GATT will result in an increase of $300 billion a year in world trade, much of which will result from application of intellectual property laws.

Intellectual property used to be the tail that failed to wag the dog in commercial transactions. Now it is the dog itself. During the past decade, intellectual property has been recognized as the dominant factor in numerous, significant commercial transactions. Recently, one investment banker from a major New York investment banking house said: "In some cases brands [*i.e.*, trademarks] represent as much as eighty percent of the value of certain companies."

For years, intellectual property has been a hidden asset whose value is only now being recognized and tapped. Why at this time? There are several reasons. First, in the United States, the merger and acquisition activity of the past decade has raised awareness of the importance of intellectual property in valuing companies in financing deals. For example, when Grand Metropolitan of Great Britain acquired Pillsbury for $5.7 billion, it did so in large part to acquire such powerful global brands as Burger King®, Green Giant®, and Haagen-Dazs®.

Second, the high cost of introducing new brands into the marketplace and the high failure rate of new brands is enhancing perceptions about the value of already established franchises. For example, the domestic launch in the United States of a new soap brand is a $100 million venture, of a new cigarette brand $300 million. Add to this the heavy cost of promoting new brands in the initial years. In the United States ten thousand new products are introduced annually. Of these, eighty percent fail. Fewer than one percent will ever obtain annual sales of $15 million. Consequently, active existing brands, especially those with global reputations, are indeed very valuable.

Third, the stepped up pace of negotiating new trade agreements, such as NAFTA and GATT, is resulting in the increased internationalization of intellectual property. For example, global trademarks are a by-product of increased trade between countries, with goods and services bearing such marks flowing more freely across national borders as a result of the new trade pacts.

The purpose of this book is to serve as an intellectual property advisor to international business professionals and their counsel, and to help them explore intellectual property questions in distinctly business settings. Presently, no single text treats the subject of intellectual property from a primarily commercial context. This is the first work to do so, and it does so from an interdisciplinary perspective. The contributors to the book include domestic and international lawyers, accountants, the director of a large corporation's intellectual property unit, a financial rating specialist, appraisers of intellectual property assets and academics. The strength of this book lies in the breadth of experience brought to this project by its contributors, all of whom are recognized experts in their respective practice areas.

The book is also international in scope. We have called upon the expertise of numerous professionals around the world. Where possible, we have tried to present international laws on the intellectual property issues we consider significant. We have necessarily been constrained, however, by the limited size of this project. Nevertheless, the issues in those countries not treated here are similar, if not identical, to the issues presented. Thus, this book will help the internationalist, whether or not his or her country's laws are discussed within the four corners of this work.

The book is presented in four parts. Part I, "Accounting, Finance, and Valuation," contains several chapters discussing how intellectual property can be measured, accounted for and valued. If intellectual property is to realize its full commercial potential, international standards of measuring, valuing and accounting for intellectual property must be found.

Part II, "Protecting Intellectual Property," discusses the various domestic and international laws used to protect intellectual property assets. We live in a time where economic security has been equated with national security, and where intellectual property is considered a form of national wealth. Thus, protecting intellectual property is not just important to private persons, whether individuals or companies, but also to national governments, whose global influence may well be determined by the level of international intellectual property protection their citizenry receive.

Part III, "Commercial Exploitation of Intellectual Property," treats the status of intellectual property in business transactions from the corporate user's perspective. This Part discusses how intellectual property is managed in such commercial activities as mergers and acquisitions, licensing and bankruptcy.

Part IV, "Other Commercial Exploitation: Taking a Security Interest in Intellectual Property," discusses U.S. and foreign laws on the use of intellectual property as loan collateral. The use of intellectual property as a source of collateral, such as designer trademarks in the fashion industry, is a recent idea whose time has come. Since intellectual property can easily be a corporation's most valuable asset, there is no logical reason why such asset, in the form of secured collateral, cannot be used to support substantial financings.

The tremendous value that intellectual property has always had, coupled with the recent realization of the magnitude of such value, has cast intellectual property in a new role as a dynamic and dominating factor in commercial transactions. Problems in valuing, measuring and collateralizing intellectual property may exist, but intellectual property's newly realized commercial value will inevitably overcome such problems. There is simply too much money at stake to permit continued ambiguity in the use of intellectual property in commercial deals. The General Editors hope this book contributes to better understanding the unique role of intellectual property in commercial transactions.

March 1994   Melvin Simensky
New York, New York   Lanning G. Bryer

SUMMARY TABLE OF CONTENTS

Brazil
    LUIZ HENRIQUE O. DO AMARAL
    PETER D. SIEMSEN
Canada
    GERVAS W. WALL
Germany
    WILHELM J.H. STAHLBERG
    ANDREAS EBERT-WEIDENFELLER
Hungary
    EVA SZIGETI
Israel
    NEIL J. WILKOF
    AARON S. LEWIN
Italy
    DOMENICO DE SIMONE
    GIOVANNI GUGLIELMETTI
Japan
    EIICHIRO KUBOTA
Korea
    SOON YUNG CHA
    YOON KUN CHA
Mexico
    HORACIO RANGEL-ORTIZ
Taiwan
    KWAN-TAO LI
    DAISY WANG
    C.T. CHANG
    C.W. TING
    JULIA HO
United Kingdom
    MARK LEWIS
    MORAG MACDONALD
Venezuela
    GABRIEL BENTATA

DETAILED TABLE OF CONTENTS

OVERVIEW: INTELLECTUAL PROPERTY—THE NEW GLOBAL CURRENCY

Colleen Spring Zimmerman
Leslie J. Dunlop

CHAPTER 4
THE RATING AGENCY VIEW OF INTANGIBLE ASSETS *115*
THOMAS W. HOENS

PART II PROTECTING INTELLECTUAL PROPERTY *141*

CHAPTER 5
IMPERATIVE STRATEGIES FOR PROTECTING INTANGIBLE ASSETS:
THE U.S. MARKET *143*
AL J. DANIEL, JR.

PART III   COMMERCIAL EXPLOITATION OF INTELLECTUAL PROPERTY

CHAPTER 8

THE ACQUISITION AND DISPOSITION OF INTELLECTUAL PROPERTY IN COMMERCIAL TRANSACTIONS: THE U.S. PERSPECTIVE   289

SAMUEL FIFER
CAROL ANNE BEEN

CHAPTER 10

OVERVIEW: INTELLECTUAL PROPERTY—THE NEW GLOBAL CURRENCY

Colleen Spring Zimmerman, Esq.
Leslie J. Dunlop, Esq.
Fasken Campbell Godfrey
Toronto, Ontario

INTRODUCTION

In the modern economy, intellectual property is fast emerging as a new source of wealth and power. The foundations of the economy have shifted away from the traditional industries of cars, steel, mining, and textiles to high-technology, information-based industries. As the manufacturing base that once defined the North American market is eroding or moving to less developed nations where costs are lower, it is being replaced by idea-based industries, commonly referred to by the buzzword "information technology." A recent study by a Canadian economist noted that the fastest growing industries in North America fall into four categories: computers and semiconductors, instrumentation, health and medical, and communications.[1] The success of these industries is based on knowledge and innovation, rather than manufacturing might.

Various forces are responsible for this shift. One factor is the rapid rate of technological developments, notably in the areas of semiconductor chips, computer software, and biotechnology. New products are entering the market at breathtaking speed—automatic teller machines, facsimile machines, cellular telephones, smart cards, and laptop computers. Personal computers and networks are replacing the mainframe. Advances in biotechnology are allowing scientists to create mice susceptible to cancer, oysters that are edible all year, and new varieties of plants with greater nutritional value and higher yields. New technologies are being developed that revolutionize both the workplace and the home. Fiber-optic cables and laser technology with the capacity to carry a wide range of information—voice, visual, and data—are having a tremendous impact on the advertising, entertainment, telecommunications, publishing, health care, and education sectors, among others. Direct broadcast satellites, referred to by cable companies as "death

The authors would like to thank Ian Kyer of Fasken Campbell Godfrey for his very valuable assistance with this Overview.

[1] Nuala Beck, *Shifting Gears, Thriving in the New Economy* (Toronto: Harper Collins Publishers Ltd., 1992) p. 66.

1

stars," have arrived on the broadcasting scene, with the capacity to provide hundreds of channels to television viewers. The cable companies have responded to this technological challenge with digital-video compression, which has the capacity to compress as many as four channels into the space previously occupied by one and also permits viewers to access hundreds of channels.

As a result, the composition of world trade is changing. Commerce in intellectual property has become an even greater component of trade between nations. Dynamic changes in the United States economy are indicative of this trend:

1. The movie industry employs more people than the auto industry,[2]
2. Revenues from video games have surpassed those of the movie industry,[3]
3. The travel service industry is bigger than the petroleum and steel industries combined,[4]
4. The software industry, which was almost insignificant before the 1980s, is now growing by 25% per year and is bigger than the auto parts industry,[5]
5. The information technology and communications sectors grew to be close to 10% of the U.S. gross domestic product in 1992,[6]
6. The biotechnology industry in the United States employs more people than the entire machine tool industry,[7] and
7. The United States ran a $12 billion surplus in its trade in ideas in 1990.[8]

A second force propelling the modern information-based economy is the "globalization" of the world economy. Enhanced communications technologies have played a major role in this restructuring. Marshall McLuhan, a recognized commentator on the role of communications in this century, coined the term "Global Village" to characterize the impact of television on societies.[9] The world economy has become more closely integrated as technological leaps in computerization and data-transfer telecommunications have made it possible for companies to coordinate the activities of their distant plants, divisions, and subsidiaries and to link those activities with buyers and suppliers. "Global" corporations are emerging, with integrated international strategies rather than a series of "domestic" subsidiaries.[10] The elimination of barriers to trade and the formation of free trade zones, under the auspices of the General Agreement on Tariffs and Trade (GATT), the North American Free Trade Agreement (NAFTA), and the European Community, is creating a "global marketplace" for goods and services.

Another force underlying the modern economy is the emergence of a new global mass culture, driven by communications technologies. The telecommunications and entertainment industries—television, movies, and other mass entertainment media—offer manu-

---

[2] Ibid., p. 69.
[3] *The Toronto Star* (24 July, 1993).
[4] Beck, *Shifting Gears*, p. 69.
[5] Ibid., p. 68.
[6] Ibid., p. 68.
[7] Ibid., p. 69.
[8] "Policing Thoughts," *The Economist* (22 August, 1992); 55.
[9] Marshall McLuhan, *War and Peace in the Global Village: An Inventory of Some of the Current Spastic Situations That Could Be Eliminated by More Feed Forward* (Toronto: Bantam Books, 1968).
[10] For a discussion of this development, see Michael Porter, *Competition in Global Industries* (Boston: Harvard Business School Press, 1986).

facturers and marketers new opportunities to place brand and product "images" before the public. The mass media is fueled by advertisers exporting not only a product, but an image of American culture desired by consumers worldwide. They are doing so in the form of well-known American consumer products, such as video games, rock music, designer T-shirts and sunglasses bearing famous trademarks, and local franchised outlets of American fast food chains. Although there may not be many common features among Red Square in Moscow, the thirteenth-century parliament buildings in The Hague, and rural Illinois, they do share one notable element—the golden arches of McDonald's.

Ironically, the emergence of new technologies has permitted unauthorized copying and counterfeiting on a much larger scale than ever before, undermining the value of the creator's work. Much of this copying has taken place in the countries of the Third World, which justify their poor standards and inadequate enforcement of intellectual property rights by the need for access to Western technologies. Losses arising from counterfeiting of trademarked goods and piracy have led developed countries to press for international, enforcement mechanisms. The United States has reported losses exceeding $60 billion per year from these activities[11] and, in the absence of international enforcement mechanisms, has amended its trade laws to permit retaliation against countries that provide inadequate protection of intellectual property rights.

As a result of these forces, intellectual property rights are increasingly being recognized as valuable assets to be protected and exploited. This trend is apparent on corporate, national, and international levels. Control of information technology, and the intellectual property rights therein, translates into economic power and wealth that is recognized and can be exploited on an international scale in the new world economy. In this sense, intellectual property is becoming a new global currency.

Corporations are quickly developing intellectual property portfolios, recognizing that these assets are valuable and can be exploited through licensing. Mounting global competition has made the protection of intellectual property rights much more significant in shaping corporate strategies. Businesses are realizing that their valuable intellectual property assets may form collateral against which to borrow money. Accountants are devising new methods of valuation to recognize intellectual property assets on the company's balance sheet. Joint ventures are forming to maximize research, development, and marketing efforts. The owners of valuable intellectual property rights are litigating to enforce these rights and protect their value. In the United States, the number of lawsuits over intellectual property increased by nearly two-thirds from 1980 to 1988.[12]

The rapid rate of technological change and the globalization of the world economy are also thrusting intellectual property issues onto political agendas. Different countries, often with very diverse histories and cultures, have created similar legal systems and justifications for protecting intellectual property. Governments recognize the need to protect intellectual property rights to stimulate innovation. Policymakers argue that the protection and enforcement of intellectual property rights foster the development and transfer of technology and inventions that are essential for economic growth, stimulate international trade and the exchange of goods and services, and create a favorable climate for foreign investment. Trademark protection encourages competition by differentiating sources of goods and services. Copyright protection enriches a culture's art and literature and recently has become the primary means to protect computer software. Patent protection promotes public disclosure of useful inventions and ideas. New legislation is

---

[11] "The Ideas Business: Economy of the Mind," *The Economist* (23 December, 1989); 99.
[12] Ibid.

being enacted in many countries, often in response to pressures from trading partners, that recognizes and protects new forms of intellectual property, such as biotechnology and semiconductor chips, and provides for new types of rights, such as the "moral rights" of creators. As one commentator has remarked, a country's legislative scheme for intellectual property rights and its participation in various international negotiations on intellectual property can play a pivotal role in fostering innovation in its economy.[13]

Intellectual property, which confers property rights on certain forms of information, has always had an international dimension. The flow of information, intangible by nature, is not constrained by national borders. Whereas laws are by their nature regional or national, intellectual property, through various treaties, is international. The need for comprehensive international agreements governing intellectual property became evident in the nineteenth century with the formation of the Union of Paris for the Protection of Industrial Property[14] (the Paris Convention) in 1883 and the Berne Convention for the Protection of Literary and Artistic Works[15] (the Berne Convention) in 1886. These treaties have continued to expand both in membership and in the scope of the minimum rights that the contracting parties have agreed to protect in their national laws. Additional treaties have been formed to govern other forms of intellectual property.

Although intellectual property has long had this international aspect, it is increasingly seen as pivotal to world trade. For the first time in the more than 40 years since the formation of the GATT, trade-related intellectual property rights (TRIPs), were on the table in the recent GATT negotiations to ensure national and international protection and enforcement of intellectual property rights. The United States, taking an aggressive stance against violations of international standards by less developed nations, has been the driving force behind efforts to harmonize intellectual property rights and adopt international enforcement mechanisms through the GATT's Uruguay Round of trade liberalization talks. Under the TRIPs agreement, which resulted from Uruguay Round, members will have to provide minimum standards for intellectual property protection and enforcement or face trade retaliation.

At the same time, international efforts to provide minimum standards of intellectual property protection are being made in North America and in Europe. NAFTA will gradually eliminate all tariffs on goods traded between the United States, Canada, and Mexico. Similarly, the goals of the European Community are to facilitate trade, prevent disturbances to competition, and generate harmony among member countries. In both instances, member countries have been directed to amend their intellectual property laws to implement the international agreements to eliminate those nontariff barriers to trade.

The increasing value and importance of intellectual property has generated various tensions within the legal structures of the new world economy. One issue is where the line should be drawn between the legitimate and desirable goal of providing incentives to encourage research and development, on the one hand, and, on the other, fostering the

---

[13] Murray G. Smith, ed., "Editor's Introduction," in *Global Rivalry and Intellectual Property, Developing Canadian Strategies* (Toronto: The Institute for Research on Public Policy, 1991), p. 4.

[14] The Paris Convention for the Protection of Industrial Property (known as the Paris Convention) was concluded in Paris in 1883 and ultimately revised in Stockholm in 1967. For the text, see Marshall A. Leaffer, ed. *International Treaties on Intellectual Property* (Washington DC: The Bureau of National Affairs, Inc., 1990), p. 20.

[15] The Berne Convention for the Protection of Literary and Artistic Works (known as the Berne Union or Berne Convention) was first established in 1886 in Berne, Switzerland, and has been revised five times with two additions. For the text, see Leaffer, *International Treaties*, ibid at p. 342.

use of monopoly positions with consequent higher prices, the potential for stifling competition, and the limiting of the dissemination of technology.

A second debate is emerging between the developed and developing countries about the protection of intellectual property. Greater protection of intellectual property increases the cost to consumers in nations that import technology. Although the United States runs a healthy trade surplus in ideas each year, most other developed countries, not to mention developing countries, pay more for technology licenses and copyrights than they earn from them. The economic goals of the developing world and the rights of the intellectual property owner often conflict. Strengthened intellectual property rights are perceived by some to hamper the diffusion of knowledge from the developed to developing nations. These tensions run through much of the discussion that follows.

This Overview is not intended as an exhaustive analysis of recent national and international developments in intellectual property law. Rather, it highlights some current trends and issues that illustrate the increasing value and importance of intellectual property as an economic asset and as a tool in commerce, in contrast to the pressures these trends and issues exert on the legal dimensions of the global economy. It first outlines basic ways in which intellectual property is protected and the rationale underlying such protection. Next discussed are various trends in the marketplace and in the courts that reflect the extension and exploitation of the value of intellectual property. Then international developments involving intellectual property are considered. The concluding section touches on some of the tensions arising from the international move toward greater protection of intellectual property rights.

THE LEGAL SCHEME FOR PROTECTING INTELLECTUAL PROPERTY

Intellectual property laws exist to protect the results of innovation and creation. Intellectual property rights do not exist in the absence of legal protection. The worth of the intellectual property right does not lie in the particular idea or technology, although clearly these may have significant commercial value of their own. Rather, the value lies in the owner's ability to prevent others from exploiting the idea or technology. The legislative schemes for protecting intellectual property rights reflect a policy decision by governments to leave the economic value of intellectual property in the hands of its owner and its owner's financial partners. As a starting point, therefore, it is useful to provide a brief definition of each of the various rights protected by law and the policy underlying such protection.

Intellectual property rights are generally monopolies mandated by statute, enabling the owner to prevent others from using and/or producing the protected invention, technology, or creative work. The monopoly rights conferred upon the owner, allowing the owner to exclude competing products or processes from the market, translate into economic power. The basic tools of intellectual property protection are trademarks, copyrights, patents, industrial designs, and trade secrets. In addition, new intellectual property rights are being recognized in response to advancing technological developments. These rights are governed internationally through various treaties that attempt to harmonize the laws of their members and to provide uniform solutions to certain problems arising from international legal diversity.

Trademarks and Service Marks.   Trademarks and service marks (often referred to collectively as trademarks) are names or designs, or both, that distinguish the owner's goods and services from those of others. No one other than the trademark owner may use the protected trademark or any similar mark that would lead to confusion in the mind of the public. Trademarks exist primarily to protect the reputation of a producer of goods or provider of services. In doing so, they provide businesses with an incentive to maintain, upgrade, and develop new goods and services. Enforcing trademark rights protects the owner's investment in advertising and other forms of goods and service differentiation.

In many countries, trademarks are entitled to both statutory protection and protection arising automatically through use. However, the most effective trademark rights are statutory trademark registrations. Registration serves as constructive notice to the public of the registrant's ownership claim in the trademark and creates an obligation for others to make certain that a newly adopted trademark does not conflict with a registered mark. The registrant may also avail itself of a broad range of remedies in an infringement lawsuit. The term of protection is not generally limited, provided the trademark continues to be used.

Patents.   Patents protect the functional elements of an invention or technology and are available to protect a product or process. A patent describes an invention and, in exchange for disclosure, gives the inventor or owner the right to exclude others from making, using, or selling the invention. To be patentable, an invention must possess a minimum degree of novelty and nonobviousness. If the invention is obvious to persons skilled in the field of the invention in view of prior disclosures (called prior art), a patent will be denied. Patents are granted for a term, and once the patent expires, the technology falls into the public domain.

Society expects to gain certain advantages from granting patents to industrial innovators. The first is greater innovation and technological growth, achieved by rewarding inventors for the uncertain and expensive process of research and development. A second advantage is greater technology transfer and distribution. A patent requires public disclosure of the technical steps leading to the new product or process. Other companies may use the information, providing they respect the patent or upon its expiration. By issuing patents, a society also avoids costly duplication of research by industry, through the distribution of information. Finally, through patents, new technologies may create benefits that improve technical efficiencies in related companies and industries.[16]

Copyrights.   Copyright protection exists for all original works (literary, dramatic, musical, or artistic) fixed in any tangible means of expression. Copyright provides the owner with the right to prevent a variety of unauthorized uses, such as the reproduction of a literary work or the public performance of a piece of music. Copyrights have become the most widely accepted means of protecting computer software. Unlike patents, copyrights do not prevent others from using or copying ideas embodied in the work, but only protect the form or expression of those ideas. Furthermore, the independent creation of the same or a similar work is not prohibited as long as there is no direct copying involved, again a contrast to patent protection. The term of copyright protection is limited, generally to 50 years after the author's death, at the end of which the work enters the public domain.

Copyright exists to reward creators for creating works and disclosing them to the public and to foster a cultural sensitivity and identity. Copyright protection has become more

---

[16] For a discussion of the economic implications of patent protection see Keith E. Markus, "Economic Analysis of Intellectual Property Rights: Domestic and International Dimensions" in *Global Rivalry and Intellectual Property*, supra, note 13 at p. 119.

urgent in recent years owing to the proliferation of efficient, inexpensive, high-quality copying techniques (such as photocopying and audio and video reproduction). The proliferation of pirated copies produced in developing countries and exported throughout the world has eroded the profits of publishers, music and film producers, and software developers, among others.

Moral Rights.   Originally a European concept, moral rights of authors and artists are being recognized by other countries, such as Canada, in copyright legislation. Moral rights are addressed in Article 6 bis of the Berne Convention, but not all countries have adhered to this Article.

Moral rights are related to, but independent of, copyright. They generally provide the author or artist of a copyrighted work with the right to be identified as the creator of the work by name or pseudonym, or conversely, the right to remain anonymous. Moral rights also confer upon an author or artist the right to prevent his or her work from being distorted or mutilated, or from being associated with a product, service, cause, or institution in a manner likely to cause prejudice to the creator's reputation. Moral rights give authors and artists greater control over the use of their works, even if they no longer own the copyright in those works.

In Canada, moral rights apply to any copyrighted work.[17] The United States has recently introduced moral rights protection, but has limited it to works of fine art, such as paintings and drawings. Protection extends only to works produced in single editions or in limited editions of 200 or fewer copies.[18] The concern about adopting moral rights in the United States hinges on the fact that moral rights are artistic rather than economic in nature. Thus, the fear about their adoption is that moral rights will give artists the right to prevent copyright authors from exercising their economic rights, thereby frustrating trade and commerce.

A justification for implementing moral rights legislation in Canada, and for that matter universally, was articulated by a subcommittee of the Canadian House of Commons studying the revision of Canada's copyright law prior to the amendments to Canada's new copyright legislation in 1988. In its report to the Canadian House of Commons entitled "A Charter of Rights for Creators," the subcommittee stated:

> Moral rights should have as much importance as economic rights. . . . We live in an advertising age. No one would dispute that advertisers must obtain a person's consent before using that person to endorse a product. Individuals cannot be forced to publicly endorse products, services, causes or institutions against their will. But such a situation might occur indirectly where the individual is an author and a work is used without the author's consent as part of an advertisement, even though a publisher or collective has licensed the use. The traditional rights of reproduction or radio communication may not be sufficient to control such uses as they may be owned by third parties who have no particular interest in protecting the personality of the author. . . .
>
> The sub-committee believes that such uses go beyond the normal economic exploitation of creative works and that authors alone should have the right to decide whether they wish, even indirectly through the use of their works, to endorse a particular product, service, cause or institution.[19]

---

[17] *Copyright Act (Canada)*, R. S. C. 1985. c. C-30, § 14.1.

[18] Moral rights were introduced in the United States by the Visual Artists Rights Act, which took effect on June 1, 1991, enacted as part of the Judicial Improvements Act of 1990, Public Law 101-650.

[19] "A Charter of Rights for Creators," in *Minutes of Proceedings in Evidence of the Subcommittee for the Standing Committee on Communications and Culture on the Revision of Copyright* (Ottawa: Canada House of Commons, 1985), p.6.

Industrial Designs.   Industrial design is similar to copyright protection and protects the designers of the ornamental aspects of useful articles—the features of shape, configuration, pattern, or ornament in a finished useful article—that are decorative rather than functional. Only the owner may reproduce the design. As in the case of copyrights and patents, industrial design protection is for a limited term, after which the protected design may be exploited by the public.

Trade Secrets.   Technology or other information that is not patentable may be protected as a trade secret. Trade secret protection is different from that of the other forms of intellectual property. Protection is not mandated by statute (although in some cases it has now been codified); rather, it derives from common-law principles of tort and contract law. Its rough equivalent in civil law systems is the concept of "unfair competition." Trade secrets are not limited in time, provided the protected information is kept confidential. Confidentiality is usually achieved by limiting access and restricting use, often by contract.

Unlike patent and copyright protection, trade secret protection does not contribute to the public benefit by promoting disclosure and diffusion of technological developments. The rationale underlying trade secret protection is simply to allow inventors to protect the value of their time and investment. Trade secret protection does not confer any monopoly and is not generally considered a property right. Protection may be lost if another party can independently develop the protected work or the work is generally disclosed to the public, whether or not by the inventor.

Trade secret pretection may be used alone or combined with other forms of protection, such as copyright for computer software, to provide additional safeguards. It is often used as an alternative to patent protection, when the owner does not wish to disclose the technology. A number of states within the United States have codified trade secret protection. Other jurisdictions continue to protect trade secrets under common law principles.

International Treaties.   The major treaties dealing with intellectual property do not attempt to unify national laws. The fields of trademark, patent, and copyright law are too complicated, and the many issues that arise too controversial for a worldwide consensus except on certain basic principles.

Rather, the treaties attempt to harmonize the laws of member states. To harmonize the law means to reconcile national legal systems without necessarily achieving a uniform result. Generally, harmonization has been achieved on issues of formalities, such as the procedures for filing claims for intellectual property rights.[20]

The two major multinational intellectual property treaties are the Paris and the Berne Conventions. The Paris Convention was concluded in 1883 and revised in Stockholm in 1967, superseding a complex system of bilateral treaties. Administered by the World Intellectual Property Organization,[21] it includes provisions relating to inventions, trade names, trademarks, service marks, industrial designs, utility models, indications of source, appellations of origin, and the repression of unfair competition. Its objectives are to secure legal protection for industrial property and encourage uniformity of law. The Paris Convention also encompasses a series of special agreements covering a broad range

---

[20] Leaffer, *International Treaties*, supra, note 14 at p. 5.

[21] The World Intellectual Property Organization is a specialized agency of the United Nations that administers the Paris Convention and Berne Convention.

of intellectual property, such as the Patent Co-operation Treaty,[22] and the Madrid Agreement[23] covering trademarks. On January 1, 1990, 100 states were party to the Paris Convention, including Canada, the United States, and Mexico.[24]

The Berne Convention was established in 1886 and is also administered by the World Intellectual Property Organization. It has undergone two additions and five revisions. The goal of the Berne Convention is to ensure that all authors of works published in member states, irrespective of their nationality, are treated without discrimination under the national law of a member state and without being subjected to any formalities. The Convention covers a broad range of subjects, encompassing "literary and artistic works [that] shall include every production in the literary, scientific and artistic domain whatever may be the mode or form of its expression."[25] The forms of expression include choreography, painting, architecture, compilations, and derivative works. The Berne Convention requires that a work be protected without formalities outside the country of origin, although it does not govern protection of works within a member country of origin. As of January 1, 1990, 84 states were party to the Berne Convention, including Canada, the United States, and Mexico.[26]

The founding members of the Paris and the Berne Conventions intended to create a permanent, independent, legal entity open to all countries. Both Conventions were designed to adapt to changes in world conditions and, in so doing, have been revised periodically. Each Convention operates on the principle of national treatment, under which each country affords nationals of other member states the same protection that it affords its own nationals. This national treatment eliminates problems associated with the principle of reciprocity, which would require Country A to grant citizens of Country B the same treatment that Country B granted citizens of Country A. Both conventions establish minimum substantive standards that each country must recognize in its national laws. These minimum standards avoid imbalances that could be created from the application of national treatment. Although each Convention began with a small number of minimum rights, new rights have been added with each revision.[27]

Other international conventions include the European Patent Convention,[28] which creates a system for examining and granting patents originating from participating countries, and the Universal Copyright Convention,[29] which is administered by UNESCO as an alternative to the Berne Convention. The Universal Copyright Convention was

---

[22] The Patent Co-operation Treaty creates a union for cooperation in filing, searching, and examining patent applications. Rather than creating an international patent, it allows for the filing of separate applications in the member countries. The treaty was completed in June 1970 and entered into force on January 24, 1978. For the text, see Leaffer, *International Treaties*, supra, note 14 at p. 79.

[23] The Madrid Agreement Concerning the International Registration of Marks is a special union within the Paris Convention. It entered into force on April 14, 1891. Designed to simplify the procedures for filing for trademarks and service marks in different countries, it provides for the international registration of trademark by a single filing in one language, together with the payment of a single fee. For the text, see Leaffer, *International Treaties*, supra, note 14 at p. 229.

[24] Leaffer, *International Treaties*, supra, note 14 at pp. 5, 6, 17–19.

[25] The Berne Convention, Article 2, par. 1.

[26] Leaffer, *International Treaties*, supra, note 14 at pp. 6–7, 339–341.

[27] Ibid., pp. 7–8.

[28] The European Patent Convention was signed on October 5, 1973, and came into force on October 7, 1977. For text, see Leaffer, *International Treaties*, supra, note 14 at p. 143.

[29] The Universal Copyright Convention was signed and entered into force on September 6, 1952, and was revised in Paris in 1971. For text, see Leaffer, *International Treaties*, supra, note 14 at p. 381.

created because various countries were not party to the Berne Convention. In addition, treaties governing integrated circuits and plant varieties have been formed, among others.

INTELLECTUAL PROPERTY AS A NEW SOURCE OF WEALTH

Intellectual property rights, protected by the legal structures previously described, are emerging with dramatic force as a new source of wealth. Recent trends in the marketplace, the courts, and legislation indicate the growing significance of intellectual property as an asset with commercial value. Evidence of the economic value of brand names, or trademarks, can be seen daily in the grocery store. Legislators and courts appear to be extending the reach of intellectual property rights, thereby increasing the value of such rights to their owners. Pharmaceutical companies are a notable example. Specialized courts and tribunals have been created to resolve disputes over intellectual property. Collective societies and private enforcement agencies have been formed to exploit and enforce these valuable rights on behalf of their owners. These and other examples of the increasing importance of intellectual property are discussed in greater detail in the following paragraphs.

The Value of the Brand.   Trademarks, or brand names as they are often referred to in the consumer products industries, may often be a business's most valuable asset. Companies invest substantial resources into developing brand-loyal customers. In many cases, the brands that were popular 25 years ago are still the leaders today. In the category of food blenders, for example, one survey indicated that consumers still rank General Electric as the number one brand—20 years after the company stopped manufacturing the product.[30]

An investment banker from a major New York investment firm recently stated that a company's brand names may, in some cases, represent as much as 80% of a company's value.[31] One well-known example is the Marlboro trademark for cigarettes, which industry sources have valued at $40 billion worldwide.[32] Owned by Philip Morris, whose portfolio also includes the well-known Cheezwhiz, Maxwell House, and Kraft trademarks, Marlboro cigarettes are said to be the world's most popular product, and its distinctive red and white label is equivalent to legal tender in many countries.

Brands names sparked some of the biggest takeover battles of the 1980s. The extension of successful brands to new products and courtroom battles over popular trademarks indicate that trademarks are a strategic asset for many companies. Franchising and merchandising depend on well-known trademarks. The recent success of private-label and generic brands, however, is a countervailing trend suggesting that, at least in a recession, established brands face a challenge and may not be as valuable as they once were.

Mergers and Acquisitions.   The mergers and acquisitions of the 1980s were, in many cases, driven by the intellectual property assets of the target. Examples include the $6.2 billion breakup of Beatrice and the $5.7 billion acquisition by Grand Metropolitan of the

---

[30] "The Purest Treasure," *The Economist* (7 September, 1991): 67.

[31] Ian Jay Kaufman, Melvin Simensky, and Lanning G. Bryer, "International Laws on Security Interests in Intellectual Property: The Sequel," *Trademark World* (July/August 1991): 30.

[32] Ibid.

Pillsbury Company, owner of Burger King, Green Giant, and Haagen Dazs.[33] Kohlberg, Kravis & Roberts paid a premium of $21.7 billion above book value when it spent $25 billion for RJR Nabisco.[34] Philip Morris purchased Kraft for $12.9 billion, four times its book value.[35] Nestlé acquired Rowntree, owner of the trademarks Smarties, Polo, Kit Kat, and Black Magic, for $4.5 billion, five times its book value.[36] In these cases, the premium paid was for the trademarks, rather than for the physical assets.[37]

"Brand Stretching."   A recent study by the United States Trademark Association concluded that it is cheaper in the United States for companies to bring out new products using existing, well-known trademarks registered for other products and capitalize on brand recognition, than to develop a new trademark to launch a new consumer product.[38] Although launching a new brand may cost as much as $75 to $100 million, many new products fail whereas "tried and true" trademarks endure.[39] This practice of extending trademarks to new products, known as "brand stretching," has become common. Though risky—if the new product does not succeed, it could harm the reputation of the original product—if successful, it is a cheaper way of marketing and advertising.

One example of successful brand stretching is the extension of the trademark Sunkist from the orange juice market into frozen juice bars and vitamin C tablets, where the brand's image of health and freshness was credible.[40] McDonald's Corporation has expanded its line of fast-food products from its originally successful hamburger to Chicken McNuggets and, recently, McPizza, again a logical extension. Guiness has introduced a new Tanqueray Sterling vodka to accompany its well-known gin.[41]

Other attempts have been less successful owing to basic problems with the "fit" between the brand's core product and the new item. For example, Levi Straus's attempt to expand into a line of men's suits failed and simultaneously damaged the company's jeans sales.[42] Less successful still are attempts to transfer the value of a premium brand to a down-market product. Cadillac's efforts to attract lower-income car buyers with its cheap Cimarron model in the early 1980s hurt its reputation as a producer of luxury cars.[43]

Protection of Brand Image.   Many companies are starting to recognize the value of brands and the necessity of taking a long-term view toward preserving their image. Tactics such as price promotions, coupons, and discounts, spawned by the pressure to generate short-term gains in sales, ultimately have a negative impact on a brand's value. In an effort to avoid the negative impact of short-term marketing strategies, some companies, such as Colgate-Palmolive and Canada Dry, have introduced "brand equity managers" who are charged with taking a long-term view to protecting a brand's image.[44] Coca-Cola has even ventured beyond the services of traditional advertising agencies to preserve and promote

[33] "Brand-Stretching Can Be Fun—And Dangerous," *The Economist* (May 5, 1990) 17.
[34] *The Globe and Mail Report on Business* (12 April, 1993).
[35] "The Purest Treasure," supra, note 30.
[36] Ibid.
[37] Ibid.
[38] Ibid.
[39] Ibid.
[40] Ibid.
[41] "Brand-Stretching Can Be Fun," supra, note 30.
[42] Ibid.
[43] "The Purest Treasure," supra, note 30.
[44] Ibid.

the image of its valuable brand, announcing in 1991 that it was engaging Creative Artists Agency, which represents many of the world's biggest film stars, as its global media advisor.[45]

Incidents reflecting badly on a brand's image can be devastating to the owner. The uproar in the summer of 1993 involving allegations that syringes had been found in cans of Pepsi's cola caused Pepsi to consider a product recall. Although it was ultimately shown that the allegations were fabricated, Pepsi had to engage in an extensive public relations campaign to reassure consumers and clear its name. Although the costs of such a program are enormous, companies must weigh them against the long-term national and international damage to their trademarks that could occur if such controversies persist.

An example of the great lengths to which a company will go to protect the image of its brand is the case of Tylenol analgesics. When tampering with its product resulted in the death of at least seven consumers in 1989, Tylenol pulled its product from the shelves and created new packaging that was less susceptible to tampering. Again, the potential for long-term damage to the reputation associated with the company's valuable trademark was perceived to outweigh the short-term costs of the product recall.

Trademark Wars.   Another indicator of the value of a trademark is the number of major "trademark wars" that break out between competitors. The success of one company's marketing efforts is often exploited by its competitors, who steal the company's trademark and distinctive packaging or labeling. Companies will go to great lengths to protect their valuable trademarks, often litigating at substantial cost to prevent competitors from imitating their distinctive identifiers.

The recent Canadian case involving Molson Breweries, Miller Brewing Company, and Labatt Brewing Company is an example. Molson, which has the rights to market Miller beer in Canada, accused Labatt of misappropriating its trademark and the distinctive packaging for its Miller Genuine Draft beer in the sale and marketing of Labatt Genuine Draft. Miller began marketing its highly successful Miller Genuine Draft in the United States in 1986. Molson, under license from Miller, began to market Miller Genuine Draft beer in Canada early in 1992. However, before Molson could launch its product in Canada, Labatt began selling its own Labatt brand Genuine Draft. As a result of the similarity in the trademarks and packaging of the two products, Molson sued Labatt for unfair competition and passing off, and applied for an interlocutory injunction application to prevent Labatt from marketing Labatt Genuine Draft, which was dismissed.[46]

At the same time, Molson began a public relations battle against Labatt. Molson produced advertisements stating that it "believed that Labatt had copied the overall look and feel of 'Miller Genuine Draft' " and said, "While Labatt could not copy the great taste of Miller Genuine Draft, we think that you will agree they copied just about everything else." As part of its campaign, Molson ran a contest offering prizes to contestants who identified three similarities in the packaging of the products. Labatt retaliated by seeking its own injunction to stop the advertisements, the injunction application was dismissed. The outcome of the action will be determined at trial.[47]

A new battle between the brewery giants has now arisen in the U.S. and Canada over the new "ice" beer. Labatt developed a new process for manufacturing beer using

---

[45] "Soda-Pop Celebrity," *The Economist* (September 14, 1991) 75.

[46] *Molson Breweries v. Labatt Brewing Co.* (1992), 44 C.P.R. (3d) 242 (F.C.T.D.).

[47] This summary of the proceedings appear in an article by David Steinberg in the Fasken Campbell Godfrey *Intellectual Property Bulletin*, vol. 1, no. 2, September, 1992.

patented technology that enables Labatt to cool the beer sufficiently during brewing that ice crystals form. Intending to name its new product Ice Beer, Labatt was beaten to the market by Molson, which came out with its own Canadian Ice beer just weeks before Labatt had planned to launch its product. With both products now in the market, it remains to be seen how the dispute will be resolved.

Franchising and Merchandising.   Another indicator of brand power is the expansion of well-known trademarks into new markets. Franchising depends for its success on the value of a well-known trademark. McDonald's Corporation's distinctive "Golden Arches" are internationally renowned, and its entry into Russia and China is a classic example of the power of that company's distinctive trademark to bridge cultural and economic boundaries. Other examples of international franchises include Baskin-Robbins and Kentucky Fried Chicken.

The exploitation of trademarks has become an industry in itself. The impact of merchandising can be seen in the range of perfumes, eyewear, and other products bearing the trademarks of famous clothing designers or manufacturers of sports equipment. Guccio Gucci, the manufacturer of the Gucci watch, has licensed its famous trademark for use on products ranging from shoes, luggage, purses and wallets, to perfume.

The proliferation of T-shirts, lunch boxes, stuffed animals, china figurines and other products bearing well-known characters from film or television is further evidence of the value of these intellectual property rights, or "properties," as they are often referred to in merchandising deals. Perhaps the best-known success in the merchandising business is Walt Disney Company. Mickey and Minnie Mouse, Sleeping Beauty, Winnie-the-Pooh, Princess Jasmine, and Beauty and the Beast grace an array of products including clothing, watches, jewelry, games, figurines, umbrellas, and dishes. Walt Disney Company operates theme parks from California to Japan, evidence of its international renown and of the value of its intellectual property rights. Disney has also acquired a hockey franchise, calling its team the Mighty Ducks. Disney was motivated in part by the tremendous growth in the sale of sports-related merchandise and the success of teams like the Los Angeles Kings and the Chicago Bulls. These teams make an enormous percentage of their money from licensing. Marvin Miller, former executive director of the Major League Baseball Players Association, in his book, *A Whole New Ballgame*, tells the story of the development of licensing by the Players Association. When he joined the Association in the 1960s, only a few superstar players made more than $100,000 a year. At the moment, by licensing the pictures and other likenesses of players for products, including orange juice and breakfast cereals, each player earns more than $100,000 a year from licensing fees alone.[48]

The willingness of courts to protect a name or trademark beyond the specific product or service for which the mark has acquired its reputation has a direct impact on the licensing activities of the owners of valuable marks. Recently, a court in the United Kingdom protected the rights of a licensee of a trademark who was using the mark not on the products for which the mark was registered, but, rather, on products in a related industry. The court allowed the licensee to its right in the trademark it had established in the licensed goods against third parties, thereby protecting the investment of the licensee and extending the value of the trademark.[49]

[48] Marvin Miller, *A Whole New Ballgame: The Sport and Business of Baseball* (New York: Birch Lane Press, 1991) pp. 148–149.

[49] *Mirage Studios v. Counter-Feat Clothing Co. Ltd.*, F.S.R. 145 (V.C.) (1991).

A Canadian court has followed this lead in *Paramount Pictures Corp. v. Howley*.[50] This decision expands the protection available to famous trademarks in circumstances in which a pattern of licensing in an industry is recognized by the public.

The case concerned the merchandising potential of the film *Crocodile Dundee*, distributed by Paramount Pictures. Howley went to see the film immediately upon its release. Paramount had not expected the film to be so successful and did not have any merchandising arrangements when the film opened. The film was an immediate popular success in Canada, taking in $23 million at the box office within two weeks of its release. During those two weeks, Howley had filed a trademark application for Crocodile Dundee for sportswear and other products. His trademark showed a surfing crocodile wearing a hat similar to the hat worn by the lead in the movie. The crocodile was holding a can of Fosters beer and saying, "Come 'ave a Fossi with me and me mates." At that time, Paul Hogan, the actor who played the lead in the movie, was advertising Fosters beer on Canadian television. The trademark also showed the words "Crocodile Dundee" in the same script and colors as those used by Paramount in its newspaper advertisements. Howley then licensed his trademark to a third party for T-shirts.

Although there had been no material merchandising by Paramount of the *Crocodile Dundee* film at the time in issue, the court found that Paramount derived an important part of its revenue from licensing merchandise bearing images from its films. It was not disputed that the use of the "Crocodile Dundee" character and trademarks in a *film* would have violated Paramount's rights, but the court went further, allowing Paramount to stop a person from applying "Crocodile Dundee" to clothing even though Paramount was not using "Crocodile Dundee" in this manner.

Crucial to the court's decision was its analysis of the film industry and the role of trademarks and copyrighted characters in that industry. The court commented that over the past 15 years licensing had increased greatly in the film industry and that both distributors of T-shirts and the purchasing public were well aware of the practice.

Because the public had come to recognize an industry pattern of licensing, Paramount was entitled to extend its rights in its trademark and prevent the use of the trademark in clothing, despite not having used the mark for clothing itself. By its decision, the court strengthened the rights of trademark owners in the merchandise licensing industry and increased the value of these assets.

The Challenge of Private Labels and Generics.   Recent events may suggest, however, that after many years of building up the value of brand names, manufacturers are losing consumer loyalty. Philip Morris was the first to signal that premium brands might not be as secure as they were thought to be in the 1980s. In 1993, Philip Morris cut the price of its Marlboro cigarettes acknowledging that its product was threatened by competition from generic labels, as well as by an unexpectedly weak economy. The price cut caused the shares of Philip Morris to fall on the financial markets.[51]

These events triggered concern among other brand-name manufacturers and further volatility on the stock market. Following the price cuts by Philip Morris, Proctor & Gamble (the maker of Pampers and Luvs, the world's best-known disposable diapers) cut its product prices.[52] Other owners of premium brands, including Kraft and Quaker Oats,

---

[50] (1992), 5 O.R. (3d.) 573 (Gen. Div.)
[51] *The New York Times* (3 April, 1993).
[52] *The Washington Post* (15 April, 1993).

were similarly prompted to cut their prices or put a halt to planned increases.[53] At the same time, the price fall of Philip Morris shares was quickly followed by a drop in share prices for various manufacturers of consumer products. Analysts reasoned that if consumers were reaching for cheaper generic brands of cigarettes, what was to stop them from choosing other generic or store-brand consumer products, such as toothpaste, breakfast cereal, canned tomatoes, or bleach?[54]

The once-powerful premium brands are now clearly facing a challenge from generic or private-label brand products. The improved quality of these products, together with the prolonged recession, has made price a more significant consideration for consumers and has reduced the impact of traditional brand loyalty. Retailers and grocery stores are establishing their own private lines of products. Private-label groceries are well established in Europe and have become more popular in recent years. In Germany, private labels typically cover discount and inferior quality products, such as toilet paper.[55] But in the United Kingdom, chains such as Marks & Spencer (with its St. Michael label), Sainsbury, and Tesco have developed sophisticated private-label products that are seen by consumers as cheaper than, but comparable in quality to, well-known brands and that sometimes even sell at a premium over branded products. Their example is being followed by grocery chains throughout much of Europe, particularly in France.[56]

In North America, generic or store brands have until lately been associated with lower-quality alternatives to branded products. In the United States, however, Safeway has recently developed a new line of soft drinks, which it claims is competing well against Coca-Cola and Pepsi.[57] Sainsbury, which acquired the New England grocery chain Shaws, has concentrated on developing an up-market line of privately labeled products.[58] In Canada, Loblaws has produced its President's Choice line of products, which has been so successful that the trademark now denotes premium quality, rather than discount, products.

Ironically, some leading manufacturers, including Philip Morris, H.J. Heinz and Campbell's Soup, have started to produce their own generic brands, which compete with their regular brands, in an attempt to maintain market share.[59] IBM has taken the same approach with computers. Leading tire and automotive manufacturers, such as Goodyear, Michelin, and B.F. Goodrich, now manufacture products sold under private labels, such as Monarch, Lee, and Star, and for large department stores such as Sears. In Canada, well-known tire and automotive-parts makers manufacture a range of automotive products sold by the Canadian Tire Corporation under its well-known Motomaster label.

Most commentators agree that the financial markets have overreacted to what they see as threats facing the traditional premium brands. Although brand loyalty may be eroding slightly, it is still significant among consumers and a valuable source of economic power. Other analysts have argued that the shift toward lower-priced, generic brand products may be more than just a by-product of the recession and that loyalty to many brands may have been permanently affected by the emergence of generic and store-brand products. Interestingly, private-label brands may become as valuable as premium brands. The

---

[53] *The Financial Times* (6 May, 1993).
[54] "What's in a Name", *Industries in Transition* (April 1993).
[55] *The Financial Times* (6 May, 1993).
[56] Ibid.
[57] Ibid.
[58] Ibid.
[59] Ibid.

success of brands such as Marks & Spencer's St. Michael label or Loblaws' President's Choice line of products in Canada suggests that trademarks will always be capable of becoming valuable economic assets, whether they are intended to signify "premium" or "value-priced" products.

The Value of Patents.   The dramatic increase in the number of patents applied for and obtained is further evidence of the increased importance of intellectual property to businesses. In 1992, the United States Patent Office received 185,446 patent applications, more than in any previous year, and granted 109,728, almost twice as many as a decade ago.[60] In Japan the number of patent applications nearly doubled between 1980 and 1987.[61] Recognizing the growing importance of patents, Canada has finally granted a contract to IBM to automate the records of the Patent Office for filing and prosecuting patent applications and to improve the dissemination of technology—the policy underlying patent protection.

The scope of patent protection is expanding. In a recent collaboration, a consortium of the "Big Three" American car makers, General Motors Corporation, Ford Motors Company and Chrysler Corporation, were awarded their first joint patent. The three companies have embarked on several joint research and development programs, which only a few years ago would have been illegal under U.S. antitrust laws, in an attempt to gain a competitive advantage over Japanese rivals. The patent was awarded for a new process for producing car components from liquid, molded composites, which may replace the use of steel in the interior body structure of some vehicles. The patent is seen as a milestone for the industry's research and development efforts.[62]

Patent protection is also extending to previously unpatentable subject matter. In 1980, the United States Supreme Court held for the first time that living matter was patentable, granting patent protection to a microorganism that, when genetically engineered, was capable of successfully "eating" oil spills. In rejecting the decision of the lower court, which had maintained that the invention was not patentable because it was alive, the Supreme Court stated that the range of patent laws was intended to encompass "anything under the sun that is made by man."[63]

Soon after this decision, the United States Board of Patent Appeals considered a patent application covering oysters which, because of their sterility, do not use their body weight to reproduce and, therefore, remain edible year-round. The Patent Examiner rejected the application. However, the Board of Patent Appeals affirmed the Patent Examiner's rejection, but disagreed with the conclusion that oysters were not patentable solely because they were living organisms, reiterating that patent laws should be given wide scope to include human-made life forms.[64] In the wake of the decision, the United States Patent Office announced that it would accept applications for patents on "non-naturally occurring, non-human, multi-cellular living organisms, including animals," thereby extending the reach of patent protection to plants and animals. Human beings were held not to be patentable subject matter owing to the constitutional prohibition on property rights in humans.[65]

---

[60] John Seabrook, "Flash of Genius: Annals of Invention," *The New Yorker* (11 January, 1993) 38.

[61] "The Ideas Business: Economy of the Mind," supra, note 11.

[62] *The Financial Post* (14 April, 1993).

[63] *Diamond v. Chakrabarty*, 447 U.S. 303 (1980), at p. 309.

[64] *Ex parte Allen*, 2 U.S.P.Q. (BNA) 1425 (PTO Bd. App. int. 1987).

[65] 1077 Official Gazette Patent Office 24 (April 7, 1987).

These decisions spurred the growth of the biotechnology industry in the 1980s, because they sustained the possibility of patenting microorganisms. As of 1989, more than 75 patents on multicellular organisms were pending at the United States Patent Office.[66] The first patent on a multicellular, living organism was issued by the United States Patent Office in 1988.[67] Known as the Harvard onco mouse, the patented mouse is a genetically altered mouse highly susceptible to cancer. Protection for the onco mouse was recently granted by the European Patent Office.[68]

Some countries have also considered whether higher forms of plant life can be patented. In 1985, the United States Patent Office granted a patent for a new variety of corn plant whose seeds contained high amounts of an essential amino acid nutrient, thereby making the seeds useful for animal feed.[69]

The law in Canada is not as advanced as it is in the United States. Although patents have been granted to protect lower levels of life forms, such as bacteria, viruses, yeasts, molds, and protozoa, the Supreme Court of Canada has made it clear that novel, hybrid plant species developed through cross-breeding will not be granted patent protection under the current Patent Act.[70] One issue for the court was whether an invention can be reproduced simply by reading the instructions to the patent. This issue has now been addressed by amendments to the Patent Act[71] that permit deposit of samples of the life forms, thereby making it possible to check the sample against the claims in the patent. The court also said that a plant variety that results from "cross-breeding" is a chance transformation and not a predictable result of human intervention and, therefore, is not patentable subject matter.

Granting biotechnology patents on multicellular organisms has ramifications for agriculture, health care products, and the chemical industry. For example, it is conceivable that cattle and hogs will be significantly genetically altered to provide higher yields of meat with greater nutritional value, poultry will be genetically altered to maximize meat, egg, and feather production, and dairy cows will be altered to produce maximum yields of milk. It is likely that patents will be issued in the future for major row crops, such as soybeans and corn, and that genetic engineering will lead to the development of disease-resistant high-yield crops. Biotechnological innovations may reduce the need for herbicides and insecticides. In addition to biotechnology companies, seed companies and nurseries may seek patent protection for new plant varieties.[72]

The debate on this issue has been taken up by various lobby groups, such as Greenpeace, animal welfare groups, and farmers. Greenpeace has protested that the proposals will hand control of the world's genetic heritage to multinational corporations that will be the quickest to file patents and the fiercest in defending them. This group complained that patents could make it profitable to manufacture "natural" foods and flavorings, such as cocoa, depriving millions of Third-World farmers of their livelihoods. Animal welfare groups have raised emotional and ethical issues revolving around the fear that patents on

---

[66] Marsha L. Montgomery, "Building a Better Mouse—And Patenting It: Altering the Patent Law to Accommodate Multicellular Organisms," *Case Western Reserve Law Review*, vol. 41, 231 at p. 232.

[67] U.S. Patent No. 4,736,866.

[68] Granted May 13, 1992. See *World Intellectual Property Report*, vol. 7, no. 4, p. 91.

[69] Ex parte *Hibbard*, 227 U.S.P.Q. (BNA) 443 (PTO Bd. App. and Int., 1985).

[70] *Pioneer Hi-Bred Ltd. v. Commissioner of Patents* (1989), 1 S.C.R. 1623.

[71] *Intellectual Property Law Improvement Act* (Canada) S.C. 1993, c. 15, s. 38.1.

[72] Edmund J. Sease, "From Microbes, to Corn Seeds, to Oysters, to Mice: Patentability of New Life Forms," 38 *Drake Law Review* 551, (1988–89).

animals will make people less sensitive to their suffering. Farmers fear that such patents might force them to pay license fees on their animals and seeds. Research and development companies, on the other hand, have argued that without patents, much genetic engineering is not worth the expense.[73]

The European Parliament has declared its "resolute opposition" to the European Patent Office's decision to protect the Harvard mouse and has called upon the European Patent Office to remove the patent. Although the resolution has no legal effect on the European Patent Office, it signals the European Parliament's intention to carry on the battle for restructuring the patentability of life forms in the European Community. The assembly has approved the European Community's proposal on legal protection for biotechnological patents, but has requested amendments that would prohibit patents on animals "subject to unnecessary suffering," as well as patents on the human body or parts of the human body.[74]

Recent developments in the pharmaceutical industry in Canada are a striking example of the tremendous economic power patents can confer. Amendments to the Canadian Patent Act[75] have significantly increased protection for pharmaceutical companies. As a result of the most recent amendments, the patent holders now enjoy patent protection for 20 years from the date of application, an increase from 17 years. Patent protection is now available for a medicine itself, rather than just for the process of making the medicine, as was previously the case. Moreover, the compulsory licensing provisions, which permitted generic drug companies in Canada to obtain compulsory patent licenses from pharmaceutical companies through an application to the Canadian Patent Office, have now been eliminated.

Under these licenses, generic drug companies could import and manufacture drugs otherwise protected by patent, in return for royalties. The licensing was intended to reduce barriers to pharmaceutical markets, increase competition, and lower prices for the benefit of Canadian consumers and taxpayers. Now, drug patent owners will not face competition from the generic drug companies for the duration of the patent protection in Canada.

The result is that generic drug companies will have a longer wait to get their cheaper versions on the market. In exchange, the pharmaceutical companies have agreed to increase their research-and-development spending in Canada. The theory is that patent protection in Canada will cause drug companies to earn more money because of less competition from the generic manufacturers. More money will lead to more research and development, and more research and development will lead to more effective drugs.[76]

The Canadian legislators have attempted to balance the monopolistic rights granted to pharmaceutical companies by extended price review and regulation by the Patented Medicines Prices Review Board.[77] The Board may require a patent owner to produce

---

[73] "Survival of the Quickest," *The Economist* (24 November, 1990): 72.

[74] *World Intellectual Property Report* 7, No. 4 (1993): 91.

[75] Patent Act Amendment Act (Canada), 1992, S.C. 1993, c.2, which came into force on February 15, 1993.

[76] Eric Reguly, "Drug Companies May Be Courting New Backlash," *The Financial Post* (19 February, 1993).

[77] The Patent Amendment Act continues the Patented Medicines Prices Review Board, which has the power to control excessive pricing and the duty to report yearly to the Canadian Parliament on the overall research and development relative to sales of pharmaceutical companies. The Board has the power to investigate and regulate excessive pricing, investigate sales and expense activities in Canada, and investigate Canadian research and development.

information on the sales price of a medicine in any market and the costs of making and marketing the medicine. If the Board finds the price for the patented drug is excessive, it may direct the patent owner to reduce the price or may set a price itself. The Board also has the power to require owners of drug patents to provide it with details on expenditures made on research and development in Canada. How this Board will exercise these broad powers remains to be seen.

The Value of Copyright—"Look and Feel" Protection for Software.   The judiciary's approach to the protection of computer software is an illustration of the difficulty in reconciling the competing policy arguments about the protection of intellectual property. The courts in this area have weighed the value of protecting the time, effort, and investment of the creator against the dangers of too much protection and the resulting stifling of competition. In doing so, they have often arrived at inconsistent results.

In most jurisdictions, copyright legislation protects the source code and object code of computer software. Courts in the United States have taken the lead, however, in extending protection beyond the code to protecting the overall structure, sequence, and organization (or the "look and feel" of the program) in cases in which the alleged infringer expended time and effort writing a different code. The extension of protection beyond the literal elements of the program requires the courts to walk a difficult line in distinguishing unprotectable ideas from protectable expression.

One of the first cases to consider protection for the structure, sequence, and organization of software was the 1978 case *Synercom Technology Inc. v. University Computing Co.*[78] In that case, Synercom had developed a computer program for structural analysis designed to solve certain engineering problems. Synercom had developed unique input formats that gave the user greater access to the program, but required less knowledge. The defendant decided to compete with Synercom and developed a competitive structural analysis program that was completely compatible with Synercom's program, using a preprocessor program that would accept Synercom's exact input formats. Synercom argued that the defendant's preprocessor program infringed its program, because it simply translated the expression of the formats to a different computer language. The court considered whether Synercom's sequence and ordering of data was a protectable expression or an unprotectable idea. The judge concluded that there had been no infringement, stating that if "sequencing and ordering is expression, what separable idea is expressed?" The judge adopted the following analogy to illustrate the difficulty in separating expression from the underlying idea:

> The familiar "figure-H" pattern of an automobile stick is chosen by an automobile manufacturer. Several different patterns may be imagined, some more convenient for the driver or easier to manufacture than others, but representing possible configurations. The pattern chosen is arbitrary, but once chosen, it is the only pattern which will work in a particular model. The pattern (analogous to the computer "format") may be expressed in several different ways: by a prose description in the driver's manual, through a diagram, photograph, or driver training film, or otherwise. Each of these expressions may presumably be protected through copyright. But the copyright protects copying of the particular expressions of the pattern, and does not prohibit another manufacturer from marketing a car using the same pattern. Use of the same pattern might be socially desirable, as it would reduce the retraining of drivers.[79]

---

[78] 462 F. Supp. 1003.
[79] Ibid., p. 1013.

The high-water mark for protection of nonliteral elements of a program was the 1986 case of *Whelan v. Jaslow*.[80] In that case, none of the code had been copied. The allegedly infringing program had been written in a different programming language and ran on a different platform. For there to be copyright infringement, there must have been copying of a protected work. The Third Circuit Court of Appeals concluded that the entire structure, sequence, and organization of the original program was protectable by copyright, and had been copied. The court noted that "by far the larger portion of the expense and difficulty in creating programs is attributable to the development of the structure and logic of the program" and that to protect this would "provide the proper incentive for programmers by protecting their most valuable efforts."[81]

The court addressed the thorny distinction between expression and idea by finding that the purpose or function of the work was the "idea" (and therefore unprotectable) and that anything necessary to effect the function was part of the idea. However, because there were a variety of program structures through which that idea could be expressed, the structure was not a "necessary incident" to the idea, and consequently, could be protected.

In this vein, the courts in the United States have also protected the user interface of a program, defined as the menus (including the structure and organization), the long prompts, the screens on which they appear, the function key assignments, the macro command and language,[82] the organization and sequencing of Nintendo's lock and key security system,[83] and a program's layouts, file names, field definitions, transaction codes, screen displays, and reports.[84] Infringement has been found where two programs were substantially similar in data flow and control flow, and the modules performed the same functions in a similar manner owing to the use of common algorithms, mathematical constants, and formulas.[85]

As this body of case law has developed in the United States, however, the courts appear to have narrowed the protection afforded structure, sequence, and organization. The 1992 decision of the Second Circuit Court of Appeals in *Computer Associates Inc. v. Altai Inc.*[86] developed what has come to be known as the "abstraction-filtration" test, which involves breaking the work into its constituent modules and subroutines, removing from these components all nonprotectable material, and, finally, comparing the "golden nugget" that remains with the allegedly infringing program. In determining what can be protected by copyright, all similarities dictated by the functional demands of the program, as well as programming tools and subroutines in the public domain, are to be ignored. Further, where efficiency of operation limits choices of program structure to a small number, such features are considered part of the "idea" and, therefore, unprotectable. To the extent that this decision limits the rights given to software authors in previous cases,

---

[80] *Whelan Associates, Inc. v. Jaslow Dental Laboratory, Inc. et al.*, 797 F.2d 1222 (1986).

[81] For a fuller discussion, see Ian Kyer "Canadian Copyright Developments: Courts Chart the Boundaries of Computer Copyright," *Computer Law Strategist* 8, No. 10 (February 1992).

[82] *Lotus Development Corporation v. Paperback Software International et al.*, 740 F. Supp. 37 (1990).

[83] *Atari Games Corp. and Tengen Inc. v. Nintendo of America Inc.*, 24 U.S.P.Q. 2d. 1015 (2d Cir., 1992).

[84] *NME Speciality Hospitals Inc. v. Friedman*, Comp. Ind. Lit. Reporter, 11, 665 (D.C.M.J., 1990).

[85] *Gates Rubber Company v. Brando American Inc.*, 24 U.S.P.Q. (2d) 1161 (D. Colo., 1992).

[86] 23 U.S.P.Q. 2d 1241 (2d Cir., 1992).

the court held that the limitations form the proper constitutional balance between protection and free competition.[87]

Critics of "look and feel" protection question whether the legal system should require computer programmers to use different user interfaces or a different structure, sequence, and organization for each product, with the resulting inefficiencies. Those who defend such protection point out the significant value of structure, sequence, and organization, as well as the time and effort that go into developing an original design, all of which is capitalized on by a programmer who copies the work of another, even if using different codes.[88]

American courts have not adopted a uniform approach to "look and feel" cases. The confusion derives, in part, from the fact that the cases are decided by the courts of different circuits, and the issue has yet to come before the Supreme Court. One American observer has commented:

> Overall, the decisions seem to indicate that the pendulum is swinging away from the broad scope of copyright protection awarded in some cases following *Whelan* . . . . They tend to bring software copyright analysis more into line with the analysis for traditional copyright works. This gives more opportunity for competition in the software industry, but will make it harder for software publishers and their lawyers to determine whether or not there is infringement.[89]

Interestingly, although the United States appears to be restricting the original scope of "look and feel" protection, the United Kingdom has recently adopted the broad protection of *Whelan*, holding in a recent case that a computer program had been infringed even where no code had been copied.[90] In contrast, in a case decided at the same time, a Canadian court adopted the more restricted approach of the *Computer Associates v. Altai* decision. The Canadian court refused to find that there had been infringement, although the program was markedly similar in function, appearance, and operation to the original work, but was written in a different programming language and was not a literal copy of the first program.[91] It remains to be seen how the courts in these countries will resolve the balancing act between protecting investment and providing opportunity for competition. What is clear, however, is that the rights of software developers in the structure, sequence, and organization of their programs are valuable assets they will strive to protect.

Personality Rights.   Many societies even give protection to a celebrity's name, voice, and likeness for the reason that the celebrity's image or personality is an asset of economic value to its owner, which others should not be permitted to appropriate and exploit. In the United States, a celebrity has a common-law right of publicity, sometimes codified in legislation, that allows him or her to control the commercial exploitation of his or her personality. The right may be transferred, licensed, and, in some states, passed on as part of the estate of deceased celebrity.

---

[87] Hillary E. Pearson, "Is Whelan Losing Its Teeth?—Recent U.S. Cases on Software Copyright," *Computer Law and Practice* 9, No. 1 (1993): 25.

[88] For a fuller discussion, see Canadian Copyright Develoopments, supra, note 81.

[89] Pearson, "Is Whelan Losing Its Teeth?", supra, note 87.

[90] *John Richardson Computers Ltd. v. Flanders and Chemtec Ltd.* (Feb. 1983).

[91] *Delrina Corporation v. Triolet Systems Inc. and Duncome* (1993), 47 C.P.R. (3d) 1 (Ont. G\Ct. Gen. Div.).

Rock stars, such as Bette Midler[92] and Tom Waits,[93] and television personalities, such as Vanna White,[94] have been able to prevent others from using their images or evoking their identities to advertise a product or service. In Canada, the nature and scope of this right have not yet been fully resolved, but a well-known football player[95] and a champion water skier[96] were permitted by the courts to prevent the use of their images. The rationale for such decisions was that the celebrities had expended time, effort, and money to develop their images and that the results of these efforts should not be appropriated without their consent.

The Protection of Intellectual Property Through Specialized Tribunals, Societies, and Private Enforcement Agencies.   The increasing importance of intellectual property rights has led many jurisdictions to recognize the need for judges with technical expertise to understand the complex issues in litigating intellectual property disputes. A recent report stressed the need for well-qualified judges knowledgeable in intellectual property, in light of the significant economic value that these assets may represent.[97] In 1972 Canada created the Federal Court to hear, among other things, trademark, patent, and copyright cases. Despite its existence, one Federal Court judge, in a frank articulation of the difficulties that a largely generalist judiciary faces when required to decide highly technical and complex patent matters, has said that a specialized patent tribunal should be created, at least to decide cases including patents for nonmechanical inventions:

> When one considers the apparent silliness of a trial by a judge who is utterly unschooled in the scientific substance of a patent, hearing conflicting testimony of so-called experts who speak the antithesis of scientific verity, and lawyers who have been engaged in the particular case for years before the trial, one knows that this field cries out for reform. It wastes the scarce resources of the court, which is not configured for getting at the truth of arcane scientific contradictions. A judge unschooled in the arcane subject is at difficulty to know which of the disparate, solemnly-mouthed and hotly-contended "scientific verities" is, or are, plausible. Is the eminent scientific expert with the shifty eyes and poor demeanor the one whose "scientific verities" are not credible? Cross-examination is said to be the great engine for getting at the truth, but when the unschooled judge cannot perceive the truth, even if he or she ever hears it, among all the chemical or other scientific baffle-gab, is it not a solemn exercise? Reform is much needed in the field of non-mechanical patents litigation.[98]

Recognizing the same problem, the United States established a new court in 1982, with judges familiar with patents specifically to handle patent appeals, rather than allow such appeals to go to the Circuit Courts of Appeal. Until then, Circuit Court judges tended to dismiss patents as invalid just to speed the process. Between 1959 and 1975, three of every four patents in Circuit Courts were ruled invalid or not infringed. The impact of the new

---

[92] *Midler v. Ford Motor Co.*, 849 F.(2d) 460 (9th Cir., 1988).

[93] *Waites v. FritoLay Inc.*, 978 F.(2d) 1093 (9th Cir., 1992).

[94] *White v. Samsung Electronics America Inc.*, 23 U.S.P.Q. 2d 1583 (9th Cir. July 29, 1992).

[95] *Krouse v. Chrysler Canada* (1972), 5 C.P.R. (2d) 30 (Ont. H.C.) rev'd (1974), 13 C.P.R. (2d) 28 (C.A.).

[96] *Athans v. Canadian Adventure Camps* (1978), 34 C.P.R. (2d) 126 (Ont. H.C.).

[97] Gordon F. Henderson, *Intellectual Property, Litigation, Legislation, and Education: A Study of the Canadian Intellectual Property and Litigation System* (Ottawa: Consumer and Corporate Affairs Canada, 1991).

[98] *Unilever plc. v. Procter & Gamble Inc.* (Federal Court Trial Division, February 9, 1993, unreported).

patent court has been to increase the value of patents. Now, three of every four patents is found to be valid or to have been infringed.[99]

Similarly, in the United Kingdom, the Patent County Court was set up in 1991 to provide a cheaper forum than the High Court for patent and design disputes between "small and medium size enterprises." Its procedure differs from that of the High Court by requiring more detailed pleadings, in which the parties set out their respective interpretations of the claims, explain how the defendant's product infringes or does not infringe, and analyze the prior art in some detail if the defendant alleges invalidity. The majority of decisions of this court so far have been in favor of the patentee.[100]

In the private realm, 10 major food companies, including General Mills, Kellogg, and PepsiCo, have signed an agreement to mediate intellectual problems with a neutral intermediary if they cannot resolve such problems between themselves within 30 days. If the dispute is not settled by the mediator, the parties can resort to court action. The participating companies hope not only to avoid high litigation costs, but also to avoid losing consumer goodwill if product packaging and marketing strategies need to be altered after lengthy court battles. The companies also hope to reduce industry friction that can be exacerbated by litigation.[101]

The formation of these specialized tribunals is an acknowledgement that intellectual property rights are valuable assets and that the adjudication of disputes involving such rights must be handled by judges who understand the technical issues involved. The tendency of these courts to uphold the validity of the intellectual property at issue increases the value of the intellectual property.

In the field of copyright, licensing bodies, known as "societies," have been formed to administer collectively the rights of copyright owners and maximize their economic value. Copyright owners become members of the society and authorize it to grant blanket licenses to users of their copyrighted works in return for royalties. This arrangement benefits both parties, allowing users quick and easy access to copyrighted material, while permitting creators to exercise rights that could not be effectively administered individually and to obtain remuneration for the use of their assets. It also eliminates drawn-out negotiations to determine royalty payments and provides the mechanisms to collect and distribute royalties and to commence copyright infringement suits when necessary.

Societies grant licenses of performing, mechanical, and synchronization rights in musical works, the rights to reproduce photographs, and the rights to photocopy literary works. The American Society of Composers, Authors and Publishers (ASCAP) was established in the United States in 1914. The equivalent in England is the Performing Rights Society (PRS), which was formed the next year, and in Canada, the society now known as the Composers, Authors and Publishers Association of Canada (CAPAC) was formed in the 1930s. These performing-rights societies were created in response to the rapid growth in the public performance of musical works. Over the years, they have come to represent copyright holders for virtually all music that is publicly performed. These associations have reciprocal contracts with other similar societies throughout the world. They use blanket license agreements with movie theaters, the organizers of public concerts, bars and night clubs, and "elevator music" and "supermarket music" companies, among others.

---

[99] "Flash of Genius," supra, note 60.

[100] *Linklater & Paines Intellectual Property News*, No. 11 (September, 1992).

[101] Ellen Joan Pollock, "Food Concerns Opt to Mediate Not Litigate," *The Wall Street Journal* (28 January, 1993) B1.

Until the late 1970s, copyright societies were generally limited to dealing with problems of the public performance of musical works. Then a number of organizations were formed to deal with the issue of photocopying. In 1978, the Copyright Clearance Centre was created by the Association of American Publishers and the Authors League of America. This voluntary association has developed the annual authorization service, which provides blanket copying licenses to participating corporations. Other organizations were formed in Europe in the 1980s. In Canada, the reprography collective is known as "CANCOPY."[102]

Canada has recently amended its Copyright Act to permit copyright societies to be used with respect to all forms of copyrighted works.[103] To qualify as a licensing body under the statute, the organization must collectively represent copyright holders in the administration of their copyrights. This collective administration must include the operation of a licensing scheme setting out the classes for which the copyrighted works may be used and the royalties, terms, and conditions on which the collective agrees to license the various exclusive rights granted to copyright holders under the Copyright Act.

As in the case of pharmaceutical patents, the new copyright legislation has attempted to introduce a system of checks and balances. To ensure that the collective exercise of rights does not lead to abusive practices, the Canadian Copyright Act established the Copyright Board,[104] a regulatory body vested with the authority to set rates after hearing interested parties.

Another reflection of the growing economic importance of intellectual property rights is the proliferation of private enforcement agencies and organizations to police intellectual property rights. Examples in the software industry include the Federation Against Software Theft (FAST), the Canadian Alliance Against Software Theft (CAAST), the Business Software Alliance, and the Software Publishers Association. The recently formed Canadian Alliance for the Responsible Use of Font Software is concerned with unauthorized copying of typefaces. These organizations are self-styled "software police," publishing information regarding copyright infringement and spearheading legal action on behalf of their members against pirates.

INTERNATIONAL DEVELOPMENTS

On the international level, as well as in the marketplace and the courts, the protection of intellectual property has become an important issue. The negotiations on "Trade-Related Aspects of Intellectual Property Rights Including Trade in Counterfeit Goods" (TRIPs) at the Uruguay Round of the GATT talks represent the first time that intellectual property rights have been addressed in the context of trade negotiations. Following this trend NAFTA unlike the earlier Free Trade Agreement between the United States and Canada, specifically addresses intellectual property rights.[105] NAFTA members must amend their intellectual property laws to offer protection that equals or exceeds the standards required by the GATT. Various directives from the Council of the European Community illustrate a similar concern with the harmonization of intellectual property laws among member states to reduce nontariff barriers to trade.

---

[102] Ian Kyer and Christopher Erickson, "Copyright Law in Canada," in Steven M. Stewart, *International Copyright and Neighbouring Rights.*, 2d ed., vol. 2 (London: Butterworths, 1993).

[103] *Copyright Act* (Canada), § 70, supra, note 17.

[104] Ibid, § 66.

[105] North American Free Trade Agreement, Chapter 17.

GATT.   The most recent round of negotiations, known as the Uruguay Round of the General Agreement on Tariffs and Trade, commenced on September 20, 1986. The Uruguay Round of negotiations resulted in a variety of trade agreements, including the TRIPs agreement, which contains provisions relating to all aspects of intellectual property.

The fact that an important trade agreement incorporates provisions dealing with intellectual property demonstrates the growing recognition of intellectual property as an important source of national revenue. The United States has pushed to put TRIPs on the table at the Uruguay Round of the GATT to counteract the losses resulting from counterfeiting and pirating. The goal of the TRIPs negotiations is to reach an agreement to establish minimum standards of national and international protection and enforcement of intellectual property rights.

The GATT proposals cover a large spectrum of intellectual property rights, including trademarks, geographic indicators, industrial designs and patents, copyrights, semiconductor integrated circuits, and trade secrets. The GATT proposals require each member country to provide national treatment to nationals of other members. Internal and border measures are mandated, including provisions for blocking infringing goods at borders, which the countries will have to implement. The agreement specifically does not introduce the doctrine of exhaustion, which would lessen the protection of the intellectual property down the distribution chain by the "exhaustion" of the rights after the first sale, although it contains a statement of principle that enforcement procedures are to be applied in such a manner as to avoid the creation of barriers to legitimate trade.

A major advantage of a multilateral agreement on intellectual property is the opportunity to enforce the obligations of each member through effective dispute settlement mechanisms. The GATT's surveillance and dispute settlement procedures would put teeth into the enforcement of intellectual property rights. The existing body for overseeing the international protection of intellectual property, the World Intellectual Property Office, does not have such mechanisms. The adoption of TRIPs would allow trade sanctions to be imposed against other GATT member nations for violation of the TRIPs agreement provisions.

The TRIPs agreement has helped to establish the significance of intellectual property in the world. The many years of steady work by intellectual property advocates around the world has raised world consciousness regarding the importance of intellectual property as a legitimate aspect of world trade.

NAFTA.   NAFTA was signed by Canada, Mexico, and the United States in December 1992 and later ratified by the legislature of each country. Unlike the earlier Free Trade Agreement between Canada and the United States,[106] NAFTA contains a chapter exclusively dealing with intellectual property. Members of NAFTA must offer intellectual property protection equal to or exceeding the requirements of GATT. Like GATT, NAFTA covers trademarks, patents, industrial designs, copyrights and related rights, semiconductor chip protection, and trade secrets. Members are required to adopt, as minimum standards, four international intellectual property conventions: the Paris Convention, the Berne Convention, the Geneva Convention for the Protection of Producers of

---

[106] The Free Trade Agreement entered into force on January 1, 1989. It is replaced by NAFTA.

Phonograms Against Unauthorized Duplication of the Phonograms,[107] and the International Convention for the Protection of New Varieties of Plants.[108]

NAFTA adopts the principle of national treatment. Detailed provisions dealing with enforcement and dispute settlement are prescribed, including mechanisms for the enforcement of intellectual property rights at international borders. The agreement contains no provision relating to the doctrine of exhaustion, and therefore the status quo is not altered. However, NAFTA requires the members to ensure that enforcement measures do not themselves become barriers to legitimate trade.

Among the more significant provisions of NAFTA are the creation of a rental right for computer programs and sound recordings, the elimination of special patent regimes for particular products, the end of patent rights discrimination based on national origin (requiring Canada to eliminate compulsory licensing requirements), and protection for encrypted program-carrying satellite signals.

The European Community.   The European Community has in place various measures to standardize the protection of intellectual property throughout the Community. The European Patent Office already exists, making it possible to file a single patent application that covers all of the member states. The Treaty of Rome,[109] in contrast to the provisions in GATT and NAFTA, endorses the principle of exhaustion, which prevents the use of intellectual property rights from restricting the flow of goods from one member state to another (although there is no similar provision respecting goods imported from outside the Community).

As part of the goal of establishing a single market, the European Community Council has introduced various directives requiring member states to harmonize their intellectual property laws. Trademark laws and software protection are among the issues that have been addressed.

The European Community Directive to harmonize the laws relating to the protection of trademarks was adopted by the member states in December 1988.[110] The Directive was to be implemented originally by December 1991, but the deadline was extended until December 1992. This deadline was not met, and several member states have failed to introduce the necessary legislation to their respective parliaments. They are in breach of their obligations under the Directive. This matter is not yet resolved.

Under the present system, a trademark owner must apply to register its mark in each jurisdiction within the European Community, complying with national rules about what is registrable, the procedures to be followed, and the level of protection granted. As a result, it is often impossible for an owner to obtain protection for the same trademark in all Community countries and to adopt a single marketing plan. The Directive introduces a

---

[107] The Convention for the Protection of Producers of Phonograms Against Unauthorized Duplication of Their Phonograms, known as the Geneva Convention, was opened for signature on October 29, 1971. It intended to address the increasing problem of record and tape piracy. For the text, see Leaffer, *International Treaties*, supra, note 14 at p. 385.

[108] The International Convention for the Protection of New Varieties of Plants confers patent or similar protection to the breeder of a new plant variety. The Convention was completed in 1961 and entered into force in 1968. Because a number of countries (including the United States) were not members of the original Convention, it was revised on Ocobter 23, 1978, to take into account various obstacles of substantive law in those states. For text, see Leaffer, *International Treaties*, supra, note 14 at p. 55.

[109] The Treaty of Rome (as amended by the Single European Act, O.J. 1987 L. 169/3 [June 29, 1987]) established the European Economic Community and entered into force on January 1, 1973.

[110] Directive 89/104/EEC.

common set of rules relating to what constitutes a trademark, what should be registrable, whether a mark can coexist with marks already on either the register of the country where the application has been filed, another national register, the Community Trade Mark Register (when it is introduced), or the International Register established under the Madrid Agreement. The Directive addresses the nature of the exclusive rights granted by registration, the limitations on those rights, and the grounds for expunging the mark from a national register. Optional provisions, including those relating to consents to overcome objections based on a prior registration and the licensing of trademarks, are also included. Spain, France, Denmark, Greece, and Italy have implemented the Directive through legislation. Other member states have not yet complied.

The proposed European Community Trade Mark is a parallel development to the harmonization of national trademark laws in European Community member states. When implemented, it will provide a single registration covering the whole of the European Community.[111]

The Council's Directive on the legal protection of computer software is another initiative[112] adopted to deal with the increasing software piracy within the Community. In the preamble to the original proposal, the Commission noted that "the size and growth of the computer industry is such that its importance in the economy of the Community cannot be overemphasized," and that "unless a legal environment is created which affords a degree of protection against the unauthorized reproduction of computer programs that is at least comparable to that given to works such as books and films, research and investment in that vital industry will be stifled as software producers will become increasingly unwilling to invest intellectual effort and financial resources in the creation of programs which can be easily copied."[113]

At the time that the Directive was introduced, there were significant differences between member states in the protection afforded to computer software. The objectives were to prevent computer piracy, promote the free circulation of computer software within the community, and allow industry to take advantage of the single market by harmonizing the law of the member states.

The legal protection of biotechnological inventions and the harmonization of member states' regulations concerning medical devices and pharmaceuticals are among the other intellectual property issues on the table for the Council.

NEW INTELLECTUAL PROPERTY LAWS

Consistent with the policy of affording greater protection to intellectual property rights, many countries have introduced new legislation to protect emerging forms of intellectual property that do not fit into the existing legal categories, often in response to pressures from trading partners. Typically, in countries considering such new legislation, there is a continuing debate about whether old laws should be adopted to take advantage of existing treaties, or whether new sui generis[114] laws should be passed. The emergence of sui generis legislation illustrates the limited ability of the traditional legislative schemes to protect intellectual property and accommodate the technological innovations and discov-

---

[111] Clifford Chance, "The European Software Directive," 1991.

[112] Directive 91/25/EEC.

[113] *Linklater & Paines Intellectual Property News*, November 1992.

[114] The term *sui generis* is a Latin term meaning: "of its own kind or class, i.e., the only one of its own kind; peculiar," defined in *Black's Law Dictionary*. 5th ed. (St. Paul, MN: West Publishing, 1968).

eries of the present age. As an example, copyright legislation in Canada still refers to "records, perforated rolls, cinematograph film or other contrivance by means of which the work may be mechanically performed or delivered."[115] This legislation was not originally intended to deal with such subject matter as computer software and electronic data bases, nor with sophisticated means of reproduction, such as photocopying. Patent legislation, originally intended to protect mechanical and chemical inventors, is not easily applied to protect microorganisms, plant varieties, and higher life forms.

The explosive growth of the computer industry has generated new laws and amendments to protect adequately the investment of developers. Semiconductor chip legislation is one such example. Protection exists in the United States under the Semiconductor Chip Protection Act,[116] which prohibits manufacturers of integrated circuits from incorporating protected topographies and prevents the importation or commercial exploitation of infringing works. The European Community Directive on legal protection of topographies of semiconductor products[117] likewise requires all member states to implement laws barring unauthorized reproduction of protected topographies. Canada has recently enacted new legislation, known as the Integrated Circuit Topographies Act,[118] in response to pressure from the United States, whose statute grants protection for foreigners only if their country of origin has adopted similar legislation.

Special protection for computer data bases is also on legislators' agendas. The European Community has issued a draft Directive on the protection of data bases, providing that electronic data bases will be protected by copyright law.[119] Also proposed is a 10-year "unfair extraction" right, which would protect the contents of an electronic data base even though they lack sufficient originality of selection or arrangement to qualify for copyright protection. This protection is to be available only reciprocally. Concern about this approach has been one factor influencing the World Intellectual Property Organization to propose a protocol to the Berne Convention to deal with computer data bases.[120]

Constant developments in biotechnology have challenged the traditional principles of patent law and, in some cases, have led to new legislation. The United States and Canada have introduced new legislation protecting plant breeders' rights, permitting breeders of new plant varieties to hold exclusive rights and receive royalties when these varieties are sold.[121] As in the case of patents, protecting plant breeders' rights has the objective of promoting innovations, while at the same time encouraging their early disclosure by granting an exclusive right in qualifying innovations for a limited period.

In most countries that grant plant breeders' rights, the laws derive from the International Convention for the Protection of New Plant Varieties[122], which was first established in the early 1960s by a number of European countries with the objective of promoting consistent protection of new plant varieties in member states. The plant breeding indus-

---

[115] *Copyright Act*, supra, note 17, § 2.

[116] Semiconductor Chip Protection Act, 17 U.S.C.A., c. 9.

[117] Directive 87/54/EEC, as extended by Directives 93/16/EEC and 93/17/EEC.

[118] Integrated Circuit Topographies Act (Canada), S.C. 1990, c. 37.

[119] The text of the European Commission's proposal for the draft Directive on Data Bases appears in the *Official Journal* C 156 (June 23, 1992). The European Parliament approved the Commission's proposal subject to certain amendments, some of which were accepted by the Commission. The amended proposal is currently before the Council for a common position.

[120] Clifford Chance, "Data Protection," 1989.

[121] *Plant Breeders' Rights Act* (Canada) S.C. 1990, c. 20.

[122] Joy D. Morrow, "Plant Breeders' Rights: An International Perspective," *Canadian Intellectual Property Review* (September 1992): 34.

try, particularly in Europe, lobbied for an international system to protect plant materials, and it was this pressure that ultimately resulted in the diplomatic conference that gave rise to the Convention.[123]

In most member states, subject matter capable of protection includes any new clone, line, hybrid, or genetic variant of a plant. To be protectable, a plant variety must be clearly distinguishable by one or more important characteristics from any other variety; it must be uniform within the group; and it must remain true to its description after repeated reproduction from generation to generation. The plant breeders' rights grant to the breeder the exclusive right to sell the reproductive material of the variety and to produce such material for the purpose of selling it. Some member countries have enacted a "farmer's exemption," permitting farmers to use seed of protected varieties that they have saved from a previous year's crop.

New methods of exploiting intellectual property may also spur new legislative amendments. For example, as intellectual property is increasingly becoming the most valuable asset of many companies, it is being used as collateral to secure loans. Accordingly, the registration of security interests (i.e., the legal vehicle used to collateralize property) against registered trademarks, copyrights, patents, and industrial designs has become a crucial concern to existing and prospective creditors. Although the current practice in some intellectual property offices is to allow registration of security interests, many questions persist about the effect of such registrations and whether additional registrations should be made in accordance with other legislative schemes, such as the Uniform Commercial Code in the United States or the Personal Property Security Act or equivalent legislation in Canada.[124] If intellectual property is truly going to be effective as collateral against which to secure financing, new legislation may be required to create a system for registering security interests in intellectual property. Committees of intellectual property lawyers are currently studying this issue in Canada, with a view to recommending legislative action.

As a result, in part, of the harmonization of intellectual property laws and the pressure from the United States to upgrade enforcement procedures, several developing countries have implemented new and improved intellectual property laws. The following list does not purport to be an exhaustive survey, but is illustrative of this trend:

- Mexico enacted a new Industrial Property Law in June 1991, which completely revamped the Mexican industrial property regime and signaled a significant step forward in Mexico's efforts to join the global economy.[125]

- Indonesia passed a new trademark law in August 1992, which came into effect on April 1, 1993. The new law enacted a new "first to file system," protection for service marks, applications based on proposed use, and cancellation actions, as well as recognition of Paris Convention priority.[126]

- Vietnam adopted new trademark legislation in March 1993, under which a "first to file system" was adopted. Vietnam is also considering new rules to remove trade-

---

[123] Ibid.

[124] Colleen Spring Zimmerman, Lise Bertrand, and Leslie Dunlop "Intellectual Property in Secured Transactions," *Canadian Intellectual Property Review* (December 1991): 74.

[125] John McKnight and Carlos Muggenburg, "Mexico's Industrial Property and Copyright Laws: Another Step Towards Linkage with a Global Economy," *International Business Lawyer* (December 1992): 573.

[126] *United States Trademark Association Bulletin*, 48, No. 9 (31 March, 1993).

marks wrongfully registered by trademark pirates and provide protection for famous marks.[127]

- Taiwan has approved sections of a new copyright agreement with the United States and revised local copyright laws to prohibit parallel imports, except in special cases, and to make it illegal to import copyrighted material without permission of the copyright owner. In addition, a task force to ensure greater enforcement of intellectual property rights protection was established to study the bringing of criminal charges and administrative punishments against software counterfeiters.[128]
- Honduras is considering new trademark and patent legislation.[129]
- The republics of the former Soviet Union, including Azerbaijan, Ukraine, and Kazakhstan, are enacting new trademark laws.[130]
- Bulgaria has enacted a new patent law offering protection in line with Western patent laws and is considering draft copyright legislation.[131]
- China has introduced a new patent law and is considering new trademark legislation.[132]
- Brazil has introduced draft patent legislation allowing patent protection for pharmaceutical products and processes.[133]

CONCLUSIONS—COUNTERTRENDS

As noted in this Overview's introduction, the increased international protection afforded intellectual property has generated various controversies. One debate focuses on the appropriate scope of protection that society should afford to intellectual property rights holders. Does the granting of monopoly rights to creators confer a benefit upon society through stimulating research, development, and innovation? At what point may this benefit be countered by losses resulting from monopolies and a stifling of competition?

In the new information economy, a good idea is the genesis of every business success story. Does that idea require monopoly protection to be successfully exploited? There is evidence that in many sectors, research and development would continue without monopoly protection afforded to intellectual property rights. Surveys have suggested that competitive pressures and business strategies relating to market structure, as well as the ability to keep valuable technology and information secrets, and the inherent difficulties that rivals may have in duplicating new technology, may be more important than patent protection to induce innovative and technological growth.

Legal borrowing of ideas spawned some of the healthiest industries of the 1980s. One example is the thriving industry that revolved around the manufacture of computer clones. IBM decided not to claim proprietary rights in its system architecture, choosing instead to create an industry standard. As a result, competitors could acquire IBM's operating system from Microsoft and microprocessors from Intel and build what was, in effect, an IBM computer. This decision created an entire industry of IBM-clone manufacturers, including COMPAQ, DELL, and ASI Research. In 1988 the number of IBM clones available in the marketplace far exceeded the number of IBM's own proprietary

---

[127] *United States Trademark Association Bulletin*, 48, No. 9 (31 March, 1993).
[128] *World Intellectual Property Organization Report*, 7, No. 6 (June, 1993).
[129] *United States Trademark Association Report*, 48, No. 7 (8 March, 1993).
[130] *United States Trademark Association Report*, 48, No. 18 (19 April, 1993).
[131] *World Intellectual Property Report*, 7, No. 5.
[132] *United States Trademark Association Report*, 48, No. 9.
[133] *World Intellectual Property Report*, 7, No. 6.

machines. Although this industry is now rife with cutthroat competition, resulting in many bankruptcies, the cause is more likely the market conditions resulting from the current recession, rather than the inability of these companies to assert monopoly intellectual property rights.

There are two possible reactions to increased competition: (1) to seek increased protection for one's valuable ideas and technology or (2) to respond with a policy of increased openness. Many companies have indeed adopted the strategy of publicizing their ideas, thereby gaining leadership of their respective markets. Microsoft, the market leader for personal computer software, has adopted this approach. This company has invested a significant amount of time and effort in explaining how its operating systems work and persuading other companies to adopt its products as standard or to use them under license at modest royalty rates, as a foundation for further innovations. This openness is in striking contrast to the protectionist approach of Apple Computer, which recently sought to protect its competitive advantage by preventing Microsoft from using a similar screen display and common structures.

Adobe has also endorsed the policy of openness. When Microsoft mounted a competitive challenge to Adobe, Adobe's response to the heightened competition was to make public (under license) the technology it had previously kept secret, seeking to set industry standards with its very popular "PostScript" language, describing how text and graphics are laid out on a page. Because it is a standard, companies use PostScript to compose publications inexpensively in their own offices and then send a ready-to-print copy to a commercial publisher for mass production. In seeking to create a standard, Adobe cannot keep its language secret or no one would be able to use it. Instead, Adobe is keeping ahead of its competitors by extending its technology (for example, to cope with color printing), advertising heavily, and diversifying into new technologies for applications software.[134]

Another striking example of this approach is the videocassette recorder industry. Originally there were two players in this market: JVC, which manufactured VHS video recorders, and Sony, which manufactured BETAMAX machines. JVC adopted an open approach, licensing its competitors to manufacture VHS recorders. JVC thereby created an industry standard for VHS, squeezing Sony's BETAMAX, which in fact had been acknowledged to be the better technology, out of the market. Sony itself now manufactures VHS machines.

Examples of industries that have thrived without intellectual property protection are discussed earlier in this chapter. Given the profusion of research currently accomplished by scientists, despite the uncertainty regarding the patentability of multicellular organisms, it is unlikely that denying patents on living organisms would halt biotechnological research. The United States Supreme Court has stated:

> The grant or denial of patents on micro-organisms is not likely to put an end to genetic research. [Furthermore], legislative or judicial fiat as to patentability will not deter the scientific mind from probing into the unknown."[135]

The success of the generic and private-label consumer products against traditional premium brands is another illustration of the success of competitive products that offer an advantage to the public (in this case value and quality), without the benefit of monopoly

---

[134] "Postscript for PostScript," *The Economist* (16 September, 1989).

[135] *Diamond v. Chakrabarty*, supra, note 63 at p. 314.

protection. The more recent trend in United States courts to limit the copyright protection available to the nonliteral elements of computer programs may also create greater opportunities for competition in the industry.

Has the protection of intellectual property gone too far? One commentator[136] has argued that it has, citing in support of his position various court decisions: In the trademark field, trade dress protection has been applied to enjoin fine art posters similar to each other only in artistic style and subject matter despite the prominent display of each artist's name,[137] and weak trademarks have been protected against dilution.[138] In the copyright field, fabric designs have been protected against specifically different designs having the same aesthetic appeal,[139] and music has been protected against the use of electronically altered sound bites (called sampling).[140] In the patent field, patents on computer software and on genetically engineered animals, such as the onco mouse, have generated emotional and ethical debates over the appropriate reach of intellectual property laws. Many business leaders feel ambivalent about the strengthening of intellectual property rights. Although they are interested in obtaining exclusive rights for their creations and inventions, they are concerned that a competitor might already have rights in the same work, of which they may be unaware for years until they are presented with a patent suit.

A case involving a small company, Arrhythmia Research, illustrates the negative impact of overprotecting intellectual property. In most countries, software is protected by copyright. A United States federal court recently upheld Arrhythmia's patent on the calculations its software performed to analyze electrocardiograms for signs of impending heart attack. In so doing, the court effectively knocked down most of the barriers to patenting computer software.[141]

Under patent law, unlike other forms of intellectual property protection, it is no defense against a charge of infringement to show that the inventor came up with an idea independently, without any knowledge of the patented innovation. The Arrhythmia case has alarmed managers in America's booming software industry. They are concerned that many programmers will have devised similar solutions to the same problem, or made the same calculations to solve different problems. Other high-technology industries have similar concerns. In 1990 semiconductor firms were shocked when a basic patent on the microprocessor was awarded to Gilbert Hyatt, an independent inventor who had worked from his home in Los Angeles. Roger Billings, another independent inventor, who spent much of the 1980s working on hydrogen-powered vehicles, claims an equally broad patent on the idea of getting computers to share work over networks. In both cases, royalties worth hundreds of millions of dollars are at stake.[142]

The granting of monopoly rights creates the potential for abuse. One dramatic example is the NutraSweet case, which came before the Canadian Competition Tribunal in

---

[136] William M. Borchard, "Stifling Creating by Overprotecting Intellectual Property," *Trademarks America* (May, 1993).

[137] *Romm Art Creations Ltd. v. Simcha International Inc.*, 786 F. Supp. 1126.

[138] For a discussion of this topic see Elizabeth C. Bannon, "The Growing Risk of Self-Dilution," *The Trademark Reporter*, 82, No. 4 (July/August 1992): 570.

[139] *Peter Pan Fabrics Inc. v. Martin Wiener Corp.*, 274 F.(2d), 487.

[140] *Grand Upright Music Ltd. v. Werner Bros Records, Inc.*, 780 F. Supp. 182.

[141] *Arrhythmia Research Technology v. Lorazonix Corp.*, 958 F.(2d) 1053 (Fed. Cir., 1992).

[142] "Policing Thoughts," *The Economist* (22 August, 1992).

1990.[143] NutraSweet was, at the time, one of two producers of artificial sweetener. Its customers were primarily food and beverage manufacturers who used aspartame as an ingredient in their sugar-free products. Coca-Cola and Pepsi Cola were the largest purchasers of the product. NutraSweet's patents expired in 1987 in Canada, but subsisted to 1992 in the United States.

It was alleged that NutraSweet had used its well-known trademark to prevent competition in the market for aspartame by paying an allowance to customers who displayed the trademark. Exclusive purchasing requirements were imposed on major customers who agreed to use the trademark. The Tribunal also found that NutraSweet had used its United States patents to foreclose competition in Canada, through a series of rebates on exports from the United States intended to induce importers to use only NutraSweet's aspartame in products prepared by them in Canada. These practices prevented or lessened competition substantially.

A judge of the United States Ninth Circuit Court of Appeals has recently made the point that intellectual property rights are imposed at the expense of future creators and of the public at large. Accordingly, legislative schemes for protecting these rights have incorporated a system of checks and balances.

> The relatively short life of patents; the longer, but finite, life of copyrights; copyright's idea-expression dichotomy; the fair use doctrine; the prohibition on copyright facts; the compulsory license of television broadcasts and musical compositions; federal pre-emption of over-broad state intellectual property laws; the nominative use doctrine in trademark law; the right to make sound alike recordings.[144]

In his dissenting reasons, the judge made the following compelling comment on the counterproductive results of too much protection:

> Overprotecting intellectual property is as harmful as underprotecting it. Creativity is impossible without a rich public domain. Nothing today, likely nothing since we tamed fire, is genuinely new; culture, like science and technology, grows by accretion, each new creator building on the works of those who came before. Overprotection stifles the very creative forces it is supposed to nurture.[145]

Thus, although intellectual property rights may translate into economic power and wealth for their owners in the new world economy, at some point society's need for reasonable and fair access to intellectual property will outweigh the owner's proprietary interests. Social policy will intervene to transfer the value of these assets back from the owner to the public. To invoke the image in the title of this Overview, although intellectual property may be a new global currency, it is, indeed, a heavily regulated currency.

Not all countries have endorsed stronger protection for intellectual property. International tensions have arisen between technology-producing nations and those that are importers of technology. The newly industrialized Asian countries and the fledgling economies of Eastern Europe have less than adequate intellectual property protection and enforcement laws. In the new global economy where information is a key economic asset, countries such as the United States are worried that their best ideas and technologies are being stolen by low-cost countries, such as Brazil, China, Thailand, and India.

---

[143] *Director of Investigation Research v. The NutraSweet Company* (1990), 32 C.P.R. (3d) 1 (Comp. Trib.).

[144] Dissenting opinion of Judge Kozinski in *White v. Sampson Electronics America, Inc.*, No. 90-55840, 1993 WL 73915 18 March, 1993.

[145] Ibid.

These countries, in the words of one author, "ride the high seas of trade as intellectual property pirates, duplicating pharmaceuticals, music tapes, videos, books and computer software and selling them for little more than the cost of production."[146] Producers of intellectual property want strong protection and enforcement laws. At the GATT negotiations, the United States is pushing for strong international standards and enforcement mechanisms. As noted above, in response to United States pressure, many countries have introduced national legislation to strengthen and improve their intellectual property protection.

However, although the United States may have succeeded in building a consensus for the concept that intellectual property rights should be enforced worldwide, no one yet agrees on what those rights should be. On the contrary, countries may be moving apart. In the field of data base protection, for example, the United States Supreme Court recently ruled that factual compilations had to have some degree of originality to be copyrighted. Telephone directories, which are merely alphabetical collections of names, cannot be protected.[147] The European Commission, on the other hand, is considering a data base directive that grants protection, in part based on the amount of effort taken to assemble the facts, regardless of originality.[148] A proposed protocol to the Berne Convention would clarify levels of protection and ensure consistency around the world with respect to data bases. Interestingly, the United States and Canada do not support the proposal. They fear that if the exercise fails, those who challenge data base protection will say that existing laws do not protect them.

Developing countries often argue that strengthened intellectual property rights will impede the diffusion of knowledge from developed countries, amounting to a new, sophisticated form of colonialism. These countries objected to the United States proposals at the TRIPs portion of the GATT negotiations as a disguised attempt to preserve for the developed world activities that are knowledge intensive.[149] Many also state that the costs of strengthening their intellectual property systems would be considerable. The main costs would include the administration and enforcement associated with reform, increased payments for foreigners' proprietary knowledge, additional domestic research and development, economic displacement of pirates, and the loss in consumer surplus generated by the anticompetitive aspects of such measures.[150]

Further strengthening patent protection would increase the right of foreign and domestic innovators to charge higher monopoly prices, thereby transferring monopoly rents to foreign producers. There is also a perception that foreign owners might abuse patent rights. If, for example, innovators chose not to supply a product under patent to the local economy, it could not be consumed there nor could it be produced domestically. For this reason, many developing nations have introduced compulsory licensing and do not give national treatment to foreigners in the provision of patents.[151]

---

[146] "Developing World Fears Loss of Sovereignty," *The Globe and Mail* (5 July, 1993).

[147] *Feist Publications Inc. v. Rural Telephone Services Co*.y, 111 S. Ct. 1282.

[148] Chance, "Data Protection,"

[149] Carlos Alberto Primo Braga, "The North-South Debate on Intellectual Property Right," in *Global Rivalry and Intellectual Property: Developing Canadian Strategies*, ed. Murray Smith (Toronto: The Institute for Research on Public Policy, 1991), p. 173.

[150] Keith E. Maskus, "Economic Analysis of Intellectual Property Rights: Domestic and International Dimensions, in *Global Rivalry and Intellectual Property: Developing Canadian Strategies*, ed. Murray Smith (Toronto: The Institute for Research on Public Policy, 1991), p. 119.

[151] "The Developing World Fears Loss of Sovereignty," *The Globe & Mail* (5 July, 1993).

The immediate costs of stronger intellectual property laws in the Third World would be borne by specific sectors, such as the pharmaceutical industry. One report has stated that India's pharmaceutical prices would rise tenfold under the Dunkel proposals. The recent GATT proposals for patenting seeds and other life forms is another critical issue to farmers, particularly in Third World nations. One organization in India, opposed to patent protection for genetic resources, has commented that the Green Revolution—the phenomenon in the 1960s whereby new hybrid seeds and chemical fertilizers boosted Asia's food production—would not have succeeded had farmers been prohibited from saving seeds between harvests. Nearly two-thirds of the 600,000 tons of seeds planted every year in India come from interfarm sales, which would not be permitted under the Dunkel proposals of the GATT. Instead, farmers would have to buy seeds every season from distributors. There is also a fear that patent holders would not be interested in propagating low-value crops, such as millet, and that the entire orientation of research would shift from trying to serve basic human needs to only what is patentable and profitable.[152]

Stronger intellectual property rights will not necessarily benefit everyone. One commentator has argued that the benefits a country extracts from the protection of intellectual property rights will tend to increase as the country develops. The costs associated with reform will be immediately felt, whereas the benefits will take time to materialize. Accordingly, the economic effects of strengthening intellectual property rights will vary significantly across the developing countries.[153] Intellectual property is clearly a more stable currency in developed countries than it is in the developing world.

Although intellectual property rights are becoming increasingly valuable assets strengthened by forces in legislation, the courts, and the marketplace, there are countervailing pressures and tensions that raise the question of where the appropriate level of protection lies. The balance must reflect the interests of creators and inventors, without stifling innovation or resulting in anticompetitive acts.

Germane to this theme is a quotation from a paper presented at a recent Canadian conference entitled *Global Rivalry and Intellectual Property: Developing Canadian Strategies*:

> Our message must be clear: economic development and international trade are enhanced by minimum standards of protection and enforcement of intellectual property rights. Only by establishing such standards can we ensure adequate incentives for the people who do the inventing and the creating. But alone, standards will not protect intellectual property rights. Dispute settlement mechanisms, uniformly applied and enforced, must go hand in hand with standards. They must carry appropriate redress, including clear penalties.
>
> Against this must be balanced society's need for reasonable and fair access to intellectual property. Without that, we will not get the synergistic use of research and development across international borders that will nurture entrepreneurs of technology. Beyond that, remembering that tomorrow's locus of business value is not known, there is the need for regulatory flexibility, . . . adaptability, [and] balance.[154]

---

[152] Ibid.

[153] Markus, "Economic Analysis of Intellectual Property Rights," supra, note 17 at p. 124.

[154] Robert A. Ferchat, "Global Rivalry in Innovation and High Technologies," in *Global Rivalry and Intellectual Property: Developing Canadian Strategies*, ed. Murray Smith (Toronto: The Institute for Research on Public Policy, 1991): p. 25.

PART I

ACCOUNTING, FINANCE, AND VALUATION

CHAPTER 1

QUANTITATIVE METHODS OF VALUING INTELLECTUAL PROPERTY

Russell L. Parr
Gordon V. Smith

AUS Consultants
Valuation Services Group
Moorestown, New Jersey

Intellectual property has taken center stage as the driving force behind wealth creation for individuals, corporations, and nations. For a business, it represents the difference between being a commodity company chasing slim profit margins and a fast-growth company that almost mints money. In our competitive economic environment, profits are eventually driven downward to the lowest level at which a fair return can still be extracted from participation in a mature market. Above-average profits are not often sustainable for long periods. Competitors are quick to recognize and enter high-profit markets. New entrants in such a market force lower selling prices and squeeze profitability. This microeconomic process is efficient in general, but can be a bumpy one for market participants along the way. Attractive profit levels often attract more competitors than the market will bear. When supply exceeds demand, the corresponding reduction in selling prices can make the entire industry unprofitable for continued competition. After the inevitable shakeout the profitability of the industry tends toward the lowest point at which a fair return can still be earned, and a once promising industry evolves into a group of commodity producers. Previous glories of above-average profits become only memories. Keystone intellectual property, however, can change this scenario and deliver sustained superior profits. This chapter discusses the ways in which intellectual property contributes to corporate value and how intellectual property value can be quantified.

1.1 ACTIVE INTELLECTUAL PROPERTY

When above-average profits are generated consistently, intellectual properties are responsible. Active intellectual properties are categorized as those that are directly responsible for generating sustained amounts of above-average profits. Active intellectual properties work to control costs of production or introduce product characteristics that command premium selling prices. Sometimes intellectual property contributes by commanding a premium selling price on a consistent basis, regardless of competitor actions. Well-recognized trademarks are good examples. Two polo shirts of identical material and construction quality can differ in selling price by as much as $25. Customers are consistently willing to pay more money for the Polo logo. The same can be said for other consumer goods, such as Sony televisions, Toro lawn mowers, Maytag kitchen appliances, and some of the Japanese automobile offerings. As long as the entire amount of premium is not spent on image-creating advertisements, net profits are enhanced.

Production costs savings constitute another area in which active intellectual properties are a source of enhanced earnings. Typical production costs involve the purchase of raw materials such as steel, plastics, glass, rubber, chemicals, and other basic product components. Production costs also derive from the wages of manufacturing labor, the cost of production machinery, and the manufacturing facility's utility expenses.

There are various ways that intellectual property can directly contribute to controlling production costs:

1. Reduction in the amount of raw materials used
2. Substitution of lower-cost materials without sacrifice of quality or product performance
3. Increases in the amount of production output per unit of labor input
4. Improved quality, which reduces product recalls
5. Improved production quality, which reduces waste or finished product rejects
6. Reduced use of electricity and other utilities
7. Production methods that control the amount of wear and tear on machinery and thereby reduce the amount of maintenance costs and production downtime for repairs
8. Elimination of manufacturing steps and investment in the machinery previously used in the eliminated process

1.2 PASSIVE INTELLECTUAL PROPERTY

Enhanced profitability can also be derived from passive intellectual property, whereby profits are not directly enhanced by premium selling prices or cost savings. These intellectual properties can be just as valuable, but their contribution to earnings enhancement is more subtle. Even when active contributions to earnings are not present, intellectual property can provide a company with above-average profits. The Quaker State trademark is an example. A dominant position in a market allows the company to enjoy a consistently large sales volume. A quart of Quaker State Motor Oil does not typically sell at a premium price in comparison with other brands. Yet the trademark still contributes greatly to high profits by attracting a loyal following. The large sales volume generated by these customers provides a predictable basis for planning all aspects of manufacturing and operations, which in turn allows the enhancement of profits through optimum efficiency.

When an organization can rely on large and consistent production volumes, operating efficiencies are possible, which generally lead to enhanced profits. Typical synergies associated with large production volumes include the following:

1. Raw materials can be purchased at large-order discounts. Suppliers are likely to offer discounts to customers that place large orders. A cost savings is the result.
2. Manufacturing efficiencies can be introduced throughout each step of the process.
3. Selling expenses can be more controllable, with fewer sales people covering large accounts.

4. Retail efficiencies can include special arrangements with distributors or discounts in the purchase of retailers' shelf space.

5. Regulation and compliance costs can be spread over a larger production base, along with other fixed overhead costs.

6. Large volumes can allow companies to provide utility companies with guaranteed energy purchases, which may be obtained at a bulk rate discount.

1.3 EMERGENCE OF INTELLECTUAL PROPERTY EXPLOITATION STRATEGIES

Strategic alliances will dominate the corporate landscape far into the future as the primary strategy for creating corporate value. At the core of these strategies will be intellectual property—especially technology and trademarks. Licensing deals and joint ventures are becoming the dominant strategies for optimization of intellectual property exploitation.

Intellectual properties, such as patented technology and world class trademarks, are at the very core of corporate achievement. The success of Microsoft has nothing to do with buildings or manufacturing equipment. The foundation of the company's success is the intellectual property associated with the disk operating system (DOS) software. Similarly, it does not matter how many sewing machines are owned by Ralph Lauren until he comes up with another design to which he affixes the Polo trademark.

These intellectual properties capture huge market shares, command premium prices, and hold customer loyalty. They are also in scarce supply and expensive to create. Companies that possess such assets will grow and prosper. Those without access to intellectual property will stagnate for a while in low-profit commodity businesses and eventually fade out of existence.

D. Bruce Merrifield, professor of entrepreneurial management, the Wharton School of the University of Pennsylvania, explained that wealth is no longer derived from possessing physical resources:

> Wealth no longer can be measured primarily in terms of ownership of fixed physical assets that can be obsolete in a few years. . . . Wealth instead will be measured, increasingly, in terms of ownership of (or time-critical access to) knowledge-intensive high value-added, technology-intensive systems.[1]

Of special interest is Merrifield's parenthetical mention of the time-sensitive nature of intellectual property. Not only do companies need such knowledge-based assets, but they need them right now. Product life cycles are shortening, and new products must be introduced more frequently. Less time is available between product introductions, and so time has become one of the primary forces driving the trend toward strategic alliances. Time is also a major force that drives intellectual property value, royalty rates, and joint venture equity splits.

(a) Corporate Value Derived from Intellectual Property.   A comparison of stock market values with accounting book values for selected companies indicates that the investment

---

[1] D. Bruce Merrifield, "Economics in Technology Licensing," *Les Nouvelles: The Journal of the Licensing Executive Society* (June 1992).

Company	Price per Share	Book Value per Share	Price as a Multiple of Book Value
Merck & Company	$35.38	$4.21	8.4
Microsoft Corporation	$92.50	$8.04	11.5
Coca-Cola Company	$42.63	$2.99	14.3

Exhibit 1.1 Intellectual property companies.

community recognizes the value of intellectual properties.[2] Expenditures that are made for land, factory buildings, office headquarters, truck fleets, and manufacturing equipment are all capitalized and presented as assets on the balance sheet. Funds spent to acquire or build these assets become part of the equity of the company to the extent that their value exceeds liabilities. Stock prices typically include the value of these assets. A question arises, however, about the extent to which the market price of a stock reflects the intellectual properties of trademarks and technology. Just as for fixed assets, funds are expended to build trademarks through advertising. Other funds are used to create trade secrets and technology through research and development efforts. Although these expenditures are not recorded on the balance sheet, the assets are indeed quite real. Nonetheless, the market recognizes these assets and reflects their value in stock prices. When valuable technology, trademarks, and other intellectual properties are part of an unregulated business, they contribute to the earnings of the company far above the contribution of the fixed assets. Stock prices reflect this earnings power and trade above the book value of the stock, sometimes substantially.

Stock prices for three companies possessing significant intellectual property, as well as a ratio of the stock price to the accounting book value of each company, are presented in Exhibit 1.1. *Book value* is the amount of monetary and fixed assets associated with each share of stock, but omits the value of intellectual property. The stock prices trade at multiples of book value for the companies listed. This phenomenon does not exist simply because investors like the names of these companies, but because they recognize the intellectual property value of the companies not reflected in the accounting book value.

Microsoft Corporation is a worldwide personal computer software company possessing leading operating systems software. The Coca-Cola soft-drink company owns the most famous trademark in the world. Merck & Company is a pharmaceutical company possessing drug patents, FDA approvals, and the finest research capabilities.

(b) Corporate Value Delivered by Trademarks. A regression analysis of advertising expenditures was conducted to see whether the market recognizes the long-term value of trademarks that are being created and maintained by advertising expenditures.[3] The analysis compared the market-to-book-value ratio of selected companies with the amounts spent on advertising. Analysts found that advertising expenditures are seen as asset-building investments that deserve recognition in the stock price. Companies that spend the most on advertising are either creating or maintaining valuable trademarks. It

---

[2] Russell L. Parr, *Investing in Intangible Assets: Finding and Profiting from Hidden Corporate Value* (New York: John Wiley & Sons, 1991), p. 52.
[3] Ibid.

follows that companies spending the most money have some of the best-known names. The question is, Do well-known trademarks contribute to stock performance? The answer is definitely yes.

Philip Morris recently provided a strong example of how brand names and stock prices intermingle. Many of the leveraged buy-outs of the 1980s involved companies that possessed the most widely known brands. The huge prices paid for these companies ($25 billion for RJR Nabisco) were partially justified by a belief that the acquired brands could be managed more aggressively, meaning that product prices could be raised faster. This tactic worked for a while; however, consumers will only pay so much, and not pay a penny more, to keep an "old friend" brand product around the house. A modest premium is tolerable, but the price ceiling can quickly be reached when alternative products of equal utility are available. Enter quality generics and house brands.

In an attempt to thwart market share advances of discount cigarettes, Philip Morris recently announced a 20% price cut of its premier Marlboro brand cigarettes. Discount cigarettes have demonstrated tremendous growth, currently at 36% of the market from a standing-still start in 1981, with some analysts predicting a 50% market share by the end of the decade. The price difference for a pack of cigarettes is substantial. House brands are priced at $1.00, whereas premium brands such as Marlboro were priced at $2.40 a pack. The price cut by Philip Morris is expected to reduce pretax tobacco profits by $2 billion from the $5.2 billion it earned last year. In response to the announcement investors pushed the stock downward by 23% in one day, and Philip Morris lost nearly $13 billion of value—all of which is considered to be a reduction in the value of the brand name. The Marlboro brand will still sell at a premium over discount cigarettes and will surely retain a large number of brand-loyal consumers. However, an upper boundary for the price that consumers are willing to pay for mystique and image has apparently been found. Jack Trout, a marketing consultant, told *The Wall Street Journal*, "This shows that even the biggest and strongest brands in the world are vulnerable."[4] The stock price of Philip Morris continues to reflect the strength of the Marlboro brand.

(c) Corporate Value Delivered by Technology.   Another example, using research and development (R&D) expenditures, confirms that the marketplace reflects the value of intellectual property in stock prices. A regression analysis of R&D spending for selected pharmaceutical companies was performed with the market-to-book-value ratio for the same companies.[5] As spending levels grow, the market rewards the company price with a higher market-to-book multiple—not because investors reward endless spending, but because valuable intellectual properties are being created.

The primary benefit derived from the continuous nurturing of intellectual properties is best exemplified by the technology of the pharmaceutical industry. An analysis of six pharmaceutical companies showed that continued support of research efforts is rewarded. The number of patents awarded to these companies when compared with the 10-year compounded rate of return earned by investors shows that superior investment returns are associated with the research efforts that yielded patents.

Huge value comes from possessing proprietary intellectual property. Without it, all that remains is an idle manufacturing plant where employees aimlessly wander.

---

[4] "Cigarette Burn: Price Cut on Marlboro Upsets Rosy Notions About Tobacco Profits," *The Wall Street Journal*, 5 April 1993, p. 1.

[5] Parr, *Investing in Intangible Assets*, p. 55.

1.4 FACTORS THAT DRIVE STRATEGIC ALLIANCES: TIME, COST, RISK

Companies typically seek to expand product lines, increase market share, minimize new product development costs, expand market opportunities internationally, and reduce business risks. They seek to create corporate value for investors. Intellectual property, however, is even more important. Without intellectual property profits are low, growth is lacking, and corporate value is lost. Corporate managers realize today more than ever that access to intellectual property is key to their ability to create corporate value and, more important, essential to continued corporate survival. The forces driving the licensing and joint venturing of intellectual property include time savings, cost controls, and risk reduction.

(a) Too Expensive on Your Own.   Even the largest companies cannot fund all the intellectual property programs that they may desire. Research programs can run into hundreds of millions of dollars annually, and trademark costs can reach billions of dollars. A major force behind the desire to form strategic alliances is the high level of investment needed to create new intellectual properties. The following list gives an indication of the amounts required to create, acquire, or protect keystone intellectual property:

- Pharmaceutical companies spend almost $250 million to develop and commercialize a new drug.
- Hoffman LaRoche paid $300 million to Cetus Corporation for the polymerase chain reaction technology.
- Philip Morris spends more than $2 billion annually on advertising programs to support the continuing recognition of its portfolio of brand names.
- A film producer paid $9 million for the television rights to the new book *Scarlet*.

One of the first major joint ventures of the 1990s was the combination of pharmaceutical product lines from DuPont with the distribution network of Merck & Company. The new joint venture company, DuPont-Merck, is equally owned by the two companies. DuPont had a product line of drugs but needed help with international distribution. The time and cost required to create its own network of sales staff was a formidable obstacle to fast growth and return on the research effort that DuPont had in the new drug line. Part of DuPont's worries included the remaining patent life associated with some of their drug products. By the time a self-created distribution network could be established, some of the valuable products would be off-patent. Full exploitation of patents required that sales be maximized during the premium price years before generic products hit the market. DuPont needed a way to tap its full market potential—fast.

Merck has annual sales of more than $6.5 billion. It also has one of the largest research and development budgets in the world. Even so, Merck has limitations as to the number of new drugs it can discover, investigate, develop, and commercialize. Access to a new line of already commercialized products was a great attraction for Merck.

The DuPont-Merck joint venture saved DuPont both time and money. It gave this company immediate access—a vital point made by D. Bruce Merrifield—to an international distribution network. Simultaneously, Merck gained immediate access to a whole new product line that would have cost enormous amounts of time and money to develop. This joint venture is a classic case of how the factors of time and cost drive strategic alliances founded on access to intellectual property. It also illustrates how strategic combinations of key intellectual property can reduce the investment risk associated with new ventures. If DuPont had attempted to build its own international distribution network, the cost would have been high, the time needed long, and there was no assurance that the company would successfully construct a network that could move the goods. Merck enjoyed a reduction in investment risk by gaining access to the profits associated with the DuPont product line. If Merck had embarked on its own plan to duplicate the DuPont product line, there was no assurance that it would have been completely successful. Furthermore, there was the risk that the Merck product line could have ultimately infringed on the DuPont product line. The two companies saved research funds, gained immediate access to commercialized intellectual property, and reduced business risk. Judy Lewent, chief financial officer at Merck & Company, told *The Wall Street Journal* that the Merck-Dupont deal "added about a third to our research capacity."[6]

The cost to establish and maintain first-class trademarks is no different. Huge sums of money are required, and customer recognition takes time. One of the first mega-launches of a new product in the cosmetics industry was Yves Saint Laurent's 1978 Opium party to introduce his new fragrance. In attendance were Cher, Truman Capote, several BBC correspondents, the crew of *60 Minutes*, and leaders of the fashion industry. The party cost $250,000, which in 1978 was a staggering amount for a single party to launch a new product. The total launch budget was $500,000. It seems that those were inexpensive times; similar launch budgets now range between $20 and $25 million.

(b) Impossibility of Mastering All Necessary Tools.   A battery that stores electricity mechanically instead of chemically may be the breakthrough needed to make electric-powered automobiles a reality. Conventional chemical-based batteries currently available have a range of potential of 100 miles at the most. The new technology, however, may possibly power a car for 600 miles on a single charge. This innovation is the product of American Flywheel Systems, a company composed of scientists formerly of the Environmental Protection Agency and military aerospace researchers. The new battery is referred to as a flywheel electromechanical battery, which stores energy kinetically. It operates on the same principle that drives the ancient potter's wheel. A heavy mass rotates at a very high speed inside a vacuum enclosure, suspended by magnetic bearings and controlled by sophisticated electronics.

The first electric car was created 100 years ago, but its chemical batteries required frequent recharging. The old batteries also involved toxic wastes, subjected other car components to corrosives, and introduced the potential for explosion. Flywheel batteries were studied in the 1970s but could not be perfected until recently. For the flywheel battery to become a reality, advanced technological development in three separate fields of science were required: composite materials, computers, and electromagnetics.

A confluence of these three critical technologies was needed to make the flywheel battery a viable technology. Lightweight but strong materials, such as graphite, DuPont's Kevlar, the Japanese-made Technora, and fused silica, have recently come into being. In 1990 the Army tested a flywheel battery that used graphite components having a tensile strength of 52,000 pounds per square inch. Graphite now available has a tensile strength of 1 million pounds per square inch. The second critical breakthrough has occurred in computer power. Faster computers allow the performance of millions of calculations and

---

[6] "Financial Prescriptions for Mighty Merck," *The Wall Street Journal,* 30 June 1992, p. A17.

the simulation of thousands of prototypes. This development allows scientists to turn ideas into working machines more quickly. The third direct scientific advance involved the development of magnetic bearings. The electromagnetic fields they support allow objects to spin in vacuums without friction.

All of these technologies are needed for one product idea. But what company can master all the necessary science alone? None—and that is why we are seeing more strategic alliances.

The critical technologies that will cause extensive and fundamental restructuring in major segments of business are highly complex and cost vast sums to investigate and develop. According to Merrifield and others, these include the following:

Advanced Materials
- Electronic materials
- Ceramics
- Composites
- High-performance metals
- High-performance alloys

Biotechnology
- Diagnostics
- Medical instruments
- Drug delivery systems
- Molecular biology therapies

Information Processing and Storage
- Microelectronics
- High-performance computer networks
- Data storage
- Sensor and signal processing
- Computer simulation

Manufacturing Techniques
- Computer-integrated processing
- Microfabrication capabilities
- Systems management technologies
- "Smart" processing equipment

Transportation Systems
- Aeronautics
- Surface-transport technologies

Energy and Environmental Technologies
- Long-distance power transmission
- Pollution minimization systems
- Waste management technologies

1991	
Corporation	Number of Agreements
IBM	136
AT&T	77
Hewlett-Packard	65
Sun Microsystems	45
Daimler-Benz AG	44
Motorola	43
General Electric	42
Mitsubishi	41
Siemens	39

Exhibit 1.2.   Leading strategic alliance partners.

Technology is becoming more complex. Investigating any one of these critical technology areas requires a multidisciplinary understanding of a wide variety of sciences such as physics, chemistry, and electronics. Advanced knowledge in each discipline is required, not just in one specialty combined with a superficial understanding of the others. A corporation's capabilities are often much like those of an individual. A professional architect, although expert in marina design, cannot cope with all the complexities of modern life without outside assistance. Tax preparation services, medical treatment, lawn care, and many other areas of individual expertise may have to be acquired from others in order for the architect to cope. Corporations too have their specific areas of expertise, but to deliver the products of tomorrow these specialized corporations will need to incorporate into their products advanced aspects of different technologies. This will take specialized knowledge that they do not possess and require them to obtain outside assistance through strategic alliances.

Speaking to *The Wall Street Journal* about pocket-size cellular telephones, in which wireless telecommunications technology must be integrated with portable computing, information services, and satellite technology know-how, John Sculley, chief executive officer of Apple Computer, Inc. said, "No one can go it alone anymore."[7]

(c) Strategic Planning with an Intangible Basis.   Popular forms of strategic alliances include the following:

Technology licensing,

Trademark licensing,

Research and development contracts,

Marketing agreements,

Manufacturing contracts,

Supply agreements, and

Minority equity purchases.

---

[7] "Getting Help: High-Tech Firms Find It's Good to Line Up Outside Contractors," *The Wall Street Journal,* 29 July 1992, p. A1.

The trend is not at all limited to small companies that might be expected to be the most needy. It is usually the lack of capital, distribution networks, manufacturing expertise, or other proprietary know-how that drives small companies to the arms of strategic partnerships with large companies. But huge multinational corporations are also embracing the new trend. Four of the most active participants in strategic alliances during 1991 were IBM, AT&T, Hewlett-Packard, and Digital Equipment Corporation. Exhibit 1.2 was presented in the first quarter 1992 issue of *Corporate Venturing*, a publication of Venture Economics of Newark, New Jersey. It shows the number of strategic alliances in which the 10 most active companies engaged during 1991.

The same issue of *Corporate Venturing* reported that the most active strategic partnering industry was the computer software and service industry, which completed 661 of the 5,080 deals that were monitored during 1991. Industrial products and equipment took second place with 625 deals. Polymers, industrial chemicals, and specialty metals were also hot areas for strategic alliances.

The number of strategic alliances with foreign-based companies is growing, and Japan is the most active partner as U.S. companies seek to gain access to the Japanese marketplace. In 1991, 753 deals were counted between U.S. and Japanese companies, involving semiconductors, therapeutic biotechnology, and mobile communications.

Dow Chemical Corporation is making strategic alliances a cornerstone of its growth plans. The Dow board of directors felt that the company possessed a portfolio of projects and businesses that addressed relatively mature markets. It was decided that growth would come only through an aggressive search for new opportunities founded on emerging technologies. The company identifies discontinuity throughout the world and then develops products that fill the gaps. The search for product technology includes developing alliances with universities, start-up companies, and federal laboratories.

Upjohn realized that it could not entirely rely on internal sources to support new product development. Therefore, it created the Technology Partnership Program (TPP) to seek out strategic alliances with development-stage companies that possess technologies and products related to health care therapeutics. TPP's mission is to gain access to technologies that will complement existing licensing and acquisition programs. Through this program, Upjohn gains access to the desired technologies. In return, its partners realize a variety of benefits, which can include financial assistance, manufacturing capabilities, access to marketing prowess, and research assistance.

Genentech created the Technology Venture Program in order to take advantage of emerging technologies from around the world. The program focuses on gaining access to promising technologies in commercial gene therapy products. The goals of the program are (1) to expand the current product portfolio of the company whereby Genentech's commercialization expertise can take emerging technology to market, (2) to seek partners with complementary technology that would allow Genentech to accelerate the introduction of products that are being internally developed, and (3) to participate in technological areas that are outside the current Genentech focus of expertise.

It seems that management leaders have finally returned to a tight business focus. Possibly the leveraged buy-out (LBO) debt burdens hanging around many corporate necks have forced clear thinking as to how to get the most out of the businesses that these managers know how to run best.

Clearly, as seen in the preceding discussion, keystone intellectual property is driving economic success and corporate value. The next question centers on quantification of value. Three generally accepted approaches are available for valuing property. There are *only* these three methods. Many variations can be described, but all valuation methods that aim to establish monetary values are derived from the cost, market, and income approaches. Each is discussed in the following sections of this chapter.

1.5 COST APPROACH

The cost approach seeks to measure the future benefits of ownership by quantifying the amount of money that would be required to replace the future service capability of the subject intellectual property. The assumption underlying this approach is that the cost to purchase or develop new property is commensurate with the economic value of the service that the property can provide during its life. The cost approach does not directly consider the amount of economic benefits that can be achieved nor the time period over which they might continue. It is an inherent assumption with this approach that economic benefits indeed exist and are of sufficient amount and duration to justify the developmental expenditures.

First discussed are the general concepts of the cost approach as it typically applies to the valuation of fixed assets These include production equipment, office furnishings, truck fleets, and many other tangible items used in a business enterprise.

(a) General Cost Approach Principles. If the price of a new computer-controlled machine tool were set at a level exceeding the present value of the future economic benefits of owning the machine, then none would be sold. Likewise, if there are limited future benefits associated with intellectual property ownership, then the property would not be desirable. In both cases it is doubtful that development efforts and costs would be undertaken.

If the opposite is true, however, and demand for the machine or specific intellectual property is strong and economic benefits can be derived from owning the property, then the costs to develop it could be justified. Most often a company is concerned with determining the value of an existing property, whether it be a machine or intellectual property. When it first identifies the costs needed to create the property, the aggregate amount does not reflect the effects on the utility of the property that have accumulated as the property has aged. This involves the concept of depreciation and the associated diminution in value.

(b) Depreciation. It is rare that anyone is called upon to render an opinion of value on brand-new property. Most often the concern is with the value of property that is in use. The cost approach nearly always brings with it the complexity of quantifying the reduction from "brand-new" value as the result of depreciation. The passage of time depreciates the value of most property. Although intellectual property is not typically affected by "wear and tear," time can still cause obsolescence to creep up on intellectual property, so that at some point in the future no value remains.

A cost approach valuation usually begins *either* with a determination of the current cost to obtain an unused replica of the subject property—Cost of Reproduction New (CRN)— or the cost of obtaining a property of equivalent utility—Cost of Replacement (COR). When there is a difference between these two amounts, it is usually because COR represents a less costly substitute, one element of functional obsolescence.

The next step is to reflect *physical depreciation*,[8] since presumably the subject is not new. How much of the future service is gone as a result of wear and tear? If the replica is not "state-of-the-art," or suffers from design or operating deficiencies that reduce its desirability when compared with similar properties available in the marketplace, then *functional obsolescence*[9] must be reflected to obtain Replacement Cost Less Depreciation (CORLD). The process can be stated as a formula:

Cost of Reproduction New (CRN)

or

Cost of Replacement (COR)

Less: Physical Depreciation
Less: Functional Obsolescence

Equals: Replacement Cost Less Depreciation (CORLD)

The last element necessary to determine fair market value by the cost approach is to reflect *economic obsolescence*,[10] the third in the "Big Three" of depreciation factors. It is similar in concept to "highest and best use" as applied to real estate. This concept is based on the assumption that property devoted to business use achieves full fair market value only when it is capable of contributing to the earnings of that business, and when those earnings are capable of providing a reasonable rate of return on all the property devoted to the enterprise.

In other words, a brand-new, state-of-the-art production line for Hula Hoops has a low fair market value, because it is devoted to a business that is unlikely to earn a return that would be adequate to justify an investment at its replacement cost less physical and functional depreciation. Thus the fair market value of assets in a business is dependent to some degree on factors that arise entirely outside the particular circumstances of the individual asset. The fair market value of an asset can be significantly degraded by the economics of the business to which it is devoted. The extent to which it is degraded depends on the type of asset it is. Distinctly unique assets may suffer considerably, because they have little use outside the particular business. Other assets that have general use may suffer in value only to the extent of the costs that would be incurred to remove them from the business and transport and install them in a new business and location for use in a more profitable industry.

If the owner of a manufacturing plant is consistently unable to generate adequate earnings from the facility, then he or she would liquidate the investment and seek alternate investment opportunities. Examples of such actions are reported daily in the financial press in announcements of plant closings or sales of complete operating divisions. Thus we are continually reminded that the fair market value of a business and individual assets within that business are dependent on their earning power.

---

[8] The reduction in value from wear and tear on assets derived from normal use.

[9] The reduction in value caused by changing conditions that make assets less useful; e.g., computer keypunch machines that remain in top working condition may have lost all their value because they no longer have a viable function in the new world of advanced computing.

[10] The reduction in value caused by changing economic conditions that render previously useful assets less desirable to own; e.g., lower oil prices have made shale oil recovery equipment processes almost worthless.

The preceding equation can now be completed to describe the full course of the cost approach in determining fair market value:

Cost of Reproduction New (CRN)

or

Cost of Replacement (COR)
Less: Physical Depreciation
Less: Functional Obsolescence
_____
Equals: Replacement Cost Less Depreciation
Less: Economic Obsolescence
_____
Equals: Fair Market Value

In this formula, one begins with the cost of a new replica of the subject property and, after considering all forms of depreciation, ends with an indication of fair market value by the cost approach.

The cost approach is especially useful for appraising highly specialized property, such as a foundry, a reservoir, a steel mill, a coal-unloading facility, a nuclear reactor, a telephone switching center, a power plant, an electric substation, or a satellite space station.

The cost approach is also very useful as a valuation method for certain intangible assets, such as certain types of computer software, an assembled work force, or research and development programs. It is often used when other valuation methods are not applicable or to allocate values among assets that may have been valued in total by another means.

(c) Cost Versus Value.   Cost is not the same as value. Unless economic benefits can be earned from ownership of a property, the value must be relatively low, regardless of the amounts needed to develop the property. Consider the trademark "Dusenburg." This automobile name still has solid national recognition among many people in the United States. The cost to create an automobile name of similar strength could easily be tens of millions of dollars, perhaps even hundreds of millions. Yet current ownership of this name is not likely to contribute much in the way of profits for today's car seller. In fact, the name could be a detriment; association with an old and discontinued product probably would not inspire consumers.

Many fixed assets have a value that is relatively independent of the business or industry in which they are used. One company's delivery trucks can be used in another business or industry. The economics of a specific industry, however, do not affect fixed asset values as severely as they do some types of intellectual property. The value of trademarks and patents are usually very closely aligned with the economic condition of the business or industry in which they are used. Redeployment of a brand name to another industry is not necessarily easy to accomplish. The economic fate of a trademark or patent may be exactly parallel to that of the business in which it is used.

(d) Applying the Cost Approach to Intellectual Property.   The starting point in using the cost approach is to obtain an estimate of the cost to produce a new replica of the intellectual property. One method is a trending of historical costs.

(i) Historical Cost Trending.   Some corporations keep detailed records of the costs that were incurred in the development of a specific intangible asset. Restatement of these historical costs in current dollars provides an indication of the total cost that would have to be invested in order to reproduce the property.

In valuing a technological asset using the cost approach, the information that would be important includes identification of the following:

1. Scientists and engineers who worked on the product development effort
2. Salaries and benefits of those involved with the project
3. Overhead costs for utilities and research space
4. Overhead costs for clerical support and technicians
5. Raw materials used in the development process
6. Prototype construction and testing expenses
7. Outside services for independent evaluation and certifications
8. Pilot plant expenses

The resulting indication of value from trending historical costs assumes that the property being valued is state-of-the-art. However, an intellectual property under consideration at present will have aged since the last amounts of development costs were spent. Obsolescence in one or more of its many forms may be present, requiring deductions from the trended total to reflect physical, functional, and/or economic obsolescence.

Trademarks can also be valued by trending the historical costs associated with their creation, such as for the following:

1. Concept development
2. Consulting
3. Preliminary consumer testing
4. Package designs
5. Advertising campaign development
6. Commercial planning, scripting, and recording
7. Television, radio, newspaper, and magazine spots

(ii) Re-creation Costs.   Another means by which to derive the cost to reproduce an asset is a direct estimate of the efforts and costs necessary for creating a similar asset. A lack of accurate record keeping often requires this approach.

In the case of specialized software, such a determination can be accomplished by estimating the costs associated with the following:

1. Salaries and benefits that would be paid to computer programmers
2. The length of time required for program development
3. The amount of overhead and support costs for developmental computer time, office space, utilities, clerical support, and the like
4. The time and costs associated with installation of the program on company computers and the time needed to achieve full implementation of the program

The aggregate of all of the expenses of these efforts is an indication of the cost to reproduce the asset. This procedure can be used to ascertain the costs necessary to reproduce an intellectual property in a form that is "brand-new." Adjustments for elements of obsolescence must then be considered.

(e) Cautions in Using the Cost Approach. A failure of the cost approach is that there is an absence of direct consideration of the economic benefits, and the period over which they might be enjoyed is not accurately captured in the value. This important missing element is best explained in the following examples.

During the late 1950s, the United States government spent many millions of dollars on the development of nuclear-powered aircraft. A prototype was built and tested. Unfortunately, the engines were never able to generate enough thrust for lift-off. Application of the cost approach to this technology might provide an indication of value well into eight figures. Considering, however, the potential for application of nuclear aircraft technology and the prospects for economic benefits, a cost approach indication of value would be in error. The current value of an aircraft technology that fails to get the craft airborne is zero.

Another example is a technology that was quite able to perform the desired task: extraction of oil from shale rock. At considerable expense, the U.S. government ventured once again into technological development where others feared to tread. This technology worked. It was to be part of our salvation from the death grip of OPEC. But with the steep decline in oil prices, the cost of producing shale oil became far too high. And so the technology sits on the shelf with no prospects for use in the near future. The cost approach might indicate that its value is another eight-figure bonanza, but economic conditions tell us that the shale oil technology has very little value. Someday in the distant future, conditions may require its use. Yet the current value of "zero" reflects the possibility that the use of shale oil technology may be a long way off, if ever viable.

Where economic conditions are not conducive to deriving profits, it is difficult to ascribe any value to intellectual property, regardless of the indications of the cost approach. There is also the possibility that an intellectual property can have economic potential far above that indicated by the cost approach. A patented product may have been inexpensive to create but still have significant value because of the huge demand for the product, regardless of the selling price.

It is hard to imagine that the Hula Hoop originally required an extensive research budget. The cost approach would not indicate a high value for the product. Yet the then-present value of the future economic benefits directly associated with the product would provide a much higher and more correct indication of its value.

The cost approach is not as comprehensive as the other two valuation models. Many of the most important factors that drive value are not directly reflected in the methodology and must be considered apart from the basic cost approach process:

1. The cost approach does not directly incorporate information about the *amount of economic benefits* that are associated with the property. These benefits are driven by demand for the product or service and the profits that can be generated.

2. Information about the *trend of the economic benefits* is also missing from consideration. Intellectual property providing economic benefits with an increasing growth rate can be far more valuable than that which displays a downward trend. The trend is affected by social attitudes, demographics, and competitive forces.

3. The duration over which the economic benefits will be enjoyed is yet another element, not directly considered, that has a significant effect on value. The *economic remaining life* of the property is a vital component to value conclusions.

4. The *risk* associated with receiving the expected economic benefits is not directly factored into the cost approach model. Where a high degree of risk makes realization of expectations speculative, a lower value corresponds.

5. The adjustments that are necessary to reflect the effects of *obsolescence* must be separately calculated and are often difficult to quantify.

As an example, suppose that two trademarks are being valued, with the following characteristics:

Trademark 1 is associated with a highly profitable product in a growth industry for which there is very little competition. Consumer recognition is strong, and there is a strong potential for the trademark to be extended to new product applications while maintaining an above average profit margin.

Trademark 2 is associated with a low-profit-margin product, in a declining industry that has become crowded with competition. Consumer recognition of the trademark has become blurred with that of competitors' and has almost no potential for application to other products.

If both trademarks are nationally recognized, the cost approach might easily indicate the same value for both of them. The level of research, advertising, and promotion that has gone into establishing each name might be the same. A trending of historical advertising expenses could actually provide a higher indication of value for the trademark that is associated with the low-profit product. However, the cost approach can indicate an order of magnitude to use as a starting point or as a check on the values derived from other approaches. Use of the cost approach as a means to estimate a range of value for intellectual property is fraught with potential for error.

1.6 MARKET APPROACH

One of the most unique opportunities to value a patent was presented by VLI Corporation. The company was, for the most part, based on one patented product. The product was the "Today" brand vaginal contraceptive sponge. Sales reached $17.0 million in 1986, from a standstill in 1983. The product was stocked in more than 93% of all drug stores nationwide, and in 88% of all food stores that carry contraceptives. During September 1987 the company reported that the U.S. Patent and Trademark Office denied the company's petition to reinstate the expired patent on the sponge. The original patent expired in July because the company failed to pay a newly required patent-maintenance fee on time. Although the missed payment was called "inadvertent" by the company, the Patent Office did not renew the patent.

The company was, at the time, a takeover target of American Home Products Corporation, which in July 1987 offered $7 for each of VLI's 11.9 million shares, contingent upon reinstatement of the patent. This represented a value for the company of $83.3 million. As of October 1987 (before the crash) the shares were trading over-the-counter at $4 per share. Typically, a takeover candidate trades at the price offered by the suitor, and often at a price slightly higher. The premium, above the offer price, represents speculation that another buyer may materialize with an offer of a higher amount. In this case the stock was trading below the $7 offer. The $3 difference can be viewed as the value of the patent protection. When multiplied by the number of shares, the value of the patent equals $35.7 million.

The stock market concluded that the same company, with the same product, and the same distribution system, while serving the same customers, was worth substantially less without the patent. The protection against competition was lost. As a result, competitive products could almost immediately be introduced. VLI could experience pricing pressures and a loss in sales volume. In consideration of this possibility, the market dropped the share price of the company. Another way to express the value of the patent would be to calculate the present value of all earnings that will be lost owing to the entrance of competition. In this case, the market indirectly made that calculation, with the lower stock price reflecting the potentially lost earnings.

The $3 difference may actually undervalue the patent. Somewhere within the valuation considerations that the market used to price the shares at $4, is the probability that the patent will eventually be reinstated. VLI said that company attorneys assured it that there would not be any trouble in getting the patent reinstated.

(a) General Principles of the Market Approach.   The market approach provides an indication of value by comparing the price at which similar property has been exchanged between willing buyers and sellers. When the market approach is used, an indication of the value of a specific item of intellectual property can be gained from looking at the prices paid for comparable property.

Requirements for successful use of this approach include the following:

1. The existence of an active market
2. Past transactions of comparable property
3. Access to pricing information
4. Arm's-length transactions between independent parties

Transactions of specific items of intellectual property are not common. When such transactions actually occur, the terms of the exchange are not often disclosed to the public. The most difficult aspect of the market approach as it applies to intellectual property is comparability. Even if pricing information for a specific exchange regarding a specific patent were available, the price at which the property exchanged most likely will have no bearing on the value of other patents unless positive comparability exists.

(b) Comparability.   In residential real estate, comparability is quite easy. The neighborhood, size and number of rooms, and quality of construction can all be compared with the indications of value that are established by past sales of other homes. Adjustments can be made for differences such as pools, fireplaces, and finished basements. After adjustments, a consideration of the market transactions can lead to a determination of value for the house being studied. Unfortunately, valuation is not so easy for intellectual properties such as patents and trade names. Many factors come into play. The following are some of the important factors that should be considered in seeking intellectual property comparability:

Industry characteristics
Profit history
Market share potential

New technologies

Barriers to entry

Growth prospects

Industry cycles and economics can limit the value of businesses and the intellectual property that they possess. Market transactions that are to serve as a basis for an indication of value are most useful if the exchanged property is employed within the same industry, subject to the same potentials, demographic factors, government regulation, and investment risks.

If a trademark in the cosmetics industry were to be exchanged, the price at which the transaction occurred might be a good indication of the value of other cosmetic trademarks. This assumes, however, that the influence of the other factors listed is the same. A trademark that exchanged in the steel industry would not be considered useful for valuing a cosmetics mark.

Profitability is fundamental to the existence of monetary value. Intellectual property that contributes to strong and continuing profits is very valuable. Market transactions involving trademarks in the same industry might not be useful indications of another name in the industry unless profitability measures are similar. An excellent example of this situation are sports products.

For the most part, the primary players in the sports shoe market manufacture products of almost equal quality. Each competitor has products with designs and features that are intended to enhance athletic performance. Yet some branded products have achieved substantial profits above the average achieved by the major competitors. Part of this success should be attributed to the recognizability of the trademark among consumers and the positive attributes they associate with the name. If a sports shoe trademark were to be exchanged for an amount that is disclosed, an indication of value for another trademark in the same industry might not necessarily be provided For a reasonable comparison, the profits that can be associated with the exchanged mark would also need to be above average. Therefore, although industry transactions are a fundamental factor for judging comparability, comparable profitability is also very important.

Market share can be associated with profitability. Control of a large share of a big market provides a company with enhanced profits from many economics of scale. Patented products and trademarks can contribute to maintenance of a significant market share, and this factor must be reflected in the value of the intellectual property. Intellectual property transactions may not be comparable if the market share that the property controls is not comparable.

Emerging technologies can have a significant impact on the value of intellectual property. The potential competition represented by emerging technology can affect the remaining economic life of an intellectual property. In considering intellectual property transactions as market indications of value, care must be taken to ensure that the effect of emerging technology is very similar when compared to the property being valued. The existence of research that is expected to render the subject property obsolete must be reflected in the value decision. Even within the same industry, intellectual properties may not be influenced to the same degree by emerging technology.

The computer software industry is evolving at light speed. Many software programs have an economic life of less than three years. In 1985, Fifth Generation Systems introduced the first hard disk backup program, which allowed a hard disk to be backed up to floppy disks in less than 10 minutes. This was a fantastic product for programmers. Previously, hours were spent each time a protective backup was conducted. The product was a big winner, but in less than two years 16 competing products entered the market. Many of the competitors included advanced features. The value of the original proprietary product must reflect the effect on future profits from these other programs, as well as the inroads that are expected from new products that complete backup by continuous processing using an expansion board. In looking for market transactions of comparable property, consideration must be given to the effect that derives from new products and technology. If the market transactions center on intellectual property that is free of the impact of technology gains, their use in valuing otherwise similar property is inappropriate.

Barriers to entry can enhance the value of intellectual property. Barriers include distribution networks, substantial capital investments, patents, and trademarks. FDA approval in the drug industry is a perfect example of a barrier to entry. The value of currently accepted proprietary drug products is, in a sense, supported by the hurdles that competitors must jump in order to enter the market. The time delay allows the current products to enjoy less competition, higher pricing options, and, most important, an opportunity to dominate the market. Market dominance can be achieved in many ways through advertising, establishment of customer loyalty, or the development of highly efficient production facilities. As such, intellectual property within a market that also presents high entry barriers is possibly more valuable than similar property that operates in a more open industry.

Growth prospects are directly related to value. This relationship lies in the fact that a growing income stream is more valuable than one that is flat or declining. The intellectual property from whence the income stream flows is valued according to the growth prospects of the income. Generally, higher growth can be associated with higher value, assuming that investment risks are the same. Comparable market transactions are not useful as value indicators if the properties being compared have decidedly different prospects for future income growth.

When information is available on market transactions of specific intellectual property having similar characteristics to the property under study, direct application of the market approach is possible. When the intellectual property has been exchanged as part of a package of assets, usually as part of a business enterprise, then an allocation of the purchase price among the assets is required in order to identify the amount specifically attributable to the intellectual property.

(c) Complementary Asset Investments. The following equations define the typical enterprise of which intellectual property is a part:

$$\text{Business Enterprise Value} = \text{Invested Capital}$$

$$\text{Invested Capital} = \text{Long-Term Debt} + \text{Shareholders' Equity}$$

$$\text{Long-Term Debt} + \text{Shareholders' Equity} = \text{Net Working Capital} + \text{Tangible Assets} + \text{Intangible Assets} + \text{Intellectual Property}$$

The business enterprise is defined as invested capital, which equals the value of shareholders' equity and long-term debt. This amount represents the amount originally provided to start the company. It was used to purchase machinery, establish procedures, and to create products. In many firms, the initial investment was used to develop a new product. Therefore, the market value of the business enterprise equals the value of the assets that constitute the business: net working capital, tangible assets, intangible assets, and intellectual property.

Based on this framework, the value of a specific asset can be determined if the overall value of the business enterprise is known. Allocation of the overall business enterprise value to specific categories continues until the residual amount of unallocated value can be ascribed to the asset for which the valuation is desired.

When Ford Motor Company purchased Jaguar Plc, it paid about $2 billion. In return, Ford got the whole company—lock, stock, barrel, and brand name. Many analysts say that Ford paid the entire price just to get the brand name. The manufacturing facilities were old and needed major upgrades. The work force was aging and motivated more by union rules than by product quality. The dies and tooling were worn. The product designs were in need of upgrading. The automotive technology was not state-of-the-art. After values were assigned to each of these enterprise categories, most of the purchase price was ascribed to the Jaguar brand name.

(d) Cautions in Using the Market Approach.   Comparability is needed for the market approach to be useful. It is also the most difficult element of the market approach to establish for intellectual property. The inherent uniqueness of many types of intellectual property, such as key patents and first-class brand names, make satisfactory application of this approach difficult, but not impossible.

Underlying this procedure is also the assumption that an independent third-party transaction of intellectual property reflects value optimization. It is assumed that best efforts are being made to expand application of the intellectual property and that other uses with economic potential are being studied and/or exploited. If this is not the case, then then market value indication may not be appropriate for a given assignment.

1.7 INCOME APPROACH

The value of any asset can be expressed as the present value of the future stream of economic benefits that can be derived from its ownership. The income approach can yield very credible valuation conclusions for many types of intellectual property and, at least until more market transactions are disclosed, is probably the most accurate means of valuing intellectual property.

A number of factors, fundamental to success in using an income approach, can be summarized by answering the following questions:

- What amount of economic benefit can be expected?
- How long can it be expected to continue?
- Will the amount of benefits be increasing or decreasing?
- What risk is involved with achieving the anticipated benefits?
- Can specific economic benefits be attributed to specific intellectual property?

(a) Net Cash Flow.   The future stream of economic benefits is best measured by the amount of net cash flow to be derived from employment of a property. This measure should take into account the costs of doing business as well as additional capital investment that will be needed to sustain the cash flows. After accounting for these future uses of gross cash flow, the net amount represents the economic benefits derived from ownership of the property.

The amount of future net cash flow is not determined solely by management actions. Other factors can enhance or diminish the sustainable level of these benefits. The amount of cash flow that will be available on a sustained basis is affected by *economic climate, profitability, competition*, and *capital requirements*.

(i) Economic Climates.   Economic climates are cyclical. The health of the general economy in which intellectual property is employed has a significant bearing on the amount of net cash flow that will ultimately be realized. Monetary policies, federal budget deficits, and income tax laws all contribute to the condition of the economy. Demand for the service or product derived from an intellectual property is directly related to general economic conditions. In addition to the ultimate amount of product demand, pricing pressures brought on by prevailing economic conditions will affect the net cash flows that are ultimately enjoyed.

An example of economic climate is inflation. During periods of low inflation, manufacturers are usually able to pass along directly to consumers the rising costs of raw materials and production. The contribution margin associated with an intellectual property is therefore maintained, and sometimes even increased. During periods of high inflation, however, not all of the increased production costs can be passed along to consumers without a loss in sales volume. When the economy is under severe inflationary pressures, profit margins are generally squeezed and the contribution associated with the intellectual property is also reduced.

Often, the economic climate can affect a specific industry. A health overall economy can still have pockets of weakness isolated in certain industries. In considering the amount and sustainability of cash flows from intellectual property, it is imperative to study the conditions and outlook for the specific industry in which it is used. The most advanced technology in the world may not be able to overcome certain industry conditions that limit demand for a product or service.

Where it is possible for certain forms of intellectual property to generate cash flow from a variety of industries, the diversified nature of the income stream can enhance the value of the property in comparison with other property that has limited fields of application and a nondiversified income stream.

(ii) Profitability.   In addition to the health of an economy, profitability is also an important factor: an intellectual property must be used in a business where profits are generated. Profitability affects the amount of net cash flow. It aggregates the cost elements such as wages, procurement of raw materials, conversion of raw materials, selling efforts, and the overhead involved with producing a service or product. Many variables enter into the ability to sustain a positive balance between revenues and costs.

The value of intellectual property is directly related to its ability to contribute to the attainment of sustainable profits. Intellectual property that can enhance the profitability of a product line is inherently valuable. The contribution may be process technology that saves raw materials, energy, labor, or other manufacturing inputs. Profits can also be attributed to intellectual property when process technology allows substitution of inexpensive input factors for costly inputs to achieve optimization of production costs.

The contributions made by technological property toward enhancing profits include the following:

- Reduction in the amount of raw material input that is required per unit of output.
- Reduction in the amount of electrical, gas, or steam energy used in the manufacturing process.
- Automation of part of all of the process, allowing a reduction in the amount of labor.
- Substitution of less expensive input factors for those inputs costing more, without an effect on product quality.
- Achievement of enhanced product or service attributes such as quality, reliability, or aesthetics, while maintaining the same unit production costs. Greater market share and/or a premium selling price should result.
- Reduction of the amount needed as capital investment while retaining the ability to produce adequate product quantities to satisfy demand.

Technology can also enhance economic benefits by reducing the amount of raw material waste generated by a specific process or by reducing the amount of finished product that must be rejected or reworked.

An enhanced selling price can also be evidence of intellectual property value. This outcome can be the result of technological intellectual property or can result from the strength of a trademark. Often there are products that sell for significantly more than comparable merchandise only because of the trademark on the product.

Unlimited economic benefits are not usually possible. Whenever a market exists in which the participants are enjoying above average profits, competitors enter. A patent can guard above-average profits over the length of its legal life, but the maximum protection periods from utility patent protection and from design patent protection are 17 and 14 years, respectively. This assumes that advancing technology does not obsolete the patented technology prior to its statutory expiration.

(iii) Competition. The achievement of economic benefits through the introduction of alternate products and services or by the development of superior technology can be affected by competition. The strategies of competitors can limit the *amount, duration*, and *trend* of future net cash flows. The owner of a highly profitable asset may enjoy cash flows for only a limited amount of time. Competitors are quick to recognize markets that provide enhanced profit opportunities. Their actions can diminish the growth rate of future cash flows or cause cash flows to halt abruptly with the introduction of superior products or services. Patent protection is not absolute in all cases, because competitors may be able to offer alternative technological benefits or products.

(iv) Capital Requirements. Capital requirements can reduce the amount of future net cash flows that can be realized from exploitation of an asset. The value of any asset is best measured by the cash flow that is thrown off after allowing for "reinvestment." This can take the form of plant expansions and higher working capital requirements. In fact, a very desirable characteristic of intellectual property is that it can sometimes allow the generation of earnings with *less* investment in plant and equipment. This component of value is captured when the future net cash flow is expected to be enhanced by reduced requirements for capital additions.

Clearly, the net cash flow stream is affected by many factors. An additional and significant concern is the duration over which these net cash flows will be enjoyed.

(b) Cash Flow Duration.   Technological breakthroughs can abruptly interrupt a stream of economic benefits. Governmental regulations can also cause standard business practices to become obsolete. Value is therefore very sensitive to the remaining period of time over which cash flows will be received. The duration over which net cash flow is to be received is just as important as the amount.

The economic life of intellectual property may be short because of advancing technologies, industry practices involving regular model changes, changes in social attitudes toward a product or service, and other factors. The economic benefits associated with a specific intellectual property need not be immediate for the property to have value. Many years of development and research may be required before net cash begins to flow, but the property can still have a huge value because of its potential. The value, however, is still dependent on the amount, growth rate, and timing of the economic benefits.

Typically, net cash flows are estimated by comprehensive analysis of the market for the products that can be derived from the intellectual property. It is much easier to make forecasts of net cash flows for technology that has proven to be commercially viable. Embryonic technology presents many challenges to forecasting. Still, the value of emerging technology is directly related to the present value of the future economic benefits that will ultimately be enjoyed. Forecasting net cash flows for uncertain technology is precarious. The degree of certainty with which the forecasts are viewed has much to do with the discount rate that is used in the present value calculations.

1.8 INTELLECTUAL PROPERTY PROFIT CONTRIBUTION

Quite often analysts estimate the contribution margin that is attributed to an intellectual property by using a market-negotiated royalty rate. The intellectual property contribution is estimated as the amount that the business would have to pay a third party to license similar property. The amount saved in licensing fees is considered to represent the profit contribution of the intellectual property possessed. This procedure is fraught with potential errors. The primary dangers of using royalties as a measure of the contribution are briefly outlined:

1. Royalty information regarding similar intellectual property is very rare. Seldom can a reasonable comparison be found, and still more seldom is third-party royalty rate information available.

2. Royalty rates that are available may reflect specific licensing clauses that affect the royalty rate that was negotiated. The effect of license agreement clauses on the negotiated royalty rate may be quite appropriate for the conditions under which the property is being licensed, but may correlate very poorly with the conditions associated with outright ownership.

3. Many royalty rates were negotiated by legal experts with insufficient consideration for business risk and investment rates of return.

4. Many "industry" royalty rates were established years ago, reflecting economic conditions, business risks, and investment rates of return that are no longer appropriate.

5. Royalty rates provide the licensor with only a portion of the overall intellectual property contribution. The licensee also expects to enjoy a portion of the economic benefits of the property, as well as compensation for investing in the complementary assets that are required to exploit the intellectual property. Some have suggested that the licensor receives only 25% of the economic benefit that the property contributes. Use of a market royalty such as this would result in a conclusion of value for the intellectual property at only 25% of its true value.

Care must therefore be exercised if royalty rates are to be used as an estimate of the contribution of an intellectual property.

(a) Discount Rate.   The valuation component that measures the compensation of the investor for the commitment of capital is the discount rate. A capital commitment causes an investor to give up other investment opportunities and assume the risks associated with a particular investment. Factors that affect this component of value include inflation, liquidity, real interest rates, and measures of relative risk.

The discount rate is used to translate the future economic benefits into present value. The following equation shows that the discounted future cash flows equal the value of the underlying technology:

$$V = \frac{CF1}{(1 + i)} + \frac{CF2}{(1 + i)^2} + \frac{CF3}{(1 + i)^3} + \ldots$$

Where:

V = the value of the intellectual property,

CF = the amount of net cash flow during each successive time period, and

i = the required rate of return on the intellectual property.

If the future cash flows are expected to grow at a constant rate, introduction of this factor into the model, along with algebraic wizardry, provides a useful form of this equation as follows, where g represents a constant growth rate that is expected:

$$V = \frac{CFo\,(1 + g)}{i - g}$$

When the growth rate is expected to be higher than the discount rate, i, the equation is not useful and specific projections for each year are necessary. The discount rate is affected by many factors beyond the scope of a single chapter. However, a general overview of this topic is presented in the following paragraphs.[11]

The required rate of return that investors demand for bearing certain levels of investment risk includes *inflation, liquidity, real interest rates*, and a *risk premium*.

---

[11] More details are available in Gordon V. Smith and Russell L. Parr, *Intellectual Property: Licensing and Joint Venture Profit Strategies* (New York: John Wiley & Sons, 1993).

(i) Inflation. Inflation can diminish the purchasing power of the future economic benefits that are provided by an investment. The discount rate that is used must include assumptions about inflation to compensate for this loss of purchasing power. Expectations of a higher inflationary climate mandate a correspondingly higher rate of return. The higher rate is needed to compensate for the negative effects on the purchasing power of the expected cash flow.

(ii) Liquidity. Another risk that must be considered is liquidity. Liquidity represents the relative difficulty with which an investment can be quickly converted into cash. Many financial securities can be traded on active public exchanges for cash at any time. Intellectual property investments, especially during embryonic development, do not possess this strong characteristic of investment liquidity. Additional return to the investor is warranted and should be reflected in the discount rate when liquidity is lacking.

(iii) Real Interest. Real interest represents the component of return on investment associated with sacrificing the use of invested funds—the reward for deferring consumption in favor of investment. In its pure form and in a risk-free environment, the real interest rate has been shown to be about 3%. The typically higher rates that are paid by investments reflect compensation for the risk elements introduced by inflation, illiquidity, and risk premiums.

(iv) Risk Premium. Risk premium is the added amount of return that investors demand for the assumption of risk in excess of real interest in a risk-free investment—the possibility of loss and/or an unanticipated variability in earnings. The amount of risk premium varies according to the type of property and the industry. An element of risk already discussed is the likelihood of competitive technologies that could make the owned property obsolete. Computer software products are an example of intellectual property that quickly loses out to improved and more powerful products within a very short time. Compensation for this risk requires a premium. Another consideration in determining a risk premium is the versatility of the intellectual property. The feasibility of property to be easily redeployed to other business activities reduces the negative impact should the initial concept fail. Property that cannot be redeployed elsewhere may become completely valueless with the total loss of the original investment.

(b) Assessing Risk. The income approach for valuation is based on the concept that a dollar to be received in the future is worth less than a dollar currently in hand. A high discount rate reflects a high risk of receiving the future dollars. The current value of risky future dollars is therefore lower as the discount gets higher. If the risk of receiving the future dollars is low, then the dollars are worth more. A high discount rate is associated with risky investments. The higher the discount rate, the lower the present value of the future cash flows. As the discount rate (the required rate of return) decreases, the indicated value of the underlying property increases.

A proper perception of risk is needed in considering the development or acquisition of intellectual property. If a too-high perception of risk is used, then a low value will result. The outcome may be a decision to forgo development or to pass by an acquisition. A competitor with a "clearer" perception of risk may then be able to obtain an advantage by developing or acquiring the intellectual property, thus gaining an edge.

Too often we see the opposite side of this situation. The amount of investment risk is not at all properly judged, and a lower required rate of return is used in the discounting process. The resulting value is very high. In the case of an acquisition, the euphoria of capturing the acquisition target is quickly followed by reality. Ultimately, divestment at a substantial loss likely follows.

In general, analysis of the financial securities marketplace can serve as a starting point. By looking at the rates of return that investors require from various industry investments, each having its own unique risk factors, an appropriate rate can be comparatively determined. For emerging technology, the analysis should concentrate on the return requirements of professional venture capitalists.

The present value of the future net cash flows thus indicates the value of intellectual property when an appropriate discount rate is used to reflect the risk of the investment. The net cash flows that are discounted must reflect the direct contribution of an intellectual property.

1.9 PRODUCT LIFE CYCLE

Product life cycle theory assumes that the diffusion of a product into the economy follows a pattern comprising four stages:

Introduction

Growth

Maturity

Decline

The time period over which this pattern is completed varies significantly by industry and product. It can span as little as one year, as in the electronics industry, where new products are constantly being introduced, or can span many years, as in the aircraft industry, where new designs take decades to perfect.

During the introductory stage, sales volume is usually low and the product or service is highly priced. At this point consumers are not well informed as to the benefits associated with the new product, and a process of education is required. Once proven, the product or service gains acceptance and greater sales volume is generated. Manufacturing techniques can be improved as economies of scale resulting from larger production volumes are achieved. These cost reductions can allow a lower selling price, which helps to further expand the market. If the product is patented, above average profits can be protected from the encroachment of competitors. Without patent protection, pricing pressure during the growth stage may deteriorate the above-average profit margins that are enjoyed during the introductory stages.

At maturity, the overall market for the product or service is well established and further penetration by the industry producers is slow. Pricing pressures become significant if patent protection is lacking or has expired.

Decline can begin as advances in technology introduce new product and service offerings that erode the demand for an established product. Pricing pressure and reduced demand can cause the product or service to assume the characteristics of a commodity.

The compact disk and compact disk players provide an excellent example. When first introduced, a basic compact disk player was priced at $1,000 and more. It had very few operating features other than the ability to play a compact disk. Disks were priced at almost $20 each. Demand for these products was at first limited to adventurous music lovers with high levels of discretionary income. As their superior fidelity became well known, demand for these products increased and the manufacturing economies of scale allowed pricing reductions for market expansion. Many manufacturers entered the market and added features such as scanning, remote control, preprogramming of selections, and so on. Today a compact disk player with extensive features can be purchased for less than $250. The compact disks cost less than $12. The market is well defined and well into the growth stage of the product life cycle.

At the same time, the effect on the long-playing vinyl record has been extraordinary. Almost every record store in the country has dramatically reduced the shelf space allotted to LPs. Sales of turntables are rapidly declining. Prices of LP records are severely reduced, and selections are becoming very limited. In less than five years the purchase of LP records may require the same diligence as that required to find parts for a 1962 Rambler.

The value of technology follows the pattern of life cycle theory. While compact disk and compact disk player manufacturing technology can be argued as being very valuable, the value of LP record and turntable technology is breathing its final gasp.

In valuing intellectual property, attention to product life cycle theory and defining the stage at which one finds the subject property are most important. The critical question: Is your intellectual property providing access to a fast-growing, highly profitable industry or leaving you in a crowded commodity-oriented environment that is in decline?

Valuation is only one aspect of intellectual property analysis. Determining the value of intellectual property is necessary when it is being used as the down payment for entrance into a joint venture. Exploitation activities include licensing deals in which intellectual pricing questions must be answered. The rest of this chapter provides criticism of the most popular methods for establishing royalty rates (rental for use of intellectual property). The methods are easy to apply but badly flawed.

1.10 ROYALTY RATES

Some of the more commonly used royalty rate development models are presented in this section, along with highlights of their primary deficiencies.

(a) The 25% Rule.   Fully stated, the "25% method" calculates a royalty as 25% of the gross profit, before taxes, from the enterprise operations in which the licensed intellectual property is used. At best, this method of royalty determination is crude. *Gross profit* has never been accurately defined where this rule is discussed. Gross profit based on a generally accepted accounting principles definition includes the direct costs of production. These include raw material costs, direct labor costs, manufacturing utility expenses, and even depreciation expenses of the manufacturing facilities. All of the costs and expenses associated with conversion of raw materials into a final product or service are captured. Because this is most likely the area of greatest contribution from intellectual property, consideration of the amount of gross profit in setting a royalty is reasonable. However, it fails to consider the final profitability that is ultimately realized with the licensed property. Absent from the analysis are selling, administrative, and general overhead expenses.

An argument for eliminating these expenses from the analysis might center on the idea that value of intellectual property, such as manufacturing technology, should not be measured—with respect to royalties—by analysis of business areas in which it has no direct input. A more broadened view, however, shows that an intellectual property royalty can be affected by the selling expenses and other support expenses that are part of the commercialization. Intellectual property that is part of a product or service that requires little marketing, advertising, and selling effort can be more valuable than a product based on intellectual property that requires the use of national advertising and a highly compensated sales staff.

Two patented products may cost the same amount to produce and yield the same amount of gross profit. Yet one of the products may require extensive and continuing sales support, whereas the other does not. The added costs of extensive and continuing sales efforts make the first product less profitable to the licensee. Although the two products may have the same gross profit, it is very unlikely that they would command the same royalty.

The profit level after consideration of the nonmanufacturing operating expenses is a far more accurate determinant of the contribution of an intellectual property. The royalty for specific intellectual property must reflect the industry and economic environment in which the property is used. Some environments are competitive and entail many support costs which reduce net profits. Intellectual property that is used in this type of environment is not as valuable as property in a high-profit environment in which fewer support costs are required. A proper royalty must reflect this aspect of the economic environment in which it is to be used. A royalty based on gross profit cannot accomplish this portion of the analysis.

The 25% rule also fails to consider the other key royalty determinants of risk and fair rates of return on investment. The percentage of gross profit that should ultimately go to the licensor is considered by most advocates of the 25% rule to be flexible. Where licensees must heavily invest in complimentary assets, a lower percentage of gross profit may be more proper. If very little investment is needed, then a royalty based on the majority of gross profits may go to the licensor.

Intuitively, this methodology seems to be correct, yet is unsatisfying because it provides no clue as to quantifying a relationship between licensee capital investment and the percentage of gross profit that goes to royalty.

Too many important factors cannot be reconciled by this royalty rate methodology. Using the 25% method in negotiating a royalty rate is very difficult. There are many factors to be considered in selecting an appropriate split of gross profits. Unstructured consideration of such factors, absent a formalized investment analysis, is bound to omit from consideration the effect of some very important elements. The 25% rule is not really even useful as a general guide with which to begin negotiations.

(b) Industry Norms.   The royalty rate determination methodology based on industry norms misses even more of the important elements than the 25% rule. Here, consideration of the profitability of the enterprise using an intellectual property is lacking, in addition to the other failures of the 25% rule. The industry norms method focuses on the rates that others are charging for intellectual property licensed within the same industry. Investment risks, net profits, market size, growth potential, and complimentary asset requirements are all absent from direct consideration. The use of industry norms places total reliance on the ability of others to consider and interpret correctly the many factors affecting royalties. Any mistakes made by the initial setting of an industry royalty are passed along.

Changing economic conditions, along with changing investment rate of return require-ments, are also absent from consideration in using industry norms. A royalty established only a few years earlier is probably inadequate to reflect the changes in the value of the licensed property and the changes that have occurred in the investment marketplace. Even if an industry norm royalty rate was a fair rate of return at the time it was established, there is no guarantee that it is still valid. Value, economic conditions, rates of return, and all of the other factors that drive a fair royalty have dynamic properties. They change constantly, and so must the underlying analysis that establishes royalties.

(c) Return on R&D Costs.   In determining a reasonable royalty, consideration of the amount that was spent on development of the intellectual property could be terribly misleading. The main theme of the analysis presented throughout this book concentrates on providing a fair rate of return on the value of the intellectual property assets. The amount spent in research and development is rarely equal to the value of a property. A proper royalty should provide a fair return on the *value* of the asset, regardless of the costs incurred in development.

The underlying value of intellectual property is based on the amount of future economic benefits. Factors that can limit such benefits include the market potential, the sensitivity of profits to production costs, the period of time over which benefits will be enjoyed, and the many other economic factors that have been discussed. The develop-ment costs do not reflect these factors in any form. Basing a royalty on development costs can completely miss the goal of obtaining a fair return on a valuable asset.

(d) Return on Sales.   A royalty rate that is based on net profits—return on sales—as a percentage of revenues has several primary weaknesses. The first difficulty is determina-tion of the proper allocation of the profits between the licensor and the licensee. A precise and quantifiable method for dividing net profits is rarely specified when this royalty rate methodology is described. Another area of weakness is the lack of consideration for the value of the intellectual property that is invested in the enterprise, as well as a lack of consideration for the value of the complimentary monetary and tangible assets that are invested. Finally, this method fails to consider the relative investment risk associated with the intellectual property.

1.11 SUMMARY

The determination of a royalty rate for a license agreement or profit split for a joint venture should be at such a level as to provide an amount that represents a fair rate of return on the value of the investment in the intellectual property, with respect to the amount of investment risk accepted. The earnings that are attributed to intellectual property must consider any enhanced earnings enjoyed by the business and must also consider the amount invested in the complementary assets of net working capital and tangible assets.

A royalty rate must consider at least:

1. Investment rates of return available from alternative forms of investment possess-ing comparable elements of risk
2. The value of the intellectual property that is the subject of the licensing

3. The amount of complementary monetary and tangible assets required to commercialize the intellectual property

4. The relative investment risk associated with the complementary monetary and tangible assets

5. The investment risk associated with the intellectual property introduced by factors such as advancing and competing technology, industry economics, governmental regulations, and other factors

Intellectual properties in the form of trademarks and patents can dramatically contribute to earnings. The return on monetary and fixed asset investments can be propelled to extraordinary levels with the introduction of intellectual property.

Of the three methods for valuing property, the income approach is currently the best alternative. The market approach can provide an indication of value, but the required marketplace data is scarce. The cost approach has limited usefulness.

The extraordinary importance of intellectual property has made patents, trademarks, and copyrights valuable investment assets. The methods needed to quantify such values are evolving and typically become just as complex as the latest version of semiconductor chips. The same is true of intellectual product licensing price analysis. Rules of thumb are just not good enough anymore. Because intellectual property represents the future of industries and nations, investment analysis will dominate its valuation and pricing from now on.

CHAPTER 2

FINANCIAL ACCOUNTING AND REPORTING CONSIDERATIONS

Donald T. Nicolaisen, CPA

Price Waterhouse
New York

Michael A. Diamond, CPA, PhD

University of Southern California
Los Angeles, California

2.1 INTRODUCTION

Although a broader definition may exist, intellectual property is often separated into three main categories: trademarks, copyrights, and patents. With the growth of global markets, and their ever-increasing reliance on technology, intellectual property currently enjoys a position of great significance. In fact, it is often the primary factor leading to many of today's business mergers, acquisitions, and joint ventures. Many companies today also consider their market image, reputation, technological advantages, and investments in skilled employees and management as being among their most valuable resources: all are intangible assets.

The world's financial markets readily recognize that intellectual property is a valuable asset for a great many companies. Nevertheless, the current accounting and reporting requirements in the United States often do not allow recognition of these assets in a company's financial statements. Thus, stock market studies frequently show a divergence between the market values of a company's technology and the recorded book values of its assets. For many companies, particularly those in the technology or service sector, the book values of tangible net assets are often only a small fraction of total market capitalization.

(a) Accounting Objectives. The accounting system presently followed for intellectual property is perhaps best considered within the context of the broader objectives of financial reporting within the United States, a primary objective of which is to provide readers of financial statements with useful and reliable information to facilitate their investing and lending decision-making processes. To achieve this objective, information reported must be relevant, understandable, and reliable. Moreover, its usefulness is almost always enhanced if the information is prepared consistently with comparable information of similar enterprises. However, identification and measurement uncertainties surrounding intangibles have made it difficult to develop accounting information that reflects all these attributes.

To illustrate, substantial resources may have been expended by an enterprise in developing its intellectual property, but because of the uncertainties of cost measurement or of recovery, the U.S. accounting model usually dictates that no asset be reflected in the balance sheet. Thus the value of such investments is not necessarily evident in reading a company's financial statements. Similarly, a reduction in such investment may not be apparent, during a period of declining earnings, if expenditures on investing activities are reduced to help mitigate the fall in reported earnings.

(b) Key Criteria for Asset Recognition.   Financial Accounting Standards Board (FASB) Statement of Concepts, No. 6 defines an asset as follows:

> Assets are probable future economic benefits obtained or controlled by a particular entity as a result of past transactions of events.

An asset has three essential characteristics:

1. It embodies a probable future benefit that involves a capacity, singly or in combination with other assets, to contribute directly or indirectly to future net cash inflows,
2. A particular entity can obtain the benefit and control others' access to it, and
3. The transaction or other event giving rise to the entity's right to or control of the benefit has already occurred.

Before recognition of an asset as such, U.S. accounting standards require that there be an ability to measure the asset and provide information that is both relevant and reliable. *FASB Statement of Concepts, No. 5* states that to be reliable, information must be "sufficiently free of error and bias to be useful" to financial statement users. This need for both relevancy and reliability quite often, as acknowledged in FASB *Statement of Concepts, No. 6*, requires some trade-off if the perceived relevance warrants a tolerable amount of uncertainty. It is this balance between relevance and reliability that must be weighed carefully whenever the recognition of intellectual property is considered.

2.2 INTELLECTUAL PROPERTY ACQUIRED IN BUSINESS COMBINATIONS

As discussed in section 2.1, the criteria necessary for an asset to be recognized are that it entails probable future economic benefits and its historical cost can be reliably determined. The one time when the cost or value of intellectual property is crystallized and can be objectively measured is at the point at which an asset changes hands. It is at this point that the value of purchased intellectual property represents its historical cost to the acquiring company. In this case, U.S. accounting principles require asset recognition.

Accounting Principles Board Opinions No. 16 and No. 17 (APB 16 and 17) set forth the accounting for purchased intangibles. Basically, the standards require that all intangibles acquired in a business combination be recognized as assets. Intangible assets are defined as nonmonetary assets lacking physical substance that are held for the continuing benefit of the business. Such definition, of course, includes intellectual property of all types.

Intangible assets are grouped in two broad categories, those that are separately identifiable and those that are not. Identifiable assets are those capable of being acquired or disposed of separately, without necessarily acquiring or disposing of other elements of a business. Generally, intellectual property in the form of trademarks, copyrights, and patents are thought of as identifiable intangibles. And it is this segregation that drives the accounting for the asset acquired.

U.S. accounting standards require that intangible assets be recorded at cost on the date acquired. When such assets are acquired in combination with other assets (such is usually the case in a business combination), cost is determined based on an allocation of the total cost of the acquisition to all the assets acquired and all the liabilities assumed. First, cost is assigned to identifiable assets (both tangible and intangible) and to liabilities based on the relative fair values of each at the date of acquisition.

Fair value is generally defined in accounting as the price at which an asset can be sold, or a liability settled, in an arm's-length transaction between unrelated parties. The determination of fair value often requires the use of independent appraisals as evidence of the underlying fair value of an asset.

Any difference between the total cost assigned to identifiable assets (including specifically identifiable intangibles), less the cost of the liabilities assumed in a business combination, is recognized as the cost of unidentifiable intangibles, usually referred to as "goodwill." APB 17 requires that the cost of identifiable intangible assets not be included in the cost assigned to goodwill. In addition, APB 17 prohibits the immediate write-off of such assets, whether through the income statement or directly to equity. An exception relates to research and development in process, which must be expensed as costs are incurred.

2.3 DIRECT ACQUISITION OF INTELLECTUAL PROPERTY

The accounting for the direct acquisition of intellectual property from third parties is essentially the same as that required for the acquisition of intellectual property in connection with a business combination. The only substantive difference is that in a direct acquisition, the cost of the asset acquired is usually determinable directly; that is, allocations are not necessary. In a direct acquisition, APB 17 requires that cost be measured by "the amount of cash disbursed, the fair value of other assets distributed, the present value of amounts to be paid for liabilities incurred, or the fair value of consideration received for stock issued."

2.4 COSTS INCURRED TO CREATE AND MAINTAIN INTELLECTUAL PROPERTY

(a) **General Charges.** Costs to maintain and create intellectual property are often incurred in situations other than the acquisition of assets, whether by purchase or in a business combination. As discussed earlier in sections 2.2 and 2.3, the accounting for costs incurred in acquiring intellectual property from others is clearly specified; they are to be recognized as assets. But when such similar costs are incurred internally to develop or enhance the value of such assets, the accounting rules are less specific; however, recognition as assets is quite limited.

APB 17 specifies that the "costs of developing, maintaining, or restoring intangible assets which are not specifically identifiable, have indeterminable lives, or are inherent in a continuing business and relate to an enterprise as a whole—such as goodwill—should be deducted from income when incurred." The accounting statement does not, however, address the accounting for costs associated with intangible assets that are identifiable, have determinate lives, or are incremental. In theory many of these costs may meet the definition of an asset—that is, probable future economic benefits as a result of past transactions or events.

In establishing whether costs incurred to create or maintain intangibles or intellectual property meet the criteria for recognition as an asset, several obstacles are likely to arise. First, there may be difficulty in determining objectively the cost of the transactions that yield these assets. Second, the benefit, if any, which is to be realized from the expenditure may not be clearly identifiable. Some costs, such as legal fees, registration costs, and other expenditures directly related to securing rights such as patents or copyrights, may be reliably established and capitalized if it is clear that the rights will in fact result in future economic benefits. When such costs are capitalized, any recognition criteria and accounting practice are to be applied consistently. However, for many other identifiable intangibles, neither the transactions nor the related costs will be capable of reliable identification or estimation. Therefore, a great many internally developed intangibles will not meet the criteria for recognition as an asset.

Frequently, the costs incurred to develop or maintain intellectual property are considered under the rubric of "research and development" activities. The accounting for those types of costs are discussed in the paragraphs that follow.

(b) Deferred Charges—Research and Development Costs.   Research and development (R & D) activities entail a wide range of expenditures. Specialized areas, such as research and development conducted under contractual arrangements or in specialized industries (e.g., mineral exploration and extraction) are often subject to specific rules and thus are not considered in this chapter.

For U.S. accounting purposes, R & D activities are typically categorized as either research or development, although some activities have elements of both:

1. *Research* may be defined as investigation directed toward the advancement of knowledge in general or in a specific area, with the aim of developing a new product or service or significantly improving an existing product or process.

2. *Development* is generally thought of as the translation of research findings toward the introduction or improvement of specific commercial products or processes.

Primarily because of the uncertainty of realization of research and development activities, *Statement of Financial Accounting Standards, No. 2* (FAS 2), "Accounting for Research and Development Costs," requires that research and development costs be expensed as incurred. Such costs include salaries, wages, and other benefits provided to employees who carry out the research and development activities. Tangible assets such as materials, equipment, and facilities that have an alternative future use may be capitalized and depreciated over their estimated useful lives. If they do not have an alternative future use and, hence, no separate economic value, FAS 2 requires that the costs of such assets be expensed when incurred. FAS 2 also requires that the cost of any research and development in process which is acquired from others be expensed when acquired.

If a product or process under development does achieve commercial viability, then some direct, incremental costs (e.g., legal fees to obtain patents) may be capitalized as assets. However, costs that are deferred should be limited to those directly related to and incremental to the new product or process. Thus, costs incurred to maintain an asset, including salaries and other personnel costs of administrative and clerical employees, would not normally qualify for capitalization. Similarly, any costs that would be incurred regardless of whether the company was engaged in the development of intellectual property, such as allocated administrative overhead, generally cannot be capitalized.

2.5 AMORTIZATION OF INTELLECTUAL PROPERTY

Whenever intellectual property is recognized as an asset, generally accepted accounting principles require that the cost of the asset be allocated in some systematic manner to the periods expected to benefit from the use of the asset. This is required because, as stated in APB 17, "the Board believes that the value of intangible assets at any one date eventually disappears." Therefore, APB 17 requires that the cost be amortized over the estimated useful life of the asset on a straight-line basis, unless another systematic approach (such as accelerated amortization) is more appropriate.

APB 17 lists factors to be considered in estimating an appropriate useful life. The following are examples:

1. Legal, regulatory, or contractual provisions may limit the maximum useful life.
2. Provisions for renewal or extension may alter a specified limit on useful life.
3. Effects of obsolescence, demand, competition, and other economic factors may reduce a useful life.
4. A useful life may parallel the service life expectancies of individuals or groups of employees.
5. Expected actions of competitors and others may restrict present competitive advantages.
6. An apparently unlimited useful life may in fact be indefinite and benefits cannot be reasonably projected.

Although evaluation of these factors should result in the development of a reasonable estimate of the useful life of an asset, APB 17 goes on to limit arbitrarily the maximum life that may be used to 40 years. The Board set this arbitrary period because, in its view, even in situations in which the life of an asset is indeterminate, its value eventually disappears.

2.6 IMPAIRMENT OF INTELLECTUAL PROPERTY

Like any other asset, intellectual property may become impaired. APB 17 requires companies to evaluate continually the periods of amortization of intangible assets to determine whether a change in estimate is necessary. The standard also notes that, in some circumstances, an estimate of value and future use may indicate that an immediate write-down is necessary. The standard does not, however, specify when such a write-down is required or how it should be measured.

At the time this chapter was written, the Financial Accounting Standards Board (FASB) was working on a major project intended to deal with the identification of and accounting for impaired assets, including intangibles. The outcome of this project will provide specific guidelines on when and how an impairment in value of intellectual property is to be recognized. The FASB's proposal is to recognize impairment whenever estimates of future cash flows (on an undiscounted basis) from such asset, or group of assets, is less than the book value of the asset.

2.7 APPLICATION OF RECOGNITION AND AMORTIZATION CRITERIA

(a) **Patents.** A patent is an exclusive right to a design, idea, or similar asset, which is usually conferred by law, allowing the holder generally to produce and to market the asset without being infringed by others for a specified period of time. The majority of costs associated with internally developed products to be patented are related to research and development activities and, as such, usually must be expensed as incurred. The types of costs that may qualify to be capitalized for internally developed patents generally relate to registration costs, including technical drawings made specifically for purposes of registration. Sometimes unrecovered costs of successfully defending patents are capitalized in practice.

An unsuccessful legal case or the continued infringement of patents by competitors generally would be indicative of an impairment in value. In determining the useful economic life for purposes of computing amortization, the period over which the product is expected to be commercially viable (i.e., produce positive cash flows) should be used if shorter than the legal term of the patent. In today's high-technology economy, a shorter life is frequently warranted.

(b) **Trademarks.** A trademark is a distinctive name or logo connected with either a specific product or a business, which usually can be legally protected like a patent. Costs for internally developed trademarks that may meet the criteria for capitalization include registration fees and certain design costs, such as external fees paid to a design consultant. The decision to capitalize such costs is dependent on whether the commercial viability of the product to which they are connected has been established.

A trademark's continuing value to a business may also be built up or enhanced over a period of years or decades by significant advertising and other marketing activities in which customer loyalty is established. However, the identification of the specific activities that led to the creation of this added value and the measurement of the historical cost of these activities are almost always, in the case of internal generation, so uncertain as to prohibit their recognition as assets. In addition, the American Institute of Certified Public Accountants (AICPA) recently issued a Statement of Position that, except in very limited situations, would prohibit the capitalization of advertising costs.

The period of amortization is usually established by reference to the commercial life of corresponding connected products, as well as by any limit on the length of legal protection. The discontinuance of the use of a trademark in connection with a commercially viable product would be evidence of impairment and of the need to write off the related costs.

(c) **Copyrights.** A copyright usually confers an exclusive right to control publication, distribution, or performance of written, musical, or other works. The costs of establishing a copyright are typically capitalized and amortized over the period of expected revenue generation, which is usually significantly shorter than the copyright life. It is normally prudent practice to write off the costs over the period of the first edition of the work.

SOURCES AND SUGGESTED REFERENCES

Accounting Principles Board. *APB Opinion, No. 16*, "Business Combinations." New York: APB, 1970.

_____. *APB Opinion, No. 17*, "Intangible Assets." New York: APB, 1970.

American Institute of Certified Public Accountants. *Statement of Position, No. 93-7*, "Reporting on Advertising Costs." New York: AICPA, 1993.

Choi, Fererick D.S. *Handbook of International Accounting*. New York: John Wiley & Sons, 1991.

Financial Accounting Standards Board. *Statement of Financial Accounting Standards, No. 2*, "Accounting for Research and Development Costs." Stamford, CT: FASB, 1974.

_____. *Statement of Financial Accounting Concepts, No. 5*, "Recognition and Measurement in Financial Statements of Business Enterprises." Stamford, CT: FASB, 1984.

_____. *Statement of Financial Accounting Concepts, No. 6*, "Elements of Financial Statements." Stamford, CT: FASB, 1985.

CHAPTER 3

AMORTIZATION OF INTELLECTUAL PROPERTY FOR U.S. FEDERAL INCOME TAXES

Raymond F. Gehan
Paul F. Herrera

Deloitte & Touche
New York, New York

3.1 THE REVENUE RECONCILIATION ACT OF 1993

(a) Introduction.   On August 6, 1993, Congress passed, and on August 10, 1993, the president signed, the Omnibus Budget Reconciliation Act of 1993. Title VIII of the Act is the Revenue Reconciliation Act of 1993.

The new law provides for a 15-year uniform amortization period for most purchased intangibles, including goodwill. The provision generally applies to property acquired after the date of enactment of the new law. However, taxpayers may elect to apply the new law to all property acquired after July 25, 1991. Alternatively, they may elect to apply prior law (rather than the provisions of the new law) to property that is acquired after the date of enactment of the new law if the property is acquired pursuant to a binding written contract that was in effect on the date of enactment. The following is a summary of the relevant portions of the Conference Committee Report released on August 4, 1993.

(b) Section 197—Intangible Assets.   The new law allows an amortization deduction with respect to the capitalized costs of certain intangible property (defined as a § 197 intangible) that is acquired by a taxpayer and that is held by the taxpayer in connection with the conduct of a trade or business or an activity engaged in for the production of income. The amount of the deduction is determined by amortizing the adjusted basis of the intangible ratably over a 15-year period that begins with the month in which the intangible is acquired. No other depreciation or amortization deduction is allowed with respect to a § 197 intangible that is acquired by a taxpayer.

In general, the new law applies to a § 197 intangible acquired by a taxpayer, regardless of whether it is acquired as part of a trade or business and applies to a § 197 intangible that is treated as acquired under § 338. The new law generally does not apply to a § 197

The authors wish to thank Stephen T. Taniguchi, also of Deloitte & Touche, for his assistance with this chapter.

intangible that is created by the taxpayer if the intangible is not created in connection with a transaction that involves the acquisition of a trade or business or a substantial portion thereof.

No inference is intended as to whether a depreciation or amortization deduction is allowed under prior law with respect to any intangible property that is either included in, or excluded from, the definition of a § 197 intangible. In addition, no inference is intended as to whether an asset is to be considered tangible or intangible property for any other purpose of the Internal Revenue Code.

The term *§ 197 intangible* is defined as any property that is included in any one or more of the following categories:

- Goodwill and going concern value
- Certain specific types of intangible property that generally relate to work force, information base, know-how, customers, suppliers, or other similar items
- Any license, permit or other right granted by a governmental unit or an agency or instrumentality thereof
- Any covenant not to compete entered into in connection with the direct or indirect acquisition of an interest in a trade or business
- Any franchise, trademark, or trade name

(i) Goodwill and Going Concern Value.   Goodwill is the value of a trade or business that is attributable to the expectancy of continued customer patronage, whether resulting from the name of the trade or business, the reputation of the trade or business, or any other factor. Going concern value is the additional element of value of a trade or business that attaches to property by reason of its existence as an integral part of a going concern. Going concern value includes the value that is attributable to the ability of a trade or business to continue to function and generate income without interruption, notwithstanding a change in ownership. Going concern value also includes the value attributable to the use or availability of an acquired trade or business, for example, the net earnings that otherwise would not be received during any period were the acquired trade or business not available or operational.

(ii) Work Force.   The term *§ 197 intangible* includes a work force in place (sometimes referred to as an agency force or an assembled work force), the composition of a work force (for example, the experience, education, or training of a work force), the terms and conditions of employment, whether contractual or otherwise, and any other value placed on employees or any of their attributes. Thus, for example, the portion of the purchase price of an acquired business that is attributable to the existence of a highly skilled work force, or the cost of acquiring an existing employment contract or a relationship with employees or consultants (including key employee contracts), is to be amortized over the 15-year period.

(iii) Information Base.   The term *§ 197 intangible* includes business books and records, operating systems, and any other information base including lists or other information with respect to current or prospective customers (regardless of the method of recording such information). Thus, for example, the portion of the purchase price of an acquired business that is attributable to the intangible value of technical materials, training manuals or programs, data files, and accounting or inventory control systems, is to be

amortized over the 15-year period. Further, the cost of acquiring customer lists, subscription lists, insurance expirations, patient or client files, or lists of newspaper, magazine, radio, or television advertisers, is to be amortized over the 15-year period.

(iv) Know-How. The term *§ 197 intangible* includes any patent, copyright, formula, process, design, pattern, know-how, format, or any other similar item. Also included are package designs, computer software, and any interest in a film, sound recording, videotape, book, or other similar property, except as specifically provided otherwise in the law.

(v) Customer-Based Intangibles. The term *customer-based intangibles* is defined as the composition of market, market share, and any other value resulting from the future provision of goods or services pursuant to relationships with customers (contractual or otherwise) in the ordinary course of business. Thus, for example, the portion of the purchase price of an acquired business that is attributable to the existence of a customer base, circulation base, undeveloped market or market growth, insurance in force, investment management contracts, or other relationships with customers that involve the future provision of goods or services, is to be amortized over the 15-year period. Customer-based intangibles include the deposit base or any similar asset of a financial institution. Thus, for example, the portion of a purchase price of an acquired financial institution that is attributable to the checking accounts, savings accounts, escrow accounts, and other similar items is to be amortized over the 15-year period.

(vi) Supplier-Based Intangibles. The term *supplier-based intangibles* is defined as the value resulting from the future acquisition of goods or services pursuant to relationships (contractual or otherwise) in the ordinary course of business with suppliers of goods or services to be used or sold by the taxpayer.

Thus, for example, the portion of any purchase price of an acquired business that is attributable to the existence of a favorable relationship with persons who provide distribution services (for example, favorable shelf or display space at a retail outlet), the existence of a favorable credit rating, or the existence of favorable supply contracts, is to be amortized over a 15-year period.

(vii) Other Similar Items. This category includes any other intangible property that is similar to work force, information base, know-how, customer-based intangibles, or supplier-based intangibles.

(viii) Licenses, Permits, and Other Rights Granted by Governmental Units. The term *§ 197 intangible* includes any license, permit, or other right granted by a governmental unit or any agency or instrumentality thereof (even if the right is granted for an indefinite period or is reasonably expected to be renewed for an indefinite period). Thus, for example, the capitalized cost of acquiring from any person a liquor license, a taxicab medallion (or license), an airport landing or takeoff right, a regulated airline route, or a television or radio broadcasting license, is to be amortized over the 15-year period. The issuance or renewal of a license, permit, or other right granted by a governmental unit is to be considered an acquisition of such.

(ix) Covenants Not to Compete and Other Similar Arrangements. The term *§ 197 intangible* includes any covenant not to compete (or other arrangement to the extent that it has

substantially the same effect as a covenant not to compete) entered into in connection with the acquisition of an interest in a business.

Any amount paid or incurred under a covenant not to compete in connection with the acquisition of a trade or business is chargeable to the capital account and is amortized ratably over 15-years. In addition, any amount paid or incurred under a covenant not to compete in a subsequent year is to be amortized ratably over the remaining months in the 15-year period.

An arrangement that requires the former owner of an interest in a business to continue to perform services that benefit the business is considered to have substantially the same effect as a covenant not to compete, to the extent that the amount paid to the former owner under the arrangement exceeds the amount that represents reasonable compensation for the services actually rendered by the former owner.

(x) Franchises, Trademarks, and Trade Names.   The term *franchise* is defined to include any agreement that provides one of the parties to the agreement the right to distribute, sell, or provide goods, services, or facilities, within a specified area. The renewal of a franchise, trademark, or trade name is treated as an acquisition. As under existing law, a deduction is allowed for amounts that are contingent on the productivity, use, or disposition of a franchise, trademark, or trade name only if (1) the contingent amounts are paid as part of a series of payments that are payable at least annually throughout the term of the transfer agreement and (2) the payments are substantially equal in amount or payable under a fixed formula. (See § 1253[d][1].) Any other amount, whether fixed or contingent, that is paid or incurred on account of the transfer of a franchise, trademark, or trade name is chargeable to the capital account and is to be amortized ratably over the 15-year period.

(c) Exceptions to the Definition of § 197 Intangible.   The new law contains several exceptions to the definition of the term *§ 197 intangible*, several of which apply only if the intangible property is not acquired in a transaction that involves the acquisition of assets that constitute a trade or business or a substantial portion thereof. The determination of whether acquired assets constitute a substantial portion of a trade or business is to be based on all of the pertinent facts and circumstances, including the nature and the amount of the assets acquired, as well as the nature and amount of the assets retained by the transferor. It is not intended, however, that the value of the assets acquired relative to the value retained is determinative of whether the acquired assets constitute a substantial portion of a business. However, the acquisition of a franchise, trademark, or trade name does constitute the acquisition of a trade or business or a substantial portion of a trade or business.

(i) Interests in a Corporation, Partnership, Trust, or Estate.   The term *§ 197 intangible* does not include any interest in a corporation, partnership, trust, or estate, whether or not such interests are regularly traded on an established market.

(ii) Interests Under Certain Financial Contracts.   The term *§ 197 intangible* does not include any interest under an existing futures contract, foreign currency contract, notional principal contract, interest rate swap, or other similar financial contract, whether or not such interest is regularly traded on an established market. Not excluded is an interest under a credit card servicing contract or other contract to service indebtedness issued by another person, or any interest under an assumption reinsurance contract.

(iii) Interests in Land.   The cost of acquiring an interest in land is to be taken into account under existing law and includes a fee interest, life estate, remainder, easement, mineral rights, timber rights, grazing rights, riparian rights, air rights, zoning variances, and any other similar rights. An interest in land does not include an airport landing or takeoff right, a regulated airline route, or a franchise to provide cable television services.

(iv) Certain Computer Software.   The term *§ 197 intangible* does not include computer software (whether acquired as part of a trade or business or otherwise) that (1) is readily available for purchase by the general public, (2) is subject to a nonexclusive license, and (3) has not been substantially modified. Nor does the term include computer software that is not acquired in a transaction that involves the acquisition of assets that constitute a trade or business or a substantial portion of a trade or business.

The term *computer software* is defined as any program (i.e., any sequence of machine-readable code) that is designed to cause a computer to perform a desired function. The term includes any incidental and ancillary rights with respect to computer software that (1) are necessary to effect the legal acquisition of the title to, and the ownership of, the software and (2) are used only in connection with the software. The term *computer software* does not include any data base or similar item (other than a data base or item that is in the public domain and that is incidental to the software, for example, a dictionary feature used to spell-check), regardless of the form in which it is stored.

If a depreciation deduction is allowed with respect to computer software that is not a § 197 intangible, the amount of the deduction is to be determined by amortizing the adjusted basis ratably over a 36-month period that begins with the month the software is placed in service. The cost of any computer software that is taken into account as part of the cost of computer hardware under existing law is to continue to be taken into account in such manner. In addition, the cost of any computer software that is currently deductible under existing law is to continue to be taken into account in such manner.

(v) Certain Interests in Films, Sound Recordings, Videotapes, Books, and Other Similar Property.   The term *§ 197 intangible* does not include any interest (including an interest as a licensee) in a film, sound recording, videotape, book, or other similar property (including the right to broadcast or transmit a live event) if the interest is not acquired in a transaction that involves the acquisition of assets that constitute a trade or business or a substantial portion of a trade or business.

(vi) Certain Rights to Receive Tangible Property or Services.   The term *§ 197 intangible* does not include any right to receive tangible property or services under a contract (or any right to receive tangible property or services granted by a governmental unit or by an agency or instrumentality thereof) if the right is not acquired in a transaction that involves the acquisition of assets that constitute a trade or business or a substantial portion of a trade or business.

If a depreciation deduction is allowed with respect to a right to receive tangible property or services that are not § 197 intangibles, the amount of the deduction is to be determined in accordance with regulations to be promulgated by the Treasury Department. It is anticipated that the regulations may provide that, in the case of an amortizable right to receive tangible property or services in substantially equal amounts over a fixed period that is not renewable, the cost of acquiring the right will be taken into account ratably over such fixed period. It is also anticipated that the regulations may provide that, in the case of a right to receive a fixed amount of tangible property or services over an unspecified period, the cost of acquiring such right will be taken into account under a method that allows a deduction based on the amount of tangible property or services received during a taxable year, compared with the total amount of tangible property or services to be received.

For example, assume that a taxpayer acquires from another person a favorable contract right of such person to receive a specified amount of raw materials each month for the next three years (which is the remaining life of the contract) and that the right to receive such raw materials is not acquired as part of an acquisition of assets that constitute a trade or business or a substantial portion thereof (i.e., such contract right is not a § 197 intangible). It is anticipated that the taxpayer may be required to amortize the cost of acquiring the contract right ratably over the three-year remaining life of the contract.

(vii) Certain Interests in Patents or Copyrights.   The term *§ 197 intangible* does not include any interest in a patent or copyright which is not acquired in a transaction that involves the acquisition of assets that constitute a trade or business or a substantial portion of a trade or business.

If a depreciation deduction is allowed with respect to an interest in a patent or copyright and the interest is not a *§ 197 intangible*, then the amount of the deduction is to be determined in accordance with regulations to be promulgated by the Treasury Department. It is expected that the regulations may provide that if the purchase price of a patent is payable on an annual basis as a fixed percentage of the revenue derived from the use of the patent, then the amount of the depreciation deduction allowed for any taxable year with respect to the patent equals the amount of the royalty paid or incurred during such year. See *Associated Patentees, Inc. v. Commissioner*, 4. TC 979 (1945).

(viii) Interests Under Leases of Tangible Property.   The term *§ 197 intangible* does not include any interest as a lessor or lessee under an existing lease of tangible property (whether real or personal). The cost of acquiring an interest as a lessor under a lease of tangible property, wherein the interest as lessor is acquired in connection with the acquisition of the tangible property, is to be taken into account as part of the cost of the tangible property. For example, if a taxpayer acquires a shopping center that is leased to tenants operating retail stores, the portion (if any) of the purchase price of the shopping center that is attributable to the favorable features of the leases is to be taken into account as a part of the basis of the shopping center and is to be taken into account in determining the depreciation deduction allowed with respect to the shopping center.

The cost of acquiring an interest as a lessee under an existing lease of tangible property is to be taken into account under present law (see § 178 of the Code and Treas. Reg. § 1.162-11[a]) rather than under the provisions of the new law. In the case of any interest as a lessee under a lease of tangible property that is acquired with any other intangible property (either in the same transaction or in a series of related transactions), however, the portion of the total purchase price that is allocable to the interest as a lessee is not to exceed the excess of (1) the present value of the fair market value rent for the use of the tangible property for the term of the lease over (2) the present value of the rent reasonably expected to be paid for the use of the tangible property for the term of the lease.

(ix) Interests Under Indebtedness.   The term *§ 197 intangible* does not include any interest (whether as a creditor or debtor) under any indebtedness that was in existence on the date

that the interest was acquired. Thus, for example, the value of assuming an existing indebtedness with a below market interest rate is to be taken into account under existing law, rather than under the new law. In addition, the premium paid for acquiring the right to receive an above-market rate of interest under a debt instrument may be taken into account under § 171 of the Code, which generally allows the amount of the premium to be amortized on a yield-to-maturity basis over the remaining term of the debt instrument. This exception for interests under existing indebtedness does not apply to the deposit base and other similar items of a financial institution.

(x) Professional Sports Franchises.   The term *§197 intangible* does not include a franchise to engage in professional baseball, basketball, football, or other professional sport, nor any item acquired in connection with such a franchise. Consequently, the cost of acquiring a professional sports franchise and related assets (including any goodwill, going concern value, or other § 197 intangibles) is to be allocated among the assets acquired as provided under existing law (see, for example, § 1056 of the Code) and is to be taken into account under the provisions of existing law.

(xi) Purchased Mortgage Servicing Rights.   The term *§ 197 intangible* does not include purchased mortgage servicing rights which are not acquired in connection with the acquisition of a trade or business. Any depreciation deduction allowable with respect to such excluded rights must be computed on a straight line basis over a period of 108 months.

(xii) Certain Transaction Costs.   The term *§ 197 intangible* does not include the amount of any fees for professional services, or any transaction costs, incurred by parties to a transaction with respect to which any portion of the gain or loss is not recognized under Part III of Subchapter C (see for example, *INDOPCO, Inc. v. Commissioner*, 112 S.Ct 1039 (1992).

(xiii) Regulatory Authority Regarding Rights of Fixed Term or Duration.   The new law authorizes the Treasury Department to issue regulations that exclude a right received under a contract, or granted by a governmental unit or an agency or instrumentality thereof, from the definition of a § 197 intangible if (1) the right is not acquired in a transaction that involves the acquisition of assets that constitute a trade or business and (2) the right either (a) has a fixed duration of less than 15 years or (b) is fixed as to amount and the cost is properly recoverable under a method similar to the unit of production method.

(xiv) Exception for Certain Self-Created Intangibles.   The new law generally does not apply to any § 197 intangible that is created by the taxpayer if the § 197 intangible is not created in connection with a transaction that involves the acquisition of assets that constitute a trade or business or a substantial portion thereof.

   For purposes of this exception, a § 197 intangible that is owned by a taxpayer is to be considered created by the taxpayer if the intangible is produced for the taxpayer by another person under a contract with the taxpayer that is entered into prior to the production of the intangible. For example, a technological process or other know-how that is developed specifically for a taxpayer under an arrangement with another person, pursuant to which the taxpayer retains all rights to the process or know-how, is to be considered created by the taxpayer.

The exception for self-created intangibles does not apply to the entering into or renewal of a contract for the use of a § 197 intangible, for example, the capitalized costs incurred by a licensee in connection with entering into a contract for the use of know-how or another § 197 intangible.

In addition, the exception for self-created intangibles does not apply to (1) any license, permit, or other right that is granted by a governmental unit or an agency or instrumentality thereof, (2) any covenant not to compete (or other similar arrangement) entered into in connection with the direct or indirect acquisition of an interest in a trade or business (or a substantial portion thereof), or (3) any franchise, trademark, or trade name. Thus, for example, the capitalized costs incurred in connection with the development or registration of a trademark or trade name are to be amortized over the 15-year period.

(d) Special Rules

(i) Determination of Adjusted Basis.   The adjusted basis of a § 197 intangible that is acquired from another person is generally to be determined under the principles of existing law that apply to tangible property that is acquired from another person. Thus, for example, if a portion of the cost of acquiring an amortizable § 197 intangible is contingent, the adjusted basis of the § 197 intangible is to be increased as of the beginning of the month that the contingent amount is paid or incurred. This additional amount is to be amortized ratably over the remaining months in the 15-year amortization period that applies to the intangible, as of the beginning of the month that the contingent amount is paid or incurred.

(ii) Treatment of Certain Dispositions of Amortizable § 197 Intangibles.   Special rules apply if a taxpayer disposes of a § 197 intangible that was acquired in a transaction or series of related transactions and, after the disposition, the taxpayer retains other § 197 intangibles that were acquired in such transaction or series of related transactions. For this purpose, the abandonment of a § 197 intangible or any other event that renders a § 197 intangible worthless is to be considered a disposition of a § 197 intangible.

First, no loss is to be recognized by reason of such a disposition. Second, the adjusted bases of the retained § 197 intangibles that were acquired in connection with such transaction or series of related transactions are to be increased by the amount of any loss that is not recognized. The adjusted basis of any such retained § 197 intangible is increased by the product of (1) the amount of the loss that is not recognized solely by reason of this provision and (2) a fraction, the numerator of which is the adjusted basis of the intangible, as of the date of the disposition, and the denominator of which is the total adjusted bases of all such retained § 197 intangibles, as of the date of the disposition.

For purposes of these rules, all persons treated as a single taxpayer under § 41(f)(1) of the Code are treated as a single taxpayer. Thus, for example, a loss is not recognized by a corporation upon the disposition of a § 197 intangible if after the disposition a member of the same controlled group as the corporation retains other § 197 intangibles that were acquired in the same transaction (or a series of related transactions) as the § 197 intangible that was disposed of. It is anticipated that the Treasury Department will provide rules for taking into account the amount of any loss that is not recognized as a result of this rule (e.g., by allowing the corporation that disposed of the § 197 intangible to amortize the loss over the remaining portion of the 15-year amortization period).

These special rules do not apply to a § 197 intangible that is separately acquired (i.e., a § 197 intangible that is acquired other than in a transaction or a series of related transactions that involve the acquisition of other § 197 intangibles). Consequently, a loss may be recognized upon the disposition of a separately acquired § 197 intangible. In no event, however, is the termination or worthlessness of a portion of a § 197 intangible to be considered the disposition of a separately acquired § 197 intangible. For example, the termination of one or more customers from an acquired customer list, or the worthlessness of some information from an acquired data base, is not to be considered the disposition of a separately acquired § 197 intangible.

(iii) Special Rule for Covenants Not to Compete.   A covenant not to compete (or other arrangement to the extent such arrangement has substantially the same effect as a covenant not to compete) shall not be considered to have been disposed of or to have become worthless until the disposition or worthlessness of all interests in the trade or business or a substantial portion thereof that were directly or indirectly acquired in connection with such covenant (or other arrangement).

Thus, for example, in the case of an indirect acquisition of a trade or business (e.g., through the acquisition of stock that is not treated as an asset acquisition), a covenant not to compete (or other arrangement) entered into in connection with the indirect acquisition cannot be written off faster than on the straight line basis over 15 years (even if the covenant or other arrangement expires or otherwise becomes worthless) unless all the trades or businesses indirectly acquired (e.g., acquired through such stock interest) are also disposed of or become worthless.

(iv) Treatment of Certain Amounts That Are Properly Taken into Account in Determining the Cost of Property That Is Not a § 197 Intangible.   The new law does not apply to any amount that is properly taken into account under present law in determining the cost of property that is not a § 197 intangible. Thus, for example, no portion of the cost of acquiring real property that is held for the production of rental income (for example, an office building, apartment building, or shopping center) is to be taken into account under the new law (i.e., no goodwill, going concern value, or any other § 197 intangible is to arise in connection with the acquisition of such real property). Instead, the entire cost of acquiring such real property is to be included in the basis of the real property and is to be recovered under the principles of existing law applicable to such property.

(v) Modification of Purchase Price Allocation and Reporting Rules for Certain Asset Acquisitions.   Sections 338(b)(5) and 1060 of the Code authorize the Treasury Department to promulgate regulations that provide for the allocation of purchase price among assets in the case of certain asset acquisitions. Under regulations that have been promulgated pursuant to this authority, the purchase price of an acquired trade or business must be allocated among the assets of the trade or business through the residual method.

Under the residual method specified in the Treasury regulations, all assets of an acquired trade or business are divided into the following four classes: (1) Class I assets, which generally include cash and cash equivalents, (2) Class II assets, which generally include certificates of deposit, U.S. government securities, readily marketable stock or securities, and foreign currency, (3) Class III assets, which generally include all assets other than those included in Classes I, II, and IV (such as furniture, fixtures, land, buildings, equipment, other tangible property, accounts receivable, covenants not to compete, and other amortizable intangible assets), and (4) Class IV assets, which include intangible assets in the nature of goodwill or going concern value. The purchase price of an acquired trade or business (as first reduced by the amount of the assets included in Class I) is allocated to the assets included in Class II and Class III, based on the value of the assets included in each class. To the extent that the purchase price (as reduced by the amount of the assets in Class I) exceeds the value of the assets included in Class II and Class III, the excess is allocable to assets included in Class IV.

It is expected that the present Treasury regulations that provide for the allocation of purchase price in the case of certain asset acquisitions will be amended to reflect the fact that the new law allows an amortization deduction with respect to intangible assets in the nature of goodwill and going concern value. It is anticipated that the residual method specified in the regulations will be modified to treat all amortizable § 197 intangibles as Class IV assets, and that this modification will apply to any acquisition of property to which the new law applies.

(vi) General Regulatory Authority.   The Treasury Department is authorized to prescribe such regulations as may be appropriate to carry out the purposes of the new law, including such regulations as may be appropriate to prevent avoidance of the purposes of the new law through related persons or otherwise. It is anticipated that the Treasury Department will exercise its regulatory authority, where appropriate, to clarify the types of intangible property that constitute § 197 intangibles.

(e) Effective Date

(i) In General.   The provisions of the new law generally apply to property acquired after the date of enactment of the new law. As more fully described in the following paragraphs, however, a taxpayer may elect to apply the new law to all property acquired after July 25, 1991. In addition, a taxpayer who does not make this election may elect to apply existing law (rather than the provisions of the new law) to property acquired after the date of enactment of the new law, pursuant to a binding written contract in effect on the date of enactment of the new law and at all times thereafter until the property is acquired. Finally, special "antichurning" rules may apply to prevent taxpayers from converting existing goodwill, going concern value, or any other § 197 intangible for which a depreciation or amortization deduction would not have been allowable under existing law, into amortizable property to which the new law applies.

(ii) Election to Apply Bill to Property Acquired After July 25, 1991.   A taxpayer may elect to apply the new law to all property acquired by the taxpayer after July 25, 1991. If a taxpayer makes this election, the new law also applies to all property acquired after July 25, 1991, by any taxpayer who is under common control with the electing taxpayer at any time during the period that began on August 2, 1993, and ends on the date that the election is made.

The election is to be made at such time and in such manner as may be specified by the Treasury Department, and the election may be revoked only with the consent of the Treasury Department.

(iii) Elective Binding Contract Exception.   A taxpayer may also elect to apply existing law (rather than the provisions of the new law) to property acquired after the date of

enactment of the new law if the property is acquired pursuant to a binding written contract that was in effect on the date of enactment of the new law and is at all times thereafter until the property is acquired. This election may not be made by any taxpayer who is subject to the previously described election who applies the provisions of the new law to property acquired before the date of enactment of the new law.

The election is to be made at such time and in such manner as may be specified by the Treasury Department, and it may be revoked only with the consent of the Treasury Department. It is anticipated that the Treasury Department will require the election to be made on the timely filed federal income tax return for the taxable year that includes the date of enactment of the new law.

(iv) Antichurning Rules.   Special rules (antichurning rules) are provided by the new law to prevent taxpayers from converting existing goodwill, going concern value, or any other § 197 intangible for which a depreciation or amortization deduction would not have been allowable under existing law, into amortizable property to which the new law applies.

The new law also contains a general anti-abuse rule that applies to any § 197 intangible that is acquired by a taxpayer from another person. Under this rule, a § 197 intangible may not be amortized under the provisions of the new law if the taxpayer acquired the intangible in a transaction of which one of the principal purposes is to (1) avoid the requirement that the intangible be acquired after the date of enactment of the new law or (2) avoid any of the antichurning rules (described in the preceding paragraph) that are applicable to goodwill, going concern value, or any other § 197 intangible for which a depreciation or amortization deduction would not be allowable but for the provisions of the new law.

(f) Annual Reports

(i) Report on the Implementation and Effects of the New Law.   It is intended that the Treasury Department will conduct a continuing study of the implementation and effects of the new law, including effects on merger and acquisition activities (including hostile takeovers and leveraged buyouts). It is expected that the study will address effects of the legislation on the pricing of acquistions and on the reported values of different types of intangibles (including goodwill). It is also intended that the Treasury Department report the initial results of such study as expeditiously as possible but no later than December 31, 1994. The Treasury Department is expected to provide additional reports annually thereafter.

(ii) Report Regarding Backlog of Pending Cases.   The purpose of the new legislation is to simplify the law regarding the amortization of intangibles. The severe backlog of cases in audit and litigation is a matter of great concern and any principles established in such cases will no longer have precedential value due to the new law. Therefore, the Internal Revenue Service is urged in the strongest possible terms to expedite the settlement of cases under prior law. In considering settlements and establishing procedures for handling existing controversies in an expedient and balanced manner, the Internal Revenue Service is strongly encouraged to take into account the principles of the new law so as to produce consistent results for similarly situated taxpayers. However, no inference is intended that any deduction should be allowed in these cases for assets that are not amortizable under prior law.

In addition, it is intended that the Treasury Department report annually to the House Ways and Means Committee and the Senate Finance Committee, regarding the volume of pending disputes in audit and litigation involving the amortization of intangibles and the progress made in resolving such disputes. It is intended that the report will also address the effects of the new law on the volume and nature of disputes regarding the amortization of intangibles. It is intended that the first such report shall be made no later than December 31, 1994.

3.2 PRIOR LAW AND REGULATIONS

(a) Determinable Useful Life

(i) General Rules.   With respect to depreciable and amortizable property, the Internal Revenue Code provides:

> There shall be allowed as a depreciation deduction a reasonable allowance for the exhaustion, wear and tear (including a reasonable allowance for obsolescence)—
>
> **1.** Of property used in the trade or business, or
> **2.** Of property held for the production of income.[1]

The Treasury Regulations go on to state as follows:

> *Useful Life*—For the purpose of section 167 the estimated useful life of an asset is not necessarily the useful life inherent in the asset but is the period over which the asset may reasonably be expected to be useful to the taxpayer in his trade or business or in the production of his income. This period shall be determined by reference to his experience with similar property taking into account present conditions and probable future developments. Some of the factors to be considered in determining this period are:
>
> **1.** Wear and tear and decay or decline from natural causes,
> **2.** The normal progress of the art, economic changes, inventions and current developments within the industry and the taxpayer's trade or business,
> **3.** The climatic and other local conditions peculiar to the taxpayer's trade or business, and
> **4.** The taxpayer's policy as to repairs, renewals and replacements.
>
>   Salvage value is not a factor for the purpose of determining useful life.
>   If the taxpayer's experience is inadequate, the general experience in the industry may be used until such time as the taxpayer's own experience forms an adequate basis for making the determination. The estimated remaining useful life may be subject to modification by reason of conditions known to exist at the end of the taxable year and shall be redetermined when necessary regardless of the method of computing depreciation. However, estimated remaining useful life shall be redetermined only when the change in the useful life is significant and there is a clear and convincing basis for the redetermination.[2]

The regulation that specifically pertains to intangible assets provides:

> *Intangibles*—If an intangible asset is known from experience or other factors to be of use in the business or in the production of income for only a limited period, the length of which can be estimated with reasonable accuracy, such an intangible asset may be the subject of a depreciation

---

[1] § 167(a).
[2] Reg 1.167(a)-1(b).

allowance. Examples are patents and copyrights. An intangible asset, the useful life of which is not limited, is not subject to the allowance for depreciation. No allowance will be permitted merely because, in the unsupported opinion of the taxpayer, the intangible asset has a limited useful life. No deduction for depreciation is allowable with respect to goodwill.[3]

(ii) Patents and Copyrights.   The regulations also provide specifically for the depreciation of patents and copyrights, as follows:

> *Depreciation of Special Cases*—(a) Depreciation of patents or copyrights. The cost or other basis of a patent or copyright shall be depreciated over its remaining useful life. Its costs to the patentee includes the various Government fees, cost of drawings, models, attorney's fees and similar expenditures . . . . If a patent or copyright becomes valueless in any year before its expiration, the unrecovered cost or other basis may be deducted in that year.[4]

The legal life of a United States patent is 17 years.

Where separate values of a group of interdependent patents—the remaining useful lives of which are of different periods—cannot be determined, depreciation may be determined on the average life of the patents.[5]

(iii) Patent Applications.   The courts hold that because an invention or patent application is a property right, when it ripens into a patent, depreciation should be allowed from the date of the granting of the patent, based on the value of the invention or patent application on the date the right was acquired. The value can be written off over a 17-year period dating from issuance of the patent, or such shorter economic life, if justified.

(iv) Copyrights.   In the case of copyrighted material published before 1978, the U.S. copyright term was for 28 years, and copyrights could be renewed for a second term of 28 years.

In the case of works created after 1977, the copyright term is for the life of the author plus 50 years. The copyright term for joint works created after 1977 is the life of the last surviving author plus 50 years. Where works made for hire are created after 1977, the copyright period is 75 years from the date of first publication, or a term of 100 years from the year of creation, whichever expires first. In general, these same rules apply to works created before, but not published or copyrighted before, 1978. If a copyright is in its first 28-year term on January 1, 1978, the copyright may generally be renewed for 47 years, provided application for renewal is made within one year before expiration of the first term (this would give a total of 75 years). Similarly, if the copyright is in its second 28-year term on January 1, 1978, the copyright may generally be renewed for an additional 19 years (for a total of 75 years).[6]

In light of regulations discussed previously, it is clear that depreciation may be based on a determinable economic useful life, rather than the legal useful life, of the copyright.

(v) Engineering Drawings.   Designs, drawings, models, and patterns are depreciable where their period of usefulness can be estimated with reasonable accuracy. In such case, their cost will be recovered by way of depreciation allowances spread over the period of their useful life.

---

[3] Reg 1.167(a)-3.
[4] Reg 1.167(a)-6.
[5] *Lanova Corp.*, 17 TC 1178 (1952).
[6] 17 USC 302-304.

(vi) Trademarks, Trade Names, and Franchises.   The general rule with respect to trademarks and trade names is that they are not amortizable. Costs of acquiring a trade name are not amortizable because a trade name does not have a determinable life, there being no restrictions on the time or method of its use.[7] However, the Internal Revenue Code provides special rules that apply to the deduction or amortization of fixed sum payments and contingent payments that are made in certain transfers of a franchise, trademark, or trade name.[8]

The term *franchise* includes an agreement that gives one of the parties to the agreement the right to distribute, sell, or provide goods, services, or facilities, within a special area.[9] It does not include a franchise to engage in a professional sports league such as a football, basketball, or baseball league.[10] It does, however, include other sports enterprises, such as golfing, bowling, and other sporting enterprises, as a trade or business.[11]

The term *trademark* includes any word, name, symbol, device, or any combination thereof, adopted and used by a manufacturer or merchant to identify his or her goods and distinguish them from those manufactured or sold by others; whereas the term *trade name* includes any name used by a manufacturer or merchant to identify or designate a particular trade or business or the name or title lawfully adopted and used by a person or organization engaged in a trade or business.[12]

An amount paid or incurred on account of a transfer, sale, or other disposition of a franchise, trademark, or trade name that is (1) contingent on its productivity, use, or disposition and (2) part of a series of payments that are paid not less frequently than annually over the entire term of the transfer agreement and are substantially equal in amount, is currently allowed as a deduction.[13]

On the other hand, if a transfer of a franchise, trademark, or trade name is made in discharge of a sum agreed upon in the transfer agreement, and if the transferor retains any "significant power, right or continuing interest" with respect to the subject matter of the franchise, trademark, or trade name, then:

1. In the case of a single payment of $100,000 or less, the amount paid is amortizable ratably over 10 years or over the period of the transfer agreement, whichever is shorter.[14]

2. In the case of a single payment of more than $100,000, the amount paid is amortizable ratably over 25 years.[15]

3. In the case of a payment which is one of a series of approximately equal payments made over the period of the agreement or a period of more than 10 years, the amounts are deductible in the year paid.[16]

The term "significant power, right or continuing interest" includes, but is not limited to, rights (whether expressly stated in the agreement or implied in fact from the conduct of the parties) with respect to the franchise, trademark, or trade name that is transferred:

---

[7] *H.M. Stiles*, TC Memo 1967-100.

[8] § 1253.

[9] § 1253(b)(1).

[10] § 1253(e).

[11] Committee Reports on P.L. 91-172.

[12] 15 USC 1127 and Proposed Reg § 1.1253-2(b) and (c).

[13] § 1253(d)(1).

[14] § 1253(d)(2)(A)(i).

[15] § 1253(d)(2)(B) and (d)(3)(B).

[16] § 1253(d)(2)(A)(ii).

1. A right to disapprove any assignment of the transferred interest, or of any part thereof,

2. A right to terminate the transferred interest at will,

3. A right to prescribe the standards of quality of products used or sold, or of services furnished, and of the equipment and facilities used to promote such products or services,

4. A right to require that the transferee sell or advertise only the products or services of the transferor,

5. A right to require that the transferee purchase substantially all of his or her supplies and equipment from the transferor or from suppliers designated by the transferor,

6. A right to payments contingent on the productivity, use, or disposition of the subject matter of the transferred interest where the estimated amount of such payments constitutes more than 50% of the total estimated amount the transferee has agreed to pay the transferor in consideration for the transferor,

7. A right to prevent the transferee from removing equipment outside the territory in which the transferee is permitted to operate,

8. A right to participate in a continuing manner in the commercial or economic activities of the transferred interest, such as, for example, by conducting activities with respect to a transferred franchise such as sales promotion (including advertising), sales and management training, employee training programs, holding national meetings for the transferee, or providing the transferee with blueprints or formulae, and

9. Any other right that permits the transferor to exercise continuing, active, and operational control over the transferee's trade or business activities.[17]

(vii) Package Design Costs. The term *package design* means an asset that is created by a specific graphic arrangement or design of shapes, colors, words, pictures, lettering, and so forth on a given product package, or the design of a container with respect to its shape or function.

Because package designs generally have useful lives greater than one year, package design costs generally must be capitalized. For these purposes it is irrelevant whether a package design was created in-house, created by an independent contractor, or purchased from a third party who produced it.

In general, the cost of package designs may not be amortized because their useful lives cannot be ascertained.[18]

However, to minimize disputes regarding the useful lives of individual package designs, the Internal Revenue Service, as a matter of administrative convenience, will allow taxpayers to elect to deem the useful lives of certain package designs to be 60 months.

As a condition to a taxpayer's electing to deem the useful lives of certain of its package designs to be 60 months, the taxpayer must first change its method of accounting for package design costs to a capitalization method. If the package design is disposed of or abandoned within the 60-month period, the taxpayer is permitted to deduct the unamortized portion of the costs in the year of disposition or abandonment.[19]

---

[17] Proposed Reg § 1.1253-2(d).
[18] Rev Rul 89-23, 1989-1 CB 85.
[19] Rev Proc 89-17, 1989-1 CB 827.

(viii) Publication Rights.   The income forecast method and the straight line method are acceptable methods for computing the depreciation allowance for book manuscripts. The sliding scale method cannot be used.[20]

(ix) Software.   Revenue Procedure 69-21 provides guidelines to be used in connection with the examination of federal income tax returns involving the cost of computer software.[21]

For the purpose of the Revenue Procedure, *computer software* includes all programs or routines used to cause a computer to perform a desired task or set of tasks, and the documentation required to describe and maintain those programs. Computer programs of all classes, for example, operating systems, executive systems, monitors, compilers and translators, assembly routines, and utility programs, as well as application programs, are included. *Computer software* does not include procedures that are external to computer operations, such as instructions to transcription operators and external control procedures.

Cost of Developing Software.   The costs of developing software (whether or not the particular software is patented or copyrighted) in many respects so closely resemble the kind of research and experimental expenditures that fall within the purview of § 174 of the Internal Revenue Code as to warrant accounting treatment similar to that accorded such costs under that section. Accordingly, the Internal Revenue Service will not disturb a taxpayer's treatment of cost incurred in developing software, either for his or her own use or to be held by the taxpayer for sale or lease to others, where:

1. All of the costs properly attributable to the development of software by the taxpayer are consistently treated as current expenses and deducted in full, in accordance with rules similar to those applicable under § 174(a) of the Code, or

2. All of the costs properly attributable to the development of software by the taxpayer are consistently treated as capital expenditures that are recoverable through deductions for ratable amortization, in accordance with rules similar to those provided by § 174(b) of the Code and the regulations thereunder, over a period of five years from the date of completion of such development or over a shorter period where such costs are attributable to the development of software that the taxpayer clearly establishes has a useful life of less than five years.

Cost of Purchased Software.   With respect to costs of purchased software, the Service will not disturb the taxpayer's treatment of such costs if the following practices are consistently followed:

1. Such costs are included, without being separately stated, in the cost of the hardware (computer), and such costs are treated as a part of the cost of the hardware that is capitalized and depreciated, or

2. Such costs are separately stated, and the software is treated by the taxpayer as an intangible asset, the cost of which is to be recovered by amortization deductions ratably over a period of five years or such shorter period as can be established by the taxpayer as appropriate in any particular case if the useful life of the software in his or her hands will be less than five years.

---

[20] Rev Rul 79-285, 1979-2 CB 91.
[21] 1969-2 C.B. 303.

(b) Methodologies for Determining the Useful Lives of Intangible Assets.   As stated earlier, § 1.167(a)-3 of the Income Tax Regulations provides that if an intangible asset is known from experience or other factors to be of use in a business for only a limited period, the length of which can be estimated with reasonable accuracy, such an intangible asset may be the subject of a depreciation allowance. No allowance will be permitted merely because, in the unsupported opinion of the taxpayer, the intangible asset has a limited useful life.

Rev. Rul. 74-456 provides that in order for an intangible asset to be amortizable, the taxpayer must prove that the asset has value, separate and apart from goodwill, and has a limited useful life, the duration of which can be ascertained with reasonable accuracy.[22] Although this sometimes poses a difficult task for the taxpayer, there are several court decisions in which the taxpayer has met its burden of proof and has been allowed to amortize the value of the intangible assets.

Holden Fuel Company v. Commissioner[23]

Computing & Software, Inc. v. Commissioner[24]

Los Angeles Central Animal Hospital, Inc. v. Commissioner[25]

National Service Industries v. United States[26]

Sirovatka v. Commissioner[27]

Metro Auto Auction of Kansas City, Inc. v. Commissioner[28]

Business Service Industries, Inc. v. Commissioner[29]

Citizens & Southern Corporation v. Commissioner[30]

Colorado National Bankshares, Inc. v. Commissioner[31]

Analysis of the useful lives of acquired intangible assets can be performed by recognized actuarial and statistical methods. The use of such methods to determine useful lives of intangible assets has been approved by the Court of Appeals in *Super Food Services, Inc. v. United States*.[32] In that case, the intangible asset displayed a definite and consistent pattern of termination that would have been discernible as of the date of acquisition.

(i) Survivor Curves.   Actuarial and statistical approaches are applied to create a survivor curve for a group of assets. Survivor curves illustrate the relationship between the rate of retirement of assets retired from the group and the current age of the existing assets remaining in the group. The performance of this type of statistical study requires that records be available that indicate the acquisition date of all existing assets, and the acquisition date and termination date of all retired assets.

---

[22] 1974-2 C.B. 65.

[23] 73-2 USTC 9514 (CA-6).

[24] 65 TC 223 (1975).

[25] 68 TC 269 (1977).

[26] 73-2 USTC 9703 (DC, GA).

[27] 47 TCM 1 (1983).

[28] TC Memo 1984-440.

[29] TC Memo 1986-86.

[30] 91 TC 463 (1988), aff'd 91-1 USTC 50,043 (CA-11).

[31] TC Memo 1990-495, aff'd 1993-1 USTC 50,077 (CA-10).

[32] 69-2 USTC 9558 (CA-7).

(ii) Turnover Method. As an alternative, if the data necessary to determine a survivor curve analysis is not available, a turnover study is used to determine the useful life. A turnover study analyzes the annual amounts of additions, retirements, and year-end balances of the assets in the group for a period of years.

The following excerpt from *Depreciation*, by Grant and Norton,[33] explains the turnover methodology that can be used in developing the remaining life of an intangible asset:

> Often the data required for actuarial studies are not available. If so, it is not possible to obtain survivor curves. However, it still may be possible to use a turnover study to get an estimate of the average service life.
>
> Such study requires annual figures for acquisitions, retirements, and balances in service for the class of property unit under consideration. These figures should extend over a period of years at least equal to the average service life, preferably longer. This type of information often is directly available from accounting records. It permits the determination of the turnover period, which is defined as the time required to exhaust the amount of property existing as of a given date by subtracting therefrom all subsequent retirements of the same class of plant. All retirements are subtracted; this applies to property actually included in the balance at the given date and retirements of subsequent additions.[33]

(iii) Attrition Rate Studies. Finally, if data to perform a turnover study is not available, then an attrition study can be performed. This approach has been described in and approved by the Tax Court in *Business Service Industries, Inc.* and other cases.[34] In an attrition study, the number of assets that are retired annually is compared with the beginning-of-year balances to calculate an attrition rate. The reciprocal of the attrition rate yields the useful life of the asset.

(c) Amortization Methods

(i) Straight Line. The generally acceptable method of amortization of intangible assets is the straight-line method, under which the cost or other basis of the asset is amortized over its useful life in equal annual (or monthly) installments.

(ii) Income-Forecast Method. The Internal Revenue Service has addressed the question of the proper method of depreciating the cost of leased or rented television films, taped shows for reproduction, and motion picture films for federal income tax purposes.[35]

The IRS concluded that the so-called income-forecast method is readily adaptable in computing depreciation, without producing any serious distortion of income, and constitutes an acceptable method for computing a reasonable allowance for depreciation under § 167(a). The method requires the application of a fraction, the numerator of which is the income from a film for the taxable year, and the denominator of which is the forecasted or estimated total income to be derived from the film during its useful life, including income from foreign exhibition or other exploitation of the film. The term *income* for purposes of computing this fraction means income from the film less the expense of distributing it.

---

[33] Eugene L. Grant and Paul T. Norton, Jr., *Depreciation* (New York: Ronald Press, 1955), pp. 75–76.

[34] TC Memo 1986–86.

[35] Rev Rul 60-358, 1960-2 CB 68, as amplified by Rev Rul 64-273, 1964-2 CB 62.

In addition, books, patents, and sound recordings used to produce income in a manner similar to television and movie films may use the income forecast method of computing depreciation.[36]

For purposes of the income-forecast method, the estimate of income from motion picture films produced in the United States and originally released for theatrical exhibition after 1970 does not have to include any estimated revenue from future television exhibition of the films. However, if a domestic TV exhibition arrangement is entered into before the cost of the motion picture has been depreciated down to a reasonable salvage value, an estimate of income from TV exhibition is to be made at that time.

In addition, the estimate of income from a television series or a film made for TV released after 1970 does not have to include any estimated income from domestic syndication of the series or film. However, if a domestic syndication arrangement is entered into before the TV series or film has been depreciated down to a reasonable salvage value, an estimate of income from domestic syndication is required to be made at that time.[37]

(iii) Sliding-Scale Method.   Depreciation of the cost of films and film rights under the sliding-scale method was approved in the Tax Court case *Kiro, Inc.*[38] In that case, a percentage of the cost was allocated to each showing, depending on the number of showings. The percentages were set up on a graduated or sliding scale, with higher rates for the earlier showings. The straight-line method, however, was required for some film contracts where there was no limit on the number of showings and the station did not establish the number of expected showings.

The sliding-scale method cannot be used for book manuscripts, patents, or master sound recordings.[39]

(iv) Associated Patentees Case.   In many instances, the purchase price of a patent is tied to the future revenue derived from the use of the product. Under these circumstances, depreciation is allowed under Reg. 1.167(a)-3, but the computation of depreciation cannot be determined by dividing basis by useful life, because basis is unknown. In such case, the depreciation allowed equals the amount of the royalty, paid or accrued during the tax year, that is considered a capital expenditure made to acquire the patent. (See *Associated Patentees, Inc.*[40])

3.3 IRS COORDINATED ISSUE PAPERS

(a) Purpose and Legal Status.[41]   Coordinated Issue Papers set forth the current thinking of the Internal Revenue Service under prior law with respect to key industry compliance issues and were designed to be used by revenue agents in examining tax returns. A key purpose of the papers was to establish examination conformity within industry categories; that is, to ensure that key industry issues were raised in all cases, on a consistent basis, and subsequently resolved using the guidance provided.

---

[36] Supra, note 20.

[37] Rev Proc 71-29, 1971-2 CB 568.

[38] 51 TC 155 (Acq).

[39] Rev Rul 79-285, 1979-2CB 91.

[40] 4 TC 979 (1945), Rev Rul 67-136, 1967-1 CB 58.

[41] Internal Revenue Service Industry Specialization Program Coordinated Issue Papers, Obtained by Bureau of National Affairs, Inc., Report No. 95, May 15, 1992.

Once they were issued, revenue agents were instructed to give the Industry Specialization Program (ISP) papers to taxpayers with tax returns under examination in which the issue was raised. In addition, the Internal Revenue Service determined that the papers may be obtained under the Freedom of Information Act.

The Coordinated Issue Papers were designed primarily to ensure consistency in ISP examinations by identifying key industry issues that should be raised, and therefore they served as audit guidance, advising revenue agents to examine certain issues. The documents set forth the Service's current "thinking" as to its practice, but they clearly were not revenue rulings or regulations and, therefore, were not official pronouncements of IRS position.

(b) Application to Intellectual Property. Of the 68 published ISP Coordinated Issue Papers, only a few relate to the amortization of intangible assets for federal income tax purposes. None discuss intellectual property such as patents, copyrights, trademarks, and trade names. However, the IRS theory and rationale spelled out in the papers in which amortization was denied to other intangible assets is useful in understanding the IRS position with respect to intellectual properties that do not have a legal life, such as nonpatented technology, secret processes, drawings, formulas, know-how, and so forth.

The Coordinated Issue Papers that cover amortization, and the intangible assets that are discussed, are as follows:

- Covenants not to compete
- Employment contracts
- Order backlog
- Assembled work force
- Market-based intangibles
- Customer-based intangibles
- Core deposit intangibles
- Package design costs
- Cable customer subscription lists

The IRS view was that allowance for depreciation for purchased intangible assets turns on a two-pronged factual inquiry: (1) whether the intangible has an ascertainable value separate and distinct from any goodwill or going concern value obtained in the acquisition and (2) whether it has a limited useful life that can be determined with reasonable accuracy.

In these Coordinated Issue Papers the IRS takes the position that where an intangible asset is acquired as part of an ongoing business, with characteristics such as no change in name, location, or personnel, so that the taxpayer could be seen as stepping into the shoes of the seller and expecting continued patronage by the existing group of customers, and has the ability to function and generate operating revenues without interruption as a result of the change of ownership, the conclusion is that the intangible is goodwill, or is inextricable from goodwill.

3.4 LEADING INTANGIBLE ASSET AMORTIZATION COURT DECISIONS

(a) Newark Morning Ledger Co. v. United States.[42] The Newark Morning Ledger Co. was the successor to Herald Company, which had acquired Booth Newspapers, Inc. in 1976.

---

[42] 945 F.2d 555, 91-2 USTC 50,451 (CA-3), reversed and remanded S Ct 93-1 USTC 50, 228.

Booth operated newspapers in eight Michigan communities, with 460,000 total subscribers. The purchase price of $328,173,154 was allocated among the various assets acquired, including $67,773,000 for "paid subscribers" and $26,337,152 for goodwill and going concern value.

Newark presented a statistical analysis of the remaining lives for the subscribers for each of the eight newspapers. The resulting lives ranged from 14.7 to 22.2 years for daily subscribers and 14.7 to 23.4 years for Sunday subscribers.

In valuing the paid subscribers, Newark used the income approach. The future income attributable to the acquired subscribers list was developed based on a statistical study of the number of subscribers expected to remain active in future years. Net revenues from the remaining subscribers each year were discounted back to the acquisition date. The resulting value of the subscribers was thus computed to be $67,773,000.

Newark argued that the "paid subscribers" were separate and distinguishable from goodwill by reason of the fact that the useful lives could be estimated with reasonable accuracy.

The Internal Revenue Service accepted the estimates of the remaining useful lives of the subscriber lists and did not dispute the estimated values computed using the income approach. However, the IRS claimed that in order to claim an amortization deduction for an intangible asset, the taxpayers must not only demonstrate that the value and the life could be reasonably estimated, but must also show that the asset had a value that was separate and distinct from goodwill.

The District Court found in favor of the taxpayer and allowed the amortization deduction. The IRS appealed the decision to the Third Circuit Court of Appeals. The IRS argued that the applicable law was that, in order to qualify for amortization, an intangible asset must both (1) have an ascertainable value separate and distinct from goodwill and (2) have a limited useful life, the duration of which can be ascertained with reasonable accuracy. The IRS asserted that in the *Newark* case the second test had been met, but that the first test had not.

The Court of Appeals agreed with the IRS and held that, even though the subscriber list may have a limited useful life that can be ascertained with reasonable accuracy, its value was not separate and distinct from goodwill.

The Supreme Court reversed and remanded the Court of Appeals in a five to four decision on April 20, 1993. The Court held that an intangible asset with an ascertainable value and a limited useful life, the duration of which can be ascertained with reasonable accuracy, is depreciable under § 167 of the Code. The fact that it may also be described as the expectancy of continued patronage is entirely beside the point.

The Court reasoned that goodwill is not amortizable intangible property because its useful life cannot be ascertained with reasonable accuracy. It must follow that if a taxpayer can prove with reasonable accuracy that an asset used in the trade or business or held for the production of income has a value that wastes over an ascertainable period of time, then that asset is depreciable under § 167, regardless of the fact that its value is related to the expectancy of continued patronage. The significant question for purposes of depreciation is not whether the asset falls within the core of the concept of goodwill, but whether the asset is capable of being valued and whether that value diminishes over time.

The 460,000 paid subscribers constituted a finite set of subscriptions, existing on a particular date. The asset was not composed of constantly fluctuating components; rather, it consisted of identifiable subscriptions, each of which had a limited useful life that could be estimated with reasonable accuracy according to generally accepted statistical principles.

The Supreme Court also upheld the income approach used by the taxpayer to value the paid subscribers at $67,773,000. This amount was arrived at by computing the present value of the after-tax subscription revenues to be derived from the paid subscribers, less the cost of collecting those revenues, and adding the present value of the tax savings resulting from the depreciation of the subscribers.

The Internal Revenue Service had taken the view that the only value attributable to the paid subscribers was equivalent to the cost of generating a similar list of new subscribers, which was about $3 million.

The Supreme Court stated that the IRS had mischaracterized the asset as a mere list of names and addresses. The uncontroverted evidence presented at trial revealed that the paid subscribers had substantial value over and above that of a mere list of customers. These subscribers were seasoned; they had subscribed to the paper for lengthy periods of time and represented a reliable and measurable source of revenue. In contrast to new subscribers, who had no subscription listing and who might not last beyond the expiration of some promotional incentives, the paid subscribers at issue here provided a regular and predictable source of income over an estimable period of time. The cost of generating a list of new subscribers was irrelevant, for it represented the value of an entirely different asset.

Although it was possible to estimate the direct cost of soliciting additional subscribers, those subscribers, if obtained, were not and would not have been comparable, in terms of life characteristics or value, to the paid subscribers acquired. The cost of generating such marginal subscribers would not reflect the fair market value of the existing subscribers as of the date of acquisition.

(b) Citizens and Southern Corporation and Subsidiaries v. Commissioner.[43]   During 1981 and 1982, Citizens and Southern (C&S) acquired nine banks located throughout Georgia. C&S allocated the purchase price among the various assets, including $41,785,070 for the core deposit base and $10,496,372 for goodwill and going concern value.

To value the core deposit base, C&S first determined the survival probabilities of the accounts based on an examination of the historical rate of closure. Next, the balances of each age group of accounts at the valuation date were multiplied by the survival probabilities shown in the runoff table. C&S then multiplied the net investable balances by a spread rate to arrive at the projected earnings from each of the age groups in each of the future years. Finally, C&S discounted the projected earnings from each of the age groups in each of the future years to present value. C&S also conducted impairment studies in 1983, 1984, and 1985 to determine whether the value of the deposit base asset had become materially impaired. The depreciation deduction for tax purposes in each year was equal to the present value at the acquisition date of the projected income stream for the taxable year.

The Internal Revenue Service disallowed the depreciation deductions on the grounds that the amount paid was for the purchase of goodwill and going concern value, which are nondivisible assets with undeterminable lives. The IRS contended that C&S's position failed to consider the case law interpreting goodwill and that, as a threshold matter, C&S must establish that the deposit base was an asset separate and distinct from goodwill. The IRS also contended that C&S was claiming a deduction for the cost of purchased, terminable-at-will customer relationships and that any value attributable to these relationships was a component of goodwill, because C&S had no right to the funds but merely

---

[43] 91 TC 463 (1988), aff'd per curiam, 900 F2d 266, 91-1 USTC 50, 451 (CA-11).

expected that, because there was a preexisting business relationship, the customers would remain at the bank.

The Court decided that the fact that a deposit account had no fixed termination date and was terminable at will did not as a matter of law prevent C&S from factually showing that the deposit base had an ascertainable cost basis separate and distinct from goodwill and that it had a reasonably ascertainable useful life.

The Court stated:

> At the onset, it is crucial to focus on exactly what petitioner valued and depreciated. Petitioner examined only the income that it expected to derive from the use of the balances of the core deposit accounts existing at the acquisition dates. Although petitioner certainly hoped that during the period between the acquisition of a bank and the closure of an account the average balance in the account might increase, petitioner did not take this into account. Petitioner also did not include any income that would be derived from future accounts. The life and value of deposit base was based solely upon the core deposits acquired in the purchase.
>
> Moreover, the economic value attributable to the opportunity to invest the core deposits can be valued. The value is based solely upon the core deposits acquired in the purchase. The fact that new accounts may be opened as old accounts are closed does not make the deposit base self-regenerative.
>
> The value of deposit base rests upon the ascertainable probability that inertia will cause depositors to leave their funds on deposit for predictable periods of time. We conclude that deposit base has an ascertainable cost basis separate and distinct from the goodwill and going concern value.

The Court also allowed the accelerated method of depreciation, under which the amount of depreciation each year is equal to the present value on the acquisition date of the projected cost savings for the year. The C&S method was based on the contribution the current year's cost savings made to the value of the deposit base, and thus the method of depreciation resulted in a fair allocation of the basis of the asset to periods in which the benefit was realized.

(c) Colorado National Bankshares, Inc. v. Commissioner.[44]   Colorado National Bankshares, Inc. purchased seven banks in 1981 and 1982 and claimed amortization deductions for the core deposit intangibles of the acquired banks. Colorado National defined core deposits as deposit liabilities on which no or low interest rates were paid, specifically interest-free checking accounts, interest-paying checking accounts (NOW accounts), and savings accounts. The buyer intended to reinvest the core deposits at higher rates of interest. The spread between the interest paid on the core deposits and the rate at which the buyer reinvested the assets represented a positive income stream to the bank. Colorado National claimed the present value of these future income streams as an intangible asset that could be amortized.

The Internal Revenue Service disallowed the deductions on the theory that the core deposit intangibles should be considered part of the goodwill of the acquired banks. The Tax Court held in favor of Colorado National, and the Tenth Circuit Court of Appeals affirmed the decision.

The appellate court reiterated the general rule that a two-step analysis must be performed to determine whether a taxpayer may validly claim an amortization deduction for an intangible asset. The taxpayer must demonstrate that the intangible asset (1) has an ascertainable value independent of goodwill and (2) has a limited useful life, the duration of which can be ascertained with reasonable accuracy. The Tenth Circuit stated that Colorado National had presented the Tax Court with substantial evidence and that the Tax Court found that the core deposit intangibles were separate and distinct from

---

[44] Supra, note 31.

goodwill, and had both an ascertainable value independent of goodwill and a limited useful life.

This conclusion is reinforced by relevant regulatory treatment of goodwill and core deposits. Although not necessarily controlling for income tax purposes, in the absence of an income tax regulation, it is certainly pertinent evidence that the Financial Accounting Standards Board, the Securities and Exchange Commission, and the Office of the Comptroller of the Currency all require banks to record their core deposits as assets separate and apart from goodwill.

For purposes of calculating an appropriate purchase price and as part of regulatory submissions required for the purchases, Colorado National conducted detailed and thorough studies specifically identifying and estimating the value of the assets of the banks it proposed to acquire. It also estimated the lives of the core deposits and the income likely to result from their reinvestment.

The Tenth Circuit distinguished the Third Circuit's holding in the *Newark Morning Ledger*[45] case, in which the taxpayer attempted to depreciate approximately $68 million, a sum attributable to the future profits it hoped to derive from the future patronage of 460,000 at-will newspaper subscribers. Calling that case a totally different situation, the Tenth Circuit stated that when dealing with core deposits, the Tax Court has consistently held that a taxpayer who demonstrates a reasonably ascertainable value and a limited useful life for these assets may claim a valid amortization deduction. (See *IT&S of Iowa, Inc. v. Commissioner*[46] and *Citizens and Southern Corp. v. Commissioner*.[47])

The Court stated that it declined to adopt the Third Circuit's very expansive view of goodwill as expressed in the *Newark Morning Ledger*.[48] However, in a footnote, the Court also stated that a determination of whether subscriber lists are amortizable would be fact specific, and it expressed no opinion as to whether such assets would, in fact, be amortizable.

The Court also noted that neither the Internal Revenue Service, the Treasury Department, nor Congress has promulgated a specific and uniform definition of goodwill, and although case law establishes that goodwill constitutes "the expectancy of continued patronage, for whatever reason," this amorphous and general definition provides little practical guidance to taxpayers and courts asked to define the parameters of the amortization deduction.

In summary, the Court of Appeals declined to accept the Internal Revenue Service's absolute prohibition on amortizing core deposits for many reasons, the most important of which were:

1. Sufficient evidence demonstrating that these core deposits have a life expectancy that can be determined with reasonable accuracy,

2. The Tax Court's factual determination that these core deposits are not self-regenerating,

3. The reasonableness of the Tax Court's consistent pronouncements on this very question,

4. The lack of a workable and useful definition of goodwill,

5. The adequacy of the residual method of calculating goodwill,

---

[45] Supra, note 42.
[46] 97 TC 496 (1991).
[47] Supra, note 43.
[48] Supra, note 42.

6. The necessity of substantial additional time, effort, and expense to produce income from the core deposits, and

7. The fact that the core deposits could have been severed and transferred apart from the goodwill of the banks in question.

3.5 GENERAL ACCOUNTING OFFICE REPORT TO THE JOINT COMMITTEE ON TAXATION

On August 9, 1991, the General Accounting Office, in response to the Joint Committee's request, issued a report on how the purchase price for acquired businesses was being allocated among intangible assets. Following is the Excecutive Summary of that report.

(a) **Purpose.**[49] One of the oldest controversies between taxpayers and the Internal Revenue Service is the extent to which taxpayers can deduct the price they pay for intangible assets, such as customer or subscription lists. The opportunities for disputes to arise intensified during the 1980s, when business acquisition activity increased and led to a growth in the reported values of intangible assets from about $45 billion in 1980 to $262 billion in 1987. As a result, billions of dollars of potential tax deductions and, therefore, tax revenues are still affected by decisions on whether tax deductions for intangible asset costs are permitted.

Recognizing the importance of this tax issue, the Joint Committee on Taxation asked the General Accounting Office (GAO) for information on the types of deductible intangible assets, the asset values and useful lives claimed, and the industries affected. GAO also explored various proposals for revising intangible asset tax rules, which have not significantly changed since 1927.

(b) **Background.** Current tax rules allow taxpayers to deduct the cost of assets through periodic tax deductions, known as depreciation or amortization. Tangible assets, such as buildings and equipment, are depreciated over specific statutory periods. For intangible assets, however, the rules are more complex. The general rule is that tax amortization deductions are taken over the useful life of each intangible asset. Taxpayers determine the specific useful life for each intangible asset separately.

Purchased goodwill and other intangible assets without determinable useful lives are not amortizable. The tax value of goodwill is the amount by which the purchase price exceeds the fair market value of the acquired company's individual assets, including identified intangible assets. Certain other intangible assets can be amortized over statutorily assigned useful lives. For example, patents may be amortized over a 17-year period, unless the taxpayer can show a shorter life.

The taxpayer's determination of useful life is questioned only when the IRS performs an audit. The IRS frequently contends that many intangible assets are, in fact, purchased goodwill and not amortizable. Taxpayers, however, assert that the assets are not goodwill, the determined useful lives are accurate, and the intangible assets are eligible for amortization. As a result, the IRS and taxpayers must resolve disagreements on a case-by-case basis. Unresolved issues are ultimately decided by the courts on the basis of facts and circumstances. Court decisions have varied and have led to inconsistent treatment for similarly situated taxpayers.

---

[49] *Tax Policy: Issues and Policy Proposals Regarding Tax Treatment of Intangible Assets*, Report to the Joint Committee on Taxation, United States General Accounting Office, August 1991.

An analysis of purchased intangible asset taxation also requires a familiarity with the treatment of costs incurred in creating such assets. Generally, costs of creating long-lasting assets are included, or capitalized, in the cost basis of the asset and deducted over the asset's life. Because some intangible assets, such as goodwill, are not normally considered distinct or traceable assets by taxpayers, most costs of creating them, such as advertising expenses, are usually deducted in the year incurred, rather than capitalized and amortized over the life of the asset. The result of these tax rules is that purchased goodwill is treated less favorably than other purchased assets, whereas the costs of creating goodwill are treated more favorably than the costs of creating other assets. This unusual result must be kept in mind in devising solutions to the problems of intangible asset tax rules.

(c) Results in Brief. GAO analyzed tax data that the IRS had gathered in 1989 on all its unresolved, or open, purchased intangible assets cases. Taxpayers in nine industry groups had claimed deductions for 175 types of purchased intangible assets that they identified as different from goodwill and valued at $23.5 billion. The IRS most frequently challenged the classifications rather than the useful lives and/or values that taxpayers assigned to these intangible assets. These disagreements occurred in most industries and primarily stemmed from differences in the tax treatment of goodwill, which is never amortizable, and other intangible assets that are amortizable.

GAO believes that the disagreements between the IRS and taxpayers over which intangible assets may be amortized will continue unless changes are made in the current rules. Recognition of all intangible assets that waste away over time and the development of guidelines for their amortization would help to prevent such disputes and provide uniform treatment for all taxpayers.

(d) GAO's Analysis.

(i) Taxpayers Amortized Numerous Purchased Intangible Assets.   GAO's analysis is based on data gathered by the IRS in 1989 from all open cases involving purchased intangible asset issues in its examination, appeals, or litigation units. Generally, these cases involved tax years 1979 to 1987. To illustrate and analyze the conflicts these issues generate, GAO grouped the assets in the following seven categories:

1. *Customer- or market-based assets.* Taxpayers valued this category at $10.5 billion; it was the largest category of intangibles. Examples included stable pools of deposits, called core deposits, held by financial institutions, and newspaper and magazine subscription lists. On average, taxpayers amortized these assets over 8.8 years. The IRS's proposed adjustments totaled $4.1 billion.

2. *Contract-based assets.* Taxpayers valued this category at about $3.7 billion; the category included assets supported by specific contracts, such as covenants-not-to-compete and leases. On average, taxpayers amortized these assets over 6.3 years. The IRS's proposed adjustments totaled $1.2 billion.

3. *Technology-based assets.* Taxpayers valued this category, which included assets such as computer software, drawings, and technical manuals, at $2.2 billion. On average, taxpayers claimed amortization over 6.4 years. The IRS's proposed adjustments totaled $665 million.

4. *Statutory-based assets*. Taxpayers valued such assets at $3.5 billion. These assets had specific, statutorily defined amortization periods that could be elected in lieu of useful lives. Examples included patents and copyrights, and the average amortization period was 10.6 years. The IRS's proposed adjustments totaled $341 million.

5. *Work-force-based assets*. Taxpayers valued these assets at $1.1 billion. Assets in this category related to existing work forces and included trained staff and technical expertise. On average, taxpayers amortized these assets over 6.6 years. The IRS's proposed adjustments totaled $866 million.

6. *Corporate organizational/financial assets*. Taxpayers valued these assets, which related to the organizational structure and the financial-based assets of a company, at $1.3 billion. Examples included acquisition costs, legal and auditing fees, and favorable financial arrangements. The average amortization period was 7.5 years. The IRS's proposed adjustments totaled $358 million.

7. *Unidentifiable assets*. This category included $1.2 billion of intangible assets that GAO could not classify because of an insufficient level of detail in the IRS data. The average amortization period was 8.9 years, and the IRS's proposed adjustments totaled $498 million.

(ii) The IRS Calls Intangible Assets Goodwill in 70% of Cases.   In 70% of the cases in which taxpayers claimed that intangible assets had a determinable useful life, the IRS claimed that the assets were, in fact, goodwill and not amortizable. In total, the IRS's proposed adjustments of about $8 billion on the basis of its evaluation of the value, useful life, or classification of intangible assets. The final outcome of these cases will depend on the IRS's or the courts' interpretation of facts related to each asset.

(iii) Tax Policy Considerations.   In GAO's opinion, conflict between taxpayers and the IRS regarding which purchased assets are amortizable is likely to continue. The fact- and circumstance-based nature of the controversy leads to costly disagreements between taxpayers and the IRS and to inconsistent treatment for similarly situated taxpayers. A legislative change, similar to the changes made to the tangible asset rules to address these same problems, is needed. Keeping the current tax rules would mean accepting frequent and costly disagreements between taxpayers and the IRS, with the courts acting as the final arbiter.

When these conflicts arise, they are caused by the disparity between the tax treatment of (1) goodwill and other nonamortizable intangible assets without determinable useful lives and (2) amortizable intangible assets with taxpayer-determined useful lives. This disparity gives taxpayers an incentive to establish values and useful lives for purchased intangible assets other than goodwill.

The current tax treatment of goodwill and similar intangible assets fails to recognize the economic benefits that wasting intangible assets contribute over time. These assets are consumed over time, even if a precise period cannot be determined. Denying amortization deductions does not result in an accurate determination of taxable income, because expenses are not properly matched to income generated. Recognition of these economic benefits over time for tax purposes can be accomplished by establishing specific statutory cost-recovery periods for purchased intangible assets similar to those now used for tangible assets.

Providing specific cost-recovery periods could, therefore, result in a more accurate measurement of income. It could also eliminate conflicts resulting from the nondeductibility of purchased goodwill and disagreements over the estimated length of useful lives.

Administrative concerns, such as the appropriate identification of the categories to which particular intangible assets belong and the calculation of asset values, should be considered in choosing the lengths of cost-recovery periods and category definitions. These conflicts were not significant when compared with conflicts over goodwill, but could grow in importance as the number of categories eligible for amortization and the span of cost-recovery periods increase.

The potential revenue consequences of this proposal depend on specific design components. For example, a cost-recovery system could gain revenue, be revenue neutral, or lose revenue, depending on the specific useful lives established. Statutory recovery periods for purchased intangible assets would also raise the question of the proper tax treatment of the costs incurred in creating intangible assets. Any new rules covering the costs of created intangible assets may also affect revenues.

(iv) Matters for Congressional Consideration.   Congress should consider revising the current tax law to provide for amortization of purchased intangible assets, including goodwill, over specific statutory cost-recovery periods.

(v) Agency Comments.   The views of responsible agency officials were sought during the course of GAO's work and have been reflected in the report where appropriate. They generally agreed with the facts presented.

3.6 INTERNATIONAL TAX ISSUES

In the international tax context, the most important issue with respect to intangible property generally concerns which member of the multinational group should own the intangible. There are many factors that impact on this central question, including:

- Local country income tax implications,
- Withholding tax implications,
- Intercompany transfer pricing implications, and
- Rules applicable to the transfer of intangible property.

This section addresses these issues primarily from a U.S. federal income tax perspective and includes comments regarding other countries as appropriate.

It should be noted that U.S. statutory changes in the 1980s have drastically altered the legal landscape in the case of a U.S. owner of an intangible seeking to house the intangible offshore. The key planning techniques that remain available in this regard relate to the development of new intangibles and the allocation of their ownership through "cost sharing" arrangements.

(a) Local Income Tax Implications.   In deciding where to house the intangible (i.e., in which country ownership should be established), consideration should be given to whether the local jurisdiction allows amortization of the intangible for income tax purposes. The earlier sections 3.1 and 3.5 of this chapter discuss the U.S. income tax amortization rules for intangible property.

(i) Amortization

Canada.[50] Intangibles that have a fixed expiration date (e.g., patents and copyrights) are treated as depreciable property, and their costs may generally be written off on a straight-line basis over the life of the intangible (i.e., useful life, not legal life).

Intangible property that has an indefinite life (e.g., goodwill) can be deducted under Canada's capital property rules. These rules allow 75% of the cost of an intangible to be amortized on a declining-balance basis using a 7% rate.

The costs of all eligible capital property are included in a pool. When capital property is sold, 75% of the proceeds is credited to the pool. If there is a negative balance in the pool at the end of the taxable year, the negative balance must be included in taxable income.

France.[51] Intangible assets are generally not depreciable or amortizable for income tax purposes. However, patents may be written off over their useful lives.

In limited circumstances, a provision for a permanent reduction in the value of goodwill may sometimes be deducted. Software development expenses may be written off as incurred or amortized over a maximum of five years, and software purchases may be amortized over their expected lives or in 12 equal monthly installments.

Germany.[52] Intangible assets developed by a company itself cannot be capitalized and therefore cannot be amortized. Acquired intangible assets, such as patents, trademarks, and copyrights, may generally be amortized over their legally protected lives or, if shorter, their useful lives. Acquired goodwill must be amortized for tax purposes over a 15-year period, using the straight-line method.

Japan.[53] Intangible assets, including patents, trademarks, and copyrights, can be amortized over their useful lives using the straight-line method. Goodwill may be charged to current expense, or may be amortized over five years.

The Netherlands.[54] Generally, intangible assets whose value diminish over time may be amortizable for Dutch corporate income tax purposes. Intangibles (e.g., purchased goodwill and patents) may be amortized over their useful lives. In practice, a five-year write-off period is acceptable for goodwill.

United Kingdom.[55] The United Kingdom does not technically allow depreciation or amortization to be deducted for income tax purposes. Instead, deductions for intangibles are allowed through the U.K. capital allowance system.

The capital allowance given each year is called a "writing-down allowance." For example, an annual allowance of 25% on a declining-balance basis is given for capital expenditures incurred on the acquisition of patent rights.

(ii) Example. To illustrate the local tax impact of the decision of where to house an intangible, assume that a U.S. corporation with a Japanese subsidiary has decided to acquire a business located in Country X for $100 million. Further assume that the only asset of the business is goodwill, that the business will be conducted in branch form in Country X, and that business reasons prevent a joint venture acquisition.

---

[50] *Deloitte Touche Tohmatsu International World Tax Planner*, December, 1993.
[51] *Deloitte Touche Tohmatsu International World Tax Planner*, December, 1993.
[52] *Deloitte Touche Tohmatsu International World Tax Planner*, December, 1993.
[53] *Deloitte Touche Tohmatsu International Tax and Business Guide: Japan*, May 1991.
[54] *Deloitte Touche Tohmatsu International Tax and Business Guide, Netherlands*, March 1992.
[55] *Deloitte Touche Tohmatsu International Tax and Business Guide, United Kingdom*, March 1992.

In deciding whether the U.S. corporation should acquire the business directly or through its Japanese subsidiary, consideration should be given to whether the acquiring corporation will be able to claim a tax deduction in its host country for the acquired goodwill.

If the Japanese subsidiary acquires the business, its tax deductible amortization during the first five years will be $100 million. If, on the other hand, the U.S. corporation acquires the business, current U.S. tax law may prevent it from claiming any tax deductible amortization.

(iii) Other Local Income Tax Issues

Subpart F.   If it is decided to house an intangible in a foreign affiliate controlled by a parent in the United States or certain other countries, it is necessary to consider the U.S. Subpart F provisions or similar provisions in other jurisdictions. For example, in Canada these provisions are known as the foreign accrual property income (FAPI) provisions. In Japan, they are referred to as tax haven provisions. Generally, these provisions tax the shareholder on undistributed income earned by the foreign affiliate under specified conditions (For ease of discussion, all these provisions are referred to as Subpart F provisions).

In the United States, Subpart F provisions require that more than 50% of the stock of a foreign corporation be owned by U.S. shareholders owning 10% or more. Such a foreign corporation is referred to as a controlled foreign corporation (CFC).

If a CFC earns specified types of income (including passive royalty income), even in the absence of a dividend distribution by the CFC, the U.S. shareholders of the CFC are required to currently include their pro rata share of such income in their U.S. federal taxable income.

The current inclusion rules of Subpart F do not apply to active royalties. To be considered active, the company must be involved in the active development, marketing, and so on, of the intangible.

There are other antideferral provisions under U.S. law that may apply to U.S. shareholders of foreign corporations that earn passive income such as royalties. Generally, the active royalty exception also applies in these cases.

For example, assume that a U.S. corporation's wholly owned foreign subsidiary, A Company, incorporated in tax haven X, receives $1 million in royalty income from an unrelated Country Y corporation. Further assume that the royalty is not an active royalty, tax haven X imposes no tax on the royalty received by A Company, A Company does not incur any expenses, and A Company does not distribute a dividend to the U.S. corporation.

The U.S. corporation is a "U.S. shareholder" of A Company, as it owns 10% or more of A Company. Because A Company's stock is more than 50% owned by "U.S. shareholders" (i.e., the U.S. corporation), A Company is a CFC. Because A Company receives passive royalty income, the U.S. Subpart F provisions apply. Under these provisions, even though A Company does not distribute a dividend, the U.S. corporation is required to include the $1 million in its U.S. federal taxable income.

(b)   Withholding Tax

(i) Foreign-Owned Intangibles.   If an intangible is housed outside the United States and is licensed to an affiliate for use in the United States, U.S. withholding tax implications should be considered.

Foreign individuals and corporations that are not engaged in a U.S. trade or business are subject to taxation at a flat rate of 30% on fixed or determinable annual or periodic income (FDAPI) from U.S. sources. In addition, foreign individuals and corporations are taxable on U.S. source gains from the sale or exchange of intangible property (including patents, copyrights, goodwill, trademarks, and trade names) that is contingent on productivity, use, or disposition of the intangible at the flat 30% rate.[56]

FDAPI is defined to include royalties.[57] Royalties are considered to be from a U.S. source if the intangible is used in the United States.[58] The 30% tax is withheld at source on payments to foreign individuals, corporations, and partnerships.[59]

(ii) U.S.-Owned Intangibles. Foreign jurisdictions also generally impose withholding taxes on royalties paid to U.S. taxpayers. If the intangible property is owned by a U.S. affiliate and licensed to foreign affiliates, U.S. foreign tax credit provisions should be evaluated.

As in many foreign jurisdictions, U.S. federal income tax law allows foreign income taxes paid or deemed paid to be credited against the U.S. income tax.[60] The ability to claim credit for foreign income taxes paid or accrued is governed by the U.S. foreign tax credit limitation provisions.[61]

The United States does not impose a "per country limitation" for purposes of limiting the credit for foreign taxes. However, the United States has imposed a "basket" concept for purposes of the foreign tax credit limitation.[62] Under the U.S. basket concept, basically, the common limitation methodology used in many jurisdictions (foreign source taxable income, divided by worldwide taxable income, multiplied by local income tax) is subdivided into sublimitations for different kinds of income. Each sublimitation is calculated as foreign source taxable income for that particular basket, divided by worldwide taxable income, and multiplied by U.S. federal income tax. This limits the ability of averaging high-taxed foreign source income and low-taxed foreign source income such as royalties.[63]

Foreign source royalties (generally, royalty income from intangible property used outside the United States[64]) are typically classified in the passive limitation income basket.[65] As an exception, foreign source royalty income derived from unrelated third parties as part of a taxpayer's active trade or business (as previously discussed in section (a), part (iii)) are classified as general limitation basket income.[66]

With respect to a multinational group, another exception from the passive-income basket classification of royalty income is the "look-through" rule. Under the look-through rule, royalty income received from a controlled foreign corporation will be included by the recipient in the same limitation category from which it was deducted. If

---

[56] IRC § 871(a)(1)(D); IRC § 881(a)(4).
[57] Reg. § 1.871-7(b); Reg. IRC § 1.881-2(b).
[58] IRC § 861(a)(4).
[59] IRC § 1441(a) and (b) and IRC § 1442(a).
[60] IRC § 901.
[61] IRC § 904.
[62] IRC § 904(d).
[63] IRC § 904(d)(1).
[64] IRC § 862(a)(4).
[65] IRC § 904(d)(2)(A); IRC § 954(c)(1)(A).
[66] IRC § 954(c)(2)(A).

the controlled foreign corporation is engaged in an active trade or business, related-party royalties will generally constitute general limitation basket income.[67]

In February 1993, the Clinton Administration proposed that all royalties be classified as passive. Because royalty income generally bears little foreign tax, this proposal would have further limited the averaging of low-taxed foreign source income and high-taxed foreign source income. However, this proposal was removed during the House Ways and Means Committee negotiations.

(iii) Treaty Shopping. Because of the relatively high U.S. domestic withholding tax rate and the U.S. foreign tax credit limitation provisions, many taxpayers have sought to interpose a corporation in a foreign jurisdiction with favorable treaty and/or local withholding tax rules between the licensor and licensee, where one of them is the United States.

The Netherlands/U.S. income tax convention provides a zero withholding tax rate on royalties. Moreover, the Netherlands domestic income tax rules do not require withholding on royalty income. Thus, the Netherlands has often been used in structuring multinational operations. For example, in the past, if a Japanese affiliate owned an intangible that would ultimately be licensed to a U.S. affiliate, the Japanese affiliate may have interposed a Netherlands corporation between the Japanese and U.S. affiliates. The Japanese affiliate would license the intangible to the Netherlands affiliate, and the Netherlands affiliate would sublicense the intangible to the U.S. affiliate.

Under the Netherlands/U.S. income tax convention, royalties derived from U.S. sources by the Netherlands affiliate were, arguably, not subject to U.S. income tax withholding, in contrast to 10% withholding (under treaty) between the United States and Japan.[68] The royalty paid by the Netherlands affiliate would presumably not be subject to Netherlands withholding tax under Netherlands domestic income tax law.

The IRS has long taken the position that in this situation, the royalty paid by the Netherlands company was still U.S. source and thus subject to U.S. withholding tax.[69] This situation is known as "cascading royalties." To avoid such treatment, some companies have attempted to convert the nature of the payment from the Netherlands to something other than royalty income.

The IRS has attacked other back-to-back structures that attempt to claim protection under the current Netherlands/U.S. income tax convention and other treaties by challenging the conduit nature of the structure. The IRS would likely take the position that if the Netherlands entity does not have complete control and custody of the payment received from the U.S. affiliate, it has not derived the income and the payment is, thus, not entitled to the benefits of the treaty.[70]

With respect to the new Netherlands/U.S. income tax convention (effective on January 1, 1994, with a transition rate permitting a January 1, 1995 effective date), the limitations on benefits provision has been significantly toughened in an attempt to prevent the previously described conduit structures.

Although the aforementioned constraints limit the ability of foreign corporations to avoid or reduce withholding taxes on royalties from the United States, it is still possible to use a "royalty company" to reduce withholding taxes from other countries. A royalty

---

[67] IRC § 904(d)(3)(A).
[68] The Netherlands/U.S. Income Tax Convention Article VIII(1).
[69] Rev Rul 80-362, 1980-2 CB 208.
[70] Rev Rul 84-152, 1984-2 CB 381.

company is a company located in a country with a wide treaty network, such as the Netherlands, which licenses the intangible from the owner and then sublicenses it to the users of the intangible. In the Netherlands, it is possible to get a ruling that defines the amount of income such a company must report.

Another possible structure to limit the amount of Dutch tax is a Dutch company that acquires an intangible—as part of a larger acquisition, for example—and then licenses the users of the intangible. The Netherlands company may then offset its royalty income with amortization deductions and interest expense.

In both structures, the parent company may be subject to current income inclusions under Subpart F provisions.

(c) Transfer Pricing. The U.S. transfer pricing rules are codified in Internal Revenue Code (IRC) § 482. The purpose of § 482 is to place controlled taxpayers on a tax parity with uncontrolled taxpayers. In cases in which transactions between members of a controlled group of taxpayers do not reflect the "true" taxable income of the members, the Internal Revenue Service is allowed to distribute, apportion, or allocate gross income, deductions, allowances, and credits between members of a controlled group of taxpayers in order to prevent the evasion of taxes or to reflect clearly the income of the members of the controlled group.[71] In determining whether transactions between members of a controlled group properly reflect the true taxable income of the members, the standard to be used has historically been the arm's-length standard.[72]

The arm's-length standard basically requires that transactions between members of a controlled group of taxpayers take place as if the members were uncontrolled (i.e., as if the related parties were dealing with unrelated third parties). Determining whether controlled transactions meet the arm's-length standard thus requires comparison, in some form, with uncontrolled taxpayers.

The difficulty in applying the arm's-length standard in general is the issue of comparability. This problem is compounded in the case of intangibles that have high profit potential, because such intangibles are generally not transferred to unrelated third parties. Thus there are few, if any, unrelated-party transactions with which to compare a related party transaction.

The following discussion attempts to describe briefly the transfer pricing law as it applies to intangible property.

(i) Prior to the Tax Reform Act of 1986. Under U.S. transfer pricing rules in existence prior to the Tax Reform Act of 1986 (TRA 86), the District Director of the (IRS) was allowed to make transfer pricing adjustments to reflect appropriately the arm's-length consideration for the sale or use of intangible property by related parties. In determining arm's-length consideration, the standard to apply was the amount that an unrelated party would have paid for the same intangible property under the same circumstances.[73]

If the transferrer also transferred the same or a similar intangible under the same or similar circumstances to an unrelated party, the consideration charged to the unrelated party was viewed as the best indicator of an arm's-length consideration. If sufficiently similar transactions with unrelated parties could not be found, the regulations provided a list of 13 factors that should be considered in determining the arm's-length price.[74]

---

[71] IRC § 482.

[72] Reg § 1.482A-1(b)(1) (Certain of the preexisting § 482 regulations were redesignated in the revision of the regulations in 1993).

[73] Reg § 1.482A(d)(1) and (2).

[74] Reg § 1.482A(d)(2)(ii) and (iii).

(ii) TRA 86. Prior to TRA 86, in spite of changes made to § 367(d) (discussed further in a later paragraph), valuable intangible property could, arguably, be transferred offshore for a nominal or no consideration (as in the case of a § 351 transfer of an intangible). Income from the intangible thus often escaped U.S. income taxation, even though the expenses of developing it offset U.S. income and in some cases a credit was allowed for conducting the research and development (R&D) in the United States.[75]

In reaction to this perceived erosion of the U.S tax base, changes to § 482 were made by TRA 86 to require that payments for the transfer of intangible property between related parties be commensurate with the income from the intangible.[76] The legislative history indicates that Congress was concerned that there was a strong incentive for U.S. taxpayers to transfer intangible property to related offshore foreign corporations.[77]

Congress believed that the arm's-length standard of pre-TRA 86 § 482 was inadequate because of the lack of comparable transactions involving high-profit-potential intangibles. Congress stated that industry norms or other unrelated-party transactions do not provide a safe-harbor minimum payment for an intangible. Instead, where taxpayers transfer high-profit-potential intangibles, Congress took the view that the compensation charged should be greater than industry averages or norms.[78]

(iii) The 1993 Temporary and Proposed Temporary Regulations. New temporary and proposed temporary regulations were issued on January 13, 1993, and the 1992 proposed regulations were withdrawn.

With respect to intangible property, the temporary regulations reiterate that consideration must be commensurate with the income from an intangible. The three methods provided in the temporary regulation to determine commensurate income are the comparable uncontrolled transaction method (CUT), the comparable profits method (CPM), and other methods.[79]

The selection of methods is subject to the best-method rule of the temporary regulations,[80] which replaces the traditional priority of methods (i.e., comparable-uncontrolled-price method first, resale-price method second, cost-plus method third, and other methods last).

Under the best-method rule, the arm's-length result must be determined by the method that provides the most accurate measure under the facts and circumstances of the transaction at issue. The factors to consider include the completeness and accuracy of the data used to apply the method, the degree of comparability between the controlled and uncontrolled transactions, and the number, magnitude, and accuracy of the adjustments required to apply the method.[81]

The CUT method may be applied if the controlled and uncontrolled transactions are comparable. Intangible transactions are comparable if they involve comparable intangible property and take place under comparable circumstances.[82]

The CPM determines whether consideration in a controlled transaction is an arm's-length price based on comparison with an "arm's-length range." The temporary regulations state that, with respect to the best-method rule, the CPM will ordinarily provide an

---

[75] IRC § 162 and IRC § 174.
[76] House Committee Report on TRA 86 at 425.
[77] House Committee Report on TRA 86 at 423.
[78] House Committee Report on TRA 86 at 425.
[79] Prop Reg § 1.482-4T(a).
[80] Temp Reg § 1.482-4T(a).
[81] Temp Reg § 1.482-1T(b)(2)(iii)(A).
[82] Temp Reg § 1.482-4T(c)(2)(i).

accurate measure of the arm's-length price unless the tested party uses "valuable, non-routine intangibles."[83]

The arm's-length range is determined by applying a single profit level indicator (PLI) of uncontrolled taxpayers engaged in the same business under comparable circumstances to the financial data of the tested party. The PLI should be derived from a sufficient number of years (generally, the year under review and the two preceding taxable years).[84] Applying the PLI of uncontrolled taxpayers to the tested party's financial data produces a range of constructive operating profits. The range of constructive operating profits constitutes the arm's-length range.[85]

With respect to the transfer of intangible property, the temporary regulations require that the form of the consideration in the controlled transaction be consistent with that which would be used in an uncontrolled transaction. The temporary regulations specify that if the transferrer retains a substantial interest in the intangible, the consideration must be in the form of a royalty. The treatment of a lump-sum payment is reserved (i.e., not discussed at this time) under the temporary regulations.[86]

The temporary regulations also provide that, except in limited instances, the consideration for intangible property may be adjusted periodically to ensure that the commensurate-with-income standard is met. The District Director of the IRS may use hindsight in determining whether the consideration in the year under audit is commensurate with income.[87]

(iv) The Final Transfer Pricing Regulations. On July 1, 1994 the IRS and Treasury Department filed the final intercompany transfer pricing regulations. The final regulations are generally effective for taxable years beginning after October 1994. However, taxpayers may elect to apply them to all open years. Such an election may become an important consideration in audits of prior years.

Although the final regulations are generally consistent with the flexibility introduced in the 1993 temporary regulations, there are many substantive changes. Most of these changes do not come as a great surprise and should be well received by taxpayers, U.S. tax treaty partners, and the OECD. It is clear that the drafters have carefully considered the public comments received in response to the 1993 temporary regulations. We believe many of the most significant problems in the prior regulations have been effectively resolved. Nonetheless the current IRS enforcement process is likely to ensure that heated controversy will continue to affect this area for years to come.

As expected, one of the major changes in the final regulations is the expanded use of inexact comparables for all transfer pricing methods. Under the temporary regulations, inexact comparables could be used in the Comparable Profits Method. The acceptance of inexact comparables for all methods is an important step forward under U.S. transfer pricing law. This will help to partially restore the importance of transactional transfer pricing in the U.S. Transactional transfer pricing is generally accepted throughout the rest of the world.

Despite the many positive changes in the final regulations, it is important to keep in perspective the serious burdens that have been placed on the multinational taxpayer in the United States. The aggressive U.S. enforcement in the transfer pricing area has significantly increased the risk of double taxation for many taxpayers. This risk is compounded

---

[83] Temp Reg § 1.482-5T(a).
[84] Temp Reg § 1.482-5T(d)(1).
[85] Temp Reg § 1.482-5T(d)(1).
[86] Temp Reg § 1.482-4T(e)(1).
[87] Temp Reg § 1.482-4T(e)(2).

by severe penalties that can apply for U.S.-based transfer pricing adjustments. Indeed, for many large multinationals which operate primarily in countries that have tax treaties with the U.S., the risk of U.S. penalties is now a primary concern.

In order to reduce these risks, the final regulations place an enormous burden on taxpayers to analyze all relevant information. Taxpayers will be required to exercise considerable judgment on a myriad of factors and issues set forth in the final regulations. Additionally, under the penalty provisions, major decisions will have to be supported by a thorough analysis that will have to be documented on a contemporaneous basis.

Guidance governing the steps that must be taken to satisfy the best method rule has been greatly expanded. The best method rule provides that an arms length result must be determined under the method that, given the facts and circumstances, provides the most reliable measure of an arms length result. No priority or presumption of correctness is given to any method. In applying the best method rule, three principal factors must be considered. First, a comparability analysis must be performed. Second, an evaluation of the quality of the data and assumptions must be considered. Third, a review of the consistency of results obtained under other methods is likely to be required.

In contrast to the temporary regulations, the Profit Split Method is now a specified method to determine pricing for transfers of both tangible and intangible property. The final profit split rules do not require the presence of non-routine intangibles, and other substantive and administrative requirements, such as a binding election, have been eliminated. While these changes would seemingly make the Profit Split Method more readily available, we believe that use of the Profit Split Method, as defined under the final regulations, will still be quite limited. However, the ability to use an unspecified profit split as an "other" method has been expanded under the final regulations, although the current penalty provisions impose stricter standards for the use of an unspecified method.

With respect to cost sharing, the temporary regulations which incorporated the 1968 cost sharing regulations, as amended, continue to apply. Thus, the changes in the cost sharing rules that were proposed in January 1992 have not been finalized. The preamble to the regulations state that future final cost sharing regulations will most likely follow the 1992 proposed regulations. The fact that the regulations have not been finalized in this area is interesting since the 1992 cost sharing proposals were one of the least controversial elements of the 1992 proposed rules.

The method to determine the price for the sale of tangible property associated with valuable intangibles (e.g., property associated with a highly valuable tradename) has been subject to much controversy. The 1992 proposed regulations explicitly stated that such property was to be treated as intangible property. The 1993 temporary regulations provided that valuable non-routine intangibles embedded in tangible property would also be tested under the intangible rules. The final regulations have changed this rule and explicitly state that the methods for tangible property should be applied, as long as the purchaser of the property does not acquire the right to exploit the intangible (other than in connection with the resale of the product). However, the embedded intangibles must be taken into account in evaluating the comparability of unrelated transactions.

The 1986 Tax Reform Act amended Section 482 to provide that in the transfer or license of intangible property, the income with respect to such transfer or license must be commensurate to the income generated from the intangible property. This provision allows IRS to make adjustments to fixed royalty rates even if the rates were at arm's length in the year that they were originally established. Many foreign governments have severely criticized this rule as being in violation of the arm's length principle. The Final Regulations show some sympathy towards this view by providing more meaningful exceptions to its application than were contained in the prior temporary and proposed regulations. These exceptions generally require that careful projections be made in writing before the intangible is transferred. The primary exception provides that adjustments are not required to be made after the fifth year, as long as the intangible property generated acceptable profits through the fifth year. This exception requires that the consideration was at arm's length within the first year and that the profits or cost savings during the first five years were within a range of between 80 and 120 percent of what was reasonably foreseeable when the related parties entered into their written agreement.

Another significant change concerns the implementation of a rule concerning the treatment of lump sum payments for intangibles. Under this rule, a royalty equivalent amount is computed based on an analysis of the present value of projected sales over the relevant period. This imputed royalty payment can qualify for the generally applicable exceptions to the rule requiring periodic adjustments.

Although the flexibility in the regulations will provide many planning opportunities, it will also result in an enormous burden on taxpayers to engage in extensive analysis to satisfy the best method rule. The number of subjective judgments that must be documented under the final regulations and the transfer pricing penalty regulations will provide IRS with extensive ammunition in the future audits. These regulations reflect the end of a long process whereby IRS has sought to change taxpayer behavior and the beginning of a new era in which transfer pricing planning is a necessary aspect of doing business in the United States for multinational companies. Clearly, taxpayers that do not take planning quite seriously face significantly increased risk in future years.

(d) Outbound Transfers of Intangible Property. Prior to the Tax Reform Act of 1984 (TRA 84), a taxpayer could arguably transfer patents, trademarks, and similar intangibles to related foreign corporations free of U.S. income tax if it could substantiate, in an advance ruling request, that tax avoidance was not the principal purpose for the transfer of intangibles to foreign affiliates.[88] As noted earlier, U.S. taxpayers could expense the costs of developing an intangible, possibly obtain the benefits of R&D credits in the United States, and then, for example, transfer the intangible to a controlled foreign corporation as a contribution to capital. The income stream from the intangible could then be received by the foreign corporation without incurring U.S. tax.

In response to this perceived loophole in the tax law, Congress amended § 367(d) to provide that, except to the extent provided in regulations to be issued by the IRS, a transfer of intangible property to a foreign corporation, as a contribution to capital of a controlled corporation, or as part of a reorganization, would be treated as a sale of the intangible in exchange for a royalty stream. This royalty stream is treated as U.S.-source income versus foreign-source income, which would result if the intangible were licensed. The combination of sales treatment under TRA 84 and the commensurate with-income standard introduced with TRA 86 significantly limited the ability of U.S. taxpayers to transfer most high-profit-potential intangible property to foreign affiliates without incurring a significant U.S. tax in connection with the transfer. As a result, transferrers of intangibles are now subject to the so-called "super royalty" rule, so that additional consideration must be paid to the transferrer where the value of an intangible increases over time.

To illustrate, assume that a U.S. corporation has developed a patent for super widgets that, when licensed, is forecasted to earn $1 billion. As opposed to licensing the super widget patent directly and subjecting the $1 billion to U.S. taxation, the U.S. corporation attempts to contribute the patent to its wholly owned subsidiary, B Company, located in Country Y. Further assume, for purposes of this example, that the royalty income

---

[88] Rev Proc 68-23, 1968-1 CB 821, § 3.02(1)(b)((iii).

received by B Company from licensing the super widget patent is an active royalty and would not be subject to the U.S. Subpart F provisions explained earlier. Also assume that B Company has a significant net operating loss that can offset the $1 billion forecasted royalty and will not incur income tax in Country Y.

What appears as a good tax-planning scheme on the surface would be defeated by the U.S. outbound super royalty rule. The U.S. corporation would be deemed to have sold the super widget patent to B Company for a $1 billion royalty stream, and the $1 billion royalty would thus be subject to U.S. taxation. Furthermore, the royalty stream would be considered U.S.-source income and thus could not be shielded by foreign tax credits.

(e) R&D Cost Sharing. Because of the previously described difficulty imposed on the deductibility for amortization of most intangible property in the United States and the limitations imposed by the super royalty rule, consideration should be given to R&D cost sharing agreements. Under R&D cost sharing, basically each member to the agreement pays its share of the R&D costs incurred in developing the intangible and is viewed as the owner of the resulting intangible. Each member's share of the R&D costs must be determined in accordance with the anticipated benefits to be derived from utilizing the intangible.

Because each member is treated as having developed and owning the resulting intangible, there is no transfer or license of the intangible. Cost-sharing payments are deductible by the payers (and possibly available for credit under local rules). The recipient of the payment treats the cost-sharing amount as a reimbursement of cost. Thus, generally, withholding tax should not be imposed.

The proposed U.S. transfer pricing rules specifically provide for the use of R&D cost-sharing agreements.[89] The cost-sharing provisions of the 1992 proposed regulations were left intact under the 1993 temporary and proposed temporary regulations. Under the proposed regulations, in order for an agreement to be viewed as a qualified cost-sharing agreement, the agreement must meet the following requirements[90]:

1. The agreement must be between two or more eligible participants,
2. The agreement must be contemporaneously written at the formation of the cost-sharing arrangement,
3. The agreement must provide for sharing of costs and risks among eligible participants in return for a specified interest in any intangible that may be produced,
4. The agreement must reflect a reasonable effort by each eligible participant to share all costs and risks of developing the intangible, including the costs and risks of less successful and unsuccessful projects, such that each eligible participant's share of the costs and risks is proportionate to the benefits each reasonably anticipates it will receive from the exploitation of the intangible developed under the agreement, and
5. The agreement must meet specified administrative requirements.

The validity of cost-sharing arrangements will likely figure prominently in future tax controversies. In particular, the fourth requirement, relating to the relationship between costs borne and expected benefits, will likely be of particular sensitivity in future tax examinations.

---

[89] Prop Reg § 1.482-2(g).
[90] Prop Reg § 1.482-2(g)(2)(i).

CHAPTER 4

THE RATING AGENCY VIEW OF INTANGIBLE ASSETS

Thomas W. Hoens, CPA

Fitch Investors Service, Inc.
New York, New York

4.1 WHAT IS A RATING?

In their book, *The New Corporate Bond Market*, authors Wilson and Fabozzi define a rating as "an indicator or assessment of the issuer's ability to meet its principal and interest payments in a timely manner in accordance with the terms of the issue."[1] Raymond Carty, vice president of Fitch Investors Service, in an interview with *Bondweek*, put it very succinctly when he said, "A rating is an informed credit decision regarding the quality of a bond; it's not a pricing or trading decision." The article went on to state that ratings "are expert opinions of long-term credit quality; they are not meant to reflect or react to current market shifts."[2]

Standard & Poor's, in its debt ratings definitions, provides some basic framework for all ratings:

> The ratings are based, in varying degrees, on the following considerations:
>
> 1. Likelihood of default—capacity and willingness of the obligor as to the timely payment of interest and repayment of principal in accordance with the terms of the obligation;
> 2. Nature of and provisions of the obligation;
> 3. Protection afforded by, and relative position of, the obligation in the event of a bankruptcy, reorganization, or other arrangement under the laws of bankruptcy and other laws affecting creditor's rights.

In the United States, ratings are issued by Nationally Recognized Statistical Rating Organizations (NRSROs). The Securities and Exchange Commission is the regulatory agency that determines whether a company may hold itself out to the public as an NRSRO. Currently, six companies are so designated, four of which are recognized to assign ratings to all classes of obligations: Fitch Investors Service, Moody's Investors Service, Standard & Poor's, and Duff and Phelps Credit Rating Co. The ratings assigned by these agencies are widely followed by investors, issuers, regulators, and others for a

---

[1] Richard S. Wilson and Frank J. Fabozzi, *The New Corporate Bond Market: A Complete and Insightful Analysis of the Latest Trends, Issues, and Advances* (Chicago: Probus Publishing Company, 1990), p. 23.

[2] Raymond Carty, "Institutional Investor," *Bondweek* (3 August 1992): 7.

Fitch	Standard & Poor's	Moody's	Duff & Phelps
		Investment Grade	
AAA	AAA	Aaa	AAA
AA+	AA+	Aa1	AA+
AA	AA	Aa2	AA
AA−	AA−	Aa3	AA−
A+	A+	A1	A+
A	A	A2	A
A−	A−	A3	A−
BBB+	BBB+	Baa1	BBB+
BBB	BBB	Baa2	BBB
BBB−	BBB−	Baa3	BBB−
		Speculative Grade	
BB+	BB+	Ba1	BB+
BB	BB	Ba2	BB
BB−	BB−	Ba3	BB−
B+	B+	B1	B+
B	B	B2	B
B−	B−	B3	B−
CCC+	CCC+	No Equivalent	No Equivalent
CCC	CCC	Caa	CCC
CCC−	CCC−	No Equivalent	No Equivalent
CC+	No Equivalent	No Equivalent	No Equivalent
CC	CC	Ca	No Equivalent
CC−	No Equivalent	No Equivalent	No Equivalent
C+	No Equivalent	No Equivalent	No Equivalent
C	C	C	No Equivalent
C−	No Equivalent	No Equivalent	No Equivalent
DDD	No Equivalent	No Equivalent	No Equivalent
DD	No Equivalent	No Equivalent	DD
D	D	No Equivalent	No Equivalent

Exhibit 4.1.   Comparative rating symbols.

variety of purposes. Two other agencies, IBCA and Thompson BankWatch, have limited recognition and issue ratings only on commercial paper and bank debt.

Rating symbols, first introduced by Fitch in 1922 in its bond guide, have come into universal acceptance as a shorthand designation of the credit quality of a particular issue.[3] The categories range from a high of AAA to a low of D. The top four categories (AAA, AA, A, and BBB) constitute the investment-grade ratings, whereas the rest (BB, B, CCC, CC, C, and D) are noninvestment-grade, "speculative," or simply "junk" ratings. See the comparative rating symbols of the major rating agencies in Exhibit 4.1[4] and the rating definitions in Exhibit 4.2.

---

[3] *Note*: Of the major rating agencies, only Moody's uses a different nomenclature: (Aaa, Aa, A, Baa) for investment grade and (Ba, B, Caa, Ca, and C) for speculative grade ratings. In addition, although Fitch, S&P, and Duff use a plus (+) or minus (−) to subdivide ratings from AA to CCC, Moody's uses a numerical system of 1, 2, 3 for high, medium, and low within the grades Aa to B.

[4] Note that for purposes of this chapter only industrial bond ratings are considered. Commercial Paper, CDs, Insurance Claims Paying, Preferred Stocks, and other types of ratings are not addressed.

The following are the corporate bond rating definitions for each of the major Nationally Recognized Statistical Rating Organizations (NRSRO)

Rating Symbols	Fitch Investors Service	Standard & Poor's	Moody's Investors Service	Duff & Phelps
AAA	Bonds considered to be investment grade and of highest quality. The obligor has an exceptionally strong ability to pay interest and principal, which is unlikely to be affected by reasonable foreseeable events.	Debt rated AAA has the highest rating assigned by Standard & Poor's. Capacity to pay interest and repay principal is extremely strong.	Bonds that are rated Aaa are judged to be of the best quality. They carry the smallest degree of investment risk and are generally referred to as "gilt edged." Interest payments are protected by a large or exceptionally stable margin, and principal is secure. Although the various protective elements are likely to change, such changes as can be visualized are most unlikely to impair the fundamentally strong position of such issues.	Highest credit quality. The risk factors are negligible, being only slightly greater than risk-free U.S. Treasury debt.
AA	Bonds considered to be investment grade and of very high credit quality. The obligor's ability to pay interest and repay principal is very strong, although not quite as strong as bonds rated AAA. Because bonds rated in the AAA and AA categories are not significantly vulnerable to foreseeable future developments, short-term debt of these issues is generally rated F-1+.	Debt rated AA has a very strong capacity to pay interest and principal and differs from the highest rated issues only in small degree.	Bonds that are rated Aa are judged to be of high quality by all standards. Together with the Aaa group, they comprise what are generally known as high grade bonds. They are rated lower than the best bonds because margins of protection may not be as large as in Aaa securities, or fluctuation of protective elements may be of greater amplitude, or there may be other elements present that are somewhat larger than for the Aaa securities.	High credit quality. Protection factors are strong. Risk is modest but may vary slightly from time to time because of economic conditions.

Exhibit 4.2. Rating Definitions

Rating Symbols	Fitch Investors Service	Standard & Poor's	Moody's Investors Service	Duff & Phelps
A	Bonds considered to be investment grade and of high credit quality. The obligor's ability to pay interest and repay principal is considered to be strong, but may be more vulnerable to adverse changes in economic conditions and circumstances than for bonds with higher ratings.	Debt rated A has a strong capacity to pay interest and repay principal, although it is somewhat more susceptible to the adverse effects of changes in circumstances and economic conditions than debt in higher rated categories.	Bonds that are rated A possess many favorable investment attributes and are to be considered as upper-medium-grade obligations. Factors giving security to principal and interest are considered adequate, but elements may be present that suggest a susceptibility to impairment sometime in the future.	Protection factors are average but adequate. However, risk factors are more variable and greater in periods of economic stress.
BBB	Bonds considered to be investment grade and of satisfactory credit quality. The obligor's ability to pay interest and repay principal is considered to be adequate. Adverse changes in economic conditions and circumstances, however, are more likely to have adverse impact on these bonds and, therefore, impair timely payment. The likelihood that ratings of these bonds will fall below investment grade is higher than for bonds with higher ratings.	Debt rated BBB is regarded as having an adequate capacity to pay interest and repay principal. Whereas it normally exhibits adequate protection parameters, adverse economic conditions or changing circumstances more likely to lead to a weakened capacity to pay interest and repay principal for debt in this category than in higher rated categories.	Bonds that are rated Baa are considered as medium-grade obligations, (i.e., they are neither highly protected nor poorly secured). Interest payments and principal security appear adequate for the present, but certain protective elements may be lacking or may be characteristically unreliable over any great length of time. Such bonds lack outstanding investment characteristics and, in fact, have speculative characteristics as well.	Below average protection factors, but still considered sufficient for prudent investment. Considerable variability in risk during economic cycles.
BB	Bonds are considered speculative. The obligor's ability to pay interest and repay principal may be affected over time by adverse economic	Debt rated BB has less near-term vulnerability to default than other speculative issues. However, it faces major ongoing uncertainties and exposure to	Bonds that are rated Ba are judged to have speculative elements; their future cannot be considered as well assured. Often the protection of interest	Below investment grade, but deemed likely to meet obligations when due. Present or prospective financial protection factors fluctuate according to

	changes. However, business and financial alternatives can be identified which could assist the obligor in satisfying its debt service requirements.	adverse business, financial, or economic conditions, which could lead to inadequate capacity to meet timely interest and principal payments. The BB rating category is also used for debt subordinated to senior debt that is assigned an actual or implied BBB-rating.	and principal payments may be very moderate, and thereby not well safeguarded during both good and bad times over the future. Uncertainty of position characterizes bonds in this class.	industry conditions or company fortunes. Overall quality may move up or down frequently within this category.
B	Bonds are considered highly speculative. Although bonds in this class are currently meeting debt service requirements, the probability of continued timely payment of principal and interest reflects the obligor's limited margin of safety and the need for reasonable business and economic activity throughout the life of the issue.	Debt rated B has a greater vulnerability to default, but currently has the capacity to meet interest payments and principal repayments. Adverse business, financial, or economic conditions will likely impair capacity or willingness to pay interest and repay principal. The B rating category is also used for debt subordinated to senior debt that is assigned an actual or implied BB or BB-rating.	Bonds that are rated B generally lack characteristics of the desirable investment. Assurance of interest and principal payments or of maintenance of other terms of the contract over any long period of time may be small.	Below investment grade and possessing risk that obligations will not be met when due. Financial protection factors will fluctuate widely according to economic cycles, industry conditions, and/or company fortunes. Potential exists for frequent changes in the rating within this category or into a higher or lower rating grade.
CCC	Bonds have certain identifiable characteristics which, if not remedied, may lead to default. The ability to meet obligations requires an advantageous business and economic environment.	Debt rated CCC has a currently identified vulnerability to default and is dependent on favorable business, financial, and economic conditions to meet timely payment of interest and repayment of principal. In the event of adverse business, financial, or economic conditions, it is not likely to have the capacity to pay interest	Bonds that are rated Caa are of poor standing. Such issues may be in default, or there may be present elements of danger with respect to principal or interest.	Well below investment-grade securities. Considerable uncertainty exists as to timely payment of principal, interest, or preferred dividends. Protection factors are narrow, and risk can be substantial with unfavorable economic/industry conditions, and/or with unfavorable company developments.

Exhibit 4.2. (Continued)

Rating Symbols	Fitch Investors Service	Standard & Poor's	Moody's Investors Service	Duff & Phelps
		and repay principal. The CCC rating category is also used for debt subordinated to senior debt that is assigned as actual or implied B or B- rating.		
CC	Bonds are minimally protected. Default in payment of interest and/or principal seems probable over time.	The rating CC typically is applied to debt subordinated to senior debt that is assigned an actual or implied CCC rating.	Bonds rated Ca represent obligations that are speculative to a high degree. Such issues are often in default or have other marked shortcomings.	No Equivalent.
C	Bonds are in imminent default in payment of interest or principal.	The rating C typically is applied to debt subordinated to senior debt that is assigned an actual or implied CCC-debt rating. The C rating may be used to cover a situation where a bankruptcy petition has been filed but debt service payments are continued. The rating CI is reserved for income bonds on which no interest is being paid.	Bonds that are rated C are the lowest rated class of bonds, and issues so rated can be regarded as having extremely poor prospects of ever attaining any real investment standing.	No Equivalent.
D	Bonds are in default on interest and/or principal payments. Such bonds are extremely speculative and should be valued on the basis of their ultimate recovery in liquidation or reorganization of the obligor. DDD represents the highest potential for recovery on these bonds, and D	Debt rated D is in payment default. The D rating category is used when interest or principal payments are not made on the date due even if the applicable grace period has not expired, unless S&P believes that such payments will be made during such grace period. The D rating	No Equivalent.	Defaulted debt obligations. Issuer failed to meet scheduled principal and/or interest payments.

represents the lowest potential
for recovery.

also will be used upon the filing
of a bankruptcy petition if debt
service payments are
jeopardized.

Source: Fitch Rating Register, January 1993; *Standard & Poor's Rating Guide*, January 1993;
Moody's Bond Record, January 1993;
Duff & Phelps Rating Register, October 1992

Exhibit 4.2. (*Continued*)

Although ratings represent "informed credit decisions" of a team of financial professionals they are, when all is said and done, a subjective opinion, and opinions will vary among analysts. During the rating process many quantitative and qualitative factors are weighed to arrive at the final letter-grade designation and no two analysts can be expected to assign each factor the same weight. In spite of this, given the broadness of each rating category, issues generally will carry an equivalent rating from each of the major agencies, however differences ("split ratings") will occur. It is therefore important for a user of ratings to try to understand the analyst's underlying rationale[5] for the particular letter-grade ratings assigned to an issue.

Ratings are very useful gauges of credit quality. However, they have some major inherent limitations on their usefulness. In their bond rating definitions, Moody's has highlighted some of the overall limitations on the use of ratings:

Limitations to Uses of Ratings

Bonds carrying the same rating are not claimed to be of absolutely equal quality. In a broad sense they are alike in position, but since there are a limited number of rating classes used in grading thousands of bonds, the symbols cannot reflect the fine shadings of risks which actually exist. Therefore, it should be evident to the user of ratings that two bonds identically rated are unlikely to be precisely the same in investment quality.

As ratings are designed exclusively for the purpose of grading bonds according to their investment qualities, they should not be used alone as a basis for investment operations. For example, they have no value in forecasting the direction of future trends of market price. Market price movements in bonds are influenced not only by the quality of individual issues but also by changes in money rates and general economic trends, as well as by the length of maturity, etc. During its life even the best quality bond may have wide price movements, while its high investment status remains unchanged.

The matter of market price has no bearing whatsoever on the determination of ratings which are not to be construed as recommendations with respect to "attractiveness." The attractiveness of a given bond may depend on its yield, its maturity date or other factors for which the investor may search, as well as on its investment quality, the only characteristic to which the rating refers.

Since ratings involve judgments about the future, on the one hand, and since they are used by investors as a means of protection, on the other, the effort is made when assigning ratings to look at "worst" potentialities[6] in the "visible" future, rather than solely at the past record and the status of the present. Therefore, investors using the rating should not expect to find in them a reflection of statistical factors alone, since they are an appraisal of long-term risks, including the recognition of many non-statistical factors.

Though ratings may be used by the banking authorities to classify bonds in their bank examination procedure, Moody's Ratings are not made with these bank regulations in view. Moody's Investors Service's own judgment as to desirability or non-desirability of a bond for bank investment purposes is not indicated by Moody's Ratings.

Moody's Ratings represent the mature opinion of Moody's Investors Service, Inc., as to the relative investment classification of bonds. As such, they should be used in conjunction with the description and statistics appearing in Moody's Manuals. Reference should be made to these statements for information regarding the issuer. Moody's Ratings are not commercial credit ratings. In no case is default or receivership to be imputed unless expressly so stated in the Manual.

Ratings Changes

The quality of most bonds is not fixed and steady over a period of time, but tends to undergo change. For this reason changes in ratings occur so as to reflect these variations in the intrinsic position of individual bonds.

---

[5] Including an understanding of how a firm's intangible assets were factored into the rating decision.

[6] This would include an analysis of the risks, technological as well as competitive, to a firm's portfolio of intangible assets.

A change in rating may thus occur at any time in the case of an individual issue. Such rating change should serve notice that Moody's observes some alteration in the investment risks of the bond or that the previous rating did not fully reflect the quality of the bond as now seen. While because of their very nature, changes are to be expected more frequently among bonds of lower ratings than among bonds of higher ratings, nevertheless, the user of bond ratings should keep close and constant check on all ratings—both high and low ratings—thereby to be able to note promptly any signs of change in investment status which may occur.[7]

The Fitch Rating Guide provides a final caveat with respect to ratings:

Fitch ratings are not recommendations to buy, sell, or hold any security. Ratings do not comment on the adequacy of market price, the suitability of any security for a particular investor, or the tax-exempt nature or taxability of payments made in respect to any security.

Fitch ratings are based on information obtained from issuers, other obligors, underwriters, their experts, and other sources Fitch believes to be reliable. Fitch does not audit or verify the truth or accuracy of such information. Ratings may be changed, suspended, or withdrawn as a result of changes in, or the unavailability of, information or for other reasons.[8]

4.2 MAJOR FACTORS USED IN A RATING DECISION

In assessing the credit quality of various debt obligations of industrial companies, rating agencies consider a wide range of information, both qualitative and quantitative. The following outline lists some of the major factors:

I. Industry risk profile
   A. Industry maturity
   B. Basis of competition
   C. Intangibles
II. Assessment of the company's competitive position within industry
   A. Historical financial analysis
      1. Revenue and earnings (profitability)
         a. Diversity, magnitude, consistency, outlook
         b. Accounting policies: liberal/conservative, off-balance-sheet exposure
         c. Degree of operating leverage
         d. Coverages of interest and fixed charges
         e. Profit margins: gross, operating, pretax, net
         f. Returns: total capital, equity, assets, and so on
      2. Cash flow
         a. Magnitude, stability, diversity of operating cash flow
         b. Coverages of debt service
         c. Future debt service requirements
         d. Coverages of fixed charges
         e. Capital expenditure requirements
         f. Dividend policy
         g. Operating/nonoperating sources and uses of cash
      3. Liquidity
         a. Receivable mix and quality

---

[7] *Moody's Bond Record*, January 1993, p. 3.
[8] *Fitch Rating Register*, January 1993, p. i.

        b. Inventory mix and quality

        c. Working capital to sales

        d. Inventory and receivable days outstanding

        e. Accounts payable terms and days outstanding

   4. Leverage

        a. Appropriateness of capital structure

        b. Ability to access the financial markets (debt and equity)

        c. Financial leverage, and risk-adjusted leverage

        d. Off-balance-sheet liabilities

        e. Impact of Intangibles

        f. Priority of claims

        g. Recorded and unrecorded intangibles

        h. Total debt to total capital

B. Management

   1. Character

   2. Depth and breadth

   3. Degree of control

C. Forecasts

   1. Underlying assumptions

        a. Macro economic

        b. Industry assumptions

        c. Company specific

        d. Optimism

   2. Sensitivity of forecasted results to changes in key variables

        a. Effect on cash flow

        b. Effect on coverages

        c. Effect on leverage

        d. Level of "cushion" available if events do not adhere to the assumptions in the forecast

D. Bond/note/issue specific

   1. Seniority of ranking within the capital structure

   2. Purpose for the financing (use of proceeds)

   3. Collateral, if any

        a. What is it?

        b. Where is it?

        c. Marketability

        d. Creditor access to the collateral

        e. Liquidation value

   4. Term of the financing

   5. How will the financing be repaid?

   6. Covenant protection

   7. Default provisions

   8. Presence, or absence, of any parent/affiliate guaranties

The relative weight that these factors, among others, receive during the rating process will vary, depending on the industry being considered. For example, geographic diversity of revenue sources can be a critical factor in the retailing industry, yet it is almost irrelevant in the aerospace industry. Similarly, being recognized as the low cost producer is a decisive competitive advantage in commodity-type businesses, such as metals and mining companies, whereas in high-value-added businesses, such as branded consumer goods, there is considerably less emphasis on this issue.

In investment decisions, including the assignment of ratings, quantitative factors tend to carry significantly more weight in the decision process than those of the "soft," or "subjective," qualitative considerations. The unscientific rationale for this is probably that financial analysts, including rating agency types, tend to be a numerically inclined group of people. Stock prices, revenues, margins, earnings per share, leverage ratios, and so forth can be charted; statistics can be calculated and performances compared. This is clearly home turf for the number crunchers. Intangibles,[9] on the other hand, are a decidedly subjective, but nonetheless crucial, factor in financial analysis.

GAAP (generally accepted accounting principles) has proven itself unable and unwilling to address the full range of intangibles encountered in business situations. This sentiment is clearly stated in the Financial Accounting Standards Board's SFAC No. 5:[10]

A statement of financial position *does not purport to show the value of a business enterprise* but, together with other financial statements and other information, should provide information that is useful to those who desire to make their own estimates of the enterprise's value. As a result of limitations stemming from uncertainty and cost-benefit considerations, *not all assets and not all liabilities are included in a statement of financial position*, and some assets and liabilities that are included are affected by events, such as price changes or accretion, that are not recognized. Statements of financial position also commonly use different attributes to measure different assets and liabilities.

Uncertainty and related *limitations of financial accounting put the burden of estimating values of business enterprises and of investments in them on investors, creditors, and others. Information about components of earnings and comprehensive income often plays a significant part in that analysis.* For example, investors may use that information to help estimate "earning power," or other amounts that they perceive as representative of long-term earning ability of an enterprise, as a significant step in comparing the market price of an equity security with its "intrinsic value." *Those estimates and analyses are part of financial analysis, not financial reporting, but* financial accounting facilitates financial analysis by, among other things, classifying financial statement information in homogeneous groups."

The Financial Accounting Standards Board (FASB) also addressed the scope of financial reporting in the SFAC No. 1 when it stated:

Accrual accounting provides measures of earnings rather than evaluation of management's performance, estimates of "earnings power," predictions of earnings, assessments of risk, or confirmations or rejections of predictions or assessments. *Investors, creditors, and other users of the information do their own evaluating, estimating, predicting, assessing, confirming, or rejecting.* For example, procedures such as averaging or normalizing reported earnings for several periods and ignoring or averaging out the financial effects of "nonrepresentative" transactions and events are commonly used in estimating "earnings power." However, both the concept of "earnings power"

---

[9] Intangibles such as trademarks, patents, and the like are not alone in this situation. Human resource accounting and debtholder protection afforded by covenants or security are similarly misunderstood and misinterpreted by analysts.

[10] Financial Accounting Standards Board, *Statement of Financial Accounting Concepts, No. 5*, "Recognition and Measurement in Financial Statements of Business Enterprises" (Norwalk, CT: FASB, December, 1984), pars. 27 and 28 (author's emphasis).

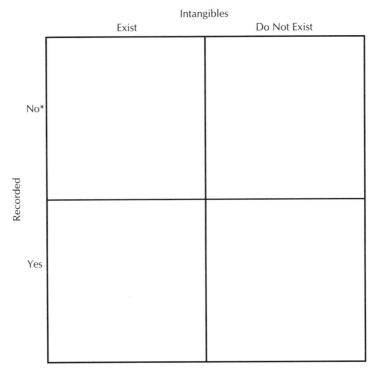

*Also includes under-reported intangibles

Exhibit 4.3 Decision matrix

and the techniques for estimating it are part of financial analysis and are beyond the scope of financial reporting.[11]

Imperfect as it is, however, GAAP is all an analyst has to work with in assessing financial performance and enterprise value. The goal, then, for financial analysts is to devise a simple method, which uses reported GAAP results, to quantitatively evaluate the impact of intangibles on a company.

4.3 EFFECT OF GAAP ON REPORTED RESULTS

What results can be expected when GAAP is applied to financial statements of companies with and without intangibles? Is there any useful information from financial reporting that financial analysts can use in assessing creditworthiness on a consistent basis among firms when significant intangibles are involved?

Under generally accepted accounting principles, an internally created intangible such as a new patent, trademark, and the like is afforded no balance sheet presentation as an asset. All research and development costs are expensed as incurred, as are all marketing expenditures. Reported intangibles, in material amounts, primarily arise as the result of an acquisition, either of a product line or of an entire company. The net effect of these

---

[11] Financial Accounting Standards Board, *Statement of Financial Accounting Concepts, No. 1,* "Objectives of Financial Reporting by Business Enterprises" (Norwalk, CT: FASB,), par. 48 (author's emphasis).

rules of financial reporting is that financial analysts are confronted with four possibilities, as presented in Exhibit 4.3.

In simple terms, intangibles either exist or they do not. Similarly, on a GAAP basis, intangible assets are either recorded as assets or they are not. Assuming that only these possibilities exist, the question is, what should an analyst expect to see as reported GAAP results in each situation?

According to SFAC No. 6, "Assets are probable future economic benefits obtained or controlled by a particular entity as a result of past transactions or events." And, among other things, they involve "a capacity . . . to contribute directly or indirectly to future net cash inflows."[12] Therefore, all other things being equal, a company that possesses intangible assets should have a greater level of net cash flow and, by extension, profitability, than it would without intangibles.

An example of this phenomenon can be seen in the pharmaceutical industry. At about the time that any particular drug's patent protection has expired or a drug has been rendered outdated by a competitor's product, the price of the drug and its profitability will fall dramatically. Such was the case with SmithKline's leading ulcer product, Tagamet, which had sales of approximately $1 billion before the introduction of Zantac by Glaxo PLC.[13] The resultant loss in sales and profitability eventually led to the merger of Smithkline and Beecham. In other words, the loss of an intangible such as patent protection or, in this case, a competitive advantage, resulted in SmithKline's loss of substantial amounts of income and cash flow, so that its continued existence as an independent company was no longer feasible.

Furthermore, the company that has recorded intangibles will have more assets and more total capital (Total capital = Shareholder's equity + Total debt) than it will with unrecorded intangibles. The before-and-after balance sheet of any leveraged buy-out will demonstrate this point.

Exhibit 4.4 shows a spreadsheet of RJR Nabisco before and after acquisition. Note that the only thing that changed between February 8, 1989, and February 9, 1989, was the ownership of RJR Nabisco; yet $18.8 billion of assets were created overnight and have since been certified as such by RJR's auditors. Did these assets just appear out of thin air? Hardly. These assets not only "existed" before the acquisition—they formed the rationale for the bulk of the purchase price. However, until the acquisition these were unrecorded assets under generally accepted accounting principles.

In summary then, the chart shown in Exhibit 4.3 can be filled in with the following observations about intangibles and GAAP, as shown in Exhibit 4.5.

4.4 QUANTITATIVE METHODS OF EVALUATING INTANGIBLES

Financial analysts use several methods, both qualitative and quantitative, to consider the value of intangibles in their decisions. In a rating agency the qualitative factors, including intangibles, tend to be used as modifiers of the rating that would be assigned through a strictly quantitative analysis. However, there are quantitative methods that can be used by rating agencies and other financial analysts to assess more accurately the impact of intangibles, both recorded and unrecorded, on the financial results of companies.

---

[12] Financial Accounting Standards Board, *Statement of Financial Accounting Concepts, No. 6,* "Elements of Financial Statements" (: FASB,), pars. 25–26.

[13] Zantac has accounted for almost half of Glaxo's $2 billion in annual revenue, clearly qualifying as a significant level of cash flow and profitability.

	Actual	Pro Forma	
Current assets*	$6,181	$ 7,164	
PP&E, net	6,149	6,149	
Goodwill, trademarks, and other	5,421	23,238	
Total Assets	$17,751	$36,551	← +$18.8 billion
Notes payable and CMLTD	$760	$ 5,760	
Other current liabilities	3,520	3,441	
Total Current Liabilities	4,280	9,201	
Long-term debt	4,975	17,430	
Other noncurrent liability and deferred income taxes	2,677	2,072	
Redeemable Pfd	125	0	
Common equity	5,694	7,848	
Total Assets	$17,751	$36,551	
Total capital**	$11,554	$31,038	← +$19.5 billion

*Note: Increase in current assets primarily relates to a revaluation of ending inventory.
**Total capital = total interest-bearing debt + preferred and common equity.
Source: RJR Nabisco Company Filings.

Exhibit 4.4. RJR Nabisco, Inc.: Actual and pro forma summary balance sheets, December 31, 1988.

Intangibles

	Exist	Do Not Exist
No*	Higher income and cash flow / Lower total capital	Lower income and cash flow / Lower total capital
Yes	Higher income and cash flow / Greater total capital	Lower income and cash flow / Greater total capital

Recorded

*Also includes under-reported intangibles

Exhibit 4.5 Decision matrix with observations

The three major quantitative methods are the cost, market value, and income methods.

(a) Cost Method. The cost method values intangibles at the costs incurred to create them. It is also the method preferred by GAAP.[14] However, this is not a very practical method for financial analysts in general, and especially for rating agency purposes, for several reasons:

1. It is all too often possible, even with high-priced professional assistance, to overpay for something. To recall the name of any failed leveraged buy-out (for instance, Allied/Federated, Hills Department Store) or "acquisition-from-hell"[15] is to see the shortfall of this approach. Some of these examples have since opted for the "prepackaged bankruptcy" route. Wall Street even has its own pet phrase for these mistakes, preferring to refer to them as "good companies with a bad balance sheet."

2. It is virtually impossible for an outsider to ascertain what any intangible really costs to produce.

3. Even if it were possible to determine the underlying cost, it would be impractical to use that information in any decision-making process because, for the most part, it is irrelevant. The formula for Coca-Cola Classic is arguably one of the most valuable trade secrets of all consumer products. It was created in the late 1800s, at about the same time that Dr. Pepper was created. Assume that these two products cost the same to create. What possible bearing does that have on today's value for Coca-Cola Classic or Dr. Pepper? Should an investor in the 1990s expect to pay the same price for either trademark? Hardly.

4. Unfortunately, the accounting profession has yet to deal effectively with the valuation, including the potential impairment, of intangibles.[16]

It is for these reasons that "leverage reported under GAAP is meaningless for consumer products companies because brand assets are not on the balance sheet."[17] The limitations of the cost method as a rational basis for financial analytical use could be extended almost ad nauseam, but the point is made.

(b) Market Value Method. Generally, the market value method calls for an analyst to assess the future profitability, or cash flow, from an intangible and then "present value" that stream of earnings or cash using some appropriate discount rate. This is known as the discounted cash flow method. Alternatively, for a publicly held company, such as The

---

[14] It is this method that preserves the financial accounting principles of objectivity and historical cost basis.

[15] Such as in the early 1980s, when Exxon, the largest U.S. oil company, diversified into the office equipment business and purchased the three then-leading manufacturers: Vydec (word processors), Quix (electronic typewriters), and Quip (facsimile machines). A few hundred million dollars later, Exxon quietly exited that business.

[16] In 1980 the trucking industry was deregulated. Up until that time trucking firms used to buy and sell routes (intangibles). Deregulation had the effect of eliminating any rational basis for valuing these intangibles. However, it was not until the FASB promulgated SFAS No. 44 that trucking firms were ultimately forced to write off these investments.

[17] Thomas W. Hoens, quoted in A. Ourusoff with M. Ozanian, P. Brown, and J. Starr, "What's in a Name: What the World's Top Brands Are Worth," *Financial World* (1 September 1992): 46.

Coca-Cola Company, an analyst could use the current market equity value (equity method) to value the company's intangibles.

The discounted cash flow approach is the most analytically correct method, but it is also the most complex. Therefore, it is almost impossible for an outside analyst, using GAAP information, to compute a discounted cash flow valuation with any degree of accuracy. Second, the method is very sensitive to the selection of the discount rate and terminal value of the intangible being measured. This method, however, is quite relevant for management in its internal capital allocation schemes, and for fixing a price in buy-sell agreements.

The equity method is far easier to perform, but it provides an answer only on a consolidated basis for a company, and then only for one with an actively traded stock. It also assumes that the stock price is fairly valued. The equity method will yield no clue as to the allocation of intangible value among divisions or products of the company. In the RJR example, the analyst would still be left with the question of how to allocate the intangible value among the trademarks Oreo, Winston, Salem, Camel, Teddy Grahams, and so forth.

(c) **Income Method.**   The income method, although not as analytically superior as the discounted cash flow method, is the preferred method for rating agency use. The income method shares the simplicity of the equity method without its drawbacks. This method uses a multiple of operating earnings, or capitalization rate, to impute a value to the organization as a whole and, by extension, to the intangibles. Like the discounted cash flow method, it is based on the presumption that intangibles have value as a function of their profitability, not their cost. It differs from the discounted cash flow method, however, in that it uses historical results rather than forecasted results, and is therefore far easier to compute.[18]

One feature of the income method is its reliance on operating earnings (EBIT, or earnings before interest and taxes) as a starting point.[19] Not only do all companies report this number in their financial statements, but it is also required for segment reporting as well, thereby facilitating understanding by external financial analysts. Internal corporate management accounting systems will report divisional and/or product line income statements to the EBIT line. This, in turn, allows for an internally consistent allocation of intangible value to be made across diverse product lines. Clearly, this method achieves the previously stated goal of using GAAP-reported results to quantify the value or contributions of intangibles to a company. And it is this ease of use, profitability basis, and internally consistent results that make the income method a good, though not perfect, benchmark measure of intangible value.

4.5 HOW A RATING AGENCY USES THE INCOME METHOD

How, then, does a rating agency factor the presence of intangibles into its analysis? To answer this question, recall that a rating agency's objective is to form a credit opinion

---

[18] This is not to suggest that the income method cannot be used in forecasts; it most certainly can and is. Rather, it means that forecasts are not a prerequisite for its calculation, as is the case with the discounted cash flow method.

[19] This does, however, create an opportunity for manipulating the results in the presence of management fraud, such as has been charged in the cases of *Chambers Development*, *Leslie Fay*, and *Phar-Mor*, for example. A more analytically correct application of the income method would use operating cash flow as the basis for capitalization. The benefits to be derived from this alternative are probably outweighed by its cost to implement.

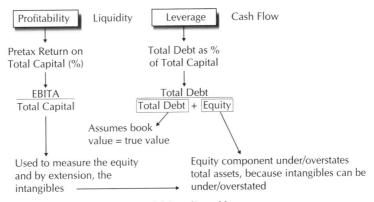

Exhibit 4.6 Rating agency model for adjusted leverage

regarding the quality of a bond; it is not a pricing or trading decision. Ratings are an indicator or assessment of the issuer's ability to meet its principal and interest payments in a timely manner in accordance with the terms of the issue.

In a rating decision there are four major quantitative areas of analysis: profitability, cash flow, liquidity, and leverage. In considering a debt rating, it is axiomatic that—all other things being equal—the greater the leverage, the lower the credit quality. Yet, as previously noted under GAAP, assets are understated in the presence of unrecorded intangibles, which results in leverage being overstated for the same reason.

In analyzing a particular company or industry, if intangibles are thought to play a substantial role, then, according to an earlier observation (See Exhibit 4.5), income and cash flow will be enhanced while leverage will be overstated. By using the income method to compute an adjusted leverage, it is possible then to compare the leverage[20] of such disparate companies as The Coca-Cola Company, which has no recorded intangibles, and RJR Nabisco and Dr. Pepper/7-Up, which by virtue of their leveraged buy-outs (LBOs) have material amounts of intangible assets.[21] Furthermore, the results will be consistent with traditional leverage analysis.

4.6 THE MODEL

From a consideration of the previously discussed effects of intangibles on GAAP results and an application of ratio analysis, a change can be made in the traditional leverage calculation (see Exhibit 4.6).

Traditionally, leverage is calculated as a percentage:

$$\text{Total debt/total capital} = x\%,$$

where total capital is defined as total debt plus total stockholder's equity. Total stockholder's equity is defined as total assets minus total liabilities.

---

[20] In certain industries, however, such as cable television and bottling, it is has become an accepted industry standard to gauge leverage as a function of cash flow.

[21] In addition, as a side benefit, it is also possible to gain some insight into whether Kohlberg, Kravis, & Roberts (KKR) overpaid for its acquisition of RJR Nabisco.

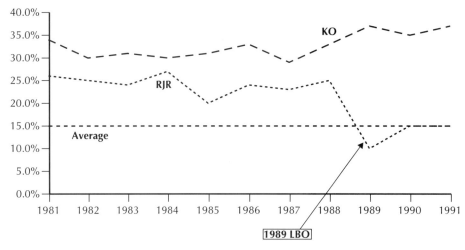

Exhibit 4.7 The Coca-Cola Company and RJR Nabisco pretax return on total capital, 1981-1991.

One of the key measures of profitability, pretax return on total capital, calculates the unlevered return to all the providers of capital. The average annual pretax return on total capital[22] for all rated industrial companies over the last 10 years is approximately 15%. However, in the presence of substantial unrecorded intangible assets, such as those of The Coca-Cola Company, this measure will reach near astronomical heights on a sustainable basis (see Exhibit 4.7).

If the pretax return on total capital is set equal to a constant, in this case 15%, then profitability will, in turn, define a value for appropriate "adjusted" total capital. Feeding this adjusted total capital into the leverage equation results in an adjusted leverage which, unlike cash flow multiples, provides a consistent result with historical leverage calculations.

(a) Why 15%?   In the model (Exhibit 4.6) 15% is used as a benchmark rate of return in the pretax return on total capitalization equation. This "appropriate" rate of return drives the model and provides the adjusted total capital on which the adjusted leverage is, in turn, calculated.

How did the 15% capitalization factor arise? In a survey of rated industrial companies over the last 10 years, excluding regulated utilities and financial institutions, 15% was found to be the average rate of return on total capital.[23] As an average, then, a 15% factor is useful as a benchmark[24] for valuing intangibles over a broad spectrum as is found within an industry or a company with multiple trademarks, such as RJR Nabisco. This is quite

---

[22] Pretax return on total capital is defined here as operating profit (EBIT) divided by total capital, where total capital equals total debt plus total shareholders equity. In order to exclude the effects of acquired intangibles from the calculation, intangible amortization expense is added back to operating profit (EBITA).

[23] The survey used more than 800 industrial companies rated by Standard & Poor's. Results were for the period 1981 through 1991, as reported by Compustat. Return on total capital was defined as (earnings before interest and taxes + intangible amortization)/(average total debt + average stockholder equity).

[24] So long as the user is consistent in its application, the model will yield similar results, regardless of the capitalization factor chosen. The absolute value of adjusted leverage will change, whereas the ranked order of adjusted leverage will remain constant.

($ in millions)	Intangible Assets $	Total Assets $	Intangibles as a % of Total Assets %	Trademarks
American Brands Inc.-Del.	3,373.8	15,115.5	22.3%	Benson & Hedges, Pall Mall, Jim Beam, Acco, MasterLocks
Coca-Cola Co. (The)	303.7	10,222.4	3.0%	Coca-Cola, Diet Coke, Minute Maid, Hi-C
CPC International Inc.	677.6	4,510.3	15.0%	Skippy, Mazola, Thomas's English Muffins
General Mills Inc.	81.0	4,305.0	1.9%	Olive Garden, Red Lobster, Cheerios, Betty Crocker, Wheaties
Heinz (H.J.) Co.	1,179.3	5,931.9	19.9%	"57 Varieties," Weight Watchers, Star-Kist
Kellogg Co.	49.8	3,925.8	1.3%	Kellogg's, Mrs. Smith's, Eggo
Pepsico Inc.	5,932.4	18,775.1	31.6%	Pepsi, Taco Bell, Kentucky Fried Chicken, Frito-Lay, Doritos
Philip Morris Cos. Inc.	18,662.0	47,384.0	39.4%	Marlboro, Kraft, General Foods, Miller Beer
Procter & Gamble Co.	2,882.0	20,468.0	14.1%	Cheer, Spic & Span, Tide, Charmin, Pampers, Crest
Quaker Oats Co.	446.2	3,016.1	14.8%	Gatorade, Aunt Jemima
Ralston Purina Co.	486.3	4,632.1	10.5%	Chex, Everready Batteries, Puppy Chow, Wonder Bread, Beech-Nut
RJR Nabisco Hldgs. Corp.	22,540.0	32,131.0	70.2%	Winston, Salem, Oreos, Teddy Grahams, Planters, LifeSavers
Sara Lee Corp.	(a)	8,122.0	(N.A.)	Hanes, Playtex, L'Eggs, Sara Lee, Hillshire Farms

(a) No figure reported
Source: Compustat and Lotus One Source.

Exhibit 4.8. Intangible assets as a percentage of total assets of selected consumer products companies.

133

| | ($ in millions) | | | | |
Name	Total Debt	Total Equity	Total Capital (1)	Leverage (2)	Debt Rating (3)
Kellogg Co.	464.3	2,159.8	2,624.1	17.7%	AAA
Coca-Cola Co. (The)	2,287.6	4,425.8	6,713.4	34.1%	AA
Sara Lee Corp.	1,772.0	2,894.7	4,666.7	38.0%	AA–
American Brands Inc.-Del.	3,282.5	4,316.0	7,598.5	43.2%	A
Procter & Gamble Co.	6,080.0	7,736.0	13,816.0	44.0%	AA
Heinz (H.J.) Co.	1,902.5	2,367.4	4,269.9	44.6%	AA
General Mills Inc.	1,122.4	1,370.9	2,493.3	45.0%	A+
CPC International Inc.	1,381.7	1,630.6	3,012.3	45.9%	A
Quaker Oats Co.	814.7	905.8	1,720.5	47.4%	A+
Philip Morris Cos. Inc.	16,900.0	12,512.0	29,412.0	57.5%	A
Pepsico Inc.	8,034.4	5,545.4	13,579.8	59.2%	A
RJR Nabisco Hldgs. Corp.	14,337.0	8,419.0	22,756.0	63.0%	BBB–
Ralston Purina Co.	2,248.4	895.2	3,143.6	71.5%	A–

(1) Total Capital = Total Debt + Total Equity.
(2) Leverage = Total Debt/Total Capital.
(3) Rating = Senior Debt Rating—Standard & Poor's, as of Jan. 1993.
Note: All figures are as of 1991 year-end results per Compustat.

Exhibit 4.9.   Reported comparison of GAAP leverage and senior debt rating.

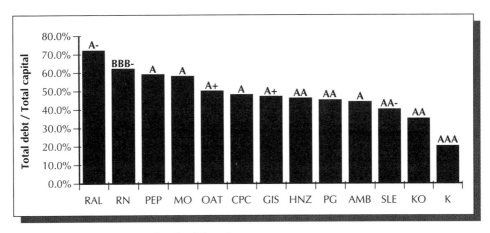

Exhibit 4.10 GAAP leverage and senior debt rating.

adequate for the needs of a rating agency attempting to quantify leverage in the presence of significant intangible assets.

(b) Example of the Model. Exhibits 4.8 through 4.14 provide an example of how the model would be used to adjust reported leverage for a variety of consumer product companies. The figures in Exhibit 4.8 are based on the companies' reported amounts per GAAP. Reported intangibles range from a low of 1.3% of assets for Kellogg to a high of 70% for RJR Nabisco Holdings Corp. Exhibits 4.9 and 4.10 then rank the companies based on their reported leverage (Total Debt/Total Capital) and include their senior debt rating. It is interesting to note here that BBB-' rated RJR Nabisco Holdings Corp. appears to be less leveraged than 'A-' rated Ralston Purina. Exhibit 4.11 calculates the reported pretax return on total capital for the selected companies. The results range from a high of almost 40% for The Coca-Cola Co. and Kellogg Co., both companies with minimal reported intangibles, to a low of 15.3% for RJR Nabisco Holdings, which since its 1989 LBO has all of its intangibles reported on its balance sheet.

In Exhibit 4.12, the adjusted total capital for each company is calculated. Based on its operating results, Philip Morris Co. would have its total capital increased by $31.7 billion due to unreported or under-reported intangibles. Amazingly this adjustment is in addition to the $18.7 billion of intangibles already present on the company's GAAP balance sheet (Exhibit 4.8). The results of using this adjusted total capital figure in the leverage equation are shown in Exhibits 4.13 and 4.14. When ranked based on adjusted leverage, RJR Nabisco's 'BBB-' falls into place relative to its peers. However, other companies such as Procter & Gamble Co. appear to be more highly leveraged than lower rated competitors. Because it is possible that factors other than leverage can account for the rating disparity, the reader is encouraged to carefully study the rating rationale published by the appropriate agency.

(c) Caveats and Observations. Of all the caveats that could be stated concerning this model, the greatest is this: "Do not ever lose sight of the fundamentals of good credit." The analysis of intangibles, and their effect on reported leverage, is but one aspect of the rating process, albeit an important one.

($ in millions)

		Total Debt	Total Equity	Total Capital	Operating Profit	Amortization Expense	Pretax Return on Total Capital
American Brands Inc.-Del.	AMB	3,282.5	4,316.0	7,598.5	1,502.0	75.9	20.8%
Coca-Cola Co. (The)	KO	2,287.6	4,425.8	6,713.4	2,567.8	(a)	38.2%
CPC International Inc.	CPC	1,381.7	1,630.6	3,012.3	821.4	(a)	27.3%
General Mills Inc.	GIS	1,122.4	1,370.9	2,493.3	934.0	(a)	37.5%
Heinz (H.J.) Co.	HNZ	1,902.5	2,367.4	4,269.9	1,119.3	40.3	27.2%
Kellogg Co.	K	464.3	2,159.8	2,624.1	1,044.9	(a)	39.8%
Pepsico Inc.	PEP	8,034.4	5,545.4	13,579.8	2,286.2	208.7	18.4%
Philip Morris Cos. Inc.	MO	16,900.0	12,512.0	29,412.0	8,667.0	499.0	31.2%
Procter & Gamble Co.	PG	6,080.0	7,736.0	13,816.0	3,099.0	(a)	22.4%
Quaker Oats Co.	OAT	814.7	905.8	1,720.5	508.6	22.4	30.9%
Ralston Purina Co.	RAL	2,248.4	895.2	3,143.6	856.5	(a)	27.2%
RJR Nabisco Hldgs. Corp.	RN	14,337.0	8,419.0	22,756.0	2,865.0	609.0	15.3%
Sara Lee Corp.	SLE	1,772.0	2,894.7	4,666.7	1,025.0	(a)	22.0%

(a) Insignificant figure per Compustat.
Pretax Return on Total Capital = (Operating Profit + Intangible Amortization Expense)/(Total Capital).

Exhibit 4.11. Calculation of pretax return on total capital.

($ in millions)

	Reported Total Capital	Operating Profit (EBIT)	Intangible Amortization	EBITA	Adjusted Total Capital	Increase in Total Capital
American Brands Inc.-Del.	7,598.5	1,502.0	75.9	1,577.9	10,519.3	2,920.8
Coca-Cola Co. (The)	6,713.4	2,567.8	(a)	2,567.8	17,118.7	10,405.3
CPC International Inc.	3,012.3	821.4	(a)	821.4	5,476.0	2,463.7
General Mills Inc.	2,493.3	934.0	(a)	934.0	6,226.7	3,733.4
Heinz (H.J.) Co.	4,269.9	1,119.3	40.3	1,159.6	7,730.3	3,460.5
Kellogg Co.	2,624.1	1,044.9	(a)	1,044.9	6,966.0	4,341.9
Pepsico Inc.	13,579.8	2,286.2	208.7	2,494.9	16,632.7	3,052.9
Philip Morris Cos. Inc.	29,412.0	8,667.0	499.0	9,166.0	61,106.7	31,694.7
Procter & Gamble Co.	13,816.0	3,099.0	(a)	3,099.0	20,660.0	6,844.0
Quaker Oats Co.	1,720.5	508.6	22.4	531.0	3,540.0	1,819.5
Ralston Purina Co.	3,143.6	856.5	(a)	856.5	5,710.0	2,566.4
RJR Nabisco Hldgs. Corp.	22,756.0	2,865.0	609.0	3,474.0	23,160.0	404.0
Sara Lee Corp.	4,666.7	1,025.0	(a)	1,025.0	6,833.3	2,166.6

(a) Insignificant figure per Compustat.
EBITA = Operating Profit plus Intangible Amortization Expense
Adjusted Total Capital = EBITA/15%
Increase in Total Capital = Adjusted Total Capital minus Reported Total Capital.

Exhibit 4.12. Calculation of adjusted total capital.

	($ in millions)			Debt/Total Capital		
	Total Debt	Reported Total Capital	Adjusted Total Capital	Reported	Adjusted	Rating
Kellogg Co.	464.3	2,624.1	6,966.0	17.7%	6.7%	AAA
Coca-Cola Co. (The)	2,287.6	6,713.4	17,118.7	34.1%	13.4%	AA
General Mills Inc.	1,122.4	2,493.3	6,226.7	45.0%	18.0%	A+
Quaker Oats Co.	814.7	1,720.5	3,540.0	47.4%	23.0%	A+
Heinz (H.J.) Co.	1,902.5	4,269.9	7,730.3	44.6%	24.6%	AA
CPC International Inc.	1,381.7	3,012.3	5,476.0	45.9%	25.2%	A
Sara Lee Corp.	1,772.0	4,666.7	6,833.3	38.0%	25.9%	AA−
Philip Morris Cos. Inc.	16,900.0	29,412.0	61,106.7	57.5%	27.7%	A
Procter & Gamble Co.	6,080.0	13,816.0	20,660.0	44.0%	29.4%	AA
American Brands Inc.-Del.	3,282.5	7,598.5	10,519.3	43.2%	31.2%	A
Ralston Purina Co.	2,248.4	3,143.6	5,710.0	71.5%	39.4%	A−
Pepsico Inc.	8,034.4	13,579.8	16,632.7	59.2%	48.3%	A
RJR Nabisco Hldgs. Corp.	14,337.0	22,756.0	23,160.0	63.0%	61.9%	BBB−

Exhibit 4.13. Calculation of adjusted leverage.

138

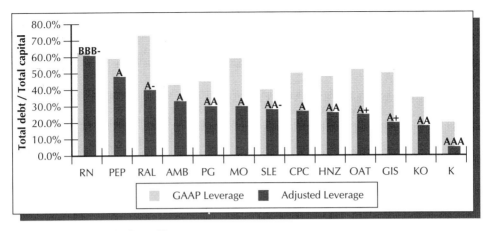

Exhibit 4.14 GAAP and adjusted leverage

From a rating agency viewpoint, the longer a company has unfettered use of an intangible and the greater the profitability derived from that intangible, then the greater the value a rating agency will ascribe to it when assessing the firm's overall leverage position (see Exhibit 4.15).

The results of this benchmark calculation, like any other, must be interpreted in its proper context. Valuing intangibles for rating agency purposes, or for any other reason, for that matter, cannot be performed in a vacuum. The analyst must take care to ascertain that the value ascribed to the intangible has a life at least as great as that of the debt instrument being considered. This would include an understanding of competitive environment as

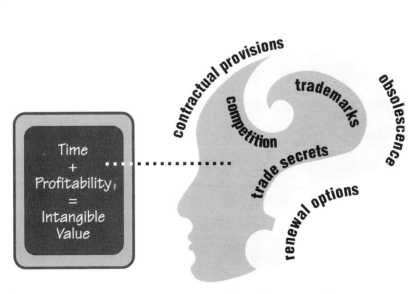

Exhibit 4.15 Conceptual Framework of Intangibles Rating Agency Value

well as the advent of new technologies.[25] Consider a high-tech company, such as Intel. A new generation of computer chip will yield spectacular results, which, in turn, will drive the adjusted leverage down. However, the duration of this enhanced value creation is remarkably fleeting. Similarly, a successful drug patent will also yield enhanced profitability, but only until the expiration date, when generic companies are free to compete against the product. The importance of looking beyond the benchmark results to the underlying portfolio of trademarks cannot be overstated.

Similarly, trademarks have value only when commercially exploited by a going concern. As credit quality deteriorates, and financial default or Chapter XI protection appears as a real possibility, the value ascribed by a rating agency to the intangible assets of a company will be substantially diminished.

By design, the rating agency method ascribes value only to intangibles of proven commercial success. Those that have yielded above-average profitability, such as the trademarks Oreo, Coca-Cola, Budweiser, Duracell, Marlboro, Avon, Raid, and Puppy Chow, fulfill this criterion and, as a result, can support some degree of financial leverage. New or promising creations that are in development or early stages of commercialization are afforded no value in the model. The analyst must factor this "product pipeline" into any analysis.

Finally, intangibles are not "free assets." They require maintenance, just like any other asset, if they are to retain their value to the enterprise. Disregard of this rule was one of the underlying flaws in the retailer LBOs of the 1980s. Allied/Federated became so overleveraged that it could not afford the annual expenditures required to maintain its trademarks. Each year The Coca-Cola Company and its bottler network spend more than $4 billion in advertising and marketing to maintain their trademark. Similarly, Philip Morris spends more than $2.4 billion to maintain its Marlboro, General Foods, Kraft, and other trademarks.

---

[25] Depending on its materiality to the analysis, it might be appropriate to use other valuation methods, such as discounted cash flow. The return-on-capital approach has its greatest validity when used as a benchmark of intangible value.

PROTECTING INTELLECTUAL PROPERTY

CHAPTER 5

IMPERATIVE STRATEGIES FOR PROTECTING INTANGIBLE ASSETS: THE U.S. MARKET

Al J. Daniel, Jr., Esq.

Frankel & Abrams
New York, New York

5.1 INTELLECTUAL PROPERTY RIGHTS, PROTECTION, AND EXPLOITATION

(a) Introduction

(i) History of Intellectual Property Rights. This chapter surveys the types of protection for intellectual property that concern most businesses in the United States today. Some are based on ancient legal principles. Others reflect the emergence of technologies and services previously unknown, such as special protection for designs used in silicon chips—although this particular form of protection draws heavily on copyright principles.

In the United States some rights to intellectual properties, such as copyrights and patents, are based exclusively on statutes passed by the Congress of the United States. Rights to others, such as trademarks and trade names, may be protected both under federal laws and statutes and under the common law of the individual states. The rights to some properties, such as trade secrets, and some forms of rights against unfair competition, are protected primarily by the common law of individual states. This chapter principally examines the federal laws of the United States, which protect intellectual property, except where state laws are of particular significance or are the primary source of protection for certain kinds of rights.

People today live and work in a global economy. Intellectual property rights are in the forefront of many of the fastest growing areas of global trade in goods and services, such as silicon chips, computer software, and audio and video recordings. This chapter focuses on intellectual property laws in the United States, but it is often important for people in business to also be aware of changes in the international agreements affecting protection for intellectual property.

Some international treaties and agreements make it relatively easy to obtain protection in other countries for different kinds of intellectual property created in the United States, when exploited abroad. The form and extent of global protection varies considerably, from little or none to substantial, depending on the kind of property and the particular country involved. Adequate legal protection for newer technologies has often lagged behind the development of such products and services.

More than one hundred nations of the world are members of the General Agreement on Tariffs and Trade (GATT), the major international agreement that is the touchstone for global trade.[1] The Uruguay Round of Multilateral Trade Negotiations under the GATT began in 1986 and final agreement was reached on December 15, 1993.

One of the proposals in the Uruguay Round was, for the first time, to add protection of intellectual property to this international agreement. This proposal would require member countries to afford broader and more effective protection (generally equivalent to that afforded their own nationals, i.e., national treatment) for the intellectual property rights of persons and companies in other countries, when exploited in such member countries.[2]

Other international agreements affect intellectual property rights as well. The United States-Canada Free Trade Agreement has expanded the protection and trade of intellectual property between the United States and Canada.[3] The North American Free Trade Agreement (NAFTA) was signed by President Bush in late 1992. Agreement among the three parties—the United States, Canada, and Mexico—was finally reached late in 1993.

(ii) Choosing the Right Protection.   Different forms of protection may be available for different aspects of the same products or services. For example, a packaged computer software program usually involves several forms of protection. The program itself can generally be protected by copyright, and sometimes by patent law, the product name and logo can be protected by trademark law, and other aspects of the program may be protected as trade secrets.

It is important to understand the basic principles of the different types of intellectual property in order to ensure that appropriate protection is obtained. For example, patents provide protection for new products or processes themselves, if they are highly original and give their creators a monopoly in the use of those ideas for a period of time. However, the product or process must be disclosed to the public, and after the period of exclusive patent protection has expired, anyone can use and exploit them.

The same product or process can be protected indefinitely as the "trade secret" of a particular person or business, for example, the formula for Coca-Cola. The creator or owner of a trade secret must *keep* the information secret and protect it through agreements with those who have access to the secret and through vigilant enforcement of those agreements.

Ideas themselves cannot be copyrighted, but an individual's particular expression or discussion of an idea can be copyrighted and others cannot use that particular expression without the author's permission.

---

[1] General Agreement on Tariffs and Trade, Oct. 30, 1947, 61 Stat. A-11, T.I.A.S. No. 1700, 55 U.N.T.S. 194 (hereinafter GATT).

[2] Completion of the Uruguay Round of negotiations was delayed in large part because of disputes between the United States and the European Community concerning the intellectual property provisions and disputes involving agriculture. The Uruguay Round was finally concluded on December 15, 1993. *Final Act Embodying the Results of the Uruguay Round of Multilateral Trade Negotiations* (GATT Doc. MTN/FA) (15 Dec. 1993). It includes an *Agreement on Trade-Related Aspects of Intellectual Property Rights Including Trade in Counterfeit Goods*. The *Final Act* will become effective when it is approved by GATT members at a ministerial meeting of the GATT in Marrakech on April 15, 1994. These intellectual property provisions are discussed in depth in Al J. Daniel, Jr.'s "Intellectual Property in the Uruguay Round: The Dunkel Draft and A Comparison of United States Intellectual Property Rights, Remedies, and Border Measures", 25 *N.Y.U. J. Int'l Law & Politics*, 801 (1994).

[3] Anderson and Fried, "The Canadian-U.S. Free Trade Agreement in Operation," 17 Canada-U.S. L.J. 397 (1991).

Copyright in a work is created and protected from the moment the work is "fixed" in some tangible or perceivable form. Neither registration nor government approval is required to create the author's copyright.

In contrast, trademarks and trade names, until very recently, could be created only by their use and association with a particular business or product. Congress recently amended the Trademark Act to allow registration of a trademark based on an *intent* to use the mark, if it is then actually used in commerce within six months (extendable for an additional six months).[4] In most cases, trademarks are registered on the basis of actual use in commerce.[5]

(iii) Application, Registration, and Notice of Transfer.   Proper applications, registrations, and notices of transfers of interests are usually essential for the most complete protection of intellectual property rights. For example, there can be *no* patent protection without an application to the United States Patent and Trademark Office (PTO) "by the inventor" and the ultimate issuance of letters patent by that Office.[6] It is the issuance of the patent by the PTO that actually *creates* the patent rights of the inventor.[7] Patent applications are confidential, but the patents are made public when issued, with limited exceptions.[8] The priority of claims to inventions, a sometimes complex question, depends substantially on the date of filing of the patent application.[9]

Formalities and registration are not generally required to create and protect copyrights. A copyright exists from the time a protectable work is "fixed" in a tangible form.[10] Thus, an author's copyright in a book or story is protected from the moment it is first put on paper or in a computer file. However, registration of a copyrighted work is almost always advisable to obtain the maximum protection and all the remedies provided by the Copyright Act. In most cases, no copyright infringement action can be brought unless the work has been registered (with exceptions for foreign works protected under the Berne Convention).[11] Similarly, no statutory damages or attorney's fees can be awarded for copyright infringement unless a work has been registered, with limited exceptions.[12]

Registration of a trade or service mark with the PTO also provides important additional advantages, including prima facie evidence of validity, incontestability after five years (except for specified defenses), and constructive notice nationwide of the ownership and use of the mark for particular goods or services.[13]

(iv) Exploitation of Intellectual Property Rights.   There are a variety of ways to exploit intellectual property rights, depending on the nature of the rights involved and the goals

---

[4] 15 U.S.C. § 1051(b).

[5] 15 U.S.C. § 1501(a).

[6] 35 U.S.C. § 111. There is a limited exception, when the inventor refuses to apply or cannot be found. 35 U.S.C. § 118.

[7] 35 U.S.C. § 101.

[8] 35 U.S.C. § 122. There is a provision for confidentiality of patents in which the United States government has an interest where national security interests might be adversely affected. 35 U.S.C. § 181.

[9] 15 U.S.C. §§ 102, 119.

[10] "Copyright protection subsists . . . in original works of authorship fixed in any tangible medium of expression." 17 U.S.C. § 102(a).

[11] 17 U.S.C. § 411.

[12] 17 U.S.C. § 412. However, there are bills pending in Congress that would eliminate the requirement of registration as a condition for obtaining statutory damages and attorney's fees, among other things. Copyright Reform Act of 1993, H.R. 897 and S. 373, 103d Cong., 1st Sess.

[13] 15 U.S.C. §§ 1057(b) and (c), 1115(a) and (b).

and objectives of the owner. Owners can exploit the rights themselves. For example, the owner of various patents may manufacture and sell products that are themselves patented or made through the use of patented processes. The owners may also license others to manufacture products using those patents in return for royalty payments. Similarly, owners of copyrights may themselves publish and sell their copyrighted works or authorize others to do so in exchange for lump sum or periodic royalty payments.

(b) Copyrights

(i) Background. The Constitution of the United States authorizes the Congress "to promote the . . . useful Arts, by securing for limited Times to Authors . . . the exclusive Right to their respective Writings."[14] The Congress early recognized the importance of copyright and enacted the first copyright law in the United States in 1790.[15] The law has been substantially revised at four points in our history—in 1831, 1870, 1909, and, most recently, in 1976—usually in response to new and changing technologies.

The 1976 Copyright Act provides that the federal law of copyright preempts any laws of the states that are "equivalent to any of the exclusive rights" protected by federal copyright law, so that there would be a single, nationwide system of copyright protection.[16] Thus, the courts have ruled that some state laws or common-law remedies have been preempted by the Copyright Act and are thus unenforceable in particular circumstances. For example, a state software licensing statute and a state law claim of tortious interference with contracts were held preempted where they were being used to protect state law rights that the courts held were equivalent to the exclusive rights protected by the Copyright Act.[17]

Copyright law can be exceedingly complex, with numerous pitfalls for the unwary and ill-advised.[18] The complexity derives in part from the abstract nature of many copyright concepts, the complexity of the Copyright Act, the divisibility of the numerous rights that constitute copyrights, the long duration of the rights, the issues involving renewal of copyrights for works created or renewed under the prior Copyright Act of 1909, and the right of authors or their heirs to terminate grants of rights or transfers after a period of years.

(ii) What Can Be Copyrighted? The Copyright Act establishes copyright protection "in original works of authorship fixed in any tangible medium of expression."[19] Each word in this phrase is pregnant with meaning and each must be satisfied in order to create a copyright. The work must be original, meaning that it was created by the author—that is,

---

[14] U.S. Const. art. I, § 8, cl. 8.

[15] Act of May 31, 1970, 1 Stat. 124.

[16] 17 U.S.C. § 301(a). This power of federal preemption derives from the Supremacy Clause of the Constitution. U.S. Const. art. VI, cl. 2.

[17] See *Vault Corp. v. Quaid Software, Ltd.*, 847 F.2d 255 (5th Cir. 1988) (Louisiana software license statute preempted); *Harper & Row Pubs., Inc. v. Nation Enterprises*, 723 F.2d 195 (2d Cir. 1983), *rev'd on other grounds*, 471 U.S. 539 (1985) (New York law of tortious interference preempted).

[18] The recognized authoritative treatise on copyright is M. Nimmer and D. Nimmer, *Nimmer on Copyright* (1992), a comprehensive multivolume work that is frequently relied on by the courts. It contains detailed analysis of all provisions of the Act, appendices of statutes, and various copyright-related forms. A less exhaustive, but more compact treatise of three volumes is P. Goldstein, *Copyright* (1989).

[19] 17 U.S.C. § 102(a).

it "originated" with the author, not someone else—but it need not be *highly* unique or creative, which is required for some other forms of intellectual property protection, such as patents.[20] For example, an unlimited number of authors could independently write, publish, and copyright their own descriptions or impressions of the Chrysler Building in the morning sunlight in Manhattan, even if each article was very similar or even identical.

A work must be *fixed* in some tangible way in order to create a copyright. Authors cannot simply come up with brilliant ideas for books or songs and carry them around in their heads or sing them and thus obtain copyright protection. The works must be written down, recorded, encoded on a computer disk, or in some other way "fixed in a tangible medium of expression . . . from which they can be perceived, reproduced, or otherwise communicated."[21]

The Copyright Act specifies the most common categories of works of authorship in which copyrights subsist; these include many that are immediately familiar, such as literary works, music, and movies.[22]

A work is considered to be a "collective work" if it contains a number of independent works that "are assembled into a collective whole," such as a magazine or encyclopedia.[23] The collective work and the individual works within it can be separately copyrighted.

Another category of work of some significance is a "compilation," which may include collective works. A compilation collects and assembles preexisting material or data, which may or may not be separately copyrightable, in such a way that it meets the criteria for a work of authorship. The Supreme Court recently addressed the limits of copyright in a compilation, when it held that the names, towns, and telephone numbers in a telephone book were not copyrightable because they were not selected, coordinated, or arranged in an original way.[24] The Court reiterated the basic principle that facts themselves cannot be copyrighted, but that a particular compilation of facts, if selected, coordinated, or arranged in a sufficiently original way, can be copyrighted.

There can also be a copyright interest in a collective work (assuming it meets the minimum requirement of a work of authorship), which is separate from the copyright in each of the works in the collection.[25] Thus, there can be a separate copyright in a collection of short stories, while each individual author retains copyright in each story. Of course, consent of the author of each story would be required to include it in the collection.[26]

---

[20] See "Patents," in section 5(1)(d), later in this chapter.

[21] 17 U.S.C. § 102(a).

[22] Works of authorship include the following categories:

(1) literary works;
(2) musical works, including any accompanying words;
(3) dramatic works, including any accompanying music;
(4) pantomimes and choreographic works;
(5) pictorial, graphic, and sculptural works;
(6) motion pictures and other audiovisual works;
(7) sound recordings; and
(8) architectural works.

17 U.S.C. § 102(a).

[23] 17 U.S.C. § 101.

[24] *Feist Publications, Inc. v. Rural Telephone Service Co., Inc.*, 111 S.Ct. 1282, 1289–1290 (1991).

[25] 17 U.S.C. § 201 (c).

[26] 17 U.S.C. § 201 (c).

The Copyright Act also has provisions further defining the scope of exclusive rights in other specific types of copyrighted works, including sound recordings,[27] nondramatic musical works,[28] computer programs,[29] noncommercial broadcasting,[30] transmissions of television superstations and networks,[31] and architectural works.[32]

It is critical to understand what the Copyright Act does *not* protect. *No* copyright can be created in "any idea, procedure, process, system, method of operation, concept, principle, or discovery, regardless of the form in which it is described, explained, illustrated, or embodied in such work."[33]

Thus, a manufacturer cannot protect a new and revolutionary manufacturing process by simply writing it down and copyrighting it. Copyrights would exist only in the written description of the process, not in the process itself.[34]

Similarly, a trademark would only protect a *mark* related to a process, not the *process*. Once the process is publicly disclosed in writing, it enters the public domain and anyone can use it, unless it is protected by a *patent*. The process could also be protected as a trade secret if properly protected as such, as explained later in this section, in (f). These examples illustrate the importance of choosing the appropriate form of intellectual property protection.

Works may be created by a single author or by many authors. A work is "joint work" if it was "prepared by two or more authors with the intention that their contributions be merged into inseparable or interdependent parts of a unitary whole."[35] However, the fact that a person provided research, ideas, and other assistance in the creation of a work does not necessarily make that person a coauthor.[36]

(iii) The Bundle of Rights Called Copyrights.   The author of a work entitled to copyright protection has a *bundle* of specific rights, not just a single right. Each right can be separately conveyed or licensed to others, and each right has more or less value, depending on the nature of the copyrighted work and a host of market and other variables. The Copyright Act itself contains a list of the exclusive rights encompassed by "copyrights":

> The owner of copyright . . . has the exclusive right to do and to authorize any of the following:
> (1) to reproduce the copyrighted work in copies or phonorecords;
> (2) to prepare derivative works based upon the copyrighted work;
> (3) to distribute copies or phonorecords of the copyrighted work to the public by sale or other transfer of ownership, or by rental, lease, or lending;
> (4) in the case of literary, musical, dramatic, and choreographic works, pantomimes, and motion pictures and other audiovisual works, to perform the copyrighted work publicly; and

---

[27] 17 U.S.C. § 114.

[28] 17 U.S.C. § 115–116A.

[29] 17 U.S.C. § 117.

[30] 17 U.S.C. § 118.

[31] 17 U.S.C. § 119.

[32] 17 U.S.C. § 120.

[33] 17 U.S.C. § 102(b).

[34] 17 U.S.C. § 102(b). Some fundamental forms of expression, such as mathematical formulas, and widely known information, such as calendars, measures, and rulers, cannot be copyrighted as such.

[35] 17 U.S.C. § 101.

[36] *Childress v. Taylor*, 945 F.2d 500 (2d Cir. 1991) (actress who provided research and other assistance to a playwright, not a joint author of the play).

(5) in the case of literary, musical, dramatic, and choreographic works, pantomimes, and pictorial, graphic, or sculptural works, including the individual images of a motion picture or other audiovisual work, to display the copyrighted work publicly.[37]

For each of the rights specified in § 106 of the Copyright Act, the author can negotiate whatever form of compensation the market and the author's reputation will bear, including a lump sum payment and/or royalties based on sales.

For example, a popular novelist such as Stephen King would have the following exclusive rights in a novel he has written: (1) publish the book in hardcover, (2) publish the book in paperback, (3) serialize the book, or excerpts, in a magazine, (4) write a theatrical script, (5) make a motion picture based on the book, and (6) make audio recordings of a reading of the book, just to name a few possibilities. King may do any and all of these things himself or, by contract, he may authorize others to do so. There are similar opportunities to exploit the works of musical composers and performers, or the creators of copyrighted designs used in fabrics for clothing or for other purposes. "Derivative works" are works based on preexisting copyrighted works. Anyone who creates a derivative work, for example, a movie based on a Stephen King story or novel, would be a copyright infringer unless the derivative work was authorized by King.

The importance of these separate rights can vary substantially, depending on the particular kind of copyrighted work involved. For example, the reproduction rights for a unique painting, even by a famous artist, would probably be less valuable than the reproduction rights for a popular graphic design or a popular song by a famous rock star.

Copyrights are completely separate from ownership of the material objects in which a particular copyrighted work may be embodied, such as a book, record, or motion picture film. Thus, the copyrights or the objects in which the copyrighted work is embodied can be separately and freely transferred.[38] For example, a particular copy of a motion picture film can be freely sold, but ownership of the film itself does not give its owner the right to *show* the film in public. Similarly, legal ownership of a written copy of a play does not authorize the owner of the copy to produce the play on Broadway.

The broad range, complexity, and long duration of these copyrights easily give rise to numerous disputes and litigation concerning the extent of the rights granted by an author.[39]

The Copyright Act describes other exclusive rights for particular types of copyrighted works, which have enormous economic value in mass markets. For example, the owners of copyrights in pictorial, graphic, and sculptural works also have the exclusive right to important industries as diverse as fine china, illustrated T-Shirts, and textiles, in which copyrights are widely used to protect particular images and designs.[40]

A "license" generally refers to the authorization by the owner of intellectual property rights for another to use the protected rights in a particular way. The terms of a license (which is simply a contract) are usually negotiated between the parties, and the owner of the rights is usually free to refuse to grant any license at all.

Some intellectual property laws provide for "compulsory licenses" under specific circumstances. This generally means that persons other than the owner of the rights can use them without consent of the owner, if the statutory requirements are met, usually by

---

[37] 17 U.S.C. § 106.

[38] 17 U.S.C. § 202.

[39] See, e.g., *King v. Innovation Books, Inc.*, 976 F.2d 824 (2d Cir. 1992) (concerning use of short story author's name in movie credits).

[40] See, e.g., *Folio Impressions, Inc. v. Byer California*, 937 F.2d (2d Cir. 1991).

accounting for the uses and paying royalties to the owner of the rights. The Copyright Act authorizes compulsory licenses for recordings of nondramatic musical works and certain television transmissions.[41]

For example, the composer of a song has a copyright in the music and lyrics and initially has absolute control over whether and by whom the music will be published, recorded, or publicly performed, under § 106 of the Act.[42]

If that composer authorizes the music to be recorded and conveys exclusive copyrights in that particular recording to a record company, as is common in the popular music industry, at least two significant consequences flow. First, the record company then *owns* the rights in that particular recording and has the right to make copies of the recording in phonorecords, to make derivative works from *that* particular recording, and to sell or rent copies of the recording, under § 114 of the Act.[43] In return for the right to make the recording and ownership of the master recording, the record company generally agrees to account for sales and pay specified royalties to the copyright owner of the musical composition and to the artist who performed the work for the recording (who is often the same person), either in the recording agreement or in separate so-called mechanical license agreements.[44]

The second consequence is that once *any* recording of a nondramatic musical work has been made and sold to the public *with the authorization of the owner of the musical work*, "any other person may . . . obtain a compulsory license to make and distribute phono-records of the work" by complying with § 115 of the Act.[45] This compulsory license provision applies only to the making of records for sale for home use; it does not apply to other uses, such as in commercial jingles or for synchronization in motion pictures.

Section 115 (the compulsory license provision) requires the person desiring to make a second or subsequent recording of the work to send a written notice of intention to obtain a compulsory license to the copyright owner of the work, either before the new recording is made, or within 30 days after recording and before distribution of the new recording.[46] If the notice requirement is satisfied, the person making the new recording must account for and pay specified royalties to the owner of the musical work on a monthly basis.[47]

Failure to comply with the compulsory license requirements, for example, by failure to comply with the notice requirements or by failure to account for or pay royalties, makes manufacture, distribution, or sale of the new recording an act of infringement and subjects any infringers to the substantial remedies provided for in the Copyright Act.[48]

In practice, statutory compulsory licenses are not widely used in the recording industry, because of the statutory royalty rate and the relatively onerous monthly accounting and payment provisions. Instead, individual license terms are negotiated and reached

---

[41] 17 U.S.C. §§ 115, 116, and 119.

[42] 17 U.S.C. § 106.

[43] 17 U.S.C. § 114.

[44] See, e.g., *Peer International Corp. v. Pausa Records, Inc.*, 909 F.2d 1332 (9th Cir. 1990), *cert. denied*, 111 S.Ct. 1019 (1991); Harris v. Emus Records Corp., 734 F.2d 1329 (9th Cir. 1984).

[45] 17 U.S.C. § 115 (author's emphasis). In general, the permission of the copyright owner is required before another person can perform a copyrighted musical or literary work, or exercise any of the protected rights under § 106 in connection with a copyrighted work. An agreement containing such permission by the copyright owner is often referred to as a "license," i.e., a license to use the work without being charged with copyright infringement.

[46] 17 U.S.C. § 115(b) (1).

[47] 17 U.S.C. § 115(c).

[48] 17 U.S.C. § 115(b) (2) and (c) (5). See *Peer International Corp. v. Pausa Records, Inc.*, *supra*, at note 44.

between the party seeking to record the work and the copyright owner, either directly or, more often, through the Harry Fox Agency, which represents a large number of music publishers in the United States.[49] These negotiated licenses normally contain a termination provision similar to that in § 115 of the Act, discussed earlier.

The Act contains a separate procedure for obtaining a compulsory license provision for "public performance of works on a coin-operated phonorecord player."[50] The statutory license fees must be deposited with the Register of Copyrights, who transmits them to the Copyright Royalty Tribunal.[51] However, the affected parties may also enter into negotiated license agreements regarding public performances on coin-operated players, which supersede the compulsory license provisions.[52]

There are special royalty provisions regarding the use of copyrighted works in noncommercial broadcasting.[53] Extensive and detailed special provisions, concerning both royalties and restrictions, apply to copyrighted works that are broadcast or transmitted on television. The details of these provisions vary, depending on the means of transmission and many other variables,[54] and are beyond the scope of this chapter.

Congress established a new licensing provision for digital audiotape (DAT) machines and tapes in the Audio Home Recording Act of 1992.[55] This new addition to the Copyright Act requires that payment of copyright royalties on DAT machines and tapes be made and that they must be manufactured in such a way that only a single DAT tape can be made of any particular compact disc.

(iv) Notice of Copyright and Deposit of Works with the Library of Congress.   The familiar notice of copyright, such as "© 1993 Megabuck Publishers, Unltd.," is no longer a mandatory requirement for protection of a published copyrighted work in the United States, as of March 1, 1989.[56] Formal notice on the copyrighted work has not been required in most other countries for many years. Compliance with the notice requirement is still important for the validity of works created in the United States prior to the effective date of the Berne Implementation Act in 1988, that is, March 1, 1989. However, the omission of proper notice on works created prior to 1988 can be cured or has limited

---

[49] S. Shemel and M. Krasilovsky, *This Business of Music*, 6th ed. (New York: Billboard Books, an imprint of Watson-Guptill Publications, 1990), pp. 241–243.

[50] 17 U.S.C. § 116(b) (1).

[51] 17 U.S.C. § 116(c). The Copyright Royalty Tribunal is an independent legislative-branch body with five members that is authorized to periodically establish royalty rates under the compulsory license provisions, § 115 and § 116 of the Act. It also determines "reasonable terms and rates of royalty payments" under § 118. 17 U.S.C. § 801. Final determinations of the Tribunal are subject to judicial review in a United States court of appeals. 17 U.S.C. § 810. The proposed Copyright Reform Act of 1993 would abolish the Tribunal and replace it with ad hoc arbitration panels.

[52] 17 U.S.C. § 116A.

[53] 17 U.S.C. § 118.

[54] 17 U.S.C. § 119.

[55] Pub. L. 102–563, 106 Stat. 4327.

[56] 18 U.S.C. § 401(a). Formal copyright notice was mandatory under the Copyright Act until the United States adhered to the Berne Convention for the Protection of Literary and Artistic Works, one of the principal international copyright agreements, effective March 1, 1989. Berne Convention Implementation Act of 1988, Pub. L. 100–568, 102 Stat. 2853 (Oct. 31, 1988). The Universal Copyright Convention, Article III(1), to which the United States is also a signatory, permits nations, by local law, to require a formal copyright notice; a few nations still require such notice. See M. Nimmer and D. Nimmer, *supra*, at note 18.

adverse effect in specified circumstances.[57] A work is considered to be published when copies are offered or distributed to the public "for sale or other transfer of ownership or by rental, lease, or lending."[58]

Nevertheless, it is advisable to continue to use the appropriate notice of copyright where at all possible. Inclusion of proper copyright notice not only publicizes to the world the owner's claim to copyright in a work, it also has important evidentiary weight in the event the owner is required to bring suit to enforce the copyright. If proper notice of copyright is given on the work, an alleged infringer may not attempt to mitigate copyright damages by claiming that the infringement was innocent.[59]

In general, proper copyright notice includes the symbol ©, the word "copyright," or the abbreviation "Copr.," plus the year of first publication and the name of the copyright owner. The form of notice used to indicate copyright in sound recordings is a "P" in a circle, such as "℗Smog City Records, Inc." The Copyright Act and regulations of the Copyright Office should be consulted, because there are special notice provisions for particular kinds of works.[60]

The Copyright Act generally requires that two copies of every copyrighted work be deposited with the Library of Congress within three months after publication, but the Register of Copyrights is authorized to issue, and has issued, regulations exempting some works from deposit and providing alternative means for others.[61] Failure to comply with this requirement *does not* affect the validity of a copyright, but fines can be imposed if works are not deposited within three months after a demand for deposit has been made by the Register of Copyrights.[62]

---

[57] 17 U.S.C. §§ 405 and 406. Section 405 provides that failure to include a proper copyright notice for works prior to the effectiveness of the Berne Implementation Act will not adversely affect copyright (1) if the notice was missing from only a small number of copies, (2) the work was registered prior to or within five years of publication and a reasonable effort is made to add proper notice to the works, or (3) the failure to include the notice resulted from violation of a written requirement of the owner that distributed copies should bear proper notice.

Section 406 limits the effect of errors in names or dates where copyright notices are required on pre-Berne Act works. A copyright notice that incorrectly names a person who is not the copyright owner does not adversely affect the true owner's rights. However, an innocent infringer who relied on the erroneous notice has a defense to an infringement claim, if the infringer establishes that he or she was misled by the improper notice and acted under rights supposedly granted by the person named in the erroneous notice, unless the true owner had previously registered the work, or the person named in the notice has recorded a writing with the Copyright Office showing the name of the true owner. Section 406 contains other provisions dealing with the consequences of error in copyright notices.

[58] 17 U.S.C. § 101.

[59] 17 U.S.C. § 401(d).

[60] The Copyright Act or regulations of the Register of Copyrights specify the manner in which copyright notices should be made on different kinds of works. 17 U.S.C. §§ 401 (b) and (c) and §§ 402–406.

[61] 17 U.S.C. § 407. The Register of Copyrights is the official who heads the United States Copyright Office. The exemption and special deposit regulations are too detailed and lengthy to summarize fully, and the current regulations should be consulted for each particular kind of work involved. 37 C.F.R. § 202.19–202.23. A random sample of works exempted from deposit are greeting cards, on-line data bases, three-dimensional sculptural works, and advertising material, id., although deposit of some of these items may be required if the work is registered. Id. at § 202.20 (c). Special exemptions may be requested, and photographs in lieu of deposit of some works are permitted. Id. at §§ 202.19(e) and 202.21.

[62] 17 U.S.C. § 407(d).

(v) Registration of Copyright. Registration of a work with the Copyright Office is not a mandatory requirement to establish copyright in a work, whether the work is published or unpublished. However, registration is almost always advisable.

First, with limited exceptions, registration is a mandatory requirement for copyright owners in order to bring any lawsuit for copyright infringement.[63] Second, registration is a condition for a copyright owner to be eligible to recover statutory damages and attorney's fees in a copyright infringement action. The availability of statutory damages is a significant advantage. The copyright owner can elect to recover statutory damages even when he or she does not submit proof of actual damages. Statutory damages *must* be awarded in an amount between $500 and $20,000 per violation, or up to a maximum of $100,000 per willful violation; the exact amount is decided by the court.[64] Third, if a work is registered before or within five years of publication, the certificate of registration "shall constitute prima facie evidence of the validity of the copyright and of the facts stated in the certificate."[65] If registration occurs after five years, the court, in any infringement action, has discretion to decide what weight, if any, to give to the registration certificate.[66]

Failure to register a work does not permanently prevent a copyright owner from pursuing an infringement claim, since a work can be registered at any time. The courts have held that the registration requirement can be satisfied even after a lawsuit has commenced.[67]

(vi) Fair Use and Other Limitations on an Author's Exclusive Copyrights. There are a number of general and specific limitations on the exclusive rights given to copyright owners. The broadest is the principle of "fair use," which allows *anyone* to use a copyrighted work without permission of the author under circumstances specified in the Act.[68] The fair use provision allows a person to use any of the otherwise protected rights of copying or reproduction "for purposes such as criticism, comment, news reporting, teaching (including multiple copies for classroom use), scholarship, or research" without being liable for copyright infringement.[69]

Although these categories of uses are fairly specific, there are four discretionary factors that must be considered to determine whether a particular use of copyrighted material without permission is a fair use. These factors include consideration of (1) the

---

[63] 17 U.S.C. §§ 411 and 412. Registration is not required to bring an infringement action in at least two circumstances: (1) where the work originates in a country other than the United States and is protected under the Berne Convention; or (2) when an author of certain visual works sues to protect the author's rights of attribution or integrity protected by the Visual Artists Rights Act of 1990. 17 U.S.C. § 106A (Pub. L. 101–650, 104 Stat. 5128, added § 106A to the Copyright Act). Bills have been introduced in Congress which would eliminate the registration requirement as a condition of pursuing infringement litigation. See Copyright Reform Act of 1993, *supra*, at note 12.

[64] 17 U.S.C. § 504(c)(1) and (2).

[65] 17 U.S.C. § 410(c).

[66] Id.

[67] Parties have been allowed to amend their pleadings to allege a registration obtained while a case was pending in court. *ISC Bunker Ramo Corp. v. Altech, Inc.*, 765 F. Supp. 1308 (N.D. Ill. 1990). Where the Copyright Office has refused to register a work for which an application was duly filed, the applicant for registration may still sue for infringement, and the court will also determine whether the work was entitled to registration under 17 U.S.C. § 411(a). *Esquire, Inc. v. Ringer*, 591 F.2d 796 (D.C. Cir. 1978), *cert. denied*, 440 U.S. 908 (1979).

[68] 17 U.S.C. § 107.

[69] Id.

particular use, (2) the nature of the protected work, (3) the quantity and substance of the work used, and (4) the effect on the economic market for the protected work.[70]

The subjectivity of these factors has led to much controversy and litigation, in the most obvious fields of news reporting and publication. For example, *Time* magazine sued the Bush Reelection Campaign for copyright infringement for using an image of then-Governor Bill Clinton on a copyrighted cover of the magazine in a television advertisement in the last weeks of the 1992 presidential campaign. The Bush advertisement consisted solely of the *Time* cover with an announcer's voice-over.[71] *Time* contended that this was not a fair use of its copyrighted cover, and that the cover had been subtly modified as well.[72] The correct legal answer to this dispute will never be known, inasmuch as the case was settled when, after being sued, the Bush Campaign said it would stop running the ad.

In another case, however, the Supreme Court of the United States held that it was not a fair use for *The Nation* magazine to publish extensive quotations from unpublished memoirs of President Ford without permission.[73] The Court found *The Nation*'s use to be a commercial one, which had the effect of substantially diminishing the market value of President Ford's memoirs. This was evident from the fact that *Time* magazine subsequently declined to go through with its contract with President Ford to serialize his memoirs.[74]

Fair use issues may arise in more clearly commercial spheres as well. The Supreme Court in 1984 held that "time-shifting," copying of copyrighted movies and other material from television by individuals with videocassette recorders, was a fair use in the famous Sony Betamax case.[75] In this case, the industries involved in the production and presentation of copyrighted movies and other materials claimed that Sony was a contributory infringer because, the plaintiffs said, Sony knew that its Betamax machines would be used to make unauthorized copies of copyrighted materials.

On a purely practical level, the Betamax case shows an industry already overwhelmed by a new technology. The use of VCRs to copy television material was already so widespread that it was not likely to be preventable. The Court might have thought it unfair to impose a copyright "user fee" on Sony long after the use was a well-established public phenomenon.[76]

---

[70] In determining whether the use made of a work in any particular case is a fair use, the factors to be considered shall include—

   (1) the purpose and character of the use, including whether such use is of a commercial nature or is for nonprofit educational purposes;

   (2) the nature of the copyrighted work;

   (3) the amount and substantiality of the portion used in relation to the copyrighted work as a whole; and

   (4) the effect of the use on the potential market for or value of the copyrighted work.

(17 U.S.C. § 107).

[71] *Time, Inc. v. Bush Quayle '92 General Committee, Inc. et al.*, Civ. Action No. 92-2299 (D.D.C.).

[72] Id., Complaint §§ 6–17.

[73] *Harper & Row, Publishers, Inc. v. Nation Enterprises*, 471 U.S. 539 (1985).

[74] Id.

[75] *Sony Corp. of America v. Universal City Studios, Inc.*, 464 U.S. 417 (1984).

[76] The industry encompassing producers of copyrighted works was much better prepared when DAT recorders were later being developed for the mass consumer market. The industry believed DAT machines would make it easy to make copyright-infringing copies of compact disc musical recordings. Unlike its belated challenge to the use of VCRs to copy copyrighted materials, the industry anticipated the potential popularity of DAT machines and tapes and persuaded Congress to enact the Audio Home Recording Act of 1992, which requires payment of copyright royalties on each such machine and DAT tape and imposes a variety of obligations of importers of such merchandise to facilitate enforcement of the Act. Pub. L. 102–563, 106 Stat. 4327.

The fair use defense may arise in "artistic" realms as well. The Second Circuit rejected a fair use parody defense by the artist Jeff Koons. The court held that he intentionally created a sculpture called *String of Puppies* based on a copyrighted photograph entitled *Puppies* made by a professional photographer.[77] The court found that Koons's purpose in using the copyrighted photograph was commercial; he had made four sculptures, three of which had been sold for a total of $367,000. The artist's claim of parody escaped the court; it found that his motive was a bad-faith desire to make money based on another's copyrighted work and that none of the other factors relevant to fair use weighed in favor of Koons.[78]

However, the Supreme Court recently issued a new decision involving the "fair use" issue in a case involving a rap music version of Roy Orbison's popular song "Pretty Woman."[79] The Court reversed the court of appeals' holding that the rap version by the group 2 Live Crew was not protected fair use because of its commercial nature. The Supreme Court held that this was only one of several factors to be considered. The Court's decision analyzes the role of parody in fair use, and discusses the relevant factors in detail. It held that a work of "parody must be able to 'conjure up' at least enough of that original [work] to make the object of its critical wit recognizable."[80] The Supreme Court concluded that the rap version was a parody (which concurring Justice Kennedy questioned) and was thus eligible for fair use protection, but the Court remanded the case for further evidentiary proceedings. The Court emphasized that there is no "bright-line" rule for deciding when a parodist can establish a fair use defense to a claim of copyright infringement.[81] Nevertheless, not every claim of parody will be protected: "context is everything, and the question of fairness asks what else the parodist did besides go to the heart of the original."[82]

(vii) Ownership of Copyrights.   A copyright belongs initially to the author or authors of a work.[83] If, however, the work is considered a "work for hire" under the Copyright Act, the copyright belongs to "the employer or other person for whom the work was prepared," unless otherwise provided for in a signed document.[84]

The question of whether a work was "made for hire" is a sometimes difficult, and often litigated, one. It also affects other issues, such as the rights of heirs of the author and the renewal of copyright terms, which is still an important issue for works created prior to the effective date of the 1976 Copyright Act.

Section 101 of the Copyright Act defines the phrase "work made for hire" in two alternative ways. First, it includes "a work prepared by an employee within the scope of his or her employment."[85] This definition describes the traditional common-law employer-employee relationship. The Act's second definition of a "work for hire" includes a list of nine specific kinds of works which, even if created by an independent

---

[77] *Rogers v. Koons*, 960 F. 2d 301 (2d Cir.), *cert. denied*, 113 S. Ct. 365 (1992). This case also illustrates the use of the full panoply of copyright infringement remedies, which are discussed later, in section 5.2 of this chapter.

[78] Id. at 308–312.

[79] *Campbell v. Acuff-Rose Music, Inc.*, 114 S. Ct. 1164 (1994).

[80] Id. at 1176.

[81] Id. at 1170.

[82] Id. at 1176.

[83] 17 U.S.C. § 201(a). Where there is more than one author, they are co-owners. Id.

[84] 17 U.S.C. § 201(b).

[85] 17 U.S.C. § 101.

contractor, can be considered a work for hire, for example, "a work specially ordered or commissioned for use as a contribution to a collective work, as a part of a motion picture or other audiovisual work," or for other specified purposes. However, to satisfy this second definition, "the parties [must] expressly agree in a written instrument signed by them that the work shall be considered a work made for hire."[86]

The Supreme Court recently construed the Act's definition of "work for hire" in a case involving conflicting claims to the copyrights in a sculpture.[87] The sculpture was created by an artist for a nonprofit organization, the Community for Creative Non-Violence (CCNV), for use in a holiday display to "dramatize the plight of the homeless" in Washington, D.C.

The Court held that the Act's definition indicates that "a work for hire can arise through one of two mutually exclusive means, one for employees and one for independent contractors."[88] The Court stated:

> To determine whether a work is for hire under the Act, a court first should ascertain, using principles of general common law of agency, whether the work was prepared by an employee or an independent contractor. After making this determination, the court can apply the appropriate subsection of § 101 [defining "work for hire"].[89]

The Court applied the general principles of agency and concluded that the artist was an independent contractor, not an employee of CCNV. CCNV had not paid the artist any salary or benefits, and it paid no payroll or other taxes. The Court rejected other possible tests of employment based either on actual control or the right to control the end product. However, the Court remanded the case for a determination of whether CCNV and the artist were *joint* authors, because of CCNV's involvement with the design of the sculpture.

(viii) Transfer of Copyright Ownership and Termination of Transfers and Licenses by the Author.   Copyrights are personal property rights that can be freely sold, transferred, and licensed. They "may be transferred in whole or in part by any means of conveyance or by operation of law, and may be bequeathed by will or pass as personal property by the applicable laws of intestate succession."[90]

The Copyright Act contains its own "statute of frauds" in § 204 (a):

> A transfer of copyright ownership, other than by operation of law, is not valid unless an instrument of conveyance, or a note or memorandum of the transfer, is in writing and signed by the owner of the rights conveyed or such owner's duly authorized agent.[91]

The transfer of an "exclusive license" or transfer of any other "exclusive" right by a copyright owner, even when it is limited as to time or place, is defined as a "transfer of copyright ownership" in § 101 of the Act. Thus, any such "exclusive license" must comply with the Act's "statute of frauds" in § 204(a).

Nonexclusive licenses are not covered by the statute of frauds provision and can be created orally or be implied from the conduct of the parties.[92] It is almost always advisable

---

[86] Id. (author's emphasis).

[87] *Community for Creative Non-Violence v. Reid*, 490 U.S. 730 (1989).

[88] Id. at 743.

[89] Id. at 750–751.

[90] 17 U.S.C. § 201(d)(1).

[91] 17 U.S.C. § 204(a).

[92] Nimmer and Nimmer, *Nimmer on Copyright*, vol. 3, § 10.03 (A), p. 10–38.

to have a signed writing when the transfer or grant of any significant interests in copyrights are involved, to avoid both inadvertent and intentional disputes as to the extent of the rights granted.

Original documents (or certified copies of originals) that transfer copyright ownership or other documents relating to copyrights can, and in most cases should, be recorded in the Copyright Office.[93] Recordation both memorializes the event and provides constructive notice to the world of the facts set forth in the document.[94] Compliance with recordation requirements also gives priority to the earlier executed document in the event of conflicting transfers.[95]

The Act prevents involuntary governmental action to take the copyrights of the original copyright author, except as permitted by federal bankruptcy laws.[96]

(ix) Duration of Copyrights. Calculation of the term of copyright is somewhat complicated owing to the relatively new Copyright Act, which became effective January 1, 1978, the continued existence of works created under the 1909 Copyright Act, and recent amendments of the current Act.[97] Copyrights endure for varying periods of time, depending on whether the protected works were created before or after that date and, in some cases, depending on the kind of author involved.

There are four broad categories of works for which the lengths of copyrights are calculated differently: (1) works created on or after the effective date of the current Copyright Act, (2) works that were created before the effective date of the current Act, January 1, 1978, but that were not previously published or copyrighted, (3) works still in their *first* 28-year term under the 1909 Act on the effective date of the new Act, and (4) works in their *renewal* term of 28 years or registered for renewal prior to the effective date.

First, copyrights in works created on or after January 1, 1978, are covered by the term established by the 1976 Copyright Act. The term of copyrights in such works is the life of the author plus 50 years, subject to the following special rules.[98]

When such works are created by two or more authors (except for works for hire), the copyrights endure for the life of the last surviving author plus 50 years.[99] The copyrights for works for hire, anonymous works, and pseudonymous works endure 75 years from the year of first publication or 100 years from the work's creation, whichever comes first.[100]

Second, works that were created, but were not published or copyrighted prior to the effective date of the new Act on January 1, 1978, endure for the life of the author plus 50 years, with two provisos.[101] In no case will such a copyright expire prior to December 31,

---

[93] 17 U.S.C. § 205(a).

[94] 17 U.S.C. § 205(c).

[95] 17 U.S.C. § 205(d) and (e).

[96] As to these individual copyrights, "no action by any governmental body or other official or organization purporting to seize, expropriate, transfer, or exercise rights of ownership with respect to the copyright, or any of the exclusive rights under a copyright, shall be given effect under this title except as provided under Title 11 [of the United States Code]." 17 U.S.C. § 201(e).

[97] The Copyright Amendments Act of 1992, Pub. L. No. 102–307, 106 Stat. 264, clarified and modified portions of § 304 of the 1976 Act, 17 U.S.C. § 304(a).

[98] 17 U.S.C. § 302 ff.

[99] 17 U.S.C. § 302(b).

[100] 17 U.S.C. § 302(c). This provision allows the true authors of anonymous or pseudonymous works to reveal their identities by registration with the Copyright Office prior to the expiration of the special terms for anonymous or pseudonymous works, and the terms of copyright for these works then are controlled by the normal rules in 17 U.S.C. § 302(a) and (b).

[101] 17 U.S.C. § 303.

2002. If the work is published on or before that date, the term continues until December 31, 2027.[102]

Third, the current 1976 Copyright Act originally provided that works in their first 28-year term under the 1909 Act would endure for that period of time and be subject to a renewal term of 47 years.[103] This provision was amended in 1992 to make renewal registration optional for some works, as explained in a subsequent paragraph.

Fourth, works that were in their renewal term under the 1909 Act or that were registered for renewal during specified dates prior to January 1, 1978, have an extended term of 75 years from the date the copyright was first secured.[104] The term of copyright for works created *prior* to January 1, 1978, is thus 75 years from the date the work was created.[105]

Finally, the 1992 amendment to the Copyright Act makes renewal registration optional for works with copyrights obtained between January 1, 1964, and December 31, 1977.[106] Although renewal registration for such works is not mandatory, failure to so register them significantly restricts the copyright owners' remedies, as discussed earlier. In addition, failure to obtain renewal registration of an original work covered by the 1992 amendment also means that a party authorized to exploit a derivative work during the first term of copyright in the original work can continue to do so during the renewal term of the original work without such exploitation resulting in infringement.[107]

Obviously, proper and timely renewal of copyright was critical under the 1909 Copyright Act. Failure to renew, through oversight or negligence, resulted in valuable properties entering the public domain after their initial term of 28 years had expired, to the great loss of their prior owners.[108]

Even after the 1992 amendment to the Act, which makes renewal registration optional for some works, it is important to determine whether a work subject to a renewal term has in fact been registered for renewal. This includes works that were created and published or registered in unpublished form prior to January 1, 1978. Proper registration should be verified when considering possible acquisition of such a work or when involved in a copyright infringement dispute or litigation. A renewal application must be filed with the Copyright Office within the allowable time frame, *and* the application must be filed in the name of the person *entitled* to renew the rights under the statute.

The right of renewal is only an expectancy during the life of the author under the 1909 Act. If the author survives to the beginning of the renewal term, a conveyance of renewal

---

[102] Id.

[103] 17 U.S.C. § 304(a).

[104] 17 U.S.C. § 304(b). Works created under the prior Copyright Act of 1909 had a first term of 28 years. The copyright could be renewed for a second term of 28 years, *if* a renewal application was filed with the Copyright Office within a year of expiration of the first term. Copyright Act of 1909, § 24.

[105] The manner of calculating the term varies, depending on whether the work was in its original or renewal term on that date. 17 U.S.C. § 304.

[106] Pub. L. 102–307, § 102(g) (2), 106 Stat. 266, 17 U.S.C. § 101 note.

[107] 17 U.S.C. § 304(a) (4) (A).

[108] For example, no renewal copyright term was sought for the motion picture *A Star Is Born*, and it entered the public domain upon expiration of its first 28-year term, despite the fact that the film's owner still held a common-law copyright in the unpublished underlying story and screenplay. *Classic Film Museum, Inc. v. Warner Bros., Inc.*, 597 F.2d 13 (2d Cir. 1979). Similarly, the 1948 Italian film *The Bicycle Thief* entered the public domain in the United States when a renewal application was not filed in the name of the copyright owner. *International Film Exchange, Ltd. v. Corinth Films, Inc.*, 621 F. Supp. 631 (S.D.N.Y. 1985).

rights to another party is valid and enforceable.[109] If, however, the author dies prior to the renewal term, the right of renewal passes to designated statutory successors—the widow, widower, children, executors, or next of kin succeeds to the right of renewal—not to the person to whom the author purportedly conveyed the renewal rights.[110]

Ownership of renewal rights in a particular work can be of critical importance to owners of separate copyrights in derivative works based on a prior work. Unless the author of the underlying work is living at the beginning of any copyright renewal term, no purported conveyance of renewal rights or licenses by the author of the original work are effective. "A copyright renewal creates a new [copyright] estate [and] the new estate is clear of all rights, interests or licenses granted under the original copyright."[111]

The complexity of the problems involved in copyright renewal terms can be especially difficult when successive derivative works are involved. Consider, for example, a 1951 case involving conflicting claims to motion picture rights in *G. Ricordi & Co. v. Paramount Pictures*.[112] The dispute involved successive works based on a story entitled *Madame Butterfly*, which originally appeared as a novel written by John Luther Long. The novel was published in the *Century Magazine* and copyrighted by the Century Company. The copyright owner of the novel gave oral consent to its use in a play written by David Belasco, and the owner of the rights in the novel and the play then gave permission for the creation of an opera based on the novel and the play, with music and lyrics by Giacomo Puccini. Ricordi & Co., the owner of the rights in the opera, sued Paramount Pictures, the owner of the renewal rights in the novel, to determine which party owned the right to make a *Madame Butterfly* motion picture.[113] The court held that because Paramount owned the rights in the novel, Ricordi could not use the original story to make a motion picture version of its opera. On the other hand, the court held that even though Paramount owned the rights in the novel, it could not make a motion picture that contained any of the copyrighted elements of Ricordi's operatic version without Ricordi's consent.

The Supreme Court addressed a more recent dispute concerning motion picture rights and copyright renewal for the famous film *Rear Window*, starring Jimmy Stewart.[114] The author of the original story, which was published in *Dime Detective Magazine*, assigned the motion pictures rights to another party. Those rights were subsequently acquired by Jimmy Stewart and Alfred Hitchcock, who formed a production company and made the popular movie *Rear Window*, based on the story.

The author of the story had agreed to renew the copyright in the story and assign the motion picture rights in the renewal term; however, he died before the renewal copyright term matured. The author's executor sold the renewal rights to Abend, who sued the owners of *Rear Window* for infringement.

The Supreme Court held that the owners of rights in the movie could not continue to exploit the copyrights in the original story without permission of the new owner of the renewed copyrights in the original story. The Court explained the congressional purpose in establishing the renewal term rights:

[109] *Fisher Music Co. v. M. Witmark & Sons*, 318 U.S. 643 (1943).

[110] 17 U.S.C. § 304(a). *Miller Music Corp. v. Charles N. Daniels, Inc.*, 362 U.S. 373 (1960).

[111] *G. Ricordi & Co. v. Paramount Pictures*, 189 F.2d 469, 471 (2d Cir.), *cert. denied*, 342 U.S. 849 (1951) (footnote omitted).

[112] Id.

[113] The copyrights in the play entered the public domain because no copyright renewal application was filed. id., 189 F.2d at 471.

[114] *Stewart v. Abend*, 495 U.S. 207 (1990).

> The renewal provisions were intended to give the author a second chance to obtain fair remuneration for his creative efforts and to provide the author's family a "new estate" if the author died before the renewal period arrived.[115]

Renewal rights do not revert to the statutory successors for some categories of works. For example, the proprietor of the copyright, not the actual author, has the right to the renewal term if the original work was created as a work for hire or was originally copyrighted by the proprietor of the work or by a corporation that acquired the work other than as assignee or licensee of the author.[116]

(x) Right of Authors and Heirs to Terminate Transfers of Copyrights and Licenses at Specified Times.   It is also important to be aware, in evaluating copyrights, that the author and specified successors have the right to *terminate* transfers of either an original or a renewal term of copyright at specified times.[117] This termination right does not apply to a work made for hire.[118]

The theory underlying these recapture provisions is simple. The economic value of many copyrightable works, such as books, music, motion pictures, or computer software, often cannot be known or predicted in advance. Congress determined that authors and heirs should be able to recapture their copyrights and have the opportunity to negotiate new, and presumably more lucrative, terms for the exploitation of their copyrights when the works have withstood the test of time in the marketplace.[119]

The possible existence of such termination rights should be investigated and considered when acquisition of longstanding copyrighted material is contemplated, because this can substantially affect the value of such works.[120]

For a grant or transfer of copyright occurring on or after January 1, 1978, termination can be effective within a 5-year period beginning 35 years after execution of the grant (or, if publication rights are involved, beginning 35 years after the grant or 40 years after publication, whichever is shorter).[121]

If a transfer involving a work that was in its first or renewal term on January 1, 1978, termination can be effective at any time during the 5-year period at the end of 56 years after copyright was originally established or beginning on January 1, 1978, whichever comes later.[122]

For termination of rights under either § 203 or § 304, notice of the effective date must be given between two and ten years prior to the chosen effective date of termination.[123]

---

[115] Id., 495 U.S. at 220.

[116] 17 U.S.C. § 304(a).

[117] 17 U.S.C. §§ 203 and 304(c)(1) and (2).

[118] Id.

[119] This purpose is explained in the House Report on the 1976 Copyright Act. H.R. Rep. No. 94–1476, 94th Cong., 2d Sess. 124–128 (1976).

[120] See *Bourne Co. v. MPL Communications, Inc.*, 675 F. Supp. 859 (S.D.N.Y. 1987) (a publisher that owned copyrights in a song had to repurchase the rights after proper termination under Section 304(c)); Melniker & Melniker, *Termination of Transfers and Licenses Under the New Copyright Law*, 22 N.Y.U. L. Rev. 589 (1977); Curtis, *Caveat Emptor in Copyright: A Practical Guide to the Termination-of-Transfers Provisions of the New Copyright Code*, 25 Bull. Cpyrt. Soc'y 19 (1977–1978).

[121] 17 U.S.C. § 203(a)(3).

[122] 17 U.S.C. § 304(c)(3).

[123] 17 U.S.C. §§ 203(a)(4)(A) and 304(c)(4)(A).

Where the original copyright owner has conveyed all copyrights, the author cannot defeat the recapture rights of the statutory beneficiaries by purporting to establish a trust by will, where the author had retained no rights to bequeath.[124]

These recapture rights are limited in one significant respect. Under § 304(c)(6)(A), "a derivative work prepared under authority of the grant before its termination may continue to be utilized under the terms of the grant after the termination," although new derivative works may not be created based on the terminated grant.

The Supreme Court has held that this provision means that a music publisher who had licensed numerous recordings of a particular song under a grant of right prior to termination under § 304(c) is entitled to continue to receive royalties payable for numerous licensed recordings of the song, despite the termination. The owner of the recaptured copyright is, of course, entitled to receive its share of royalties under the terms of the prior agreement with the music publisher.[125]

(xi) Enforcement of Copyrights—Judicial and Other Remedies.   Owners of copyrights can sue alleged infringers of those rights in an appropriate United States District Court. Numerous potential remedies are available in a private civil action brought by the owner of the rights, including a temporary restraining order, temporary and permanent injunctions, actual damages, profits of infringers attributable to the infringement, statutory damages to be determined by the court, destruction of infringing goods, costs, and attorneys' fees.[126] In addition, owners of copyrights registered with the Copyright Office can file an application with the United States Customs Service to have goods infringing the copyright owners' rights completely excluded from entry into the United States, as explained in detail in § 11.4, Customs Service Protection, *infra*.[127]

The available remedies for owners of intellectual property rights seeking to enforce their rights against infringers are discussed in detail in § 11.3, Enforcement and Remedies.

(c) Trademarks

(i) Background and Overview.   Trade and service "marks" and "trade dress" are often *the* most valuable assets a company has, both literally and figuratively.[128] The global importance and recognition of trademarks is self-evident. Marks such as "Sony," "Coca-Cola," or "Chanel," for example, immediately conjure up particular products, or notions of quality and style, among consumers worldwide. Such marks can serve as substantial collateral for loans and lines of credit. Proper valuation of such marks is crucial in mergers or acquisitions involving companies with widely known and popular marks.[129]

Trademarks in one form or another are centuries old and are based largely on common sense. Some individuals or groups make products or provide services that are better or more desirable than others. And some other people would rather steal another's mousetrap rather than make a better one. One of the fundamental principles underlying the use

---

[124] *Larry Spier, Inc. v. Bourne Co.*, 953 F.2d 774 (2d Cir. 1992).

[125] *Mills Music, Inc. v. Snyder*, 469 U.S. 151 (1985).

[126] 17 U.S.C. §§ 501–505 and 509–510.

[127] 19 C.F.R. Subparts D-F. This right of exclusion also applies to products or works infringing trademarks and protected silicon chip mask works. 19 C.F.R. Part 133 and 17 US.C. § 910.

[128] One of the leading practitioner's reference works in this field is J. McCarthy, *Trademarks and Unfair Competition*, 2d ed. (1984).

[129] Melvin Simensky, "Enforcing Creditors' Rights Against Trademarks," 79 *Trademark Rep.* 569, 569 (1989).

of trademarks is protection of the reputation of producers of particular goods or services from those who seek to get a free ride by making cheap imitations of another's goods and passing them off to the public as the real thing. This principle derives from the medieval guild systems of Europe and the ancient commercial worlds of the Middle East and Asia.

Unlike copyrights and patents, rights in trademarks can continue indefinitely, as long as the trademark is used and properly protected from infringement. However, trademark rights can be lost by failure to use or protect them. Marks are protected by giving other persons notice, actual or constructive, of rights in a particular mark. Actual use of a mark in commerce remains the keystone to trademark protection.

In general, trademarks can be transferred only with the goodwill of a business to which the mark relates. A trademark is not a separate asset that can be transferred or retained "in gross," except in the limited situation where the former owner of the business can show an intention "within a reasonable time after the sale of the other assets" of the business.[130] Thus, although trademarks are generally referred to as one of the several aspects of "intellectual property," a company does not "own" trademarks in the same sense that it owns an interest in real estate or in copyrights.[131]

The Trademark Act of 1946 (known as the Lanham Act) is the United States law governing trade and other marks nationwide.[132] It is administered by the United States Patent and Trademark Office (PTO). The Lanham Act defines a "mark" broadly to include "any trademark, service mark, collective mark, or certification mark."[133] The widely used § 43(a) of the Act protects against infringement of registered marks; it also provides a remedy for a wide range of other unfair trade practices and unfair competition. A trade *name*, that is, the name of a company or business, cannot be registered for protection under the Lanham Act, only the goods or services that the company provides and the trade dress associated with them.

Federal registration of a mark under the Lanham Act is not required in order to create or protect a mark in the market within which a company does business. However, there are significant advantages to registration of marks with the PTO.[134] This chapter assumes that, in most circumstances, such registration is advantageous.

---

[130] *Berni v. International Gourmet Restaurants of America*, 838 F.2d 642 (2d Cir. 1988). In the absence of such circumstances, the former shareholders of an Italian corporation that operated a restaurant in Rome lacked standing to challenge the registration and use of the mark in the United States. Id.

[131] Trademark law is an aspect of the law of unfair competition. "There is no such thing as property in a trade-mark except as a right appurtenant to an established business or trade in connection with which the mark is employed." *United Drug Co. v. Theodore Rectanus Co.*, 248 U.S. 90, 97 (1918).

[132] 15 U.S.C. § 1051 ff. The Trademark Act implements the obligations of the United States as a party to the Paris Convention for the Protection of Industrial Property (Stockholm 1967). The Paris Convention is the principal international agreement governing patents, trademarks, and unfair competition, to which industrialized countries have adhered. Provisions of the recently concluded Uruguay Round of GATT negotiations would obligate GATT members to comply with specified trademark and other provisions of the Paris Convention. See *supra*, note 2.

[133] 15 U.S.C. § 1127.

[134] There are two registers of trademarks maintained by the PTO, the Principal Register and the Supplemental Register. References in this chapter to registration of marks will mean registration on the Principal Register, unless otherwise stated. Marks registered on the Principal Register obtain maximum protection. 15 U.S.C. § 1051 ff. Some marks that do not, or do not yet, qualify for registration on the Principal Register may nevertheless be registered on the Supplemental Register. 15 U.S.C. §§ 1091–1096. For example, marks that are merely descriptive of certain goods may be registered on the Supplemental Register even though the mark has not acquired "secondary meaning" and is thus not registrable on the Principal Register. These terms are explained in subsequent paragraphs.

Registration protects a mark nationwide and provides nationwide constructive notice of the registered owner's rights. A certificate of registration of a mark on the Principal Register is treated as prima facie evidence that the mark is valid and enforceable, and places the burden of proof on the party who is allegedly infringing the mark.[135] In addition, after a mark has been registered with the PTO for five years, it becomes "incontestable," meaning that there are only a limited number of grounds on which a mark can be challenged or invalidated.[136]

In the United States (and in many other nations) it is now possible to protect a mark by filing an application with the PTO based on an *intent* to use a particular mark in commerce; the mark must then be used in commerce within a specified period of time. This procedure provides important protection in areas of commerce where a substantial amount of lead time is required to develop new products or services.

Depending on a particular company's business plans, it may also be advisable to apply to register a mark in one or more states within the United States. In addition, it may be advantageous to apply to register a mark in the foreign countries where the company expects to sell its products or services.

Prompt action must be taken against trademark infringement, including a lawsuit if necessary, to prevent unauthorized use. Vigilant protection of a mark is essential because rights in a mark can be lost, under certain circumstances, if they are not protected. If suit becomes necessary, the prevailing trademark owner can obtain injunctive relief, damages, lost profits, and attorneys' fees, as well as other forms of relief that are discussed in later paragraphs.

Although the PTO plays a key role in protecting and determining the validity of rights in trade and other marks, it is the federal courts that ultimately have the power to decide issues of ownership and infringement of marks.

(ii) Types of Protectable Trade and Service Marks.   The Trademark Act defines various kinds of "marks" that can be protected under the Act.[137] A "trademark" can be "any word, name, symbol, or device, or any combination thereof" that a person actually uses in commerce or has applied to use "to identify and distinguish his or her *goods*, including a unique product, from those manufactured or sold by others and to indicate the source of the goods, even if that source is unknown" (author's emphasis).[138]

A "service mark" is identical to a trademark, except that it refers to a mark used in connection with the rendering of *services*.[139] Service marks are of particular importance to the radio, television, and entertainment industries because "titles, character names, and other distinctive features of radio or television programs may be registered as service marks" even if they are used to advertise a sponsor's goods.[140]

A "certification mark" can be created by a person or organization that intends to allow third parties to use the mark to identify goods or services that "certify regional or other origin, material, mode of manufacture, quality, accuracy, or other characteristics of such person's goods or services or that the work or labor on the goods or services was performed by a member of a union or other organization."[141] For example, the mark

---

[135] 15 U.S.C. § 1057(b).
[136] 15 U.S.C. § 1065.
[137] 15 U.S.C. § 1127.
[138] Id.
[139] Id.
[140] Id.
[141] Id.

"Approved by Underwriters Laboratories" identifies a product that meets the specification of, or has been tested by, the Underwriters Laboratories.

A "collective mark" refers to a mark "used by the members of a cooperative, an association, or other collective group or organization" and includes a mark that reflects membership in a particular organization.[142] Intent-to-use applications can also be used for collective marks.[143]

(iii) Trade Dress.   Although it is a concept not specifically defined in the Trademark Act, trade dress is recognized as protectable. Specific parts of a product's trade dress may be trademarked; however, trade dress refers to the "total image of a product" and can be protected regardless of whether any particular part of the trade dress has been registered.

The Supreme Court of the United States recently held that trade dress can be "inherently distinctive" and protectable under § 43 of the Lanham Act, without proof that the trade dress has acquired secondary meaning, that is, that it has come to be associated with the source of a particular product.[144]

(iv) Words or Symbols Usable as Marks.   The Lanham Act generally permits registration of any trade or service mark that can distinguish the goods or services of one person from those of another—*unless* the mark falls within a list of exceptions.[145]

First and foremost, a mark cannot be registered if (1) it is sufficiently similar to a mark already registered or in use in the United States or (2) it is "likely, when used on or in connection with the goods of the applicant, to cause confusion, or to cause mistake, or to deceive."[146] The meaning of this exception is somewhat in the eye of the beholder. It generates numerous disputes in administrative proceedings before the PTO and in the courts, as explained in subsequent paragraphs.

There are other important exceptions to registrability that relate primarily to the character of the word or symbol chosen by the applicant. Some of these exceptions are at the heart of the sometimes arcane law of trademarks. For example, a mark cannot be registered if it is:

1. "Merely descriptive or deceptively misdescriptive" of the goods or services,

---

[142] Id.

[143] Id.

[144] *Two Pesos, Inc. v. Taco Cabana, Inc.*, 112 S. Ct. 2753 (1992) (distinctive design and decor of chain of Mexican-style restaurants protectable as trade dress). The Supreme Court quoted from various lower courts' definitions of the term "trade dress," including the following: "It 'involves the total image of a product and may include features such as size, shape, color, or combinations, texture, graphics, or even particular sales techniques.'" Id. at 2775 n. 1.

[145] 15 U.S.C. §§ 1052 and 1053. Some of the exceptions to registrability established by Congress relate to the *content* of certain types of marks, concern individual privacy interests, or involve governmental symbols. For example, a mark cannot be registered which "consists of or comprises immoral, deceptive, or scandalous matter," falsely suggests a connection with a particular person or institution, encompasses the flags or coats of arms of governmental bodies, "consists of or comprises a name, portrait, or signature identifying a particular living individual," without his or her consent, "or the name, signature, or portrait of a deceased President of the United States during the life of his widow, if any, except by the written consent of the widow." 15 U.S.C. § 1052(a)-(c).

[146] 15 U.S.C. § 1052(d). The identical exceptions are applicable to service marks. 15 U.S.C. § 1053.

2. "Primarily geographically descriptive or deceptively misdescriptive" of the goods or services (except for approved marks of regional origin), or

3. "Primarily merely a surname."[147]

Some of these exceptions appear formidably incomprehensible. In the context of specific examples, they *usually* make sense. For example, no one can register the word *apple* as a trademark to describe the fruit that grows on a tree, because it simply describes what it is. But a company can, and one has done so successfully, register the word "Apple" to identify a particular brand of computer. In the context of computers, the word "Apple" is not descriptive at all; it is highly arbitrary and thus protectable as a trademark.

Trademark law has developed a hierarchy of categories to help separate marks that are protectable from those that are not.[148] In a recent case, the Supreme Court relied on a "classic formulation" of the classification of trademarks, articulated by Judge Friendly.

> Arrayed in an ascending order which roughly reflects their eligibility to trademark status and the degree of protection accorded, these classes are (1) generic, (2) descriptive, (3) suggestive, and (4) arbitrary or fanciful. The lines of demarcation, however, are not always bright. Moreover, the difficulties are compounded because a term that is in one category for a particular production may be in quite a different one for another, because a term may shift from one category to another in light of differences in usage through time, because a term may have one meaning to one group of users and a different one to others, and because the same term may be put to different uses with respect to a single product.[149]

Thus, for trademarks, context is everything.[150] A court of appeals recently illustrated the point by quoting a leading commentator:

> "The word 'apple' would be arbitrary when used on personal computers, suggestive when used in 'Apple-a-Day' on vitamin tablets, descriptive when used in 'Tomapple' for combination tomato-apple juice and generic when used on apples." 1 J. T. McCarthy, Trademarks and Unfair Competition § 11:22, at 498–99 (2d ed. 1984).[151]

A brief description of these different categories follows.

(v) Generic Marks. "A generic mark is one that refers, or has come to be understood as referring, to the genus of which the particular product is a species."[152] However, a mark is not considered generic simply because it "is also used as a name of or to identify a unique product or service."[153]

Thus, the word *apple* cannot be used as a trademark for the fruit of this name. A word can *become* a generic description of a product or service, even if it once was a protected mark, such as "Aspirin," once a protected mark of the Bayer Company. The product was

---

[147] 15 U.S.C. § 1052(e).

[148] *Two Pesos, Inc.*, 112 S.Ct. at 2757; see *Bristol-Myers Squibb Co. v. McNeil-P.P.C., Inc.*, 973 F. 2d 1033, 1039 (2d Cir. 1992) (battle between giants involving claimed infringement of trade dress of "Excedrin PM" by "Tylenol PM").

[149] *Abercrombie & Fitch Co. v. Hunting World, Inc.*, 537 F.2d 4, 9 (2d Cir. 1976) (footnotes omitted) (opinion of Friendly, J.) (involving use of mark "Safari" for sports clothing).

[150] *Bristol-Myers Squibb Co.*, 973 F.2d at 1041.

[151] Id.

[152] Id.

[153] 15 U.S.C. § 1064(3).

so successful that it became the generic name for the product among the general consuming public, through the failure of Bayer to prevent the use of the mark in that way.

In some cases, where a trademark has become so successful that the courts have concluded that it has become a generic term, the courts have reached a Solomonic judgment to allow its general use, but have required that the newly generic term be accompanied by an identification of the manufacturer when made by those other than the originator. Thus, the trademark "Thermos" was held to have become generic as a description of a vacuum bottle, but the makers of such bottles other than King-Seeley were required to preface descriptions of their products with their own names as well as the word "thermos" and could not use the term "Original" in connection with "thermos."[154]

(vi) Descriptive Marks.   The Lanham Act forbids registration of a mark that is "merely descriptive,"[155] that is, one that merely describes what the product or service is. However, a descriptive term can *become* a protectable mark if it acquires a "secondary meaning" (i.e., by becoming associated in the mind of the consuming public with a particular *source* of the product or service).[156] The criteria for establishing that a mark has acquired secondary meaning are described in a later paragraph.

(vii) Suggestive Marks.   A suggestive mark, one that falls somewhere between a merely descriptive mark and an arbitrary or fanciful mark, can be protected without proof of secondary meaning.[157] A suggestive mark " 'requires imagination, thought and perception to reach a conclusion as to the nature of the goods.' "[158]

(viii) Arbitrary or Fanciful Marks.   An arbitrary mark is one in which a familiar word or term is used in an unexpected way, such as the use of "Apple" or "Macintosh" to refer to particular computers. A fanciful mark is one in which a word is "invented solely for . . . use as [a] trademark."[159] For example, the mark "Exxon" is an invented word used to refer to a particular brand of gasoline and petroleum products.

(ix) "Secondary Meaning": Protection of Otherwise Descriptive Marks and Trade Dress.   Marks that would ordinarily be considered merely descriptive and thus unworthy of trademark protection can sometimes acquire a "secondary meaning," which connects them to particular goods or services. When a word can be shown to have acquired secondary meaning, it can be registered and protected under the Lanham Act. Secondary meaning is present when, in the words of the statute, a descriptive mark has "become distinctive of the . . . goods [or services] in commerce."[160] Five years of "substantially exclusive and continuous use" of a descriptive mark for particular goods or services establishes "prima facie evidence" that the mark has become distinctive.[161]

A person attempting to show that a descriptive mark has acquired secondary meaning "must show that the primary significance of the term in the minds of the consuming public

---

[154] *King-Seeley Thermos Co. v. Aladdin Industries, Inc.*, 321 F.2d 577 (2d Cir. 1963).
[155] 15 U.S.C. § 1052(e).
[156] *Abercrombie & Fitch*, 537 F.2d at 10.
[157] *Bristol-Myers Squibb Co.*, 973 F.2d at 1040.
[158] *Abercrombie & Fitch*, 537 F.2d at 11 (citation omitted).
[159] Id. at 11 n. 12.
[160] 15 U.S.C. § 1052(f).
[161] Id.

is not the product but the producer.''[162] The concept of secondary meaning is relevant only to descriptive marks and trade dress.

(x) Likelihood of Confusion—The All-Purpose Test for Registrability, Infringement of Marks, and False Designations of Origin. Likelihood of confusion is the test applied in a variety of contexts to determine whether a mark should be registered when there is a prior similar mark, whether there has been infringement of a registered mark under § 32 of the Lanham Act, and whether there has been a false designation of origin under § 43 (a) of the Act.

> The trier of fact must consider and balance the factors set forth in *Polaroid Corp. v. Polarad Electronics Corp.*, 287 F.2d 492, 495 (2d Cir.), *cert. denied*, 368 U.S. 820 (1961) to determine the "likelihood of confusion." The *Polaroid* test examines eight factors, including the strength of the senior user's mark, the degree of similarity between the two marks, the proximity of the products, the likelihood that the senior user will bridge the gap between the products, the sophistication of buyers, quality of defendant's product, actual confusion, and the defendant's bad faith in adopting the mark. *Polaroid, supra*, 287 F.2d at 495. This list, however, is not exhaustive. Each factor must be balanced with the others to determine the likelihood of confusion.[163]

(xi) Benefits of Registration—Nationwide Protection and More. It is advisable to obtain registration of marks whenever possible and feasible. Registration provides several important benefits. First, both the application for registration and final registration provide constructive notice to others of the claim of ownership of the mark.[164] An application or registration does not protect a mark absolutely, because it can be challenged in an administrative proceeding before the PTO or in court by a competitor.[165] However, a registered mark becomes incontestable after five years of continuous use.[166] This does not make the right in the mark absolute, but it limits the kinds of challenges that can be made against the mark, as explained subsequently.[167] The applicant for registration of a mark, as well as opponents, may obtain judicial review of the approval or denial of registration of the mark.[168]

The application process for a mark should include a search for prior users of the same or a similar mark for the same or a similar product or service. This may avoid a futile

---

[162] *Kellogg Co. v. National Biscuit Co.*, 305 U.S. 111, 118 (1938) ("shredded wheat" referred to the product, not to the producer that previously held a patent on the manufacturing process).

[163] *Nikon Inc. v. Ikon Corp.*, 987 F.2d 91, 94 (2d Cir. 1993) (application to register mark "Ikon" denied by PTO because of similarity to "Zeiss Ikon" mark; after settlement with "Zeiss Ikon," Nikon opposed registration of defendant's "Ikon" mark and brought suit claiming violations of Lanham Act; court found likelihood of confusion).

[164] 15 U.S.C. §§ 1057(c) and 1072.

[165] Persons who believe they would be injured by registration of a mark can oppose it before the PTO or file a petition to cancel after registration under specified circumstances. 15 U.S.C. §§ 1063 and 1064. The Commissioner of Patents and Trademarks can also declare an "interference" when there appear to be conflicting users of the same mark, unless the registered mark has become incontestable. 15 U.S.C. § 1066. An administrative appeal can be taken to the Trademark Trial and Appeal Board from the decision of a trademark examiner in the PTO. 15 U.S.C. § 1070.

[166] 15 U.S.C. § 1065.

[167] 15 U.S.C. § 1115.

[168] 15 U.S.C. § 1071(a) and (b). There are two alternative methods for obtaining judicial review. Under one method, the United States Court of Appeals for the Federal Circuit reviews the administrative record made before the Commissioner of Patents and Trademarks or of the Trademark Trial and Appeal Board. 15 U.S.C. § 1071(a). Alternatively, a person authorized to seek judicial review under the Act may file a civil action in a United States District court and obtain a de novo decision on a new record. 15 U.S.C. § 1071(b). An adverse party has the right to compel a trial de novo even if an appeal to the Federal Circuit court has initially been sought. 15 U.S.C. § 1071(a) (1).

application, the burden and expense of defending a mark against a claim of infringement, and possibly the expense of losing a mark, if the trademark search reveals that there is a prior and valid user.

Registration also affords a critical right for persons or companies who contemplate international marketing of their goods or services. Under international conventions to which the United States is a party, a citizen or resident of the United States who files an application for registration of a mark in the United States obtains priority as of that date if that person files for registration in another country that is party to the same international conventions or has a reciprocal agreement with the United States.[169] The process and benefits of registering marks in other countries are discussed in Chapter 6.

An additional benefit of registration relates to protection from counterfeit imported merchandise. Once a mark is registered with the PTO, the mark can be recorded with the United States Customs Service. The Customs Service will then refuse to allow importation of goods with counterfeit names or marks. This is one of many protections which registration of marks provides.[170]

(xii) Renewal of Registration. A certificate of registration of a mark is effective for 10 years, but registration can be renewed indefinitely if the mark continues to be used and does not become generic.[171] The PTO will cancel a registration unless an affidavit of continued use is filed during the year prior to the sixth anniversary of each current registration certificate.[172] Registration of a mark must be renewed during the last six months of each 10-year term.[173]

(xiii) Registration Based on Actual Use of Marks. The most common method of acquiring rights in a mark is by actually *using* the mark in connection with particular goods or services. This was the *only* basis for obtaining registration of a mark under the Lanham Act until it was amended in 1988 to allow intent-to-use applications, as explained in the following paragraph.[174] An application for registration based on *use* of a mark must contain (1) a drawing of the mark, (2) a verified statement as to when the mark was first used and the kinds of goods or services with which the mark is used, and (3) a statement of belief that the applicant is the owner of the mark and is not aware of any use of the mark by others in connection with goods or services in such a manner as to be likely "to cause confusion, or to cause mistake, or to deceive."[175]

(xiv) Registration Based on Intent-to-Use Application. An application for registration of a mark can now be made on the basis of an *intent* to use the mark (ITU application), rather than on the basis of actual use in commerce, as a result of an amendment to the Lanham Act, effective 1989.[176] Thus, a mark can now be reserved prior to the often expensive and lengthy process of developing a new product or service.

An ITU application is similar to an application based on actual use. The application must specify the mark, include a drawing, describe the goods or services with which the

---

[169] 15 U.S.C. § 1126(d).
[170] 15 U.S.C. § 1124.
[171] 15 U.S.C. §§ 1058 and 1059.
[172] 15 U.S.C. § 1058.
[173] 15 U.S.C. § 1059.
[174] 15 U.S.C. § 1051(a).
[175] Concurrent use of the same mark is permitted under limited circumstances. Id.
[176] Trademark Law Revision Act of 1988, Pub. L. 100–667, 102 Stat. 3935.

mark is to be associated, and include a verified statement that the applicant does not believe that anyone else is already using the mark or has the right to use it in connection with the same goods or services.[177] Within six months after the ITU application has been allowed by the PTO, a verified statement must be filed stating that the mark has actually been used in commerce.[178] An extension of an additional six months may be allowed to file the verification of actual use.[179]

The United States was the last developed nation to adopt an intent-to-use registration provision.[180] Congress recognized that, prior to adoption of the ITU system, United States businesses were at a serious international disadvantage. U.S. companies could not reserve a mark with an ITU application before making the very substantial investment often required to bring a product or service with international potential to market.[181]

In sharp contrast, companies in other countries could file an intent-to-use application for a mark in their home country and obtain priority for that mark not only in their home market, but in the United States and other countries as well, under various international agreements that recognize and give priority to foreign registrations, as most nations in the developed world do.[182]

(xv) Administrative Proceedings Before the Patent and Trademark Office.   There is a substantial administrative process involved in the determination by the Patent and Trademark Office of an application to register a mark, oppositions to registration, requests for cancellation, and determination of a so-called interference, that is, a circumstance where there appears to be a likelihood of confusion between a registered mark and a mark proposed for registration.[183] Detailed regulations of the PTO, as well as the Lanham Act, govern this process of trademark prosecution.[184]

Registration applications are ordinarily reviewed in the first instance by a trademark examiner, an employee of the PTO, who may reject, recommend modification, or approve an application for publication. If the application is initially rejected by the examiner, the applicant may reply to the objection or amend within six months and have the application reconsidered by the examiner. Upon publication of the proposed registration of the mark in the *Official Gazette*, a government publication, interested parties may oppose registration.[185] After publication of the application and consideration of any

---

[177] 15 U.S.C. § 1051(b).

[178] 15 U.S.C. § 1051(d)(1).

[179] 15 U.S.C. § 1051(d)(2).

[180] England adopted an intent-to-use provision in 1938; Canada has had one since 1954. See S. Rep. No. 100–515, 100th Cong., 2d Sess. 5 (1988).

[181] The Senate Report on the 1988 Act explained:

> The Lanham Act's preapplication use requirement . . . creates unnecessary legal uncertainty for a U.S. business planning to introduce products or services into the marketplace. It simply has no assurance that after selecting and adopting a mark, and possibly making a sizable investment in packaging, advertising and marketing, it will not learn that its use of the mark infringes the rights another acquired through earlier use. In an age of national, if not global, marketing, this has a chilling effect on business investment. This effect is not merely theoretical, but is real. And it can be costly: Marketing a new product domestically can often exceed $30 million for a large company and can consume the life-savings of an individual or small entrepreneur.

S. Rep. No. 100–515, at 5–6.

[182] Id.

[183] 15 U.S.C. §§ 1062–1070.

[184] 37 C.F.R. § 2.1 et seq.

[185] 15 U.S.C. § 1062.

opposition, the PTO issues a certificate of registration for an application based on actual use of the mark or a notice of allowance, if based on an intent-to-use application.[186]

Certain trademark matters are determined by the Trademark Trial and Appeal Board, such as a declared interference, opposition to registration, an application for a concurrent use, or an application for cancellation of a registered mark.[187] Such proceedings, called "inter partes proceedings," are conducted like administrative trials governed by the Federal Rules of Civil Procedures, which are otherwise applicable to cases in a United States district court.[188]

The Trademark Trial and Appeal Board can also hear ex parte appeals to any final decision of a trademark examiner.[189]

Decisions of the Commissioner of the Patent and Trademark Office and of the Trademark Trial and Appeal Board are subject to judicial review, either in the United States Court of Appeals for the Federal Circuit or in a United States district court.[190]

(xvi) Registered Marks Incontestable After Five Years—With Exceptions.   A registered mark becomes incontestable after it has been registered for five consecutive years and the required affidavit of continued use is filed within one year after each five-year period of use, with limited exceptions.[191] One exception is that a mark can be challenged at any time if it "becomes the generic name for the goods or services, or a portion thereof."[192] A mark can still be challenged if it has been abandoned, was obtained by fraud, or is knowingly used in a deceptive way.[193]

Section 33(b) of the Act declares an incontestable mark to be "conclusive evidence of the validity of the mark" and of the registrant's ownership and right to use it in commerce, subject to specified defenses, including acquisition of registration by fraud, abandonment, genericism, and deceptive use, among others. There is also a "limited geographic use" defense available to a person who has used a mark identical to the incontestable one within a limited geographic area, if the use was made in good faith prior to registration of the incontestable mark, even if the owner of the incontestable mark was the first user. In that situation the limited conflicting use will be allowed to continue, but cannot expand beyond that limited area.[194] However, the geographic extent of the permitted use in such a case may be disputed.[195]

Yet an incontestable mark cannot be challenged on the ground that the mark is "merely descriptive," as the Supreme Court held in a case involving the service mark "Park 'N Fly," which was used for a chain of parking lots adjacent to airports.[196]

(xvii) Display of Notice of Registration or of Application for Registration.   The Lanham Act permits, but does not require, a registered trademark to be accompanied by a notice of

---

[186] 15 U.S.C. § 1063(b).
[187] 15 U.S.C. § 1067.
[188] 37 C.F.R. § 2.116.
[189] 15 U.S.C. § 1069.
[190] 15 U.S.C. § 1071.
[191] 15 U.S.C. § 1065.
[192] 15 U.S.C. § 1065, by reference to 15 U.S.C. § 1064(3).
[193] Id.
[194] *Thrifty Rent-A-Car System v. Thrift Cars, Inc.*, 831 F.2d 1177 (1st Cir. 1987).
[195] *Uno's Pizza, Inc. v. Pizzeria Uno Corp.*, 722 F. Supp. 971, 976–977 (W.D.N.Y. 1989).
[196] *Park 'N Fly, Inc. v. Dollar Park & Fly, Inc.*, 469 U.S. 189 (1985).

registration.[197] Notice may be given in one of three forms: (1) "Registered in U.S. Patent and Trademark Office," (2) "Reg. U.S. Pat. & Tm. Off.," and (3) the familiar "R" within a circle—®.[198]

It is not mandatory to include a notice of registration with a mark, but it is strongly recommended. Failure to include a notice of registration precludes a claim for profits of the infringer or damages in a suit for trademark infringement, unless it can be shown that the infringer actually knew the mark was registered.[199]

(xviii) General Protection from False Designations of Origin and False Descriptions of Goods and Services Under § 43(a) of the Lanham Act. Section 43(a) of the Lanham Act provides an all-purpose judicial remedy designed to offer protection from false designations of the origin of goods or services and from false and misleading descriptions or statements in advertising, packaging, or otherwise, in interstate or international commerce.[200] This powerful remedy is available regardless of whether the claim involves a registered mark. Section 43(a) is a widely used federal remedy for unfair and deceptive practices and is particularly useful in protecting the rights of authors, artists, and performers.[201] It creates the right to bring such a claim in a United States District Court regardless of the usual impediments to federal jurisdiction, such as diversity of citizenship and a minimum claim of $50,000.[202]

(xix) Other Judicial Remedies for Protection of Trademarks. In addition to § 43(a), the Lanham Act provides powerful remedies for the protection of registered trademarks.[203] The relief available under § 43(a) and for registered marks includes injunctions[204] and monetary relief, which can include recovery of the plaintiff's damages, the infringer's profits, costs, and, in an "exceptional case," attorney's fees.[205] Special remedies are available where the intentional use of counterfeit goods is involved. The court is *required* to award three times the plaintiff's damages or the infringer's profits, where intentional counterfeits are involved, plus attorneys' fees, unless there are "extenuating circumstances."[206] Finally, the Lanham Act provides that all goods, labels, and plates, molds, or other devices used to make the infringing goods, whether involving infringement of a registered mark or violations of § 43(a) of the Act.[207]

Remedies are discussed in more detail in section 5.2, "Judicial Remedies for Infringement of Intellectual Property Rights."

---

[197] 15 U.S.C. § 1111.

[198] Id. This notice provision was included in the Lanham Act by an amendment, effective January 2, 1975, to reflect the change in the name of the Patent Office to the Patent and Trademark Office. Pub. L. 93–596, 88 Stat. 1949. Previously registered marks may continue to use the forms of notice previously authorized by this section of the Lanham Act.

[199] 15 U.S.C. § 1111. However, use of a registration symbol prior to actual registration of a mark with intent to mislead or deceive, can result in cancellation of a mark. *Copeland's Enterprises, Inc. v. CNV, Inc.*, 945 F.2d 1563 (Fed Cir. 1991).

[200] 15 U.S.C. § 1125(a).

[201] Diana Pinover, "The Rights of Authors, Artists and Performers Under Section 43(a) of the Lanham Act, 83 *Trademark Rep.* 38 (1993).

[202] 15 U.S.C. § 1121(a).

[203] 15 U.S.C. § 1114.

[204] 15 U.S.C. § 1116.

[205] 15 U.S.C. § 1117(a).

[206] 15 U.S.C. § 1117(b).

[207] 15 U.S.C. § 1118.

(d) Patents

(i) Background.   Patent protection in the United States derives from the Constitution, which empowers Congress to "promote the Progress of Science and useful Arts, by securing for limited Times to . . . Inventors the exclusive Right to their respective . . . Discoveries."[208]

Congress passed the first patent statute in 1790.[209] The Patent Act itself has been stable over the decades, the last major revision having been made in 1953. The Supreme Court of the United States recently observed that "today's patent statute is remarkably similar to the law as known to Jefferson in 1793."[210] The Act has been substantially revised only three times since then. Significant developments in patent law have emerged in large part from the courts. Patents, like copyrights and trademarks, have an ancient lineage.

In the United States, the federal government has the exclusive power to grant patent rights. After a patent is granted, the basis and operation of the patented invention is made public. The exclusive rights created by a patent last for 17 years and cannot be renewed.[211] Once the patent expires, the product or process enters the public domain and can be copied and freely used by anyone.

Depending on the philosophical and economic conditions of the times, the granting of patents has been looked upon favorably as a source of incentive for productive creativity, or unfavorably as an undesirable monopolistic practice. The modern limitation of patent monopolies derives from the Statute of Monopolies, which was enacted by the English Parliament in 1623 to limit the abuses resulting from Royal patents.[212]

Patent protection is the exclusive domain of federal law, which preempts any attempts by individual states to provide patentlike protection for designs and concepts that cannot be protected by federal patent law or for which a patent has expired. For example, the Supreme Court held that a Florida law that protected a particular unpatented boat hull molding process was preempted by federal law and could not be enforced.[213] The Court reiterated the well-established principle that "ideas once placed before the public without the protection of a valid patent are subject to appropriation without significant restraint."[214] The Florida law thus could not prevent a competitor from duplicating the hull by "reverse engineering." Other legal principles, such as protection of trade secrets or unfair trade laws that prevent deceptive practices, would not necessarily be preempted in such a situation.[215] However, it cannot be an unfair practice merely to copy an unpatented product.[216]

---

[208] U.S. Const. art. I, § 8, cl. 8.

[209] 1 Stat. 109.

[210] *Bonito Boats, Inc. v. Thunder Craft Boats, Inc.*, 489 U.S. 143, 148 (1989).

[211] 35 U.S.C. § 154. Patents involving compositions or processes subject to approval under the Food, Drug, and Cosmetic Act may be extended for the period during which they were subject to review before marketing, for up to five years. Id., §§ 155 and 156.

[212] 21 Jac. I, c. 3 (1623). The Statute "curtailed . . . the [practices] of the Crown in granting monopolies to court favorites in goods or businesses which had long before been enjoyed by the public." *Graham v. John Deere Company of Kansas City*, 383 U.S. 1, 5 (1966). See *Sears, Roebuck & Co. v. Stiffel Co.*, 376 U.S. 225, 229 (1964).

[213] Id. *Bonito Boats*, 489 U.S. at 156–168.

[214] Id. at 156.

[215] Id. at 154–155.

[216] Sears, Roebuck, 376 U.S. at 232–233 (not improper to copy pole lamp); *accord, Compco Corp. v. Day-Brite Lighting, Inc.*, 376 U.S. 237 (1964) (permissible to copy particular type of light fixture for which patent denied).

The Patent Act is administered in the Patent and Trademark Office (PTO) by a Commissioner under the supervision of the United States Department of Commerce.[217]

(ii) Things New and Useful—What Can Be Patented?   The Patent Act provides: "Whoever invents or discovers any new and useful process, machine, manufacture, or composition of matter, or any new and useful improvement thereof, may obtain a patent therefor, subject to the conditions and requirements of this title."[218] This disarmingly simple language is essentially identical to the Patent Act of 1793, written by Thomas Jefferson.[219] However, virtually every word in this definition requires interpretation of Talmudic proportion. The principles may be relatively easy to describe but are often difficult to apply in specific situations. Such an effort not only requires knowledge of the legal principles and the administrative process, it also requires a high degree of scientific and other knowledge about the state of the art in the particular field involved.[220]

The general categories of patentable subject matter are (1) processes, (2) machines or compositions of matter ("utility" patents),[221] (3) invented or discovered and asexually reproduced varieties of plants,[222] and (4) "any new, original and *ornamental* design for an article of manufacture."[223]

In addition to falling within one of the four patentable categories, the subject matter must meet the affirmative statutory requirements that it be "new and useful."[224] A patent application must briefly describe the current state of the art in the particular area involved, and specify how the claimed product or process constitutes a "new and useful" improvement over the current art, as discussed in the following paragraph.[225]

(iii) Things New but Not Useful—Design Patents.   Certain kinds of designs can be patented under the Patent Act, but contrary to the rule for product and process patents, designs may *not* be patented unless they are "new, original and *ornamental*."[226]

---

[217] 15 U.S.C. § 6(a). The Commissioner and the PTO are also responsible for registration of trademarks under the Lanham Act.

[218] 35 U.S.C. § 101.

[219] *Diamond v. Chakrabarty*, 447 U.S. 303, 308 (1980).

[220] Thus, patent lawyers generally have scientific training as well as law degrees and tend to specialize in patent law exclusively. Attorneys may not be registered to practice before the PTO in prosecuting patent applications unless they have the requisite scientific training and have passed a written examination or have worked "in the patent examining corps of the [PTO]" for at least four years. 37 C.F.R. § 10.7(b).

[221] 35 U.S.C. § 101.

[222] 35 U.S.C. § 161.

[223] 35 U.S.C. § 171 (author's emphasis).

[224] 35 U.S.C. § 101.

[225] 35 U.S.C. § 112; 37 C.F.R. §§ 1.71 and 1.75.

[226] 35 U.S.C. § 171. It is important to note that in the United States, only *ornamental* designs can be protected (author's emphasis). At least 12 European countries provide for protection of industrial designs, and the European Community has considered such legislation. *Green Paper on the Legal Protection of Industrial Design, Working Document of the Services of the Commission* 111/ F/5131/91-EN (June 1991). For example, a car manufacturer in France can protect the design of a car's fender, thus limiting the aftermarket sources for such auto parts which thrive in the United States and elsewhere. There have been proposals for such design protection in the United States. H.R. 1790, 102d Cong., 1st Sess. (Ver. 3, introduced Dec. 20, 1991). The proposal has pitted two giants against one another. The automobile industry generally supports such proposals; they are opposed by the insurance industry because its costs and those of consumers would be increased.

(iv) Plant Patents—Growing Things Made or Modified by Humans.   The Plant Patent Act of 1930 is codified within the Patent Act. It provides that "whoever invents or discovers and asexually reproduces any distinct and new variety of plant, . . . subject to certain conditions, can obtain a patent for the plant."[227] The primary criterion is that the plant be in some way made or modified by humans. A new variety of plant found growing in the wild cannot be patented.

The Supreme Court explained where the line is to be drawn between works of nature and works of humankind:

> Patents cannot issue for the discovery of the phenomena of nature. . . . The qualities of these bacteria [involved in that case], like the heat of the sun, electricity, or the qualities of metals, are part of the storehouse of knowledge of all men. They are manifestations of laws of nature, free to all men and reserved exclusively to none. He who discovers a hitherto unknown phenomenon of nature has no claim to a monopoly of it which the law recognizes. If there is to be invention from such a discovery, it must come from the application of the law of nature to a new and useful end.[228]

Protection for new plants under the Plant Patent Act is distinct from the protection available for other living organisms that may be patented as a "manufacture" or "composition of matter" under the general category of patentable subject matter.[229] This specific patent protection for plant varieties was enacted during the Great Depression to stimulate the nascent plant breeding industry, which was being supported in part by agricultural colleges established under the Morrill Land Grant Act.[230]

(v) Exceptions to Patentability—Ideas and Laws of Nature in the Abstract.   There are also exceptions to patentability that have been developed by the courts, consistent with the underlying purposes of the patent clause in the Constitution and the Patent Act. A fundamental idea or principle can be employed to create a patentable process or product, but an idea or principle in the abstract cannot be patented. The Supreme Court has explained this exception in a variety of ways:

> "While a scientific truth, or the mathematical expression of it, is not patentable invention, a novel and useful structure created with the aid of knowledge of scientific truth may be." That statement followed the longstanding rule that "an idea of itself is not patentable. . ." "A principle, in the abstract, is a fundamental truth; an original cause; a motive; these cannot be patented, as no one can claim in either of them an exclusive right. . . . Phenomena of nature, though just discovered, mental processes, and abstract intellectual concepts are not patentable, as they are the basic tools of scientific and technological work.[231]

---

[227] 35 U.S.C. § 161. There is also a separate Plant Variety Protection Act of 1970, which provides "plant variety protection" for "the breeder of any novel variety of sexual reproduced plant (other than fungi, bacteria, or first generation hybrids)." 7 U.S.C. § 2402(a). This statutory scheme is similar in structure to the Patent Act, but it is administered by the United States Department of Agriculture. If an application for plant variety protection meets certain novelty and other requirements, a certificate of ownership of the variety is issued which establishes the owner's right to exclude others from the sale, importation, or other use of the variety for a term of 18 years. 7 U.S.C. § 2483 (a) and (b).

[228] *Funk Bros. Seed Co. v. Kalo Inoculant Co.*, 333 U.S. 127, 130 (1948).

[229] 35 U.S.C. § 101. See *Diamond v. Chakrabarty*, 447 U.S. 303, 307 (1980) (genetically engineered bacterium patentable subject matter under § 101).

[230] Application of Bergy, 596 F.2d 952, 981–982 (CCPA 1979), *aff'd sub nom Diamond v. Chakrabarty*, 447 U.S. 303 (1980).

[231] *Gottschalk v. Benson*, 409 U.S. 64, 67 (1972) (citations omitted).

Thus, the Court held that the Patent Office properly refused to patent the claimed invention of "a method for converting binary-coded decimal . . . numerals into pure binary numerals" in connection with digital computers, which was, in essence, a mathematical formula called an algorithm.[232] The Court pointed out that the applicant did not seek to patent a particular process that used a scientific principle, but to patent "any use of the claimed method in a general-purpose digital computer of any type."[233] In essence, the applicant sought to patent the mathematical formula itself. This, the Court held, went beyond the pale of the Act's protection.[234]

Similarly, the Supreme Court held that William F. B. Morse, the inventor of the telegraph, had exceeded the limits of patentability in a case involving the extent of his rights in the telegraph.[235] The Court upheld Morse's patent claims in various aspects of his *apparatus*, but rejected the following part of his claim:

> "I do not propose to limit myself to the specific machinery or parts of machinery described in the foregoing specification and claims; the essence of my invention being the use of the motive power of the electric or galvanic current, which I call electro-magnetism, however developed, for marking or printing intelligible characters, signs or letters, at any distances, being a new application of that power of which I claim to be the first inventor or discoverer."[236]

The Court rejected this claim as comparable to a hypothetical claim by Fulton to "the exclusive right to use the motive power of steam, however developed, for the purpose of propelling vessels," simply because he had invented a particular method of using a steam engine.[237] In short, the Court said Morse "claims an exclusive right to use a manner and process which he has not described and indeed had not invented, and therefore could not describe when he obtained his patent. The claim is too broad, and not warranted in law."[238]

In a subsequent case, however, the Court rejected a challenge to Alexander Graham Bell's claim of a patent in the *process*, which he described, of transmitting speech through the use of electricity, distinguishing it from Morse's.[239]

There may sometimes be completely different ways of reading a particular patent claim with completely different conclusions as to patent eligibility. Thus, in one case, five justices of the Supreme Court saw a claim that described a process for transforming "raw, uncured synthetic rubber, into a different state or thing."[240] Four dissenting justices, however, perceived no patentable subject matter; they saw nothing more than a different "solution of the mathematical problem or formula used to control" the temperature in the mold.[241]

Although patent claimants have encountered difficulty in obtaining patent protection for claims related to computer programs, such programs can be protected under the

---

[232] Id. at 64.

[233] Id. The Court addressed the patentability of algorithms in a subsequent decision and reached a similar result. *Parker v. Flook*, 437 U.S. 584, 594 (1978) (no "inventive application" of mathematical formula shown).

[234] The Court's analysis in its line of cases on algorithms has been criticized. D. Chisum & M. Jacobs, *Understanding Intellectual Property*, Patents, § 2C[1][F], at 2–34 (Matthew Bender, 1992).

[235] *O'Reilly v. Morse*, 15 How. (56 U.S.) 62, 112 (1853).

[236] Id.

[237] Id. at 113.

[238] Id.

[239] *The Telephone Cases*, 126 U.S. 1, 533–534 (1888).

[240] *Diamond v. Diehr*, 450 U.S. 175, 184 (1981).

[241] Id. at 208.

Copyright Act and under the Semiconductor Chip Protection Act if their requirements are met.[242]

Establishing that a patent claim involves one of the categories of patentable subject matter is the first step. Next, it must be determined whether the claimed patentable subject matter has "utility"—that it is "useful." Finally, it must be established that the claim meets two other conditions for patentability: (1) novelty, that is, that the supposed invention is not already known or in use, and (2) nonobviousness, that is, that the claimed invention is not such an obvious next step to anyone knowledgeable in the particular field, that it does not qualify for patent protection.[243]

(vi) Utility of Claimed Patent.   For a process, product, or other subject matter to be patentable, the claim must show that it is "useful." The requirement of "utility" is contained both in the Constitution and in the Patent Act.[244] In most circumstances, this requirement is not difficult to meet. It is satisfied if it is shown that "a new product or process [is] 'capable of being used to effect the object proposed.' "[245] Justice Story stated the requirement succinctly: the Court "does not look to the degree of utility; it simply requires that the [claimed invention] shall be capable of use, and that the use is such as sound morals and policy do not discountenance or prohibit."[246]

The usefulness necessary to satisfy this requirement is fairly modest. The claimed invention "need not be the best or the only way to accomplish a certain result, and it need only be useful to some extent and in certain applications."[247] Described another way, "to violate [the utility requirement,] the claimed device must be totally incapable of achieving a useful result."[248]

However, quackery cannot be patented, in part because it does not meet the "utility" requirement. Thus, the United States Court of Appeals for the Federal Circuit (the Federal Circuit), which reviews PTO decisions, held that a patent claim for a device that supposedly produced more energy than it consumed, lacked utility. The court stated that "the claimed device was a 'perpetual motion machine', and that perpetual motion is impossible for it violates either the first or second law of thermodynamics."[249]

(vii) Prior Art.   The point of reference for determining novelty and nonobviousness, as well as other critical patent principles, is called "prior art," a term of art itself in patent law. In one respect, prior art generally refers to the body of knowledge reasonably available to a person familiar with the particular field. It has more particular and complex meaning in the context of the determination of novelty and nonobviousness.

(viii) Patent Condition No. 1—Novelty.   A patent claim must present something new and, in general, the claimant must be the first to achieve the claimed result; the claim must establish what is referred to as "novelty."[250]

---

[242] *See* § _____, above at _____.
[243] 35 U.S.C. §§ 102 and 103.
[244] Const. art. I, sec. 8; 35 U.S.C. § 101.
[245] *Stiftung v. Renishaw PLC*, 945 F.2d 1173, 1180 (Fed. Cir. 1991) (citation omitted).
[246] *Bedford v. Hunt*, 3 Fed. Cas. 37 (No. 1217) (C.C.D. Mass. 1817).
[247] Id.
[248] *Brooktree Corp. v. Advanced Micro Devices, Inc.*, 977 F.2d 1555, 1571 (Fed. Cir. 1992).
[249] *Newman v. Quigg*, 877 F.2d 1575, 1577 (Fed. Cir. 1989), *cert. denied*, 495 U.S. 932 (1990);
[250] 35 U.S.C. § 102.

The Patent Act establishes a detailed scheme of seven priorities and conditions for determining novelty.[251] For example, a person cannot obtain a patent if

(a) *the invention was known or used* by others in this country, or patented or described in a printed publication in this or a foreign country, *before the invention . . . by the applicant, . . .* or

(b) the invention was patented or described in a printed publication in this or a foreign country or in public use or on sale in this country, more than one year prior to the date of the application for patent in the United States, or . . . .

(e) the invention was described in a patent granted on an application for the patent by another filed in the United States before the invention . . . by the applicant, . . . or on an international application by another who has fulfilled [certain] requirements before the invention . . . by the applicant, . . . or . . . .

(g) before the applicant's invention thereof the invention was made in this country by another who had not abandoned, suppressed, or concealed it.[252]

It is often the case that more than one person is involved in pursuing a particular line of research and development in the hope of being the first to develop a patented process or product. A famous example involves the telegraph. William F.B. Morse was held to have been the inventor and entitled to the telegraph patent, even though inventors in England, Germany, and France were very close behind Morse with their similar devices.[253] Under the Patent Act, Morse would have been entitled to the patent even if he was not literally the *first* to invent the telegraph, if none of his competitors had previously applied for a patent for the device and had not previously published a description of that device.[254]

The issue of novelty is often raised by a defendant in a patent infringement case, whereby the defendant claims that the plaintiff's patent is invalid because of "anticipation," meaning that one of the disqualifying events described in § 102 of the Patent Act had occurred before the plaintiff's invention. The inquiry in determining whether a patent claim has been anticipated is an inquiry into the prior art, as described in § 102.[255]

However, for prior art to anticipate and invalidate a particular patent, "all of the elements and limitations of the claim [must be] found within a single prior art reference."[256]

(ix) Patent Condition No. 2—Nonobviousness.   In addition to satisfying the novelty requirements in § 102 of the Act, a patent cannot be granted if the step from the known prior art to the claimed patent is obvious. Thus, a patent cannot be obtained

if the differences between the subject matter sought to be patented and the prior art are such that the subject matter as a whole would have been obvious at the time the invention was made to a person having ordinary skill in the art to which said subject matter pertains.[257]

---

[251] 35 U.S.C. § 102.

[252] 35 U.S.C. § 102 (author's emphasis).

[253] *O'Reilly v. Morse*, 15 How. (56 U.S.) at 107–111.

[254] Id. at 110–111.

[255] One suggested approach to analyzing the prior art as relevant to § 102 "is to view it as having limits in four dimensions—(1) *source* . . . ; (2) *place* . . . ; (3) *time* . . . ; and (4) *person.* . . . An item is prior art only if it falls within the limits in all four dimensions." Chisum and Jacobs, *Understanding Intellectual Property*, Patents § 2C[5], at 2–84–2–85 (emphasis in original).

[256] *Scripps Clinic & Research Foundation v. Genentech, Inc.*, 927 F.2d 1565, 1576 (Fed. Cir. 1991).

[257] 35 U.S.C. § 103.

However, a patent cannot be denied merely because an invention is simple. "Simplicity is not inimical to patentability."[258]

The Supreme Court has described the relevant factors for determining nonobviousness:

> Under § 103, the scope and content of the prior art are to be determined; differences between the prior art and the claims at issue are to be ascertained; and the level of ordinary skill in the pertinent art resolved. . . . Such secondary considerations as commercial success, long felt but unsolved needs, failure of others, etc., might be utilized to give light to the circumstances surrounding the origin of the subject matter sought to be patented. As indicia of obviousness or nonobviousness, these inquiries may have relevancy.[259]

For example, the Federal Circuit recently upheld Symbol Technologies's patent for its popular aim-and-shoot laser scanner in an infringement case. There the defendant argued that the aim-and-shoot feature of the device was obvious and therefore not patentable.[260] Symbol and others had prior patents for laser scanners, but none had the new features of the challenged device—its handle, trigger, and aim-and-shoot feature. The new patent was nonobvious "in light of the prior art because the . . . references did not disclose or suggest the 'aim and shoot' feature. . . . "[261] As the court pointed out, the defendant's expert had been involved in the scanner industry since its inception, and it had never occurred to him to develop a point-and-shoot scanner. The court also considered the great commercial success of the challenged scanner as supporting its finding of nonobviousness.[262]

(x) Contents of Patent Applications.   A patent application must be made by the inventor (with limited exceptions) under oath and must contain (1) a specification and (2) a drawing.[263] The PTO may require a model when it is considered appropriate, and, where a composition is involved, a specimen may be required.[264] In general, the applicant must claim under oath to be the inventor.[265] When there are joint inventors, each must join in the application and take the required oath.[266] If an inventor refuses to sign a patent application or cannot be found, an assignee of the patent or a person with a sufficient proprietary interest in it can apply on behalf of the inventor.[267]

The specification describes what the claimed patent is and how it is made and operates:

> The specification shall contain a written description of the invention, and of the manner and process of making and using it, in such full, clear, concise, and exact terms as to enable any person skilled in the art to which it pertains, or with which it is most nearly connected, to make and use [it], and shall set forth the best mode contemplated by the inventor of carrying out his invention.
>
> The specification shall conclude with one or more claims particularly pointing out and distinctly claiming the subject matter which the applicant regards as his invention.[268]

---

[258] *In re Oetiker*, 977 F.2d 1443, 1447 (Fed. Cir. 1992).
[259] *Graham v. John Deere Co.*, 383 U.S. at 17–18.
[260] *Symbol Technologies, Inc. v. Opticon, Inc.*, 935 F.2d 1569, 1576–1579 (Fed. Cir. 1991).
[261] Id. at 1577.
[262] Id.
[263] 35 U.S.C. § 111.
[264] 35 U.S.C. § 114.
[265] 35 U.S.C. § 115.
[266] 35 U.S.C. § 116.
[267] 35 U.S.C. § 118.
[268] 35 U.S.C. § 112.

Virtually all of the words in the provision have significant bearing on whether a patent claim will be approved and will determine the extent of the patent. The PTO and the courts generally dissect the specification and the claim with exquisite care to resolve issues of validity and infringement. For example, the enablement requirement derives from this provision and means that the description of the patent must be sufficiently clear and specific that one knowledgeable in the field can duplicate the claimed patent.[269]

Preparation of a proper specification and claim is an art in itself and requires an intimate knowledge of the claimed invention and of the prior art to which it relates. Competent professional advice is essential to filing a proper patent application.

(xi) Patent Application in Foreign Country—Establishing Priority in the United States. Patent applications should generally be filed promptly. Unless an inventor files a patent application within 12 months after creation of the invention, there is a risk that someone else may be able to use or claim rights in the invention, despite the inventor's claim.[270]

A U.S. patent application filing date can be established by filing a patent application in a foreign country, if that country affords reciprocity to U.S. citizens, and if a U.S. application is then filed within 12 months after the foreign application.[271]

A patent application under this provision will be denied if, more than a year prior to the U.S. application, the invention was "patented or described in a printed publication in any foreign country" or if the invention "had been in public use or on sale in this country."[272] Timely filing of a patent application in such circumstances is, therefore, essential to ensure that patent rights are not irretrievably lost.

(xii) Confidentiality of Patent Applications. An application for a patent is generally treated as confidential by the PTO.[273] Thus, information concerning a *pending* application will not be released to others without the consent of the applicant except in "special circumstances."[274]

Information about a patent application may be disclosed in the context of an "interference" proceeding before the PTO, in which there may be one or more persons who claim to be the creator of the same invention. Then the process changes from an ex parte claim of the applicant before the PTO examiner and becomes an adversarial proceeding before the Board of Patent Appeals and Interferences, in which such information may be disclosed to the contending parties, as in a federal court case.[275]

(xiii) Patent Applicant's Obligation of Candor. Because the issuance of a patent grants a monopoly for a period of time, and because the application process is largely ex parte (that is, involves only the patent claimant and the PTO examiner), the patent applicant and those involved in filing and prosecuting the application bear a duty to be candid in all respects concerning the application. This duty is included in the PTO's Rules of Practice: "A duty of candor and good faith in dealing with the [PTO]" is imposed on all persons substantively involved with the claim.[276] The duty "includes a duty to disclose to the

---

[269] *Newman v. Quigg*, 877 F.2d 1575 (Fed. Cir. 1989), *cert. denied*, 110 S.Ct. 2173.
[270] 35 U.S.C. § 102(b).
[271] 35 U.S.C. § 119.
[272] 35 U.S.C. § 119.
[273] 35 U.S.C. § 122.
[274] Id.
[275] 35 U.S.C. § 135; 37 C.F.R. § 1.651.
[276] 37 C.F.R. § 1.56(a), as amended January 17, 1992, 57 Fed. Reg. 2034.

Office all information known to that individual to be material to patentability."[277] The recently amended rule defines the phrase *material to patentability* as follows:

> (b) . . . Information is material to patentability when it is not cumulative to information already of record or being made of record in the application, and
>
> (1) It establishes, by itself or in combination with other information, a prima facie case of unpatentability of a claim; or
>
> (2) It refutes, or is inconsistent with, a position the applicant takes in:
>
> (i) Opposing an argument of unpatentability relied on by the Office, or
>
> (ii) Asserting an argument of patentability.
>
> A prima facie case of unpatentability is established when the information compels a conclusion that a claim is unpatentable under the preponderance of evidence, burden-of-proof standard, giving each term in the claim its broadest reasonable construction consistent with the specification, and before any consideration is given to evidence which may be submitted in an attempt to establish a contrary conclusion of patentability.[278]

An applicant who plays cat and mouse with the PTO in connection with a patent claim runs several substantial risks. If found out, the patent claim may be rejected or the patent itself invalidated, if previously granted. Violation of the duty may provide a defense in a patent infringement action.[279] In extreme cases, it can even be the basis of an antitrust claim against a patent holder who has violated the duty of candor.[280]

(xiv) Examination and Determination of Patent Applications by the PTO.   A completed patent application is assigned to a patent examiner in the PTO in one of several specialty groups.[281] The patent examiner then studies the application, considers the prior art in the particular field involved, and determines whether a patent should be granted.[282] It is possible for an application to be approved without modification, but it is more common for there to be a period of give-and-take between the applicant and the examiner, who may seek and obtain additional information from the applicant. The applicant may also be asked to modify or narrow the claimed invention in the course of this process.

Members of the public may submit protests to the PTO objecting to the granting of a particular application, including whatever information or publications are considered appropriate.[283] The examiner may give this information such weight as is appropriate, but the applicant is not required to respond directly to a public protest.[284] Anyone, except a party to an interference proceeding, may also petition for public use proceedings, asserting that the claimed patent was in public use more than a year prior to the patent

---

[277] Id.

[278] Id., at § 1.57(b) (2).

[279] *Argus Chemical Corp. v. Fibre Glass-Evercoat Co., Inc.*, 759 F.2d 10 (Fed. Cir. 1985) (patent unenforceable because of inequitable conduct where information as to sales more than a year prior to application was withheld).

[280] *Walker Process Equipment, Inc. v. Food Machinery and Chemical Corp.*, 382 U.S. 172 (1965) (patent obtained by fraud may be basis of Sherman Act antitrust claim); *Senza-Gel Corp. v. Seiffhart*, 803 F.2d 661 (Fed. Cir. 1986) (patent misuse established by showing of antitrust tying arrangement and established defense to patent infringement claim).

[281] 35 U.S.C. § 131; 37 C.F.R. § 1.101.

[282] 35 U.S.C. § 131.

[283] 37 C.F.R. § 1.291.

[284] Id.

application.[285] The Commissioner then decides whether a public use proceeding is to be conducted and, if so, appoints an officer to take testimony.[286]

The examiner ordinarily issues what is called an "Office Action," which describes the official action taken by the PTO. If at first an application is rejected by the PTO examiner, the applicant must be notified in writing with a statement of reasons for the rejection.[287] The applicant may ask the examiner to reconsider the patent application, with or without amending the application, within six months of the initial denial.[288]

There are various avenues of review or other courses of action available if the application is finally rejected or other adverse action is taken. If the examiner has twice rejected any claim in the patent application completely, the applicant's only choice is to appeal to the Board of Patent Appeals and Interferences.[289] If the examiner takes other adverse action but does not reject the application, the applicant may petition the Commissioner to review the decision of the examiner.[290] Amendments may be made to an application at various stages of the process in an effort to accommodate the views of the examiner and obtain approval.[291]

(xv) Administrative Appeals to the Board of Patent Appeals and Interferences. The Board of Patent Appeals and Interferences is an administrative adjudicatory body that, among its various functions, hears appeals from rejected patent applications and decides disputed patent claims in interference proceedings.[292] The procedures before the Board are similar to those in a federal court of appeals.

The applicant who appeals to the Board first files a brief that describes the status of the claims involved, the claimed invention, and the issues to be reviewed and presents an argument containing the applicant's contentions in favor of the claim.[293] An appendix is also submitted, which contains a copy of the patent claims involved.[294]

The primary examiner who decided the fate of the patent application may file an answer to the appellant's brief before the Board, explaining the basis of the examiner's action and responding to the applicant's brief. The appellant may respond to the examiner's answer in a reply brief.[295] Oral argument may be requested by the appellant.[296]

The Board may affirm or reverse the action taken by the examiner, in whole or in part, or remand the claim to the examiner for further proceedings.[297]

In addition, the Board may reject an appeal on other grounds known to it that were not part of the examiner's decision.[298] If the Board affirms on a new ground, the appellant then has two courses of action. The appellant may amend the patent claim and have the matter reconsidered by the examiner, whose decision is then subject to another appeal to

---

[285] 37 C.F.R. § 1.292(a).
[286] Id.
[287] 35 U.S.C. § 132; 37 C.F.R. §§ 1.107-1.108.
[288] 35 U.S.C. § 133; 37 C.F.R. §§ 1.111 and 1.112.
[289] 35 U.S.C. § 134; 37 C.F.R. § 1.113.
[290] 37 C.F.R. §§ 1.113 and 1.181.
[291] 37 C.F.R. §§ 1.115 and 1.116.
[292] 35 U.S.C. § 134; 37 C.F.R. § 1.191.
[293] 37 C.F.R. § 1.192.
[294] 37 C.F.R. § 1.192(c) (7).
[295] 37 C.F.R. § 1.193(a) and (b).
[296] 37 C.F.R. § 1.194.
[297] 37 C.F.R. § 1.196(a).
[298] 37 C.F.R. § 1.196(b).

the Board.[299] Alternatively, the appellant may ask the Board to reconsider its rejection on the new ground it has determined.[300]

If the Board determines that the patent claim should be granted in amended form, that decision is binding on the examiner and the applicant is allowed to amend his or her application accordingly, unless the examiner determines there are new grounds for rejection.[301]

If the Board issues an unfavorable decision, the appellant may make one request for reconsideration.[302]

(xvi) Issuance of Patent. If the PTO determines that all requirements for a patent have been met, it sends written notice to the applicant, including a statement of the amount of the issue fee required to be paid within three months.[303] If the applicant does not pay the required amount within that time, the application will be considered abandoned.[304] The patent may also be issued to an assignee of record of the inventor.[305]

A letter patent is issued in the name of the United States, contains a short description of the patent, and states the term of 17 years. It describes the owner's "right to exclude others from making, using, or selling the invention throughout the United States," or, if it is a process, the right to prevent others from using the process or from importing goods made by that process.[306] The specification and drawings are attached and are a part of the patent.[307]

The normal term of 17 years may be extended for the period of time during which a product or process was subject to review under the Federal Food, Drug, and Cosmetic Act and could not be exploited, up to a limit of 5 years in specified circumstances.[308]

(xvii) Judicial Review of Decisions of the Board of Patent Appeals and Interferences. There are two ways in which judicial review of decisions of the Board of Patent Appeals and Interferences may be obtained—either in the Federal Circuit court of appeals on the administrative record before the Board, or in a trial de novo, that is, on the basis of the evidence introduced at trial in a United States district court.[309]

Any appeal is taken to the United States Court of Appeals for the Federal Circuit by giving notice of appeal to the Commissioner and filing a statement of reasons with the Patent and Trademark Office.[310]

An appeal to the Federal Circuit may be taken by the patent applicant or by any party to an interference proceeding.[311] If there has been an interference proceeding and one party appeals to the Federal Circuit, an adverse party in the proceeding may elect to have

---

[299] 37 C.F.R. § 1.196(b) (1).
[300] 37 C.F.R. § 1.196(b) (2).
[301] 37 C.F.R. § 1.196(c).
[302] 37 C.F.R. § 1.197(b).
[303] 35 U.S.C. § 151.
[304] Id.
[305] Id.
[306] 35 U.S.C. § 154.
[307] Id.
[308] 35 U.S.C. §§ 155 and 156(g) (6).
[309] 35 U.S.C. §§ 141 and 145.
[310] 35 U.S.C. §§ 141 and 142.
[311] 35 U.S.C. § 141.

the case tried de novo in a district court by giving notice to the Commissioner within 20 days of the filing of a notice of appeal to the Federal Circuit.[312]

(xviii) Marking Products with Notice of Patent. It is not mandatory that a notice of patent be included on products protected by a patent.[313] However, proper notice *should* be given in virtually all cases. Failure to give notice can significantly reduce the damages that can be recovered in the event of patent infringement.[314] An appropriate notice consists of the word "Patent" or "Pat." followed by the patent number, either on the article itself or on its packaging.

Failure to include notice of patent protection on the product means that the patent owner can recover damages for patent infringement only for the period *beginning* when the infringer is put on notice of infringement and lasting as long as the infringement continues.[315] Thus, appropriate notice of patent rights should always be included on a product or its packaging.

(e) Semiconductor Chip Protection Act. The Semiconductor Chip Protection Act of 1984 (the Chip Act) was enacted by Congress to protect circuit designs and provide for reciprocity with other countries affording similar protection.[316] Only a brief description of the statute is included here, because it is so similar in structure to the Copyright Act and because it applies to a single industry only, although an extremely important one.

This special statute was enacted because not all aspects of chip design were fully protectable under other intellectual property regimes. However, it is possible for different aspects of a single chip to be protected by the Copyright Act and the Patent Act, as well as by the Chip Act.

The Chip Act is structured much like the Copyright Act, and registrations under the Chip Act are administered by the Register of Copyrights.[317] The Act protects the "mask work," which is "fixed or encoded" in a semiconductor chip product.[318] Mask works are called "layout designs" or "topographies" in some countries.

A mask work is defined in the Act as

A series of related images, however fixed or encoded—
   (A) having or representing the predetermined, three-dimensional pattern of metallic, insulating, or semiconductor material present or removed from the layers of a semiconductor chip product; and
   (B) in which series the relation of the images to one another is that each image has the pattern of the surface of one form of the semiconductor chip product.[319]

A recent Federal Circuit decision involving a claim of infringement under the Chip Act describes mask works in more concrete terms:

Chip design layouts embody the selection and configuration of electrical components and connections in order to achieve the desired electronic functions. The electrical elements are configured in

---

[312] Id.
[313] 35 U.S.C. § 286(a).
[314] Id.
[315] 35 U.S.C. § 287(a).
[316] 17 U.S.C. §§ 901–914.
[317] 17 U.S.C. § 908.
[318] 17 U.S.C. §§ 901, 902.
[319] 17 U.S.C. § 901(a)(2).

three dimensions, and are built up in layers by means of a series of "masks" whereby, using photographic depositing and etching techniques, layers of metallic, insulating, and semiconductor material are deposited in the desired pattern on a wafer of silicon. This set of masks is called a "mask work," and is part of the semiconductor chip product.[320]

In addition to meeting these requirements, a certain level of originality, beyond that which is commonplace in the industry, is required in order to register a work.[321]

As under the other intellectual property regimes, the owner of a mask work is given certain exclusive rights, including the rights to reproduce the mask work and to import or distribute the chips in which the mask work is contained.[322] These exclusive rights can be enforced by actions for infringement, as under the Copyright Act, Lanham Act, and Patent Act.

"Reverse engineering" on mask work or chips is an express defense to a charge of infringement under the Chip Act.[323] Thus, another person can attempt to work backward from the functioning of a protected chip and mask work in order to duplicate it, as long as the protected work is not simply copied and thus infringed.

> In performing reverse engineering a person may disassemble, study, and analyze an existing chip in order to understand it. This knowledge may be used to create an original chip having a different design layout, but which performs the same or equivalent function as the existing chip, without penalty or prohibition. Congress was told by industry representatives that reverse engineering was an accepted and fair practice, and leads to improved chips having "form, fit, and function compatibility with the existing chip, thereby serving competition while advancing the state of technology.[324]

Remedies for infringement of rights protected under the Act, which can be substantial, include damages, profits, costs, and attorney's fees.[325] Remedies are discussed in more detail in section 5.2, later in this chapter.

(f) Trade Secrets. Trade secrets of a business can be protected under the laws of the individual states of the United States. There is no federal statutory law that defines and protects trade secrets as such.[326] However, more than 30 states have enacted the Uniform

---

[320] *Brooktree Corp.*, 977 F.2d at 1561.

[321] 17 U.S.C. § 902(b).

[322] 17 U.S.C. § 905.

[323] 17 U.S.C. § 906(a).

[324] *Brooktree*, 977 F.2d at 1565.

[325] A jury award of $25 million in damages for infringement of a mask work protected under the Chip Act, and patents, was upheld by the Federal Circuit, rejecting a claim of legitimate reverse engineering. Brooktree, 977 F.2d at 1565. See *Sega Enterprises Ltd. v. Accolade, Inc.*, 758 F. Supp. 1392 (N.D. Cal. 1992) (preliminary injunction against copyright infringement by U.S. company which claimed it had "reversed engineered" new software for Japanese video entertainment system).

[326] Any disclosure of trade secrets required in federal litigation or in various administrative proceedings can be restricted by protective orders, under appropriate circumstances. See, e.g., 19 U.S.C. § 1333(h) (U.S. International Trade Commission can issue administrative protective orders in connection with its proceedings); F.R.Civ.P. 26(c)(7) (trade secrets can be protected in discovery proceedings in federal court). Further, "trade secrets and commercial or financial information obtained [by any government agency] from a person [which is] privileged or confidential" cannot be disclosed to the public by federal agencies under the Freedom of Information Act, 5 U.S.C. § 552(b)(4).

Trade Secrets Act (the Trade Secrets Act); thus, the laws in those states are very similar or identical.[327]

The Uniform Trade Secrets Act defines a trade secret as follows:

"Trade secret" means information, including a formula, pattern, compilation, program, device, method, technique, or process, that:

(i) derives independent economic value, actual or potential, from not being generally known to, and not being readily ascertainable by proper means by, other persons who can obtain economic value from its disclosure or use, and

(ii) is the subject of efforts that are reasonable under the circumstances to maintain its secrecy.[328]

The United States Court of Appeals for the Second Circuit in New York has described the definition of trade secrets in the *Restatement of Torts* § 757, comment b (1939), as "the most comprehensive and influential."[329] That *Restatement* comment defines the term as follows:

A trade secret may consist of any formula, pattern, device or compilation of information which is used in one's business, and which gives him an opportunity to obtain an advantage over competitors who do not know or use it.

The range of information and objects that can be the subject of trade secret protection is extremely broad. A trade secret can be as simple an item as a company's customer list or as complex as a formula for a product or a manufacturing process.[330] Somewhere in between, but protectable as a trade secret, may be the particular manner of interaction between different components of a computer software program.[331]

It is not necessary that trade secrets be protectable under any of the other statutory intellectual property schemes, such as those for copyrights or patents. In fact, trade secrets often cannot satisfy the requirements for other forms of protection.

The criteria for determining whether certain information constitutes a trade secret under New York law are as follows:

(1) The extent to which the information is known outside of his business; (2) the extent to which it is known by employees and others involved in his business; (3) the extent of measures taken by him to guard the secrecy of the information; (4) the value of the information to him and to his competitors; (5) the ease or difficulty with which the information could be properly acquired or duplicated by others.[332]

---

[327] The Uniform Trade Secrets Act was adopted by the National Conference of Commissioners on Uniform State Law, a private organization that had developed and issued a number of proposed laws that it encourages the states to adopt in order to establish more uniformity in the laws of the states. A well-known treatise on trade secrets is R. Milgrim, *Milgrim on Trade Secrets* (1990).

[328] Uniform Trade Secrets Act § 1(4).

[329] *Integrated Cash Management Services, Inc. v. Digital Transactions, Inc.*, 920 F.2d 171, 173 (2d Cir. 1990) (citation omitted). The *Restatement of Torts* is one of many restatements of different areas of the law issued by the private American Law Institute since the 1930s. They are widely relied upon by the courts in the absence of or in addition to precedential court decisions.

[330] See, e.g., *A.F.A. Tours, Inc. v. Whitchurch*, 937 F.2d 82 (2d Cir. 1991); *Defiance Button Machine Co. v. C & C Metal Products Corp.*, 759 F.2d 1053, 1063 (2d Cir.), *cert. denied*, 474 U.S. 844 (1985) (customer lists protected as trade secrets).

[331] *Integrated Cash Management*, 920 F.2d at 173–174.

[332] Id. at 173 (citation omitted).

Clearly, all information used in a business cannot qualify as a trade secret. Thus, one court rejected a trade secrets claim of an individual who worked as an independent corporate acquisition "finder," who sought to protect information he provided about the availability and attractiveness of a particular company for acquisition by a larger company. The court reached this conclusion for the simple reason that the finder "had no control over . . . disclosure" of the information inasmuch as he had obtained the information from the company itself, which was, of course, free to tell others, even if there was something distinctive about the finder's presentation or analysis.[333]

There are distinct advantages to protecting proprietary business information as trade secrets, rather than seeking a patent, for example. If properly protected, trade secrets can be exploited exclusively for an indefinite period of time. In contrast, patents and copyrights have limited terms of exclusive rights and require public disclosure of the information.

Thus, trade secrets may be the most appropriate form of protection for much proprietary business information. Moreover, a company's trade secrets may sometimes be its most valuable asset. One obvious example is the closely guarded secret formula for Coca-Cola, particularly when combined with its famous trademark.

Inevitably, trade secrets will be revealed to at least a few employees of a company in the course of their employment, whether through using customer lists, in dealing with customers and suppliers, or in manufacturing products. Trade secrets can be protected from disclosure by employees by requiring them to sign agreements not to disclose trade secrets during or after their employment. A duty not to disclose may also be inferred from the circumstances, although it is generally preferable to have such an agreement in writing.

There are a variety of judicial remedies available to the owner of a trade secret who believes it has been improperly disclosed or used. The Trade Secrets Act specifically provides for injunctions against actual or threatened improper use of trade secrets.[334] Under special circumstances, injunctions may require that continued use of a trade secret be coupled with payment of a reasonable royalty.[335]

Damages can also be recovered under the Trade Secrets Act to compensate an owner of a trade secret for misappropriation, including recovery of both actual losses by the owner "and the unjust enrichment caused by misappropriation that is not taken into account in computing actual loss."[336] Punitive damages can be awarded for "willful and malicious appropriation" up to double the amount of actual damages.[337]

Several recent cases illustrate the significance of trade secrets and the available judicial remedies. In *Integrated Cash Management*, the plaintiff seeking to protect its trade secrets was a computer software company with a successful combination of integrated computer utility programs. Several former employees and a consultant terminated their relationships with the plaintiff and immediately started working with a competitor.[338] The competitor soon produced and began to sell a remarkably similar product. The plaintiff company had spent millions of dollars in developing its product, and the former employees and consultant had signed agreements not to disclose confidential or proprietary information when they left their employment with the plaintiff. Based on the facts

---

[333] *Lehman v. Dow Jones & Co., Inc.*, 783 F.2d 285, 299 (2d Cir. 1986).
[334] Trade Secrets Act § 2(a).
[335] Id. at § 2(b).
[336] Id. at § 3(a).
[337] Id. at § 3(b).
[338] *Integrated Cash Management*, 920 F.2d at 173–174.

presented at trial, the court ruled that the defendants had misappropriated the plaintiff's trade secrets and granted injunctive relief.

The court stated the following requirements for establishing misappropriation of a trade secret:

> A plaintiff . . . must prove: "(1) it possessed a trade secret, and (2) defendant is using that trade secret in breach of an agreement, confidence, or duty, or as a result of discovery by improper means."[339]

The court held that the particular way in which the utility programs were integrated and worked together was a trade secret and that the defendants had breached their agreements not to reveal or use them. Injunctions were issued against the new employer of the individuals who had developed the new program, which permanently prevented its sale. The individuals were barred from working on any comparable product for their new employer for six months.[340]

In another case, a travel agency sought an injunction, as well as actual and punitive damages, against a former employee who had led tours for it for some 17 years, for using confidential customer lists and tour information in a competing business.[341] The former employee had no written agreement and claimed that the lists and information had been freely disseminated. The trial court had dismissed the case on jurisdictional grounds, but the appellate court ruled that jurisdiction was present and that a trial was necessary because the former employer claimed that the lists were marked confidential when distributed to hotels for preregistration of tour customers and were never sold or traded to others. The court noted that the measure of the plaintiff's damages would be its losses resulting from the misappropriation "or by the profits unjustly received by the defendant."[342]

Many businesses have information that qualifies as trade secrets wholly apart from other forms of intellectual property. Appropriate steps should be taken to ensure that such information is properly protected against unauthorized dissemination and that appropriate judicial remedies will be available in the event of misappropriation by others.

5.2 JUDICIAL REMEDIES FOR INFRINGEMENT OF INTELLECTUAL PROPERTY RIGHTS

Each statutory intellectual property scheme—whether for copyrights, trademarks, patents, or silicon chips—contains a wide range of effective judicial remedies for protection of owners of intellectual property rights.[343] The remedies in these various schemes are quite similar, though not identical. The appropriate act must be consulted to determine the available remedies for a particular claim. For purposes of this survey, the various types of remedies are explained, together with examples of their use in particular cases.

(a) Injunctive Relief. Each act provides for various types of injunctive orders that a court can issue to prevent the alleged or confirmed infringer from committing acts of infringe-

---

[339] Id. at 173.

[340] Id. at 173.

[341] *A.F.A. Tours, Inc. v. Whitchurch*, 937 F.2d 82 (2d Cir. 1991).

[342] Id. at 87.

[343] Copyright Act, 17 U.S.C. § 501 ff.; Lanham Act, 15 U.S.C. § 1111 ff.; Patent Act, 35 U.S.C. § 281 ff.

ment in the present or in the future.[344] These include temporary restraining orders and preliminary and permanent injunctions. The remedies of a temporary restraining order and preliminary and permanent injunctions are generally available in civil actions in United States district courts under the Federal Rules of Civil Procedure.[345] A temporary restraining order can be obtained for a period of up to 10 days (renewable for an additional 10 days), without prior notice to the party to be restrained or to the party's attorney, upon a showing that it is necessary to prevent irreparable harm that would result from the delay required for notice and an opportunity to be heard.[346] A preliminary injunction, however, can be issued only after notice to the adverse party and a hearing on the request for an injunction can be consolidated with a hearing on the merits of the case.[347] Injunctive relief can be obtained when monetary damages cannot provide a fully adequate remedy, which is often the case. The party seeking a temporary restraining order or preliminary injunction must provide security to protect the adverse party from injury resulting from a wrongful order or injunction, that is, one ultimately found to be without merit.[348] Both injunctive and monetary relief may be obtained in an appropriate case.

(b) Actual Damages and Lost Profits.   Various remedies provide for an award of damages to the owner of intellectual property rights as monetary compensation for the infringement of protected rights. These include recovery of the owner's actual damages resulting from the infringement, including lost profits, and the right to recover the infringer's profits resulting from the acts of infringement.[349]

Congress has provided procedural devices intended to make it easier for the owner of rights to obtain monetary compensation. Thus, in order to recover the infringer's profits, the owner needs only to prove the infringer's gross profits; then the burden shifts to the infringer to prove the amount of costs and expenses that can be deducted from the gross profits.

(c) Statutory or Enhanced Damages.   The owner of infringed copyrights may choose to recover statutory damages, as an alternative to proving actual damages. The exact amount of statutory damages is determined by the discretion of the court within maximum and minimum limits set by Congress.[350] Other schemes give courts authority to enhance actual damages where counterfeiting or other circumstances make it appropriate.[351]

(d) Impoundment of Infringing Goods and Manufacturing Equipment.   Several of the acts provide specific remedies designed to remove infringing goods from the marketplace and

---

[344] Copyright Act, 17 U.S.C. § 502; Lanham Act, 15 U.S.C. § 1116(a); Patent Act, 35 U.S.C. § 283.

[345] F.R.Civ.P. 65.

[346] F.R.Civ.P. 65(b).

[347] F.R.Civ.P. 65(a).

[348] F.R.Civ.P. 65(c).

[349] Copyright Act, 17 U.S.C. § 504(a) and (b); Lanham Act, 15 U.S.C. § 1117; Patent Act, 35 U.S.C. § 284 (adequate damages required; not less than a reasonable royalty for use of patent plus interest).

[350] Copyright Act, 17 U.S.C. § 504(c) (statutory damages of $500–$20,000 per ordinary infringement; up to maximum of $100,000 per willful infringement; minimum of $200 per unintentional infringement; damages can be remitted where infringer had reasonable belief that infringing use was a fair use).

[351] Lanham Act, 15 U.S.C. § 1117(a) and (b); Patent Act, 35 U.S.C. § 284 (court may treble actual damages found).

prevent their further manufacture, either temporarily or permanently. Thus a court may, on a proper showing, order that goods, such as copies or records that are alleged to infringe copyrights, as well as goods used to manufacture them, be impounded pending a final determination of the merits of the claim. If a final judgment or decree of infringement is entered, the court can order these goods to be destroyed or otherwise disposed of.[352]

(e) Costs and Attorney's Fees. The acts generally provide for the recovery of specified items of costs.[353] The circumstances under which reasonable attorney's fees may be awarded to the prevailing party vary, depending on the particular language of the pertinent act. Under the Copyright Act, attorney's fees are almost routinely awarded to the prevailing party.[354] The Supreme Court recently held that a prevailing defendant in a copyright infringement case is to be considered eligible for a discretionary award of attorney's fees under the same standard as a prevailing plaintiff, rejecting the dual standard previously applied by some courts.[355] However, under the Lanham Act and the Patent Act, Congress has provided that attorney's fees may be awarded only "in exceptional cases," and fees under these acts are therefore not routinely awarded to the prevailing party.[356]

(f) Criminal Remedies. Congress has also made it a federal crime to infringe specified intellectual property rights under certain conditions, either in the specific intellectual property acts or in the federal criminal code. For example, "any person who infringes a copyright willfully and for purposes of commercial advantage or private financial gain" can be fined up to $250,000 and imprisoned for up to five years.[357] The same penalties can be imposed upon anyone who "knowingly traffics in a counterfeit label affixed or designed to be affixed to a phonorecord, or a copy of a motion picture or other audiovisual work."[358] A similar criminal penalty applies to anyone who "intentionally traffic[s] or attempt[s] to traffic in goods or services and knowingly use[s] a counterfeit mark on or in connection with such goods or services."[359] These criminal provisions also permit forfeiture and destruction or other disposition of infringing goods and, for counterfeited copyrights, related manufacturing equipment.[360] The Copyright Act, among others, provides that the customs laws governing seizure and forfeiture "of vessels, vehicles, merchandise, and baggage" shall also apply to cases of copyright infringement as well.[361] Similarly, compensation can be awarded to informers in connection with such forfeitures.[362]

---

[352] Copyright Act, 17 U.S.C. § 503; see also Lanham Act, 15 U.S.C. § 1118.

[353] Copyright Act, 17 U.S.C. § 505; Lanham Act, 15 U.S.C. § 1117(a). There is no specific provision in the Patent Act for an award of costs, but costs are generally "taxed against the losing party" in federal litigation under F.R.Civ.P. 76(c).

[354] Copyright Act, 17 U.S.C. § 505 ("the court may also award a reasonable attorney's fee to the prevailing party as part of the costs").

[355] *Fogarty v. Fantasy, Inc.*, 114 S. Ct. 1023 (1994).

[356] Lanham Act, 15 U.S.C. § 1117(a); Patent Act, 35 U.S.C. § 285.

[357] 17 U.S.C. § 506(a).

[358] 18 U.S.C. § 2318(a).

[359] 18 U.S.C. § 2320.

[360] 18 U.S.C. §§ 2318(d) and 2320(b).

[361] 17 U.S.C. § 509(b).

[362] Id.

The Patent Act includes a criminal penalty of $500 per violation for a variety of offenses relating to goods or advertising, counterfeiting or imitating patent marks, patent numbers, and false or misleading representations regarding patents or patent applications.[363] This provision has a private enforcement remedy: "Any person may sue for the penalty, in which event one-half shall go to the person suing and the other to the use of the United States".[364] It is also a crime to forge or counterfeit letters patent or pass such documents as genuine.[365]

(g) Examples of Civil Remedies in Litigation. A few recent cases illustrate the range of civil remedies available for infringement of intellectual property rights.

In *Rogers v. Koons* (previously mentioned under "Copyrights" in this Chapter), the visual artist Jeff Koons, known as a painter and sculptor (among other things), purchased a copyrighted postcard photograph in a gift shop, which portrayed a couple holding a litter of eight German shepherd puppies; the photograph was made by professional photographer Art Rogers.[366] Koons tore the copyright mark off of the photograph and sent it to an Italian studio, which carved four life-size sculptures called *String of Puppies* based on the photograph. As work on the sculptures progressed, Koons repeatedly urged the Italian workers to make the sculpture look more like Rogers' photograph. Three of the four sculptures were sold for a total of $367,000, and the fourth was still being exhibited at the time of the lawsuit.

Rogers learned of the sculptures by chance and sued Koons and his New York City art gallery for copyright infringement. The trial court granted summary judgment for Rogers, finding that Koons' infringement of the copyrighted photograph was willful and in bad faith.[367] The amount of damages was not specifically determined. However, the court of appeals stated that on remand, the trial court should determine the amount of the photographer's actual damages, which could be measured by Koons's profits. Rogers proved that Koons' gross profits for sale of three of the infringing sculptures had been $367,000, and the burden then shifted to Koons to prove his deductible expenses and to attempt to prove that part of the sale price of the sculptures was attributable to his reputation and concomitantly high prices, rather than to the infringement, a recognized legal principle.[368] The court of appeals also noted that Rogers could still elect to have the trial court determine statutory damages, instead of seeking actual damages. The court of appeals also stated that, "given Koons' willful and egregious behavior, we think Rogers may be a good candidate for enhanced statutory damages pursuant to 17 U.S.C.

---

[363] Patent Act, 35 U.S.C. § 292.

[364] Id. at § 292(b). This is called a *qui tam* remedy. *Boyd v. Schildkraut Giftware Corp.*, 936 F.2d 76, 79 (2d Cir.), *cert. denied*, 112 S.Ct. 378 (1991).

[365] 18 U.S.C. § 497. It may possibly be useful to know that there is a short list of federally protected objects, characters, names, and slogans, including "Smokey the Bear," "Woodsy Owl," "Give a Hoot, Don't Pollute"; the design of a federally approved military cremation urn; likenesses of various federal seals, including that of the United States, the president and vice president; the Golden Eagle Insignia; and marks and goods protected under the Olympic Charter Act. 18 U.S.C. §§ 710–715, and 2320(d) (1) (B).

[366] 960 F.2d 301 (2d Cir.), *cert. denied*, 113 S.Ct. 365 (1992).

[367] The trial court rejected all of Koons' defenses, including the claim that he had not "copied" the photographic work, only the idea; and that Koons' use was a fair use, within the meaning of copyright law, because his sculpture was parody or satire. Id. at 307–312.

[368] Id. at 313.

§ 504(c)(2)," the provision that allows statutory damages up to $100,000 per violation for willful infringement.[369]

Finally, the court of appeals upheld the district court's order that Koons turn over the fourth unsold sculpture (as authorized by the Copyright Act) to Rogers. Incredible as it may seem, Koons had disobeyed the permanent injunction requiring him to turn over the sculpture and had shipped it to a gallery in Germany. The court of appeals upheld the finding that Koons was in contempt of court for ignoring the turnover order. The gallery, as well as Koons, was found liable for infringing profits.[370]

Another recent copyright case illustrates the effective use of a class action of the statutory damages remedy in a suit against a record company.[371] The plaintiffs were owners of the copyrights in various musical compositions that had already been recorded. They were thus subject to the compulsory license provisions in the Copyright Act that allows others to record the same songs, either upon compliance with the statutory compulsory license provision or upon obtaining a negotiated license from the copyright holders or their agents.[372] In this case, Pausa Records obtained negotiated licenses from the Harry Fox Agency (an agency that represents numerous copyright owners for this purpose).

The Harry Fox licenses provided for quarterly accounting and payment of royalties and stipulated that the licenses could be terminated upon 30 days' notice for failure to account and pay royalties, and that further use of the copyrighted works thereafter would constitute acts of infringement. The record company failed to pay, and a notice of termination was given. The court granted summary judgment in favor of the copyright owners, finding 80 acts of infringement. The court also imposed the then-maximum statutory penalty for willful infringement of $50,000 per infringement, resulting in a total award of $4,000,000. The proof of willfulness was surprisingly simple and was decided on summary judgment; the court found that "Pausa's conduct in ignoring the revocation was unreasonable, and that its further use of the plaintiff's copyrighted works thereafter was willful as a matter of law within the meaning of section 504(c)(2) [of the Copyright Act]."[373]

A third case, involving semiconductor chips, illustrates various remedies available for patent infringement and mask work infringement under the Semiconductor Chip Protection Act, and the discretion of the trial court in deciding whether to enhance damages for willful infringement and whether to award attorney's fees.[374]

Brooktree designs, manufactures, and sells semiconductor chips used for computer graphics displays. Advanced Micro Devices, which was found to have infringed Brooktree's product, is one of the five largest chip manufacturers in the United States and, at the time, had sales some 30 times greater than Brooktree's.

A jury found that Advanced Micro had willfully infringed Brooktree's patent and its registered chip mask works; the jury awarded damages of more than $25,000,000, after a seven-week trial. Despite the finding of willful patent infringement, the trial court denied

---

[369] Id.

[370] Id. at 306.

[371] *Peer International Corp. v. Pausa Records, Inc.*, 909 F.2d 1332 (9th Cir. 1990), *cert. denied*, 498 U.S. 1109 (1991).

[372] 17 U.S.C. § 115.

[373] *Pausa Records*, 909 F.2d at 1336.

[374] *Brooktree Corp., supra.*

Brooktree's request for enhanced damages and attorney's fees, both of which are permitted, but not required under the Patent Act, and the Federal Circuit affirmed.[375]

The court of appeals held that the district court did not abuse its discretion by concluding that the evidence of willfulness was not strong and that enhanced damages and attorney's fees were not warranted.[376] The Federal Circuit also affirmed denial of attorney's fees under the Semiconductor Chip Protection Act, even though it recognized that it was modeled on the Copyright Act and that fees generally *are* awarded to the prevailing plaintiff under that Act. Nevertheless, the court affirmed the trial court's denial of fees, primarily because this was a case which presented new and difficult legal issues, which Advanced Micro defended in good faith.[377]

Thus, although the courts have very powerful remedies available to protect intellectual property rights, they also have wide discretion in determining when and how to employ these remedies.

5.3 CUSTOMS SERVICE EXCLUSION OF GOODS THAT INFRINGE U.S.-BASED INTELLECTUAL PROPERTY RIGHTS

It might not be apparent from a stroll down Fifth Avenue near Tiffany's or a walk along the bazaar of Canal Street in Manhattan, but the United States Customs Service has power under the Tariff Act of 1930 and various intellectual property laws to prevent the importation into the United States of merchandise that would infringe the rights of owners of trademarks, copyrights, and mask works in the United States and to prevent the entry of counterfeit or pirated goods. Importation or sale of goods that were made by a process patented in the United States are also acts of patent infringement, in the absence of authorization from the patent owner.

This scheme is intended to protect the rights of owners of intellectual property *in* the United States. Thus, except for goods brought in for personal use, the Tariff Act provides that:

> It shall be unlawful to import into the United States any merchandise of foreign manufacture if such merchandise, or the label, sign, print, package, wrapper, or receptacle, bears a trademark owned by a citizen of, or by a corporation or association created or organized within the United States, and registered in the Patent and Trademark Office *by a person domiciled in the United States* . . . if a copy of the certificate of registration of such trademark is filed with [the Customs Service], . . . unless written consent of the owner of such trademark is produced at the time of entry.[378]

Section 42 of the Lanham Act also makes it unlawful to import trademarked goods without the consent of the U.S. owner of the trademark, under specified circumstances.[379]

The Copyright Act has various provisions intended to protect owners of U.S. copyrights from importation of infringing or unauthorized copies or phonorecords.[380] As with trademarks, the owners of U.S. copyrights can notify the Customs Service, as well as the

---

[375] Id., 977 F.2d at 1581–1582.
[376] Id.
[377] Id., 977 F.2d at 1582–1583.
[378] 19 U.S.C. § 1526 (author's emphasis).
[379] 15 U.S.C. § 1124.
[380] 19 U.S.C. §§ 602 and 603.

Postal Service, of their rights and have infringing or unauthorized goods denied entry into the United States. The owners may, however, be required to first obtain a court order.[381]

Another provision of the Copyright Act forbids the importation and distribution of nondramatic literary material in the English language by an author who is a national or domiciliary of the United States, unless it was manufactured in the United States or Canada (with specified exceptions and conditions).[382] This provision has been upheld as legitimate economic protection for the printing industry against various constitutional challenges under the First and Fifth Amendments.[383] Essentially identical protection from imports is available for mask works under the Semiconductor Chip Protection Act.[384]

The Tariff Act allows the owners of trademarks registered in the United States Patent and Trademark Office to prevent, under some circumstances, the importation into the United States of goods with identical marks.[385] This provision may also apply to exclude some "gray market" goods under some circumstances. The Supreme Court has defined a gray-market good as "a foreign-manufactured good, bearing a valid United States trademark, that is imported without the consent of the United States trademark owner."[386] Where a foreign trademark owner has sold the rights to import and sell such trademarked goods in the United States to an independent U.S.-based company, gray-market goods can be excluded.

The Customs Service has detailed regulations implementing these provisions.[387] Section 133.2 of the Customs Service Regulations specifies the contents of the application. Section 133.21 describes the circumstances under which gray-market imports can be excluded.

The gist of this rule is that, generally, U.S. retailers can acquire bona fide trademarked goods abroad from sources other than authorized dealers, import them into the United States, and sell them in competition with the identical goods sold in the United States by importers who acquire the goods from authorized dealers, *if* they are not owned or controlled by the foreign trademark owner.[388]

Many discount retailers, such as Kmart and 47th Street Photo, were parties in U.S. Supreme Court cases involving various challenges to the Customs Service's common ownership regulations. The U.S. Supreme Court, in large part, upheld the validity of the Customs Service's regulations. The Court's decision described various import arrangements, some of which permitted exclusion of gray-market goods and others which did not, under the regulations.[389]

The Supreme Court upheld two of the Customs Service's regulations under which a U.S.-based trademark owner cannot exclude gray-market goods. In the first scenario, gray market goods cannot be excluded where the foreign and U.S.-based trademarks are owned by the same company. In the second, the goods cannot be excluded where the foreign and domestic marks are owned by companies which are parent and subsidiary

---

[381] Id. at § 603(b) (1).

[382] 19 U.S.C. § 601.

[383] *Authors League of America, Inc. v. Oman*, 790 F.2d 220 (2d Cir. 1986).

[384] 19 U.S.C. § 910(c).

[385] 19 U.S.C. § 1527.

[386] *Kmart Corp. v. Cartier, Inc.*, 486 U.S. 281, 285 (1988).

[387] 19 C.F.R. Part 133.

[388] 19 C.F.R. § 133.21 (c) (1) and (2).

[389] *Kmart Corp.*, 486 U.S. at 285. This decision was based solely on the Court's analysis of the Tariff Act provision, 19 U.S.C. § 1526, and did not involve construction of the Lanham Act.

companies or are subject to "common ownership and common control."[390] However, in the third situation, the Court held that gray market goods could be excluded if they were manufactured abroad under a license form the U.S.-based trademark owner; the Court invalidated a Customs Service regulation which had not allowed exclusion of gray market goods in this scenario.[391]

However, The Custom Service's common ownership regulations have been held *not* to apply in preventing a U.S. owner of certain trademarks to exclude importation of goods with identical marks made abroad by a related company, where it was demonstrated that the domestic and imported goods were not in fact identical. Thus, Lever Brothers was able to prevent the importation of British versions of two of its popular products, Shield soap and Sunlight dishwashing detergent. Although the marks and logos of the foreign and domestic products were essentially identical, and the U.S. and British companies were related, the court found that the formulations of the products were designed to meet the peculiarities of the different markets and were not in fact identical products. Thus, the U.S. Lever Brothers Compnay was held entitled to exclude the gray-market goods.[392]

A similar scheme of exclusion by the Customs Service applies to copyrighted works.[393] The U.S. Chip Act also provides for exclusion of allegedly infringing mask works and chips by the Customs Service, the Postal Service, court order, or an order of the International Trade Commission under § 337 of the Tariff Act, 19 U.S.C. § 1337.[394]

5.4 CLEARING INTELLECTUAL PROPERTY RIGHTS

It is particularly important to investigate possible existing rights in a trademark or trade name, possible copyrights, or patents before making a substantial business investment in creating, using, or acquiring intellectual property. This inquiry is comparable to the necessity of a title search when dealing in real estate. The expense and possible delay entailed is usually well worth the investment and may be essential to ensure that rights can be lawfully created or acquired. In some circumstances, it may also be a requirement to obtain insurance to protect against adverse claims.

The Patent and Trademark Office and the Copyright Office have vast public records available to search and will also conduct a search and provide copies of documents on file. The charges for their services and copies are generally reasonable, but the process is relatively slow, often taking six to eight weeks or more to respond to a simple request.

Various private companies also provide extensive search and report services for intellectual property rights. They will search, prepare reports, and provide copies of relevant documents. They can also provide information from the appropriate offices of all of the states of the United States, where trademarks and trade names may be locally registered, as well as information on international intellectual property rights.

The services of these search companies are substantially more expensive than those available from the government offices, but their reports and the needed documents are available much sooner. Normal response time is usually within five business days, and for a price, of course, they can respond with expedited service, often on the same day they receive a request.

---

[390] 19 C.F.R. 133.21 (c) (1) and (2).

[391] Kmart Corp, supra, 486 U.S. at 288–289 and note 2.

[392] *Lever Bros. Co. v. United States*, 796 F. Supp. 1 (D. D.C. 1992), following preliminary analysis of court of appeals in prior appeal, id., 877 F.2d 101 (D.C. Cir. 1989).

[393] 19 C.F.R. Subparts D-F.

[394] 17 U.S.C. § 910.

Other sources and private agencies may be relevant to other aspects of intellectual property. For example, licenses to use copyrighted musical compositions in recordings and movies can often be obtained from organizations such as Broadcast Music, Inc. (BMI) the American Society of Composers, Authors and Publishers (ASCAP), and the Harry Fox Agency, which represent numerous artists or copyright owners and are authorized to enter into licensing agreements on their behalf.

As with other aspects of these highly technical fields, competent advice and knowledge of the industry are essential in order to fully protect intellectual property rights and to avoid infringing the rights of others.

CHAPTER **6**

IMPERATIVE STRATEGIES FOR PROTECTING TRADEMARK ASSETS: THE INTERNATIONAL MARKET

Ian Jay Kaufman, Esq.

Ladas and Parry
New York, New York

6.1 NECESSITY OF TRADEMARK PROTECTION

Obtaining trademark protection outside the United States often involves significantly different factors than obtaining protection within the United States, primarily because trademark protection is still largely governed by national law. Where treaties exist, they are usually limited by geography or, to a great extent, ultimately cognizant of and dependent on the individual national laws of the member countries. Notwithstanding the modern drive toward "harmonization," that is, the effort to minimize the distinctions between national laws, the legal systems of the world fall primarily into two categories: common law and civil law.

The common law, one of the many legacies bestowed by the British Empire on those territories where "the sun never set," comprises the body of those principles and rules of action derived from custom, usage, and judicial decisions recognizing and enforcing the same, in contrast to those legal principles derived from legislation. The so-called beneficiaries of this legal tradition include the United States, Australia, South Africa, India, Hong Kong, and Israel.

The traditions of civil law date back to Roman times, from whence they spread to the European continent and were subsequently carried abroad on Spanish, French, and Portuguese ships of exploration and conquest. The emphasis of civil legal systems rests heavily on codified legislation, as opposed to precedents of judicial decision and custom.

The historical development of both legal traditions has resulted in such modern-day dichotomies as evident in Canada, where Quebec's civil-law tradition and culture exist side by side with those of the other provinces, and in the United States, where Louisiana has retained its civil-law system, notwithstanding the common-law tradition of the remaining 49 states.

The same dichotomy has presented challenges in modern efforts toward harmonization, an important example of which is illustrated in the European Community (EC) Directive to harmonize the trademark laws of the member states. EC members comprise

The author gratefully acknowledges the assistance of Bharati Bakshani, an associate at Ladas & Parry, in the research and preparation of this chapter.

both common-law and civil-law countries, and the Directive has, among other things, introduced the common-law concept of "acquiescence"[1] to civil-law countries.

Insofar as trademarks are concerned, the civil/common-law dichotomy may be summed up as follows: Common-law jurisdictions generally do not require registration of a trademark for a user of that mark to claim a proprietary right in the mark (although infringement actions almost always require registration). Civil-law jurisdictions, however, generally grant rights in a trademark only upon registration. The party who registers first, that is, "wins the race to the Register," obtains priority of the registration in the mark, although exceptions are generally made in cases of "well-known" marks or in obvious cases of bad faith.

Under both legal systems, registration is imperative for securing a monopoly to use a mark, as well as the rights to license, assign, or create a security interest in the mark.

6.2 SELECTION OF TRADEMARKS SUITABLE FOR INTERNATIONAL MARKETS

Companies that want to expand their horizons beyond their national borders by offering their products or services in foreign markets must, among the myriad of other international business decisions, consider the selection of their trademarks very carefully. Although use and registration of a slightly suggestive trademark for the home market may be desirable, the same mark may not be received favorably by foreign consumers and patent offices.

Distinctiveness is a basic requirement for registration of a trademark in many countries. However, some countries may permit registration of a mark which, albeit not currently distinctive or distinctive per se, may become distinctive when used over a number of years so as to create a sufficient reputation and recognizability by consumers. Marks that are only "capable of distinguishing" are usually more difficult and more costly to register. Some countries that follow British law even create a separate register for marks that are considered only "capable of distinguishing."[2]

The name of a company, individual, or firm may be registrable, although some countries may require the name to be presented in a special or particular manner or may not allow registration of such designations as "Inc." or "Co." This is very important when a company's name and primary trademark are the same (e.g., Kodak), in which case the mark is referred to as a "house mark." Brazil has even created a special procedure for registration of such marks. It is advisable to register such marks as commercial names in those countries in which it is possible to do so, thereby securing protection for a broader range of goods and services than a trademark registration will provide.

As to the selection of a trademark, it has been found that invented words constitute the best kind of trademarks in many respects. They are prima facie distinctive, and imitations

---

[1] *Black's Law Dictionary* defines *acquiescence* as "conduct recognizing the existence of a transaction, and intended in some extent at least, to carry the transaction, or permit it to be carried, into effect."

[2] See *Kerly's Law of Trade Marks and Trade Names* 12th ed., edited by T.A. Blanco White and Robin Jacob (London, Sweet & Maxwell: 1986), pp. 73, 127, for commentary on Parts A and B of the Register.

can be prevented easily. What constitutes an invented word may be a matter of some debate in certain trademark offices.[3] Although the presence of a word in a dictionary may be relevant to demonstrate that the word is not invented, its absence from the dictionary will not always be determinative of its invention. Mere combinations of words or slight variations in spelling or letter order may not be sufficient to qualify as inventions if the same idea would be conveyed to the consumer by the words in their ordinary form. The same may be said for phonetic equivalents or alternate spellings (e.g., *Lite* for *Light*).

Invented words may be coined in various ways. One way is to take the first letters of the words forming the applicant's trading name and join them with suitable vowels to constitute a pronounceable word. Another method is to add a suitable prefix or suffix to the descriptive word or delete certain letters from the word. A third method is to take two words, join them together, and then delete or add a few letters so as to make this innovation readable as a single word distinct from the original words. Whether the resulting word is really an invented word is a question of fact.[4]

If a mark is a geographical name, it may not qualify for registration. However, the mere fact that a proposed mark also denotes some location or geographical feature may not cause objection, unless it appears that the goods have some connection with that particular place. Thus "Southpole" could, in most jurisdictions, serve as an acceptable trademark for calculators. If the only significance of a word is a geographical one, the word is considered to be a geographical name in its ordinary significance.[5]

A surname may also be excluded from registration. However, if the mark is both a rare surname and an ordinary word with a specific meaning that is much more commonly known, the mark may be considered not to be objectionable.

Words that are clearly laudatory or descriptive do not qualify for registration.[6]

Pictorial or device marks—for example, representations of common objects such as animals—and graphic designs may constitute distinctive marks if the representation has no reference to the character or quality of the goods they identify. A device must contain some striking feature that will fix itself in the minds of consumers so as to enable them to remember the device and identify the goods bearing the mark (e.g., The Mercedes circle and spoke device). Device marks are particularly useful, either alone or with a word mark, in countries of low literacy where consumers may recognize a device more easily than a mere word mark.

---

[3] For example, *Sardovy*™ in re (1924) 41 R.P.C. 171. Sardovy was held to be invented and registration allowed in respect to a mixture of sardines and anchovies; *Dustic*™ in re (1955), 72 R.P.C. 151. Dustic, for industrial adhesives, was held to be invented. The objection that it was merely a misspelling of "does stick" and had a direct reference to the character and quality of goods was overruled. The word was derived from the first two letters of "Dundas," and the termination "stic" for "stick" was commonly used for adhesives.

[4] See P. Narayanan, *Trade Marks and Passing-off*, 3d ed. (Calcutta, Eastern Law House: 1981), p. 120.

[5] For example, *Livron*™ (1937), 54 R.P.C. 161. The word "Livron," originally registered as an invented word for tonic medicines, was canceled on the ground that at the time of registration it was a geographical name of a town in France where similar goods were manufactured.

[6] For example, *Orwoola*™ in re (1909), 26 RPC 837. The trademark Orwoola, registered in respect of "woolen material" with a disclaimer of the words "all wool," was expunged from the Register on the ground that the word was merely a combination of the words "all wool" misspelled. These words, being purely descriptive, were not adapted to distinguish woolen goods.

Ordinary letters and numerals may not be considered registrable, even though it may be common practice among traders to use their company initials. However, a monogram consisting of three or more letters may be considered registrable, particularly if it forms a pronounceable word.

Marks must not be offensive to morality. The use of "OPIUM" for perfume was initially considered scandalous but, nevertheless, was able to achieve acceptance in all but a very few jurisdictions. The outstanding, yet from a historical perspective understandable, failure in obtaining registration for the "OPIUM" mark was Hong Kong. In addition, a mark must not contain a negative connotation within a particular jurisdiction. For example, "Mist" may play well in English markets but means "manure" in German, and "Totes" is the phonetic equivalent of "dead" in German. Marks that are subject to ridicule can be disastrous.

6.3 INTERNATIONAL LICENSING AND ASSIGNMENT RECORDALS

(a) Recordal of Licenses.   The recording of license agreements is often an essential procedure in the licensing of an intellectual property right. The law of most civil-law jurisdictions provides for the independent recording of license agreements. The British Trademark Act of 1938 and the law of most countries following British law have adopted a special procedure—the Registered User Procedure. This Procedure requires the proprietor and licensee to file with the Registrar certain documents indicating the relationship of the parties and the terms and conditions of the license, particularly with respect to control exercised by the proprietor. On the basis of the facts disclosed, the Registrar will determine whether he or she will enter the licensee as a registered user of the trademark concerned. The Registered User Procedure also permits a registered user application to be filed simultaneously with a trademark application, based on the proposed use by the licensee.

In several civil-law and British-law countries licensing is recognized. Recordation is optional but advisable, as use of a trademark by a recorded licensee usually protects the validity of the trademark from attack by a third party, based on cancellation for nonuse.

(b) Recordal of Assignments.   An important requirement in connection with assignments is that the deed of assignment be recorded in the Trademark Office. It is generally provided that only a recorded assignment is valid, as against third parties. The effect of failure to record is that the unrecorded assignee cannot prevail against a third party who may have obtained a subsequent assignment of the same trademark, so long as the third party had no knowledge of the previous assignment. The recordal of an assignment is constructive notice as against a subsequent assignee.

In addition, it is possible for a company's competitor to begin using the same or a similar mark. The competitor may claim that because the assignment was not recorded, it was assumed that the unrecorded assignee was using the mark adversely to the owner of record in the Trademark Office, and that the latter acquiesced to such adverse use. The competitor may claim that, deducing that the owner had abandoned the mark, he or she could freely adopt the abandoned property.

The law of a number of countries considers the absence of recordal as likely to have these consequences and imposes an obligation on the assignee to record his or her assignment within a certain term. The legal consequences are that a late recording will be refused or, at least, sanctioned with the payment of fines.

The British Trade Marks Act of 1938 imposes an obligation on the assignee to register his or her title. The Registrar will then make such an entry on the Register.[7] Any person aggrieved by the failure or omission to make such an entry may petition to expunge the mark from the Register.[8] An assignment for which no entry has been made in the Register will not be admitted in evidence in any court as proof of title to a trademark, unless the court otherwise directs.[9] No time limit is fixed generally for the recordal of an assignment. However, if the assignment is made without the goodwill of the business, application for recording must be made within six months from the date the assignment is made, unless the Registrar grants an extension.

These provisions are generally applicable in all British-law countries. However, there are some civil-law countries in which the requirements are even stricter. For instance, in China (Taiwan) all assignments must be recorded within one year from the date of the deed of assignment.

6.4 INTERNATIONAL INTELLECTUAL PROPERTY TREATIES

(a) Background. Originally, trademark rights were severely limited in their geographical scope, inasmuch as each nation possessed its own law and practice independent of all others. Not until the late nineteenth century did nations consider cooperating in order to protect the rights of their nationals in neighboring countries. When these nations also recognized that the trademark rights afforded by their neighbors differed significantly from their own, the desire grew to ensure that nationals of one nation would not be greatly disadvantaged by the laws or practices of another nation. This desire formed the early roots of "harmonization" of intellectual property laws.

(b) Paris Convention. One of the most far-reaching examples of an attempt at uniform treatment of trademark owners and international trademark law, and creation of a multinational regime governing intellectual property rights, was the Paris Convention for the Protection of Industrial Property of March 20, 1883. The Paris Convention became effective on March 7, 1884. This Convention has undergone several revisions, the most recent being the Stockholm Amendment of July 14, 1967. Today, more than 100 countries are members of the Paris Convention.[10]

---

[7] U.K. Trade Marks Act, § 25.

[8] Id., § 32.

[9] Id., § 25.

[10] The following countries are Members of the Paris Convention as of January 1, 1993: Algeria, Argentina, Australia, Austria, Bahamas, Bangladesh, Barbados, Belgium, Benin, Brazil, Bulgaria, Burkina Faso, Burundi, Cameroon, Canada, Central African Republic, Chad, Chile, China, Congo, Cote D'Ivoire, Croatia, Cuba, Cyprus, Czech Republic, Democratic People's Republic of Korea, Denmark, Dominican Republic, Egypt, Finland, France, Gabon, Gambia, Germany, Ghana, Greece, Guinea, Guinea-Bissau, Haiti, Holy See, Hungary, Iceland, Indonesia, Iran (Islamic Republic of), Iraq, Ireland, Israel, Italy, Japan, Jordan, Kenya, Lebanon, Lesotho, Libya, Liechtenstein, Luxembourg, Madagascar, Malawi, Malaysia, Mali, Malta, Mauritania, Mauritius, Mexico, Monaco, Mongolia, Morocco, Netherlands, New Zealand, Niger, Nigeria, Norway, Philippines, Poland, Portugal, Republic of Korea, Romania, Russian Federation, Rwanda, San Marino, Senegal, Slovakia, Slovenia, South Africa, Spain, Sri Lanka, Sudan, Surinam, Swaziland, Sweden, Switzerland, Syria, Togo, Trinidad and Tobago, Tunisia, Turkey, Uganda, Ukraine, United Kingdom, United Republic of Tanzania, United States of America, Uruguay, Vietnam, Yugoslavia, Zaire, Zambia, and Zimbabwe.

(c) Other Treaties.   In addition to the Paris Convention, nations have adopted other treaties of a limited bilateral or multilateral nature. These include the treaty between France and Italy; the Benelux Treaty, which creates one registration covering the territories of Belgium, the Netherlands, and Luxembourg; and the OAPI arrangement,[11] which created one registration covering Cameroon, Central African Republic, Chad, Congo, Benin, Gabon, Guinea, Mali, Ivory Coast, Mauritania, Senegal, Togo, Burkina Faso, and Niger. Other conventions also harmonize laws and grant certain reciprocal rights, for example, the Pan American Convention of 1929, the Central American Convention, and the Decision of the Andean Pact Countries.

(d) The Madrid Agreement.   In 1891, the Madrid Agreement Concerning the International Registration of Marks arose out of the Paris Convention. The Madrid Agreement is a special arrangement under the Paris Convention, and only countries party to the Paris Convention join the Madrid Agreement. The Agreement entered into force in 1892 with only five member countries: France, Spain, Switzerland, Tunisia, and Belgium. Today, more than 100 years later, 33 countries[12] are members of the Madrid Agreement.

The Agreement was signed in Madrid on April 14, 1891, and was revised in Brussels on December 14, 1900, in Washington on June 2, 1911, at The Hague on November 6, 1925, in London on June 2, 1934, in Nice on June 15, 1957, in Stockholm on July 14, 1967, and amended on October 2, 1979. As of January 1, 1989, only the texts as revised at Stockholm in 1967 (Stockholm Act) and at Nice in 1957 (Nice Act) are applicable.

A single set of regulations dated April 22, 1988, which entered into force on January 1, 1989, governs the application of both the Nice and Stockholm Acts.

The Madrid Agreement extends the general principles adopted by the Paris Convention by establishing trademark protection through registration with the intermediary of a Central Registration Bureau. This Bureau is located in Geneva, Switzerland, and administered by the World Intellectual Property Organization (WIPO), an organ of the United Nations. The working language of the International Bureau is French.

The Agreement originally intended to provide for an International Registration, but fell far short of that goal in two respects: the lack of international acceptance thwarted any attempt at a truly "international" registration, and the Central Bureau's mere forwarding of a uniform application to the various member countries, rather than registering them in national trademark registers, precludes this from being an actual "registration" system.

Under the Agreement, any person or legal entity with a mark registered in his or her country of origin or domicile may obtain protection for that mark in all other contracting countries by submitting a single application, filed in one language. This registration has a uniform duration of 20 years in all the contracting countries. The total fee established by the regulations governing the Agreement is less than the sum of the national fees that would be required to be paid if a national filing were made in each of the countries party to the Agreement. Therefore, at least initially, international filing reduces costs, particularly secondary costs such as translation costs and agents' fees.

---

[11] African Intellectual Property Organization arising out of the Libreville Agreement (1962) as revised at Bangui (1977).

[12] The following countries are Members of the Madrid Agreement as of January 1, 1993: Algeria, Austria, Belgium, Bulgaria, China, Croatia, Cuba, Czech Republic, Democratic People's Republic of Korea, Egypt, France, Germany, Hungary, Italy, Liechtenstein, Luxembourg, Monaco, Mongolia, Morocco, Netherlands, Poland, Portugal, Romania, Russian Federation, San Marino, Slovakia, Slovenia, Spain, Sudan, Switzerland, Ukraine, Vietnam, and Yugoslavia.

If it is in the correct form, the application is entered on the International Register, and pro forma applications are transmitted by the Bureau to all member countries designated by the applicant. Those countries then have a period of 12 months in which to reject (if necessary, provisionally) the application. In the absence of a rejection or a "provisional objection," the mark is deemed registered in the designated countries.

Before being registered internationally, a mark must have been registered nationally with the national office of the applicant's country of origin.[13] Merely filing a national application in the country of origin is insufficient, except in those rare countries where filing constitutes registration. In the countries where the filing of a mark is followed by a procedure of examination and then registration, which is largely the case today, it is only when the mark has been registered nationally that international registration can be sought at the International Bureau.

This requirement establishes a significant difference, amounting to a practical discrimination, between countries party to the Agreement. In Monaco, for instance, the very act of filing constitutes the registration of a trademark. In Spain, the mark is subject to examination by the Patent Office with regard to registrability and anticipation, and the registration may not be effected for a considerable time after the filing of the application. As a result, a trademark owner in Monaco may apply for international registration almost immediately after filing an application, whereas a Spanish trademark owner may have to wait for months or years until he or she achieves local registration.[14]

International registration can be obtained for those goods and services covered by national registration in the country of origin, or for a part of those goods and services, but not for any expansion of coverage beyond the "home" or "basic" registration.

The country of origin is not left to the applicant's discretion. The Agreement provides that the country of origin is the member country of the Agreement where the applicant has a real and effective industrial or commercial establishment.[15] If no such establishment in a member country of the Agreement exists, the country of origin can be the member country in which the applicant has his or her domicile (or headquarters). If the applicant satisfies neither of these criteria in a member country, the country of origin is deemed to be the country of which the applicant is a national, provided that country is a member of the Agreement.

International registration has no effect in the country of origin.[16] A mark is protected in that country under the general provisions of the national law.

The currently applicable Nice and Stockholm Acts allow any contracting country at any time to declare that the protection resulting from international registration will extend to that country only at the express request of the owner of the mark.[17] At the present time, all member countries of the Madrid Agreement have chosen this route, so that international registration now becomes effective only in countries for which protection is expressly requested or "designated."[18]

Marks that are recorded in the International Register, reported to the offices of the countries concerned, and published by the International Bureau, are subject to the same

---

[13] Article 1 (2) and (3) of the Madrid Agreement.

[14] S.P. Ladas, *Patents, Trademarks, and Related Rights: National and International Protection* (Cambridge, Mass., Harvard University Press: 1975), p. 1436

[15] Madrid Agreement, Article 1 (3).

[16] Id.

[17] Article 3 bis, Nice and Stockholm Acts of the Madrid Agreement.

[18] Madrid Agreement, Article 3 ter (1).

rules as marks filed at the national level.[19] These marks are protected in each of the designated countries from the date of international registration, unless a national authority refuses or invalidates protection in that country's territory. Where a country is designated subsequent to international registration, the mark has protection from the date on which that extension was recorded in the International Register.[20]

As a step toward harmonization, the international classification of goods and services for the registration of marks was established by the Nice Agreement of 1957. This Agreement, revised at Stockholm in 1967 and at Geneva in 1977, has been adopted by all members of the Madrid Agreement. Its classification tables are periodically reviewed by a committee of experts and revised to reflect the changing technologies. The classification of goods and services under the international system is not binding on the member countries in determining the scope of protection afforded to a mark.[21]

The publication of an international registration is made in the periodical *Les Marques Internacionales*, which is issued by the International Bureau. There is no provision for national publication.

Under the Nice and Stockholm Acts, the protection resulting from international registration remains dependent on the protection afforded the "home" or "basic" registration for a period of five years from the date of international registration. Therefore, if the home registration terminates for any reason within that period, all registrations based on it also cease, regardless of whether the reason for the home registration's elimination emanates from a third country. This provision is referred to as "central attack."

If, within five years from the international registration date, the home registration is canceled or its coverage of goods and services is limited voluntarily or ex officio, the office of the country of origin must request that the International Bureau either cancel the international registration or enter a corresponding limitation in the list of goods or services covered by that registration. The International Bureau may in this regard act only upon the request of the office of the country of origin.

Judicial proceedings may be instituted in the home country against the basic registration before the five-year period expires. In that case, the home country must send the International Bureau, ex officio or at the plaintiff's request, a copy of the complaint or other documentary evidence that an action has commenced, including the decision of the court. The International Bureau then enters an appropriate notice in the International Register.[22]

After the five-year dependency period has expired, the international registration may be attacked only under the individual national laws where the international registration has been extended. However, renewal, changes in proprietorship details, and the like may still be effected in all designated countries by a single filing at the International Bureau.

Further, the fee schedule may be changed by the competent bodies of the Madrid Agreement.[23] The required fees are expressed in Swiss francs and must be paid in that currency.

Upon receipt of an application for international registration forwarded from the Trademark Office of the home or basic country, the International Bureau checks on whether the application complies with the provisions of the Agreement and the regula-

---

[19] Id., Article 4(1).
[20] Id., Article 3 ter 2, last sentence.
[21] Id., Article 4(1).
[22] Id., Article 6(4).
[23] Madrid Agreement: Stockholm Act, Article 12(4); Nice Act, Article 10(4).

tions. The International Bureau is not, however, expected to check on whether the mark in the international registration application will be found acceptable under the individual laws of the designated countries. For example, if the Bureau receives an International Service Mark Application, it will not check on whether each designated country accepts service marks for registration.

If the application does not comply with the provisions of the Agreement and the regulations, the Bureau defers the application and notifies the national office. If the application is not put in order within three months from the date of notification, the International Bureau allows a further period of three months for it to be put in order. If the application is not put in order within the second three-month period, it is deemed abandoned and any official fees already paid are reimbursed.[24]

Most Madrid Agreement countries today subject marks that have been internationally registered to an administrative examination governed by national law and practice (the form of examination varies). The designated countries are entitled to refuse protection in whole or in part.

The International Bureau cannot express an opinion as to the basis of a refusal or intervene in any way in settling the refusal or the substantive problems raised by such refusal. Responses to decisions of refusal should be prepared by the owner of the mark, or the owner's agent, and addressed to the refusing national authority within the time limit and under the conditions indicated in the refusal notice. Where, as in some countries, the assistance of a local agent is mandatory, that obligation is mentioned in the notice of refusal. Once a notice of refusal has been issued from any of the national offices, the applicant must then proceed with the case under national law and practice.

International registration may be invalidated at any time, wholly or in part, by the competent administrative or judicial authority of a country, with respect to the territory of that country. An international mark may not be invalidated without affording the owner of the mark the opportunity to defend his or her rights.[25]

Protection can be refused to a mark recorded in the International Register only for reasons applicable to a national registration filing under the Paris Convention.[26] The Paris Convention states that the conditions for the filing and registration of trademarks are determined in each country of the Convention by its domestic legislation.[27] It further establishes that every trademark duly registered in the country of origin, as is always the case with international registrations, is accepted for filing and protected as in the other countries of the Convention, subject to the cases of refusal or invalidation referred to in the Article 26.[28]

Thus, the authority of a designated country may invoke the same grounds to support its decision to refuse or invalidate an international registration, as it would assert against the owner of a national application or registration subject to the provisions of the Paris Convention.[29]

A mark may also be refused because it is likely to infringe rights previously acquired by a third party. For example, it may be identical or similar to a mark that has already been registered on behalf of a third party for identical or similar goods. Or the mark may be

[24] Rule 11(3) of the Regulations Under the Madrid Agreement Concerning the International Registration of Marks.
[25] Madrid Agreement, Article 5(6).
[26] Id., Article 5(1).
[27] Article 6(1), Paris Convention.
[28] Id., Article 6 quinquies.
[29] Id.

devoid of any distinctive character, consisting exclusively of a sign or indication that may be used in trade to designate the kind, quality, quantity, intended purpose, value, or place of production, or that has become customary in the trade practices of that country.

Changes affecting the international registration of a mark must be reported to the International Bureau for recording in the International Register. Such changes include the following:

1. Territorial extension subsequent to international registration,
2. Transfer and partial assignment,
3. Cancellation,
4. Renunciation,
5. Limitation of the list of goods and services, and
6. Others, including changes in name and address of the owner.

The term of an international registration is 20 years and may be renewed indefinitely, each time for a period of 20 years from the date of expiration of the preceding period.[30]

Because of certain provisions, such as the necessity for a valid home registration, and the possibility of "central attack," whereby cancellation of a basic registration in the first five years causes the entire international registration to fall, many commercially important nations have not adhered to the Agreement. These countries include the United States, Japan, the United Kingdom, Denmark, and Canada.

WIPO endeavored for several years to draft a new treaty that would ameliorate the "objectionable" provisions of the Madrid Agreement. This was an effort to bring about acceptance by those nations that had refused to adhere to the Agreement and simultaneously maintain the tenets of the existing treaty to accommodate the current Madrid members.

As the actuality of a Community Trademark (CTM)—discussed later, in section 6.6—came closer, the pressure on WIPO to strengthen "the Agreement" and broaden its membership increased. Such urgency was caused by the realization that the alternative would have been the decline of the Agreement's importance.

WIPO proposed other versions of the Agreement for possible acceptance. For instance, the CTM office could be designated as another *pays intéressé*, or designated jurisdiction, of the Madrid Agreement, and a CTM registration could be a "basic" registration on which a "Madrid" international registration would be founded. This proposition is referred to as the "linking provision."

This proposal was closer to the mark, particularly as the United Kingdom indicated its interest. Arpad Bogsch, director general of WIPO, left a mid-1989 United States Trademark Association (USTA) meeting with the understanding that the United States, at least as represented by the membership of USTA, might accept this proposal upon further serious consideration.

In December 1988, the notion of a single protocol similar to Protocol B, providing for a link with the CTM, was proposed. At that time, a diplomatic conference was also scheduled for June 1989. The diplomatic conference resulted in the adoption of a treaty entitled "Protocol Relating to the Madrid Agreement Concerning the International Registration of Marks."[31] This Protocol would apply the amendments only to the present

---

[30] Madrid Agreement, Article 7(1).
[31] The Protocol with Comments by WIPO is printed at 28 Industrial Property, p. 411 (1989).

nonmember countries who chose to adhere. However, it would not apply to the current Madrid members who had expressed satisfaction with the existing Agreement and were not inclined to accept changes.

(e) The Madrid Protocol. The objectives of the Protocol were to make the Madrid system more attractive to more countries, especially the four EC nonmembers,[32] to create a link with other intergovernmental trademark systems, especially the proposed CTM, and to safeguard the continuation of the existing Agreement.

The striking revision of the Agreement in the Protocol is the requirement of only a basic application instead of a granted registration as a "basis" for an international application, resulting in a treaty for international application, not registration. If the eventual basic application should not mature into a registration, the applicant would have an opportunity to reapply nationally, but retain the priority date of the original application as filed in Geneva at WIPO. This proposal was suggested by the Netherlands delegation and has come to be known as the "Dutch proposal." This version also mitigates the procedure of central attack, although it does not remove it.

Each article in the Protocol covers the same subject matter as the Agreement and parts of the Protocol, even adopted the wording of the Agreement *mutatis mutandis*.[33] The Protocol, however, presented four main changes:

1. *Basis for an international registration (IR).*[34] It was accepted that an IR may be based on a home application as well as on a home registration without requiring that the home application mature to registration. Thus, an unmatured home application enables the applicant to file nationally, retaining the priority of the original international filing date. This protects an applicant whose home application is undergoing a lengthy examination process. During this application period, the applicant may file an international application with the International Bureau. However, if the national application on which it was based is refused during the international application process, the applicant may file in each foreign jurisdiction individually. The new national applications would be given the original international filing priority date despite the actual foreign filing date.

2. *Time limit for giving notice of refusal.*[35] The Agreement's time limit of 12 months, within which a national office must notify WIPO if an IR is unacceptable in its country, was generally acceptable to the existing members of the Agreement, especially because some of them do not examine applications. This time limit was clearly unacceptable to countries such as the United Kingdom, Ireland, and Denmark, where an extensive examination is undertaken by the national office. Consequently, the proposal to extend the 12-month period to an 18-month period was accepted in the Protocol. Therefore, Article 5(2) (c) of the Protocol provides that the period for refusal is 12 months, unless a contracting party makes a declaration that the 12-month period is replaced by an 18-month period. A contracting party

[32] The European Union member states not party to the Madrid Agreement are Denmark, Greece, Ireland, and the United Kingdom.

[33] *Black's Law Dictionary* defines *mutatis mutandis* as "with the necessary changes in points of detail, meaning that matters or things are generally the same, but to be altered when necessary, as to names, offices, and the like."

[34] Protocol, Article 2.

[35] Id., Article 5.

may also declare that it will provide notification of a refusal after the 18-month period. Before those 18 months expire, however, the national office may be required to notify the International Bureau that oppositions may be filed against the trademark and to provide notification of refusal based on an opposition no later than 7 months from the date on which the opposition period began.

3. *Fees*.[36] A national office can declare that instead of the current system of supplementary and complementary fees operating under the Madrid Agreement, it proposes to charge the applicant for an IR extended into its country. The fee may be equivalent to what the national office would have charged a national applicant for a 10-year term. A clause was inserted in Article 8 requiring each national office to pass on any savings realized as a result of adopting the IR system.

4. *Transformation*.[37] The concept of central attack was generally accepted without demur. However, it was modified to allow for the possible transformation of an IR into a series of national applications in the designated countries in the event of a successful central attack on the basic home registration upon which the IR is based. These transformed national applications would have to be filed within three months from the date on which the IR was canceled, and the goods and services listed in the application must have been covered by the list of goods or services contained in the original IR.

In addition to the four major differences, there are other significant differences between the Protocol and the Agreement:

5. *Effect of registration*.[38] The original draft of this Article stated that the effect of an IR was the same as if the mark had been registered by the national office from the date of registration in the International Register. Recognizing that there could be problems with this, the conference altered the Article so that the effect is the same as if the mark had been filed at the national office. Only when refusal has not been reported within the time allowed will the mark be, in effect, registered.

6. *Central attack*.[39] The basic concept of central attack remains unchanged, namely, that an IR will fail if the basic home application or registration on which it is based is canceled in the first five years of its life. This applies whether cancellation is the result of a successful action by a third party or done voluntarily by the mark's owner. However, it was pointed out, particularly by some of the nongovernment organizations, that because an IR can now be based on an application, complications could arise if the basic home application still remains pending after the five-year period of dependency has elapsed. If the application is subsequently refused, and if in the meantime an IR were obtained, that IR would have been obtained on a "false basis." Consequently, measures were introduced into this Article to permit the five-year period to be extended if an application on which an IR is based is the subject of refusal proceedings that commence before the five-year period expires.

---

[36] Id., Article 8.
[37] Id., Article 9 quinquies.
[38] Id., Article 4.
[39] Id., Article 6.

In addition, the term for registration of a mark is reduced from 20 to 10 years.[40]

7. *The safeguard clause.*[41] Article 9 safeguards the existing Madrid Agreement by ensuring that it parallels the Protocol. As originally drafted, if a country was party to both the Madrid Agreement and the Protocol, the Protocol requirements would have no effect in that particular country. There was considerable discussion at the conference over this Article. In particular, doubts were expressed about the need to continue with the duality of systems. The conference members agreed that the Article could eventually be dropped or modified if this was agreed upon by a three-quarters majority in the Assembly. Such a vote could occur at least 10 years after the Protocol came into force, and at least 5 years after a majority of the existing members of the Madrid Agreement had ratified the Protocol.

8. *Link with the European Community Trademark.*[42] A link is provided for by the stipulation that any intergovernmental organization, such as the EU, may become party to the Protocol. To do so, the organization must have a regional office for the registration of marks within its own territory, or at least one of the member states of that organization must be a party to the Paris Convention.

9. *Denunciation.*[43] Tunisia "denounced" the Madrid Agreement in April 1988, causing considerable discussion as to the effect of this denunciation on IRs extended to or from Tunisia. The Madrid Agreement is without sufficient provision on the point, although Article 15(5) provides that existing valid extension registrations will remain valid for the normal period. Delegates to the conference wanted the Protocol to delineate the effects of a denunciation. As a result, the Article provides that in the case of a country's denouncing the Protocol, the owner of an IR has two years within which to convert the IR into a series of national registrations, all of them having the same priority date as the IR. This provision will apply whether the owner of the IR is based in the denouncing country or whether the IR has been extended into that country.

The Protocol was signed by 27 countries,[44] including most of the present members of the Madrid Agreement, and 4 countries that are members of the European Union but not of the Madrid Agreement.[45]

(f) Effective Date. The Protocol will come into effect three months after a minimum of four parties have ratified or otherwise acceded to it. The contracting parties must include at least one country that is a contracting state to the Agreement in the Stockholm version, and at least one other contracting party to the Protocol should not be a contracting state to the Agreement. The latter party may be either a noncontracting state or an organization, in the sense of Article 14(1) (b), such as the EU.

---

[40] Id., Article 6(1).

[41] Id., Article 9(6).

[42] Id., Article 14.

[43] Id., Article 15(5).

[44] Austria, Belgium, Denmark, Democratic People's Republic of Korea, Egypt, Finland, France, Greece, Germany, Hungary, Ireland, Italy, Liechtenstein, Luxembourg, Monaco, Mongolia, Morocco, Netherlands, Portugal, Rumania, Russian Federation, Senegal, Spain, Sweden, Switzerland, United Kingdom, Yugoslavia.

[45] Supra, note 32.

6.5   ADHERENCE TO THE PROTOCOL: ADVANTAGES AND DISADVANTAGES

Adoption of the Madrid Protocol by any nation will bring about significant changes in that nation's trademark registration procedure. Although adoption of the Protocol may seem to some a panacea for many ills in multinational trademark practice, a number of side effects may result from the cure.

Many countries either have recently modified or contemplate modifying their trademark laws. Included are the United States, which has amended its law to accept trademark applications on the basis of a bona fide intent to use; Japan, which has revised its trademark law with the official introduction of the International Classification system and service marks; and the members of the European Community, which have or will soon amend their laws to conform with the EC Harmonization Directive. Modifications in trademark law usually result in an increased number of trademark/service mark applications in the Trademark Office.

This phenomenon, compounded with a foreseeable onslaught of Protocol applications, will produce an additional backlog at an already overburdened trademark agency. The excess work load, coupled with the Protocol's time limitations for provisional refusals, may result in granting priority of examination to Protocol applications over national applications. It may also require additional staffing, which in turn will increase the costs of filing domestic applications.

The consequences for domestic applicants include continuous delay for processing domestic applications, additional risk of citations or objections based on prioritized Madrid registrations or applications, and the rapidly decreasing availability of marks for domestic use.

Foreign Protocol applicants may, at first glance, have the advantages of simplified procedures and fees. However, the increased numbers of applications may prompt designated country trademark examiners to issue a provisional refusal for any reason available, if only to avoid automatic registration. This will cause additional trouble and expense for the applicant, who will then be required to prove even obvious points in order to prosecute the application.

Domestic trademark law and practice may also disadvantage those basing an international application on a home or basic registration. A drawback to basing an IR on a home registration, in view of the possibility of central attack under the Protocol, arises in some countries in conjunction with common-law rights or rights based on prior use. Applicants from countries recognizing such rights are more susceptible to attack from common-law claims of priority. Such common-law attacks thereby increase the likelihood of successful central attacks.

The so-called linking provisions of the Protocol will allow multinational applicants to obtain a home registration in the European Community, provided that the EC as an organization accedes to the Protocol and that the applicant has a "real and effective industrial or commercial establishment in" a member state.[46]

Furthermore, it will be more difficult in those countries with strict examination processes, including citation of prior possible anticipations based on the Register, to obtain a home registration than in many other Madrid countries. In a commercially developed country this is especially difficult because of the number of trademark proprietors who use their marks only domestically and have no inclination to use them abroad. These purely domestic registrations block attempts to obtain home registrations. It

---

[46] Protocol, Article 2(1) (ii).

should be noted that many Madrid countries have less stringent examinations and/or no citation system, resulting in their nationals' obtaining home registrations relatively easily.

A problem experienced by companies with extensive foreign business activity results from using one mark for a product in the home market and using other marks abroad. These "foreign" marks are often unregistrable or difficult to maintain domestically, because they are not used or intended for use in the home market. They also encounter objections that bear no relation to their use in the foreign market; for example, surnames in one country may not be surnames in other countries.

A leading argument in favor of the Madrid Protocol is that the simplified procedure reduces fees expended by the applicants. Although this may be true, it may not remain true where national applications encounter any objections on the national level. Where a provisional refusal is issued, local trademark agents or attorneys must still be engaged to prosecute the application. These fees often equal those that would have been expended had the application initially been processed through the local agent, any financial savings thereby evaporating.

For applicants who may face unofficial discrimination in individual national applications, the Protocol would probably not improve the situation. Some national trademark offices under the Agreement have cited many spurious Agreement citations against national applications, veiled attempts at discriminating against foreign applicants. To overcome these citations, consents or cancellations are required, which consequently increase the cost of application.

A domestic registrant with only domestic activities would be neither benefitted nor disadvantaged by its country's accession to the Protocol. However, the situation of the multinational registrant will be changed.

Currently, it is more difficult than it was under the Madrid system for applicants to obtain rights in multiple jurisdictions. Yet once registrations are obtained, an attack on the basic registration cannot affect them. Thus, for at least the initial five-year dependency period, the rights obtained now by individual applications are more secure than those obtained through a Protocol registration, because they are not subject to central attack.

However, the conversion provision of the Protocol mitigates this situation. Under the Protocol, once a basic registration is successfully attacked, the national registrations may be converted into regular national applications. Even so, this process would involve more time, effort, and money expended by the applicant than the present system. Although the priority date could be maintained, the entire national application procedure would now have to be recommenced, with the incumbent significant costs.

Generally, the increased number of Protocol registrations combined with all the other registrations will result in an escalated number of potential "deadwood" registrations. These registrations will increase the number of opposition and cancellation proceedings, resulting in prosecution costs for trademark owners.

The Protocol also imposes time constraints on the rejection of international applications. The period in which a national office may issue a provisional refusal is 12 months, unless a contracting party declares that 18 months are required.[47] If an application is not refused within this time, the mark is deemed registered. If a refusal could result because of an opposition, a contracting party may claim additional time to notify the refusal after the 18-month period. This notification must be made to the International Bureau before the initial 18 months expire, and any notification of a refusal based on such an opposition

---

[47] Id., Article 5, p. 28.

must be made no later than 7 months from the date on which the opposition period began. These time limitations will only increase the burden on the national Trademark Offices.

Another potential consequence of the pressure, resulting from volume and time constraints, on a national Trademark Office could be the issuance of blanket refusals of an international application in every refusal category. This action would circumvent the time restrictions, as no limitations govern the issuance of replies to office actions or appeals. There would also be an additional burden on the applicant to prove a mark's registrability in every refusal category. The resulting paperwork could overwhelm the Trademark Office and add significant expense to the application process.

The Trademark Office would also need to develop a new system for distinguishing international registrations from national registrations. This can result in added record keeping, requiring more personnel and longer work hours.

Trademark practitioners will, however, have an easier task with clients seeking multiple international registrations. The number of hours spent preparing such applications, as compared with individual national applications, will be minimized. Objections to the marks at the national level will, of course, remain. It is to be expected that local attorneys and agents once engaged to assist in national practice will charge significantly higher prosecution fees when objections arise in a Protocol application. They will thus recoup the loss experienced by not having filed a national application.

Moreover, the parallel existence of the Madrid Agreement and the Madrid Protocol along with national registration and the Community Trademark will cause confusion. Under this proliferation of treaties, the practitioner will need to be cognizant of which marks are purely national, Agreement, Protocol, or Community registrations, as the rights for renewal, cancellation, and transfer recordal will vary. This situation is not helped by the absence of guidelines insisting that the national registers maintain a system for identifying them as national.

Clearing marks for trademark applicants will also be complicated. The rise in the number of registrations under the Madrid Agreement, many with broad goods specifications, has made it increasingly difficult to interpret search results. Thus, obtaining a WIPO extract to ascertain the exact protection of a registration creates additional work for the practitioner, as well as additional expense for the applicant.

The Protocol will also greatly affect the search of national Trademark Registers. The increase in applications will, undoubtedly, result in an increased uncertainty period in search results, as more applications will require more time to enter on a Register.

Furthermore, the absence of time limits for issuing a second official action or an appeal means that an application could linger for years in a designated Trademark Office after the initial official action.

Another important development that must be analyzed is the adoption of the regulations that will govern the Protocol. At its Geneva meeting on March 13, 1990, the Working Group on the Application of the Madrid Protocol debated whether a single set of regulations would govern both the Protocol and the Agreement or whether separate regulations would govern them. France argued for two different sets in order to avoid confusion. Germany and a number of others argued for a single set in order to simplify the system. Finally, the Group adopted the Italian delegation's suggestion that a single set of draft regulations would be prepared. The Draft Regulations have been considered by the Working Group of the Madrid Assembly and will be presented for adoption once a sufficient number of members ratify the Protocol.

The French have acquiesced to the admission of English as a colanguage to French for the Protocol, and the Draft Regulations now reflect this agreement. Thus, the office of origin may now prescribe the language to be used on applications that it submits to the

International Bureau. This decision will govern the language of any further correspondence, advertisement, and registration documents. Further discussions relating to the admission of any other language seem destined to failure, as the admission of just one more will reopen the issue and produce vehement arguments for the admission of several. The result of the bilingual system will be the necessity to employ additional multilingual staff at the national Trademark Offices.

WIPO applications will not be as demanding as many national offices would like them to be. The draft application form accompanying the Draft Regulations makes no allowance for specific requirements that may be necessary under national law. Examples include the requirement that applications be verified and signed by the applicant and that the applicant's first date of use or bona fide intention to use the mark be provided, the designation of a factory address, and the designation of a domestic representative for service of notice or process. One significant exception, as a result of U.S. participation and in deference to the requirements under the U.S. Trademark Law, is that a statement of bona fide intention to use may be required by a national office.

The application form will undoubtedly cause difficulties with any automated systems currently used by a national Trademark Office, necessitating vital and costly changes. This may also result in delays in retrieving data concerning Madrid applications for citation purposes.

The Draft Regulations provide that two or more natural persons or legal entities may jointly file an international application, provided that they are of the same nationality and the office of origin is the same for both. Although certain national laws allow for this, some countries place additional restrictions on such applications. For example, although U.S. trademark law allows for filing by joint applicants, U.S. Trademark Office practice requires that the joint applicants must be involved in a "doing business as" relationship, thus precluding, for example, a joint filing by a parent and subsidiary company. This national practice may create conflicts if an applicant's home office is located in a country that has less exacting standards for joint applicants.

The Draft Regulations provide for marks with color as a distinctive feature. Applications for such marks may be submitted to the International Bureau via the home office, with a color sample of the mark. Some national trademark laws either do not allow for the registration of color marks or place restrictions on the content and method of application.

The Draft Regulations do not regulate the specification of goods that may be set forth in an international application. This is left to the requirements under the national law of the home country. In certain countries, the goods must be limited to those upon which the mark has been used or for which the mark is proposed to be used. In fact, certain national Trademark Offices will not accord a priority filing date to an application whose specification of goods is too general. Could a country that demands detailed descriptions of goods and services require that Protocol applicants identify goods and services with the same specificity that they otherwise require? If not, as appears to be the case, nationals of that country will be at a distinct disadvantage with respect to the protection and coverage available. Moreover, adoption of the Protocol will, apparently, automatically necessitate the adoption of the International Classification of Goods and Services in countries where either national or no classification systems currently exist.

Just as the Draft Regulations provide no answers, the Protocol itself does not assist in answering the question of specification of goods. Article 5(1) states, "Protection may not be refused, even partially, by reason only that national legislation would not permit registration except in a limited number of classes or for a limited number of goods or services." How is this reconciled with Article 4(1)(b), which says, "The indication of classes of goods and services . . . shall not bind the Contracting Parties with regard to the determination of the scope of the protection of the mark"? Will a country be forced to accept and accord a filing date to international applications that, although meeting the requirements of the Protocol, do not meet its minimal national filing requirements?

It is expected that issues surrounding disclaimers, identification of prior registrations, use by a predecessor or related company, proof of distinctiveness, concurrent use, specimens and the specification of the mode or manner in which the mark is or is intended to be used with respect to international applications, will be addressed during examination at the national level and that no requirements on any of these issues will arise at the international filing.

The Protocol does not expressly treat the assignment of a mark along with its goodwill, as required in some countries. Certain countries do not honor assignments of trademarks without the simultaneous conveyance of the goodwill of a business. Thus, if such a country is a designated territory of an international registration, the question arises as to whether it must give effect to the assignment of an IR that does not satisfy the goodwill transfer requirements.

The Madrid Agreement was explicit in its treatment of transferring marks to parties who are not domiciliaries of contracting states. However, the Protocol merely says that such a transfer cannot be recorded on the International Register. If a mark is assigned to a person not eligible to own an international registration, it can only be assumed that the registration and rights of the assignee cease to exist.

Although, according to some, it may seem desirable for their country to become a party to the Protocol, this is not a decision that people should make lightly as they are swept up in modern trends toward international harmony in the global economy. Rather, as in the adoption of any international agreement, each country must examine the advantages and disadvantages posed to it, its national interests, and its government, by adopting the Protocol. Thus, the Protocol and its proposed regulations merit further careful scrutiny.

Recognizing the growing inclination in the United States toward acceptance of the Protocol, as well as the potential difficulties the Protocol presents, it has been suggested that the United States, as well as other leading nations, such as Japan and Canada, should not lead those rushing to join with the first wave.[48] The more sagacious approach would be careful observation of the implications in other member countries of the Protocol. Should their example prove successful, there is no reason that the "holdouts" could not join at a later date. They would not be constrained to take advantage of any specific window of opportunity and would suffer negligible detriment by what may be only a short delay. However, United States trademark law is poised for amendment to facilitate the Protocol, and a bill for adherence of the United States to the Protocol has been introduced in Congress.[49]

At a recent address to the United States Group of the Association Intérnationale pour la Protection de la Propriété Industrielle (AIPPI), Bruce Lehman, commissioner of Patents and Trademarks, advised that his office supported United States adherence to the

---

[48] See Ian Jay Kaufman, "The Madrid Protocol: Should the U.S. Join?" October 9, 1992; "The Madrid Protocol: Step Toward Harmonization," October 16, 1992; and "How the Madrid Agreement Differs from the Protocol," October 23, 1992, *New York Law Journal.*

[49] HR 2129 and S 977.

Protocol and would do everything necessary to facilitate the procedures for processing the applications at the United States Trademark Office and forward them to WIPO in Geneva.

6.6 THE EUROPEAN COMMUNITY TRADEMARK

Note: In view of the entry into force of the Maastricht Treating on European Union, the abbreviation "EU" (European Union) will be used instead of "EC" (European Community).

An economic-political creation, the European Union (EU) has also been the impetus for changes in trademark law and practice. Trademarks identify goods and services but, absent international agreement to the contrary, can be enforced only in the jurisdiction in which they are registered. Thus, trademarks registered in one member state are not automatically protected in another member state; thereby, the free movement of goods across borders is hindered and trade barriers are created.

The European Union of 12 nations[50] proposed, as part of its removal of all trade barriers by 1992, the creation of one unified trademark law with one registration system to cover the entire Union. At first it was believed that a treaty would be required; however, the European Commission concluded that it could proceed by regulation.

The Council Regulation (EC) No. 40/94 of December 20, 1993 on the Community Trademark was published in the European Union's Official Journal of January 14, 1994 (37 OJ No L11) and took effect on March 15, 1994. The Regulations consist of more than 100 sections.[51] They provide that the Community Trademark (CTM) will be registered for the entire European Union and will have identical effect throughout the Union, and that the CTM will not replace national registration systems.

As is often the case, the members of the EU have not been willing to subjugate their nationalism completely. The cumbersome result will be duality of the system: the CTM, encompassing one registration covering the 12 EU jurisdictions and potentially extending to other states that have expressed interest in joining the EU, and national registration maintained in each nation.

This duality cannot avoid resulting in claims of conflicting rights of priority.[52] When one party files an application for a Community trademark, it will be possible for a prior registrant who has a registration on the national registry of one or more of the member states to claim that this gives him or her a superior right that is sufficient to defeat the Community registration. This benefits the smaller trademark proprietors who would not wish to bear the increased costs of a Community registration.

The situation has been further complicated by the fact that the administrative body that examines Community applications apparently will not conduct a search of the national registers for possible prior rights, although there is an option for National Offices to supply search reports concerning their registers. This places the entire burden on the trademark owner to maintain an adequate watch of marks published in each member

---

[50] The 12 members of the European Community are Belgium, Denmark, France, Germany, Greece, Ireland, Italy, Luxembourg, the Netherlands, Portugal, Spain, and the United Kingdom.

[51] See, e.g., D. Wilkenson, *The Community Trademark Directive and Its Role in European Economic Integration*, 80 TMR 107 (1990) (dealing with the 1986 draft regulations).

[52] Ian Jay Kaufman, Madrid Agreement: Will Reform Proposals Attract More Members? (1990) 11 EIPR, p. 407.

state and in the EU. Although the rational motivation is to protect small enterprises from having to expend what will undoubtedly be high costs in obtaining a CTM registration against those proceeding in one or two member states, the result, at least in the first years of CTM practice, may be a higher proportion of oppositions than previously encountered in national practice.

A CTM proprietor will have exclusive rights to the use of a trademark in the entire territory of the EU. A trademark proprietor may prevent registration of marks that are identical to the proprietor's existing mark and are for identical goods or services. This is also true for marks and goods or services that are similar if there is a likelihood of confusion on the part of the public.

Where a similar mark is used for dissimilar goods or services, protection will be available where the CTM has a reputation in the EU and where use of that sign without due cause takes unfair advantage of, or is detrimental to, the distinctive character or the repute of the CTM.

Generally, the property aspects of a CTM will be governed by the law of the member state in which the proprietor has a seat or domicile, or has an establishment. Recordal of an assignment is not permitted in cases where the public is likely to be misled. Disclaimers are allowed for elements of a trademark that are nondistinctive, which is similar to the practice in the United Kingdom.

Where for a period of five years the proprietor of an earlier national registration has acquiesced in the use of a later CTM in the member state in which the earlier trademark is protected, there will be no basis for invalidating or opposing the CTM. This stipulation does not apply to use of the CTM in other member states.

Although the fee charged for filing a CTM with the Community Trademark Office (CTMO) has not been officially set, an unconfirmed source estimates the cost of filing will be in excess of U.S. $2,000.

The final obstacles to acceptance and implementation of the CTM have been removed. The summit on October 29, 1993, decided that the location of the CTMO will be Spain. At a meeting of the Council of Ministers on November 4, 1993, Alicante, a city located in eastern Spain on the Mediterranean coast, was designated as the headquarters for the CTMO. The Office has been described as "the Office for Harmonization in the Internal Market," although whether that will be its official title remains to be seen.

A decision has also been made on the question of language. Following a German proposal, it has been decided that there should be five official languages, namely, English, French, German, Italian, and Spanish. The summit decided that a translation center should be set up in the Commission's Translation Department in Luxembourg to provide translation services to the Office.

There are still some practical problems to be resolved: the implementing regulations and the nomination of the president. If everything works smoothly, the CTMO should open for the first trademark application in the second part of 1995.

6.7 THE EC HARMONIZATION DIRECTIVE

In 1988 the European Community issued a Directive to approximate the laws of member states relating to trademarks (the Directive)[53] so as to bring national practice into line, as much as possible, with the eventual CTM regulations. The Directive establishes uniform

---

[53] First Council Directive of December 21, 1988, to Approximate the Laws of the Member States relating to Trade Marks 89/104/EEC; see Industrial Property June 1989.

conditions for obtaining and maintaining trademark registration. It calls for amendment of national legislation that will harmonize national trademark laws of the member states.[54]

Because Article 1 includes service marks within the scope of the Directive, Ireland will be required to add provisions for registration of service marks. Article 2 stipulates that a trademark includes "signs such as shape of the goods or their packaging, provided that such signs are capable of distinguishing the goods." Thus, the member states, such as the United Kingdom and Germany, must provide for registration of three-dimensional objects as marks. The Directive would also eliminate the distinction between Part A and Part B of the Register, which currently exists in the United Kingdom and Ireland.

Articles 3 and 4 set out standards regarding grounds for refusal or invalidity of registration. Although the grounds are exhaustive, the member states may adopt or retain grounds that do not fall within the scope of the Directive, for example, lapse of a trademark resulting from nonpayment of quinquennial fees in Spain. Article 5 stipulates the rights conferred by a trademark, and Article 7 deals with exhaustion of the rights conferred by a trademark. Article 8 provides that a trademark may be licensed for all or part of the territory in which the mark is registered. This provision will be subject to Article 85 of the Treaty of Rome. Article 9 provides that a trademark proprietor may lose his or her rights against others after five years of acquiescence. Article 10 requires genuine use of a mark within five years of registration, and Article 12 provides grounds for revocation of a trademark.

All member countries, except Benelux, Germany, Ireland, Portugal, and the United Kingdom, have modified their laws in accordance with the Directive. The Directive deals only with the material aspects of trademark law; procedural aspects remain within the discretion of the member states.

The most important changes resulting from the Directive are the uniform definition of a trademark, service mark registration in all the member states, the introduction of user requirements in Denmark, and, in reference to Germany in particular, the ability of holding companies to own trademark rights.

6.8 THE NORTH AMERICAN FREE TRADE AGREEMENT (NAFTA)

Over the last decade, the United States has sought worldwide recognition of high standards of intellectual property protection and enforcement through unilateral,[55] bilateral,[56] and multilateral measures. Of all of these initiatives, NAFTA, negotiated in 1992 and already ratified by the United States and Mexican Congresses and the Canadian Parliament, provides the most satisfactory protection for intellectual property rights to date.[57]

Building on the work done in the General Agreement on Tariffs and Trade (GATT), specifically on trade-related intellectual property rights (TRIPs), or the Dunkel TRIPs

---

[54] Supra, note 48.

[55] The Special 301 provision of the Trade Act of 1974, 19 U.S.C. § 2411 (1988) requires the United States Trade Representative to identify any country that denies effective protection of intellectual property rights.

[56] Most of the bilateral agreements between the United States and its trade partners require high standards of protection on intellectual property, e.g., Bilateral Copyright Agreements with Indonesia and Singapore.

[57] All references to NAFTA are to the October 7, 1992, draft.

Text,[58] as they are also called, and on various international intellectual property treaties, NAFTA establishes a high level of obligations regarding intellectual property.

Chapter 17 of NAFTA establishes the rights and obligations of the three contracting parties with respect to intellectual property rights. These rights relate "to copyright and related rights, trademark rights, patent rights, rights in layout designs of semiconductor integrated circuits, trade secret rights, plant breeders' rights, rights in geographical indications and industrial design rights."[59]

Article 1701 comprises the nature and scope of obligations and reads as follows: "Each party shall provide in its territory to the nationals of another party adequate and effective protection and enforcement of intellectual property rights, while ensuring that measures to enforce intellectual property rights do not themselves become barriers to legitimate trade."[60]

To provide effective protection and enforcement of intellectual property rights, each party will have to adhere to several international treaties: The Geneva Convention for the Protection of Producers of Phonograms Against Unauthorized Duplication of Their Phonograms, 1971; The Berne Convention for the Protection of Literary and Artistic Works, 1971; The Paris Convention for the Protection of Industrial Property, 1967; and the International Convention for the Protection of New Varieties of Plants, 1978.[61]

A system for trademark protection, to be significantly effective, should include a registration system that provides for examination and prosecution of applications, publication of trademarks, opposition, and action for the cancellation of trademarks.

NAFTA provides for an effective scheme of trademark and service mark protection. Article 1708 establishes a definition for trademarks: "Any sign, or any combination of signs, capable of distinguishing the goods or services of one person from those of another, including personal names, designs, letters, numerals, colors, figurative elements, or the shape of goods or of their packaging. Trademarks shall include service marks and collective marks, and may include certification marks. A party may require as a condition for registration that the sign be visually perceptible."[62]

The inclusion of collective and certification marks is a positive step; however, it is unfortunate that there is not a further definition of the differences between these rights. It is also unfortunate that sound marks are not included.

Actual use of a trademark will not be a condition for filing an application for registration. No party may refuse an application solely on the ground that its intended use has not taken place before the expiration of a period of three years from the date of the application for registration.[63] However, NAFTA mandates a use requirement to maintain registration. In fact, the registration may be canceled for the reason of nonuse only after an interrupted period of at least two years of nonuse, unless valid reasons are shown by the trademark owner.[64]

NAFTA does not permit discrimination in granting trademark protection based on the nature of the goods or services involved.[65] It also provides that because use of a trademark

---

[58] Agreement on the Trade-Related Aspects of Intellectual Property in the Dunkel Draft.
[59] NAFTA, supra, note 57, Article 1721.
[60] Id., Article 1701, par. 1.
[61] Id., Article 1701, par. 2.
[62] Id., Article 1708, par. 1.
[63] Id., Article 1708, par. 3.
[64] Id., Article 1708, par. 8.
[65] Id., Article 1708, par. 5.

is required to maintain registration, use by another person under the control of the trademark owner (i.e., licensed use) is sufficient.[66]

Although the parties must provide an opportunity for interested persons to petition to cancel the registration of a trademark, the Agreement does not specifically provide an opposition procedure prior to registration.

Well-known trademarks are protected because of the recognition of Article 6 bis of the Paris Convention. Such protection is also extended to service marks.[67] Registration of a trademark is for a term of at least 10 years, indefinitely renewable for the same term. However, whether the term begins from the application date or from the registration date is not mentioned.[68]

NAFTA provides for contractual rights for trademark owners, including the right to assign with or without transfer of the business to which the mark belongs (i.e., the goodwill); however, it allows the imposition of conditions on licensing and assignment of trademarks.[69] The Agreement does not define the conditions of licensing. Compulsory licensing of a trademark is not permitted.

Furthermore, the text allows limited exceptions to trademark rights, such as fair use of descriptive terms, provided that such exceptions take into account the legitimate interests of the trademark owner and other persons.[70]

The parties "shall prohibit the registration as a trademark of words, at least in English, French or Spanish, that generically describe goods or services or types of goods or services to which the trademark applies."[71] Moreover, the parties "shall refuse to register trademarks that consist of or include immoral, deceptive or scandalous matter, or matter that may disparage or falsely suggest a connection with persons, living or dead, institutions, beliefs or any Party's national symbols, or bring them into contempt or disrepute."[72]

It is believed that NAFTA provides a high level of protection for trademarks that fulfill the actual requirements for adequate trademark protection, and their provisions in this area are a useful model for future negotiations.

6.9 TRADE-RELATED INTELLECTUAL PROPERTY RIGHTS (TRIPs) IN GATT

Through GATT, a substantial strengthening of intellectual property rights has been achieved. Intellectual property protection was a major component of the Uruguayan Round of multilateral trade negotiations, under trade-related intellectual property rights (TRIPs). The Dunkel Draft contains a text on TRIPs (the Dunkel TRIPs Text) that better protects intellectual property than the current regime of multilateral agreements.

NAFTA represents a major improvement in protection for intellectual property rights. Its negotiators started with the Dunkel TRIPs Text's provisions on intellectual property and built upon them.

The Dunkel TRIPs Text provides an effective system of protection for trademarks, as well as for service marks.[73] It stipulates that actual use of a trademark will not be a

---

[66] Id., Article 1708, par. 9.
[67] Id., Article 1708, par. 6.
[68] Id., Article 1708, par. 7.
[69] Id., Article 1708, par. 11.
[70] Id., Article 1708, par. 12.
[71] Id., Article 1708, par. 13.
[72] Id., Article 1708, par. 14.
[73] Dunkel TRIPs Text, supra, note 58, Article 15, par. 1.

condition for filing an application for registration.[74] It does not permit discrimination in granting trademark protection based on the nature of the goods or services involved.[75]

Publication of a trademark occurs prior to registration of the trademark, thereby affording a reasonable opportunity for actions to cancel the registration to be filed. An opportunity for interested parties to oppose a registration is not specifically included in the Text.[76]

As to the rights conferred, a registrant can prevent a third party from using a similar or identical trademark for goods or services that are identical or similar to those for which a trademark is registered, where such use would result in a likelihood of confusion.[77]

Article 6 bis of the Paris Convention is included in the Text and will apply in determining whether a trademark or service mark is well known.[78] The Dunkel TRIPs Text allows limited exceptions to trademark rights (such as fair use of descriptive terms); any such exceptions must take into account the legitimate interests of the trademark owner and other persons.[79]

As to the term of protection afforded by the Text, a trademark registration will span no less than seven years and can be renewed an indefinite number of times.[80] Furthermore, use of a trademark is not a requirement to maintain registration,[81] as it is in NAFTA.

The Dunkel TRIPs Text prohibits special requirements that encumber the use of a trademark in commerce, including requirements of use that reduce the function of the trademark as an indication of sources, or other requirements for use with another trademark.[82]

It also provides, in Article 21, for full contractual rights for trademark owners, including the right to assign a trademark with or without the transfer of the business to which the mark belongs. Conditions on licensing and assignments are allowed. It is regrettable that there is no definition of such "conditions." Finally, compulsory licensing of trademarks is not allowed.[83]

Despite some flaws, the Dunkel TRIPs Text fulfills the requirements of adequate trademark protection, and its provisions offer a useful model for the intellectual property provisions in NAFTA.

6.10 CONCLUSION

Rarely has there been an era as amorphous or as exciting as the present one or, for that matter, as challenging. No more is it business as usual, for the law and practice of today are already those of yesterday.

---

[74] Id., Article 15, par. 3.
[75] Id., Article 15, par. 4.
[76] Id., Article 15, par. 5.
[77] Id., Article 26, par. 1.
[78] Id., Article 16, par. 2.
[79] Id., Article 17.
[80] Id., Article 18.
[81] Id., Article 19.
[82] Id., Article 20.
[83] Id., Article 21.

CHAPTER **7**

IMPERATIVE STRATEGIES FOR PATENTS, DESIGN PATENTS, COPYRIGHTS, AND SEMICONDUCTOR CHIPS: THE INTERNATIONAL MARKET

John Richards, Esq.

Ladas & Parry
New York, New York

7.1 INTRODUCTION

In his 1889 novel, *A Connecticut Yankee at King Arthur's Court*, Mark Twain made the observation that "a country without . . . good patent laws was just a crab and couldn't travel anyway but sideways or backwards."

In the past decade or so the importance to the world economy of intellectual property in general, and patents in particular, has become increasingly evident. As noted in a recent United Nations report:

> Over the course of the past decade, intellectual property rights have come to play an increasingly prominent role in international policy discussions. This renewed interest has followed the growth of intangible goods in international trade and the potential abuse of intellectual property integral to the production of such goods. Both developed and developing countries have introduced legislative reform to tighten protection, and the importance of trade-related aspects of intellectual property rights has been formally recognized in the Uruguay Round of Multilateral Trade Negotiations. Intellectual property rights also bear directly on the acquisition of technology as an important catalyst of economic growth.[1]

A correlation of patent activity in and by a number of countries with other features of their economies is set forth in Exhibit 7.1. From this data a number of conclusions can be drawn:

1. The total number of patent applications filed in a country has some relationship to its gross domestic product (GDP). However, the total number of patent applications filed in Japan is much greater than might be expected, based on its GDP alone.

---

[1] *Intellectual Property Rights and Foreign Direct Investment.* UN Publication ST/CTC/SER. A/24 (March 1993).

	Argentina	Australia	Brazil	Canada	China[1]	France	Germany[2]	Hungary
GDP ($bn) in 1992	76	291	403	543	416	1100	1411	30
Avg % chg/annum GDP from 80–90	−5	3.2	2.7	3.3	9.5	2.2	2.2	1.4
GDP/head ($)	2,370	17,080	2,680	20,450	370	19,480	22,730	2,780
Total exports ($bn)	9.1	41.2	31.4	133.5	61.3	215.8	396.7	7.1
% to US	15.3	11.0	20.6	75.0	8.3	6.1	NA	NA
% to Japan	NA	27.5	8.9	5.5	14.5	NA	NA	NA
Total imports ($bn)	5.3	38.4	20.4	126.5	52.6	233.8	339.9	6.1
% from US	18.8	23.5	25.5	64.6	12.3	8.1	NA	NA
% from Japan	NA	18.1	6.3	7.0	14.2	NA	NA	NA
Total PA filed 1991	NA	27,435	12,769	38,380	11,423	79,075	109,187	9,950
% from US	NA	32.68	33.82	42.21	13.54	25.54	20.29	25.74
% from Japan	NA	6.46	2.35	10.95	7.69	15.60	14.67	2.17
% from local res	NA	29.37	18.48	6.56	64.54	20.0	39.75	22.29
% change 86–91	NA	41.4	52.8	38.3	42.6	34.4	26.8	79.0
PA filed in US by res of each country 1992	59	905	115	3,975	133	4,757	10,851	86
% change 87–92	28.3 f	−12.1 f	38.5 f	29.4	62.2 f	16.9	−.9 f	−52.5

Exhibit 7.1 Relationship between trade and patent statistics: PA = Patent applications.

	India[3]	Indonesia	Israel	Italy	Korea	Malaysia	Mexico	Philippines
GDP ($bn) in 1992	295	101	51	971	231	42	215	44
Avg % chg/annum GDP from 80–90	5.4	6.3	3.2	2.4	10.1	5.1	1.1	.9
GDP/head ($)	350	560	10,970	16,850	5,400	2,340	2,490	730
Total exports ($bn)	16.1	25.7	11.6	182.2	65.0	29.0	26.8	8.2
% to US	16.1	13.1	29.8	7.6	29.8	16.9	69.3	37.8
% to Japan	9.5	42.5	7.2	2.3	19.4	15.3	5.8	20.4
Total imports ($bn)	20.5	21.8	15.1	193.6	69.8	27.1	29.8	12.2
% from US	12.0	11.5	17.8	5.1	26.6	16.9	68.0	19.1
% from Japan	8.0	24.3	NA	2.3	24.3	24.1	4.5	19.5
Total PA filed 1991	3,595	1,336	3,717	53,300	36,154	2,427	5,271	1,921
% from US	29.12	29.49	37.42	31.74	21.45	41.00	58.56	50.13
% from Japan	3.31	12.80	1.96	11.50	20.32	15.49	2.88	8.59
% from local res	32.24	4.04	29.24	2.65	36.66	4.37	10.70	7.65
% change 86–91	2.8	114.4	1.9	57.9	156.0	890.6	31.6	NA
PA filed in US by res of each country 1992	56	15	747	2,345	1,444	24	104	10
% chg from 87–92	154.5	275.0 f	46.2	14.2	464.1	200.0 f	36.8 f	−41.2 f

Exhibit 7.1 (*Continued*)

	Singapore	Taiwan	Thailand	United Kingdom	Venezuela	Japan	USA
GDP ($bn) in 1992	34	157	79	924	51	3,141	5,446
Avg % chg/annum GDP from 80–90	7.0	7.3	7.6	2.7	0.7	4.1	3.2
GDP/head ($)	12,310	7,700	1,420	16,070	2,560	25,430	21,700
Total exports ($bn)	52.6	67.2	22.9	183.6	17.3	280.4	393.0
% to US	22.0	32.4	23.0	12.5	52.0	31.5	—
% to Japan	9.9	12.4	17.0	NA	3.2	—	12.4
Total imports ($bn)	60.5	54.7	32.9	222.6	10.2	216.8	495.3
% from US	16.0	23.0	11.0	11.4	46.1	22.3	—
% from Japan	20.2	29.2	31.0	5.4	3.9	—	18.1
Total PA filed 1991	1,014	NA	1,987	95,533	1,361	380,453	177,388
% from US	NA	NA	41.07	23.86	53.56	5.45	—
% from Japan	NA	NA	18.67	14.88	0.73	—	21.76
% from local res	NA	NA	4.03	25.39	17.12	88.34	50.19
% change 86–91	NA	NA	186.3	30.1	-19.0	17.9	44.9
PA filed in US by res of each country 1992	76	2,957	24	4,537	58	38,135	105,571
% chg from 87–92	100.0	128.0	200.0 f	-12.3 f	65.7	52.4	41.4

[1] For China, GDP figures are actually GNP figures.
[2] First 5 lines for Germany pertain only to West.
[3] India GDP/head is calculated for the year ending 3/31/90.
f = figures fluctuate.
NA = not available.

Exhibit 7.1 (*Continued*)

2. In all countries except Japan and the United States, more patent applications were filed by residents of foreign countries than by residents of the countries themselves.

3. The faster a country's GDP grows, the more likely it is that its nationals will file patent applications outside their own country (as evidenced by the growing trend of foreign-originating patent applications filed in the United States). This is particularly true in relation to the rapid increase of U.S. patent applications originating from Korea and Taiwan in recent years.

4. Based on a comparison of the percentage of imports from the United States and from Japan and the number of patent applications originating in the United States and in Japan, the interest in filing patent applications in foreign countries appears to be strongest in countries between which substantial trade relations exist. However, it is interesting to note that United States nationals seem surprisingly more interested in filing patent applications in East and South East Asia than do the Japanese.

5. Of the major industrialized countries (the G7 countries) only Japan ($+52\%$) and Canada ($+29\%$) increased their number of filings in the United States by more than 20% over the period between 1987 and 1992, and the number filed originating from Germany (-1%) and the United Kingdom (-12%) actually fell.

The patent system may be traced back to a practice of medieval times, when monarchs and princes granted monopolies in respect to the sale of certain products. Indeed, the very name "letters patent" stems from this practice, inasmuch as these were open letters issued by a monarch to his subjects at large, for example, to grant a monopoly or create a new barony, in contrast to his private correspondence. On occasion, the monopolies granted by such letters patent were for new inventions.[2]

In 1624, as part of the skirmishing between Parliament and the Crown leading up to the English Civil War, the English Parliament passed the Statute of Monopolies. This had the effect of limiting the power of the Crown to the granting of monopolies to inventions only for limited periods (14 years—the duration of two training periods for craft apprentices) and, most important, only for "manners of new manufacture" that were introduced into the realm by the recipient of the monopoly. Such grants were, however, conditioned on their not being "mischievous to the state" (for example, by raising prices of commodities) or "generally inconvenient." Patents granted for monopolies under such terms played a significant role in the Industrial Revolution. The English system was followed in the American colonies, leading to the United States making specific provision for a federal patent system in Article 1, Section 8, of the Constitution:

> The Congress shall have power . . . to promote the progress of science and useful arts, by securing for limited time to authors and inventors the exclusive right to their respective writings and discoveries.

The first United States Patent Act was enacted in 1790.

Other countries were less swift to adopt patent laws, but starting with the French law of January 7, 1791, the next hundred years saw patent laws introduced in most major countries, a trend that has continued throughout the twentieth century (the most recent countries to adopt such laws include Moldova and the United Arab Emirates). Today the

---

[2] The world's first patent law for the purpose of encouraging inventions is generally thought to be a Venetian law of March 19, 1474, which provided inventors with an exclusive right to use their inventions for 10 years.

two probably most significant countries without patent laws are Albania and Nepal, and the first of these two is likely to introduce such laws soon.

The philosophical underpinning of patent and, to a lesser extent, copyright systems has been a matter for debate over the years. The original English approach to the development of inventions, which was followed in the American Constitution, was to place emphasis on the advantage to society as a whole. Section 1 of the French law of 1791 took a somewhat different approach: "All new discoveries are the property of the author; to assure the inventor the property and temporary enjoyment of his discovery, there shall be delivered to him a patent for five, ten or fifteen years." The emphasis here was on the inventor's having property in his discovery—on the inventor's rights in the invention rather than on the benefits to society. Today this approach is of limited importance in the patent field but is still significant in the area of copyright, where the Anglo Saxon approach is focused heavily on the bundle of economic rights associated with control over whether others are entitled to copy a work. The French approach, in contrast, focuses more on the moral rights of authors—a fact that is emphasized by the general use of the term *droit d'auteur* (literally, "author's rights") in the French translation of the word *copyright*.

Modern thinking on the rationale for a patent system effectively sees this as a contract between the inventor and society at large.[3] This was well expressed in a report to the French Chamber of Deputies in the debates preceding adoption of the French Patent Law of 1844 (which remained in effect with little change up to the 1960s):

> Every useful discovery is, in Kant's words, "the presentation of a service rendered to Society." It is, therefore, just that he who has rendered this service should be compensated by Society that received it. This is an equitable result, a veritable contract or exchange that operates between the authors of a new discovery and Society. The former supply the noble products of their intelligence, and Society grants to them in return the advantages of an exclusive exploitation of their discovery for a limited period.[4]

As with all contracts, however, one quickly comes to look at the adequacy of the consideration given. In the case of patents the question is, What exactly does the inventor have to provide in return for his or her limited monopoly?[5]

It is possible, following the logic of the approach of the report to the French National Assembly previously quoted, to simply take the view that making the invention of itself justifies the reward. However, a more pragmatic approach has prevailed. To justify a patent, the patentee has to tell the public how to put the invention into practice and in some countries, including the United States and, up to 1978, the United Kingdom, also tell the public of the best method known to the patentee for putting the invention into practice. Early English patents made the training of apprentices a condition of the grant of a patent, although by the early eighteenth century it seems that this condition had been replaced by one that required the submission of a description of the invention to the Court of Chancery within six months of the patent grant. The United States Patent Act of 1790 provided that a specification describing the invention and, where appropriate, models of

---

[3] *The Economist* (20 November 1993): 100.

[4] Quoted in A. Casalonga "Brevets d'Invention," Libraire General de Droit et de Jurisprudence, Paris, 1949. Translation by the present author.

[5] Indeed, a recent issue of *The Economist* (20 November 1993, page 100) described the bargain as a Faustian one.

the invention, had to be submitted at the time of grant of the patent. This specification had to contain:

> A description . . . of the thing or things . . . invented . . . which specification [was] so partic-
> ular . . . as not only to distinguish the invention or discovery from other things before known and
> used, but also to enable a workman or other person skilled in the art of manufacture . . . to make,
> construct or use the same to the end that the public may have the full benefit thereof after the
> expiration of the patent term.[6]

The two limbs of this requirement—the "enablement" requirement and the "definition of the invention" requirement—subsequently became separated. The former became known as the specification or description, and the latter the claims of the application
defining the legal monopoly. Separate claims, which became a requirement in the United
States in 1836, increased in importance after the 1870 Act. However, separate claims
became mandatory in the United Kingdom only in 1883, and it was not until 1968 that they
were required in France.

By the end of the nineteenth century the courts in both the United States and the
United Kingdom had come to view the claims as an essential part of the consideration
given by the inventor upon the grant of a patent. It was up to the inventor to define the
boundaries of his or her monopoly so that members of the public would be able to know
easily whether any act they might contemplate would trespass on forbidden turf. At times
this requiremenrt for a precise definition at an early stage in the development of an
invention can clearly be unfair to the inventor and, in the United States at least, its
harshness has been mitigated by the so-called doctrine of equivalents, whereby for
reasons of equity a patent may sometimes be construed more broadly than is strictly
justified by the precise wording of the claims.

Other countries, however, have taken different views. As noted, France required the
presence of claims only relatively recently, and the approach to patents in Belgium and
Italy was similar. Before the adoption of the separate-claims requirement, the courts in
these countries would look to the description as a whole and, from this, determine
whether the invention described had been used by an alleged infringer. German patent
laws, on the other hand, required separate claims from an early date, but their purpose
was rather different from the "metes and bounds" approach of the Anglo-American
tradition. In Germany little consideration was given to the public's right to be able to
determine what was or was not lawful (indeed, German commentators have never really
accepted the contract theory of the patent system at all, preferring to regard it as simply an
application of the power of the state to order matters for the general good). In Germany
the purpose of a patent claim was to set forth the inventive concept of the invention and
point out specifically how the invention differed from what was known before, rather than
simply providing a definition of something new without having to point out what was new
about it, as has been the Anglo-American tradition. In Germany, it was up to the court to
determine whether an alleged infringement had used the same inventive concept—often a
somewhat subjective decision.

Many countries have over the years added a further requirement to the consideration
to be given by the patentee, namely, that an invention must be worked practically within
the particular country so as to provide a practical backup to the written description. Such
requirements are today regarded as anathema by many Americans. However, the U.S.
patent laws contained such features for inventions of foreign origin from 1832 to 1836.

---

[6]U.S. Patent Act, 1790.

After this date the requirement was dropped, but application fees were based on the nationality of the inventor: $30 for a U.S. citizen, $500 for British subjects, and $300 for all other aliens (from 1792 to 1832 nonresident aliens had been barred from receiving U.S. patents at all).

The other side of the contract today is the grant of exclusive use to an invention by the state. It is important to note that in almost all patent systems the patent does not grant the owner the right to use his or her own invention—merely the right to prevent others from using it. Thus, if a person invents an improvement to a previously patented invention, a license from the owner of the patent on the basic invention (the "dominating patent") is required before that person can work his or her own invention. This basic concept was made quite clear early in the history of the United States patent system. Section 2 of the 1793 Act states:

> Any person who shall have discovered an improvement in the principle of any machine, or in the process of any composition of matter, which shall have been patented, and shall have obtained a patent for such improvement, he shall not be at liberty to make, use, or vend the original discovery, nor shall the first inventor be at liberty to use the improvement."

Many countries have taken the view that such provisions may hamper the development of improvement of the basic invention and have included provisions in their laws providing for compulsory licensing of the basic patent or, in some cases, compulsory cross-licensing in such situations. The desirability of such schemes is still a hot topic of international discussion today.

A point on which there is less dispute (although surprisingly short terms are still stipulated in some countries) is that the duration of a patent should be long enough to encourage investment in research. The duration of U.S. patents was originally 14 years, the same as in the English Statute of Monopolies. The U.S. Act of 1836 provided for the possibility of an extension for a further period of 7 years if the patentee could show that he or she had been inadequately remunerated. In 1861 the term was fixed at 17 years from the time of grant, with no possibility of extension, and has so remained until now. Internationally, however, a 20-year term from the time of filing the patent application (a duration first chosen by the French in 1844) seems to be becoming the norm.

7.2 THE INTERNATIONAL PATENT SYSTEM

As can be seen in the preceding references to nineteenth-century developments in the United States patent system, the system was not always regarded as a means for development of international trade and foreign business. The United States was not alone in discriminating against foreigners, and matters came to a head in connection with the Vienna International Exposition of 1873. At that time the patent law of Austria-Hungary had a provision similar to that in the United States Act of 1832, requiring the working of an invention within a country for one year in order to maintain validity of any patent issued for it. Foreign inventors were reluctant to exhibit at the Exposition for fear that by exhibiting their inventions and being unable to work them within the Austrian-Hungarian Empire within the prescribed one-year period, they would, in effect, be giving their inventions away. *Scientific American*, on December 23, 1871, commented on the situation as follows: "It was almost equivalent to prohibition to require that the locomotive engines of Great Britain, the telegraph instruments of the United States, and the printed muslins of France shall be manufactured on Austrian soil within a year from securing the patent."

The article went on to note that the Austrian law meant that "the value of Austrian patents issued to Americans and other foreigners can be easily escheated to the benefit of the Austrian public." Following representations by the American minister in Vienna, the Austrian authorities passed a special law in an attempt to protect foreign inventions from loss of rights by exhibiting at the Exposition and convened an international congress in Vienna to discuss ways of improving international protection for inventions. A number of resolutions were passed, including one to the effect that the "natural rights" of the inventor should be protected by the laws of all "civilized nations," but no legally enforceable treaty was agreed to. A similar congress accompanied the Paris International Exposition of 1878. This occurred in the wake of the creation of a number of international organizations during the 1870s, including the Universal Postal Union, the International Red Cross, and the International Bureau of Weights and Measures. At the time there were high hopes that a treaty could be drafted to create a worldwide patent system. But it was not to be. Following further conferences in Paris in 1880 and 1883, the best that could be achieved was a convention prescribing how member states could treat nationals of other states and laying down certain minimum provisions as to various aspects of what is now known as intellectual property law, including patents, designs (which in most of the world are regarded as a separate species under intellectual property law), and trademarks.

(a) The Paris Convention for Protection of Industrial Property.   On July 7, 1884, the Paris Convention for the Protection of Industrial Property[7] came into effect, one month after the submission of the requisite number of ratifications of the treaty drafted at the 1883 congress. The original member states were Belgium, Brazil, Ecuador, France, Guatemala, Italy, the Netherlands, Portugal, Salvador, Serbia, Spain, Switzerland, Tunis, and the United Kingdom.[8] Today most major countries are members. The most significant exceptions are India, Taiwan, Pakistan, Thailand, Colombia, and Venezuela.

The basic provisions of the original text were as follows:

1. That no discrimination should be effected between inventions made by a country's own citizens and those made by citizens of other member states of the Convention.

2. A right of priority—that is, there should be a period during which, after a patent application has been filed in one member country of the Convention, applications could be filed in other member countries claiming the date of the first filed application as a "priority date." The effect is that publication or use of the invention after that priority date could not be used to defeat a patent application filed under the Convention in any other member country after the priority date. Originally, the term within which priority had to be claimed was six months from the first filing, which was extended to one year by a revision of the Convention effected in Brussels in 1900. This right of priority was originally subject to a limitation, namely, that any country could provide that anyone who had started to use the invention during the priority period had a right to continue to do so. This possibility was ended in 1934 by the London Revision of the Convention.

3. Preclusion of the possibility of revocation of a patent simply because the patentee imported the patented product into the country—although countries were permit-

---

[7] *Industrial property* is a term traditionally used in Europe to refer to utility patents, designs, and Trademarks. Over the last 20 years or so, it has been largely superseded by the term *intellectual property*, which includes additional topics, such as copyright and trade secrets.

[8] Ecuador, Guatemala, and Salvador withdrew before the end of the nineteenth century.

ted to revoke a patent if the invention was not worked within the country. The ability of states to limit patent rights for nonworking of the invention has been watered down over the years. The present provision, adopted at Lisbon in 1958, permits states to grant nonexclusive, nontransferable compulsory licenses for the abuse of patent rights, including failure to work the invention in the country without any legitimate excuse before the expiration of the later of a four-year period running from the filing date of a patent application or a three-year period running from the grant of a patent arising therefrom. Revocation of a patent still remains a possibility, but only if two years have elapsed from the grant of a compulsory license and there is still no actual working.

The Convention has been revised a number of times over the years. In addition to the effected changes noted earlier are a number of other important revisions.

The Brussels Revision of 1900 clarified the circumstances in which nationals of countries other than members of the Convention could take advantage of its provisions by adding to the list of possible beneficiaries those "who have real and effective industrial establishments" in the territory of a country "that is a member of the Convention."

The Washington Revision of 1911 first set out the maximum number of formalities a country could impose on an applicant wishing to claim priority under the Convention and made provision in the Convention for "utility models." These constitute a form of patent protection granted in many countries for shorter terms than provided by full patents. They are often subject to lower standards of what qualifies as an invention or to less extensive examination than is required for full patents. Typically, protection by utility model is confined to inventions of things, and only to things having defined shapes and not to process inventions.

The Hague Revision in 1925 made the provision of a grace period for payment of renewal fees mandatory and provided for exclusions from infringement in case of an invention's temporary presence within a country's territory (for example, inventions employed on ships, aircraft, etc.).

The London Revision of 1934 effected, among other things, the following:

1. Rights to claims of multiple priority from different applications,
2. A clarification that the original application from which priority was claimed need contain only a description of the invention in question and not necessarily a claim to that invention, and
3. The rights of inventors to be named in the patent.

The Lisbon Revision of 1958 included the following changes:

1. The rights to claim partial priority in a patent application and to claim multiple priorities from applications in different countries were established.
2. The right of an applicant voluntarily to divide a patent application was established.
3. The rejection of a patent application or declaring a patent to be invalid on the ground that use of the invention is unlawful, was prohibited.
4. It was established that any compulsory license granted under a patent must be nonexclusive.

A subsequent revision at Stockholm in 1967 effected little substantive change but remodeled the administration of the Convention to facilitate its being taken over by a new agency of the United Nations—the World Intellectual Property Organization (WIPO)—with headquarters in Geneva.

This change in administration led to an increase in member states of the Convention, but has also resulted in further developments becoming hindered by UN-style politicization. An attempt to effect further revision of the Convention at Nairobi in 1979 failed to achieve anything. Developing countries wished to amend the compulsory license provisions so as to permit the grant of exclusive compulsory licenses (i.e., those that would prevent even the patent owner from exploiting an invention in a country where such a license had been granted—a far cry from the French Revolutionary principle that an invention "belongs to its inventor," as set out in the original French Patent Act discussed earlier). Initially, only the United States opposed this move. Eventually, however, after substantial prodding by European industry, the European governments followed the United States in opposition and the conference terminated in disarray. The other useful improvements in the Convention that had been scheduled for consideration were never even properly discussed.

(b) Patent Cooperation Treaty. Even in light of the previously discussed difficulties, it cannot be said that there have been no recent developments in international patent matters. By far the most important has been the adoption of the Patent Cooperation Treaty (PCT), promulgated under the auspices of WIPO and signed in Washington in 1968. This treaty came into effect in 1978. The main objective of the PCT is to reduce the initial costs of filing for patent protection worldwide. In effect, by payment of a relatively small fee, an inventor can purchase an option on whether to proceed with a full foreign filing program. By taking full advantage of the provisions of the PCT, such costs may be delayed up to 18 months from the date on which they would otherwise normally be incurred, and, it is hoped, the inventor can make a better evaluation of whether the cost is justified.

Chapter 1 of the PCT provides that by filing a so-called international application (which itself may claim Paris Convention priority and, thus, be filed up to one year after the original "home country" filing), an inventor can have an international search carried out before incurring the cost of foreign filing. For U.S. residents and nationals the international search may be carried out either by the U.S. Patent and Trademark Office or by the European Patent Office (EPO) in Munich. Once this is received, the applicant has the option of either requesting an international preliminary examination or proceeding directly with national filing. If an international preliminary examination is required, this must be requested within 19 months of any claimed priority date. If this is not done, then, within 20 months of the claimed priority date, the applicant must proceed with filing in the countries in which he or she is interested or forfeit all rights. If an international preliminary examination is requested, the relevant authority will carry out an examination and report on whether the application as claimed is novel, possesses an inventive step, and complies with requirements for having an "industrial application." Typically, one exchange of views with the examiner is permissible during this phase. For United States applicants, the relevant international preliminary examination authority is the United States Patent Office or, if the European Patent Office has carried out the international search, it may be the European Patent Office. If an international preliminary examination is requested, the period within which an inventor must proceed with the actual foreign filing is 30 months from the claimed priority date. Thus, filing an international application, it may be possible to defer the high cost of foreign filing up to 30 months from the claimed priority date.

The costs of having searches and examinations carried out in the European Patent Office are higher than the costs for those carried out in the U.S. Patent Office. Thus, the cheapest way to defer foreign filing costs is to file an international application and have both the search and the examination carried out by the U.S. Patent Office. However, because a search carried out by the U.S. Patent Office, when acting as an international search authority, is generally identical to the search carried out on an equivalent application originally filed in the U.S. Patent Office, it is probable that the same examiner will handle the international preliminary examination phase of a PCT case that handled the basic U.S. case from which priority is claimed. Thus, proceeding in this way may not enable the applicant to obtain the full benefits of the PCT that can be secured by having a preliminary view of some second searching and examining authority before incurring the cost of foreign filing. Thus, if an applicant is confident of the commercial potential of an invention, but wishes to obtain a second opinion on patentability before foreign filing, then use of the EPO search and examination might be desirable. In any case, at the end of the 30-month period, the inventor must proceed with "completion" of the PCT application in each of the countries in which he or she is still interested, including the filing of translations where necessary. It should be noted that the PCT system differs from that of some countries (including the United States) in one important aspect. Under the PCT, an international application is published 18 months after the earliest claimed priority date. This procedure eliminates the possibility, which exists in the United States, of an applicant's keeping an invention secret until he or she sees whether a patent will be granted for it.

Major countries that are still not members of the Patent Cooperation Treaty include those mentioned earlier that are not members of the Paris Convention and, with the notable exception of Brazil, most countries in Latin America.

(c) Further International Treaties.   Neither the revisions of the Paris Convention nor the Patent Cooperation Treaty have addressed the ideals of those visionaries who, prior to the 1883 Paris Convention, aspired to a worldwide patent system or at least one in which major features of the laws were substantially the same in all major countries. Thus, countries have different rules on what can and cannot be patented, how long a patent monopoly should last, whether grant should be delayed if third parties object, and exactly how broad the rights granted to a patentee should be. Two recent developments have addressed the objective of reducing these differences.

(i) Trade-Related Intellectual Property Issues Under GATT.   Under strong pressure from the United States it was agreed that the current (Uruguay) round of negotiations for amendment of the General Agreement on Tariffs and Trade (GATT) included consideration of trade-related intellectual property issues (TRIPs). Simultaneously, and to some extent competitively, WIPO has been sponsoring negotiations for a Patent Harmonization Treaty.

The TRIPs Agreement reached during the Uruguay Round of GATT negotiations and signed at Marrakesh on April 15, 1994 included the following provisions:

  1. Patents will be available and enjoyable without discrimination as to the place of invention, the field of technology, and whether the product is imported or produced locally. (The first of these requirements will necessitate a change in U.S. laws that in some respect discriminate against inventions made abroad).

2. The only types of inventions that countries can exclude from patentability are those whose exploitations would prejudice public order or morality and those involving diagnostic, therapeutic, or surgical methods for the treatment of humans or animals, new strains or races of plants or animals, or essentially biological processes for the production of plants and animals. Countries taking advantage of this provision to preclude the grant of patent for new plants must, however, provide some alternative means of protection for such plants.

3. Compulsory licenses or other "official licenses" are to be permitted only after consideration of the individual situation in which such a license is requested and, except in cases of national emergency, are subject to a number of conditions, including the following:

   a. The requester of the license has used its best efforts to obtain a voluntary license on reasonable commercial terms.

   b. The license will be terminated if the circumstances leading to its grant have ceased and are unlikely to recur.

   c. The holder of the compulsory license pays adequate compensation for its right to use the invention.

   d. Determination of the amount of adequate compensation is subject to independent review.

   e. Where such a license is granted in order to enable the use of the subsequent patented invention, the license shall be granted only if the later invention is "an important technical advance of considerable economic significance" relative to the document patent and the owner of the document patent is entitled to a cross-license under the secured patent.

4. The minimum duration of a patent is to be 20 years from its filing date.

5. A requirement that in patent infringement trials involving patents granted for processes, there will be a presumption that a product that *could have* been made by the process *was* made by the patented process if either (a) the product itself is new or (b) there is a substantial likelihood that the product was made by the patented process and reasonable attempts made by the patentee have been unable to find out exactly what process was used. (Few foreign countries have discovery proceedings similar to those available to parties in U.S. litigation, so that obtaining proof of infringement of a process patent is often very difficult in foreign countries.)

(ii) WIPO Harmonization Treaty.   The second major treaty currently under consideration is WIPO's harmonization treaty. Here there is much less agreement between the negotiating countries. The key issue is whether the United States is willing to give up its "first-to-invent" rule and adopt a "first-to-file" rule, as used by most other countries and, if so, what concessions the United States should obtain from the rest of the world in return. Under a pure first-to-invent rule, in a case where there are two conflicting patent applications for the same invention, the patent is, in theory, granted to the applicant who can prove that he or she made the invention first.[9]

---

[9] This used to be the law in Canada until 1989—the United States has a "modified first-to-invent" rule since the application of the first-to-invent rule in the United States has always been subject to a number of conditions, such as those that provide that in making a determination as to the first invention one should ignore those who concealed, suppressed or abandoned the inventions and those who could not prove inventive activity within the United States.

Under the first-to-file rule the patent goes to the first person to file an application for the invention at a patent office. A diplomatic conference at The Hague in the summer of 1991 failed to reach agreement on the treaty, and further consideration was delayed following the change of administration in the United States and has again been delayed by a recent announcement by the United States that it wishes to persue further bilateral negotiations before returning to consideration of world-wide harmonization.

In addition to the adoption of a first-to-file system, the draft treaty proposed by WIPO to The Hague conference included the following proposals that may require changes in the current laws of one or more major countries:

1. A one-year grace period with respect to publications emanating from the invention, stretching back, not from the application date (as is currently the case in some countries such as the United States), but from the earliest priority date claimed.

2. In cases where a prior application was on file, but not yet published at the time of the filing of a later application for the same invention, the whole contents of the earlier application can be used when considering the novelty of the later application. However, individual countries have the option of whether or not to consider the earlier application when addressing the question of whether the contents of the later application were "obvious."

3. Pending applications are to be published 18 months from their filing date.

4. Time limits are proposed within which patent offices must complete novelty searches and patentability examinations.

5. It is proposed that rights of continued use be granted to anyone who, before the priority date or filing date of the patent in question, had in good faith used the invention or "was making effective and serious preparations for such use."

6. Pregrant opposition proceedings are to be prohibited.

7. It is proposed that a provision be introduced requiring patent claims to be construed so as to cover equivalents of what is specifically claimed.

Many of these proposals are still controversial, and it remains to be seen whether the treaty will ever be adopted.

(iii) North American Free Trade Agreement.   An important regional agreement is the North American Free Trade Agreement (NAFTA), which was signed on December 17, 1992 and came into effect on January 1, 1994. This Agreement establishes a free trade area comprising the United States, Canada, and Mexico. Among the stated objectives of the Agreement is the intellectual property system section, which limits the right of member countries to declare certain categories of subject matter as being unpatentable, although it is still permissible to preclude the granting of patents for diagnostic, therapeutic, and surgical methods for treatment of humans or animals; for plants or animals; or for essentially biological processes for the production of plants or animals. Member countries are, however, required to provide for effective protection for plant varieties either by patents or by other means. They are also required to allow a process patent to be employed to prevent importation of the direct product of that process, where the process is carried out in another country. However, the Agreement does not preclude the granting of compulsory licenses in cases of where the invention is not worked (i.e., not put into operation) within the country, although it does require that an importation from

another member country be regarded as being working for this purpose. The Agreement also permits member countries to grant limited exceptions to the exclusive rights granted by a patent as long as such exceptions "do not unreasonably conflict with normal exploitation of a patent and do not unreasonably prejudice the legitimate interests of the patent owner, taking into account the legitimate interests of other persons."

Perhaps the most controversial element of the patent requirements, however, is the impact on 35 USC 104,[10] in that the Agreement requires that evidence of the making of an invention in the United States, for purposes of determining who was the first to invent the claimed subject matter, can be replaced by evidence of the making of the invention in Canada or Mexico.

The Agreement also requires member countries to provide for protection of the layout of design of semiconductor integrated circuits, essentially adopting the provisions of the Washington Treaty on this matter, but excluding those portions to which the United States raised objection and on the basis of which the United States refused to sign the Washington Treaty. Thus NAFTA does not include the Washington Treaty's proposals relating to innocent infringement, but permits member countries to require that an innocent infringer must pay a reasonable royalty for any infringing materials on hand at the point at which he or she ceases to be "innocent." Furthermore, this Agreement, unlike the Washington Treaty, precludes compulsory licensing of designs in semiconductors and also requires a minimum 10-year term of protection. Under one of the reservations to NAFTA, however, Mexico has a four-year period within which to implement the provisions relating to semiconductor chip design.

Finally, in the intellectual property area, NAFTA requires all countries to provide adequate protection for trade secrets as long as the information is secret, it has actual or potential commercial value, and its owner takes reasonable steps to keep it a secret.

7.3 SECURING FOREIGN PATENT PROTECTION

As noted earlier, the Paris Convention and PCT provide significant procedural advantages to securing patent rights, but still require that patent application ultimately be filed in the jurisdictions in which protection is sought. Each country will then examine the application in accordance with its own requirements. (Some countries, such as Japan, undertake a strict examination as to patentability; others, such as South Africa, check only on formalities; and most others carry out a reasonable examination, but, in contrast to the United States, give the applicants the benefit of the doubt at the examination stage.) In a few countries, it is still possible to secure patent protection by simply "registering" or "confirming" patents granted in other countries. This possibility exists, for example, in Hong Kong and Singapore (where the only patents that can be registered are British patents) and in Argentina and Saudi Arabia, where registration of the first foreign patent is feasible. Each country has its own rules for examination. Some, such as Canada, China, Japan, and Korea, permit the applicant to delay actual examination (which tends to be an expensive part of the procedure) for a number of years from the time of filing. For example, in China a three-year delay is possible from the date of priority; in

---

[10] 35 USC 104 is a section of the U.S. Patent Law that imposes limitations on the territories in which acts must have taken place if they are to be taken into consideration in determining who was first to make an invention. Prior to NAFTA, only acts within the United States were taken into consideration. Now acts carried out in Canada and Mexico must also be considered.

Korea, a five-year delay from the time of filing; and in Canada and Japan, a seven-year delay from the time of filing. Other countries institute examination immediately. This multiplicity of systems is, however, to some extent alleviated by three regional treaties, namely, the European Patent Convention, the African Regional Industrial Property Office, and the African Organization for Protection of Industrial Property. The first of these is discussed in greater detail later in this section. The important features, however, are that an inventor can file a single European application at the European Patent Office in Munich, which will carry out a single examination in English, and at the end of the day the applicant has the right to secure a bundle of patents in all of the countries originally designated by the applicant who are members of the Convention, following this single examination. At the point of securing national rights, however, it is necessary to translate the entire text into the language (if other than English) of the country where protection is required. The African Regional Intellectual Property Organization essentially covers most English-speaking African countries and has an organization similar to that of the European Patent Office. In this case, the regional Patent Office is in Harare in Zimbabwe and, again, at the end of the prosecution procedure a bundle of patents may be issued. The third regional organization, the African Organization for Industrial Property, comprises most French-speaking African countries. Examination of applications by this body is carried out at Yaounde in the Cameroons, and in this case a single patent covering the entire group of countries is granted.

There is a fundamental difference between the laws of almost all foreign countries (the Philippines is an exception) and the United States, namely, their approach to the question of novelty. In general, any publication before a claimed priority date, whether by the author or by a third party, can act to destroy novelty in a foreign country. This is a consequence of the so-called first-to-file rule. There are limited exceptions to this provision, in that some grace periods for publication by the author do exist, for example, in Mexico and Canada, but they generally do not exist in Europe. It is therefore very important to ensure that U.S. application has been filed before a publication of the subject matter of an invention takes place, and if an applicant is interested in filing in non-Convention countries, such as Colombia, Venezuela, Taiwan and India, that filings in these countries are effected before any such publication occurs.

Some countries, like the United States, still do not regard prior use outside the country as being a bar to patentability. In other countries, however, notably those in Europe, prior use anywhere in the world, in a way that enables the nature of the invention to be determined, will act as a bar. A brief note on the novelty requirements in a number of major countries is included in the summary of national laws later in this chapter.

Another major difference between U.S. patent practice and that of other countries in the world is that in many countries, publication of pending applications occurs 18 months from the time of filing or, if priority is claimed, 18 months from the earliest claimed priority date. This change from traditional patent practice, under which applications remained secret until they had been examined, has become much more common over the last 20 years, as a result of the delays that have occurred in the grant of patents by almost all major patent offices. The rationale for such publication is twofold: first, industries wanted to know what their competitors were doing as early as possible so that they could avoid waste of resources in pursuing areas in which competitors had already established a niche, and, second, delays in granting patents meant that for items in which low capital investment was involved, competitors could get into a market, and out of it, by copying the inventor's designs before any patent rights were issued. A concomitant of the early publication in all countries is that the owner of an application has the right to obtain compensation from anyone who uses the invention within the period between publication and the actual granting of the patent (assuming that a patent is finally granted).

One final point of importance in connection with patents is that periodic payments are required to keep patents in force. Typically, these arise in later years during the life of a patent. In some countries such payments must be made during the pendency of the application, whereas in others this is not required.

(a) The European Patent System.   The European Patent System is unusual in two respects. The first is that many European countries have grouped together in the European Patent Convention and set up a single patent office, located in Munich, that has the right to grant a patent that can have effect in all member countries of the group, subject only to compliance with certain formalities. The second is that the Treaty of Rome, which acts as a constitution for the European Economic Community (EEC), includes certain provisions that have the effect of modifying the rights of patent holders in EC member states.

(i) The European Patent Convention

Background   The European Patent Convention (EPC), in principle, has nothing to do with the Treaty of Rome. Today all EC member states are also members of the EPC. The Convention is, however, open to all European countries, and Austria, Sweden, and Switzerland, which are not yet members of the EC, are already members of the European Patent Convention. The EPC was initially designed primarily to provide a means for cutting the costs of obtaining patents, by creating the European Patent Office (EPO) to administer a single examination to produce a bundle of patents effective in the member states. A necessary corollary to the existence of the EPO was that the same standards would be applied to patents obtained via the national and the European routes. This led to a substantial harmonization of the definition of what was patentable, the terms of patents[11] (at least in the EEC countries—Austria still has different terms for domestic patents), and the way in which patents were to be interpreted.

Like those of United States, the basic EPC requirements for patentability are novelty, nonobviousness (inventive step), and utility (industrial applicability). An additional problem in Europe, however, is the inclusion in the European Patent Convention of a rather more restricted definition of what constitutes an invention than exists in the United States. These problems have, to a significant extent, been alleviated by the EPO Appeal Boards' adopting a flexible interpretation of the strict wording of the Convention, to the effect that a broad range of subject matter has been held to be patentable.

Problems of Statutory Subject Matter.   Almost all problems of statutory subject matter have arisen in three areas: inventions relating to computer programs, pharmaceuticals, and biological inventions.

---

[11] EPC, Article 63, provides that patents will run for 20 years from their filing date. A recent amendment has permitted member states to provide for extensions of this term where marketing of the patented invention is delayed by the need to obtain prior regulator's approval, as is the case for pharmaceuticals.

The EPC itself states:

The following . . . shall not be regarded as inventions:
   (a) mathematical methods; . . .
   (b) programs for computers.[12]
These prohibitions are, however, limited by the proviso that they apply only to the extent to which a European patent application or European patent relates to such subject matter "as such."

The leading case in regard to computer programs and mathematical methods is *Vicon Systems Application*,[13] which relates to a method of digitally processing images through the use of a computer. In this case the Appeal Board reversed the rejection of the Examining Division, basing its decision on the rationale that even if the idea underlying an invention may be considered to reside in a mathematical method, a claim to a technical process in which the method is used is not an attempt to obtain protection for the mathematical method as such.

The Board did, however, draw a distinction between the processing as claimed, in which a rearranged data array was produced, and a method for "digitally filtering data" which, it felt, was "an abstract notion not distinguished from a mathematical method so long as it is not specified what physical entity is represented by the data."

The Board went on to hold that a claim to a technical process that is carried out under the control of a program (whether the implementation is in hardware or in software) should be allowable under EPC, Article 52 (2) (c) and (3), because it cannot be regarded as relating to a computer program as such.

Pursuant to the *Vicon* case, a number of issues relating to the patentability of computer-related inventions have come before the Appeal Board, mainly as a result of appeals by the IBM Corporation. In one case, it was held that the bar on patentability of computer programs did not preclude the patenting of:

A data processing system having a plurality of data processors interconnected as nodes in a telecommunication network . . . each processor having an independent control system characterized in that each control system includes [a series of "means" for determining whether a transaction was in progress, "means" for transmitting this information, "means" for receiving such information, and "means" for acting on that information].[14]

The system was apparently an extension of IBM's Customer Information Control system, which is essentially a transmitter-oriented data base management concept effected by a set of programs providing the general facilities required for a great number of application programs in the area of commercial and administrative activity.

However, in *IBM/Text Processing*,[15] it was held that the only problem solved by a program to detect and correct contextual homophone errors (e.g., *there* instead of *their*) was an essentially mental one and, as such, the invention was not patentable.

A similar flexibility has been experienced in the pharmaceutical field. The Convention states in Article 52(4) that:

Methods for treatment of the human or animal body by surgery or therapy and diagnostic methods practiced on the human or animal body shall not be regarded as inventions.

---

[12] European Patent Convention, Article 52(2).
[13] [1987] OJ EPO p. 15.
[14] Data Processor Network, IBM [1990] OJEPO 5.
[15] *IBM/Text Processing* Decision T65/86 [1990] EPOR p. 181.

This position is, however, complicated by a proviso in Article 54 (5) that states that this prohibition shall not exclude patentability for any "substance or composition for use in [such] a method," even if previously known for some other purpose as long as that purpose was not a method of treatment or diagnosis practiced on a human or animal body.

This wording was apparently adopted as a compromise between various positions at the Munich Conference that gave rise to the European Patent Convention, the chairman commenting that in his view the aim was to make clear that a known substance (or a known composition) which, because it formed part of the state of the art, was no longer patentable, could nevertheless be patented for the first use in a method for treatment of the human or animal body by surgery or therapy, but that a further patent could not be granted if a second possible use were found for the same substance, irrespective of whether the human or animal body was to be treated with it.[16]

So far as known compounds having no previous "medical history" were concerned, it fairly quickly became the practice to take the express wording of the Convention as to what was patentable and draft claims in the form

<blockquote>Compound X for use in treating Y</blockquote>

or even, following the decision in *Pyrrolidone Derivatives/Hoffmann-LaRoche*,[17]

<blockquote>Compound X for therapeutic use.</blockquote>

However, this did not help in cases where the invention was a second medical use of a substance. In 1982 the issue came before the German Supreme Court in a German national application that was to be decided under the old German law (where the relevant portion of the definition of patentability required simply that the invention was new and susceptible to industrial application—there being no specific exclusions of particular types of inventions). The German Court held that even for a second medical use, the law did not bar patent claims along the lines of the form

<blockquote>Use of compound X to treat condition Y.[18]</blockquote>

When in the following year the same issue came before the same Court in a case to be decided under a new German law (which contained provisions substantially identical with those of the EPC), it saw no reason to decide the issue differently. The Court held that on its reading of the legislative history of the European Convention it did not conclude that the member states had intended to bar protection for second medical uses. Under German law a use claim was not the same as a claim to a method of treatment. Only patents to methods of treatment were barred.[19]

In the meantime, the same issue had come before the Swiss Patent Office, which had concluded that although the wording of the Convention precluded the granting of patent claims of the type allowed in Germany, it did not preclude the granting of a patent to:

---

[16] *Minutes of the Munich Diplomatic Conference*, February 10, 1985, par. 57.
[17] *Pyrrolidone Derivatives/Hoffmann-LaRoche* T 128/82 [1984] OJEPO p. 164.
[18] *Sitsosteryl-Glycosides* Case X2B 21/81, reported in English in 14 IIC 283.
[19] *Hydropyridine* Case XZB 4/83, reported in English 15 IIC 215.

> The use of compound X for the manufacture of a
> medicament for treatment of disease Y

even if compound X had previously been used for treatment of some other disease.[20]

In *Esai's Application*, the Enlarged Board of Appeals of the European Patent Office agreed with the Swiss and upheld the grant of a claim in this form while rejecting a medical-use claim of the type allowed in Germany.[21] The "Swiss formulation" has since been followed by the British[22] and Swedish courts.[23] Yet the Dutch Patent Office has refused to allow a patent in this form unless there is something novel about the form of the medicament in question itself, and not merely in its manner of use.[24]

Methods of treatment of humans or animals are, however, not necessarily unpatentable if they are carried out for reasons other than therapy or diagnosis. For example, claims to cosmetic treatments have been allowed even if a treatment has some therapeutic value, as was the case in *Appetite Suppressant/DuPont*,[25] where the allowed claim was to:

> A method of improving the bodily appearance of . . . a mammal which comprises orally administering to said mammal [a material] in a dosage effective to reduce appetite and repeating said dosage until a cosmetically beneficial loss of body weight has occurred.

The Board reasoned that although there were medical reasons to lose weight, most people wished to do this for cosmetic rather than medical reasons, and in this case the claimed invention was specifically limited to obtaining cosmetic results.

Article 53(b) of the EPC provides that patents shall not be granted for "plant or animal varieties or essentially biological processes for the production of plants or animals." The Article goes on to state, "This provision does not apply to microbiological processes or the products thereof."

On the question of protection for higher life forms, the leading case is that relating to the European patent application for the so-called Harvard mouse (a mouse particularly susceptible to cancer, and thus a valuable research tool, and the subject of the first animal patent in the United States). This application was initially rejected, but was allowed after an appeal. The Appeal Board decided that the meaning of the term *animal variety* in the EPC's prohibition could not simply be equated with *animals*, inasmuch as the linguistics of the various equally authentic texts in three languages did not permit such an interpretation. Thus, further consideration of what was meant was necessary. Moreover, the Examining Division was directed to reconsider the evidence on the question of whether the granting of patents for animals might be contrary to public order or morality.[26]

The Examining Division, after such reconsideration, issued a decision to grant a patent for the invention. The examiners noted that the claims were not directed to any particular

---

[20] *Legal Advice from Swiss Patent Office* [1984] OJ EPO, p. 581.

[21] [1985] EPOJ, p. 64.

[22] John Wyeth & Brother Ltd.'s Application [1985] RPC p. 545.

[23] *Hydropyridine/SE* reported in English [1988] OJEPO p. 198.

[24] Decision of Dutch Patent Office Appeal Board, September 30, 1987 (No. 16673), reported at [1988] EPOJ 405.

[25] Decision T 144/83 [1986] OJEPO 301.

[26] *Onco Mouse/Harvard* T 19/90 [1990] OJEPO 476. An interesting jurisprudential issue on the question of interpretation of the Convention was touched on in the Appeal Board's decision when it expressed the view that "the purpose of a law (*ratio legis*) is not merely a matter of the actual intention of the legislators at the time when the law was adopted but also of their presumed intention in the light of changes in circumstances which have taken place since then."

subspecies of animal (in fact, the claims covered all genetically modified nonhuman animals into which the appropriate genes had been introduced) and so concluded that what was claimed could not be considered to be an animal "variety."

On the question of morality and public order, the Examining Division believed that a balancing test was appropriate in every case, depending on the invention in question, with three factors needing to be considered in the present case:

1. The interest of humankind in providing remedies for dangerous diseases,
2. Protection against uncontrolled dissemination of unwanted genes, and
3. Prevention of cruelty to animals.

Because in the present case the invention opened the way to the need for fewer animals for experimentation and the invention could be practiced in such a way as to avoid widespread dissemination of genes, the Division concluded that the advantage of providing a tool for use in the fight against cancer outweighed the possible negative factors, and thus the invention was patentable.

In a subsequent, and so far unreported case, the EPO has apparently rejected an application for an animal genetically modified so as to assist in the testing of cosmetics on the ground that the application fails the "morality test."

Novelty.   The European Patent Convention defines novelty simply as that which does not form part of the state of the art.[27]

The state of the art is defined as including everything made available to the public by means of a written or oral description, by use or in any other way, before the date of filing of a European patent application or a validly claimed Convention priority date.[28] This applies to any public disclosure of the invention before the European filing date or a properly claimed priority date *anywhere* in the world.

There is still very little case law on the question of what is meant by "made available to the public." However, a recent decision has made it clear that if a product is freely distributable to the public and is capable of being analyzed or taken apart, the information that would result from such analysis is to be taken as having been made available to the public, even though the public may have had no particular reason to carry out such analysis.[29]

So far as prior unpublished copending applications are concerned, although their entire content is relevant to the question of determining novelty of a later-filed application, they are not to be used as the basis of an allegation of lack of inventive height (i.e., that the claimed invention is obvious).[30] The mere fact that the earlier case was filed by the same applicant is irrelevant in considering its prior-art effect.

It is further provided that prior disclosure as a result of an evident abuse of the applicant's rights, or at certain international exhibitions, does not constitute a novelty bar as long as an application was filed within a six-month grace period following one of these events.[31] The extent to which an experimental use that was necessarily carried out in public may act as a bar has still to be decided. Under the old German law, such use

---

[27] European Patent Convention, Article 54(1).
[28] European Patent Convention, Article 54(2).
[29] Decision G1/92 Availability to the Public (1993) OJEPO p. 277.
[30] European Patent Convention, Article 54(3).
[31] European Patent Convention, Article 55(1).

probably was not a bar. *Prout v. British Gas PLC*,[32] a British first-instance decision, has followed the German law on this point.

A certain amount of surprise has been expressed at the view taken by the EPO Appeal Boards on the question of the patentability of new uses of old materials, and it is not clear to what extent the Appeal Boards' decisions are being followed by the examiners at first instance. In two decisions, however, *Triazole Derivatives/BASF*,[33] and *Friction-Reducing Additive/Mobil Oil*,[34] the Appeal Boards have upheld the patentability of use claims where the only novelty was in the realization that operations that had been carried out in the past were exactly the same as now being claimed to have a previously unreported and unexpected effect. In one case, a known plant growth regulation was found to have an antifungal effect, and in the other a brown rust inhibitor was found to have a friction-reducing effect.

It is prudent, however, not to read too much into these decisions. For example, the use of a known material on the basis of its known properties to obtain a known effect in a new combination (i.e., what is essentially a "similar use" to the prior art) has been held to be unpatentable.[35]

Obviousness. The second major requirement for a European patent is that the invention claimed should not be obvious in light of the prior art. Prior to the European Patent Convention's coming into effect, considerable misgivings were expressed as to the standard by which obviousness would be judged.

Concern for the need for a standard of obviousness that would be acceptable in all member states was evident early in the EPO's case law. One of the earliest Board of Appeals decisions stated that "the inventive step [required by the EPO] should not be below what may be considered the average amongst the standards presently applied by the contracting states," so that patentees would have a fair degree of certainty if their patents were litigated in a national court.[36]

In implementing this approach, the EPO aimed at applying the previous German standard and adopted the so-called problem-and-solution approach to questions of obviousness.

The definitive adoption of the problem-and-solution approach followed shortly later in *Metal Refining/BASF*,[37] in which the Appeal Board stated as follows:

> When assessing an inventive step it is not a question of the subjective achievement of the inventor. It is rather the objective achievement which has to be assessed. Objectivity in the assessment of inventive step is achieved by starting out from the objectively prevailing state of the art, in the light of which the problem is determined which the invention addresses and solves from an objective point of view, and consideration is given to the question of the obviousness of the disclosed solution to this problem as seen by the man skilled in the art and having those capabilities which can be objectively expected of him. This also avoids the retrospective approach which inadmissibly makes use of knowledge of the invention, as feared by the appellant.

---

[32] [1992] FSR 478.

[33] Decision T231/85 [1989] EPOJ p. 74.

[34] Decision G2/88 [1990] EPOJ p. 93.

[35] Profile Member/Kommerling T130/89 [1991] OJEPO p. 514.

[36] Case T 01/81, *Thermoplastic Sockets* [1981] OJEPO p. 439.

[37] T 24/81, [1983] OJEPO p. 133.

One fear expressed by opponents of the problem-and-solution approach to obviousness was that such an approach would fail to deal adequately with situations where the invention lay in realizing the nature of the problem to be solved or where the art had over the years failed to appreciate a simple solution that, once pointed out, seemed obvious.

These fears have, to some extent at least, been mollified by decisions of the Appeal Boards in cases where such issues have arisen.

Nevertheless, there is an increasing tendency for examiners to try to force an applicant to define the problem solved as the providing of an "improved" widget, rather than simply an alternative one. Some support for this is found in *Hot-Gas Cooler/Sulzer*,[38] in which the Appeal Board took the view that the broad problem postulated by the appellant had already been solved, so that the only problem left was to improve upon that solution.

Sufficiency of Disclosure.   Article 83 of the European Patent Convention requires that an application must disclose the invention in a manner sufficiently clear and complete for it to be carried out by one skilled in the art, and Article 84 requires that the claims be clear, concise, and supported by the description. The Implementing Regulations flesh out these requirements to some extent by requiring that the description will, among other things:

- *Indicate* the background art that, as far as known to the applicant, can be regarded as useful for understanding the invention, for drawing up the European search report and for the examination, and, preferably, cite the documents reflecting such art,
- *Disclose* the invention, as claimed, in such terms that the technical problem (even if not expressly stated as such) and its solution can be understood, and state any advantageous effects of the invention with reference to the background art,
- *Describe* in detail at least one way of carrying out the invention claimed, using examples where appropriate and referring to the drawings, if any, and
- *Indicate* explicitly, when it is not obvious from the description or nature of the invention, the way in which the invention is capable of exploitation in industry.

Apart from these general provisions, certain specific requirements were set out in the rules for inventions relating to microorganisms.

If the initial approach of the EPO to the question of obviousness was Germanic, the approach to sufficiency was distinctly Franco-British.

From the beginning, it has been clear that claims may be drafted broadly and do not have to be limited to specifically described embodiments or examples. The EPO guidelines recognize that claims are generalizations from one or more particular examples:

> The extent of generalization permissible is a matter which the examiner must judge in each particular case in the light of the relevant prior art. Thus, an invention which opens up a whole new field is entitled to more generality in the claims than one which is concerned with advances in a known technology. A fair statement of claim is one which is not so broad that it goes beyond the invention nor yet so narrow as to deprive the applicant of a just reward for the disclosure of his invention. The applicant should be allowed to cover all obvious modifications, equivalents to and uses of that which he has described. In particular, if it is reasonable to predict that all the variants covered by the claims have the properties or uses the applicant ascribes to them in the description he should be allowed to draw his claims accordingly.[39]

---

[38] T 170/87 [1989] OJEPO p. 441.

[39] *Guidelines for Examination in the European Patent Office*, Part C, Chapter III. Paragraph 6.2

It remains to be seen how the courts in countries that have traditionally dealt with claims of much narrower scope (such as Germany and Sweden) will deal with broad claims of the type granted by the EPO.

EPO Procedures.   From a procedural point of view, the European system differs significantly from that of the United States. First, because the European system is a multinational one, an applicant must take care initially to specify the countries in which he or she is interested. A separate designation fee must be paid for each country. Although the initial application must be filed in an official language of any of the member countries, the EPO operates only in English, French, and German. Thus applications filed in any other language must be translated into one of these three promptly after filing. Second, under the EPO, although a search of prior art is carried out automatically after the filing of the application and payment of a search fee, substantive examination occurs only if the applicant so requests, and pays a further fee, after receipt of the search report. A third major difference is that the European patent application is published automatically 18 months after its filing or, where there is a claim to priority under the Paris Convention, 18 months after its priority date. If the search has been carried out by this time, the search report is published with the application. If not, the application is republished together with the search report, when this is ready.[40]

Once this publication has occured, the applicant is in principle entitled to compensation from any one who uses the invention as long as a patent ultimately issues on the application. In order to be able to claim such compensation, however, the applicant must file a translation of the claims of the application with the national patent office in any country where compensation is to be claimed, unless the language in which the application was published is an official language of that country.

Once examination is completed, the European patent is granted. This patent, however, has force only in any country where the language of the application is one of its official languages, and even in this case additional formalities, such as recording an address for service, may be required.

If the patentee still wishes for protection in any other countries (except Luxembourg), a translation into the local language must be submitted to the national patent office in question. For protection in Switzerland, this must be effected before the grant of the European patent; in all other cases it must be done within three months of the grant of the European patent.

Once a European patent has been granted, a nine-month period is provided within which third parties may file an opposition to the patent on the ground that it did not

---

[40] The concept of early publication of pending patent applications developed in Europe in the 1960s. In 1964 the Dutch Patent Office realized that it was slipping further and further behind in examination of pending applications and introduced a system of deferred examination in which an applicant could, at his or her option, defer examination for up to 7 years. (The theory was that in many cases the applicant would lose interest during this period so that the Patent Office would be spared the trouble of carrying out an examination. However, deferred examination coupled with the traditional view that patent applications should remain secret until examination had been completed presented a major problem for industry. It resulted in too much delay before knowing whether a competitor's patents would foreclose a particular line of research. The result was a compromise: applications would be published soon after filing but, as long as a patent ultimately issued, the applicant would be entitled to compensation for any use between the date of the early publication and the grant of the patent.

comply with one or more of the requirements of the EPO. At present about 10% of all European patents are opposed. Patents granted on European patent applications have a duration of 20 years from the date of filing, as long as renewal fees are paid. Supplemental Protection Certificates may possibly be granted to extend the terms of patents relating to pharmaceuticals whose first marketing was delayed as a result of the need to comply with government regulations.

Interpretation of European Patents. The final major point on which harmonization was attempted by the EPC was how claims should be interpreted so as to prevent claims granted by a single examination being held to mean different things in different countries. The "harmonized" definition of claim interpretation is a compromise between the old German view, that claims were merely guideposts and that a patentee was entitled to a monopoly in his or her inventive concept, and the British view of fairly literal interpretation. According to the Convention, the scope is to be determined by the claims, but the specification and drawings are to be used in interpreting the claims. Article 69 reads as follows:

> The extent of the protection conferred by a European patent or a European patent application shall be determined by the terms of the claims. Nevertheless, the description and drawings shall be used to interpret the claims.

Unfortunately, just before the signing of the EPC, it was revealed that the British and Germans had totally different views as to what this meant. A protocol to explain the meaning was added to the Convention.

According to the Protocol on Article 69, a "middle way" between the fairly literal interpretation of British courts and the "inventive concept" approach of the German courts was to be followed. The actual wording of the Protocol is, however, scarcely a model of clarity:

> Article 69 should not be interpreted in the sense that the extent of the protection conferred by a European Patent is to be understood as that defined by the strict literal meaning of the wording used in the claims, the description and drawings being employed only for the purpose of resolving an ambiguity found in the claims. Neither should it be interpreted in the sense that the claims serve only as a guideline and that the actual protection conferred may extend to what, from a consideration of the description and drawings by a person skilled in the art, the patentee has contemplated. On the contrary, it is to be interpreted as defining a position between these extremes which combines a fair protection for the patentee with a reasonable degree of certainty for third parties.

In the *Lady Remington* case, however, the Dusseldorf court seems not to have moved far from the traditional German approach.[41] The claim in question was in a European patent. It required a helical spring comprising a plurality of adjacent windings arranged to be driven by:

> A motor means in rotational sliding motion relative to skin bearing hair to be removed, said helical spring including an arcuate hair engaging portion arranged to define a convex side whereas the windings are spread apart, and a concave side corresponding thereto whereas the windings are pressed together, the rotational motion of the helical spring producing continuous motion of the windings from a spread apart orientation at the convex side to a pressed together orientation at the concave side and for engagement and plucking of hair from the skin of the subject, whereby

---

[41] [1990] International Review of Industrial Property and Copyright Law (11C) 572.

the surface velocities of the windings relative to the skin greatly exceeds the surface velocity of the housing relative thereto.

The alleged infringing article used a solid rubber rod that was held in an arcuate configuration and had slots therein, that was rotated so that in one position the slots closed on a hair and, as the rod rotated, pulled it out; and as the rod rotated further, the slots opened and the hair fell out.

The German court held that there was infringement. The courts of most other countries, such as the United Kingdom and Italy, did not. Thus, the issue of harmonization of claim interpretation still needs to be resolved.

(ii) The Proposed European Community Patent Convention.   The primary concern left outstanding by the European Patent Convention, so far as harmonization was concerned, was the lack of agreement between courts on questions of infringement and validity. After the grant, a European patent splits into a bundle of national patents (the EPC simply provided a common mechanism for granting a bundle of national patents), and different courts can reach different conclusions as to their validity, and thus what is regarded as obvious in one country can be the subject of a patent in another. This problem can be resolved only by the existence of Community-wide patents and a single court system for adjudicating them. This is the objective of the Community Patent Convention (CPC), first adopted in 1975 yet still not in force.

The CPC will provide for the granting of a single EC-wide Community Patent by the European Patent Office, applying the same criteria as at present, and by means of a protocol on litigation will provide a single Community-wide appellate court to adjudicate all matters of patent infringement and validity brought before national appellate courts with respect to Community patents. In addition to the definitions of what is patentable and how claims are to be interpreted, as carried over from the European Patent Convention, the CPC also provides a definition of infringement.[42] This Convention prohibits both direct and indirect infringement. The former is defined as making, using, offering, or putting on the market, the subject of an invention or the direct product thereof. It also includes the stocking or importation of a patented product or the direct product of a patented process. To assist the patentee in cases where he or she seeks to prove that an alleged infringement is the product of a patented process, the Convention provides for a reversal of the burden of proof in cases where the product is novel.[43] Indirect infringement is defined as covering both induced and contributory infringement, although it will not be an infringement to supply another with a staple commercial product unless the supplier actively induces its use for infringement. Finally, the Convention provides that certain activities are not to be regarded as infringements, including private acts, or acts done for noncommercial purposes, experimental acts, extemporaneous mixing of medicines, and uses on board ships and aircraft as permitted by the Paris Convention.[44]

Under the Litigation Protocol, litigation will be commenced before national courts, located either where infringement occurs or within the domicile of the defendant. In deciding cases brought before them, such courts will have the power to determine the validity of the patent on a Community-wide basis, but only when the issue of validity is

---

[42] CPC, Articles 25–27.
[43] CPC, Article 35.
[44] CPC, Article 37.

raised as a counterclaim in an infringement action. Appeals may be made to national appellate courts as now, but such courts will be required to refer questions of validity and infringement to the new Community Patents Appeal Court (COPAC) for a decision on such issues.[45] The Community Court will decide these issues and then return the case to the national appellate court for a decision on the case as a whole. The system will, therefore, be somewhat similar to that which applies today in cases where specific questions of Community law are referred to the European Court of Justice.

Once the Convention is fully effective, designation of any EEC country in an "ordinary" EPO application will be taken to mean that the applicant has opted for a Community patent. Ultimately, this will be expensive, because to be effective in any country, the Community patent will have to be translated into all nine official languages of the EEC.[46] Such translations can be filed centrally with the EPO. Nevertheless, the cost is likely to be considerable. Failure to file all such translations will render the Community patent void. However, if the applicant fails to file all translations in time, he or she will be given the opportunity to obtain a bundle of European patents for those countries for which translations have been filed.[47] As noted earlier, the cost factor was a major driving force behind the implementation of the European Patent Convention. It has also become a major impediment to the adoption of the Community Patent Convention, because the cost of complying with the translation requirement is seen by industry as excessive, so that, with the exception of a few bureaucrats in Brussels, few people are pushing for the CPC to come into effect.

(iii) The Effect of the Treaty of Rome on European Patent Law.   "European law," as developed under the Treaty of Rome, is applied to intellectual property matters within two main areas: first, the extent to which European law limits the exercise of intellectual property rights validly granted under the European Patent Convention or national laws and, second, the extent to which the Treaty of Rome abrogates any such laws.

Limitations Imposed by the Treaty of Rome on the Exercise of Intellectual Property Rights. Article 2 of the Treaty of Rome sets out the basic purpose of the European Economic Community, namely, the creation of a Common Market. Article 3 sets out certain necessary requirements in order to do this and includes the elimination of quantitative restrictions on the import and export of goods and of all other measures having an equivalent effect. These basic statements of purpose have enabled the European Court of Justice to distinguish between identically worded provisions in Article 30 of the Treaty itself and a Treaty between the Common Market and Portugal (in the days before Portugal became a member of the Community) in order to reach different conclusions as to whether goods should be allowed to flow freely.[48]

The basic black letter law of the EEC on Intellectual Property Rights and the Free Flow of Goods Doctrine is by now well established. In general, an intellectual property right cannot be used to prevent importation of goods from another EEC member state if the goods were first put on the market in that EEC member state, either by the holder of

---

[45] CPC Protocol on Litigation, Articles 15–17.
[46] CPC, Article 30.
[47] CPC, Article 30(6).
[48] *Polydor Ltd. et al. v. Harlequin Record Shops* [1982] 1 Comm. Mkt. LR 677.

the intellectual property right or with the holder's consent.[49] If the goods were first put on the market outside the EEC, however, this Community law does not apply, and one must look to national law for a decision (see, for example, *EMI v. CBS*[50] and *Harlequin Records v. Polydor*[51]). This formulation law has been adopted with respect to all three branches of intellectual property; for example, in the cases of *Merck v. Stephar*[52] and *Centrapharm v. Sterling*[53] for patents, in *Winthrop Products v. Centrapharm*[54] for trademarks, and in *Deutsche Gramophon* for copyright.[55]

The European Court of Justice came to these decisions by considering the interaction of the effects of Articles 30 and 36 of the Treaty of Rome. Article 30 is the operative article implementing the policy on free flow of goods mentioned in Article 3. It prohibits quantitative restrictions on imports and all measures having an equivalent effect between member states. A limited derogation from this is permitted by Article 36, which enables member states to limit the application of the Free Flow of Goods Doctrine on public policy grounds, for example, protection of public morality or public health or protection of industrial and commercial property. It is, however, specifically stated that this derogation shall not be used as a means for arbitrary discrimination or disguised restriction on trade between member states. The Court concluded in several cases that use of patent rights and other intellectual property to prevent importation of goods could be a quantitative restriction on trade between member states. Thus, the enforcement of intellectual property rights to prevent imports from other EEC member countries could be permitted only if intellectual property rights fell within the derogation of Article 36. There was never any doubt that patents and trademarks did. There was a question at one time as to whether copyright also constituted an "industrial or commercial" property right. The Court decided that it did.[56] However, the Court had to make sure that the enforcement of intellectual property rights did not constitute an arbitrary splitting up of the Common Market. It concluded that this would be the case if intellectual property rights were used to exceed what the Court regarded as being their "specific objective." A number of different formulations of what constitutes a "specific objective" have been adopted over the years, particularly in the trademark field.[57] All of them have a common component,

---

[49] The European Court of Justice's own formulation of the rule is, "The proprietor of an industrial or commercial property right protected by the law of a member state cannot rely on that law to prevent the importation of a product which has been lawfully marketed in another member state by the proprietor himself or with his consent." *Merck & Co. v. Stephar BV* [1981] 3 Comm. Mkt. LR 463.

[50] *EMI Records Ltd. v. CBS Grammofon AS* [1976] 2 Comm. Mkt. LR 235.

[51] *Polydor Ltd. et al. v. Harlequin Record Shops* [1982]1 Comm Mkt LR 677.

[52] See note 51 above. This case made it clear that the doctrine applied irrespective of whether the items in question (pharmaceuticals in this particular case) were patentable in the country of origin.

[53] *Centrafarm BV et al. v. Sterling Drug Inc.* [1974] 2 Comm. Mkt. LR 480.

[54] *Centrapharm BV v. Winthrop BV* [1974] 2 Comm. Mkt. LR 480.

[55] *Deutsche Gramophon v. Metro Grossmarkte GmbH and Co.* [1971] 1 Comm. Mkt. LR 631.

[56] See *Deutsche Gramophon* in the previous note and the more explicit statement in *Coditel v. Cire Vog* [1983] 1 Comm. Mkt. LR 49.

[57] The specific object of a patent has been held to include the exclusive right for the patent proprietor to use an invention with a view to manufacturing industrial products and putting them into circulation for the first time, either directly or by the grant of licenses to third parties, as well as the right to oppose infringements. *Allen & Hamburys Ltd. v. Generics Ltd.* [1988] 1 Comm. Mkt. LR 701.

The specific object of trademark protection has been defined variously as follows:

> The guarantee that the owner of the trademark has the exclusive right to use that trademark for the

however, in that the specific objective does not extend to give the intellectual property right holder rights beyond those exercisable up to the time of first sale of the product within the Common Market.

The primary points of interest that remain to be resolved, therefore, lie in the question of what is consent and what happens with respect to goods first marketed without the consent of the patentee or other intellectual right holder?

First it should be noted that sales under a compulsory license have been specifically held by the European Court of Justice in the case of *Pharmon v. Hoechst* not to constitute sales to which the patentee has consented. Thus, in a case where a compulsory license had been granted with respect to the sale of drugs in the United Kingdom, a Dutch patent was enforceable to prevent import of drugs purchased in the United Kingdom into the Netherlands.[58] However, in a copyright case with respect to phonograph records, where there was a scheme in the United Kingdom somewhat similar to that in the United States providing for a mechanical recording right where a copyright owner had received a royalty for records first sold in the United Kingdom at the prevailing U.K. rate, it was held that once the goods were imported into Germany there was no right to collect an increased royalty on the basis that the prevailing rate in Germany was somewhat higher than in the United Kingdom. In this case, the copyright holder had given real consent to marketing and, hence, was not entitled to a second bite at the cherry.[59] Similarly, it was held that where a patentee had a patent that was an endorsed license of right,[60] any license fixed by the government authorities under the terms of such a provision could not prohibit the licensee from satisfying his or her needs by importing from other EEC member states, nor from exporting to other EEC member states (*Allen & Hamburys v. Generics*).[61]

Another issue explored by the Court was the extent to which various rights in fact fall within the definition of industrial property rights under Article 36. As noted earlier, at one time there were those who expressed the view that copyright was not a traditional "industrial property" right, but rather an intellectual property right and, thus, was not covered. The European Court of Justice shrugged off this argument very lightly. Sim-

---

purpose of putting products protected by the trademark into circulation for the first time. *Centrafarm v. Winthrop*, [1974] 2 Comm. Mkt. LR 480;

To give the consumer or final buyer a guarantee of identity of origin of the marked product. *Pfizer v. Eurim-Pharm GmbH*, [1982] 1 Comm. Mkt. LR 406;

In *Hoffmann LaRoche v. Centrafarm*, the court did not use the words "specific object" at all, but rather referred to "specific subject matter" of a trademark right, stating that this comprised not only a guarantee to the proprietor of the mark that he or she has the exclusive right to use it for the purpose of putting a product into circulation for the first time, but also the function of guaranteeing the identity of the origin of the trademarked product to the consumer or ultimate user. *Hoffmann La Roche AG v. Centrafarm BV*, [1978] 3 Comm. Mkt. LR 217;

The specific object of copyright has been held to include:

Exclusive right of performance and exclusive right of reproduction. *Warner Bros. v. Christiansen* [1990] 3 Comm. Mkt. LR 684.

In that case the distribution right was regarded as the commercial exploitation of the reproduction right and therefore apparently part of the specific object of protection.

[58] *Pharmon v. Hoechst AG* [1985] 3 Comm. Mkt. LR 775.

[59] *Musik-Ventrieb Membran GmbH v. GEMA* [1981] 2 Comm. Mkt. LR 44.

[60] Many countries provide that annual fees for keeping a patent in force may be reduced if the patentee signifies his or her agreement to grant a license to anyone who requests one for a reasonable royalty. Such patents are said to be endorsed "licenses of right." Once a patent is so endorsed, if the parties cannot agree on license terms, they may apply to the Patnet Office for a determination of the terms to be included in the license.

[61] [1988] 1 Comm. Mkt. LR 701.

ilarly, the Court has held that national design rights (for example, the Benelux Design Right) are entitled to respect under Article 36, even though under Benelux law the person holding the design right need have contributed nothing of intellectual merit in securing protection (see *Nancy Kean v. Kreurkoop*).[62] In *Industrie Diensten v. Beele*,[63] the Court held that the Dutch right of protection against slavish imitation was sufficiently akin to an industrial or commercial property right that it was entitled to protection under Article 36. Therefore, the Court said, one who had long supplied the Dutch market with a particular type of pipe was entitled to prevent importation of copies of the pipe from Germany, notwithstanding the fact that no copyright protection for the pipe existed in the Netherlands.

The $64,000 question in this field, however, remains unanswered: namely, whether deliberate failure to secure patent protection in one EEC member state can be construed as being an implied consent, so that if a third party markets goods in such a country, they may be allowed to flow freely throughout the common market irrespective of patents in other countries. The German courts, up to the Supreme Court level, have held that there is no implied consent under these circumstances.[64] The German Supreme Court, in fact, was so confident that this was the case that it did not feel it necessary to refer the issue to the European Court of Justice (as required under Article 177 of the Treaty of Rome if there is a "question" of European law outstanding in a case that has to be decided by the highest national court). This case is of some interest in that the losing defendants took the issue to the German Constitutional Court on the question of whether the German Supreme Court should have referred the case to the European Court of Justice. The German Constitutional Court noted that there were respectable arguments for saying that failure to secure protection in other countries, when this was the result of a voluntary act by the patentee, could be regarded as an implied consent. However, under German law it was only empowered to intervene if the Supreme Court was clearly wrong in the decision it had made. The Constitutional Court could not conclude that the Supreme Court was clearly wrong, and there the matter ended.[65]

Validity of National Laws Under the Treaty of Rome.   A question also arises, however, as to whether national laws themselves can be regarded as being in breach of the provisions of Article 30 of the Treaty of Rome. Such questions arise where, for example, an object may be patentable in one country but totally unpatentable under the laws of most other EEC member states, where a right has expired in one country but remains in force in another, or where rights to restrict particular uses of a product covered by an intellectual property right are actionable in one state but not in a country where they were first sold.

The leading case in this area (and on the Free Flow of Goods Doctrine generally) is not an intellectual property law case at all, but the famous *Casis de Dijon* case.[66] Essentially, part of its holding was that until such time as there is harmonization of national laws on particular topics, such national laws should remain enforceable as long as they do not result in arbitrary discrimination and the limitations imposed are not excessive. Notwithstanding this proviso, the European Court of Justice has held in certain cases that national laws are purely arbitrary. (For example, it has struck down the German pure beer law

---

[62] [1983] 2 Comm. Mkt. LR 47.
[63] [1982] 3 Comm. Mkt. LR 102.
[64] Partially reported in English [1983] ITC 107.
[65] *In re Patented Feed Stuff* [1989] 2 Comm. Mkt. LR 902.
[66] *Rewe-Zentral AG v. Bundesmonopol Verwalting fur Bruntwein* [1979] 3 Comm. Mkt. LR 494.

dating from the sixteenth century on the ground that this was an arbitrary prevention of foreign beers coming into Germany,[67] and has also struck down provisions in various continental European laws that certain types of alcoholic beverages could be sold only in certain types of bottles[68]—the Court felt that appropriate labeling could protect the consumer equally as well as the shape of the bottle.)

In the intellectual property law field, however, national laws have for the most part been upheld. Thus, a challenge to the old British law that held that if the only prior art against a patent was a former patent more than 50 years old, the invention was in effect "repatentable" in Britain, notwithstanding the fact that the prior publication prevented protection in all other EEC member states, failed. The U.K. patent could be enforced to prevent importation from Italy, where no patent could be obtained (*Thetford Corporation v. Fiamma SpA*).[69]

In a case where copyright protection (or, more strictly, neighboring right protection) ended earlier in Denmark than in Germany with respect to certain sound recordings, the Court held that the owner of the right in Germany could enforce this right to prevent importation of records that had been freely marketed in Denmark (*EMI Electrola*).[70]

Similarly, it was held that the importation into Denmark of phonograph records that were then rented out to the public, such records having first been purchased in the United Kingdom, could be a contravention of the rental rights provisions of the Danish law, notwithstanding the fact that, at the relevant time, there were no equivalent provisions under the U.K. law. The defendants argued unsuccessfully that what was in effect a "first sale doctrine" applied to their lawful purchases in the United Kingdom, and that they were therefore entitled to use these products throughout the Common Market in any way that was authorized under U.K. law.[71] These last few decisions have provided a powerful impetus for the Commission to push forward with a more comprehensive plan for harmonization of EEC copyright laws.

The one situation so far in which intellectual property laws have been held to be inconsistent with the Treaty of Rome has been that of compulsory licensing of patents. Both the British and Italian patent laws contain provisions for the granting of compulsory licenses if a patented invention is not worked within the country. The legality of these provisions was challenged by the Commission. The European Court upheld the challenge and held that the relevant provisions of the British and Italian laws were inconsistent with the Treaty of Rome and, therefore, of no effect insofar as they distinguished between working in each of these countries and working the invention elsewhere within the Community.[72] Henceforth, working in any member state will suffice to meet any working requirement in a national law.

---

[67] *In re* Purity Requirements for Beer: *E.C. Commission v. Germany* [1988] 1 Comm. Mkt. LR 780.

[68] See, for example, Use of Champagne-Type Bottles: *EC Commission v. Germany* [1988] 1 Comm. Mkt. LR 135.

[69] [1988] 3 Comm. Mkt. LR 549.

[70] *EMI Electrola GmbH v. Patricia Irm und Export Verwaltungsgesellschaft GmbH* [1989] 2 Comm. Mkt. LR 413.

[71] *Warner Brothers Inc. v. Christiansen* [1990] 3 Comm. Mkt. LR 684. A similar result had been obtained earlier in respect to securing payments for performance of records purchased from other EC member states. *G. Basset v. SACEM* [1987] 3 Comm. Mkt. LR 173.

[72] *Commission v. The United Kingdom* and *Commission v. Italian Republic The Times* April 15, 1992.

(b) Japan

(i) Background.   The world's third major patent system is that of Japan. Cooperation between the United States, European, and Japanese Patent Offices on technical matters and on a variety of issues, such as how best to search the prior art, has now reached a high level. Annual gatherings of officials in the so-called trilateral talks seek to develop this cooperation further. However, despite such participation the Japanese system remains very different from both the United States and the European systems and has received much criticism, not all of it justified, on this account. The first major difference, and one that causes many of the other problems, is the sheer number of new applications filed in Japan each year—approximately 380,453 as compared with 177,388 filed in the United States Patent and Trademark Office in 1991. There are a number of reasons for the large numbers. First, until 1960 Japanese patents could contain only a single claim, and although today it is possible to claim multiple embodiments of the same invention in a single patent, some of the old thinking remains. Second, Japanese authorities have, since the first introduction of a patent system in 1885, promoted the filing of patent applications. Before World War I competition between prefectures as to which could file the most patent applications was encouraged. Still today, enhanced prestige attends invention. Furthermore, Article 92 of the Japanese patent law provides that anyone who has obtained a patent for an invention and finds his or her exploitation of it blocked by a dominating patent is entitled to a compulsory license to use the invention of the dominating patent if a license agreement on reasonable terms cannot be reached. Thus patent filing in Japan may be carried out not only to exclude others from using an owner's invention, but also to provide leverage to secure the owner's own right to use the invention even though it is dominated by another—a very powerful incentive to file and one expressly rejected in the United States as long ago as the 1793 Patent Act.[73]

Despite attempts to streamline operations (the Japanese Patent Office is far closer to operating an all-computer, paperless office than any other patent office) in order to deal with the vast number of applications with which it is confronted, the Japanese Patent Office really has no alternative to operating a deferred-examination system. Under the Japanese system an applicant has seven years from the filing of a patent application within which to request examination. Even after examination is requested there may still be delays of several years before it is completed. These delays have been the focus of much criticism in recent years, and the Japanese examination procedure is to be modified in 1994 in an attempt to speed up the process. Such modification, however, will be at the cost of significantly reducing the applicant's ability to amend an application in order to deal with objections made during examination.

(ii) Patentable Subject Matter.   Among the issues of substantive patent law is the definition of invention. Under Article 2(1) of the Japanese law invention is defined as "the highly advanced creation of technical ideas utilizing natural laws." This broad definition is, however, qualified by Article 29, which provides that only inventions that are useful in industry are patentable, and Article 32 of the law, which precludes the granting of patents

---

[73] This feature of Japanese patent practice, referred to as "patent flooding," is a major source of friction to the United States. See, for example, U.S. General Accounting Office *Intellectual Property Rights: U.S. Companies' Patent Experiences in Japan* (Washington, D.C.: U.S. Government Printing Office, 1993), p. 126.

for certain types of inventions.[74] Although prohibitions on the granting of patents for chemical products and medicines were removed in 1975, the law still specifically proscribes the granting of patents for inventions of products of nuclear transformations and those that are "likely to harm public order, good morals or public hygiene." On the surface, such limitations seem fairly innocuous. However, the combination of these requirements has resulted in refusal by the Japanese Patent Office to grant patents for inventions relating to new medical treatment, methods of typhoon control (on the ground that the cost of implementation was too high to be industrially applicable), business methods, essentially biological methods of breeding new plants or animals, and computer programs as such. To a significant extent, the effect of the first of these prohibitions has been mitigated by the willingness of the Patent Office to accept so-called medicine claims of the type "Medicine X for use in treating disease Y," where the only novelty lies in the use of X to treat Y. As with the European Patent Office's improvisations to deal with the same issue, many purists are unhappy with what they see as an artificial solution to the problem.

In the other major area in which concerns as to propriety of patent protection have arisen throughout the world—the question of patentability of computer software - related inventions—the Japanese Patent Office took the lead, issuing an examination standard for computer program-related inventions in April 1971. The standard focused on the requirement of Article 2 of the law, that to be patentable a "law of nature" (which the standard contrasts with laws of man—such as the rules of chess) must be used to produce a creation of "technical ideas." This approach was reemphasized in new guidelines issued in the summer of 1993. It is therefore similar to the EPO's approach, which asks, "Is there a technical problem to be solved?" The standard requires that the *shuko no inga kankei* (roughly translated as "the technique's cause-and-effect relationship") be based on a physical law of nature; then the software in question is patentable. The mere fact that the invention is expressed as an algorithm does not of itself necessarily preclude patentability.

The 1993 guidelines seek to apply this definition to computer-related inventions. According to the guidelines, the following types of inventions are patentable:

1. Utilization of a law of nature in information processing performed by software (for example, in computer control of apparatus used for other purposes, operations controlling the computer itself, video image processing, transmission error detecting, and methods of generating and displaying certain symbols)
2. Inventions using hardware resources (for example, a command input method by higher hierarchical menu selection and methods of converting Japanese phonetic letters into Chinese characters)

The guidelines specifically provide that inventions in which no law of nature is used and no hardware resources are utilized are not patentable, and give examples of unpatentable inventions, such as arithmetical methods and sales estimation methods.

Interrelated with the question of statutory subject matter is the question of inventivity (or to use the American term, "nonobviousness"). The guidelines indicate that software will not ordinarily result in an invention having sufficient inventive character to be patentable if the invention is (1) merely the application of procedures or means for

---

[74] Article 32 precludes the granting of patents for inventions of substances manufactured by nuclear transformation of atoms and of inventions that are liable to contravene public order, morality, or public health.

realizing functions of an invention in other applications, (2) simple addition or replacement by ordinary systematizing means, (3) mere realization of functions in hardware by way of software, or (4) mere computerization of clerical work in business systems. The guidelines further indicate that program languages are not considered patentable.

The position on biological inventions in Japan is still not entirely clear, because although the patent law does not preclude the granting of patents for such inventions, the existence of a Plant and Seedlings Law administered by the Ministry of Agriculture, Foresting and Fisheries has inhibited action by the Patent Office in this area. In the summer of 1993, however, the Patent Office issued new guidelines:

1. Claims to microorganisms will now require a suitable taxonomic name and a description of the microbiological properties sufficient to characterize the microorganism.

2. Similar provisions are now to be applied to patents relating to plants and seeds.

3. So far as animals are concerned, the guidelines follow the same pattern as for microorganisms and plants, but also take note of the prohibition in the Japanese law that precludes the granting of patents for anything that contravenes public order, morality, or public health. (However, the guidelines fail to indicate when this prohibition might come into effect, leaving this for subsequent consideration by an Appeal Board or court. Yet it is clear that humans are excluded from patentability).

It is to be hoped that these guidelines will clarify the situation.

(iii) Novelty.   Although the Japanese system is, like that of Europe, a first-to-file system, it has a number of similarities to the United States system that are lacking in Europe. First, as in the U.S. system, public knowledge and public use of an invention are relevant only to questions of novelty if they occur within the granting country.[75] Publications describing an invention, however, are a bar wherever in the world they occur.[76] A prior unpublished copending Japanese patent application describing the same invention is also a bar to the grant of a patent application, unless the prior application was filed by the same applicant as the later one.[77] A further aspect in which the Japanese approach to novelty is more similar to that of the United States than to the European system, is its provision of a grace period.[78] In the case of Japan, however, the grace period is for only six months prior to the filing of the Japanese application and, unlike the position in the United States, is limited only to specific acts, namely, (1) experimental use by the applicant or with the applicant's consent, and publication or presentation of the results to a meeting of an academic society certified by the Director General of the Patent Office, (2) publication contrary to the intention of the patent application[79], or (3) publication in certain certified Exhibitions. As a practical matter, the grace period is of little value.

---

[75] Japanese Patent Law, Article 29 (1) (i) and (ii).
[76] Japanese Patent Law, Article 29 (1) (iii).
[77] Japanese Patent Law, Article 29 bis.
[78] Japanese Patent Law, Article 30.
[79] Publication of a patent in the name of the inventor is not considered a publication against the will of the inventor inasmuch as it is a government publication. Hence, such a publication does not qualify for exceptional treatment under the grace period provision.

(iv) Inventive Step. Article 29 (2) of the Japanese Patent Law precludes the grant of a patent "when an invention is such that it could easily have been made prior to the filing of the patent application on the basis of the acts that could destroy novelty of any other than an earlier unpublished application by a person having an ordinary knowledge in the technical field to which the invention pertains." The Japanese Patent Office Commentary on the Act takes the view that the provision means that a patent should be granted only for "an improved invention showing remarkable progress over the prior art in terms of its purpose, constitution or effect." As a practical matter, the standard of obviousness applied by the Japanese Patent Office does not seem to differ greatly from the standards applied in the United States and Europe, although occasional problems do occur, especially with inventions of a type where actual demonstration of "progress" is difficult—such as where the invention is a new approach to an old problem.

(v) Sufficiency of Disclosure. Although the Japanese disclosure requirements are, on the surface, similar to those of the United States and Europe, their application tends to be rather more rigorous than in the other two major systems and results in the Japanese Patent Office granting only claims of more limited scope than those granted elsewhere. A report by the United States General Accounting Office to Senators Rockefeller and De Concini in July 1993 reported that more than 70% of the U.S. users of the Japanese patent system who were questioned in preparing the report had moderate to great problems in respect to the scope of claims granted in Japan (as contrasted with 27% reporting such problems in the United States Patent Office and 30% in the European Patent Office).[80]

(vi) Procedure. Under Japanese practice, patent applications are published (as *kokai*) 18 months from filing or, if priority is claimed, from their priority date. Compensation is available from those who use the invention after publication and before the grant of the patent. Examination is undertaken only following a specific request by the applicant or a third party and may be deferred up to seven years from the filing date. After examination by the Patent Office, applications are republished (*kokoku*) and are open to the filing of oppositions. Thereafter, a patent is granted.

The term of a Japanese patent is 15 years from the *kokoku* publication, subject to a proviso that the duration will not exceed 20 years from the filing date.

(vii) Protection Afforded by Patents. Japanese courts have traditionally been strict in their interpretation of patent claims, limiting them closely to the literal wording. Enforcement of patents in Japan is also hampered by lack of discovery procedures and the lack of judges with significant patent experience outside Tokyo and Osaka. However, for those with patience, satisfactory results are sometimes obtained.

(viii) Utility Models. In addition to granting patents, the Japanese system also provides for the grant of utility models for inventions that do not possess the necessary degree of invention to qualify for patent protection. Utility model protection may be granted for "devices relating to the construction configuration or structure or combination of both, of goods which can be used in industry."

---

[80] U.S. General Accounting Office, *Intellectual Property Rights: U.S. Companies' Patent Experiences in Japan.*

The novelty requirements are the same as for patents, but the standard of invention required is specifically stated to be lower than for patents. Thus, protection of this type may be a convenient means for securing protection for mechanical inventions relatively easily. Utility model protection is for a period of 10 years from publication, subject to a maximum duration of 15 years from filing the application. Contrary to the position in some other countries, however, utility model applications in Japan are subject to a full examination.

(c) **Other Countries.**   This outline offers a brief (and sometimes oversimplified) summary of the major features of patent and copyright law in a number of major countries. It specifies the conventions to which a country is a party. Information on patents is given, including term, subject matter that is inherently unpatentable, what constitutes a statutory bar as having destroyed novelty, and an indication of the costs that may be expected in a typical case over the first four years of the life of a patent and for the entire life of the patent. These figures are based on those for a 20-page case in which "optional" extras, such as excess claim fees, are kept to a minimum. The categories indicated in "Cost" for each country correspond roughly to the following figures:

	Filing	First 4 years	Life of patent
Low	<$1,750	<$2,750	<$6,000
Moderate	$1,750–3,000	$2,750–4,000	$6,000–8,000
High	$3,000–4,000	$4,000–6,000	$8,000–10,000
Very high	>$4,000	>$6,000	>$10,000

These figures include all normal costs of filing, prosecuting, and securing grants for patent applications and payment of renewal and maintenance fees to keep them in force. They do not include unusual costs, such as incurred in the case of opposition.

It should be noted that in cases where examination may be deferred until after four years, it has been assumed that such deferral will take place, and so the cost of examination and prosecution has not been included in the figures for the first four years.

Andean Pact (Bolivia, Colombia, Ecuador, Peru, Venezuela)

1. *Conventions*: None of the Andean Pact countries belong to the Paris Convention or the PCT.
2. *Patents*: Decision 344 of the Andean Pact, adopted in 1993, provides for a harmonized patent law between the member states. Major provisions are:
   a. That the term of a patent is 20 years from filing,
   b. That most types of inventions are patentable (including chemicals per se and pharmaceuticals), and
   c. Prior publication of an invention or prior use so as to disclose the invention anywhere in the world before filing in an Andean Pact country, is an absolute bar to the grant of a patent.

Argentina

1. *Conventions*: Argentina is a member of the Paris Convention, but not of PCT.
2. *Patents*:
   a. The term of a patent is currently 15 years from grant.

    b. Under the present law, patents may not be granted for chemicals having pharmaceutical activity (although other chemicals, including intermediates for the production of pharmaceutically active compounds, may be patented). Nor are patents granted for treatments of humans or animals. Legislation is currently pending that would remove the bar on patenting of pharmaceutically active compounds.

    c. Publication of an invention or use of it anywhere in the world in such manner that the public can determine its nature prior to filing in Argentina or to a validly claimed priority date is a bar to the grant of a patent.

    d. Cost: filing, moderate; 4 years, moderate; life, very low.

Australia

1. *Conventions*: Australia is a member of the Paris, Berne, and Universal Copyright Conventions and the PCT.

2. *Patents*:

    a. The term of a patent is 16 years from its filing date, subject to a possible 4-year extension for patents relating to pharmaceuticals for which marketing was delayed as a result of the need to obtain government approval.

    b. There are no significant limitations on subject matter that may be patented.

    c. Prior publication of an invention anywhere in the world prior to the earlier of a filing in Australia or a validly claimed priority date is a bar to the grant of a patent. Prior use of an invention that discloses its nature is a bar only if it occurred in Australia.

    d. Cost: filing, low; 4 years, moderate; life, moderate.

    "Petty patents" having a duration of 6 years are also available for minor inventions.

Brazil

1. *Conventions*: Brazil is a member of the Paris Convention and the PCT.

2. *Patents*:

    a. Brazilian patents run for a term of 15 years from the date of filing.

    b. All chemical products, foods and pharmaceuticals, and methods of treatment of humans and animals are currently unpatentable, although in the nonpharmaceutical area, patents may be granted for compositions comprising mixtures of chemicals that act together to produce a useful result. At present, an inventor cannot obtain a patent even for a process for producing a new compound if its intended use is as a pharmaceutical.

    c. Any publication or use disclosing the invention anywhere in the world before filing or a validly claimed priority date is a bar.

    d. Cost: filing, 4 years, high; life, high.

Canada

1. *Conventions*: Canada is a member of the Paris Convention and the PCT.

2. *Patents*:

    a. Canadian patents granted on applications filed after October 1, 1989, run for 20 years from the date of filing.

    b. The only significant limitations on what is patentable are prohibitions on the granting of patents for methods of treatment of humans or animals.

    c. Any publication or prior public use by another before filing the application or a validly claimed priority date is a bar. Any publication or public prior use by the applicant more than 12 months before filing in Canada is a bar.

    d. Cost: filing, low; 4 years, low; life, moderate.

Czech Republic

1. *Conventions*: The Czech Republic is a party to the most recent versions of all of the Paris Convention and to the PCT.

2. *Patents*:

    a. The term of a Czech Republic patent is 20 years from the date of filing.

    b. The only significant restriction on patentable subject matter is that methods of treatment of humans or animals are not patentable.

    c. Prior publication or prior use so as to reveal the nature of the invention anywhere in the world before filing in the Czech Republic or a validly claimed priority date is a bar.

    d. Cost: filing, moderate; 4 years, moderate; life, high.

Finland

1. *Conventions*: Finland has adhered to the most recent version of all of the Paris Convention and to the PCT.

2. *Patents*:

    a. Patents are granted for a period of 20 years from the date of filing.

    b. The only significant restrictions on patentable subject matter are in the fields of computer programs and medical and veterinary treatment.

    c. Patents may not be granted if before the earlier of filing in Finland or any validly claimed priority date, there has been a publication or a public use of the invention so that the public may learn the nature of the invention anywhere in the world.

    d. Cost: filing, very high; 4 years, very high; life, very high.

Finland has recently introduced a system of utility models to provide protection for "lesser" inventions.

Hungary

1. *Conventions*: Hungary has adhered to the Paris Convention and to the PCT.

2. *Patents*:

    a. Patents are granted for a term of 20 years from the date of filing.

    b. Chemical products, foods, and pharmaceuticals are still unpatentable, although compositions containing two or more chemical compounds are patentable as long as their use is not as a food or a pharmaceutical. A new law is expected to take effect in 1994 to permit protection for inventions in some of these categories.

    c. Patents may not be granted if before the earlier of filing in Hungary or any validly claimed priority date, there has been a publication of the invention or a public use of the invention so that the public may learn the nature of the invention anywhere in the world.

    d. Cost: filing, moderate; 4 years, high; life, very high.

India

1. *Conventions*: India is not a member of the Paris Convention or the PCT, although reciprocal arrangements permit priority to be claimed from applications filed in United Kingdom, Canada, Australia, and New Zealand.

2. *Patents*:
   a. The term of patents is 14 years from the date of filing except for patents relating to food or drugs, for which the term is limited to 7 years from filing or 5 years from grant, whichever is the shorter.
   b. "Substances produced by a chemical reaction," foods, medicines, insecticides, and methods of treatment of humans or animals are not patentable. A recent Patent Office directive has indicated that patents should not be granted for production of "living things," including DNA fragments.
   c. Prior publication anywhere in the world and prior public use in India are bars to the granting of a patent.
   d. Cost: filing, low 4 years, low; life, low.

Israel

1. *Conventions*: Israel is a member of the Paris Convention, but is not a member of the PCT.

2. *Patents*:
   a. The term of a patent is 20 years from the filing date.
   b. Methods of treatment of humans are not patentable.
   c. Patents may not be granted if before the earlier of filing in Israel or any validly claimed priority date, there has been a publication of the invention or a public use of the invention so that the public may lean the nature of the invention anywhere in the world.
   d. Cost: filing, low; 4 years, low; life, low.

Korea

1. *Conventions*: South Korea is a member of the Paris Convention and of the PCT.

2. *Patents*:
   a. Patents granted on applications filed after September 1, 1990, run for a period of 15 years from publication of acceptance of the application, subject to a maximum of 20 years from the filing date.
   b. The only significant limitations on protectable subject matter are medical and veterinary treatments, although use-limited "medicine" claims may be allowed.
   c. Prior publication of an invention anywhere in the world prior to the earlier of a filing in Korea or a validly claimed priority date is a bar to the grant of a patent. Prior use of the invention that discloses its nature is a bar only if it occurred in Japan. However, a limited exception to the prior publication rule exists in the case of an applicant's own publication, as long as the application is filed in Korea within six months of the publication and the Korean Patent Office is so advised.
   d. Cost: filing, high; 4 years, low; life, moderate.

Korea provides for protection by way of utility models for "minor inventions."

Mexico

1. *Conventions*: Mexico is a party to the most recent versions of the Paris Convention. It is not a member of the PCT.

2. *Patents*:

    a. For patents granted after June 28, 1991, the term of Mexican patents is 20 years from the filing date.

    b. The major prohibitions on patentable subject matter are methods of treatment of humans or animals, animal and plant species, biological processes, and genetic material.

    c. Patents may not be granted if before the earlier of filing in Mexico or any validly claimed priority date, there has been a publication or a public use of the invention so that the public may learn the nature of the invention anywhere in the world. However, prior publication by an applicant or the applicant's predecessor in title up to one year before the priority date may be excused if details of the publication are submitted to the Mexican Patent Office at the time of filing.

    d. Cost: filing, moderate; 4 years, moderate; life, very high.

Utility model protection is possible for "lesser inventions."

Russia

1. *Conventions*: Russia is a member of the Paris Convention and the PCT.

2. *Patents*:

    a. Patents are granted for a term of 20 years from the date of filing.

    b. Under the present law, there seem to be few significant bars to patentability on the ground of excluded subject matter.

    c. Patents may not be granted if before the earlier of filing in Russia or any validly claimed priority date, there has been a publication or a public use of the invention so that the public may learn the nature of the invention anywhere in the world.

    d. Cost: filing, high; 4 years, very high; life, very high.

Taiwan

1. *Conventions*: Taiwan is not a party to any international conventions relating to intellectual property. It has a reciprocal treaty with the United States relating to copyright matters only.

2. *Patents*:

    a. For patents published after January 23, 1994, the term is 20 years from the filing date.

    b. Taiwan still prohibits the granting of patents for foods, methods of treatment, and living organisms (including plasmids). Protection for microorganism inventions will become possible if and when Taiwan joins GATT and becomes bound by the TRIPs Agreement.

    c. Patents may not be granted if before the filing in Taiwan any date there has been a publication or a public use of the invention so that the public may learn the nature of the invention anywhere in the world.

    d. Cost: filing, moderate; 4 years, high; life, high.

7.4 COPYRIGHTS

(a) Background.   Copyright statutes throughout the world grant to authors certain specified bundles of rights. Such rights, fall broadly, into two groups: moral rights and economic rights. Traditionally, civil-law countries have placed greater emphasis on moral rights than those with a common-law tradition. This is understandable in view of the history of the development of the rights in the two systems. Copyright protection in almost all countries traces its origin to licensing systems imposed on book publishers after the introduction of the printing press in the fifteenth century. Royal licenses were required to produce individual books, and normally only one license was granted for a particular book, thus giving the printer holding such a license protection against sales of copies of the book by others. The English Revolution of 1688 and the French Revolution of 1789 swept away the powers of the Crown to control book publishing in this way. Thus, some new form of protection against plagiarism was required. The English took 20 years to come up with the answer to the problem and focused narrowly on economic issues. The French had a new law of broad application within four years, based philosophically on the idea that intellectual works were part of an author's personality and that he or she had moral rights therein. Copyright protection in common-law jurisdiction traces its ancestry to the Statute of Anne enacted by the British Parliament in 1709. This statute gave to the authors of books the sole right of printing and reprinting of such books for a period of 14 years from the date of first publication. In practice, the statute, for the most part, protected publishers from competition rather than gave rights to authors, inasmuch as normal practice was for the author to transfer the rights to the publisher at the time of a book's printing. Similarly, when in 1734, following a campaign by the artist Hogarth, protection was extended to the visual arts (initially it was ony engravers who obtained protection). Hence the focus on economic rights.

Civil-law antecedents are more varied. The French law of July 19, 1793, passed just after the Revolution, abolished previous licensing systems similar to those that had formerly existed in England and was widely influential. In his report to the assembly before the law was adopted, Le Chapelier made the case for protection of authors' rights in the following terms:

> The most sacred, the most unassailable, and if I may say so the most personal of all properties is the work which is the fruit of a writer's mind.[81]

The new law gave to authors of all types of writings, to composers of music, to painters and engravers "an exclusive right during their lifetime to sell, make for sale and to distribute their works and to assign this property in whole or in part." In contemporary writing this right was viewed as one of property. However, during the nineteenth century application of the legal philosophy of writers such as Immanuel Kant led to a shift in emphasis, so that an author's rights came to be seen as being associated with the author's personality. Such thinking served to focus consideration on moral rights at the time when many continental copyright statutes were being drafted. Its legacy continues today, even though modern commentators have more or less given up trying to define exactly what copyright is, other than a bundle of specific rights laid down by statute.

---

[81] "Le Moniteur Universel," January 15, 1791. Quoted in S.M. Stewart, *International Copyright and Neighboring Rights*, Butterworths [1983] at 2.10.

Throughout the nineteenth century, copyright protection was largely given only to works of a country's nationals or to works published within the granting country. Such limitations clearly led to problems of piracy, and bilateral treaties were concluded between many countries. Even these, however, proved unsatisfactory, and in 1858 a Congress of Authors and Artists called for international recognition of copyright. This body set in motion a series of conferences that ultimately led to the creation of the Berne Convention of 1886, providing for protection of copyrights of authors who were nationals of member states, in all other member states.

(b) Berne Copyright Convention. The Berne Convention has been revised several times since adoption in 1886, most recently in 1971. Copyright is by nature a bundle of individual rights traditionally divided into economic rights and moral rights, but even within these categories subject to variation between countries. (A number of considerations arise; for example: Do economic rights include a right to control commercial rental of embodiments for copyright work? Do moral rights include the right to prevent modification of a work by the owner of the physical embodiment of the work?) The Berne Convention stipulates certain minimum standards as to the protection that each member state must provide, but not an exhaustive list of such rights. Thus, Berne Convention states must ensure the following rights:

1. Moral rights, to the extent that an author has the right always to be named as the author of his or her work and to object to any distortion, mutilation, or other modification of or derogatory action in relation to the work that would be prejudicial to his or her honor or reputation (Article 6 bis).
2. An exclusive right to the owner of a copyright to authorize reproduction of the work, subject to member states being able to legislate for exceptions in special cases, "provided that such reproduction does not conflict with the normal exploitation of the work and does not unreasonably prejudice the legitimate interest of the author" (Article 9).
3. An exclusive right for the owners of copyright to control the translation of copyright works (Article 8).
4. Exclusive rights covering the public performance or recitation of copyrighted works (Articles 11 and 11 ter) and the recording of works (Article 13). Article 11 bis provides for exclusive rights over broadcasting of copyrighted works, but member states may legislate the extent to which such broadcasting rights may be exercised.
5. Copyright owners' exclusive rights to the adaptation of their works (Article 12), including the right to make cinematographic adaptations (Article 14).

It should be noted that certain rights that are common in copyright laws in some countries, such as, for example, distribution rights and rental rights, are not specifically mentioned by the Berne Convention and are thus purely matters for national law. However, the Convention specifically provides that member states may, if they wish, provide for a *droit de suit*, giving certain creators of original works of art "an interest" in any subsequent sale of a work after the first sale (Article 14 ter) by the creation of the work.

In addition to the provision of minimum standards in regard to rights, the Berne Convention also provides minimum standards as to what works are to be subject to copyright protection. However, a measure of flexibility is allowed in some circumstances, such as in connection with works of applied art and industrial designs. The provisions relating to such designs are discussed in section 7.6 of this chapter. The basic provision of Article 2 of the Convention is that copyright should exist in "literary and artistic works," which are defined as "every production in the literary, scientific and artistic domain." The Convention, however, specifically leaves it to the member states to determine whether a work must be fixed in some material form in order to enjoy the benefit of copyright (Article 2).

The Convention also leaves to member states the definition of a "work" that is entitled to protection. The problem that has attracted most attention over the past decade or so is whether computer programs may be regarded as "literary or artistic works." Many countries have responded by defining such works as being "literary" by way of statute. However, this is not the only area in which difficulties arise. A most persistent problem has been the definition of sound recordings. These are not covered by the Berne Convention but have been subject to separate conventions of their own. The first of these was the Rome Convention of 1961 for the Protection of Performers, Producers of Phonograms and Broadcasting Organizations, and the second was the Geneva Convention of 1971 for Protection of Phonograms Against Unauthorized Duplication of Their Phonograms. Although there are a respectable number of members of both these conventions, membership is nowhere near as wide as in the Berne Convention. The fact that works of this type are not covered by the Berne Convention, and in some countries fall beyond the scope of the definition of works protected by copyright, has led to their being protected by what are known as "neighboring rights" in several jurisdictions.

An essential feature of the Berne Convention is that of national treatment, which is to say that nationals of other member states should be treated no worse than a country's own nationals (Berne Article 5). This general principle is, however, subject to an important exception in the field of copyright relating to works of applied art and industrial designs and models. Article 2(7) of the Berne Convention effectively permits member states to treat the protection of such works on a reciprocal basis in some circumstances. (Where the work is protected in the country of origin only by way of special design protection and the country in which enforcement is sought also has this type of protection, protection may be on this limited basis only; otherwise, if protection in the country of origin is only on such a limited basis, full copyright rights will exist in the country where enforcement is sought, but only for a limited 25-year term).

One further note of caution is needed. Because not all countries subscribe to the same revision of a convention, care may be needed to determine which version of the convention applies in a given case. Furthermore, it is necessary to consider the date on which a convention became effective in a given country. This is particularly important in view of the fact that the United States became a party to the Berne Convention only in 1989. Thus, works created before that date in the United States (particularly if they had already fallen into the public domain here) may not be able to take advantage of full Berne Convention rights in other countries unless they were simultaneously published in another Berne Convention country, such as Canada.

The other major feature of the Convention is the provision of a minimum term of duration of copyright. The norm is 50 years from the death of the author or, in the case of an anonymous or pseudonymous work or a cinematographic work, 50 years from the date on which the work was first lawfully made available to the public. There is, however, an exception to this provision for works of applied art, whereby the prescribed minimum term is 25 years from the date of making the work (Article 7).

A notable provision of the Berne Convention is that for works of authors who are nationals of a Convention country and for works that were first published in a Convention country, no formalities are required for the existence of copyright in any other Convention country (Article 5 [2]).

As noted earlier, the Berne Convention was last amended in 1971. Most major countries of the world are now members; the most significant exception is Russia. Under the terms of the Convention, substantive amendment may be effected only by a unanimous vote of the members (Article 27). The very success of the Convention is attracting members and has, therefore, made further revision of the Convention itself difficult. There are, however, a number of issues for which many members believe further provisions are desirable, and this has led to proposals for two new agreements that could be adopted and adhered to by fewer than all of the members of the Berne Convention. The first proposal is for a new protocol to the Convention to deal specifically with protection for computer programs, data bases, "artificial intelligence," and works created by or with the assistance of computers, and to provide minimum standards in respect to rental rights, compulsory licensing of sound recordings of musical works (e.g., the United States mechanical recording rights), compulsory licensing of primary broadcasts and satellite communications, duration of protection for photographs, and communication to the public by satellite broadcasting. The second proposed agreement is a new instrument for improving the protection granted to the producers of sound recordings. It remains to be seen whether either of these proposals will be adopted.

(c) Universal Copyright Convention.   The Universal Copyright Convention came into being after World War II. It was designed mainly to provide some form of international agreement relating to copyright for those countries that did not feel that they could adhere to the relatively high standards set out in the Berne Convention or that, like the United States, felt that some formalities were desirable in order to create or maintain copyright, such formalities being forbidden under the Berne Convention. In addition to requiring national treatment, the main features of the Universal Convention are the following:

1. A requirement that each state provide "adequate and effective protection" for the rights of authors and copyright proprietors in literary, scientific, and artistic works. The exact nature of these rights is not defined. Certain rights are, however, specifically mentioned in Article IV bis, including a reproduction right, a broadcasting right, and a public performance right, and Article V provides exclusive translation rights. The Convention does not specifically include any moral rights.

2. A requirement that insofar as member states stipulate compliance with formalities in order to secure copyright protection, works of nationals of other Convention states should be deemed to have complied with such formality requirements if, from the time of first publication, all legitimate copies of a work bear a copyright notice in the form accompanied by the name of the copyright owner and the year of first publication.

3. A general minimum protection period of 25 years from the death of the author (subject to a provision that for states that did not have this provision prior to the Convention's coming into effect, an alternative term of 25 years from the date of first publication might be permitted).

(d) The Neighboring Rights Conventions. As noted earlier, the Rome and Geneva Conventions provide an international framework for matters not covered by the Berne Convention itself.

The Rome Convention of 1961 (to which the United States is not a party) stipulates that member states must provide "national treatment" to nationals or residents of other member states in respect to performers (including those whose performances are incorporated into a phonogram or are broadcast), phonogram producers, and broadcasting organizations. Member states are, however, permitted to make certain of the provisions relating to sound recordings conditional on reciprocal rights being granted to their own nationals. Certain minimum rights must be afforded in respect to these persons. Article 14 provides that the normal duration of protection for works covered by the Convention is 20 years from the date of the performance, the fixation of the sound recording, or the broadcast, as the case may be.

Unlike the Berne Convention, but like the Universal Copyright Convention, the Rome Convention provides that member states may, in respect to phonograms, make protection dependent on marking. In this case member states may require that all copies of a phonogram for which protection is asserted must bear the symbol "P" accompanied by an indication of the year of first publication, together with certain additional information about the performers and/or producers of the phonogram.

The Geneva Convention of 1971, for protection against unauthorized duplication of phonograms, was a direct response to the increasing availability of equipment for duplication of sound recordings during the 1960s. At the time of the Rome Convention in 1961, it had been thought that the rights of producers of sound recordings were adequately protected by giving them the right "to authorize or prohibit direct or indirect reproduction of their phonogram." The Geneva Convention extended this protection to importation and distribution. The United States is a party to the Geneva Convention.

The Geneva Convention is unusual in the intellectual property field in that it does not rely on "national treatment" as a basis for providing rights. The basic provision is that of Article 2, as follows:

> Each Contracting State shall protect producers of phonograms who are nationals of other Contracting States against the making of duplicates without the consent of the producer and against the importation of such duplicates, provided that any such making or importation is for the purpose of distribution to the public, and against distribution of such duplicates to the public.

However, the method of protection and the duration of protection are left to national law, as long as protection is provided for at least 20 years from the first publication of the phonogram.

(e) North American Free Trade Agreement. The North American Free Trade Agreement (NAFTA) imposes a number of obligations on its member states in respect to their copyright laws. In general, these are similar to the obligations imposed by the Berne Convention, but the following specific features are worth noting:

1. Member states must provide protection for computer programs as literary works and also provide protection for compilations of data that by reason of the selection or arrangement of their contents constitute intellectual works.

2. Member states must provide for the copyright holder to have control over the first public distribution of the original of the work and each copy thereof.

3. Member states must give the copyright owner the right to control the commercial rental of the original and copies of copyright-protected computer programs, subject to a proviso that this provision does not apply where the computer program is not itself the essential object of the rental (as, for example, in the case of a computer program controlling the timing of the sparking of spark plugs in a rental car). The Agreement contains a specific provision that the first sale of a computer program does not exhaust the copyright owner's rights in respect to subsequent rental of the program.

4. Member states must provide for free transfer to others of economic rights existing under the copyright.

5. Fair use exceptions to the copyright holder's rights are to be confined to "certain special cases that do not conflict with a normal exploitation of the work and do not unreasonably prejudice the legitimate interests of the rights holder."

6. Member states must provide proper protection for a sound recording, including control over distribution and commercial rental of copies of the recording, unless a contract between the author of the work and the producer of the sound recording provides otherwise.

(f) Revision of General Agreement on Tariffs and Trade. Provisions affecting trade-related intellectual property rights have been included in the revised version of the General Agreement on Tariffs and Trade (GATT) that, it is hoped, emerged from the Uruguay Round of negotiations. The text of any such provisions includes a number of provisions relating to copyright. Among these are the following:

1. An obligation on parties to the GATT trade-related intellectual property rights (TRIPs) agreement to comply with the provisions of the Berne Convention.

2. A requirement to treat computer programs as literary works for copyright protection purposes and to provide protection for data bases if their selection or arrangement "constitute[s] intellectual creations"

3. A requirement to give to authors of computer programs, cinematographic works, and procedures of phonograms, the rights, in certain circumstances, to control commercial rental of the originals or copies of their works

4. An obligation that, in respect to works other than photographs and works of applied art, the normal duration of copyright protection be at least 50 years from the death of the author

5. A requirement that fair use provisions and similar limitations on the exercise of copyright be confined to "certain special cases which do not conflict with normal exploitation of a work and do not unreasonably prejudice the legitimate interests of the right holder"

6. Obligations to afford certain minimum rights for the protection of performers, producers of phonograms, and broadcasting organizations

(g) General Observations on Copyright Protection Outside the United States. The fact that the Berne Convention lays down many minimum standards for copyright protection, and that under the Convention such protection arises automatically as creation of a work without need for any formality, indicates that in many countries there is already a significant degree of uniformity in copyright laws of the world. As noted earlier, however, the different philosophical approaches of the common-law and civil-law systems may result in more differences than such common adherence to the Berne Convention might suggest. For instance, the Berne Convention does not provide any definition as to the level of creativity required for copyright protection. This has been a major point of difference between the traditional Anglo-Saxon approach to copyright—basically, to quote one English judge, that "if something is worth copying, it is worth protecting"—and the continental view that rights should arise only in works that have involved some modest level of intellectual activity, typically referred to as "originality." The differences in the understanding of the term *originality* between continental and Anglo-Saxon systems have caused difficulties in the past. The traditional Anglo-American approach has been to regard *originality* simply to mean that the author of a work did not copy it from someone else, whereas under French and German law a higher standard is required. The *Feist* decision of the U.S. Supreme Court, however, shows that even in the Anglo-American tradition the idea that some measure of creativity is required for copyright protection is not totally absent. This issue was one of great significance in the drafting of the European Community's directive on protection of computer software, in which, as noted later, the common-law approach prevailed. It is not clear, however, that this will necessarily be the case in other areas of copyright protection. The difference is only a manifestation of the traditional common-law approach based on economic rights (a thing worth copying is worth protecting), as opposed to the continental view that regards the author's rights as being part of his or her personality, thus requiring some intellectual contribution for creation of any such rights.

Cinematographic works constitute another area in which philosophic differences have caused problems over the years. Based on the economic approach, it seems natural that rights should be vested in the producer of the work; after all, in a very real sense, the producer "creates" the work by putting all the pieces together. To those brought up on the European mainland, such an approach is unthinkable: Where is the intellectual or artistically creative contribution of someone who merely puts up the money and arranges for the artists to do their work? This is an issue that is still to be resolved in any general sense.

Other areas in which national laws may differ considerably include the protection of "non-core" copyright works, such as sound recordings, which are not covered by the Berne Convention, and rights for which protection is granted, in addition to those specified in the Berne Convention—for example, in respect to matters such as distribution and rental rights. A further area in which significant differences occur is that of exceptions to protection for reasons such as fair use. The details of these matters in regard to many countries are beyond the scope of this chapter. However, the following paragraphs describe the positions of the European Community and Japan and note briefly the positions of some other major countries.

(h) European Community.[82]   As noted in the discussion of patent rights in the European Community (EC), the exercise of all intellectual property rights is tempered by the "free

---

[82] The term "European Community" remains correct when dealing with issues governed by the Treaty of Rome. "European Union" should be used in the context of matters governed by the Maastricht Treaty.

flow of goods" doctrine. The Community application of this doctrine to patent rights is generally applicable to copyright.

Within the EC are two countries that are archetypical of common-law and civil-law traditions, respectively,—The United Kingdom and France. The following paragraphs consider the copyright laws of these two countries and how they differ, as well as the Community's program for effecting harmonization of EC copyright law.

(i) United Kingdom.   The 1988 United Kingdom Copyright Act provides copyright protection for:

1. Original literary, dramatic, musical, or artistic works,
2. Sound recordings, films, broadcasting or cable programs, and
3. The typographical arrangement of published editions.

The definition of *literary work* specifically includes tables, compilations, and computer programs. *Artistic works* include graphic works, phonographs, sculptures or collages (all "irrespective of artistic quality"), architectural works, and works of artistic craftsmanship.

Copyright in literary, dramatic, musical, or artistic works normally runs for a period of 50 years from the death of the author, copyright in sound recordings or films 50 years from release of the recording or film, copyright in broadcast or cable programs 50 years from the original broadcast, and copyright in typographical arrangements of published editions 25 years from their first publication.

The bundle of rights protected by copyright are the following: copying, issue of copies to the public (including the renting of copies), performance, showing or playing a work in public, broadcasting a work or including it in a cable program, making adaptions of a work, and doing any of the above in respect to such adaption. It is further provided that importation, possessing, or dealing in infringing copies and facilitating the making of infringing copies are "secondary infringements" actionable under the Act.

The U.K. Act, in provisions similar to the U.S. fair use provisions, stipulates that certain acts are not to be regarded as infringements. However, unlike the broad equity-based definition of fair use in the United States, the British statute confines its "fair dealing" exceptions to certain specified acts: research and private study, criticism, review and news reporting, and incidental inclusion of copyright material. Copying for educational purposes is permitted only to a certain limited extent. The recording of a broadcast or cable program "solely for the purpose of enabling it to be viewed or listened to at a more convenient time" is not a copyright infringement.

(ii) France.   The French law of 1793, mentioned earlier in this chapter, remained in force until 1957. Under the 1957 law, protection is provided for "the rights of authors of all intellectual works regardless of their kind, form of expression, merit or purpose," and although the law sets out a list of works that are protected, it is not intended to be all-encompassing. The debate in the national assembly on the bill made it clear that the definition was not meant to include sound recordings since these required insufficient intellectual effort. Some protection for phonograph producers was, however, apparently available under Article 1382 of the Civil Code, which provided a general right of action against unfair competition. This situation continued until 1985, when the law was amended to provide for "neighboring rights" for a variety of subjects that had not been

covered previously. These included performance rights, rights for producers of sound recordings and video recordings, and rights for telecommunications enterprises.

The amendment of the law in 1985 also helped clarify the situation by adding to the list of works for which traditional author's rights protection existed. The additional works included circus acts, cinematographic works, graphic and typographic works, and computer software.

A noteworthy feature of French law is that fixation of a work has never been a condition for securing protection.

In general, the term of copyright protection is for 50 years after the death of the author. However, the term for musical works is up to 70 years after the death of the author.

The rights afforded in France include most notably a collection of moral, as well as economic, rights. Such rights are inalienable and are "attached to [the author's] person." They include a right of divulgation (which may permit the author to refuse to divulge a work even if he or she was commissioned to produce it and has completed it), a right of attribution of authorship, and a right to insist on maintenance of the integrity of the work and of proper respect for it. The author also has a right to correct or retract his or her work even after it has been transferred to another, and even though economic rights in the work have been assigned.

Economic rights include those of reproduction and performance of a work. Such rights are, however, subject to a general right permitting copying for private purposes. Authors of sound and audiovisual works are compensated for such use from the proceeds of a levy imposed on the sale of blank audio- and videotapes.

(iii) European Community. The first issue that the European Community addressed in the copyright area was protection for computer software. A directive requiring member states to bring their laws into conformity with EC standards was adopted in 1991 and came into effect on January 1, 1993. Its main features are as follows:

1. A requirement to protect computer software and preparatory materials by copyright as literary works;[83] the term of protection is to be at least 50 years *post mortem auctoris*.[84]
2. Adoption of a common-law definition of *originality* so as to give rise to protection (i.e., to be "original" and thus subject to protection, a work merely had to be the original work of the purported owner; this contrasts with the German approach that to be "original" a work had to involve a measure of creativity).[85]
3. A definition of *infringement* to include translation and adaptation; although, unless excluded by contract, such acts may be permitted if they are needed in order to use a program for a lawful intended purpose. Similarly, the making of a single backup copy cannot be prevented.[86]
4. The express provision that rental rights are not exhausted by first sale, but all other distribution rights are so exhausted by first sale within the EC.[87]
5. The grant of a limited right to effect reverse engineering only for purposes of determining how to make the software compatible with other software. This right

---

[83] Software Directive, Article 1(1).
[84] Software Directive, Article 8.
[85] Software Directive, Article 1(3).
[86] Software Directive, Article 4.
[87] Software Directive, Article 4(c).

may be nullified by the owner of the software if he or she freely provides the necessary information to permit such interoperability.[88]

6. A requirement to make unlawful the distribution or possession for commercial purposes of devices designed to remove copy protection from a program.[89]

Independent of the special needs of computer software, the European Commission which acts as the executive arm of the EC also considered broader questions of copyright and issued a green paper. Major concerns addressed in the green paper (which was not intended to be comprehensive) included proposals for a directive relating to piracy of copyright works, in particular to safeguard producers of films and similar audiovisual works, to seek some control over high-quality recordings, such as digital audiotapes, and to prevent widespread piracy throughout the community. The Commission included a suggestion that regulation similar to that which prevents entry into the Community of counterfeit trademark goods should be extended to copyrights.

The green paper also addressed the issue of home taping, but did not really reach any conclusion apart from rejecting the suggestion that there should be a levy on the sale of blank tapes for ordinary audio cassette machines. So far as digital audiotape machines were concerned, however, it was proposed that the sale of such machines should not be allowed within the Community without some restriction built into them to prevent their use in making copyright infringements. This proposal seems to many to be somewhat unrealistic.

In addition, the green paper proposed that laws throughout the Community should be harmonized to ensure that copyright owners are given rental rights in respect to sound and video recordings. A further proposal was that there should be a directive seeking to harmonize Community law relating to data bases. The green paper, however, did not offer a conclusion as to whether such data bases should be protected by copyright or by some sui generis right, but it seems that discussions as to exactly how this should be accomplished are continuing and nothing further has been heard officially from the Commission.

In December 1990, the Commission put forward an "action program" for further development of copyright law. The proposals included the following:

1. A directive providing for rental rights for audiovisual works and a requirement for compensation to be given to copyright holders when copies of their works are supplied to the public noncommercially, such as through public libraries.

2. A directive to harmonize the duration of copyright in member states. As discussed earlier, the basic Berne Convention provision of life plus 50 years applies only to "hard core" copyrights and does not apply to several types of rights that on the Continent are referred to as "neighboring rights." It was this problem that led to the *EMI Electrola* case in which, although the term of protection for sound recordings was 25 years in both Denmark and Germany, the start dates for the protected term were different.

3. A directive to harmonize national royalty rates for "statutory" licensing schemes such as those operated by national collecting societies and that have been featured, for example, in the *GEMA* cases in which the German collecting society has tried to collect "excess" royalties for the import of recordings of a song from England,

---

[88] Software Directive, Articles 5 and 6.
[89] Software Directive, Article 7(1) (c).

where royalties to the copyright owners had already been paid, but at a rate lower than that prevailing in Germany.

4. A study of modern reprography technology to see what can be done about it.

The rental rights directive was adopted early in 1993, to come into effect on July 1, 1994. The directive, in general, gives the author the exclusive right to control rental or lending of the originals or copies of a copyrighted work. However, such rights are also given to the following persons:

1. The performer, in respect to fixation of a performance,
2. The producer, in respect to a phonogram, and
3. The producer of the first fixation of a film, in respect to films.

Such rights are, however, transferable by way of contract, although member states must provide that any contract by which an author or performer in a phonogram or film transfers his or her rights to control rental of the phonogram or the film to the producer, will be subject to the performer's receiving equitable remuneration.

Member states may make exceptions to the aforementioned provisions with respect to public lending (for example, by public libraries) as long as provision is made for authors to obtain remuneration for such lending.

A second chapter in the directive requires that member states provide the following specific rights if they are not already present in their national laws:

1. A right to performers to control fixation and reproduction of any fixation of their performances, including a right to be given to broadcasting organizations to control fixation and reproductions of fixations of broadcasts
2. A right to phonogram and film producers to control reproduction of their phonograms or films
3. Certain rights for performers and phonogram producers with respect to the broadcasting of their works
4. Exclusive rights for performers (with respect to fixations of their works), phonogram producers, film producers, and broadcasting organizations to authorize distribution of copies of their works to the public

The directive on harmonization of the term of protection was adopted on October 29, 1993, to take effect on July 1, 1995. Under its provisions member states will have to grant copyright protection for a period of up to 70 years from the death of the author for "true" copyright works, and for 50 years from production or performance for "neighboring rights."

The Commission has recently issued a proposal that the directive that already attempts to control import of counterfeit trademark goods should be extended to products covered by copyright as well.

(i) Japan.   It was not until 1899 that Japan introduced its first copyright law. The current law is that of 1970, as amended in 1985 to introduce specific provisions relating to the protection of computer software. Like the French law, the Japanese law draws a distinction between "true copyrights (author's rights) and "neighboring rights." True copyright exists only for certain specified categories of works, namely:

Novels, dramas, theses, lectures, and other literary works

Musical works

Choreographic works and pantomimes

Paintings, woodcut prints, engravings, sculptures, and other works of art

Architectural works

Maps, as well as plans, charts, models, and other figurative works of scientific nature

Cinematographic works

Photographic works

Computer program works

Works protected by a separate neighboring-rights scheme are those of performers, producers of phonograms, and broadcasting organizations. Section 4, covering such works, was introduced in the 1970 Copyright Act to permit Japan to adhere to the Rome Convention, discussed earlier in this chapter, for protection of such works.

So far as the elements of true copyright are concerned, moral rights are afforded almost the same degree of importance in Japan as they are in France. These include a right to control initial publication of a work, a right to attribution of authorship, and a right to maintain the integrity of the work. Such rights are personal, exclusive, and inalienable. In addition to these moral rights, Japanese law also provides for certain defined economic rights, namely, the right to control reproduction of a work, the right to perform a work, the right to broadcast or defuse a work by cable, the right to recite a work, and the right to exhibit a work. There is no specific right to control distribution.

The normal duration of protection for copyright works in Japan is 50 years from the death of the author. The duration of protection of neighboring rights is 20 years from the date of the performance or fixation of the sounds in question, or from the date of a broadcast if a broadcast is being protected.

The fair use provisions of the Japanese law apply generally to copyright and neighboring rights and include, for example, the production of works for private use, reproductions in libraries, quotations, reproductions in school textbooks and the like, broadcasting in schools and other educational institutions, reproduction in examination questions, reproduction in similar use in braille, performances that are not for profit, reproduction of articles on current topics, exploitation of public speeches and the like, reporting of current events, reproduction for judicial purposes, exploitation by means of translation and adaptation, ephemeral recordings by broadcasting organizations, exhibition of an artistic work by the owner of the original, exploitation of an artistic work located in open places, and reproduction required for exhibition of artistic and similar works. Such limitations on copyright, however, cannot be regarded as in any way limiting the author's moral rights, merely his or her economic rights.

As in all Berne Convention countries, copyright in Japan arises automatically upon creation of a work. However, registration has always been possible (indeed, until 1910 it was mandatory in order to enforce rights). Amendment of the law in 1985 to provide clear protection for computer programs created a special new register for program works. Such registrations of copyright are important in certain circumstances, for example, in respect to transfer of ownership and use of a copyright as a security interest.

(j) Other Countries. The following paragraphs summarize the major features of copyright law in a number of major countries. They include the conventions to which each country is a party and information on whether registration is necessary, possible, or desirable for the protection of computer software.

(i) Andean Pact (Bolivia, Colombia, Ecuador, Peru, Venezuela). All are members of both the Berne Convention (including the Paris revisions) and the Universal Copyright Convention, although Venezuela has not yet adopted the 1971 revisions). Colombia, Ecuador, and Peru are members of the Rome Convention, and Ecuador, Peru, and Venezuela are members of the Geneva Phonograms Convention.

In January 1994, Decision 351 of the Andean Pact laid down a framework for a harmonized copyright law among members of the Andean Pact. Under the harmonized law, registration is not required to give rise to copyright protection. Registration is possible in Colombia, Ecuador, Peru, and Venezuela. In Ecuador, Peru, and Venezuela, at least, the Registry has accepted computer software as being susceptible of registration. In Colombia an official opinion has been issued that computer software is protectable.

Colombia provides for an unusually long period of protection for true copyright works: 80 years from the death of the author. All other Andean Pact countries apply the Berne Convention norm.

(ii) Argentina. Although Argentina is a member of the Berne and Universal Copyright Conventions, it has not fully adopted the latest revisions of either. Argentina is also a member of both the Rome Convention and the Geneva Phonograms Convention.

Registration of copyright is normally desired but not essential for foreigners if formalities of the country of first publication are complied with. It is understood that at least one court decision has upheld the copyrightability of computer software, and the copyright office accepts registrations of computer software as literary works.

Duration of copyright is in accord with the Berne Convention norm.

(iii) Australia. Australia is a member of Berne and Universal Copyright Conventions, of the Rome Convention on neighboring rights, and of the Geneva Phonogram Convention.

No provision exists for registration of copyrighted works.

A recent change in the statute specifically provides for copyright protection for computer software.

Duration of copyright is in accord with the Berne Convention norm.

(iv) Brazil. Brazil is a member of the Berne and Universal Copyright Conventions, of the Rome Convention on neighboring rights, and of the Geneva Phonograms Convention.

Registration of copyright is optional, but if effected, establishes prima facie rights. Any registration for computer software must be made with the Patent Office.

Under the Software Protection Act, copyright in computer software is specifically provided for a period of 25 years from the first date the software is available anywhere in the world. However, sales can be made in Brazil only if the software has been registered with the Secretariat for Informatics. Works of foreign origin can be registered only if no equivalent product of domestic origin is available.

The normal duration of true copyright is for 60 years from the author's death.

(v) Canada.   Although Canada is a member of the Berne and Universal Copyright Conventions, it has not yet adhered to the most recent version of either of these. Nor has it joined the Rome or Geneva Convention.

Registration is not necessary, but is desirable to establish prima facie rights.

A 1988 amendment to the copyright law made it clear that computer programs are to be treated as literary works for the purposes of copyright protection.

Duration of copyright protection is in accord with Berne Convention norms.

(vi) China (People's Republic).   China is a member of the Berne and Universal Copyright Conventions, but is not a member of the Rome or Geneva Convention.

In general, there are no provisions for registration. However, provisions are made for registration of computer software, and registration is a prerequisite for renewing a copyright in computer software or for instituting proceedings for enforcement.

Computer software is specifically listed among the types of work for which copyright protection is available. However, special regulations apply, and the term is limited to a 25-year period, renewable once for a further 25-year period.

With the exception of these special provisions for computer software, the duration of copyright protection is in accord with the Berne Convention norms.

(vii) Finland.   Finland has adhered to the most recent versions of the Berne and Universal Copyright Conventions and is a member of the Rome Convention and the Geneva Phonogram Convention.

There is no provision for registration.

It is apparently accepted that copyright protection extends to computer software, although there do not seem to be any reported cases.

The duration of copyright is in accord with Berne Convention norms.

(viii) Hungary.   Hungary has adhered to the most recent versions of the Berne and Universal Copyright Conventions. It has also joined the Geneva Phonogram Convention, but not the Rome Convention.

There are no provisions for registration of copyright.

Amendments to the copyright law in 1983 added computer software to an exemplary list of subject matter covered by copyright.

The duration of copyright is in accord with Berne Convention norms.

(ix) Israel.   Although Israel is a member of the Berne and Universal Copyright Conventions, it has not yet adhered to the latest version of either of these. It is a member of the Geneva Phonogram Convention, but not of the Rome Convention.

There is no provision for registration of copyright.

An amendment to the Copyright Ordinance in 1988 provided for the protection of computer software as a literary work.

The duration of most copyrights is for 70 years from the death of the author.

(x) Korea.   South Korea is a member of the Universal Copyright Convention and of the Geneva Phonogram Convention. It is not a member of the Berne or Rome Convention. Korea has taken advantage of exceptions permitted to developing countries under the Universal Copyright Convention.

The Korean Copyright Law of 1987 and the Computer Program Protection Law provide protection for computer software created after July 1, 1987.

The duration of most forms of copyright protection is 50 years from the death of the author.

(xi) Mexico. Mexico is a party to the most recent versions of the Berne and Universal Copyright Conventions, as well as those of the Rome Convention and the Geneva Phonogram Convention.

Copyright protection is available for computer programs. Although formalities are not normally required for copyright protection, in the case of computer software it is necessary to file copies of a program in material form along with an explanation of the program.

The duration of copyright protection is in accord with Berne Convention norms.

(xii) Poland. Although Poland is a member of the Berne and Universal Copyright Conventions, it is not a member of either the Rome Convention or the Geneva Phonogram Convention.

Registration of copyright is not provided for.

There are no specific provisions relating to computer software, but commentators have expressed the opinion that protection exists as long as sufficient originality exists.

The duration of most copyrights is 50 years from the death of the author.

(xiii) Russia. Although Russia is a member of the Universal Copyright Convention, it is not a member of the Berne or Rome Convention nor of the Geneva Phonogram Convention.

Registration is not required, and there are no formalities for securing copyright protection. The new law enacted in 1993 makes it clear that computer programs are protected as literary works.

Under a new law that came into effect in February, 1994, the term of copyright is now in accord with the Berne Convention norms.

(xiv) Taiwan. Even though Taiwan is not a party to any international conventions relating to intellectual property, it does have a reciprocal treaty with the United States relating to copyright matters.

Registration is, in general, required for foreigners (but not for nationals); U.S. nationals may be able to obtain protection without registration in view of the wording of the prewar U.S.-China Treaty. It is recommended that registrations be obtained. The new Taiwanese copyright law specifically provides protection for computer programs in source and object code form and for scientific and engineering drawings. The law is, however, a little ambiguous as to whether three-dimensional reproductions of such drawings are infringements of the drawings.

The duration of most copyrights is 30 years from the death of the author.

7.5 SEMICONDUCTOR CHIP RIGHTS

(a) Background. With the Semiconductor Chip Act of 1984, the United States broke new ground in the intellectual property field by giving statutory recognition to a new form of protection that lay outside traditional boundaries. The need for the new right was founded on the fact that designing the layout of a semiconductor chip could involve years of work to produce a series of masks that were used to lay down the separate layers of circuits included in a chip. However, protection by way of patent law was difficult in that it might well be arguable that the design was "obvious" and protection by way of copyright was precluded, inasmuch as the products were utilitarian and lacked the necessary artistic component. As a result, the right created was in some ways a hybrid of those provided by patents and copyright, as it provided protection for the topography of the various layers of a semiconductor chip in which computer programs are encoded. Because the new right fell beyond the traditional boundaries of patents and copyrights, it was not covered by the international treaties relating to these rights, such as the Paris and the Universal Copyright Conventions. Therefore, the United States was not required to comply with the "national treatment" requirements of these conventions. Thus, under 37 USC 902, the statute made protection in the United States for works of foreign origin conditional. Protection was to be granted if the country of which the author or owner was a national granted equivalent rights in that country to works of United States origin. This led to the adoption of semiconductor chip protection laws in many countries and to a treaty, negotiated in Washington in 1989, covering such rights. The treaty has not, however, come into effect and in its present form is unlikely to be of major importance inasmuch as the United States and Japan declined to sign the final text and although the EC countries signed the text at the end of the Washington conference, they subsequently decided not to ratify their adhesion to the treaty. The primary reason for this dissent by the major countries was their belief that the treaty provided for easy dilution of an author's rights by way of compulsory licensing. Many of the less objectionable features of the treaty have, however, found their way into the intellectual property provisions of one or both of NAFTA and the TRIPs portion of the proposed revision of GATT.

The following paragraphs discuss the protection of semiconductor chips in specific jurisdictions.

(b) European Community.   The EC's Directive 87/54 on harmonization of national laws on integrated circuits requires all member states to provide for protection of semiconductor chip products. On the basis of the Directive, all EEC member states have been granted provisional protection in the United States for semiconductor chips originating from their nationals.

Council Directive 87/54 gave member states substantial leeway in determining how they would ensure that protection for integrated circuits would be achieved. As a result, a wide variety of different means for securing such protection have been adopted. In the United Kingdom and Belgium, for example, no formalities are required. Most other countries require some form of registration, and Spain and Italy have made provision to require not only registration of a chip for its protection claimed, but also compulsory marking with a suitable symbol.

The definition of what is protected includes semiconductor products, whether in final or intermediate form, that consist of a body of material including a semiconducting layer and having other layers of conducting, insulating, or semiconducting material, arranged in accordance with a predetermined three-dimensional pattern, that are intended to perform an electronic function. What is protected for such articles is their "topography." Topography is defined as a series of related images, however fixed or encoded:

1. Representing the three-dimensional pattern of the layers of which a semiconductor product is composed, and

2. In which series, each image has the pattern or part of the pattern of a surface of the semiconductor product at any stage of its manufacture.

A limitation on what is protected is found in Article 2 of the Directive, which states that there is no protection to be given for anything that is "commonplace" in the semiconductor industry and not the result of "its creator's own intellectual effort."

The Directive leaves to the discretion of the member states the determination of ownership of topography rights where the semiconductor product is designed by an employee. The Directive requires that protection is given to works created by nationals or habitual residents of any member states. It leaves to the member states the question of whether they are to provide for protection of topographies designed by those who do not fit within either of these categories, subject to a right given to the council to make a pronouncement on behalf of all member states. At present a provisional pronouncement has been made in respect to works of U.S. origin. This will undoubtedly become absolute if and when the U.S. Patent Office (USPTO) advises the president to make a proclamation giving European nationals full rights in the United States, as opposed to the interim rights they currently hold under the Semiconductor Chip Act.

Among the more interesting features of the Directive are the provisions it makes for noninfringing uses. The relevant provisions are as follows:

1. Member states may allow reproduction of topography privately for noncommercial uses.

2. Member states must permit reproduction for the purposes of analyzing or evaluating the topography itself or teaching the concepts, processes, systems, or techniques embodied in the topography. They must also provide that any new product resulting from such analysis is free from the original right, as long as the new work is the result of the new creator's own intellectual effort and does not represent a commonplace in the art. Acts that are to be regarded as infringements, subject to their exceptions, are reproductions of a topography and commercial exploitation or importation of a topography or a semiconducting chip that has been made using the topography.

Provisions are also set out for the exhaustion of rights throughout the EC after the first making of a semiconductor product by the originator, or with the originator's consent, and for the protection of innocent infringers who are merely using a prohibited product. Once such an innocent infringer has been advised of his or her infringement, however, national law must provide that the right holder should be able to obtain "adequate renumeration" for that use.

The term of a right is to be 10 years from the end of the year in which marketing of the product commenced anywhere in the world, or in countries where registration is required 10 years from the end of the year in which registration is applied for. In no case, however, will the patent protection exceed 15 years from first fixation of the work.

Any state requiring that products have a notice in order to prevent the loss of rights is to use the letter "T" as the symbol to show that such rights exist.

(c) Japan. The Japanese Act concerning the Circuit Layout of Semiconductor Integrated Circuits[90] follows the form of the United States semiconductor chip law fairly

---

[90] Law No. 43, May 31, 1985, which came into effect on January 1, 1986.

closely. There are, however, two major differences. The first is that registration of the circuit design is essential to obtain protection. The second is that, provided that registration is effected, protection is available for all such works, irrespective of the nationality of the creator of the work.

To secure registration, drawings or photographs of a circuit layout for which protection is required must be submitted to the Industrial Property Cooperation Center operating under the auspices of the Ministry of International Trade and Industry. The duration of protection is 10 years from the date of registration.

Protection is granted for the circuit layout, which is infringed either by the manufacture of a semiconductor integrated circuit by use of a protected layout or by the "transferring, leasing, displaying for the purpose of transfer or lease or importing for business purposes of objects that are to be used primarily for the imitation of a registered circuit lay out."[91]

The Japanese law makes no specific mention of any rights for owners of a chip that is subject to protection to carry out any acts of reverse engineering on the chip, although the law specifically states that protection does not extend to "the manufacture of a semi-conductor integrated circuit which is made by utilizing the registered circuit lay out for the purpose of analyzing or evaluating the semi-conductor integrated circuit."

No requirement for marking exists in Japan.

(d) Other Countries. Many other countries have now also adopted semiconductor chip protection laws. These are discussed in the following paragraphs.

(i) Australia. No registration is required, but it is desirable to designate all protected chips with a mark or label including certain information: that "eligible layout" rights exist to the design of the chip, the country and year of first commercial exploitation, and the "maker" of the layout. Protection is for 10 years from creation or first exploitation.

(ii) Canada. Registration is required to obtain protection and must be applied for within two years of the first commercial exploitation of the layout design. Protection is for a period of 10 years from first commercial exploitation or from the filing of the application for registration, whichever is the earlier.

(iii) Finland. Registration is required; protection is granted for a period of 10 years. Full protection is, however, confined to works created by nationals or residents of the EC and European Free Trade Area (EFTA) countries, Japan, and Australia. Protection for works of U.S. nationals or residents is granted only on an interim basis.

(iv) Korea. Registration is required. However, a two-year grace period exists, within which registration may be applied for after first commercial exploitation of the current design anywhere in the world. Protection is for a period of 10 years from registration or from first commercial exploitation, whichever is the earlier, and cannot exceed 15 years from the date of creation of the layout design.

(v) Sweden. Registration is not required, but protection for works of foreign origin is granted only on the basis of reciprocity. Protection is for 10 years from first commercial exploitation of the layout design.

---

[91] Law No. 43, Article 23.

7.6 ORNAMENTAL DESIGNS

(a) **Background.**   In the United States, protection of ornamental designs is dealt with under the patent statute. This is uncommon in the international context, and most countries have special laws relating to such works. In some countries, moreover, protection for some works of this type may be granted under copyright laws, and even trademark laws may be useful in providing protection of a design that is characteristic of articles from a particular source. For many years design protection was the orphan of the intellectual property world, but today all three of its major branches are moving toward the role of adoptive parents. The failure of the intellectual property community worldwide to decide exactly what type of design deserves protection and how to provide protection for such designs has led to a greater divergence between laws on the subject in various countries than there is in most other areas of intellectual property law. Four major issues are involved:

1. What should be protectable? To what extent is it "fair" that anyone's original work should be copied, however trivial that work may seem? To what extent should society be forced to pay for the privilege of using a particular design that has no artistic or technical merit, just because someone else first designed it? This is essentially the dispute that has gone on for years in this country between the automobile industry and the insurance companies and has delayed revision of the United States design law.

2.. If some form of protection is appropriate, what form should it be: statutory monopoly of the patent type, copyright or quasi-copyright (as in the new United Kingdom unregistered design right), or protection against unfair competition (slavish imitation as in continental laws or a broadened version of § 43 (a) of the United States Lanham Act)? Should protection be possible by more than one means for a given article, or should the different types of protection be mutually exclusive? If cumulation is possible, what should be the position after the expiration of one of the protection types?

3. Should all designs be treated equally? There is a recent tendency to view surface ornamentation in a different light from designs that relate to the shape of an article.

4. Should protection be granted for parts of articles, for example, spare parts for automobiles, and, if so, should the rules that apply be the same as those for other types of design?

A book of this type cannot answer all of these questions, but can only touch on the highlights in a few jurisdictions. First, however, it is important to note that international conventions on intellectual property are not particularly helpful in assisting the establishment of uniformity in this field. The Paris Convention for Protection of Industrial Property makes only a few mentions of design protection beyond the basic provision in Article 5 *quinquies* that "Industrial designs shall be protected in all countries of the Union."

Among the other provisions are that there will be a six-month priority period, from the first filing in a Convention country, for filing design registrations in other countries of the

Convention,[92] and that design registrations are not to be subject to revocation for nonworking.[93]

The copyright conventions are only a little more helpful. The Berne Convention itself, to some extent, avoids the issue of what the law should be in this area. Berne does, however, provide minimum standards for a variety of copyright concepts in the design field. The provision set out in Article 2 (7) essentially means the following:

1. If protection is granted for such works in the country of origin, all other countries in the Convention must also provide some form of protection.
2. If this request is met and the country of origin is one where protection is by special provisions for designs or models, then protection in other countries that also provide for special protection for designs and models is to be granted without formalities, but for a period of at least 25 years from creation of the work.

The provision requiring a 25-year minimum of protection for works of applied art is a modification of the earlier versions of the Berne Convention, which had limited the term of protection of works of applied art to the term of the country of origin.

The normal provision is that national treatment applies absolutely, so that any foreigner is entitled to take advantage of national law so as to secure copyright protection in another member state even if the applicant could not secure protection for that design in his or her home country. So far as works of "applied art" are concerned, however, a member state of the Berne union can, contrary to the normal provision of national treatment, restrict the protection afforded to works of foreigners to that which is provided by its own design or model laws if protection could be secured only in that way in the country of origin.

Under the Universal Copyright Convention (UCC) member states are not required to provide for protection of applied art at all, but if they do, a minimum term of 10 years is required (Article IV [3]). The UCC also contains a general provision that no member state shall be required to grant protection for a class of works for a term longer than that granted in the country of which the author is a national (Article IV [4]). The omission of any other reference to works of applied art in the UCC (which states that it applies to "literary, scientific and artistic works") is apparently deliberate, inasmuch as at the time of the original drafting of the Convention there was no consensus as to exactly what works should be protectable by copyright, some of the signatories having no protection at all for works of applied art. By the time of the 1971 revision, there was a feeling that this part of the Convention was working so well that it did not need revision.

(b) European Community

(i) United Kingdom.   The most recent attempt to deal comprehensively with all of the issues of protection for ornamental designs was in the United Kingdom.

The 1988 intellectual property legislation in the United Kingdom provides for four different vehicles by which design protection can be obtained. These are differentiated based on the degree of "artistry" involved, as follows:

---

[92] Article 4 C.
[93] Article 5 B.

1. Artistic works are the subject of copyright and have protection for a period up to 50 years after the death of the author.

2. Nonartistic aesthetic works are the province of Registered Designs and as such are capable of protection for a period of 25 years from the date of application for registration.

3. All designs, whether or not they qualify for Registered Design protection, are the subject of the new unregistered design right unless the shape of articles embodying the design is dictated solely by function. Such designs are subject to protection for a period of 10 years from the first sale of an article embodying the design anywhere in the world, subject to a maximum of 15 years from the date of the first drawing of the design.

4. If a design is dictated solely by function, protection is available only if the design is sufficiently inventive to qualify for patent protection.

For registration as a Registered Design with a 25-year term, a design must be novel as of the date of filing the application for registration (i.e., the law is of the "patent-type").

Both registered and unregistered designs are subject to certain limitations, namely the "must fit" and "must match" exclusions limiting the applications of the statute in respect of articles that either must fit or must match some other article in order to be useful. Clearly, these stipulations go some way toward dealing with the question of spare parts. They do not, however, provide for an exception from protection for all spare parts, but simply those features of a spare part that are necessary to permit it to cooperate with some other article in order to perform its function.

Unregistered design rights are subject to a further limitation, in that the owner may not refuse to grant a license on reasonable terms during the last five years of the right's existence.

Clearly, this legislation was a valiant attempt by the British to be fair to all comers. In practice, however, it seems likely to lead to a lawyer's paradise.

Other countries have been less concerned about fairness.

(ii) Mainland Nations. As to the position of the European mainland, laws are substantially divided into situations in which (1) protection under a patent-type design law and under a copyright law are mutually exclusive (as, for example, in Italy), (2) there is theoretical overlap but a fairly tough requirement is imposed to secure protection under copyright law, as in Germany, and (3) there is total overlap, such as in France.

Germany. Perhaps the best place to start is in the middle with Germany, not only because it has already been touched on briefly and because of its economic importance, but also because its law is among the most interesting. The German copyright law does not as such preclude protection for useful items. However, in the late nineteenth century Germany passed a design law, and since that time courts have had a natural tendency to try to classify works brought before them as to whether design or copyright protection is more appropriate. Thus, a tradition has developed in Germany that copyright protection can really only be secured if those who know about art regard the item in question as being "artistic."

The German position is illustrated by a pair of cases, both of which were reported in English in 1982. The first of these related to a chair designed in the United States by

Charles Eames. The Frankfurt Oberlandsgericht (Appeal Court) took note of the fact that the chair was on permanent exhibition at the Museum of Modern Art in New York and held that this should suffice to show that the cognoscenti regarded it as a work of art. Yet another decision by the German Supreme Court, also reported in 1982, held that there was no protection under copyright law in Germany for a roll stool that was the subject of design patent protection in the United States (its country of origin) inasmuch as it was clear that in any case the stool was not sufficiently "artistic" to qualify for protection under German copyright law. The Supreme Court, however, found that copying of the stool was actionable under Section 1 of the law against Unfair Competition and Article 242 of the Civil Code (the provision that requires persons to act in good faith), because the article in question was a straight copy of what was already on the market and the same technical effect could have been obtained by choosing a different design.[94]

It has been commented that recent decisions may open the way to copyright protection for a broader range of useful articles than previously (cases in which copyright has been found to exist are in the furniture field). The rationale for this opinion is that the Supreme Court has in some cases emphasized that practical utility must not be treated as indicating a lack of sufficient creative effect to produce a work of art. The Court's view that an expert's opinion on what is artistic may be useful in opening up other areas to copyright protection.

Plans for a new airport in Munich, however, were held not to qualify for copyright protection because they were insufficiently artistic. This decision was reached notwithstanding the fact that the copyright law itself provides protection for "technical drawings." The court felt that in that case the drawings represented only technical know-how and did not have the necessary creative content or originality to justify protection. This is, of course, a rather different approach from the traditional Anglo-American view of what is meant by "originality."

The German Design Law of 1876 contains a very broad and general definition of what is protectable, namely:

> Any new and original form or color pattern of a two or three dimensional industrial product destined and apt to satisfy the visual taste or aesthetic feeling and apt to be reproduced.

Case law has fleshed out this definition to some extent, making it clear that to be protectable a design must be able to serve as a patent or model for products of the handicraft industry and must have an overall aesthetic appeal. In Germany novelty is a requirement. Until recently, a designer could apply for design registration at any district court in Germany. A change of the law in 1988, however, meant that all design applications must henceforth be filed with the Patent Office in Munich. Determination of whether a design in fact fulfills the requirements of the law has, therefore, up to then been almost entirely with the courts without any centralized system being adopted. As a broad generalization, it can be concluded that designs have been denied protection if they seek to monopolize the only way to fulfill a particular technical function, but that otherwise the fact that there are technical elements in a design will not preclude protection. The Supreme Court has pointed out that the mere fact that there must be some aesthetic effect to be protectible a design does not preclude its serving a technical function.

In a fairly recent case a German distributor of body parts for cars brought an action against Ford Motors' German subsidiary to challenge Ford's design registrations in

---

[94] Decision reported in English [1982] 11C 781.

respect to a plethora of spare parts, including front fenders for the Ford Escort car. The German Supreme Court reversed the decisions of the district and appeal courts that had held the registrations to be invalid. The lower courts had taken the view that the parts by themselves lacked sufficient aesthetic effect to qualify for protection independent of the car design itself. The Supreme Court reached a contrary conclusion. In the Supreme Court's view, industrial design protection is restricted to "self contained objects which are intended and suited to appeal to the observer's aesthetic senses," merely to ensure that there were excluded from design protection objects that "by their very nature cannot serve any aesthetic function." Thus, the fact that a part was "intended . . . to reveal its inherent aesthetic effect as part of a total product" sufficed to bring the fenders in question within the definition of what was protectable. The mere fact that part of the design of the fenders was intended to achieve a practical result did not preclude the fenders from protection. Therefore, the Supreme Court remanded the case for further consideration as to whether the fenders were novel and "original."

Germany is also of interest in that it has a fairly well-developed law against unfair competition that can be used to prevent what is often referred to as "slavish imitation," as well as the famous provision of Article 242 of the Civil Code that imposes a duty of good faith on dealings in commercial transactions. Interestingly enough, this provision is in fact based on a provision in the Napoleonic code, which has never had nearly the same significance in France.

Benelux. Problems somewhat similar to Germany's have also been encountered in Benelux. Here, however, there are complications as a result of the fact that although the three Benelux countries—Belgium, the Netherlands, and Luxembourg—have a Uniform Design Law, each of them retains its own copyright law. Article 1 of the Uniform Benelux Design Law provides that "the new appearance of a product having a utility function may be protected as a design." Article 21 provides that "a design having a marked artistic character may be protected both by this law and by the copyright laws if the conditions for application of both such legislations are met." The Uniform Law also provides that designs having no marked artistic character will be outside the protection granted under copyright law. In general, a copyright will lapse at the same time as a design unless a special declaration is made to this effect.

Prior to the adoption of the Benelux law, the Netherlands had no specific design protection, and thus there was a tendency to provide worthwhile items with protection under copyright law. Belgium, however, had a design law for many years, and its courts were reluctant to afford copyright protection to useful articles. Hence the compromise wording in Article 21. The issue of what this provision meant recently came before the Dutch Supreme Court.

The Benelux Court of Justice replied to the Dutch Supreme Court's questions as follows:

1. For a design or model to receive protection under the copyright laws in accordance with Article 21, it is necessary that the design or model qualify as a work of (applied) art, that is, as a product with its own original character bearing the personal stamp of the designer.

2. A design or model that qualifies as a work of art in the aforementioned sense also satisfies the requirement that it constitute a product of (applied) art, unless the

original character of the work relates exclusively to that which is unconditionally necessary to achieve a technical result.

3. More stringent requirements would contradict the basic principles adopted by the three countries with respect to copyright protection of designs and models.

Thus, it appears that the position in Benelux will now be that any original work, using originality in its continental sense of meaning—that the work in question is something other than a mere commonplace—will be eligible for copyright protection unless that originality goes solely to achieving a necessary technical result. This would, therefore, seem to indicate that henceforth copyright protection may be obtainable in Benelux for a wider range of works than previously. The Court's reasoning in coming to its conclusion derives largely from its review of the preparatory documents used in producing the original Benelux Design Treaty. The Court concluded that the Treaty had not been intended to set a particularly high standard for the artistic quality of a design for which copyright protection was to be retained.

France.   There are three relevant laws in France, the application of which is cumulative. First, the Design Law of 1909 provides that all new designs, shapes, and industrial objects that differ from similar articles—either by a distinct and identifying pattern giving it an aspect of novelty, or through one or more external features giving it a proper and new configuration—are protectible. This definition is, however, subject to a proviso that protection will not be afforded if the article in question constitutes both a patentable invention and a new design "and the elements of novelty of said design or model are not separable from those of the invention." In this case, protection can be afforded only by patent law. The exact meaning of this provision has caused difficulties over the years. It does, however, now seem that two tests must be met for the exclusion from protection to apply: (1) the form and the inventive elements must be inseparable, and (2) the design must constitute a patentable invention. Indeed, in recent cases, there have been situations in which courts have refused to annul a design even when a patent had been granted for it pending litigation to determine whether it was valid. In France there is no general presumption of validity for patents, as there is in the United States.

The French have a special law providing for protection of designs for clothing. Today, however, this is little used, except that because it provides for certain procedural advantages, it may be used in conjunction with the general Copyright Law. The third relevant law is, of course, the general Copyright Law itself. This protects all author's rights in intellectual creations, regardless of the type and irrespective of merit. Article 3 specifically refers to works of applied art.

Italy.   At the opposite extreme to France lies Italy, where there is a clear separation between that which is protectible as a design and that which can be the subject matter of copyright protection. Section 5 of the Design Law specifically states that the Copyright Law will not apply to such designs as are protectable under the Design statute. That which is protectable under the Design Law is defined as "designs or models capable of conferring a special appearance on an industrial product with respect to shape or the particular combination of lines, colors or other elements."

The Copyright Law provides protection for the graphic arts but requires that when applied to an industrial product, they are protectable only if their artistic value is distinct from the industrial character of the product with which they are associated (a test that seems to be at least as difficult to meet as the conceptual similarity test used in this country). Yet it should be noted that Italy is the only EEC country where the law specifically makes reference to suppression of slavish imitation. This is specifically barred by Section 2598 of the Civil Code. Italian courts do, however, seem to be somewhat reluctant to find slavish imitation of features that are dictated solely by function.

EC Proposals. The Commission of the European Community has recently issued proposals for harmonization of design laws with the EC and for creation of a single design registration office (which if and when created will probably be located at Alicante in Spain).

The Commission proposes two pieces of legislation based on the consultation document. First, there is a proposed regulation to establish an EC design right analogous to the proposed EC trademark and, second, a draft directive calling for harmonization of national laws relating to designs between the member states.

The draft regulation follows the new United Kingdom Design Law in providing for both registered and unregistered design protection. In the case of the EC regulation, however, unregistered protection would last only three years from the date of first publication or public use of the design within the EC, thereby protecting, for example, novelty items that have a short life span and for which the expense of a registration proceeding would not be justified. In addition, a full registration will provide protection for an initial 5 years, renewable every 5 years up to a maximum period of 25 years. The interrelationship between the unregistered and registered rights is governed by provision of a 12-month grace period for registered rights, so that the author of a design has a 12-month period from first marketing or publication of the design within which to decide whether an unregistered 3-year period of protection will suffice, or whether registration is required to secure longer-term protection.

The new EC proposal contains no distinction between functional and aesthetic designs, although it is necessary that the design "show an individual character in the sense that it is significantly different from other designs available in the market" to secure protection. Commonplace designs may not be protected. Furthermore, the new proposal excludes protection for aspects of a design that are necessitated because the article in question must fit with some other article. This is clearly a major concession to the spare parts industry. However, an exception to the exclusion is proposed for modular products.

The draft regulation does not contain any "must match" provisions similar to that in the U.K. law, although a "repair" clause goes some way toward providing a similar exception. Under the repair clause for "complex products," the rights to reproduce a design applied to a part of a product is exclusive to the originator of the design only for the initial three years after marketing. Thereafter, spare parts manufacturers may be able to produce copies of such parts as long as the design of the part is dictated by the appearance of the complex product into which it is to be incorporated so as to restore it to its original appearance.

The proposed directive would, in broad terms, require member states to amend national laws so as to be in conformity with the proposed regulation.

(c) Canada. The 1988 revision of the Canadian statute (which up to then had been largely based on the Imperial Act of 1911) modified the relationship between copyright and industrial design protection in new §§ 46 and 46.1. For designs created after the effective date of the amendments, the old provision—that there is no copyright in a design capable of protection under the Industrial Design Act—is repealed. However, a new provision provides that there is no infringement of copyright in copying what might (the actual wording here is a little tricky) broadly be categorized as the utilitarian aspects of a product. Thus there is no infringement, for example, in applying to a useful article features dictated solely by function. It is further provided that where a useful article has been mass-produced (generally meaning at least 50 copies have been made) by or with the consent of the copyright owner, there will be no infringement of copyright if others make further copies. This provision is, however, subject to exceptions.

(d) Japan. At first sight, Japanese Design and Copyright laws may permit dual protection for ornamental designs, because the Copyright Act specifically covers "works of artistic craftsmanship." However, it appears that the Copyright Law has never been applied to provide protection for works that are intended to be mass-produced and that, as a practical matter, protection is restricted to what is provided by the design law. Under the Design Law protection is given for "the shape, pattern or color or combination of these which through the sense of sight arouses an aesthetic sensation." Furthermore, the article in question must be capable of being mass-produced by hand or by machines and must be tradable as an independent article, although components are protectable if they can be sold separately.

The Japanese Patent Office administers the Design Law, and design applications are subject to a full patent-type examination before registration is obtained. An interesting feature of the Japanese system is that it recognizes that an applicant may not be able to satisfy the examiner that the design is sufficiently aesthetic, and permits the applicant to convert an application, originally filed to secure design protection into an application for a patent or utility model.

PART III

COMMERCIAL EXPLOITATION OF INTELLECTUAL PROPERTY

THE ACQUISITION AND DISPOSITION OF INTELLECTUAL PROPERTY IN COMMERCIAL TRANSACTIONS: THE U.S. PERSPECTIVE

Samuel Fifer Esq.
Carol Anne Been, Esq.

Sonnenschein Nath & Rosenthal
Chicago, Illinois

8.1 TYPES OF INTELLECTUAL PROPERTY

In loan transactions, sales of businesses, and other corporate deals, various types of intellectual property may be transferred or used as collateral. Each item of intellectual property involved in a transaction should be identified and its value assessed to determine its role in the transaction.

(a) Trademarks. A trademark is "any word, name, symbol, or device, or any combination thereof—(1) used by a person or (2) which a person has a bona fide intention to use in commerce and applies to register on the principal register established by this [Act], to identify and distinguish his or her goods, including a unique product, from those manufactured or sold by others and to indicate the source of the goods, even if that source is unknown."[1] As explained by the Senate Committee on Patents, the purpose of trademark protection is twofold: "One [purpose] is to protect the public so it may be confident that, in purchasing a product bearing a particular trade-mark which it favorably knows, it will get the product which it asks for and wants to get. Secondly, where the owner of a trademark has spent energy, time, and money in presenting to the public the product, he is protected in his investment from its misappropriation by pirates and cheats."[2] The owner of a mark therefore has the right to exclude another from using a symbol so related to his or her own that the ordinary consumer would likely be confused as to the source or sponsorship of the goods or services.

A trademark arises upon use as a source identifier and continues as long as the mark is used to identify the goods or services. Nonuse of a mark for an extended period of time may result in abandonment of trademark rights.[3]

---

[1] 15 U.S.C. § 1127 (1982 & Supp. 1993).
[2] S. Rep. No. 1333, 79th Cong., 2d Sess., 1274 (1946).
[3] 15 U.S.C. § 1127 (1982 & Supp. 1993).

Although trademark rights exist independently of registration, registration of a mark used or intended for use in interstate commerce with the Patent and Trademark Office does confer upon the owner of a mark several significant procedural advantages. For example, registration is prima facie evidence of the validity of a mark and of the registrant's ownership of the mark.[4] Registration also is prima facie evidence that the mark is not confusingly similar to another registered mark.[5]

Once a mark is accepted for registration by the Patent and Trademark Office, it is subjected to publication to give third parties an opportunity to object to registration through an administrative opposition proceeding. Following registration, third parties objecting to registration may pursue cancellation proceedings. Registrations issued prior to November 16, 1989, are valid for a term of 20 years. Registrations issued on or after that date are valid for a term of 10 years.

Prior to the expiration of the sixth year following registration, a registrant must show that the mark is still in use for the goods or services recited in the registration, or the registration will be canceled. The registrant at that time may also establish that there are no proceedings challenging rights in the mark and thus obtain statutory "incontestability."[6] These steps are often taken through the filing of a combined affidavit or declaration.

Registration of a mark may be renewed for a period of 10 years if a renewal application is filed within six months before the expiration of registration or during the grace period of three months after expiration.[7]

A change in the federal trademark law effective November 16, 1989, enables the filing of "intent to use" (ITU) applications to reserve rights in a mark in advance of actual use. The ITU applicant has a maximum of 36 months after allowance of the application in which to demonstrate use of the mark in commerce. Once a registration is issued, the rights in the mark are deemed to arise upon the application filing date, rather than on the date use actually commenced.

The U.S. states also have independent systems of trademark registration regulated under the various state trademark statutes. Generally, state trademark registrations must be based on use within the particular state and provide the benefits of the state trademark statute. State registrations are listed in trademark data bases available nationally, which are used by entities who are investigating marks prior to adoption.

(b) Trade Names. Trade names and fictitious or assumed names identify businesses rather than products or services. Although trade names are not subject to federal trademark registration, they are protected against infringement under § 43(a) of the federal Lanham Act.[8] Trade name infringement occurs where a business's trade name is used by another as a trade name or trademark so that confusion as to the source of the business, goods, or services is likely to occur.

---

[4] 15 U.S.C. § 1115(a) (1982 & Supp. 1993).

[5] See *Lois Sportswear, U.S.A., Inc. v. Levi Strauss & Co.*, 799 F.2d 867, 871 (2d Cir. 1986) ("Registered trademarks are presumed to be distinctive and should be afforded the utmost protection").

[6] "Incontestable" marks are still subject to the statutory exceptions and the likelihood-of-confusion test in any adversarial context. 15 U.S.C. § 1065 (1988 & Supp. 1993).

[7] 15 U.S.C. § 1059 (1988 & Supp. 1993).

[8] 15 U.S.C. § 1125(a) (1982 & Supp. 1993). *Railroad Salvage of Conn., Inc. v. Railroad Salvage, Inc.*, 561 F. Supp. 1014, 1018–19, 219 U.S.P.Q. 167, 171 (D.R.I. 1983).

Trade names may also be protected under the law of some states through trademark registration. In addition, most jurisdictions require registration of fictitious or assumed names with the county or state.

Corporate names are the names of corporations and associations that are approved in connection with the organization of corporations under state laws.

(c) Copyrights. Copyrights exist in "original works of authorship fixed in any tangible medium of expression, now known or later developed, from which they can be perceived, reproduced, or otherwise communicated, either directly or with the aid of a machine or device."[9] "Works of authorship" include literary works, musical works, dramatic works, pictorial works, and sound recordings.[10] Thus, books, movies, and artwork may be subject to copyright protection, but promotional brochures, training manuals, and computer programs also may be protected by copyright and should not be overlooked. Copyright protection is not available to an idea in the absence of any particular fixed impression, nor to any process, method of operation, or discovery.[11] Copyright protection is also not available to the extent that an item or feature is solely utilitarian or wholly unoriginal (such as a plaid pattern).[12]

A copyright is not a single right, but rather a "bundle" of exclusive rights giving an owner the rights to reproduce a work, to prepare derivative works, to distribute and display copies of the work, and to perform the work in public.[13] A copyright may be infringed if any one of these exclusive rights is violated.[14]

A copyright vests at the time a work is created.[15] Works created by an individual or individuals may be solely or jointly owned;[16] works created by an employee in the course of employment are owned by the employer under the work-made-for-hire doctrine.[17] Copyrights are valid for the life of the author plus 50 years, or for 75 years from first publication of works made for hire.[18]

Prior to adoption of the Berne Convention Implementation Act (BCIA), copyright protection was lost upon publication of a work without copyright notice.[19] Under the terms of the BCIA, which took effect March 1, 1989, copyright notice is no longer necessary to preserve copyright protection.[20] However, copyright notice does confer certain procedural advantages to the copyright owner and is still recommended.[21]

---

[9] Copyright Act of 1976, 17 U.S.C. § 102(a) (1988).

[10] Id.

[11] See the discussion in "Patents," later in this chapter.

[12] See *Harper House, Inc. v. Thomas Nelson, Inc.*, 889 F.2d 197 (9th Cir. 1989).

[13] 17 U.S.C. § 106.

[14] Id., § 501(a).

[15] Id., § 302(a).

[16] Id., § 201.

[17] Id.

[18] Id., § 302(a), (c) (term varies for works created or published before 1978).

[19] Id., § 405(a) (inadvertent omission of notice).

[20] Id.

[21] For example, a defendant in a copyright infringement suit may not be able to mitigate damages based on "innocent infringement" if a notice of copyright is properly affixed to the published work. See 17 U.S.C. § 405(b). Copyright notice also serves to warn potential infringers that the owner is likely to take steps to enforce his or her copyright.

Although federal registration is not required to maintain copyright protection, it is a prerequisite to infringement litigation.[22] Moreover, registration within 90 days after publication entitles an owner to certain procedural advantages in such litigation.[23]

(d) Mask Works.   A "mask work" is a series of stencils of integrated circuitry etched onto a semiconductor chip, sometimes called "firm ware."[24] The process of producing mask works can cost millions of dollars and consume thousands of hours of engineering and technician time. However, once a mask work has been produced, the work can be duplicated through photography for a cost of less than $50,000. To guard against piracy of mask works, Congress enacted the Semiconductor Chip Protection Act (SCPA) of 1984.[25]

To qualify for protection under the SCPA, a mask work must be "fixed in a semiconductor chip product, by or under the authority of the owner of the mask work."[26] Fixation occurs where a series of masks or stencils have been employed in stenciling two-and three-dimensional features of shape and configuration onto a chip, thereby creating a "semiconductor chip product."[27] Protection is available only for mask works that are "original," with the same standards of originality as those under the law of copyright.[28]

A mask work is protected under the SCPA if it is either registered in the Copyright Office or "commercially exploited anywhere in the world."[29] Commercial exploitation is defined as distribution "to the public for commercial purposes a semiconductor chip product embodying the mask work."[30] Registration is a prerequisite for filing an infringement action under the SCPA,[31] and statutory protection under the SCPA will be lost if registration is not made within two years after the date on which the mask work was first commercially exploited anywhere in the world.[32]

As in the case of copyright protection, notice of ownership of a mask work is not required but gives the owner certain procedural advantages.[33] A mask work notice may negate the defense of "innocent infringement" in a mask work infringement action; it also provides warning that mask work rights are likely to be enforced by their owner.

(e) Patents.   Patents may be obtained for "any new and useful process, new machine, manufacture or composition of matter, or any new or useful improvement thereof."[34] The claimed invention must also be new, useful, and nonobvious, in relation to the prior art.[35] Patents fall into one of several categories, including utility, process, and design patents. Utility and process patents are valid for a period of 17 years; design patents are valid for 14

---

[22] 17 U.S.C. § 411(a).

[23] Id., § 412 (statutory damages, provided by 17 U.S.C. § 504, and attorney's fees, provided by § 505, are available only where registration is made within three months after the first publication of the work).

[24] Semiconductor Chip Protection Act, 17 U.S.C. § 901(a) (2) 1988.

[25] Id., §§ 901–14.

[26] Id., § 901(a) (1).

[27] Id.

[28] Id., § 902(b) (1).

[29] Id., § 904(a).

[30] Id., § 901(a) (5).

[31] Id., § 910(b).

[32] Id., § 908(a).

[33] Id., § 909(a).

[34] 35 U.S.C. § 101 (1988).

[35] Id. §§ 101, 103 (1988 & Supp. 1993).

years.[36] A patent cannot be obtained for a system of doing business, an arrangement of printed matter, a mental process, or a naturally occurring article, but may cover machines, manufacturing processes, computer applications, and product configurations.

Patent rights do not exist until the issuance of a patent by the United States Patent and Trademark Office. An applicant for patent rights has no right to exclude others from using or selling the claimed invention. Moreover, marking an item "patent pending" confers no legal rights but may deter a competitor from using or selling the invention. Once a patent has been issued, however, the inventor has the right to exclude others from making, using, or selling the invention in the United States during the patent term.

Generally, a patent application is filed by or on behalf of the sole inventor or joint inventors, and later assigned, most commonly to an employer. The Patent Office conducts an extensive examination process, while treating an application as confidential to preserve trade secret protection in the event that patent protection is denied.[37]

After a patent is issued, patentability may be challenged through interference proceedings in the Patent Office to determine priority or in litigation charging invalidity.[38]

(f) Trade Secrets.   A trade secret is "information, including a formula, pattern, compilation, program, device, method, technique, or process, that: (1) derives independent economic value, actual or potential, from not being generally known . . . and (2) is the subject of efforts that are reasonable under the circumstances to maintain its secrecy."[39] Trade secrets are not registered by any government office, but are maintained through their owners' precautions to preserve secrecy. A trade secret may be, for example, a formula for a chemical compound; a process of manufacturing, treating or preserving materials; the design of a machine; or a customer list.[40] The Uniform Trade Secrets Act, variations of which have been adopted in 36 states, greatly standardized the law of trade secrets by defining trade secrets and the protection accorded them.[41] Matters of public knowledge or of general knowledge within an industry cannot be appropriated as trade secrets.[42] Elements to be considered in determining what constitutes a trade secret include the extent to which the information is known outside the business, the extent to which information is known by employees involved in the business, the extent to which the information is guarded, the value of the information to the business and to its competitors, and the ease with which the information can be duplicated.[43]

Although state trade secret statutes and case law do not set forth any specific procedure to protect the confidentiality of trade secrets, the general standard is that the steps taken must be reasonable under the circumstances. Steps that may be taken to protect confidentiality include the following:

- Marking written copies of the trade secrets as confidential,
- Disclosing the trade secrets only on a need-to-know basis,

---

[36] Id., §§ 154, 173.

[37] Id., § 122.

[38] Id., § 135.

[39] Uniform Trade Secrets Act § 1(4), 14 U.L.A. 438 (1990).

[40] See Restatement (First) of Torts § 757, cmt. b (1939).

[41] Uniform Trade Secrets Act §§ 1–12, 14 U.L.A 433–67 (1990).

[42] E.g., *Taquino v. Teledyne Monarch Rubber, Inc.*, 893 F.2d 1488 (5th Cir. 1990).

[43] Restatement (First) of Torts § 757, cmt. b (1939).

- Requiring any employees, independent contractors, manufacturers, or suppliers who may come in contact with secret information to sign confidentiality agreements,
- Limiting access to manufacturing and research facilities, and
- Requiring employees to return confidential materials to the company when the materials are obsolete or no longer required for the job, or upon termination of employment.

(g) Licensing.   Intellectual property, like other forms of property, may be licensed to third parties for exploitation. A license grants the licensee the right to do certain things that otherwise may be done only by the owner. Intellectual property licenses may cover, for example, technology and related trademarks for which the licensee may pay a negotiated royalty rate, or off-the-shelf software for which the "buyer" pays a one-time user fee for a nonnegotiable license. License agreements may incorporate various provisions that impact the value of a license in a proposed transaction. A license may restrict either party's right to transfer its interests under the license or place durational restrictions defining the life of the licensing agreement. Licenses also may impose limitations on territory, use, and sublicensing.

In addition to self-imposed covenants, parties to intellectual property licenses must also be cognizant of mandatory legal restrictions placed on certain types of licensing agreements. For example, under a trademark license, the licensor must maintain adequate control over the nature and quality of the goods and services sold under the mark by the licensee, or trademark rights may be lost.[44] Both trademark and copyright licensors are under an implied good-faith obligation not to do anything that would destroy or impair the value of an exclusive licensee's rights. Patent licenses providing for royalty payments beyond the patent expiration date are unlawful per se and unenforceable.[45] "Grant-back" licenses, whereby a patent licensee must license back to the licensor any improvement patents, may violate antitrust laws if there is an intent to restrain trade.[46] Multiple-rights licenses may raise questions about their application after the licensor's rights in portions of the licensed property expire or are terminated.[47]

8.2 DUE DILIGENCE IN PREPARATION FOR TRANSFER OR COLLATERAL ASSIGNMENT OF INTELLECTUAL PROPERTY

Due diligence in the area of intellectual property can be complex, because the property at issue is intangible and may be, but is not necessarily, the subject of official recognition. Thus, intellectual property due diligence cannot be accomplished solely through a review of public records or an inventory of the client's warehouse. Thorough due diligence requires a more detailed review of a variety of resources, including the owner's files and Patent and Trademark Office and Copyright Office records.

---

[44] See, e.g., *Kentucky Fried Chicken v. Diversified Packaging, Inc.*, 549 F.2d 368 (5th Cir. 1977); *Dawn Donut Co. v. Hart's Food Stores, Inc.*, 267 F.2d 358, 367 (2d Cir. 1959).

[45] *Brulotte v. Thys Co.*, 379 U.S. 29, 32 (1964).

[46] *Transparent-Wrap Machine Co. v. Stokes & Smith Co.*, 329 U.S. 637 (1947).

[47] See *Timely Prods., Inc. v. Costanzo*, 465 F. Supp. 91 (D.Conn. 1979) (holding that because the licensing agreement did not provide for severability of the royalty rates between the patent and other services, the entire licensing agreement failed when the subject patent was invalidated even though the agreement intended to cover other ongoing services).

(a) Identification of Rights.   The first task is to identify the intellectual property rights at issue. An investigator may start by looking at the company's intellectual property files, as well as searching for intellectual property held by the company in the various data bases that contain records of patents, trademark registrations and applications, and copyright registrations. Because these data base searches provide information only in limited areas, a review of corporate files, key products, manufacturing, advertising and promotional materials, and business records, as well as interviews with persons familiar with the development, manufacturing, sales, and marketing aspects of the business may be necessary to identify unregistered copyrights, trademarks, trade names, and trade secrets.

(b) Determining Ownership of the Intellectual Property.   If any of the intellectual property rights were created by a third party and transferred to the company, it is necessary to review the propriety of the transfer and to determine whether documents were appropriately recorded in the chain of title. If any rights were not properly and completely transferred, such as the assignment of a federal trademark registration without a state registration for the same mark, the transfer should be corrected at this time. In addition, any unrecorded documents capable of recordation should be recorded and priority assessed. (See section 8.5 of this chapter, which discusses assignment of intellectual property and recordation of assignment documents).

(i) "Work Made for Hire" Doctrine.   Assignments may be of special concern where important intellectual properties—such as a computer consultant's development of custom software—are commissioned for creation by third parties. Such works may be deemed owned by the contractor or consultant, rather than by the entity that commissions the work, with the one who paid for the work left with only a nonexclusive license or joint ownership. This is in stark contrast to the situation of works created by employees in the scope of employment, which are deemed "works made for hire" under the Copyright Act and are owned by the employer as if the employer were the author.[48] Thus, it is important to review the company's relationships with independent contractors for assignments of rights in copyright works, as well as for obligations of confidentiality.

The current test for determining whether a person is an employee for purposes of the work-made-for-hire doctrine was set forth by the United States Supreme Court in *Community for Creative Non-Violence v. Reid* (hereafter, *CCNV*).[49] In *CCNV*, the Court rejected a test based on the hiring party's ability to control a work product in favor of a "conventional master-servant relationship as understood by common-law agency doctrine".[50]

Even if the work was created by an employee, it must have been created within the scope of employment to be a work made for hire. In *CCNV* the Court looked for guidance to the list of factors in the Restatement (Second) of Agency.[51] Under the Restatement, conduct of a servant is within the scope of employment if, but only if:

1. It is of the kind he or she is employed to perform,
2. It occurs substantially within the authorized time and space limits, and
3. It is actuated, at least in part, by a purpose to serve the master.[52]

---

[48] *Community for Creative Non-Violence v. Reid*, 490 U.S. 730 (1989); 17 U.S.C. § 101.
[49] 490 U.S. 730 (1989).
[50] Id., 739–40.
[51] Id., 751–2.
[52] Restatement (Second) of Agency § 228 (1958).

Whenever a hired party's status is unclear, or there is a question as to whether the employee was acting within the scope of his or her employment duties, the hiring party should have obtained or now should obtain a written assignment of the intellectual property rights.

(ii) Additional Concerns Relating to Employees.   Under patent law, the "hired to invent" and "shop right" doctrines provide employers, under some circumstances, with protections similar to those provided by the work-made-for-hire doctrine in the copyright area. Under the hired-to-invent doctrine, if an employee is initially hired or later directed to invent or attempt to invent a specific item, the employer is deemed to be the owner of the patents on the invention.[53] Under the shop-right doctrine, if an employee uses the employer's resources to conceive of and put into practice an invention, the employer is granted a royalty-free, nonexclusive, nontransferable license to use the invention.[54] Because both of these doctrines are governed by state law, the applicability of any state statutes that may regulate the assignability of inventions to employers should be reviewed. Eight states have enacted statutes that invalidate the assignment of "inventions" from employee to employer where the inventions were produced without the employer's resources, on the employee's own time, unrelated to the employer's business and research, not resulting from the employee's work for the employer, and no trade secret information of the employer was used.[55] In these states, care must be taken to draft an effective assignment provision that meets the statutory requirements, including notice of the statute to the employee.

In addition, due diligence should include review of employment agreements with employees concerning treatment of intellectual property, as well as any agreements the employees may have entered into with former employers. If an employee was previously employed by a competitor with protectable trade secrets to which the employee had access and which are implicated in the employee's current work, there may be a risk of challenge by the former employer.

(iii) Grant Funding.   The funding for a particular project may also affect the ownership rights in an intellectual property. For example, if an invention or work was created pursuant to a government grant or in conjunction with a university or other funding entity, the funder may have acquired all rights in the invention or work, or may have a nonexclusive, perpetual right to use the invention or work. Thus, a review of grant agreements and related documents, as well as university policies on intellectual property, may be necessary to determine who owns the rights to the work.

---

[53] 6 D. Chisum, *Patents* § 22.03[2] (1993).

[54] Id., § 22.03[3]. See generally, Annotation, "Application and Effect of 'Shop Right Rule' or License Giving Employer Limited Rights in Employees' Inventions and Discoveries," 61 A.L.R.2d 356 (1958).

[55] See Laura G. Lape, *Ownership of Copyrightable Works of University Professors: The Interplay Between the Copyright Act and University Copyright Policies*, 37 **Vill. L. Rev**. 223, 258 n.143 (1992) (discussing the enactment of statutes in California, Delaware, Illinois, Kansas, Minnesota, North Carolina, Utah, and Washington that invalidate employment agreements assigning employees' inventions to the employer where those agreements do not comply with the requirements set forth in the statutes); Ronald B. Cooley, *Recent Changes in Employee Ownership Laws: Employers May Not Own Their Inventions and Confidential Information*, 41 **Bus. Law**. 57 (1985) (discussing the same statutes in five of the eight states listed in the preceding citation: California, Illinois, Minnesota, North Carolina, and Washington).

(iv) Founders' Rights. In dealing with corporations with active principals, it is important to make sure that the principals have assigned their intellectual property rights to the entity. Often, in the rush to get started, companies do not realize that some intellectual property held by the founders before incorporation was never transferred to the corporation. Thus, a review of all agreements with both former and current principals is necessary to determine where ownership lies and to transfer the ownership interest to the corporation where needed.

(v) Licenses. Due diligence should include a review of both intellectual property licensed to a company, such as patents or computer software, and intellectual property licensed by the company to third parties. Because the Copyright Office records licenses in the same way it records assignments, a search of the Copyright Office records may be a first step in determining whether a copyright license exists, but rarely would such an approach be comprehensive. A thorough search of the company's files may be necessary to identify all relevant licenses. Those licenses that are expressly nonassignable may not be used as collateral.

Finally, the investigator must be alert to any other situation that may raise questions concerning where ownership of an intellectual property actually lies. For example, a review of ownership in countries outside the United States is critical, especially because foreign ownership may differ from ownership within the United States.

(c) Determining the Current Status of Intellectual Property. After identifying the various intellectual property rights at issue and establishing their ownership, the investigator must determine the current status of the intellectual property. The current status may bear directly on the value of the intellectual property in a transaction. For example, if a key patent is only months away from expiration, it is much less valuable for assignment purposes than one that has a number of years remaining until expiration. Similarly, the status of intellectual property may reveal steps that need to be taken promptly to protect certain rights. For instance, there may be a need to file an extension to keep an intent-to-use trademark application alive. In addition, the status may reflect potential problems with the intellectual property, such as a pending or threatened copyright infringement action for computer software.

Review of the status of intellectual property should include an inquiry as to whether all the necessary filings were made and fees paid in a complete and timely manner. For example, an invention should not have been in use or on sale for more than one year prior to the filing of the patent application, or patentability may be barred.[56] Some deadlines for filing or payment do allow for late filing under appropriate circumstances, such as the late filing of a patent maintenance fee or a trademark renewal.

For trade secrets, due diligence includes review of both the value to the company of maintaining the trade secrets as confidential, and the steps taken by the company to protect the confidentiality of the trade secrets.

Encumbrances on the intellectual property as well as important assignment information may be revealed through Uniform Commercial Code (UCC) searches and searches of federal patent, trademark, and copyright filings and state trademark filings.

The degree of effort needed to determine the current status of intellectual property depends on the value of the intellectual property, the importance of intellectual property to the proposed transaction, the type of intellectual property at issue, and the degree

---

[56] Patent Act, 35 U.S.C. § 102(b).

of confidence in the company's routine manner of handling its intellectual property. The typical means used to explore the current status of intellectual property are similar to, and may be used in conjunction with, those employed in the determination of ownership of intellectual property. For example, data base searches, examination of Patent and Trademark Office records, copyright title searches, and UCC searches in relevant states, in addition to review of internal files, products, and advertising, and the interviewing of relevant employees—all aid in determining the current status of intellectual property. Although data bases containing information from government files are once removed from actual Patent and Trademark Office and Copyright Office filings, their reliability is becoming generally accepted and they have often been used instead of searches of the records of the respective government offices in performing intellectual property due diligence. Of course, if any question arises, the original files of the relevant offices should be consulted.

8.3 OPINION LETTERS

Intellectual property counsel are frequently asked to provide opinion letters concerning intellectual property issues in a given transaction. The intellectual property opinion may be only one of numerous opinions covering many different aspects of the transaction, or it may be the sole opinion requested if the transactional attorney is not familiar with intellectual property issues.

(a) General Guidelines for Opinion Letters.   In issuing any opinion letter, counsel should exercise due caution in setting forth the scope and limitations of the opinion.[57] For example, counsel should specifically state the areas of law investigated, the specific facts investigated and relied upon in forming the opinion, the documents reviewed and searches conducted, the specific matters addressed, any assumptions made, any reliance on the opinion of other counsel (such as foreign counsel on foreign law issues), and the applicable law. In addition, the lawyer's capacity as general counsel, local counsel, or special counsel should be described. This description may be accompanied by a disclaimer indicating that certain matters may be outside the attorney's knowledge or experience with the client, which, if known, might limit or change the attorney's opinion.

(b) Intellectual Property Opinion Letters.   The warranties typically requested of intellectual property holders cover the same areas frequently requested for inclusion in intellectual property opinion letters: ownership, originality, validity, enforceability, no encumbrances, noninfringement of third-party rights, and noninfringement by third parties. Other issues for which an opinion may be requested include registration of material registrable rights, effectiveness of proposed security documents for attachment, perfection, and priority of the security interest. Such opinions may be given by the company's

---

[57] For general guidelines on writing opinions letters, see Committee on Legal Opinions, *Third-Party Legal Opinion Report, Including the Legal Opinion Accord, of the Section of Business Law, American Bar Association*, 47 **Bus. Law**. 167 (1991); James J. Fuld, *Lawyers' Standards and Responsibilities in Rendering Opinions*, 33 **Bus. Law**. 1295 (1978); James J. Fuld, *Legal Opinions in Business Transactions: An Attempt to Bring Some Order Out of Some Chaos*, 28 **Bus. Law**. 915 (1973).

regular intellectual property counsel whenever possible, who is likely to be familiar with the intellectual property and any relevant concerns.

Courts have held that intellectual property opinion letters must not address specific issues, such as validity and infringement, in a conclusory fashion. For example, part of a party's affirmative defense to a suit for willful patent infringement may be reliance on a competent opinion letter. However, in a case where the opinion letter was silent on the issue of validity, discussed infringement in a conclusory manner, and failed to mention infringement under the doctrine of equivalents, and the attorney giving the opinion had not even reviewed the prosecution history of the patent prior to rendering the opinion, the opinion was deemed defective and could not be relied upon by the defendant.[58] Conclusory opinions should not be given by counsel in any area of intellectual property.

Similarly, regular intellectual property counsel may be in a favorable position to give opinions as to the effective creation of a security interest or transfer because of their familiarity with the intellectual property at issue. However, because of the complicated state of the law concerning security interests in intellectual property, regular intellectual property counsel may choose to defer to other counsel more knowledgeable of secured transactions.[59] In giving an opinion that an agreement is sufficient to create a security interest in intellectual property, counsel should confirm that the security interest was granted and "attaches," as discussed in the following section of this chapter. The portion of the opinion letter relating to the effective perfection of a security interest should be written with special care. Some discussion of the currently uncertain state of the law should be included such as a statement that, because of the absence of clear authority, it is uncertain at this time how to perfect a security interest in unregistered United States copyrights, short of first obtaining copyright registrations.

The issue of priority of a security interest may be left to nonintellectual property counsel familiar with priority in other contexts. However, to the extent that the courts hold that perfection must take place through recordation of the security interest with the Copyright Office or Patent and Trademark Office, priority would be determined in view of the statutory grace periods for recordation. The priority opinion may involve assessing the application of the statutory grace period and the impact of UCC filings on multiple security interests and liens of many other claimants without limit as to jurisdiction.

8.4 SECURITY INTERESTS IN INTELLECTUAL PROPERTY

The importance of security interests in intellectual property has increased over the years as companies have become more aware of the value of intellectual property. Historically, creditors sought security interests in inventory, equipment, and consumer goods because the value of such collateral could be easily determined and, if the debtor defaulted under the security agreement, such collateral could be sold with relative ease. In contrast, the value of intellectual property was not as obvious. Its sale presented questions that did not arise in the sale of tangible goods. By the 1980s, however, companies began to realize the significant value of intellectual property. As advances in technology, increased reliance

---

[58] *Datascope Corp. v. SMEC, Inc.*, 879 F.2d 820 (Fed. Cir. 1989), *cert. denied*, 493 U.S. 1024 (1990).

[59] For guidance in writing legal opinions on security interests in personal property, see Scott FitzGibbon and Donald W. Glazer, *Legal Opinions in Corporate Transactions: Opinions Relating to Security Interests in Personal Property*, 44 **Bus. Law.** 655 (1989); Uniform Commercial Code Committee of the Business Law Section of the State Bar of California, *Report Regarding Legal Opinions in Personal Property Secured Transactions*, 44 **Bus. Law.** 791 (1989).

on computers, and a surge in licensing and merchandising activities served to increase the value of intellectual property, an economic downturn decreased the value of other property, such as real estate. Although many financings began with the expectation that tangible property would provide the key collateral, intellectual property often emerged as far more important than initially believed. Companies have realized that granting security interests in intellectual property draws on an enormous source of value to fund and facilitate commercial transactions.

Article 9 of the Uniform Commercial Code specifically governs security interests in personal property, including general intangibles such as intellectual property; however, federal law may preempt certain provisions of Article 9. As discussed later in this chapter, it is unclear which statutory framework regulates the perfection of security interests in intellectual property, and parties are advised to comply with both UCC and federal law in creating and perfecting security interests in intellectual property.

(a) The Creation of a Security Interest in Intellectual Property. A creditor generally takes a security interest in collateral of the debtor to assure repayment of a debt. The debtor signs a security agreement, which typically states that upon default the creditor has the right to take possession of the specified collateral owned by the debtor. Hence, in the event of default, the creditor may merely seize the collateral rather than having to sue the debtor for a personal judgment and then having the sheriff levy against the debtor's assets.

A security interest in intellectual property such as copyrights, patents, trademarks, and trade secrets may be accomplished through a variety of measures including collateral assignment, conditional assignment, or an outright assignment and license back to the debtor. Originally, different methods were employed because it was uncertain whether the Patent and Trademark Office or the Copyright Office would recognize anything short of an outright assignment as acceptable for recordation. However, the federal offices currently accept any of the variations for recording, and the Patent and Trademark Office recently revised its recordation forms to specifically reference security interests.

Under the UCC, a security agreement in intellectual property becomes enforceable against the debtor with respect to the collateral upon "attachment." The security interest "attaches" upon the fulfillment of three requirements:[60]

- The debtor grants the creditor a security interest in the specified property pursuant to a written security agreement,
- The debtor has rights in the property, and
- The creditor gives value in exchange for the security interest.

Typical security agreements adequately fulfill these requirements. Similarly, the Patent Act and the Copyright Act require that any transfer of an interest in patents and copyrights, respectively, be accompanied by a written note or memorandum. The Lanham Act does not require that transfers of rights in trademarks be in writing, and case law permits oral evidence of assignments.[61] Written assignments are recommended, of course, and the law of secured transactions requires security agreements to be in writing.

---

[60] U.C.C. § 9–203(1).

[61] See, e.g., *Conde Nast Publications, Inc. v. United States*, 575 F.2d 400, 198 U.S.P.Q. 202 (2d Cir. 1978); *Edwin K. Williams & Co. v. Edwin K. Williams & Co. East*, 542 F.2d 1053 (9th Cir. 1976), *cert. denied*, 433 U.S. 908 (1977).

Parties may execute several documents in major transactions. Typical documents include financing statements, credit agreements, intellectual property security agreements, and notes. Frequently, a long-form document creating a security interest in an intellectual property is executed with an attached short-form document that grants the security interest in a bare bones fashion and includes a schedule of the relevant intellectual property. The short-form document is then filed with the appropriate government office to avoid public disclosure of the details pertaining to the transaction.

Depending on the type of transaction, a security agreement may vary in length. A security agreement must include some variation of a granting clause in which the debtor grants the creditor, or an agent of the creditor, an interest in the collateral. For example, an agreement creating a security interest in general intangibles and intellectual property may include the following language:

> As security for the payment and performance of all liabilities, the Debtor hereby assigns and grants to and for the benefit of the Creditor a continuing security interest in all of the following whether now or hereafter existing, owned, licensed, leased, arising, or acquired.

The agreement then will list and describe the particular collateral, such as inventory, accounts receivable, cash accounts, real estate, and intellectual property. The agreement should define *intellectual property* and any other terms employed in the document. The agreement may either incorporate UCC definitions or use deal-specific definitions. Intellectual property, for instance, may be defined expansively as:

> All past, present, and future trade secrets and other proprietary information; trademarks, service marks, business names, designs, logos, indicia, and/or business identifiers and the goodwill of the business relating thereto and all registrations or applications for registration; copyrights and copyright registrations or applications for registration; unpatented inventions (whether or not patentable); patent applications and patents; industrial designs and industrial design applications; and license agreements pertaining to same, wherever existing, filed, issued or entered throughout the world.

Any grant of a security interest in a trademark should include the goodwill of the business associated with the trademark. Arguably, a conditional assignment of a trademark is merely a future assignment which cannot violate the rule against assigning trademarks without the associated goodwill.[62] However, if the secured creditor were to enforce the conditional assignment in the event of default, the assignment would become operative and the assignment of the trademark without the goodwill of the business would constitute an assignment in gross, resulting in the loss of trademark rights. Hence, trademark collateral always should include the goodwill of the business associated with the mark.

In addition to definitions and a granting clause, a security agreement may contain numerous other provisions. The creditor may require the inclusion of numerous warranties pertaining to intellectual property, such as ownership, originality, validity, enforceability, noninfringement of third-party rights, noninfringement by third parties, registration of material registrable rights, and no encumbrances. Moreover, security agreements may also contain various other provisions, such as inclusion of intellectual property as collateral, maintenance of intellectual property rights in full force and effect, and granting the creditor a power of attorney to handle the intellectual property.

---

[62] See, e.g., *Li'l Red Barn, Inc. v. Red Barn System, Inc.*, 322 F. Supp. 98, 167 U.S.P.Q. 741 (N.D. Ind. 1970), *aff'd per curiam*, 174 U.S.P.Q. 193 (7th Cir. 1972).

Schedules attached to the security agreement should specifically identify and describe the intellectual property collateral.

(b) Perfection and Priority.   A security interest becomes enforceable against third parties, such as other creditors, upon "perfection." The secured creditor "perfects" the security interest by recording the transaction in the appropriate government office.[63] As discussed earlier, it is unclear whether recording under the UCC or under the relevant federal statutory framework sufficiently perfects a security interest in intellectual property, or whether a security interest in unregistered copyrights may be perfected at all. Consequently, many attorneys recommend that security agreements be filed or recorded both under the UCC and with the appropriate federal agency. To file under the UCC, UCC-1 forms should be completed and filed in the appropriate state office.

Filings at the Patent and Trademark Office (PTO) require the use of a cover sheet prepared by the PTO, to which the granting documents and schedule must be attached. The Copyright Office does not require a particular cover sheet form; rather, a simple transmittal letter may accompany submission of the granting document and schedule for recordation.

Receipts of filing are provided by the state in the form of stamped copies of the UCC-1, and by the Patent and Trademark Office and Copyright Office through providing notice of recordation and reference to the location of the recorded document.

Security interests also may be recorded under some state trademark registration statutes.

Priority under the UCC is determined on a first to file basis. Priority under the federal statutes governing intellectual property is not; the grace periods allowed under the federal statutes are described in "Recordation of Intellectual Property Assignments" later in this chapter. Which priority scheme to use would depend upon whether the UCC or federal law were held to govern.

(c) Default.   Either the financing document or the security agreement should define under what conditions a debtor may be deemed to have defaulted on the loan underlying a transaction. Default is the triggering event upon which the collateral may be transferred to the secured creditor. The parties may define an event of default as the debtor's missing a certain number of payments, transferring an interest in the collateral, failing to pay taxes pertaining to the collateral, or filing a bankruptcy petition. Upon the occurrence of any event of default, depending on the type of security interest granted, the secured creditor either will automatically hold full rights in the intellectual property collateral or will need to take additional steps to acquire full rights.

Pursuant to §§ 9–504 and 9–505 of the UCC, upon occurrence of an event of default the secured creditor has the right either to keep the intellectual property in satisfaction of the obligation (strict foreclosure) or to dispose of the property by private or public auction. Upon strict foreclosure, the secured creditor takes the collateral in full satisfaction of the debt and surrenders the right to recover any deficiency from the debtor. More commonly, the secured creditor chooses to resell the collateral at a "commercially reasonable" public or private sale. By selling the collateral, the secured creditor reserves the right to recover a deficiency judgment against the debtor. Before taking either action, the secured creditor must give proper notice to the debtor.

---

[63] Patent, 35 U.S.C. § 261; Copyright, 17 U.S.C. § 205; Lanham Act, 15 U.S.C. 1060; Semi-Conductor Chip Protection Act, 17 U.S.C. § 903(c) (1).

Several provisions of the Bankruptcy Code impact security interests in general, and security interests in intellectual property in particular. Initially, the Bankruptcy Code prohibits a secured creditor from disposing of any collateral under the "automatic stay" provision.[64] Further, the trustee may employ a number of powers in collecting and distributing the debtor's assets, which may hinder realization under a security interest. For example, the trustee may use § 544(a)(1) of the Bankruptcy Code to void an unperfected security interest in collateral, or § 547 of the Code to void certain security interests as preferences.[65] In addition, the trustee may employ § 365(n) of the Code to reject a license of intellectual property as an executory contract where the debtor is the licensor of a right to intellectual property.[66] However, § 365(n)(1)(B) provides that the licensee nevertheless may choose to retain his or her contractual rights under certain types of intellectual property licenses.

(d) Termination and Release of Security Interest. Where no event of default has occurred and the loan is paid off in full, a debtor should see to it that a termination and release of the security interest is recorded in the appropriate government offices. A typical release pertaining to patents, for instance, may include the following language:

> Whereas, the obligations of the Debtor to the Creditor have been paid and satisfied in full;
> For valuable consideration and pursuant to the terms and conditions set forth in the Security Agreement and the Patent Agreement, Creditor hereby terminates and releases its security interest in the Patents and Creditor hereby assigns and transfers to Debtor, without recourse, all of Creditor's right, title, and interest in the Patents, as set forth on the attached Exhibit X.

An attached exhibit would identify all of the debtor's relevant collateral. Filing the release will clear the chain of title and avoid later problems in the event of subsequent financings or transfers concerning the intellectual property.

8.5 ASSIGNMENTS OF INTELLECTUAL PROPERTY

Although some transactions involve granting security interests in intellectual property, other transactions entail an outright assignment of intellectual property rights. Such assignments may be imbedded in larger transactions involving the sale of a business, or in smaller, independent transactions in which certain intellectual property is sold on its own, such as a trademark and associated goodwill or a copyright created by an independent contractor. As with security interests, the parties may choose to execute a detailed long-form assignment with a short-form assignment exhibit and schedule for detaching and recording with the appropriate government office.

(a) The Assignment Document

(i) Patents. The Patent Act provides that applications for patents, patents, and any interests therein are assignable by an instrument in writing.[67] Although a patent assignment typically conveys the exclusive right to make, use, or sell a particular invention, the assignment may simply convey an undivided share of the ownership of the patent. The

---

[64] 11 U.S.C. § 362 (1988).
[65] Id., § 544(a)(1), 547(b).
[66] Id., 365(n).
[67] 35 U.S.C. § 261.

written instrument should be unambiguous and demonstrate a clear intent on the part of the assignor to transfer ownership. Language such as the following is often used:

> For valuable consideration furnished by Assignee to Assignor, the receipt and sufficiency of which Assignor hereby acknowledges, Assignor hereby without reservation assigns, transfers, and conveys to Assignee and its representatives, successors and assigns forever, the entire right, title, and interest in and to the Patents and any Patent Applications shown on the attached Exhibit X including without limitation any and all rights of action for past infringement of the Patents and the right to receive payment of damages resulting therefrom, and the right to receive any patents issued on any Patent Applications.

The assignment should describe the patent(s) by number and date, name of the patent holder, and name of the invention. Furthermore, patent assignments must expressly convey the right to sue for past infringements, or that right will not be transferred.

(ii) Trademarks. Trademark assignments must include the goodwill of the business associated with the mark.[68] Because trademarks provide a source-identifying function, an assignment of a trademark without the associated goodwill, or an "assignment in gross," is invalid and may result in the loss of trademark rights. Hence, an assignment of a trademark could include language such as the following:

> For valuable consideration furnished by Assignee to Assignor, the receipt and sufficiency of which Assignor hereby acknowledges, Assignor does hereby sell, assign, and transfer to Assignee, for itself, its successors and assigns, all of its right, title and interest in and to each of such trademarks shown on the attached Exhibit X, and any registrations or applications for registration thereof, together with all of the goodwill of the business connected with the use of and symbolized by the marks, and any registrations thereof.

Rights to sue and to recover damages also should be expressly assigned, for such rights do not automatically pass with a mark. To prevent trafficking in trademarks, the Lanham Act bars assignment of intent-to-use applications in the absence of an accompanying transfer of the relevant portion of the business.[69] Trade names may be assigned in the same manner.

(iii) Copyrights. The Copyright Act requires that a transfer of copyright ownership be in writing and signed by the assignor.[70] Any written instrument of conveyance or memorandum of the transfer should satisfy the writing requirement. The copyright assignment should specify whether all rights under copyright or only a portion of them are being assigned. Typical language used to assign copyrights often includes the following:

> For valuable consideration furnished by Assignee, the receipt and sufficiency of which Assignor hereby acknowledges, Assignor hereby without reservation grants, assigns, and conveys to Assignee and its representatives, successors and assigns forever, the entire right, title and interest in and to any and all of its original works of authorship fixed in any tangible medium of expression (the "Works") together with all other material created with respect to said Works, whether registered or unregistered, including but not limited to the items listed on the attached Exhibit X, including all those reproduction and allied rights necessary and appropriate for production, distribution and exploitation of said Works in all media throughout the world in perpetuity, any and all rights of

---

[68] 15 U.S.C. § 1060.
[69] 15 U.S.C. § 1060.
[70] 17 U.S.C. § 204(a).

action against past infringement of the Works and the right to receive payment of damages resulting therefrom.

(iv) Trade Secrets.   Also assignable as personal property under general legal principles are trade secrets and other miscellaneous intellectual property. The Uniform Trade Secrets Act does not address assignment of trade secrets. Such an assignment should always be in writing, for a trade secret assignment will not be imputed in the absence of express volitional conduct by the assignor and assignee.[71] Moreover, an assignment of a trade secret or other general intangibles should include a specific identification and description of the property being assigned. The assignment also may contain provisions relating to any continuing rights of the assignor and any obligation of the assignor to maintain confidentiality of trade secrets after the assignment.

(v) Licenses.   Although intellectual property licenses frequently bar assignments, so long as a license contains no express prohibition, a licensor's or licensee's rights and obligations under a license may be assigned to third parties. To the extent assignable, an assignment of a license should adequately identify the license, the assignor, and the assignee and state whether any approval rights under the license have been exercised and how any continuing payments under the license will be made.

(b) General Provisions.   Assignments of all types of intellectual property may include various warranties pertaining to ownership, originality, noninfringement, or any other issue that the particular circumstances of the transaction require. Although many routine assignments do not include warranties, in more significant transactions intellectual property warranties are often crucial and extensively negotiated.

Assignments of intellectual property should include an acknowledgement with a notary signature, because the Patent Act,[72] the Lanham Act,[73] and the Copyright Act[74] all provide that proper acknowledgment constitutes prima facie evidence of execution.

(c) Recordation of Intellectual Property Assignments.   Recordation of assignments of intellectual property issued or registered by the Patent and Trademark Office or the Copyright Office is governed solely by federal law. The UCC, which pertains only to security interests, does not apply. The procedures for recording assignments at the Patent and Trademark Office and the Copyright Office are the same as those used to record security interests in intellectual property.

The recording provisions for assignments of intellectual property also establish priority among assignments. As a general rule, the first transfer properly recorded within the statutory grace period after execution of the transfer prevails over any later transfer. Although recordation of assignments protects assignees against subsequent purchasers, the grace period or "look-back" provisions contained in the federal statutes leave an assignee vulnerable during those few months following the assignment.

For example, § 261 of the Patent Act provides that an assignment is void against a subsequent purchaser without notice of a prior assignment unless the prior assignment is recorded within three months from its execution or prior to the date of the subsequent

---

[71] Roger M. Milgrim, *Milgrim on Trade Secrets*, § 1.02[2] 1993.
[72] 35 U.S.C. § 261.
[73] 15 U.S.C. § 1060.
[74] 17 U.S.C. § 204(b).

purchase.[75] Hence, as between two conflicting transfers, the transfer first executed most often will prevail so long as it is recorded within three months of its execution. Because of this three-month window, an assignee who receives an interest and records it on January 1 can be defeated by a competing purchaser who does not record until March 30 but received an interest on December 31. Section 1060 of the Lanham Act provides a similar three-month look-back provision.[76] In contrast, § 205 of the Copyright Act provides a one-month look-back period.[77] Because of the uncertainty created by these look-back provisions, an assignee may wish to place consideration for the assignment in escrow for the one-or three-month period following execution of the assignment against the possibility that the rights may have been previously assigned.

The PTO will record licenses of patents and registered trademarks.[78]

Most state trademark statutes also provide for recordation of assignments of state trademark registrations, and many have required forms and procedures.

Because common-law trademarks, trade names, trade secrets, and know-how are not issued by or registered in government offices, there is no place to record assignments in such intellectual property. The PTO will not record documents solely concerning unregistered trademarks. However, assignments of registered trademarks and applications for registration often mention unregistered marks that are assigned in the same document. Although there is no means of searching for an unregistered mark in PTO records, an unregistered mark listed in an assignment of registered marks and applications would show up in the recorded assignment.

The Copyright Office will record assignments of unregistered copyrights, which may be identified and searched by owner or title. The Copyright Office also records licenses of copyrights.[79]

---

[75] 35 U.S.C. § 261.
[76] 15 U.S.C. § 1060.
[77] 17 U.S.C. § 205(e).
[78] 15 U.S.C. § 1060.
[79] 17 U.S.C. §§ 205(a), 705.

CHAPTER 9

THE ACQUISITION AND DISPOSITION OF INTELLECTUAL PROPERTY IN COMMERCIAL TRANSACTIONS: THE CANADIAN PERSPECTIVE

R. Scott Jolliffe, Esq.
Andrew Kelly Gill, Esq.

Gowling, Strathy & Henderson
Toronto, Canada

9.1 INTRODUCTION

This chapter canvasses some of the practical concerns, strategies, and procedures involved in international mergers and acquisitions from the perspective of intellectual property. Although many points are relevant to local transactions, a broader approach is attempted through highlighting some of the procedural difficulties and possible maneuverings in a multijurisdictional business transaction involving intellectual property.

International business acquisitions, whether by share or asset transfer, are necessarily complex. When intellectual property considerations are included, the complexity increases substantially. The thrust of this chapter is to provide an outline for the business person and general counsel steering an international acquisition involving intellectual property, the commercial lawyer coordinating the deal, and the intellectual property lawyer responsible for the accurate identification and subsequent acquisition or disposition of the intellectual property. Therefore, the discussion is necessarily general, with specific examples offered to highlight important areas. Searching, identifying, and valuing intellectual property are covered broadly and from a nonjurisdictional perspective. The intellectual property transfer requirements necessary to complete an international business transaction vary from one jurisdiction to the next, and it would be impossible to provide a detailed analysis of even some of the more important intellectual property jurisdictions. Instead, requirements under Canadian law are offered to indicate some of the issues that may arise in transferring intellectual property within foreign jurisdictions.

9.2 OVERVIEW OF THE TRANSACTION

Business acquisitions can take many forms. The manner and type of acquisition will have a direct bearing on the strategies and procedures adopted to handle intellectual property issues. For example, a hostile share acquisition will provide the lowest level of assurance in regard to intellectual property, whereas an asset acquisition, although providing far greater assurance for the purchaser of the assets, will involve substantially more work for the intellectual property lawyer.

(a) Nature of the Business and Its Assets.   A commercial lawyer is typically retained to advise and coordinate in a major sale or purchase of a business. The lawyer should immediately become familiar with the nature of the business and the types of assets involved. Today, more frequently than ever before, a business is apt to own, license, or rent intellectual property. If intellectual property is an important part of the business, a specialist should be retained to coordinate this aspect of the transaction. Dealing with intellectual property involves special considerations often requiring strict technical compliance with relevant statutes and regulations. It is imperative that intellectual property is used, maintained, licensed, and assigned properly, inasmuch as noncompliance may destroy the property right itself.

(b) Objectives of the Parties.   Asset purchases and share purchases are the two main means of acquiring a business. The factors influencing the selection of one method over the other are highly dependent on the parties' objectives. Seldom are the influencing factors the same for both parties, as often there are advantages for one that are not present for the other.

(c) Tax Considerations.   The decision to acquire by way of asset or share transfer is often driven by tax considerations that are little affected by, and affect very little, the role of the transaction's coordinating intellectual property specialist. Although intellectual property rights are often given different tax treatment, depending on the nature and extent of the intangible right, they rarely play such a prominent role as to dictate the method of acquiring a business. However, each type of intellectual property right involved in the transaction should be carefully analyzed, as different methods of acquisition often result in different tax consequences.

It is important to recognize and deal with the tax treatment of each type of intellectual property in an effort to minimize the tax consequences of the transaction. In an asset purchase, the purchase price ascribed to each intellectual property asset is likely to be strongly influenced by the tax treatment of the asset. In Canada, the type of the intellectual property, and whether it is licensed, purchased, or assigned, often results in different tax treatment. Currently, patents and licenses for a fixed term are written off on a straight-line basis over the life of the patent or license.[1] Licenses of an indeterminate period are considered eligible capital property, three-quarters of the cost of which may be written off on a 7% declining balance basis. The often favorable tax consequences of purchasing research and development, both current and future capacity, can also be an important, though long-term, factor.[2]

---

[1] Income Tax Act, Schedule II, Class 14. The April 26, 1993, federal budget proposed adding Class 44 to Schedule II, Capital Cost Allowances, as an alternative to Class 14 but for patents only. Class 44 would introduce a new 25% declining balance capital cost allowance for all patents and rights to use patented information acquired after April 26, 1993. A 25% declining balance rate will generally provide larger deductions in the earlier years of a patent's use, given that the value of a patent often declines faster in its earlier years as new technologies are developed. Further, taxpayers will have the option of using the existing system, which could be more advantageous in cases where a patent is acquired late in its term.

[2] For an excellent discussion in this area, see Shelley J. Kamin, "Scientific Research and Experimental Development Tax Incentives," 10 *Canadian Intellectual Property Review* (1993):487.

(d) Share Versus Asset Transactions.   A common misapprehension is that share transactions are relatively simple, particularly from the standpoint of intellectual property, because there is only one asset to purchase—the shares themselves. All other assets and liabilities flow automatically by virtue of acquiring the shares. However, in an asset transaction each individual intellectual property asset must be transferred in the appropriate manner and the transfer recorded in the relevant jurisdictions. For an international asset purchase involving intellectual property in many different jurisdictions, the costs of the transfer and recordal of the new owner can become quite expensive. Nevertheless, before purchasing shares, the prudent purchaser should conduct an in-depth review of the business and its underlying intellectual property assets. Such a review is only marginally less time-consuming or expensive for intellectual property than an asset purchase review. The only significant difference arises from the disbursements incurred to record the transfer of the registered intellectual property. In share-purchase transactions, the recordal of the transfer is obviously unnecessary, whereas in international asset purchases it is unavoidable and can be costly.

9.3 INTELLECTUAL PROPERTY RIGHTS—BROADLY DEFINED

The importance of intellectual property in any international business transaction is entirely dependent on the nature of the business itself. Rarely does a transaction not involve some kind of intellectual property, as broadly defined. Proper identification of all intellectual property rights is essential at the outset of the transaction and should be followed by an assessment of the procedures for, and consequences of, transferring these rights. An intellectual property lawyer should be involved from the start of the transaction. Registered rights in trademarks, trade names, service marks, patents, copyrights, and designs are easily identifiable, and the procedures for transfer and recordal are well known. Often overlooked, however, are the myriad potential unregistered rights, entitlements, licenses, approvals, and listings that are involved in the operation of the business. The role of the intellectual property specialist is to ensure that each right involved is properly identified and that appropriate steps are taken to transfer effectively the asset to the purchaser.

9.4 DUE DILIGENCE: THE INTELLECTUAL PROPERTY AUDIT

In an international business transaction it is necessary to define intellectual property broadly, so as to ensure a scope of review that covers all possible rights and jurisdictions involved in the transaction. Not all countries allow for the same registrations, and not all recognize unregistered rights in intellectual property, whatever the form. Due diligence begins by obtaining a thorough understanding of the entity to be acquired and the applicable laws of each jurisdiction in which it does business.

Understanding why the business is being acquired is essential to structuring the transaction and putting together an effective transaction team. If the reason for the purchase is simply to acquire more manufacturing facilities, it is unlikely that an intellectual property specialist is required to play a significant role. If, however, the purchase involves existing products, know-how, and manufacturing, distribution, and marketing, it is essential to involve an intellectual property lawyer as soon as possible.

(a) Seller's Representation of Rights for Sale or License.   Representations by a vendor often provide the first meaningful disclosure of the rights available for sale or license and greatly assist in the due diligence process. It is important for the vendor to describe accurately and fully the intellectual property rights involved in the business, because mistakes discovered on the eve of closing, even minor ones, can break a deal or significantly affect the purchase price. Furthermore, representations given in the early stages of a transaction are often repeated verbatim as warranties on closing. Therefore, there can be significant exposure through a claim for damages for breach of a warranty if the representations and warranties are inaccurate and not corrected prior to closing. Likewise, from the purchaser's perspective, failing to conduct appropriate searches and reviews to confirm the vendor's representations is equivalent to purchasing land without conducting a title search.

(b) Identifying and Protecting the Rights.   The intellectual property specialist first must identify the relevant intellectual property rights being used by the business to be transferred. To be as thorough as possible, it is helpful to have the complete cooperation of both parties, including their employees, who are often the most knowledgeable about the intellectual property rights at issue. This involves conducting an "intellectual property audit." The audit identifies all intellectual property rights being used by the business, ensuring that they are properly owned, registered, and licensed by the business, and that they are being used and protected properly. Proper use is particularly important for use-dependent rights in assets such as trademarks, trade-names, know-how, and confidential information, whose continued existence in law depends on proper procedures being followed to ensure their protectability.

The specialist begins by preparing a list of questions to be asked of both parties in an attempt to elicit as much information about potential intellectual property rights as possible. The questions should be written in plain, everyday language to allow a full appreciation of the breadth of what is being sought. A list of basic questions should be aimed at eliciting information about the following intellectual property rights:

Registered Rights
- Patents
- Trademarks
- Trade names
- Copyrights
- Design patents
- Utility models
- Chip topographies
- Plant breeds
- Pending applications

Unregistered Rights
- Inventions
- Trade secrets
- Confidential information

- Know-how
- Trademarks
- Trade names
- Trade dress
- Copyrights
- Designs
- Goodwill

Rights Arising from Employment
- Ownership of inventions, copyrights, designs, opportunities
- Duties of confidence
- Fiduciary duties
- Employment agreements

Rights Arising from Third-Party Relationships
- Licenses, distributorships, and agency relationships
- Exclusivities (product acquisition and supply)
- Purchase and sale commitments

Approvals and Listings
- Government marketing and product approvals
- Packaging, labeling, advertising approvals
- Product and service listings, qualifications and restrictions
- Company listings and approvals

Intellectual Property-Related Litigation
- Cease and desist letters sent/received
- Pending or threatened litigation
- Administrative proceedings affecting intellectual property rights
- Government investigations and inquiries

The purchaser's own information on the listed intellectual property rights may be a good starting point and, for some limited forms of transactions, may be all that is necessary. More likely, however, there will be a need for much greater detail, which can be obtained only from the vendor. It is best for the intellectual property specialist to visit the business premises and physically inspect the premises, plant, personnel, and products in order to gain a good understanding of the intellectual property rights involved in the business. The investigation begins at the front door, the specialist noting the trade name and any design used, and continues through all aspects of manufacturing, marketing, and distribution. The following is a generic list of some of the subject matter for inspection:

- Products and services
- Product components, ingredients, and raw materials
- Manufacturing and packaging processes

- Manufacturing and packaging equipment
- Product design, components, shape, configuration
- Software (manufacturing and administrative)
- Packaging, containers, labeling
- Business and trade names, trademarks, trade dress
- Advertising and marketing materials
- Channels of trade: marketing, distribution and retailing relationships
- Business information, data, opportunities
- Research and development (product, process, packaging, and marketing)
- Key employees in research, design, manufacturing, distribution, and sales
- Employee relationships and agreements
- Third-party licenses, agreements, permissions, relationships
- Restrictions through financing and security
- Affiliated company interdependence (rights, technical support, licenses)
- Management and administrative support systems

(c) Ownership/Title. A skeleton list of the intellectual property owned, registered, used, and licensed by the business can now be created. The blanks can be filled in through government searches and further inquiries with a view to creating a complete and accurate summary of the business's intellectual property portfolio. Investigations as to the title and/or codification of each identified right follow, along with searches to identify any security interests registered against the rights, contractual rights, and obligations affecting the rights and the existence and extent of any licenses, permissions, and entitlements. The unnerving aspect of this part of the transaction, for both lawyer and client, is the realization that despite the enormous cost of intellectual property, it is generally impossible to guarantee proper title and what, if any, encumbrances exist.

(i) Root of Title. The root of title refers to the original legal and equitable basis upon which the right is owned. Whether the vendor has title to the right being sold, financed, or licensed is of paramount importance. Discovering the root of title is the goal of most intellectual property lawyers involved in a due diligence inquiry. To establish with any degree of certainty the root of title and to trace the proper assignment of the right to the vendor goes a long way toward assuring that proper title is being acquired by the purchaser. Ascertaining the root of title with absolute certainty is a difficult task, which depends on the nature of intellectual property right involved.

For example, copyright is solely a creature of statute in most countries around the world. However, in many countries registration of copyright is voluntary and protection arises automatically. In some countries, copyright assignments may be registered without the original right ever having been registered, creating a registered index that is misleading to those not in the know. It is important to identify the original author/creator of a copyright, as all rights belong to this person unless assigned in writing or by operation of law (employment). Even when the basic title to a copyright has been assigned to the vendor, not all ancillary rights may have been assigned. Some rights may have been retained by the original owner, or may never have been owned by the author, or have reverted back to the author by contract or operation of law. In many countries the author retains moral rights in a copyright which can never be assigned.[3] These issues with respect to ownership are particularly difficult for copyright. Nevertheless, most other intellectual property rights have their own peculiarities with respect to ownership and title, which vary from country to country.

(ii) Assignments, Licenses, and Permissions.   Uncovering the root of title is only the first step. Next, the purchaser will require an assurance or proof that the right has been properly assigned to the vendor and that the vendor has not assigned or licensed part or some or all the right to third parties. Tracing effective assignments, licenses, and permissions of intellectual property rights is also a difficult task. There is no mandatory filing of assignments or licenses for any of the intellectual property rights in many countries, making it virtually impossible to ensure that the right in question has not already been assigned or licensed. As with ownership and title, the purchaser must ultimately rely on the representations and warranties of the vendor that the whole of the right is being transferred, unencumbered by any third-party rights or entitlements.

(iii) Security Interests.   Intellectual property rights are today being pledged as security more than ever because of their increased importance and value to business. Unfortunately, in many jurisdictions the laws regarding security interests in intellectual property are as yet undeveloped, and there are still many concerns regarding pledging, registering, and enforcing such interests. Given the fundamental impact that a security agreement may have on the transfer of an intellectual property right, it is important when purchasing such property to conduct thorough searches for security interests. In some jurisdictions it is necessary to conduct searches under special financing and security interest legislation, as well as searches of the relevant intellectual property registers.[4] A review of relevant financing and security interest agreements is also important. Ultimately, however, consultation with an expert in each jurisdiction is essential to determine the extent to which the vendor's intellectual property rights may be affected by security interests.

9.5 INTERNATIONAL TRANSACTIONS

International transactions involving intellectual property should not be treated any differently than a number of national transactions. The difference and difficulty of the international transaction lie in coordinating and confirming the intellectual property rights in each relevant jurisdiction. The intellectual property specialist generally has a rudimentary knowledge of the applicable foreign laws and procedures with regard to basic intellectual property rights, but must be sensitive to the objectives of the client as to the importance of the rights, the cost of foreign transfers and registrations, and local tax consequences.

(a) Identifying and Protecting Intellectual Property Rights.   The intellectual property lawyer immediately should attempt to identify, with the assistance of the client, all foreign

---

[3] In some countries (Canada, for example) the author's moral rights can be waived.

[4] For a detailed review of Canadian law regarding intellectual property as security interests, see D. Doak Horne, "Taking Security in Intellectual Property", 1992 Canadian Bar Association (Ontario) Seminar on Secured Financing Transactions, *From Commitment to Closing: A Practical Review of the Typical Secured Financing*.

intellectual property that is involved in the transaction. This will create a list of the foreign jurisdictions that must be considered in identifying the rights, procedures, and consequences of transfer in each jurisdiction. The coordinating intellectual property specialist should then contact the appropriate foreign associates to delegate essential tasks. Depending on the complexity and importance of the transaction, the work of a foreign associate may range from simply filing the executed assignment document to actually performing a full intellectual property audit, complete with opinions as to validity, assignment, and enforceability, along with preparing the necessary documentation to be executed upon closing and completing the post-closing filing requirements within that foreign jurisdiction.

The coordinating intellectual property specialist and the client should appreciate differences in national treatment of intellectual property rights and be sensitive to the legal and practical realities of the different jurisdictions involved. Although the differences may at times seem minute, the effects can be far-reaching for both the vendor and the purchaser. Counsel are well advised to contact and rely on foreign associates instead of attempting to use their rudimentary knowledge of foreign laws in an attempt to cut costs.

(b) Foreign Associates.   In an international transaction it is usually necessary to involve foreign counsel, if only to register local assignments. On larger transactions, particularly those involving substantial foreign operations, foreign associates play a crucial role in helping to identify and create the necessary documentation to transfer the intellectual property at issue. The intellectual property specialist will likely already have a group of foreign associates that are engaged on a regular basis to prosecute and file trademarks and patents. However, large multinational corporations frequently have particular preferences for intellectual property counsel in each jurisdiction and should be consulted before foreign associates are retained on its behalf. Contacting necessary foreign associates should be undertaken as soon as possible because, even with modern communications systems, dealing with some foreign jurisdictions can be very time-consuming and the procedural complexities of each jurisdiction can differ greatly.

(c) Cost Factor.   Involving foreign counsel in the initial intellectual property audit stage is costly and may not be necessary for most transactions. However, the proper identification, documentation, and transfer of the foreign rights are essential in transactions involving substantial foreign operations. Concerns relating to validity and infringement of intellectual property rights can be properly assessed only by foreign counsel and should never be ignored. Even where foreign associates are merely filing assignment documents, the costs rise quickly because of filing fees, requirements for translations of documents, and the associates' fees. In this context counsel should discuss the relative importance of each intellectual property right to determine whether it is necessary to go through the steps of documenting and transferring title. There will be situations in which some registered trademarks, copyrights, and patents are no longer of any value, whether on a local or a global basis.

(d) International Tax Considerations.   Careful consideration must be given to the tax consequences of intellectual property transactions in each jurisdiction. The national treatment of intellectual property varies greatly, and the vendor and purchaser must carefully consider the potential tax consequences of the transaction from an international perspective. Often this entails substantial give and take between the vendor and purchaser—one party's advantage often resulting in the other's disadvantage with respect to tax consequences.

Opinions should be solicited from tax specialists in the appropriate jurisdictions. The coordinating commercial lawyer must then discuss the various options with the client and the intellectual property lawyers, inasmuch as often what is best from a tax perspective may be highly undesirable in other ways. For example, in Canada, fixed-term licenses are fully depreciable on a straight-line basis, whereas licenses with no fixed term are depreciable only at 75% inclusion at a rate of 7% per year. Such differences in tax and legal treatment can significantly affect the purchase price and the structure of the transaction. Tax counsel should be consulted in order to minimize adverse tax consequences. At the same time, it must be realized that the validity and enforceability of intellectual property rights can be seriously affected in the process of transferring title and license rights. Extreme care must be taken to obtain and evaluate the intellectual property tax consequences before committing to any particular posttransaction structure and method to transfer.

9.6 VALUATION OF RELEVANT RIGHTS

The valuation of intellectual property rights is unique among transferable assets, as it involves a combination of the traditional tools of asset valuation with a legal analysis of the rights themselves. Because the intellectual property specialist plays a crucial role in such valuations, it is important to highlight the basics of this role.

The due diligence searches and assessments are essential in the valuation of intellectual property. In particular, opinions as to the enforceability of the vendor's monopoly, including but not limited to the validity of the rights, the scope of protection afforded, infringement by and of third parties, the period of exclusivity available, and the likelihood of extending the rights through protectable improvements—all significantly affect the purchase price of such property rights.

Some transactions justify obtaining an opinion as to noninfringing alternatives, requiring the intellectual property lawyer to consider whether it is absolutely necessary to purchase or license a particular patent or technology. Are other methods available that do not infringe the patent? Is it possible to work around the patent, and what is the cost-benefit analysis of doing this, particularly in light of potential infringement actions? These are important considerations that should be canvassed by the intellectual property specialist with the client and others involved in valuing the transaction as a whole.

9.7 RIGHTS TO BE ACQUIRED: ASSIGNMENTS

The procedural and documentation requirements to assign intellectual property differ from one type of intangible to another and from one jurisdiction to another. In comparison with transfers of other types of property, the proper assignment of intellectual property and its registration with the proper government authority are expensive and time-consuming, but essential to the ongoing validity and enforceability of the property right. The assignment and registration procedures and requirements multiply in complexity for multijurisdictional transactions in which the documentation must meet the substantive, procedural, and language requirements of each particular jurisdiction.

As the procedural requirements for each jurisdiction can differ substantially and often involve time-consuming bureaucratic criteria and delays, it is important that the vendor agree to assist in the transfer of the intellectual property after the closing of the transaction. Although early preparation can prevent a great deal of unnecessary work months or years after closing, for transactions involving extensive foreign intellectual property it is highly unlikely that the purchaser will be able to record successfully all the transfers without further assistance from the vendor.

The following review of the Canadian requirements for the assignment and registration of assignments for patents, copyrights, and trademarks highlight the difficulties incumbent upon a purchaser of foreign intellectual property and the necessity of employing specialized foreign associates familiar with the requirements for transferring, using, and licensing intellectual property.

(a) Patents.   Canadian patents are creatures of statute, and it is the Patent Act[5] and Patent Rules[6] that govern any rights. Specific procedures must be followed in order to obtain, assign, license, and maintain patent protection. A patent can be transferred and acquired, either as to the whole interest or as to any part thereof, at different stages in the patent's life, and the Patent Act provides the different procedural requirements to be met at each stage.[7]

(i) Assignment of a Right to File.   The Patent Act permits the assignment of a right to file a patent application, provided certain requirements are met. In Canada, no entity other than an individual (or individuals) can be the inventor, and all Canadian patent applications must identify the individual inventors. Applications can be filed individually by the inventors or by any person to whom the inventors have assigned, in writing, the right to make an application and obtain a patent.[8] Therefore, a patent can become the property of a company only if it is assigned to the company by the individuals.[9]

---

[5] R.S.C. 1985, c. P-4, as amended.

[6] C.R.C. 1978, c. 1250.

[7] The Canadian Patent Act, § 50(1), states that "every patent issued for an invention is assignable in law, either as to the whole interest or as to any part thereof, by instrument in writing." In *Forget v. Speciality Tools of Canada Inc.* (1993), 48 C.P.R. (3d) 323 (B.C.S.C.), it was held that a co-owner may assign his or her whole interest in a patent without the concurrence of any other co-owner, but that such a cointerest may not be subdivided into two or more parts or licensed without the concurrence of all the owners of the patent. This is similar to U.K. law where the Patents Act 1977 (U.K.), c. 37, § 36(3), states that "subject to the provisions of…and to any agreement for the time being in force, where two or more persons are proprietors of a patent one of them shall not without the consent of the other or others, grant a license under the patent or assign or mortgage a share in the patent." This is to be contrasted with the U.S. patent legislation, 35 U.S.C.S., § 262, which provides that "in the absence of any agreement to the contrary, each of the joint owners of a patent may make, use or sell the patent invention without the consent of and without accounting to the other owners."

[8] Patent Rules, Form 4. In the absence of an assignment or bequest, a patent may be granted to the personal representatives of the estate of the deceased inventor. See the Patent Act, § 49(1) and Patent Rules, Form 5.

[9] A limited exception applies to inventions made by certain types of employees where the employer can claim ownership by operation of law. For example, where an employee is hired to invent, any inventions made in the course of employment belong to the employer. See *Devoe-Holbein Inc. v. Yam* (1984), 3 C.P.R. (3d) 52 (Que.Sup.Ct). For an opposite result where the court found the invention not to be within the scope of employment, see *Camstock Can. v. Electec Ltd.* (1991), 38 C.P.R. (3d) 29 (F.C.T.D.).

A purchaser of recent research and development, where patent applications have not been filed, is often in a situation of continuing dependency on the vendor so as to be able to file and prosecute the application successfully. The purchaser's application must be filed in the name of the inventor or those claiming under the inventor. To file in the name of an assignee, it is necessary to file an assignment executed in writing by the inventor. Problems in asset transfer transactions can arise when the inventor(s) has not executed an assignment document prior to closing. It is crucial that the purchaser obtain the agreement of the vendor that the vendor will take all necessary steps to secure an executed assignment from the inventor, preferably prior to closing.

When considering purchasing the right to an invention where no application for a patent has yet been filed, the purchaser should ensure, and the vendor covenant, that nothing has transpired that adversely affects the right to file and obtain valid protection for the full scope of the invention. For example, in most countries, there must not have been any public disclosure of the invention anywhere in the world prior to filing the original application. Most jurisdictions will bar an application on the basis of prior public disclosure, with the notable exceptions of the United States and Canada,[10] which both allow for a one-year grace period for filing.

In many situations, it will be important to obtain a patentability opinion from a patent attorney or agent well prior to closing. Such an opinion will open discussions on whether the invention is patentable, the available scope of protection, and its relative value in light of possible alternatives or equivalents already available on the market.

(ii) Assignment of Pending Applications and Issued Patents. Issued patents are generally freely assignable as to the whole or any part interest. Assignments of pending applications are also permitted in most countries and may be done at any time. This is an important factor, considering that an application may be pending for several years. It should be noted, however, that not all jurisdictions permit the assignment of pending applications.[11] Care should be exercised, and suitable covenants obtained, to cover jurisdictions that have special rules and requirements regarding assignments.

There may be traps for the unwary purchaser in assignments of pending applications, which must be recognized and dealt with to achieve an effective transfer. For example, it is important to check to see whether the application was filed by an assignee of the inventor and that a proper assignment from the inventor has been filed. Some patent offices permit the filing of incomplete patent applications and allow for a period of time for the filing of a proper assignment. If an assignment has not been filed prior to closing, the purchaser must obtain a covenant from the vendor to file the assignment within the necessary time limits.

(iii) Registration of Patent Assignments. Requirements for assignment of pending applications and issued patents are quite different. The assignment of a pending application must be filed prior to grant in order to have the patent issued in the name of the assignee. However, in many countries there is no mandatory requirement to register the assignment of issued patents. In Canada, for example, although a casual reading of the Patent Act

---

[10] In Canada, significant amendments to the Patent Act regarding novelty were enacted in 1987 which apply to patents issued from applications filed on or after October 1, 1987. Absolute novelty is now the general requirement, except in the case of disclosure by the inventor, for which there is a one-year period of grace. R.S.C. 1985, c. 33 (3rd supp.), §§ 28, 29.

[11] Venezuela is one example where pending applications cannot be assigned.

suggests that the recordal of all assignments is mandatory to at least preserve priority, the case law suggests that there is no sanction for not registering.[12] For this reason the prospective purchaser of a Canadian patent is unable to rely on the Patent Office records to determine with certainty the true owner of the patent. The Patent Office records provide only the names of the original patentee and any assignee who has taken steps to have the assignments recorded. There is no way to determine whether there are other assignments that have not been recorded.

(b) Copyrights.   Pursuant to virtually all copyright legislation around the world, copyright arises automatically upon the creation of a work and there are no formal requirements necessary to obtain copyright protection.[13] However, the transfer of copyright requires compliance with certain formalities. The basic premise of most copyright legislation is that the author is the first owner of copyright, except where otherwise specified. The major exceptions include commissioned works and works made during the course of employment.[14] In most jurisdictions, in the absence of an agreement to the contrary, the person commissioning the work or the employer is deemed to be the copyright owner. The owner of copyright can usually assign the right, wholly or in part, subject to territorial limitations, and for the whole copyright term or any part thereof. However, in some jurisdictions the assignment is valid only if it is in writing and signed by the copyright owner or a duly authorized agent.[15]

The purchaser of copyright should begin his or her investigation by identifying the author of the work. It must then be determined if one of the exceptions to the author's being the first owner applies, that is, whether or not the author was an employee or the work was commissioned. The major stumbling block for vendors occurs when the work was created by an independent contractor and, although there was an intention that the vendor was to be the owner of the copyright, no written assignment was ever prepared. This situation, which can cause a serious defect in title in most countries of the world, should be identified and remedied prior to closing.

A brief review of Canadian copyright law on some of these issues is instructive, if only for purposes of comparison. There are no formal requirements for registration of copyright or any assignments.[16] Copyright may be registered, providing certain procedural advantages with respect to litigation.[17] Furthermore, the Copyright Act provides that an assignment will be void as against subsequent assignees for valuable consideration without actual notice, unless such prior assignments or licenses are registered before the

---

[12] *Colpitts v. Sherwood* (1927), 2 D.L.R. 670 (B.C.C.A.), suggests that a second executed, but first registered, assignment will not have priority over an earlier but unregistered assignment where there is fraud. The difficulty of identifying a situation where a second assignment is not fraud suggests that the first executed assignment will always have priority regardless of registration.

[13] Copyright, like patent protection, is purely statutory and does not arise otherwise than under and in accordance with the copyright legislation.

[14] For example, in Canada, the Copyright Act, § 13(3), provides that where the author of a work is in the employment of another under a contract of service, and the work was made in the course of employment, the employer will be the first owner of copyright. What is considered employment under a contract of service is a question of fact and is to be contrasted with a contract for service (the independent contractor). See, for example: *Royal Doulton Tableware v. Cassidy's Ltd.* (1984), 1 C.P.R. (3d) 214 @ 230 (F.C.T.D.).

[15] In Canada, see Copyright Act, § 13(4).

[16] *Zlata v. Lever Bros. Ltd.* (1948) Que. S.C. 459.

[17] Copyright Act, §57(1).

registering of the subsequent assignment or license. Therefore, it is recommended that all purchasers of copyright register the assignment to secure a position of priority.[18]

The purchaser of a copyright must also consider the effect of reversionary rights. Where the author is the first owner, regardless of any assignment except by way of a testamentary assignment, copyright reverts to the author's estate 25 years from the death of the author.[19] Depending on many other factors, this can be an important issue when valuing a copyright.

A purchaser must also be aware that the Copyright Act reserves to the author certain moral rights, including the right to restrain any distortion, mutilation, or other modification of the work. Moral rights cannot be assigned but may be waived in whole or in part.[20] As such, subsisting moral rights may act as a limitation, and the purchaser should consider whether securing a waiver is desirable and how this should be reflected in the purchase price.

It is essential in purchasing a business to secure an assignment of all copyrights owned by the vendor.[21] The importance of such an assignment is brought home in considering that almost every originally authored work, including such everyday business devices as manuals, brochures, and commercial designs, is generally copyright protected.[22] If the purchaser ever had to assert copyright against a third party, it would be necessary to produce a written assignment of the copyright.

(c) Trademarks.   Trademarks are very technical rights that can be maintained indefinitely, but can be destroyed almost instantaneously through improper use, assignment, or licensing. A trademark must be distinctive of the wares or services of its owner from the wares or services of other parties. If a trademark loses distinctiveness, for whatever reason, it becomes unenforceable as against third parties. Distinctiveness can be lost in many different ways, and a thorough understanding of the concept of distinctiveness is fundamental to proper trademark use, licensing, and assignment.[23]

It is important to understand and appreciate that the essential function of a trademark is to identify the sole source of the goods or services bearing that mark. In theory, the rationale is that the public is assured of consistent quality if goods bearing a trademark originate from a single source. Originally, this meant that a trademark was nondistinctive and unenforceable if goods bearing that trademark originated from more than one source, even with the owner's authority and having the same quality.

The single-source theory was adequate to deal with the economies of the eighteenth and early nineteenth centuries, but the economic changes brought about by the Industrial Revolution and the explosion of the transportation, distribution, and advertising of goods

[18] An assignment of copyright may be registered without the work itself being registered.

[19] Copyright Act, § 14(1).

[20] Copyright Act, generally, §§ 14 and 28.

[21] The copyright in a work is distinct from the physical work itself, and the transfer of the physical work does not, of itself, transfer the copyright in the work. See *Underwriters' Survey Bureau Ltd. v. Massie & Renwick Ltd.* (1938) Ex.C.R. 103 @ 111; varied (1940) S.C.R. 218; leave to appeal to Privy Council refused (1940) S.C.R. 219.

[22] See, for example, *Dynabec Ltée v. Societe d'Informatique R.D.G. Inc.* (1984), 6 C.P.R. (3d) 200, aff'd 6 C.P.R. (3d) 322 (Que. C.A.); *Apple Computer Inc. v. Mackintosh Computers Ltd.* (1990) 2 S.C.R. 209. But see *DRG Inc. v. Datafile Ltd.* (1987), 18 C.P.R. (3d) 538 (F.C.T.D.), aff'd (1991), 35 C.P.R. (3d) 243 (F.C.A.).

[23] See Harold G. Fox, *The Canadian Law of Trade Marks and Unfair Competition*, 3d ed. (Toronto: The Carswell Company Limited, 1972) pp. 282–285.

and services in the twentieth century have challenged the adequacy of the theory in a modern economy. Business practices, including the use of the corporate entity, subsidiary and related companies, and licensing and joint ventures, have changed so dramatically that the single-source theory is no longer a suitable foundation upon which to determine the essence of a trademark. Yet so deeply embedded is the theory that legislators throughout much of the common-law world have attempted to cure its inadequacy by creating a patchwork of artificialities to condone modern business practices. Unfortunately, failure to comply with these numerous and often complex and costly artificialities can destroy the distinctiveness of a mark in the eyes of the court.[24] Therefore, it is essential in using, licensing, vending, or purchasing a trademark to review thoroughly the distinctiveness of the mark in question and comply with any and all requirements to correct and ensure its continued distinctiveness.

Unfortunately, few trademark owners or lawyers fully understand and appreciate the nebulous concept of distinctiveness. To add to the complexity of international transactions, each jurisdiction often has subtle distinctions with regard to the distinctiveness of trademarks. It is necessary, therefore, for the intellectual property lawyer, as well as the owner and the purchaser of a trademark, to review and comply with all procedural and substantive rules in each jurisdiction to ensure the continued distinctiveness of the trademark.

Unregistered Trademarks.   In Canada, as in many countries, there is a voluntary system of registration for trademarks, and such marks may be assigned and licensed. Unregistered trademarks arise and exist through use and are protectable in common law. The difference lies in certain procedural and substantive advantages for registered marks.[25]

Prior to the current Trade-Marks Acts, a common-law trademark could only be assigned together with all the goodwill symbolized by the mark. A naked assignment without the accompanying goodwill would vitiate the distinctiveness of the mark, making it unenforceable as against imitators. This is no longer the practice in Canada since the passage of the 1953 Trade-Marks Act, both registered and unregistered marks were deemed assignable with or without the goodwill of the business and in respect to either all or some of the associated wares or services.[26] However, where the goodwill is not transferred with the trademark, it is important to educate the public as to the change of ownership and ensure the continued distinctiveness of the trademark.[27]

There are few statutory requirements for the transfer of a registered trademark.[28] There is no required form for a trademark assignment, and there is no need for an

---

[24] Prior to recent amendments abolishing Canada's registered-user system, a series of cases discussed how licensing of a registered trademark in a manner inconsistent with the Act may cause the trademark to lose its distinctiveness and become invalid and unenforceable; see, for example, *Motel 6, Inc. v. No. 6 Motel Ltd.* (1981) 127 D.L.R. (3d) 267 (F.C.T.D.)

[25] For example, reputation of a mark is presumed by the registration, whereas reputation must be proved in common law, which can be very expensive and time-consuming. Furthermore, registered marks enjoy national rights upon issue, whereas common-law marks typically provide rights only in the territories where they are used.

[26] Trade-Marks Act, §48(1).

[27] *Wilkinson Sword (Can.) Ltd. v. Juda* (1968) 2 Ex. C.R. 137 (Ex. Ct.). In Japan, for example, although a trademark may be assigned either with or without the goodwill of the business, the transfer must be published in a daily newspaper and registration will not be effected until 30 days after such advertisement.

[28] Trade-Marks Act, § 48(3); *Trade Mark Regulations*, §§ 58(1), (2) and 36(a).

affidavit of execution or similar documentation. Any form of assignment in English or French, which is legally binding in the jurisdiction where executed, is acceptable in Canada.

It is essential that all assignments be registered, as the chain of title cannot be broken. An assignment from a party other than the recorded owner prior to the transfer will not be accepted by the Trade-Marks Office. Furthermore, use of a trademark by a purchaser without registration of the assignment may lead to nondistinctiveness and possible expungement of the mark and will inevitably delay future transfers of the mark and any related litigation.[29]

9.8 RIGHTS TO BE ACQUIRED: LICENSES

Licenses to use intellectual property can be transferred, assuming the appropriate clauses are contained in the licensing agreement. Licenses to use registered intellectual property, with the exception of registered trademarks, are relatively simple and straightforward and based for the most part on contractual principles. Patents, copyrights, and design patents are freely licensable, and assignment of any such license is solely dependent on the wording of the document.[30]

Great care must be taken, however, in purchasing a trademark license, as improper licensing or use of the trademark might vitiate the distinctiveness of the mark and make it unenforceable as against third parties. In Canada, for example, prior to the passage of the 1953 Trade-Marks Act, any licensing of trademarks would destroy the distinctiveness of the mark.[31] With the passage of the 1953 Act, licensing of registered trademarks was permitted, but only through the adoption of a rather technical registered-user procedure that was modeled after similar provisions in the British Trade-Marks Act.[32]

Under the old registered-user regime, the owner of a trademark could license the use of the trademark by registering the licensee as a permitted user under the Act. Use of the trademark by the registered user was deemed, for all purposes of the Act, to be use by the owner. The single-source theory of trademarks was maintained by this legal fiction. In theory, the Registrar of Trade-Marks was to be responsible for ensuring that the owner had some form of control over the character and quality of the goods or services. However, this registered-user regime was clearly a matter of form as opposed to substance. It was procedurally formalistic and costly, with noncompliance resulting in the unenforceability of the mark. Equally significant, the old system was out of step with modern business practices and the legal system of Canada's most important trading partner, the United States, and has since been replaced.[33] Still, from the perspective of

---

[29] However, registration is not necessary to perfect an assignment of a trademark, nor is it necessary to bring a trademark infringement action: *Coca-Cola Co. of Can. Ltd. v. Pepsi-Cola Co. of Can. Ltd.*, (1938) Ex. C.R. 263 @ 296 (Ex. Ct.), reversed on other grounds, [1940] S.C.R. 17 (S.C.C.); [1940] 2 W.W.R. 257 (P.C.)

[30] But see the discussion *supra* at note 7, regarding licensing of patents as a co-owner.

[31] *Bowden Wire Ltd. v. Bowden Brake Co. Ltd.* (1913), 30 R.P.C. 45; *Bowden Wire Ltd. v. Bowden Brake Co. Ltd.* (1913), 30 R.P.C. 580; 31 R.P.C. 385 (H.L.).

[32] The registered-user system is still followed in Britain and many other common-law countries around the world. However, unlike the Canadian courts, the courts in Britain held that the particular wording of the Trade-Marks Act permitted unregistered licensing.

[33] Bill S-17, An Act to amend the Copyright Act, the Industrial Design Act, the Integrated Circuit Topography Act, the Patent Act, the Trade-Marks Act and other Acts in consequence thereof.

the intellectual property lawyer coordinating an international business transaction involving registered trademarks, a rudimentary knowledge of the registered-user system is essential, as a number of countries still adhere to this procedure.[34]

Recent amendments to Canada's Trade-Marks Act have fundamentally changed the licensing provisions and, perhaps, the very basis of trademark law in Canada. The registered-user provisions have been replaced with quality-controlled licensing, arguably shifting the underlying theory of Canada's trademark law away from source and toward quality. Yet, the abandonment of the single-source theory is not complete by any means. The definition of a trademark as being solely an identification of source remains unchanged in the amended Trade-Marks Act.[35] As under the old registered-user system, the amendments to the Act attempt to embrace the single-source theory by creating a similar legal fiction: use of the trademark by a quality-controlled licensee is deemed to be use by the owner.[36]

A Canadian trademark owner may now license a trademark without recording the licensee as a registered user, but must comply with the requirements of the new licensing provisions. The new provisions state that use, advertisement, or display of a trademark by a licensee is deemed to have the same effect as use, advertisement, or display by the owner, provided that the use is licensed by the trademark owner and the owner has control over the character or quality of the licensee's wares or services. Thus the intellectual property specialist must now review such licensing arrangements to determine their effect on the validity of the mark. Particular attention must be paid to the following three requirements: there must be a license; the license must give the owner control of the character or quality of the licensee's wares or services; and the licensor in fact must exercise control over the character or quality of the wares or services. Failure to comply with these requirements may well lead to the nondistinctiveness of the mark and its unenforceability and will figure prominently in any due diligence search.

(a) Authority of Vendor to Grant Rights.   It is prudent to review all licenses as to, among other things, their transferability. Many license agreements do not permit assignment. Some arrangements dictate that even a change in control of the licensee terminates the agreement. In other situations, the consent of the licensor first may be required before transfer of the rights under the license to the purchaser. A purchaser acquiring intellectual property licenses must, of course, review all the license terms and, in particular, any restrictions on transfer.

(b) Scope of Rights Offered.   Registered intellectual property can be defined with relative specificity with reference to the registration number (e.g., "Trademark Registration No. xxx,xxx"). Licensing of unregistered intellectual property is more problematic however, and it is prudent to review or define carefully exactly what is being licensed. Understand that what is covered by the terms of the license will impact on almost every other clause of

---

[34] For example, both Great Britain and Australia maintain a registered-user regime. However, both countries' systems are voluntary and permit licensing without the necessity of registering the licensee as a permitted user.

[35] Section 2: " 'Trade-mark' means...a mark that is used by a person for the purpose of distinguishing wares or services manufactured, sold, leased, hired or performed by him from those manufactured, sold leased, hired or performed by others."

[36] Trade-Marks Act, § 50, as amended by Bill S-17.

the licensing agreement, including those that deal with royalties and noncompetition. Furthermore, the agreement should be reviewed as to the permitted field of use of the right being licensed, as most intellectual property rights can be assigned and licensed in part as to territory, duration, extent, use, and sublicensing, to mention just a few terms.

Restrictions as to territory, which are among the most common found in intellectual property licenses, can have a profound impact on transferability. For example, trademarks, for the most part, are national rights and are governed by national laws. An owner may have registered an identical mark in a number of different countries but licensed the use for only one country or, perhaps, only within a section of one country. Any such restriction should immediately be brought to the client's attention, as it can have a profound impact on the purchaser's existing and future business. Furthermore, certain territorial restrictions may be in violation of local antitrust laws and should be reviewed in that context. Antitrust standards differ widely among countries, and associate counsel should be consulted in this regard.

(c) Terms of Grants to Other Licensees.   The licensor's grant of licenses covering the same intellectual property right in which a client is obtaining a license should be examined for a number of reasons. First, the client may not realize that others are currently permitted to use the right and may be assume mistakenly that there will be no opportunity for direct competition. In this regard, it is important to recall that there are three main types of licensing arrangements: Nonexclusive, exclusive, and sole licenses. A nonexclusive license permits the licensor's continued use of the right and the ability to grant additional licenses to other parties. An exclusive license, to the contrary, does not permit the licensor to use the right or to grant others a right to use the right. Finally, a sole license permits the continued use of the right by the licensor, but prevents further licensing to third parties. The type of license being offered can, therefore, be a critical issue for the client. Second, from a more practical perspective, similarities and differences in the licenses can be an important bargaining consideration for the client and will, without doubt, have an impact on the final agreement.

9.9 THE LETTER OF INTENT

A letter of intent can be executed at any stage of a transaction (sale of intellectual property) and can be binding or nonbinding, depending on the intent of the parties. The letter of intent, typically drafted to open negotiations, usually establishes the framework for future negotiations and the final agreement of purchase and sale. However, if treated as a contract instead of an offer to treat, the letter of intent will bind the vendor to the purchaser.

The importance of the letter of intent in regard to intellectual property cannot be overstated. Both the vendor's and the purchaser's representations and warranties define and, therefore, limit the assets being sold and any subsequent claim for damages. First, a letter of intent defines the business being purchased. It usually begins with the purchaser including terms in the agreement and the vendor responding. Obviously, knowledge of the underlying facts and legal opinions as to the intellectual property rights involved is imperative to effective negotiations—and to the drafting of the letter of intent and the agreement of purchase and sale.

(a) Vendor's Representations and Warranties.   The vendor's representations and warranties form the backbone of the letter of intent, in that they define and limit the rights being offered for transfer. The parties must understand what is commercially important, and the lawyer must understand this in addition to the legal intricacies of the rights being transferred. Effective negotiations and final drafting of the representations and warranties necessitate a complete understanding of these two factors and their interrelationship within the overall context of the particular business transaction. Much like drafting a patent application, preparing the representations and warranties is a difficult and time-consuming task when intellectual property is involved because of the complexity and uncertainty inherent in any such transfer. Therefore, as in drafting a patent, it is wise to consider that years down the road the drafting language of the agreement may be examined scrupulously during litigation.

(i) Defining Intellectual Property.   The preliminary definition of the intellectual property being transferred sets the limits on what rights are to be discussed. Care must be taken in drafting the operating definition of the intellectual property, as it will be incorporated, by reference, in the warranties. This is of particular concern from the vendor's perspective, where it is important to restrict the warranties and, hence, the definition of intellectual property, to ownership rights whereby strong assurances as to title and validity can be obtained. The broader the definition, the more difficult it will be to define the rights and ensure that proper warranties are given.

(ii) Title.   Representations and warranties as to title are particularly important in regard to intellectual property rights, because it is generally impossible to ensure that the vendor actually has full title. The difficulties as to title must be addressed early in the transaction. Taking the appropriate steps to ensure that the vendor actually has title, and to ensure the extent and scope of that title—often impossible to quantify absolutely—are time-consuming. Therefore, the purchaser will require a representation and warranty that the vendor has title to the intellectual property. These issues will have a direct bearing on negotiations and the final purchase price.

(iii) Validity and Enforcement.   The validity and enforcement of intellectual property rights are important considerations for the purchaser. Again, the validity of the particular intellectual property right at issue is dependent on various and often extensive matters beyond the knowledge and control of the vendor. It may be that the vendor's own prior conduct has invalidated the right. For example, trademarks may be invalidated in many ways, such as through improper licensing. The vendor and purchaser should therefore carefully review all licenses, as well as the actual conduct of the licensees and the licensor/vendor in regard to quality control. Or it may be that a third party has rights to the vendor's trademark, whether it is registered or not, and has simply not yet come forward to complain of the vendor's use. These could be concurrent rights or superior rights that may result in the expungement of the trademark being purchased, along with a claim of damages for infringement.

Therefore, the purchaser will require representations and warranties that the rights are valid and enforceable. The vendor should feel uncomfortable about giving such a broad warranty and will want to restrict the warranty to the vendor's knowledge after searching its own records. The very real and important concerns regarding representations and warranties as to validity and enforcement can result in wordy clauses. Counsel would be well advised to review these carefully from a practical and theoretical perspective.

(iv) Utility.   Representations and warranties as to utility are most often provided in the assignment of new inventions or when technology is being purchased for application in a different setting. Regarding the former, the vendor will typically warrant that the invention is new, useful, and not obvious to the best of the vendor's knowledge. Regarding the latter, the vendor will want to limit any possible liability if the technology does not perform according to its specifications. This is particularly worrisome where the vendor has no knowledge of how the purchaser intends to use the technology. As such, warranties should be carefully crafted to create a definable universe. For example, a soft drink bottling machine may fill 10, 000 bottles of soda per day at the vendor's facility, but the purchaser bottles diet soda, and because of compositional differences the machine's capacity is reduced to 8, 000 bottles per day. Such a realization after the sale can be financially disastrous and often leads to litigation. Therefore, the vendor and the purchaser are advised to include suitable representations and warranties as to utility within the practical context of the technology being transferred.

(v) Noninfringement.   The purchaser of a business may require the vendor to warrant that the conduct of the business does not infringe any intellectual property rights of third parties. The vendor may or may not have performed any public searches or obtained opinion letters on infringement. In that case, the vendor again should insist on restricting any such warranty to actual knowledge and is advised to highlight the limits of the warranty by outlining the conduct of the vendor in giving such a warranty; for example, "We have searched registered patents in Canada and the United States and received opinion of counsel that our bottling technology does not infringe any of these registered patent rights." The purchaser should also request that this warranty be extended to the effect that the vendor has not received any notice or claim to infringement or, in the opposite case, will provide a schedule of such claims.

9.10 CONCLUSION

An international business transaction involving intellectual property is not substantively different from a similar local transaction. However, the former is more complex because of the multijurisdictional issues, which are often subtle but potentially devastating. When intellectual property is involved, it is essential to have an intellectual property specialist responsible for both the national intellectual property and the coordination of the necessary foreign associates. The intellectual property specialist on the transaction team should prepare a thorough checklist of intellectual property issues tailored to the specifics of the transaction and the necessary jurisdictions. Exhibit 9.1 "Considerations in Acquiring Intellectual Property Rights," provides an example of such a checklist for the Canadian component of an international transaction involving intellectual property, which can be tailored to the laws and procedures of other jurisdictions as necessary.

I. *Intellectual Property Rights—Broadly Defined*
   A. *Registered Rights*
      1. Patents
      2. Trademarks
      3. Trade names
      4. Copyrights
      5. Design patents/utility models
      6. Chip topographies/mask works
      7. Pending applications
   B. *Unregistered Rights*
      1. Inventions
      2. Trade secrets, confidential information
      3. Know-how
      4. Trade names
      5. Trademarks, trade dress
      6. Copyrights
      7. Designs
      8. Goodwill
   C. *Rights Arising from Employment*
      1. Ownership of inventions, copyrights, designs, opportunities
      2. Duties of confidence
      3. Fiduciary duties
      4. Employment agreements
   D. *Rights from Third Parties* (including the supply of products, technology, copyright)
      1. Licenses, permission to use
      2. Entitlements (use, support, improvement, exclusivity)
      3. Obligations (confidentiality, use restrictions, royalties, improvements)
   E. *Government Approvals*
      1. Product/marketing approvals
      2. Packaging, labeling, name approvals, and registrations
      3. Advertising approvals
      4. Export approvals
   F. *Subject Matter*
      1. Product per se
      2. Product ingredients/raw materials
      3. Manufacturing and packaging processes
      4. Manufacturing and packaging equipment
      5. Product design, components, shape, configuration
      6. Software (manufacturing and administrative)
      7. Packaging, containers, labeling
      8. Business and trade names, trademarks, trade dress
      9. Advertising, marketing materials
      10. Channels of trade: marketing, distribution of retailing relationships
      11. Business information, data, opportunities
      12. Research and development (product, process, packaging and marketing, advertising)
      13. Employee relationships and agreements
      14. Third-party licenses, agreements, permissions, relationships
      15. Restrictions through financing and security
      16. Affiliated company interdependence (rights, technical support licenses)
   G. *Ownership/Title*
      1. Root of title: individual creator/inventor
      2. Employee vs. independent contractor
      3. Assignments, licenses, permissions

Exhibit 9.1   Considerations in acquiring intellectual property rights.

       4. Contractual rights and obligations affecting title
       5. Registration, perfection of rights
       6. Security interests

II. *Identifying Relevant I.P. Rights*
    A. *Seller's Representation of Rights for Sale or for License*
    B. *Investigations to Isolate Relevant or Required/Desired Rights*
       1. *Searches*: Searches will depend on the nature of the I.P. right being assigned/licensed (see V to IX).
       2. *In-house/consultant review* of commercial product/process, search results and survey of industry (prior to obligations of confidence if possible) to identify:
          a. Additional essential rights/licenses/approvals/agreements required to operate vendor's business
             (1) From vendor
             (2) From third party
          b. Noninfringing substitutes
             (1) By engineering around vendor's rights
             (2) From competitive vendors/licensers
          c. Irrelevant rights
             (1) Not embodied in commercial product/process
             (2) Unrelated packaged rights
          d. Desirable additional rights (improvements)
             (1) From vendor
             (2) From third party
          e. Unregistered rights
    C. *Investigation to Identify Potential Infringement of Rights of Others* (Same as II A and B)

III. *Valuation of Relevant Rights*
    A. *Enforceability of Vendor's Monopoly*
       1. Opinion on validity of rights
       2. Opinion on infringement of third-party rights
          a. Cost of license
          b. Obligation/cost of defense/challenge
       3. Opinion on infringement by third parties
          Obligation/Cost of Enforcement
    B. *Cost of Noninfringing Substitutes*
       1. By engineering around vendor's rights
       2. By acquiring competitive rights
    C. *Period of Exclusivity Available*
       1. Eligibility for protection
          a. Obligation/cost of prosecution
          b. Opinion on likelihood of issuance
       2. Pending applications
          a. Obligation/cost of prosecution
          b. Opinion on likelihood of issuance
       3. Remaining life of existing registration
          Obligation/cost of maintenance/renewal
       4. Likelihood of improvements
          a. To extend monopoly
          b. To improve efficiency/marketability
       5. Remaining commercial life
    D. *Rights to Be Acquired: License vs. Assignment*
       1. License
          a. Confirm authority of vendor to grant rights
             (1) Title searches
             (2) Representations and warranties
          b. Consider scope of rights offered

Exhibit 9.1 **(*Continued*)**

    (1) Exclusivity
    (2) Territory
    (3) Licensed rights
    (4) Field of use
    (5) Term/terminability
    (6) Right/obligation to enforce
    (7) Benchmark performance to maintain rights
    (8) Option to expand interest
   c. Consider related contractual terms
    (1) Scope of contractual rights/obligations
     (a) Entitlement to improvements
     (b) Right/obligation to develop
     (c) Ownership of developments
     (d) Availability of support
     (e) Right/obligation to support
     (f) Tied selling
    (2) Allocation of potential liability
     (a) Infringement of third-party rights
      (i) Indemnification by vendor (available?)
      (ii) Indemnification of customers (required?)
     (b) Warranties
      (i) From vendor (available?)
      (ii) For customers (required?)
     (c) Product liability
      (i) Vendor denials
      (ii) Waivers acceptable to customers
      (iii) Insurance availability/cost
     (d) Limitation of liability
      (i) By vendor
      (ii) Acceptable to customers
  d. Consider terms of grants to other licensees
   Most favored licensee
 2. Assignment
  a. Confirm title of vendor
   (1) Search for requisite chain of title
    (a) Registered owner
    (b) Employment agreements
    (c) Complete and registrable assignments
    (d) Ability/responsibility to register chain and remedy defects
   (2) Representations and warranties
  b. Consider scope of interest/obligations offered
   (1) Exclusive/joint
   (2) Territory
   (3) All/part of rights
   (4) Field of use
   (5) Availability of improvements
   (6) Right/obligation to develop
   (7) Ownership of developments
   (8) Availability of support
   (9) Right/obligation to support
   (10) Right/obligation to enforce
   (11) Option to expand interest
  c. Consider third-party interests
   (1) Examine nature of preexisting third-party rights/obligations identified
    by vendor
    (a) Assignment/license
    (b) Exclusivity

Exhibit 9.1 (*Continued*)

(c) Territory

(d) Rights

(e) Field of use

(f) Term/terminability

(g) Assignability

(h) Entitlement to improvements

(i) Right/obligation to develop

(j) Ownership of developments

(k) Right/obligation to support

(l) Right/obligation to enforce

(m) Minimum quotas

(n) Option to expand interest

(o) Adequacy of provisions for preservation of rights

(2) Examine nature of potential liability from preexisting third-party rights/obligations

(a) Indemnification of third parties/customers from infringement of third-party rights

(b) Remaining warranties to third parties/customers

(c) Product liability waivers by third parties/customers

(d) Limitations on liability

(3) Search for other third-party interests

(a) Security interests

(i) Federal

(ii) Provincial

(b) Registration of license/assignment interests

d. Consider allocation of responsibility for preclosing activities

(1) Contractual liabilities (contracts assigned)

(a) Review of contracts

(b) Representations and warranties of full disclosure

(c) Indemnification for claims based on preclosing activities

(2) Contractual liabilities (contracts not assigned)

(a) Review of contracts

(b) Indemnification for claims based on preclosing activities

(3) Product liability

(a) Review waivers

(b) Indemnification for claims based on preclosing sales

e. Consider allocation of responsibility for postclosing activities

(1) Infringement of third-party rights

(a) Opinions

(b) Representations and warranties of vendor (if available)

(c) Indemnification by vendor (available?)

(d) Obligation of vendor to assist in defense

(2) Contractual liabilities (contracts assigned)

(a) Review of contracts

(b) Terminate/no renewal of contracts

(c) Representations and warranties of full disclosure

(3) Contractual liabilities (contracts not assigned)

(a) Review of contracts

(b) License vendor as necessary to fulfill obligations until termination or expiration of contracts

(4) Product liability

Review waivers

IV. *Other Considerations in Purchasing/Licensing Rights*

A. *Define Property with Certainty*

General descriptions with detailed schedules

Exhibit 9.1   (*Continued*)

B. *Infringement by Third Parties*
   1. Acquire right to sue for infringement
   2. Assistance in enforcement
C. *Further Assurances/Support*
   1. Initiating applications
   2. Prosecution of pending applications
   3. Transfer files and records
   4. Obligation to provide further assignments or other necessary documents to perfect title/interest
D. *Postclosing Considerations*
   Registration of Interests
V. *Copyright Considerations*
   A. *Relevant Searches*
      1. Registration/author/title/owner
      2. Registration of licenses/assignments
      3. Registration of security interests
         a. Federal
         b. Provincial
   B. *Other Relevant Considerations*
      1. Moral rights waivers
      2. Compliance with formalities in countries outside the Berne Union
      3. Date and place of first publication
      4. Citizenship of author
      5. Date of death of author
      6. If computer software, entitlement and/or access to, and location of all source codes
VI. *Patent Considerations*
   A. *Relevant Searches*
      1. Registration/inventor/title/owner
      2. Novelty/validity/infringement
      3. Registration of licenses/assignments
      4. Registration of security interests
         a. Federal
         b. Provincial
      5. Section 11 to confirm pending application
   B. *Other Relevant Considerations*
      1. Obligation to prosecute applications
      2. Responsibility for maintenance fees
      3. Date of invention
      4. Date of first public disclosure
VII. *Trademark Considerations*
   A. *Relevant Searches*
      1. Registration/registrant/mark/owner
      2. Registrability/validity
         a. Confusing business names/corporate names
         b. Confusing registrations/applications
         c. Confusing unregistered marks
      3. Registration of assignments
      4. Registration of security interests
         a. Federal
         b. Provincial
   B. *Other Relevant Considerations*
      1. Goodwill assigned with mark
      2. Notice of assignment/distinctiveness

Exhibit 9.1 (*Continued*)

       3. Proper usage
         a. Products using marks vs. description of wares
         b. Proper marking
       4. Proper licensing:
         a. Existence of license
         b. Provision for licenser's control of character or quality
         c. Actual licenser control of character or quality
         d. Proper marking

VIII. *Trade Secrets and Confidential Information Considerations*
    A. *Relevant Searches*
       1. Employment/confidentiality agreements
       2. Access records/practice
       3. Public availability of information
    B. *Other Relevant Considerations*
       1. Detailed definition of subject matter
       2. Reviewing efforts/success of vendor to maintain confidentiality

IX. *Industrial Designs*
    A. *Relevant Searches*
       1. Registration/registrant/design/owner
       2. Novelty/validity infringement
       3. Registration of licenses/assignments
       4. Registration of security interests
         a. Federal
         b. Provincial
    B. *Other Relevant Considerations*
       1. Date and place of first publication
       2. Compliance with formalities
          Marking requirements

X. *Packaging, Labeling and Advertising*
    A. Review all product packaging, labeling, and advertising for compliance and approval under relevant legislation, including:
       1. Consumer Packaging and Labeling Act
         (for consumer prepackaged goods)
       2. Food & Drugs Act
         (for food, drugs, cosmetics and medical devices)
       3. Textile Labeling Act
         (for textile products)
       4. Hazardous Products Act
         (for scheduled hazardous products, including many in common household use)
       5. WHMIS
         (for industrial/commercial use of hazardous products)
       6. Charter of the French Language
         (for products marketed in Quebec)
       7. Competition Act
         (for general false and misleading advertising claims and proper disclosure of promotional details)
       8. Provincial Consumer Protection and Business Practice Acts
         (for compliance with general provisions for advertising claims)
       9. Product-Specific Legislation
         (e.g., Tobacco Products Control Act, Liquor Licensing Acts, Agriculture Canada Regulations)
      10. Guiding Principles for Environmental Labeling and Advertising Criminal Code
         (Trading stamps (i.e., cross-couponing), counterfeiting, illegal lotteries, or promotional contests)
    B. Review and secure ownership and/or usage rights for packaging, labeling, and advertising subject matter.

Exhibit 9.1 (*Continued*)

CHAPTER 10

INTERNATIONAL AND U.S. LICENSING OF INTANGIBLES

Lanning G. Bryer, Esq.

Ladas & Parry
New York, New York

10.1 INTRODUCTION

Licensing of intellectual property has become a booming business, in both international and domestic trade. Companies today are relying on intellectual property for an increasing portion of their revenues. For instance, the president and chief executive officer of the National Semiconductor Corporation said recently that earnings in the fourth quarter of fiscal year 1992 represented the best profit performance for semiconductor operations in any quarter in the past five years. Almost half of those profits—$11 million out of $27.5 million—were attributable to the licensing of intellectual property.[1]

Moreover, a 1989 survey disclosed that the retail sales of trademarks and brand names reaped $20.5 billion.[2] Note that this figure represents the sales of products *only* in the United States and Canada. Considering that intellectual property protection is available in almost every jurisdiction throughout the world, the total sales dependent on the licensing of intellectual property is a staggering figure.

The prevalence and profitability of intellectual property licensing should not be surprising. There are several excellent reasons to undertake a licensing venture. From the licensee's perspective, licensing can, in the case of patent and know-how licensing, effect major savings in research and development costs, and in the case of trademark licensing, save the essential and expensive marketing step of achieving name recognition. If the public is already familiar with a trademark and brand name, identical or related products sold under that mark will achieve a larger market share in less time. This immediate recognition can save enormous costs in advertising. For instance, in *Advertising Age's* "Sixth Survey of Top Advertisers Outside the U.S." it was reported that in 1991 Unilever spent a total $1.6 billion in advertising, Proctor & Gamble spent $1.4 billion in 28

The author greatly appreciates the assistance of Laura Land Sigal and Ethan Stein, second-year law students, in the research and preparation of this chapter. The author is also deeply appreciative to his partner, John Richards, for his review and comment on the sub-sections relating to licensing of foreign technology and patents.

[1] "National Semi's Profits Climb, San Jose Mercury News, 18 June, 1992, 1E (quoting Gilbert F. Amelio).

[2] Gates, "Creative Licensing," *Incentive*, 1 April 1989, p. 32.

countries, and third-place Nestle spent $843.6 million in 26 countries. Combined expenditures for the top 50 advertisers listed reached $17.8 billion.

For the benefit of the licensor, licensing can extend the range and market penetration of the intellectual property owner's product. If the owner is unable to manufacture the volume of goods the market demands or lacks a marketing organization in a particular region, licensing provides an excellent vehicle for satisfying consumers' buying demands. Satisfying this need ensures the continuing and growing popularity of the particular product.

In addition, licensing is a highly desirable method of fostering cooperation between foreign corporations and domestic retailers. By licensing intellectual property to a local vendor, a foreign entity benefits from its domestic vendor's expertise in local customs and markets. The domestic licensee will probably be in a better bargaining position to obtain low-cost raw materials and labor. Easy access to local customs and patterns thereby enables the foreign company to maximize the number of markets and the success the product enjoys in those markets. Furthermore, both licensor and licensee may benefit from the exchange of know-how and trade secrets across cultural and corporate boundaries.

Licensing not only facilitates the positive goal of increasing market share, it also serves as a means of avoiding the costs of litigation. Once accused of infringing on a patent, copyright, or trademark, an alleged infringer may choose to challenge the validity of the intellectual property. This type of litigation, however, may be resolved by establishing an amicable licensing arrangement between the parties.

Considering the expense of intellectual property litigation, the alternative of paying a licensing fee becomes quite attractive. Patent litigation in particular, which engages those lawyers with specialized scientific and antitrust knowledge and entails comprehensive investigative procedures, can be expensive. Experts on licensing have estimated that moderately complex patent litigations can be expected to cost between $500,000 and $1,000,000 (in 1990 dollars) for each side. In fact, fees of several million dollars are not rare.[3] Also of concern are findings of the Federal Circuit that, in addition to the corporate entity, corporate officers who knowingly and intentionally elect to infringe a patent may themselves be guilty of contributory infringement.[4]

This chapter is a broad overview of the licensing of intellectual property, including trademarks and other marks, patents, copyrights, and hybrid combinations of intellectual property. Also included are sections discussing major franchising, high technology, antitrust, international, and sublicensing issues. This discussion is not intended to provide an in-depth analysis of all the issues and topics related to the licensing of intellectual property. Instead, the goal is to alert business people and their legal counsel to the profitable and inevitable trend of intellectual property licensing.

10.2 OVERVIEW

(a) Types of Licenses.   In addition to licenses for various types of intellectual property, several other types of licenses are used, depending on the arrangement. For example, aside from standard patent, copyright, and trademark licenses, there are franchise licenses, extension brand licenses, hybrid licenses, and sublicenses.

---

[3] Roger M. Milgrim, *Milgrim on Licensing* (1993: New York, Matthew Bender), § 2.63.
[4] Ibid., § 2.77.

In a franchise agreement, a license is granted by the owner of a trademark or trade name (the franchisor) permitting the franchisee to sell a product or service under that name or mark. In some instances, a franchise is an elaborate agreement under which the franchisee undertakes to conduct a business in accordance with the franchisor's methods and procedure, and with the franchisor's advice and technical assistance. In other instances, a franchise can be part of a more standard manufacturing, or even distribution, arrangement. In the United States, franchising accounts for well in excess of 30% of all retail sales.

Extension licenses allow a well-known trademark to be affixed to an object that is commercially related to the original product. For instance, use of the trademark "Oreo" has been extended from the traditional cookie market into the market for ice cream. The appropriate categories for extension licensing are selected on the basis of the "quality of the fit" with the franchise. The closer the fit, the more benefit the extension license will provide, because it is more likely that purchasers of a related product will recognize the trademark associated with the original product. For instance, it is much more likely that customers with a desire for ice cream will recognize and make decisions based on the Oreo trademark than would hypothetical purchasers of black and white raincoats. The reason for the difference is that ice cream is a product much more closely related to cookies than are raincoats. Furthermore, extension licenses benefit the licensor because the licensee's promotion of its own product provides additional opportunities to reinforce recognition of the trademark.

Hybrid or "multiple" licenses involve the licensing of at least two different types of intellectual property. A common example is the licensing of a patent along with a related trade secret. In the computer law area, licenses often consist of both patent and copyright rights, or trade secret and copyright rights.

A sublicense is a grant by the original licensee of rights to a subsidiary party. Most of the same concerns in the original licensing arrangement apply to the sublicense. In addition, added emphasis on issues of quality control and oversight may be appropriate because of the extended chain of authority.

(b) Marks. Of the types of intellectual property that may be licensed, the most enduring are marks. Whereas patents and copyrights have a limited life span, trademarks may be (if properly maintained) perpetually renewed. Marks include trademarks and service marks. The United States Federal Trademark Act of 1946, known as the Lanham Act, defines a trademark as "any word, name, symbol or device or any combination thereof adopted and used by a manufacturer or merchant to identify and distinguish his *goods*, including a unique product, from those manufactured or sold by others, and to indicate the source of goods, even if that source is unknown."[5] Similarly, a service mark is the distinctive word, name, symbol, device, or any combination thereof adopted and used by a manufacturer or merchant to identify his or her *services* and distinguish them from those performed by others. Finally, a trade name is a name used in trade to designate a particular business of a certain individual, company, or entity, or the place at which a business is located, or a class of goods. A trade name, however, is not a technical trademark, because it is not applied or

---

[5] 15 U.S.C. § 1127 (1982). Section 13 of the Trademark Law Revision Act of 1988 amended the definition of a trademark to include "any word, name, symbol, or device or any combination thereof used by a person of which a person has a *bona fide* intention to use in commerce and applies to register on the principal register established by this act, to identify and distinguish his or her goods, including a unique product, from those manufactured or sold by others and to indicate the source of the goods, even if that source is unknown."

affixed to goods sent into the marketplace. Consequently, a trade name may not qualify as a trademark because it is not capable of exclusive appropriation by anyone as a trademark or service mark.

Most systems of law today provide that trademarks may be licensed with the same freedom as patents. Prior to 1938, however, many countries considered it unlawful to license trademark rights. Animating these restrictions on licensing was the concern that divorcing a mark from its source would defraud and confuse consumers. Applying a mark to a product made from a different source would, it was feared, lead consumers to rely on the mark's reputation in ignorance of the fact that the product came from a different source. This practice would thus destroy the function of the trademark as a symbol of quality and identifier of source. As a result, licensing would result in the abandonment of the mark by the original source, namely the licensor.[6]

The reluctance to sanction licensing changed with the United Kingdom's passage of the Trade-Marks Act of 1938, which started the revolution affirmatively permitting the licensing of trademarks. Today most countries recognize licensing of trademarks and, for purposes of recordation, require the deposit of a certified copy of a license agreement or, in some cases, an originally executed agreement. British-law, (common-law) countries usually follow the "registered user" procedure of the Trade-Marks Act, which requires the filing of a simple registered-user application but not necessarily a trademark license agreement.[7] In civil-law countries, the law varies widely but generally requires the deposit of a certified copy of a license agreement if the parties are not related.[8]

The licensing revolution reached the United States in 1946 with the passage of the Lanham Act. The licensing of federally registered trademarks is permitted by § 5 of the Lanham Act.[9] The Act did not require registered-user procedures or the registration of license agreements. Instead, it required trademark proprietors to control the nature and quality of the licensee's products.[10] Subsequently, in 1948, the Court of Custom and Patent Appeals held that if a trademark owner retains the right to control the quality of goods sold by its licensee, there is no abandonment of trademark rights.[11] Such controlled licensing was not "naked" licensing and did not result in an abandonment of the mark.

Thus, licensing became acceptable as a result of the acknowledgement that it was possible for the licensor to exert enough control over a product to ensure that the mark retained its function as a symbol of quality. Assuming the licensor held the licensee's product to its own standards of quality, concerns about defrauding the consumer would dissipate. Control might be exercised through inspection of goods or manufacturing facilities, prescribing manufacturing processes, and other appropriate measures.

In fact, contract terms delineating the nature of the licensor's control over the licensee's products are probably the most important part of a trademark license agree-

---

[6] *Broeg v. Duchaine* 67 N.C. 2d 466 (1946); *Haymaker Sports, Inc. v. Turian* 581 F. 2d 257 (CCPA 1978). Abandonment resulting from inadequate quality control should be distinguished from abandonment that results from nonuse of a mark.

[7] Included in this group of countries are the United Kingdom, India, Israel, Australia, Hong Kong, and South Africa.

[8] Note that common-law rights in trademarks, service marks, and copyrights existed even before the Trade-Marks Act of 1938 and similar acts in other countries. Common-law rights were acquired not through abiding by statutory procedures, but by performing acts (such as use) that the common law determined conferred ownership in intellectual property.

[9] 15 U.S.C. § 1055

[10] 15 U.S.C. §§ 1055, 1127.

[11] *E.I. du Pont de Nemours & Co. v. Celanese Corp. of America*, 36 CCPA 1061, 167 F.2d. 484 (1948).

ment. The reason that control issues are so important in a licensing agreement is that although licensing is no longer a disfavored activity, it is still possible for licensing to result in abandonment and forfeiture of a mark. In the past, courts assumed that licensing was uncontrolled and would automatically result in abandonment. Now the presumption leans the other way, with courts demanding a high degree of proof before finding that a licensing arrangement is uncontrolled. These stringent standards of proof are appropriate, because a ruling of uncontrolled licensing may result in abandonment of the mark and the forfeiture of all rights.[12]

Uncontrolled licensing may also produce a lapse in the continuity of use required to prove priority, annulment of the license agreement, and the inability of the licensor to challenge the licensee's uncontrolled use.[13] In addition, the licensor may be susceptible to claims of false advertising if it fails to exercise reasonable control over a licensee who uses the mark to defraud the public.[14]

On the positive side, in a controlled licensing arrangement, a licensee's use of a mark will help establish the continuity of use the licensor is required to demonstrate in order to retain rights to the mark. Section 5 of the Lanham Act provides that "where a registered mark or a mark sought to be registered is or may be used legitimately by the related companies, such use shall inure to the benefit of the registrant or applicant." No ownership interest is transferred via the license agreement. According to J. Thomas McCarthy, Professor of Law, University of San Francisco, "the licensee is in the position of a renter of an apartment, who does not acquire real estate ownership rights, no matter how long the tenancy."[15]

(i) Related-Company Rule in the U.S.   Pursuant to the Lanham Act, if a licensor exercises valid control over the licensee, the licensee may be called a "related company" in the United States. Section 45 of the Lanham Act defines a related company as "any person whose use of a mark is controlled by the owner of the mark with respect to the nature and quality of the goods or services in connection with which the mark is used."[16] It is important to recognize that the term *related* does not apply generally to control over the company, but narrowly to control over the goods or services associated with the mark.[17] A licensing arrangement is what makes companies "related"; bonds of ownership are irrelevant. Manifestations of common ownership, such as shared stockholders or directors, are not at all indicative that companies are related for licensing purposes.[18]

In other words, a related company is one that passes the test assessing the adequacy of control in a licensing relationship. Despite the requirement of proven control, the Patent and Trademark Office will assume that sufficient control is exerted in the case of a license arrangement between a parent company and a wholly owned subsidiary. However, if the

---

[12] *Kentucky Fried Chicken Corp. v. Diversified Packaging Corp.*, 549 F.2d 368 (5th Cir. 1977); *Winnebago Industries, Inc. v. Oliver & Winston, Inc.*, 207 U.S.P.Q. 355 (TTAB 1980).

[13] *Yocum v. Covington*, 216 U.S.P.Q. 210 (TTAB 1982) (lapse in continuity necessary to prove priority of use); *Yamamoto & Co. (America), Inc. v. Victor United, Inc.*, 219 U.S.P.Q. 968 (C.D. Cal. 1982) (voiding of license); *Sheila's Shine Products, Inc. v. Sheila Shine, Inc.*, 486 F.2d 114 (5th Cir. 1973) (inability to challenge licensee's uncontrolled use).

[14] *Scotch Whiskey Assoc. v. Barton Distilling Co.*, 337 F. Supp. 595 (N.D. Ill. 1971), *aff'd in part and rev'd in part*, 489 F. 2d 809 (7th Cir. 1973).

[15] J. Thomas McCarthy, *Trademarks and Unfair Competition*. 2d. ed. (1984: New York, Clark Boardman Callaghan); see § 18:16 discussing § 1055 of 15 U.S.C. (Lanham Act, § 5).

[16] Lanham Act, § 45 (15 U.S.C. 1127).

[17] See also Roberts, *The New Trademark Manual*, 1947), p. 20

[18] Ibid., § 18:16. See *In re Raven Marine, Inc.*, 217 U.S.P.Q. 68 (TTAB 1983).

subsidiary is only partially owned by the licensor, sufficient actual control must still be demonstrated.[19]

The related-company rule also accounts for antitrust concerns. If licensing requires control by the licensor over the licensee, the licensor may exercise an inordinate amount of control over the market for the trademarked goods or services. Such control may violate antitrust principles. Therefore, the Lanham Act limits licensing to situations where the mark is "legitimately" used by "legitimately" controlled entities. Legitimacy is analyzed by evaluating whether the control exercised complies with antitrust laws. Thus, a licensee will not qualify as a related company if the quality control exercised by the licensor is so excessive as to violate antitrust laws.[20]

(ii) Quality Control.   The Lanham Act does not establish specific quality-control requirements for a trademark license. Case law suggests that a trademark proprietor must exercise *actual* control over the licensee. Mere contractual or a passive right to control will be deemed a "naked" license because, in the absence of actual control, there is inadequate assurance that the trademark can fulfill its function as a symbol of quality.[21] One court has pointed out that the language of the related-company statute refers to a company that *is controlled*, not to a company that the licensor has the mere *right* to control.[22] The majority of cases require showings of fact demonstrating actual control, not just the mere right to control.[23] In fact, even if there are no explicit contract provisions conferring the right to control, the license agreement will not be held to be "naked licensing" so long as the licensor demonstrates adequate actual control.

If adequate inspection procedures are instituted and the quality of goods is maintained, the licensor will not be held to have abandoned the mark.[24] The question, of course, is what procedures will be deemed adequate. In *Dawn Donut*,[25] the court held that the mere exchange of information between the licensor and licensee was not adequate. Further, *Dawn Donut* stated that "chance, cursory examinations of licensees' operations by technically untrained salesmen" was inadequate.[26] Regular and knowledgeable inspections that are documented are, therefore, probably the best course of action. However, the licensor need not be involved in the day-to-day activities of the licensee. Courts have not found inadequate control based solely on the fact that the licensor lacked involvement in the licensee's internal management.[27]

Ultimately, it is the consumer who determines whether quality-control measures have been effective. In *Kentucky Fried Chicken Corporation v. Diversified Packaging Corporation*, the Fifth Circuit observed that:

---

[19] Ibid., § 18:16 (citing T.M.E.P. § 1201.03 [c]).

[20] See *Philip Morris, Inc. v. Imperial Tobacco Co.*, 251 F. Supp. 362 (E.D. Va. 1965), *later op.*, 282 F. Supp 931 (E.D. Va. 1967), *aff'd*, 401 F.2d 179 (4th Cir. 1968), *cert. denied*, 393 U.S. 1094 (1969).

[21] *Kentucky Fried Chicken Corp. v. Diversified Packaging Corp.*, 649 F.2d 368 (5th Cir. 1977); *Haymaker Sports, Inc. v. Turian*, 581 F.2d 257 (CCPA 1978); *E.I. du Pont de Nemours & Co. v. Celanese Corp. of America*, 35 CCPA 1061 (1948).

[22] *Alligator Co. v. Robert Bruce, Inc.* 196 F. Supp. 377 (D.C. Pa. 1959).

[23] McCarthy, *Trademarks and Unfair Competition*, § 18:17.

[24] Ibid, § 18:17.

[25] *Dawn Donut Co. v. Hart's Food Stores, Inc.*, 267 F.2d 358 (2d Cir. 1959).

[26] *Dawn Donut*, 267 F.2d at 369.

[27] See *Union Tank Car Co. v. Lindsay Soft Water Corp. of Omaha Inc.*, 257 F. Supp. 510, (D. Neb. 1966) *aff'd sub nom.*; *Heaton Distributing Co. v. Union Tank Car Co.*, 387 F.2d 477 (8th Cir. 1967).

Retention of a trademark requires only minimal quality control, for in this context we do not sit to assess the quality of products sold on the open market. We must determine whether Kentucky Fried has abandoned quality control; the consuming public must be the judge of whether the quality control efforts have been ineffectual. We find that Kentucky Fried has sufficiently overseen the operations of its franchises.[28]

Thus, courts will analyze whether sufficient quality-control mechanisms have been instituted to nullify an accusation of naked licensing and abandonment. However, it is the consuming public that provides feedback about whether these procedures actually produce goods with sufficient quality. Through aggregate purchasing decisions that are motivated by the quality of the goods, the public informs the licensor and the licensee as to whether quality has been maintained.

(iii) Licensor and Licensee Estoppel. As discussed earlier, if a licensor fails in its duty to exercise sufficient control over the activities of a licensee, it may be held to have abandoned its mark and lose its rights in the mark. At this point, the licensor may be estopped (barred) from claiming that the licensee is infringing on its mark. This action is called "licensor estoppel."

"Licensee estoppel" in contrast, is where a licensee is estopped from challenging the validity of the licensor's mark. The rule of "licensee estoppel" arises out of the licensing arrangement of the parties and the trademark owner usually inserts a no-contest clause in the license agreement for this purpose.

In *Sheila's Shine Products, Inc. v. Sheila Shine, Inc.*,[29] the Fifth Circuit observed that licensee estoppel "is an analogue to the estoppel against a trademark owner who knowingly sits silently by while infringers use his trademark over a significant period of time." In other words, failure to exercise control implicates licensee estoppel in the same way that failure to challenge infringers works a forfeiture of rights in a trademark. Also notable is the fact that licensee estoppel has been allowed in trademark cases, but not in patent cases.[30]

(c) Patents. The right to the exclusive manufacture and sale of the products of an invention or the processes thereof is conferred by a patent. Because the authority to bestow such exclusivity derives from the Constitution itself, patents do not violate the less authoritative antitrust laws. Specifically, the Constitution gives Congress the power "to promote the progress of science and useful arts, by securing for limited times to authors and inventors the exclusive right to their respective writings and discoveries."[31]

In the United States, the reigning Patent Act of 1952 dictates that most patents will last for 17 years after the patent is issued.[32] To be patentable, a device must embody some previously unknown idea or principle. Patents are granted for inventions, but not for discoveries of laws of nature, such as gravity. Therefore, before signing a licensing agreement for a patent that is still pending, a licensee should investigate whether the claimed patent is for an invention or for a discovery that may not be patentable. Also of

---

[28] *Kentucky Fried Chicken Corp. v. Diversified Packaging Corp.*, 549 F.2d 368, 387 (5th Cir. 1977).

[29] 486 F.2d 114 (5th Cir. 1973).

[30] See *Lear v. Adkins*, 395 U.S. 653 (1969).

[31] U.S. Const., art. I, § 8, cl. 8.

[32] 35 U.S.C. § 154.

particular concern to potential licensees is the actual, rather than the claimed, utility of a patent.[33]

Assuming the device is a patentable and useful invention, licensing is a powerful option. Licensing is particularly attractive in the case of patents because many inventions require significant investment of resources during development. Through patent licensing, the inventor/licensor improves the chances of recouping and profiting from his or her investment, as well as benefiting as much as possible from the exclusive rights granted during the limited patent term.

A patent licensor occupies a powerful bargaining position because, unlike copyright or trade secret infringers, even wholly innocent patent infringers will be held liable to a patent owner. A patent owner has exclusive rights to the invention, regardless of whether a second party has produced the product independently. In contrast, copyright owners cannot prevent a second party from creating a similar form of expression; they can sue only if the infringing party has actually copied their copyrighted work. The right to sue all infringers, regardless of their innocent intentions, makes a patent a powerful and valuable asset.

As a result of the unique qualities of a patent, a patent license does not award the right to use the invention. Rather, it provides contractual assurances that the licensee will not be sued for infringing the licensor's exclusive patent rights.[34]

(i) Doctrine of Exhaustion. A patent owner's exclusive rights to the invention do not usually affect purchasers. Under the Doctrine of Exhaustion, a patent owner's rights are exhausted by sale of the invention. Providing no restrictions apply to the article, purchasers will be safe from suit.

(ii) Types of Patent Licenses. In general, patent licenses may be exclusive or nonexclusive. Both types provide assurances against infringement actions, but an exclusive license also promises that the licensor will not confer a similar patent license to another entity, nor in most cases use the invention him- or herself within the licensed territory. There are exceptions, however, such as French law, which permits use of the invention by the licensor, even after grant of an exclusive license to another.

Nonexclusive licenses are particularly appropriate if antitrust concerns are present. If one company has a dominant position in the market, acquiring an exclusive patent license for a product in that market by that company may violate antitrust laws. To counter this possibility, the patent owner may instead grant a nonexclusive license or a restricted license.[35] In addition to distinguishing between exclusive and nonexclusive licenses, there are other ways of categorizing patent licenses. For instance, a patent license may grant rights to make, use, or sell an invention. Even if a licensee has the right to make an article, it may be held liable for infringement in the event it then attempts to sell the article.

Another way of categorizing patent licenses is according to field of use. For instance, a patent for a drug may be licensed to one company to produce medicine for humans and to

---

[33] Milgrim, *Milgrim on Licensing*, § 2.12.

[34] See 35 U.S.C. § 271(a): "Whoever *without authority* makes, uses or sells any patented invention within the United States during the term of the patent therefore, infringes the patent" (emphasis added).

[35] Milgrim, *Milgrim on Licensing*, § 9.02. See text below in this chapter for a discussion of a way to restrict patent licenses.

a second company to produce medicine for animals.[36] In order to restrict either licensee's field of use, however, the licensor should be aware of antitrust principles and be careful not to impose illegal restrictions on the licensees' businesses. Another implication of field-of-use restrictions is that they may counter the doctrine of exhaustion and restrict the purchaser's use of the product. In regard to the preceding example, a purchaser or retailer might not be allowed to use the medicine formulated for animals to treat people.

Finally, licenses are also severable by territory. Patent licenses may be issued for limited and specific geographic regions in the United States. Outside the United States, however, the U.S. patent holder may not have any rights to license because patent protection is based on U.S. laws and the U.S. Constitution. Therefore, unless he or she possesses foreign patent rights, the patent owner will need to rely instead on trade secret protection.[37] The patent owner must also be aware of any antitrust issues that arise in the event the owner seeks to limit sales by licensees to a certain territory. If the patent owner wishes to limit the rights it licenses, the better method may be to limit the "make" or "use" rights, but not the "sell" rights. This method ensures that price competition, which is at the heart of antitrust concerns, is not directly affected by territorial licensing.[38]

(iii) Patent Negotiations.   In addition to the licensing options already described, there are other issues that are particularly pertinent to the process of negotiating a patent license. As in most negotiations, it is best to initiate patent negotiations in an amicable way. Thus, it is prudent to avoid offending a potential licensee by starting negotiations with a threat to initiate a suit for infringement.

Assuming there are willing negotiators on both sides, the patent owner should first analyze the investment that the party wishing to use the invention would need to make. If it is a significant sum, the party may be more willing to settle for a patent license than to lose its investment as a result of a judicial injunction.[39]

Furthermore, the patent owner should consider the value of the patent license. This value depends on a prediction of the sum that would be awarded following a court finding of patent infringement. Unfortunately, such damages are usually quite hard to predict. Licensing arrangements are, therefore, particularly attractive because they convert an inherently unpredictable situation into a contractual certainty.[40]

Regarding royalties, a patent licensor should be careful to differentiate between royalties resulting from the actual licensing of the patent and those related to disclosure of information about the invention prior to the issuance of the patent. This distinction is significant, because royalties linked to the patent itself will cease when the term of the patent ceases. However, royalties related to the trade secrets disclosed do not hinge on the patent term. Because there are no statutory limitations on these nonpatent royalties, the contract terms control the royalties, which may outlast the term of the patent. However, the characterization of these preissuance royalties is a very sensitive topic because of judicial concerns about improperly extending patent-based royalties beyond the term of the patent. It has been suggested that nonpatent royalties be described as

---

[36] See *United States v. Glaxo Group Ltd.*, 302 F. Supp. 1 (D.D.C. 1969), *judgment entered*, 328 F. Supp. 709 (D.D.C. 1971), *rev'd as to relief*, 410 U.S. 52 (1973).

[37] Milgrim, *Milgrim on Licensing*, § 2.36.

[38] Ibid., § 2.37.

[39] Ibid., § 2.75.

[40] Ibid., § 2.77.

payments for the option to take a patent license upon issuance or as payment in exchange for disclosure.[41]

(d) Trade Secrets.   Closely tied to patent licensing is the licensing of trade secrets. These licensing arrangements are related because they often reflect rights taken in different aspects of the same invention. Similarly, trade secrets also frequently coexist with copyrights in computer software.[42]

Specifically, a trade secret is a formula, pattern, device, or compilation of information that provides the owner with an advantage over business competitors who do not know or use it. Unlike patents, which are protected only by complying with national statutory procedures, trade secrets are protected automatically in most advanced countries; however, there are exceptions, most notably the laws in France and Korea, which do not extend this automatic protection. In many jurisdictions it may be necessary to demonstrate that one has taken steps to maintain secrecy, as well as to govern the use and disclosure of trade secrets. Otherwise, formalities do not serve as conditions precedent to licensing U.S.-based trade secrets outside the United States or to licensing foreign trade secrets within the United States.[43] Furthermore, express treaty provisions governing unfair competition can often support allegations of misappropriated trade secrets.[44]

Similarly, know-how is a type of industrial property encompassing methods and techniques that promote the best practices of an invention. Know-how is particularly helpful in producing innovative patented inventions. It often saves time and money that would otherwise be required in learning how to implement the patent.[45]

Negotiating Trade Secret License Agreements.   Because trade secrets are, by definition, based on limiting access to knowledge, an important part of a trade secret licensing agreement is ensuring limited disclosure by the licensee. Trade secret licensing, therefore, should include specific provisions for safeguards the licensee is required to take in protecting the trade secret.[46]

As noted, the act of disclosure of a trade secret is a valid contractual consideration. By itself, disclosure can support a contractual agreement to pay royalties. This is true even if the agreement is made in conjunction with the licensing of a patent that is expected to be issued. In fact, the consideration of disclosure of a trade secret will also support a contractual obligation to pay royalties even *after* expiration of the patent, because it is unrelated to the statutes governing patents.[47]

Despite its appeal, there are disadvantages to trade secret licensing in comparison with patent licensing. The most important distinction is that patent licenses assure licensees that no other entity will produce the patent, at least not without the licensor's consent. Trade secret licenses cannot provide such assurances, because third parties are permitted to develop or discover independently the secret formula, pattern, device, or compilation of information. Because the trade secret owner cannot challenge innocent infringers, neither can the trade secret licensee.

---

[41] Ibid., § 2.41.

[42] See section 10.5(b) in this chapter.

[43] Milgrim, *Milgrim on Licensing*, § 3.31.

[44] Ibid.; see also art. 1(1) of the Paris Convention for the Protection of Industrial Property, Oct. 31, 1958 (1962) Vol. 13 pt. 1 U.S.T. 1, T.I.A.S. No. 4931.

[45] Ibid., § 3.14.

[46] Ibid., § 3.08.

[47] See *Aronson v. Quick Point Pencil Co.*, 440 U.S. 257 (1979).

(e) Copyrights. In general, copyright protects the original expression of an idea. In analyzing a particular copyright, however, the date when it was created is crucial, because different statutory schemes govern works created at different times. These statutory schemes are discussed briefly in the following paragraphs. Actual determinations about which copyright laws apply to a particular work are quite involved. Therefore, a potential licensor or licensee is advised to consult counsel when contemplating licensing of a copyrighted work.

(i) Copyright Laws. The first statement about copyright in the United States was made in the Constitution, in the Patent and Copyright Clause.[48] Since then, Congress has implemented several Acts to carry out the intentions of the Founding Fathers, including the Acts of 1909 and 1976, and the Berne Convention Implementation Act of 1988 (BCIA).[49]

In U.S. common law, authors had perpetual and exclusive rights to their works, as long as the work was unpublished. The 1909 Act provided a limited term of protection (56 years) for works upon publication, which was considered to be an appropriate reward for authors who introduced their works to the public, but a term not so long that it would create an unacceptable monopoly. Under the 1909 Act, works that were published without proper notice would be automatically injected into the public domain and, consequently, unprotected.

Sixty-seven years later, the 1976 Act[50] attempted to abolish the common-law/statutory distinction with the overreaching prescription that works fixed in a tangible form[51] would be protected for 50 years after the death of the author.[52] Most recently, the Berne Convention Implementation Act (BCIA) aligned the United States copyright conventions with those of most other advanced nations by eradicating the role of copyright formalities as a condition precedent to copyright protection.

Thus, for works created since the BCIA, copyright protection subsists in original works of authorship fixed in any tangible medium of expression, now known or later developed, from which they can be perceived, reproduced, or otherwise communicated, either directly or with the aid of a machine or device. Furthermore, unlike patents and trademarks, copyrights are automatically protected in most advanced countries through the Berne Convention or other treaties. In the absence of express provisions about the duration of a copyright license, the assumption is that the license is coextensive with the duration of the copyright term.[53] Moreover, without express provisions, the duty to pay royalties will cease when the copyright term expires.[54]

---

[48] U.S. Const., art. 1, § 8, cl. 8. See § 2.3, Patents, which duplicates the clause.

[49] Pub.L. 100–568, § 3(a)(1), 102 Stat. 2853. The Berne Convention Implementation Act became effective in 1989.

[50] The Copyright Revision Act of 1976, 17 U.S.C. §§ 101 *et seq.*. The 1976 Act became effective on January 1, 1978.

[51] 17 U.S.C. § 102(a).

[52] 17 U.S.C. § 302(a).

[53] *Fitch v. Shubert*, 20 F. Supp. 314 (S.D.N.Y. 1937); *Viacom Int'l v. Tandem Prods., Inc.*, 368 F. Supp. 1264 (S.D.N.Y. 1974) *aff'd* 526 F.2d 593 (2d Cir. 1975). See *Manners v. Morosco*, 252 U.S. 317 (1920). Ordinarily, such an assignment or license will not terminate merely by reason of the death of the author. *In re Estate of Young*, 81 Misc. 2d 920, 367 N.Y.S. 2d 717 (1975).

[54] *April Prods., Inc. v. G. Schirmer, Inc.*, 308 N.Y. 366, 126 N.E.2d 283 (1955); *Tams-Witmark v. New Opera Co.*, 298 N.Y. 163, 81 N.E.2d 70 (1948); see cases cited in *Warner-Lambert Pharmaceutical Co. v. Reynolds*, 178 F. Supp. 655 (S.D.N.Y. 1959) (holding *contra re* trade secret); cf. *Rose v. Bourne, Inc.*, 176 F. Supp. 605 (S.D.N.Y. 1959) *aff'd* 279 F.2d 79 (2d Cir. 1960); *In re Latouche's Estate*, 198 N.Y.S.2d 489 (N.Y. Surr. 1960).

(ii) Licensing and the Copyright Act of 1976. Parties to a licensing agreement should pay close attention to the Copyright Act of 1976. First, by protecting any expression fixed in a tangible form, this Act bypassed formal registration procedures as a condition precedent to copyright protection.[55] For works created under the 1976 Act and prior to the BCIA, however, formalities are still required as a condition precedent to copyright litigation.

As a result of the changed determination of when copyright first attaches to a work, it is quite likely that such rights may inure in many works related to the contemplated licensing agreement. For instance, copyright may apply to a user manual associated with a device subject to a patent licensing agreement. Moreover, inasmuch as the 1976 Act states that copyright attaches to works at the moment they are created and fixed in a tangible form, licenses of unregistered copyrighted works are entirely valid. However, if the licensing parties do wish to record their agreement, the Copyright Office will accept exclusive and nonexclusive licenses for recordation.[56]

(iii) Divisibility of Rights in a Copyright. The 1976 Act also signified that the United States would join the rest of the world in recognizing the divisibility of copyright.[57] Prior to this Act, the United States had abided by the theory of unity of copyright. Under this theory, licensees, including exclusive licensees, were not usually regarded as copyright proprietors. Therefore, notices affixed in their names were invalid. As a result, publication with the invalid notice of the licensee's name would inject the work into the public domain.[58]

The 1976 Act, however, declared that copyright is divisible. Therefore, copyright licenses may be granted along territorial and other dividing lines. In fact, it may theoretically be possible to make all copyright licenses exclusive by dividing the rights in copyrights along fine lines.

Although the rights inherent in a copyright apparently are divisible, the copyright itself is probably not divisible. Nimmer and Nimmer assert that an exclusive licensee does not receive a new copyright, just the protection and remedies of the licensor's copyright. Although an exclusive copyright owner may be mentioned as a "copyright owner," this phrase refers merely to the right to pursue remedies, not to the ownership rights in the copyright itself.[59] "Such copyright owners" do, however, have the right to resell their rights to copy and pursue appropriate remedies.

(iv) Exclusive Licenses. As in assignments, exclusive copyright licenses transfer the power to exercise rights in the copyright. The transfer of such rights provides the exclusive

---

[55] Note that although it is not mandated by statute, there are practical reasons that a copyright owner might want to pursue formal registration. A copyright owner who is not a citizen of a Berne country or is a citizen of the United States must register before bringing suit. Also, after the BCIA, an owner of a registered copyright has the advantages of being able to claim attorney's fees and statutory damages, as well as a presumption of valid copyright. Further, a defense of innocent infringement is foreclosed in a case involving a registered work.

[56] 17 U.S.C. § 205. Any document "pertaining to a copyright" may be recorded in the Copyright Office. Such documents must bear the actual signature of the person who executed it, or be accompanied by a sworn or official certification that it is a true copy of the original, signed document. Upon receipt of such a document, together with the prescribed fee, the Register of Copyrights is required to record the document and return it with a certificate of recordation.

[57] 17 U.S.C. § 101. Note that the notion of the indivisibility of copyright still pertains to works created before the effectiveness of the 1976 Act.

[58] Melville B. Nimmer and David Nimmer, *Nimmer on Copyright* (1993: New York, Matthew Bender), § 10.02[B][2].

[59] Ibid., § 10.02(C)(1).

licensee with the right to copy the work.[60] As a result, the copyright licensee has the right to sue other parties for infringing on its exclusive right to copy the work.

Now that copyright is divisible and more exclusive licenses can be granted, there are more exclusive licensees who have the standing to sue. Note, however, that the narrower the exclusive license, the narrower is the scope of rights that the licensee can use as a basis for standing to sue an infringer.[61]

Disputes may also arise if the parties have not clearly delineated the parameters of the rights included in the license. Most cases have held that the intent of the parties governs in decisions about the scope of rights. Yet this approach is problematic, because parties often do not have or do not manifest any intent whatsoever regarding the scope of rights.[62] Nevertheless, collateral rights that permit full enjoyment of the express rights granted in the license are usually assumed. For example, a license to record a musical work has been held to imply the collateral rights to distribute and sell the resulting records.[63]

(f) Hybrid Licenses. Hybrid licenses involve the licensing of at least two types of intellectual property. As might be expected, hybrid licenses are very complex. A high degree of skill must be applied in negotiating and drafting hybrid licenses so as to avoid the loss or impairment of some of the intellectual property rights, as well as to ensure long-lasting royalties.

Hybrid licenses often involve patents, because licensors often seek to base royalties not only on the patent, which expires after the limited patent term, but on a more lasting type of intellectual property. One common type of hybrid license includes a trademark that is associated with a patent. Through hybrid licensing, patent owners retain trademark rights even after their patent rights cease at the end of the patent term. For example, trademark rights in the original Coke bottle were retained even after the design patent expired.

A second type of hybrid licensing involving patents is patent and trade secret licensing. Trade secret protection may often guard the best processes for operating a patent device. It is obviously in the best interest of the patent licensee to license the pertinent trade secret as well. Keeping this fact in mind, the licensor therefore should limit, as much as possible, the information it reveals during patent prosecution. Of course, this can be tricky as failure to disclose material and necessary information could lead to a successful claim of invalidity. Nevertheless, by avoiding unnecessary disclosure, the licensor can claim related information as a trade secret and use it to negotiate for added consideration from the licensee.

Third, computer software licensing often involves hybrid licensing of copyrights and trade secrets. The copyright license permits the licensee to make limited copies of the work, but prohibits the licensee from using reverse engineering and other processes to copy the idea of the software program. The trade secret license establishes terms to protect any secrets inherent in the software.

10.3 LICENSE AGREEMENT TERMS

The provisions of license agreements are, of course, extremely important. They are particularly significant in determining the remittance of royalties, enforceability of an

---

[60] Nonexclusive licenses, however, do not transfer ownership of the rights to copy.

[61] Nimmer and Nimmer, *Nimmer on Copyright*, § 10.02(A).

[62] Nimmer and Nimmer, *Nimmer on Copyright*, § 10.10(B).

[63] *Royal v. Radio Corp. of America*, 107 U.S.P.Q. 173 (S.D.N.Y. 1955).

agreement between the parties or against third parties, and maintenance and protection of the underlying intellectual property rights. The following paragraphs discuss recommendations regarding basic licensing provisions and the Statute of Frauds.

(a) Basic Licensing Provisions

(i) Definition of the Property. The intellectual property right must be clearly defined (clearance and protection of the property right should have previously been undertaken or should be under way). If possible, registration or application numbers should be used for identification, and specimens of relevant trademarks should be attached to the agreement as exhibits.

(ii) Exclusive and Nonexclusive Licenses. The grant of a license should indicate whether it is exclusive or nonexclusive. If it is exclusive, the agreement should indicate whether the bar on the issuance of other licenses also includes a bar on the licensor's own use of the intellectual property.

Furthermore, in the case of an exclusive license in the U.S., a provision should be included stating whether the licensee may manufacture or sell competing products. Although this type of provision may be a restrictive covenant, it is usually permitted if the exclusive license gives the licensee a competitive advantage.

A provision relating to exclusivity may be expressed in terms of "sole" or "exclusive" licenses. Under a sole license, the licensor reserves the right to use the intellectual property right him- or herself but agrees to grant no other licenses. Alternatively, under an exclusive license, the licensee is given an exclusive right to use the intellectual property right, which is exclusive even as to the licensor. To prevent any possibility of ambiguity, the parties are advised to include additional descriptions when using the terms *sole* and *exclusive*.

(iii) Quality Control. Provisions establishing control by the licensor over the licensee should include the following:

- The standards and specifications with which the licensor expects the licensee to comply,
- The licensor's right to inspect the licensee's premises, manufacturing processes, and finished products, and
- The licensor's right to regularly receive, review, and approve samples of the licensed products.

For trademark licenses, the licensor should take the added precaution of maintaining active files to verify the quality of the licensee's goods and services. These files are helpful in defending against accusations that the public has been defrauded or misled.

(iv) Geographic Designation. The territory or scope of the license should be clearly defined.

In general, this does not create a problem, however, as discussed before in connection with licensing in the European Community, problems can arise in connection with the grant of territorially restricted licenses within a trading block.

(v) License Incentives.   Since in most countries the grant of an exclusive license precludes the licensor from itself being active in the licensed territory, it is normal practice in such licenses to include provisions to try to ensure that the licensee develops the market in its licensed territory. Such clauses may include best-effort clauses, sometimes tied to a specific market development plan and/or provisions for payment of minimum royalties after the license has been running for a year or two. Minimum royalty provisions commonly increase over a period of a few years to a maximum value. Licenses may be terminated if such minimum royalty payments are not made or a lesser penalty may be imposed, for example converting an exclusive license into a nonexclusive one.

(vi) Improvement.   In technology licensing, consideration of what rights the one party may have to use improvements made by the other is an important issue that needs to be resolved at the outset. Care needs to be taken in drafting such provisions, however, since anti-trust authorities worldwide are nervous about clauses that require a licensee to assign rights in improvements it makes to the original licensor since such provisions may serve to augment the market power of the licensor in an unjustified and anti-competitive manner. Current law in the United States, the EC and Japan permits such a provision provided that the grant back of rights by the licensee to the licensor of an improvement made by the licensee is non-exclusive.[64] Under current U.S. law grant back of exclusive rights to a licensor that already has a dominant position in the market may give rise to an anti-trust violation and intermediate situations require a rule of reason analysis.[65] The position in Japan and the EC on exclusive grant-back is more strict than in the United States and will be discussed below.

(vii) Duration of the License.   Although, in principle, there is no limitation on the duration for which a license may run, there may be restrictions on the periods for which particular types of royalty may be charged. For example, the United States Supreme Court has outlawed the payment of full patent royalty rates after the patent in question has expired,[66] although in cases where the license was granted at a time when it was unclear whether a patent would ever be granted, so that the existence of a patent was not clearly part of the consideration for the grant, a different rule may apply.[67] The rule against patent rate royalty payment, which continues after the expiration of the patent in question, also exists in the European Community.

(viii) Tie-In Clauses.   There is a tendency for owners of patents for process inventions to try to capitalize on the return they obtain from licensing the technology by requiring the licensee to purchase unpatented materials (for example, raw materials used in the process) from the licensor as a condition for the grant of the licensee. This is known as a "tie-in." At one time, the prevailing opinion in the United States was that such clauses were *per se* anti-trust violations.[68] Following the anti-trust revolution of the 1980s, the position today is probably not quite so clear. However, except in cases where it is obvious that the licensor has little or no market power in the relevant market, even when subjected

---

[64] *Transparent Wrap Machinery Corp. v. Slopes & Smith Co.*, 329 U.S. 637 (1947).

[65] *Hartford Empire Co. v. U.S.*, 323 U.S. 386 (1945).

[66] *Brulotte v. Thys Co.*, 379 U.S. 29 (1964), *reh'g denied*, 379 U.S. 985 (1965).

[67] See, e.g., *Aronson v. Quick Point Co.* 440 U.S. 257. (1979)

[68] See, e.g., *International Salt Co. v. U.S.*, 332 U.S. 392 (1947).

to a rule of reason analysis, courts tend to be unsympathetic to such clauses and a careful analysis of all relevant issues should be undertaken before they are included in a license agreement. The position in the EC and Japan is a little more settled, as discussed in Section 10.7(a).

(ix) Sublicensing Restrictions.   Provisions should be included delineating any restrictions on sublicensing or assigning the intellectual property rights conferred by the license. From the licensor's perspective, it is usually advisable to provide that no assignment or further license is permitted without the prior written approval of the licensor.[69]

(x) Termination.   Clauses should be included to govern the termination or expiration of the license, and renewal or cancellation of the agreement prior to expiration. Reasons for cancellation may include noncompliance, bankruptcy,[70] insolvency, or assignment of rights for the benefit of creditors. Termination may also be allowed in the case of impossibility of performance (i.e., because of a force majeure or an unexpected governmental action).

(xi) Royalty Provision.   A license agreement need not include or provide for payment of royalty fees in order to be valid. Nevertheless, most licenses in an arms-length transaction include clauses governing royalty fees, such as:

- The time and amount of payments and, in international agreement provisions relating to the currency in which payments are to be made, if necessary, the means used for conversion between currencies;
- Definition of the net sales against which the royalties are to be calculated,
- The requirement that the licensee keep accurate and complete accounting records,
- The right of the licensor to inspect the licensee's records, and
- In international agreements, contingency plans in the event of foreign exchange control regulations that interfere with the remittance of the royalties to the licensor.

(xii) Infringement Procedures.   A provision should be inserted relating to the possible infringement of the intellectual property rights and who is to assume discretion and control of any possible litigation. The clause may provide that an action shall be at the discretion of the licensor and that any litigation will be under the full control of the licensor. The licensor may also retain sole discretion to bring an action in the name of the licensee.

The licensee, however, is usually motivated to pay for the license so as to obtain the right to use the intellectual property without being sued and to have superior rights of such use against third parties. Therefore, the licensee may seek to ensure that the value of the license is maintained by requiring that the licensor institute suits against infringing third parties.

(xiii) Typical Contract Clauses.   The aforementioned recommended clauses are particular to intellectual property licensing. Yet because an intellectual property license is a contract

---

[69] Note that if the contract is silent, courts have held that there is no preclusion on sublicenses or assignment of rights.

[70] Termination provisions in the event of the filing of a bankruptcy have been held to be invalid and are subject to the trustee's ability to assume or reject the agreement.

like any other, clauses that should be included in contracts in general should be included here as well. Some (but clearly not all) clauses that are wisely included are as follows:

1. Choice-of-law clauses stating the governing law of the contract and jurisdiction clauses stating how and where a dispute will be adjudicated, (for example, by reference to a designated court or by arbitration, and if by arbitration, what arbitration procedures will be used, and in international agreements, what language will be used); and

2. The availability of attorney's fees as part of a damages award. This provision is particularly important in patent licensing, in which attorney's fees are likely to be quite substantial.[71]

(b) Statute of Frauds. In general, oral license agreements may be deemed unenforceable under the Statute of Frauds if not performed within one year. In New York, for instance, the length of contractual liability has been held to be the deciding factor as to whether an oral agreement will be upheld or invalidated under the Statute of Frauds.

For copyright licenses, exclusive licenses should be recorded and signed by the parties, in accordance with the Statute of Frauds. Exclusive licenses now require a writing because of the Copyright Act of 1976, which extended the writing requirement from assignments to exclusive licenses.[72] Under the 1976 Act exclusive licenses also resemble assignments, in that they are considered to convey property rights and may therefore be conveyed as gifts as well as by sale.[73]

Considering that the purpose of the Statute of Frauds is to ensure that the parties are careful and thoughtful when making long-term agreements, the writing requirement for exclusive copyright licenses makes sense. Unless there are express provisions indicating otherwise, exclusive copyright licenses are assumed to last for the term of the copyright, which generally is the lifetime of the author plus 50 years.[74] Because the 1976 Act confers copyright protection to all works fixed in a tangible form, the writing requirement applies regardless of whether the works have been registered.

In contrast to exclusive licenses and assignments, oral or implied *nonexclusive* licenses of copyrights are still valid under the 1976 Act. Moreover, if no consideration is provided, nonexclusive licenses may be revoked.[75]

10.4 FRANCHISING

In a recent year, franchising accounted for $717 billion in retail sales, or 34% of all sales in the United States. In the last decade, the number of franchise outlets has more than doubled to 533,000. There are 2,200 franchisors and 7.7 million franchise employees

---

[71] Milgrim, *Milgrim on Licensing*, § 2.79.

[72] Nimmer and Nimmer, *Nimmer on Copyright*, § 10.03 (A).

[73] Ibid., § 10.02 (B)(5).

[74] 17 U.S.C. § 302(a). This copyright term is modified if it is a jointly authored work, a work made for hire, or an anonymous or pseudonymous work.

[75] Id., § 10.02 (B)(5) (comparing *Freedman v. Select Information Systems, Inc.*, and 1983 Copyright Law Decisions [CCH] ¶ 25, 520 [N.D. Cal. 1983] [state law controls in view of congressional silence on this issue]).

(6.9% of the total nonagricultural domestic work force).[76] Congress has even predicted that franchises will handle *half* of all domestic retail sales in the year 2000.[77]

This tremendous success is based in part on the strong convergence of interests of franchisees and franchisors. Franchisees benefit from immediate name recognition, the expertise of a national corporation, and a well-developed, tested product. Franchisors benefit from the deeper market penetration produced by numerous outlets, local expertise about the market and sources for raw materials, and committed management on-site.

In general, for a franchise to be worthwhile to the parties involved, the nature of the business should require multiple units and quality control at the point of sale. Given these conditions, the franchisor will have sufficient reason to share profits with the franchisee. Furthermore, sophisticated knowledge of the business should be required of franchisees. Lack of such knowledge by some individual franchisees may injure the entire franchise operation.[78]

Assuming that the benefits of a franchising operation outweigh any anticipated problems, several types of franchises can be created. The following paragraphs discuss the centrality of trademarks to franchises, a description of different types of franchises, an investigation of applicable laws, and recommendations for franchising terms.

(a) Trademarks and Franchises.   One court has asserted that the franchise system is anchored by trademarks, inasmuch as they serve to identify the source of the product or service that is sold by each franchise outlet.[79] Usually it is not copyrights or patents, but trademarks, that motivate customers to frequent franchises.[80]

Because trademarks are essential to franchises, franchise agreements often include express provisions governing the use and misuse of trademarks. In fact, unauthorized sales by franchisees have been held to be valid grounds for terminating the franchise agreement.[81] If there are no express provisions specifically outlining the extent of permissible sales, the franchisee's sale of products that are not specifically authorized will usually not be held to be an infringement.[82] As might be expected, the franchisee must also stop using the franchisor's trademarks after the franchise agreement expires.

(b) Types of Franchises.   Several types of franchise arrangements are frequently made. The following are descriptions of business format franchises, product or distributorship franchises, and manufacturing license franchises.

(i) Business Format Franchises.   Perhaps the best-known type of franchise is the business format franchise, in the form of the fast-food restaurants that millions of consumers

---

[76] Kaufmann (quoting International Franchise Association Educational Foundation, Inc./ Horwath International, Franchising in the Economy 1988–1990, pp. 1, 11.)

[77] *Franchising in the U.S. Economy: Prospects and Problems, Before the House Committee on Small Business*, 100th Cong., 5 (1990).

[78] David J. Kaufmann, "An Introduction to Franchising and Franchise Law," *Franchising 1992*, (PLI Com. Law and Prac. Course Handbook Series No. A4-4367, 1992: New York, Practicing Law Institute).

[79] *Susser v. Carvel Corp.*, 206 F. Supp. 636, 640 (S.D.N.Y. 1962), *aff'd*, 332 F.2d 505 (2d Cir. 1964), *cert. dismissed*, 381 U.S. 125 (1965).

[80] W. Michael Garner, "Trademark Basics for Franchisors", *Franchising 1992*, (PLI Com. Law and Prac. Course Handbook Series No. A4–4367, 1992: New York, Practicing Law Institute).

[81] *Franchised Stores of New York, Inc. v. Winter*, 394 F.2d 664 (2d Cir. 1968); *Baskin-Robbins Ice Cream Co. v. D&L Ice Cream Co., Inc.*, 576 F. Supp. 1055 (E.D.N.Y. 1983).

[82] *Terry v. International Dairy Queen, Inc.*, 554 F. Supp. 1088, (N.D. Ind. 1983).

frequent. This type has been primarily responsible for the exponential growth in franchises in the United States during the last few decades.[83]

Business format franchises are sometimes also called "package" franchises, because they provide franchisees with everything they need to conduct their business in accordance with the standards of the franchise chain. In general, business format franchisees benefit from a uniformly identified trademark and service mark, trade dress, and advertising. In addition, franchisees receive standard operating plans and procedures and, sometimes, equipment, raw materials, supplies, and finished products as well. In exchange, when franchisees deliver services and goods to customers, they identify themselves as part of the franchisor's chain of operations. Franchisees are also required to comply with the dictates of the franchise chain to maintain its good reputation.

(ii) Product or Distributorship Franchises. Although not as readily recognized by the public, product franchises, or distributorship franchises, actually constitute a statistically more significant type of franchise. In 1990 these franchises, which include car dealers and gas stations,[84] accounted for 70% of all franchise sales.[85] In general, product or distributorship franchises distribute goods that are produced by the franchisor.

(iii) Manufacturing License Franchises. A third type of franchise is the manufacturing license franchise. This type includes soft drink bottlers, for example. Manufacturing license franchises are defined by the use of a patent, formula, or know-how in producing a product that is subsequently sold under the franchisor's trademark. In the soft drink industry, the syrup is a trade secret that is licensed to bottlers. The franchisees then bottle the soft drink and sell it, using the licensor/franchisor's trademark.

(c) Franchise Laws. Until fairly recently, there were no laws particular to franchise agreements. In general, the most pertinent laws were the antitrust laws and the Lanham Act governing trademarks. Section 43 of the Lanham Act forbids false advertising and, specifically, the false designation of origin. This section applies not only to misuse of trademarks, but to misuse of symbols, design elements, and characters as well.[86]

In 1970, however, the first franchise law was enacted in California. Today franchise disclosure and registration laws exist in most states in this country. One category of state franchise laws ensures that the franchisees are knowledgeable about the contracts they form. As a prerequisite to any franchise activity, the franchisor is legally required to provide and register a disclosure document. This document must contain any information that is necessary for franchisees to make informed investment decisions. Offering somewhat more limited protection, a number of states have presale disclosure requirements, but do not require registration. A second group of laws, applicable in 17 states, protects franchisees from arbitrary termination or nonrenewal.[87]

At the federal level, there are two laws specific to franchises: the Federal Trade Commission (FTC) Rule and the Uniform Franchise Offering Circular (UFOC). The FTC rule requires descriptions of the marks being franchised, details about registration

---

[83] U.S. Department of Commerce, *Franchising in the Economy* (Washington, D.C.: U.S. Government Printing Office, 1986), p. 3.

[84] Ibid.

[85] Ibid.

[86] *20th Century Wear, Inc. v. Sanmark-Stardust, Inc.*, 747 F.2d 81 (2d Cir. 1982), *cert. denied*, 470 U.S. 1052 (1985); *Johanna Farms, Inc. v. Citrus Bowl, Inc.*, 468 F. Supp. 866 (E.D.N.Y. 1978).

[87] Kaufmann, "An Introduction to Franchising".

and litigation procedures undertaken, reports on any limitations imposed on the franchisee's use of the mark (e.g., geographic limitations or limits on sales of other products), and explanations of territorial exclusivity provided to the franchisee.[88] These disclosures may be contained in a prospectus, the format of which is dictated by the *Compliance Guide* issued by the FTC. Furthermore, under the UFOC, Item XIII requires a description of the licensed marks and symbols and their status in courts and with the Patent and Trademark Office.[89] Also included in the UFOC is the requirement that franchisors reveal any legal defects in the marks being franchised.

Another relevant type of laws are business opportunity laws, which have been enacted by 23 states. Business opportunity laws require registration and disclosure for all new business ventures. Because franchises are by nature new business ventures, their activities may be covered by these laws. In some states, however, franchises are specifically excluded because they must already comply with similar federal and state laws.

(d) Terms of the Agreement.   As in all license agreements involving trademarks, franchise agreements should include detailed provisions to protect the trademark from both infringement and misuse.

There are, however, some licensing terms that are especially important to franchise agreements. In particular, terms governing know-how should be included. Franchisees receive franchisors' know-how through training and operating manuals.[90] Although both may be confidential, operating manuals are most likely to contain confidential information, such as trade secrets. Because these manuals are usually extremely comprehensive in their description of the standard procedures for implementing the franchised business, it is very important that they include express contract provisions to protect any confidential information they contain. It is recommended these provisions be kept simple by incorporating a presumption that all information franchisors call confidential is confidential. This presumption can be rebutted by another party showing that the information called "confidential" by the franchisor is in the public domain or that it was disclosed to the franchisee before the agreement was executed. The benefit of this approach is that it eliminates the need to have detailed and complex lists of what information qualifies as confidential.[91]

The fact that franchisees gain intimate knowledge of the workings of the franchisor's business has still further relevance. With such detailed information, franchisees could be in a position to compete very effectively with the franchisor after the franchise agreement ends. Therefore, franchisors should require franchisees to sign covenants not to compete, which may be enforced even after the termination or expiration of the agreement. Such covenants not to compete must, of course, be carefully drafted so as not to violate the antitrust laws.

Furthermore, employees of a franchisee also have access to the franchisor's confidential information and know-how. Provisions should therefore be designed to cover employees as well. Franchisors often require franchisees to use employee contracts that mirror the franchise agreement.

---

[88] FTC Franchise Rule (*Disclosure Requirements and Prohibitions Concerning Franchising and Business Opportunity Ventures*), 16 C.F.R. § 436 (1979).

[89] UFOC Guidelines, *Business Franchise Guide* (Commercial Clearing House, Incorporated Chicago.) ¶ 5813.

[90] Kaufmann, *An Introduction to Franchising*.

[91] Ibid.

10.5 LICENSING OF ADVANCED TECHNOLOGY

Businesses involved in applying or producing advanced technology have special reasons to consider licensing.

First, discovering or inventing advanced technology may involve a considerable financial investment, often greater than for other business enterprises. Because of the significant amount of resources required, it makes sense to include numerous investors in the venture. Licensing offers a convenient method to assure investors a return on their investment without transferring or dividing ownership in the final invention.

Licensing may also be used for advanced technology if the web of intellectual property rights is complex and the laws uncertain. Computer software licensing exemplifies this type of advanced technology licensing. Software includes many different types of intellectual property, and the laws and regulations governing software are still being developed. To sort out this confusing situation, software owners often choose to license their wares, because licensing gives them an opportunity to establish contractual obligations with the software consumer. Depending on how well the license agreement is drafted and whether there are any surprising new legal developments, software licensors should be able to hold licensees to contractual agreements, even if problems would otherwise have arisen regarding the intellectual property rights at issue.

The following paragraphs discuss two types of advanced technology licenses: biotechnology and computer software licenses.

(a) Biotechnology Licensing. As of 1980, the U.S. Supreme Court determined that patent protection covered genetically engineered microorganisms.[92] Thirteen years later, it was estimated that total annual revenues in this industry would reach $8 billion.[93] Biotechnology is big business. But before developers capitalize on a biotechnology product, millions of dollars must be invested in research. Money must also be set aside to pay the highly trained and specialized intellectual property attorneys who will prosecute the resultant patent. In addition, marketing may be costly, especially for pharmaceuticals aimed at public consumption.

As a result of these expenses, it is not surprising that many biotechnology developers choose to license their products.[94] Licensing provides a vehicle for gathering investors and assuring them a share in the ultimate profits. Yet because biotechnology is often predicated on a future outcome, the potential licensee should make a well-informed, considered assessment of the risk involved before investing.

Biotechnology Licensers.   Although many biotechnology developers have financial reasons for licensing, others have unique motivations. Licensing by universities or nonprofit research organizations is, of course, often motivated by financial considerations. These institutions may also wish to license if the research was originally undertaken for reasons of public interest (e.g., discovering a cure for AIDS). Once the public interest goal has been met, the university or nonprofit organization may license the discovery so as to avoid becoming entangled in marketing or the complicated approval procedures of the Food and Drug Administration.

---

[92] *Diamond v. Chakrabarty*, 447 U.S. 303 (1980).

[93] Michael W. Glynn, "Biotechnology Licensing and Protection" *Technology Licensing and Litigation 1993*, (PLI Patents, Copyrights, Trademarks, and Literary Property Course Handbook Series, No. G4–3897).

[94] See section 10.2 (c) in this chapter for a discussion of patent licensing.

Biotechnology companies, on the other hand, may opt for licensing for both financial and other reasons. In order to gain funds to pursue other avenues of biotechnology research, the company may license discoveries it has already made. The company may also need to license to collect the capital to market its product. For some companies, the discovery may not coincide well with the rest of their business. Instead of changing the nature of its business, a company may retain both its character and expected revenues through licensing the product.

Finally, like all other licensors, biotechnology licensors may license in order to settle a dispute amicably. Patent disputes are particularly probable in the biotechnology arena. Numerous disputes arise because of the tremendous amount of research activity in the field combined with the slow pace of review by the Patent and Trademark Office. Because approval of patents lags considerably behind discovery, patent owners may be surprised to find that they need permission to use a related patent in order to practice their own invention. As an alternative to litigating to "unblock" these patents or losing the ability to practice the patent altogether, licensing is an ideal solution.

(b) Computer Software Licensing. One of the current pressing issues in intellectual property law is determining the best type of protection for computer software. Some practitioners assert that copyright protection is adequate, others say patent protection is necessary, and some advocate a combination of copyrights, patents, and even trade secrets. As it is uncertain that these intellectual property rights will be upheld in court, it is advisable to bind the software user through the contractual terms included in a license.

(i) The "Fair Use" Problem in Copyright. The dilemmas confronted by the computer software industry are illustrated by *Sega Enterprises Ltd. v. Accolade Inc.*[95] In that case, the Ninth Circuit held that the purchaser's disassembly of Sega Enterprises' access codes was a fair use. (Disassembly of access code, a.k.a. reverse engineering, provides information about how the software operates. Through learning how the original software works, computer programmers can replicate the software without copying it directly and infringing its copyright. Reverse engineering therefore enables a competitor to produce a competing product.) Because Sega had sold its product to the public, both its copyright and its trademark infringement claims were unsuccessful. Accolade's reverse engineering was protected by the Fair Use Doctrine. In a similar case, *Atari Games Corp. v. Nintendo of America, Inc.*, the Federal Circuit also held that reverse engineering was a fair use of copyright.[96]

The courts determined that reverse engineering was deemed fair use and not infringement of the copyright because of the Doctrine of First Sale.[97] Spurred by the Doctrine Against Restraints on Alienation, the Doctrine of First Sale allows purchasers to resell or transfer the work, although they may not copy it. This Doctrine applies only to owners of copyrighted works, however, and not to renters or licensees. Yet once ownership and not mere possession is transferred, new owners can treat the work as their own for most purposes.[98] Included in their ownership prerogatives is the right to make "fair use" of the work.

---

[95] 977 F.2d 1510 (9th Cir. 1992).

[96] 975 F.2d 832 (Fed.Cir. 1992).

[97] See 17 U.S.C. § 109.

[98] Note that transfer of a copyright may be accomplished through a contract. The original owner can therefore impose restrictions on use of the copyrighted work as part of the contract.

Some observers believe that software licenses are no longer necessary,[99] because of Congress's passage of the Computer Software Rental Amendments Act in 1990.[100] However, the main purpose of this Act is to prohibit the leasing of computer programs without the consent of the copyright owner.

For the foregoing reasons, most software licenses include provisions prohibiting the disassembling, decompiling, reverse engineering, distribution, renting, re-creation, and modification of software. Boilerplate license and contract terms, in particular sublicensing and territorial restrictions, may be included in the license agreement as well.[101] Furthermore, software owners may be able to recoup additional and more significant damages under contracts than under copyright statutes.

(ii) Trade Secrets and Software Licenses. By retaining ownership, the software licensor may be able to claim trade secret privileges. However, licensors need to be aware of the possibility that federal copyright statutes will preempt assertions of federal or state trade secret rights. In the case of *Computer Associates International, Inc. v. Altai, Inc.*,[102] the court found preemption in part, but not entirely. Clearly, the question of copyright preemption of trade secrets in the context of software licensing is not very predictable.

With this proviso, software licensors seeking to maintain trade secrets in the software should include express provisions to that effect in the license. These provisions should reflect the general concerns governing trade secrets, such as a requirement that the licensor will keep the information confidential by limiting disclosure.[103]

(iii) The Software License Agreement. As discussed earlier, a software license should impose restrictions on use, such as reverse engineering, that are pertinent to software. The license may also provide specifications regarding many types of intellectual property, including copyrights, patents, trade secrets, and perhaps even trademarks. Furthermore, software licensing related to multimedia can become extremely complex, as many parties and variations of intellectual property are usually involved. The licensor might also consider provisions governing ownership rights in any modifications that are made to the software during the license term.

Like other licenses, a software license may be granted within narrow limits. Specifically, a license may govern specific types of media, such as compact discs or on-line services. The field of use may be limited to particular customers or employees of a corporation, or the software may be used only on certain types of computers (e.g., home versus powerful office computers). The license agreement may define the form of the software, for example, object or source code. Also like other licenses, software licenses

---

[99] William H. Neukom and Robert W. Gomulkiewicz, "Licensing Rights to Computer Software," *Technology Licensing and Litigation 1993*, (PLI Patents, Copyrights, Trademarks, and Literary Property Course Handbook Series, No. G4-3897). These authors, who are attorneys at the Microsoft Corporation, do not believe this themselves, but mention that other people maintain this position.

[100] Pub.L. No. 101–650, 104 Stat. 5134 (codified at 17 U.S.C. § 109(b)).

[101] As is the case in any restrictions on use, drafters of the license agreement need to be aware of the applicable antitrust laws.

[102] See Nos. 91–7893, 91–7935, 1992 U.S.App. LEXIS 33369 at *85 (2d Cir.1992) amending Nos. 91–7893, 91–7935, 1992 U.S.App. LEXIS 14305; 23 U.S.P.Q.2D (BNA) 1241 (holding that the copyright infringement claim preempted the trade secret claim, but that the trade secret claim did apply to the "extra element" of a duty under state law and contract).

[103] See section 10.2 (d) in this chapter for a general discussion of trade secrets.

may limit the duration of the license term, state grounds for termination or nonrenewal, and restrict transfers or sublicenses.

Although such divisibility is common to all intellectual property licenses, there are several divisions that are particularly common to software licenses. First, a software license may be granted to only one person who is using only one computer, or to one person using the software on more than one computer, but not simultaneously (e.g., an office computer and a laptop). Rather than linking the license to a person, it may instead be linked to a computer. In this case, the license may apply to only one computer, to only the central computer in a network, or to all computers in a network. Alternatively, the license may apply to all computers at a site, and the computers or concurrent users at the site may be recounted periodically. Assuming cooperation between the licensing parties and the availability of the necessary technology, metering may account for each use of the software. Metering is advantageous to the licensee because the fees charged will most directly reflect actual use.

(iv) Shrink-Wrapped Software Licenses.   Whatever the precise combination of terms in a software license, the license itself is often "shrink-wrapped." Currently, computer software is mass-marketed and is being sold to more and more individual consumers for home use. As a result of these changes, it is becoming less likely that there will be direct contact between the licensor and the licensee. To overcome this difficulty in contracting, software companies have been resorting to shrink-wrapped licenses.

Shrink-wrapped licenses often include terms dictated by the software licensor with the mass-marketed product. These terms may be printed on the outside of the software package or on a plastic bag sealing the computer disk. If the consumer is not dealing with a physical object such as a computer disk, but with a transmission via modem and telephone, the licensor may instead require the inclusion of a password or a response to an inquiry about acquiescence to the terms of the license.

In general, the purpose of shrink-wrapped licenses is to require an affirmative act by consumers to demonstrate that they will abide by the terms of the licensing contract. Most companies also invite consumers who do *not* wish to abide by the licensing agreement to return the product for a full refund within a set period of time.

The validity of shrink-wrapped licenses has been, and will likely continue to be, the subject of intense legal debate. In *Step-Saver Data Systems v. Wyse Technology*,[104] the court upheld a shrink-wrapped license because there had been communications in addition to the point where the "shrink-wrapped" seal was broken. This case, therefore, does not decide the issue of whether breaking the seal on a shrink-wrapped license would be, by itself, sufficient to uphold a contract. As this is a rapidly changing and complex area of the law, software licensors are advised to consult counsel before assuming that placing a shrink-wrapped license on their products is adequate protection of their rights.

10.6 ANTITRUST

Intellectual property rights and antitrust laws are engaged in a basic conflict. Patent, trademark, and copyright laws confer a limited legal monopoly on the intellectual property owner. In contrast, antitrust laws, at least in the United States, seek to prevent one or more parties from dominating or unreasonably controlling any industry or pre-

---

[104] 939 F.2d 91 (3d Cir. 1991).

dominant portion of an industry. Antitrust laws therefore use government and private enforcement to prevent restraint of trade.

There are several antitrust laws of particular interest to intellectual property practitioners. For instance, the goal of § 1 of the Sherman Act is to keep two or more parties from contracting, combining, or conspiring to restrain trade or commerce. An example of such a restraint of trade is the fixing of prices for unpatented goods. Section 2 of the Sherman Act declares that monopolization or attempts to monopolize are unlawful. This section pertains to licensing, because the licensing of trade secrets, trademarks, or patents to a company that is dominant in its field may be construed as an attempt to create a monopoly in that area. Even if licensing of these rights does not create a monopoly under § 2, it may lead to unfair competition and, instead, violate § 2 of the Clayton Act.[105]

In view of these regulations, it is prudent to be cognizant of possible violations under § 3 of the Clayton Act in contemplating patent or know-how licensing. Section 3 prohibits requiring that a lessee or purchaser not use or deal in tangible goods or services of the lessor's or seller's competitor as a condition precedent to lease or sale of tangible matter. If the effect of this type of restriction is to limit competition, then the limitation may violate § 3. Although § 3 applies to tangible matter only, it is relevant to intellectual property licensing because it may pertain to the other aspects of the licensing arrangement. Moreover, § 3 creates "a conceptual force field which puts in a poor light clauses that prevent a licensee from using goods, machines or supplies of another."[106]

Section 4 of the Clayton Act provides for the remedy of treble damages in the event of injury resulting from a violation of the anti-trust laws.[107] The sanction of treble damages is intended to serve as a deterrent against repeated violations and a warning to potential violators, as well as to satisfy private complaints.[108] Section 4 is not, however, intended to provide a remedy of treble damages for all injuries resulting from anti-trust violations and recent decisions have focused on the defendant's "anti-trust injury" in evaluating the application of Section 4.[109]

The Federal Trade Commission (FTC) Act, § 5(a) in particular, is also applicable to intellectual property licensing.[110] This section prohibits unfair methods of competition. Although many acts that would be governed by §§ 1 or 2 of the Sherman Act would likewise fall under the ambit of § 5(a) of the FTC Act, some that are not governed by § 2 may still be prohibited by § 5(a). For example, the FTC is quite diligent about scrutinizing franchising arrangements to see whether they constitute unfair competition.

Furthermore, the U.S. Supreme Court has developed a "rule of reason" to assess the impact of restraints on interstate commerce. The rule of reason, as defined in *Standard Oil Co. v. United States*,[111] focused on whether the defendant's conduct resulted in an unreasonable restraint of interstate commerce. The finding of whether a defendant's conduct creates an unreasonable restraint on interstate commerce must be determined by the trier of fact. In reaching its decision, the trier of fact must consider all of the facts and circumstances, including the economic conditions of the industry and the effect of the defendant's conduct on competition. In particular, the court should consider several

---

[105] 15 U.S.C. § 13.

[106] Milgrim, *Milgrim on Licensing*, § 7.01.

[107] 15 U.S.C. § 15.

[108] *See* 10 Von Kalinowski, Antitrust Laws and Trade Regulation at § 115.01.

[109] *Brunswick Corp. v Pueblo Bowl-O-Mat, Inc.*, 429 U.S. 477, 97 S. Ct. 690, 50 L Ed. 2d 701 (1977).

[110] 15 U.S.C. § 45 (a) (1).

[111] 221 U.S. 1 (1911).

factors, including the purpose of the restriction, the market power of the supplier, the strength of interbrand competition, the effect of the restriction on the market, and any offsetting procompetitive benefits.[112] As a general rule, territorial restrictions have been found to violate the Sherman Act where they form part of a broader conspiracy to restrain trade or monopolize.[113]

(a) Trademarks. Because a trademark functions to identify the origin of goods or services in one source, it may be considered an exclusive right, that is, a monopoly. A trademark has been characterized as "tantamount to a gift of exclusive ownership of the use of an English word."[114] In the sense of an "exclusive right," trademarks can be characterized as a kind of "property."

The view of the Department of Justice in connection with trademark licensing appears consistent with its position on patent licensing. Specifically, the *International Antitrust Guide* takes the position that a system of exclusive territorial trademark licenses "is not inherently illegal."[115] Yet, exclusive trademark licensing may become an antitrust violation where it has "the purpose or effect of territorial allocation."[116]

(i) Trademarks: Symbols of Goodwill. According to one case, "there is no such thing as property in a trademark except as a right appurtenant to an established business or trade in connection with which the mark is employed."[117] This exclusive "property" right of a trademark is generally created by public perception in the marketplace; it is a direct result of the mental state of the consumer. Thus, a trademark has no existence, and no status as property, apart from the goodwill of the product or service it symbolizes.[118] This element of a mental state in the definition of the property right is unique to trademark property rights and is not a feature present in other forms of property, such as real estate or patents.

Safeguarding a trademark does, however, have antitrust implications. To retain this property right, the trademark owner must prevent consumer confusion about the source of the trademarked goods.[119] To prevent confusion, the trademark owner must control the licensee's use of the mark. The fact that maintenance of a trademark right demands dramatic and pervasive supervision by the owner implicitly creates grounds for conflict with U.S. antitrust laws. In this regard, there are four types of controls that trademark owners frequently use to protect a trademark's reputation: (1) purchasing, (2) price, (3) territory, and (4) customer. Significantly, U.S. antitrust laws restrict all four controls if they have an anticompetitive effect.

---

[112] See B. Hawk, *U.S. Common Market and International Antitrust: A Comparative Guide* (Englewood Cliffs, N.J.: Prentice-Hall, 1986), p. 4.

[113] *U.S. v. Imperial Chemical Industries*, 100 F. Supp. 504, 592–93 (S.D.N.Y. 1951).

[114] *Majestic Manufacturing Co. v. Majestic Electric Appliance Co.*, 79 F. Supp. 649 (N.D. Ohio 1948), *aff'd* 172 F.2d 862 (6th Cir. 1949).

[115] See Case F, Department of Justice Guidelines: International Operations, Antitrust Enforcement Policy.

[116] Id.

[117] *United Drug Co. v. Theodore Rectanus Co.*, 248 U.S. 90, 97, 63 L. Ed. 141, 39 S. Ct. 48 (1918), *superseded by statute* as stated in *Foxtrap, Inc. v. Foxtrap, Inc.*, 671 F.2d 636; See also *American Steel Founderies v. Robinson*, 269 U.S. 372 (1926).

[118] *Prestonettes, Inc. v. Coty*, 264 U.S. 359, 68 L.Ed 731, 44 S. Ct. 350 (1924); *Coca-Cola Bottling Co. v. Coca-Cola Co.*, 269 F. 796 (D.C. Del. 1920).

[119] *International Order of Job's Daughters v. Lindeburg & Co.*, 633 F.2d 912 (C.A.Cal. 1980), *cert. denied* 452 U.S. 941 (9th Cir. 1982); See *Kentucky Fried Chicken Corp. v. Diversified Packaging Corp.*, 549 F.2d 368 (9th Cir. 1977).

(ii) Purchasing Control.   Trademark owners frequently seek to control their licensees' purchases of raw materials and products necessary to manufacture finished goods. This control system of purchasing is justified by the trademark owner as a necessary element of product uniformity and quality standards. Yet such a system has been held to violate the antitrust laws. For example, in *Federal Trade Commission v. Brown Shoe Co.*,[120] the United States Supreme Court held licensing arrangements that "take away freedom of purchasers to buy in an open market" to be in direct conflict with the policies of the Sherman and Clayton Acts, and with § 5 of the FTC Act.

However, subsequent to *Brown Shoe*, U.S. courts reviewed other licensing and franchising arrangements and in some instances allowed restrictive buying arrangements. In *Susser v. Carvel Corp.*, the district court upheld a franchise operation in which the Carvel Corporation granted franchisees and licensees the right to use their "Carvel" trademarks for an entire soft ice cream business.[121] The franchisees were required to purchase all ingredients of the end products sold to the consumer from Carvel or other designated sources. The court held that these requirements were not per se illegal under the antitrust laws, in the absence of a showing that the franchisor occupied a dominant position in the market or that a substantial amount of commerce in the "tied" products would be foreclosed.[122] On appeal, the U.S. Court of Appeals for the Second Circuit concluded that the district court was fully warranted in holding that, in the context of the Carvel franchise system, the restriction that no non-Carvel product be sold at the retail level was "reasonably necessary for the protection of Carvel's good will."[123] The court stated:

> Antitrust laws . . . [do not] proscribe a trademark owner from establishing a chain of outlets uniform in appearance and operation. Trademark licensing agreements requiring the sole use of the trademarked item have withstood attack under the antitrust laws where deemed reasonably necessary to protect the good will interest of the trademark owner and such agreements certainly are not unlawful *per se* under the antitrust laws.[124]

The *Carvel* decision became one of the leading trademark cases in the licensing area. Frequently cited, *Carvel* reaffirmed that a trademark owner has an affirmative duty to maintain sufficient control over manufacture of the product in order to sustain the owner's original position as guarantor to the consumer that the goods bearing the trademark are of the same nature and quality as those manufactured by the owner.[125]

In analyzing antitrust issues, though, it is important to read the *Carvel* decision in conjunction with the decision handed down in *Siegal v. Chicken Delight, Inc.* That decision limited the use of purchasing restrictions for quality-control purposes. The facts of the case involved a franchise agreement that licensed Chicken Delight's trade name, trademark, and method of operation in return for the franchisee's promise to purchase all

---

[120] 384 U.S. 316, 321 (1966).

[121] 206 F. Supp. 636 (S.D.N.Y. 1962), *aff'd* 332 F.2d 505 (2nd cir. 1964), *cert. granted* 379 U.S. 885 (1964), *cert. dismissed* 381 U.S. 125 (1965).

[122] 206 F. Supp., 646. In a "tying arrangement" the sale of one item is coercively "tied" to the customer's purchase of another product. Where it is necessary (as was the case in *Carvel*) that licensees use particular supplies in preparing or producing the final product, the franchisor can tie the availability of such supplies to the sale of the franchise license or trademark right.

[123] 322 F.2d 505, 517.

[124] Id., 517.

[125] 206 F. Supp., 641.

cooking equipment, as well as dip spice mix and paper packaging, solely from Chicken Delight. All of these products would be sold at specified prices.[126] Chicken Delight, Inc., like Carvel Corporation, argued that the tie-ins were necessary to ensure quality control and protect goodwill. The district court ruled that the tie-in of the paper products was unjustified, and the jury found inadequate justification for the other purchase requirements.[127] Damages were awarded to recompense the franchisees for payments exceeding the fair market value of the supplies.

Licensors and franchisors can protect themselves from antitrust allegations by providing quality specifications. Then the licensees can purchase from whatever sources they choose, provided that the products meet certain quality standards.[128]

Alternatively, the franchisor may designate a number of acceptable sources from which franchisees may purchase supplies. As long as there are a sufficient number of such approved sources, antitrust laws are not violated because "franchisees retain the option to shop around."[129]

Note the caveat, however, that manufacturer franchisors are entitled to require franchisees to use a mark only in connection with goods that they supply. In this case, the mark acts to identify the source, which is the manufacturer franchisor. No purchase occurs, because the franchisee is merely a distributor of the franchisor's products. Therefore, antitrust concerns are not at stake.[130]

(iii) Price Controls.   Under a variety of statutes, certain types of concerted arrangements have been found to be unreasonable per se. Such arrangements include horizontal and vertical price fixing. Specifically, § 1 of the Sherman Act, which applies to both interstate and foreign commerce, declares unlawful any contract, combination, or conspiracy in restraint of trade.[131] Section 2 of the Sherman Act prohibits monopolization, attempts to monopolize, and conspiracies to monopolize.[132] Section 2(a) of the Robinson-Patman Act[133] (amending the Clayton Act) prohibits price discrimination under certain conditions.

With the recognition of the "per se"[134] rule, there is little that a trademark owner can do contractually to establish a certain price level. Under the so-called Colgate Doctrine,[135] a seller may suggest a resale price as long as he or she does not solicit the buyer's agreement to fix prices or does not use coercive methods to achieve this result. The licensor could refuse to do business with a licensee who does not follow the licensor's suggested resale price. However, the licensor would have to cease doing business with the licensee without providing any threat to cease dealing, lest the licensor be accused of

---

[126] 311 F. Supp. 847 (N.D.Cal. 1970), modified on appeal 448 F.2d 43 (9th Cir. 1971), *cert. denied* 405 U.S. 955 (1972).

[127] Id., 850–51.

[128] McCarthy, *Trademarks and Unfair Competition*, § 18:19 (citing Wilson, "Legal Problems in Franchising: The Enforcement Agencies," *Franchising Today* [1969]: 154, 157).

[129] *Kentucky Fried Chicken*, 549 F.2d at 378.

[130] Id.

[131] 15 U.S.C. § 1 (1982).

[132] 15 U.S.C. § 2 (1982).

[133] 15 U.S.C. §§ 13b, 21a, known as the Robinson-Patman Anti-Discrimination Act.

[134] The rationale for the "per se" rule is that the marketplace determines whether prices are reasonable, with the implication that any agreement that undermines the market is inherently unreasonable. Notwithstanding the foregoing, not all business arrangements that affect price competition are illegal "per se."

[135] *U.S. v. Colgate & Co.*, 250 U.S. 300 (1919).

coercion. The mere suggestion of the licensor's acting in association with other licensees may successfully be challenged in a court of law.[136]

Trademark licensors frequently assert that the goodwill appurtenant to their trademarks will be diluted or lost if the products bearing the trademarks are subject to price reductions. Arguably, such concern justifies prescribing the licensees' resale prices. Although this is an interesting argument, it has not been established that uniformity of price is a legitimate licensor interest merely because uniformity of quality is a legitimate interest. In fact, even arrangements with foreign or domestic competitors to fix prices in foreign markets have been held illegal where there is an effect on U.S. domestic or foreign commerce.

Price-fixing has been held to be one of the more burdensome and anticompetitive restrictions, which partially explains the domestic per se ban on resale price maintenance or vertical price-fixing. Few courts or commentators question trademark owners' legitimate business interests in the prices at which their trademarked products are sold. Yet the question remains whether this restriction is essential to maintain the goodwill of a trademark or to promote the quality of a product associated with the trademark.

It is the author's contention that this restriction does not really interfere with preservation of the integrity of a trademark. In the event that a trademark owner believes that a price publication is necessary to elicit buyer interest, the owner is free to establish a fair market value for goods that he or she sells directly. The owner can then distribute promotional literature advertising that the price is subject to local variation for goods sold by licensees. Thus, the issue of selling price does not directly impact on the quality of the product. The author further observes that whatever public perception or goodwill is ultimately associated with a trademark will rise and fall on the quality associated with the manufacture, sale, and distribution of the product rather than its price.

(iv) Territorial Controls.   Trademark license agreements that provide for a division of markets among licensees fall within the scope of the Sherman and Clayton Acts.[137] In the case of territorial controls, trademark owners typically argue that it is easier to trace violations of quality standards if licensees' sales are confined to a narrow geographical area. However, it is questionable whether provisions for exclusive territories for product sales and trademark use are absolutely essential for the trademark owner to maintain the quality standards necessary to comply with the requirements of the Lanham Act.

The legitimacy of territorial controls in a trademark licensing agreement was considered in the seminal Supreme Court case of *Timken Roller Bearing Co. v. U.S.*[138] In this decision, the agreement at issue established exclusive marketing areas that prevented the licensor (American Timken) and the licensees (British and French Timken) from selling in each other's territories. The agreement also required British Timken and French Timken to manufacture and sell antifriction bearings only under the terms of the agreement and under the trademark "Timken." In reaching its decision, the United States Supreme

---

[136] *U.S. v. Parke, Davis & Co.*, 362 U.S. 29 (1960); *Monsanto Co. v. Spray-Rite, supra* at 767–68. The Supreme Court in *Monsanto* held that the correct standard is whether or not there is "direct or circumstantial evidence that tends to exclude the possibility of independent action by the manufacturer and distributor."

[137] *Timken Roller Bearing Co. v. U.S.*, 341 U.S. 593 (1951); *Denison Mattress Factory v. Spring-Air Co.*, 308 F. 2d 403 (5th Cir. 1962); 7 *Von Kalinowski*, Antitrust Laws and Trade Regulation at § 59.06[3].

[138] 341 U.S. 593 (1951).

Court held that provisions in an agreement providing for exclusive marketing areas constituted a restraint of trade in violation of the Sherman Act.[139]

(v) Customer Control. United States courts scrutinize arrangements that attempt to control the terms and conditions under which licensees must operate, including the customers to whom the licensees will sell. For example, courts have struck down restrictions that interfere with the right of licensees to sell to a specific category of customers.

In particular, the United States Supreme Court considered the propriety of these vertical territorial and customer restrictions in *U.S. v. General Motors* in 1966.[140] In that case, the Court condemned joint action by a manufacturer and its dealers to maintain and enforce vertically imposed marketing restrictions. It declared that such actions were a per se violation of the antitrust laws. However, because the Court based its opinion on the existence of an unlawful conspiracy, it did not expressly consider or condemn the restrictions.[141]

Furthermore, a sale by manufacturer/licensor to a dealer/licensee would bar limitations on the licensee. The reason for such a prohibition is that any restrictions would probably violate the Sherman Act. In this regard, sales to dealers/licensees are distinguishable from consignments, because title passes in the first, but not the second, type of transaction.

(b) Patent Licensing and Antitrust Laws. Analysis under the antitrust laws contemplates a balancing of patent interests and their possible effect on market competition. "When the patented product is so successful that it creates its own economic market or consumes a large section of an existing market, the aims and objectives of patent and antitrust laws may seem, at first glance, wholly at odds. However, the two bodies of law are actually complementary, as both are aimed at encouraging innovation, industry and competition."[142] As noted earlier, in section 10.2(c)(ii) of this chapter, companies that already enjoy a dominant market position must take care when acquiring patent licenses to not run afoul of antitrust laws. Potential licensors, then, should carefully take account of what possible antitrust constraints are inherent in any potential licensing situation. The very strength of the property rights in patents may elicit greater antitrust constraints.

There is also a somewhat complicated relationship between the Misuse Doctrine and antitrust laws. When a patent owner goes beyond the limits of the patentee's statutory rights, it is called "patent misuse." Although the courts lack a general theory for resolving the question of whether a particular practice of a patentee is to be treated as proper means

---

[139] *Timken*, 341 U.S. 593. Please, note, however, that the Congress of the United States passed the Foreign Trade Antitrust Improvements Act of 1982 to clarify the law regarding extra-territorial applications of the Sherman and FTC Acts, and to limit anti-trust exposure arising from foreign suits. The Sherman and FTC Acts apply to foreign transactions only when the activities cause "direct, substantial, and reasonably foreseeable" injuries to United States import or export commerce, and the activities must otherwise violate the Sherman Act. The 1982 Act, of course, has not ended anti-trust disputes in this area, especially with regard to the showing needed for the "direct, substantial, and reasonably foreseeable" effect standard. Von Kalinowski at § 5.02[2]. *See also* 1982 Foreign Trade Antitrust Improvements Act, Pub. L. No. 97–290, § 408, codified at 15 U.S.C. § 45(a)(3).

[140] 384 U.S. 127 (1966); See also *United States v. White Motor Co.*, 194 F. Supp. 562 (N.D.Ohio 1961) (District Court entered summary judgment condemning vertically imposed territorial and customer restrictions as per se violations of § 1 of the Sherman Act.)

[141] *U.S. v. General Motors Co.*, 384 U.S. at 145–47.

[142] See, e.g., *Atari Games Corp. v. Nintendo of America, Inc.* 897 F.2d 1572, 1576 (Fed. Cir. 1990).

of exercising its statutory patent rights,[143] both antitrust laws and the Misuse Doctrine center on this question. The Federal Circuit recently stated in *Mallinckrodt, Inc. v. Medipart, Inc.* that "the concept of patent misuse arose to restrain practices that did not in themselves violate any law, but that draw anticompetitive strength from the patent right, and thus were deemed to be contrary to public policy. The policy purpose was to prevent a patentee from using the patent to obtain market benefit beyond that which inheres in the statutory patent right."[144]

Under the Misuse Doctrine, a patent owner cannot obtain relief for patent infringement and cannot enforce a license agreement that increases the licensed patent's scope. However, patent misuse may be "purged," and the owner may then enforce the license or patent.[145] In 1988 Congress amended Patent Act § 271(d) to find "misuse" only if the offending practice violates the antitrust laws.[146] It has yet to be determined how this amendment will be treated in case law.

The most important provisions of the antitrust laws that relate to patent activities are §§ 1 and 2 of the Sherman Act, §§ 3 and 7 of the Clayton Act, and § 5 of the FTC Act. As stated earlier, § 1 of the Sherman Act renders illegal every contract, combination, or conspiracy in restraint of interstate or foreign trade or commerce.[147] Section 2 makes monopolists, or those who seek to monopolize interstate or foreign trade or commerce, guilty of a misdemeanor.[148] Section 3 of the Clayton Act provides that it is illegal to sell or lease commodities on condition that the purchaser or lessee will not deal with the products of the seller's competitors, where the effect of this condition may be to lessen competition or create a monopoly.[149] Section 7 does not allow the acquisition of stock or assets if this would substantially lessen competition or possibly create a monopoly.[150] Finally, § 5 of the FTC Act prohibits unfair competition and unfair or deceptive practices in commerce.[151]

In considering all of these statutory guidelines, it must always be remembered that "a particular license restriction is seldom considered in isolation by the judiciary, but usually is viewed against the background of the motivation of the patent owner in issuing the license embodying the restriction."[152] The totality of the circumstances under which a license agreement arises is the key to determining whether particular restrictions are valid.

Royalties, which relate to either the number of units sold or the actual value of sales subject to license, are paid for patents to have the patentee relinquish its exclusive right to practice the invention. Patent royalties are not applicable to time periods predating the patent's issue date, inasmuch as the exclusive rights that are statutorily given to a patent do not arise until the patent's issuance. However, preissuance royalty payments for patents can be justified as contractual payment on nonpatent grounds.[153] License agree-

---

[143] See, generally, Donald S. Chisum, *Patents* (1993: New York, Matthew Bender), § 19.04[2].
[144] 976 F.2d 700, 704 (Fed. Cir. 1992).
[145] See, e.g., *United States Gypsum Co. v. National Gypsum Co.*, 352 U.S. 457 (1957).
[146] Pub. L. 100–703, 102 Stat. 4674, 4676 (Nov. 19, 1988).
[147] 15 USC § 1.
[148] 15 USC § 2.
[149] 15 USC § 14.
[150] 15 USC § 18.
[151] 15 USC § 45.
[152] Raymond C. Nordhaus, *Patent-Antitrust Law*, 3d rev. ed. (New York, Law & Forms, 1976), § 4–3.
[153] See Milgrim, *Milgrim on Licensing*, § 8.08.

ment provisions that require a licensee to pay royalties for practices postdating the expiration of a patent are also unenforceable.[154]

Under antitrust principles, there is an almost universal recognition that price-fixing practices are prohibited. Under patent law, though, there is an exception to this general rule: a patentee that manufactures a product may "fix" a minimum manufacturing-licensee resale price for the product.[155] This exception has been narrowed by subsequent decisions, however, so it is advisable to avoid price-fixing arrangements.[156]

License "packaging" involves a licensee's taking several licenses in intellectual property, usually being permitted to take some that he or she wants on the condition that other, less desirable, ones are also taken. So long as there is no overreaching or other objectionable use of leverage by the licensor, which would constitute misuse,[157] this type of packaging has been accepted. Clearly, if a product has many patentable aspects, it is common for the parties to license all of the patents in a package rather than granting a patent-by-patent license of each element of the product. These packages should be formed by explicit recitals in the license agreement.[158]

"Complex licensing" involves combinations of different types of intellectual property. For a combination of two patents, as stated, there is no antitrust violation so long as the licensee is not coerced into taking unwanted patents in order to receive wanted patents. Mandatory coupling of several patents is not a problem, however, in the case of products for which practice of each patent requires practice of the others.[159] For a "patent plus trademark" license, there is an inherent problem: because of the possible perpetual duration of marks, coupled with the limited duration of patents, requiring a licensee to take such a license could be held to constitute misuse of the patent.[160]

Another practice, known as "patent pooling," involves an agreement between patent owners by which each agrees not to assert its patents against the others. These may be executed by covenants not to sue or exchange of licensing agreements. Depending on the extent of these pools and the purposes to which they are put, they can be acceptable under the antitrust laws, or may instead be a violation of them. The legality of such pools may be determined under the "rule of reason," whereby it is determined whether the conduct is violative of the underlying policies of the antitrust laws.[161] If a pool is entered into for anticompetitive purposes, it may violate Sherman Act §§ 1 or 2 or may constitute patent misuse. Patent pools may also violate the antitrust laws where the purpose is to prevent

---

[154] *Brulotte v. Thys Co.*, 379 U.S. 29 (1964), *reh'g denied*, 379 U.S. 985 (1965); *Meehan v. PPG Indus., Inc.*, 802 F.2d 881 (7th Cir. 1986).

[155] See, e.g., *United States v. General Electric Co.*, 272 U.S. 476 (1926); *In re Yarn Processing Patent Validity Litigation*, 541 F.2d 1127 (5th Cir. 1976), *cert. denied*, 433 U.S. 910 (1977); *Prestole Corp. v. Tinnerman Prods. Co.*, 271 F.2d 146, (6th Cir. 1959), *cert. denied*, 361 U.S. 964 (1960).

[156] Milgrim, *Milgrim on Licensing*, § 8.12.

[157] See, e.g., *Rocform Corp. v. Acitelli-Standard Concrete Wall, Inc.*, 367 F.2d 678 (6th Cir. 1966); *Beckman Instruments, Inc. v. Technical Development Corp.*, 433 F.2d 55 (7th Cir. 1970), *cert. denied*, 401 U.S. 976 (1971)

[158] Milgrim, *Milgrim on Licensing*, § 8.27.

[159] See *International Mfg. Co. v. Landon*, 336 F.2d 723 (9th Cir. 1964), *cert. denied*, 379 U.S. 988 (1965).

[160] See, e.g., *Switzer Bros. v. Locklin*, 297 F.2d 39 (7th Cir. 1961).

[161] See Justice White's opinion in *Standard Oil Co. v. United States*, 221 U.S. 1 (1911), which is a seminal exposition of the rule of reason.

technological developments.[162] Patent pooling may, in addition, violate § 7 of the Clayton Act, which forbids acquisitions of assets if they lead to anticompetitive results.[163]

"Cross-licensing" agreements, like patent pooling, are also analyzed under the rule of reason.[164] The passage of the National Cooperative Research Act of 1984[165] (NCRA) will certainly influence the development of cross-licensing and pooling arrangements in intellectual property. The intentions of the NCRA are summarized in the following list.

1. The Act eliminates application of any per se rule of illegality to joint research and development ventures and requires the courts to apply a rule of reason to test such ventures.[166]

2. Parties engaged in joint research and development ventures can obtain immunity from treble damage liability for conduct in the course of their joint venture by notifying the Department of Justice and the Federal Trade Commission and permitting publication of a notice of the proposed joint venture in the Federal Register.[167]

3. The Act provides for the recovery of attorneys' fees from an unsuccessful claimant for damages resulting from the joint venture's conduct to the extent that the claimant's assertion of the claim was "frivolous, unreasonable, without foundation or in bad faith."[168]

The NCRA also states that courts will consider "all relevant factors affecting competition, including, but not limited to, effects on competition in properly defined, relevant research and development markets."[169]

10.7 INTERNATIONAL LICENSING

Most systems of law today provide that trademarks may be licensed with the same freedom as patents. However, prior to 1938 many countries considered the licensing of trademark rights to be unlawful. The passage of the Trade-Marks Act of 1938 in the United Kingdom marked the start of the licensing revolution by which the United Kingdom and, gradually, other countries that followed U.K. trademark law affirmatively permitted the licensing of trademarks.

The United States recognized licensing in the Lanham Act of 1946, but the law did not incorporate any requirement of registered user or the registration of license agreements.

---

[162] See *United States v. Automobile Manufacturers' Ass'n*, 307 F. Supp. 617 (C.D. Cal. 1969), *aff'd in part sub nom.*; *Grossman v. Automobile Mfrs. Ass'n*, 397 U.S. 248 (1970), *modified*, 1982–3 CCH Trade Cas. para. 65,088 (C.D. Cal. 1982).

[163] See *Dairy Foods, Inc. v. Farmer's Coop-Creamery*, 298 F. Supp. 774, 777 (D. Minn. 1969): "Patents are assets and where two large business concerns own patents which may be similar in scope and decide not to compete but to put both into a common corporation or pool of which each owns 50% of the stock, such may tend to lessen competition."

[164] *Duplan Corp. v. Deering Milliken, Inc.*, 540 F.2d 1215 (4th Cir. 1976) (settlement of patent litigation by cross-licensing agreement would be lawful if entered into to unblock conflicting patent claims).

[165] 15 U.S.C. §§ 4301–4305.

[166] See 15 U.S.C. § 4302.

[167] See 15 U.S.C. §§ 4303, 4305.

[168] 15 U.S.C. § 4304(a)

[169] 15 U.S.C. § 4302.

Instead, the Lanham Act requires that the proprietor of the trademark control the nature and quality of the licensee's products.[170] Section 1055 of the Act provides that "where a registered mark or a mark sought to be registered is or may be used legitimately by the lay companies, such use shall inure to the benefit of the registrant or applicant," and § 1127 defines a related company as "any person [including a juristic person] whose use of a mark is controlled by the owner of the mark with respect to the nature and quality of the goods or services on or in connection with which the mark is used." Accordingly, the Lanham Act permits a trademark proprietor to license his or her trademark to anyone, provided that the proprietor retains control over the nature and quality of the goods or services in connection with the use of the trademark.

In some civil-law jurisdictions, case law recognized the lawfulness of licensing even before 1938, whereas in other countries, such as France (in 1857) and Spain (in 1929), the licensing of trademarks was already lawful under statute.

(a) Limitations on Technology Licensing.   The limitations imposed by U.S. anti-trust laws on technology licensing in the United States have been discussed above. Similar limitations on freedom of contract exist in many other countries. It is not possible to discuss these in detail in a work of this type; however, a brief overview of the position in the European Community and Japan follows.

(i) European Community.   The European Community presents particular problems in technology licensing as one is confronted not only with classified anti-trust problems, but also the intention of the Treaty of Rome eliminates, as far as possible, the notion of national boundary splitting of the EC. Article 2 of the Treaty of Rome provides for the basis of the European Economic Community, namely, the creation of a Common Market. Article 3 sets out certain necessary requirements and includes the elimination of quantitative restrictions on the import and export of goods and of all other measures having equivalent effect. These basic statements of purpose have enabled the European Court of Justice to distinguish between identically worded provisions in Article 30 of the Treaty itself and a Treaty between the Common Market and Portugal (in the days before Portugal became a member of the Community) for the court to reach different conclusions on whether goods should be allowed to flow freely.[171]

The basic black letter law of the EEC on Intellectual Property Rights and the Free Flow of Goods doctrine is well established. One cannot, in general, use an intellectual property right to prevent importation of goods from another EEC member state if the goods were first put on the market in that state by the owner or with his consent.[172] If the goods were first put on the market outside the EEC however, this black letter community law does not apply and one has to look to national law for a decision.[173] This formulation of black letter law has been adopted in respect of all three branches of intellectual property, for example,

---

[170] 15 U.S.C. 1055, 1127.

[171] *Polydor Ltd. et al. v. Harlequin Record Shops* (1982) 1 Comm. Mkt. LR 677.

[172] The European Court of Justice's own formulation of the rule is "the proprietor of an individual or commercial property right protected by the law of a member state cannot rely on that law to prevent the importation of a product that has been lawfully marketed in another member state by the proprietor himself or with his consent." *Merck & Co. v. Stephar BV* (1981) 3 Comm. Mkt. LR 463.

[173] See, for example, *EMI Records Ltd. v. CBS Grammofon AS* (1976) 2 Comm. Mkt. LR 235; and Polydor Ltd. et al. v. Harlequin Record Shops (1982) 1 Comm. Mkt. LR 677.

in the case of *Merck v. Stephar*[174] and *Centrafarm v. Sterling*[175] for patents, *Winthrop Products v. Centrafarm*[176] for trademarks, and in *Deutsche Gramaphon*[177] for copyrights.

The free flow of goods doctrine imposes certain problems when licensing intellectual property rights, as one can never assure a licensee of absolute exclusivity within a licensed territory unless the licensed territory is the entire EC, which is often not the case.

The Treaty of Rome contains two anti-trust provisions: Article 85, which is generally similar to Section 1 of the Sherman Act, and Article 86, which resembles Section 2 of the Sherman Act.

Under EEC law, all agreements in breach of Article 85(1) of the Treaty of Rome as a result of their anti-competitive nature and adverse effect on trade between the member states are void unless they have been exempted. There are two types of exemptions: (a) group exemptions promulgated by the Commission for certain classes of agreement and (b) specific exemptions issued after consideration of the facts of the case. Few specific exemptions are actually granted because the bureaucracy has an enormous backlog of requests.

Thus, as a practical matter, the twin pillars of EEC technology licensing law are the group exemptions granted by the European Commission under Article 85(3) of the Treaty of Rome for (1) patent and (2) know-how licensing, although for arrangements between relatively small enterprises, protection may also be found in the Notice on Minor Agreements.[178]

Patent Group Exemption.[179]   The basic provision of the patent group exemption, which came into effect in 1985 is the grant of an exemption to patent license agreements that confer a certain measure of exclusivity on the licensee as long as certain prohibited clauses are not present. The group exemption also provides a list of clauses that are not regarded as being anti-competitive in themselves and that therefore do not require an exemption.

The basic provisions on exclusivity are set out in Article 1 of the basic regulation. An exemption is granted thereby making permissible clauses in agreements that impose any of the following obligations:

a. on the licensor not to grant other licenses in the licensed territory or to exploit the invention him/herself in the licensed territory so long as at least one of licensed patents remain in force;

b. on the licensee not to exploit the licensed invention outside its own territory in other countries within the Common Market where parallel patents exist and where exploitation in such other countries is reserved to the licensor or other licensees;

c. on the licensee not to sell at all in any EEC territory where parallel patents exist for five years from the date of first sale of the product within the EEC; and

---

[174] See note 172. This case made it clear that the doctrine applied irrespective of whether the items in question (pharmaceuticals in this particular case) were patentable in the country of origin.

[175] *Centrafarm BV et al. v. Sterling Drug Inc.* (1974) 2 Comm. Mkt. LR 480.

[176] *Centrafarm BV v. Winthrop BV* (1974) 2 Comm. Mkt. LR 480.

[177] *Deutsche Gramaphon v. Metro Grossmarkte GmbH and Co.* (1971) 1 Comm. Mkt. LR 631.

[178] O.J.C. 231/2 (Sept. 12, 1986).

[179] Patent License Group Exemption (Regulation 2349/84).

> **d.** on the licensee not to establish an active sales policy (for example, by advertising or establishing branches or distribution depots) in other EEC territories where parallel patents exist at any time during the lives of the patents in such territories.

Except for obligations on the licensor not to license other parties and obligations on the licensee not to manufacture or use the product in territories where other parties are licensees, the exemption referred to above only applies if the licensee manufactures the licensed product itself or has it manufactured by a sub-contractor.

The exemption will, however, not apply at all if certain prohibited clauses provided in Article 3 are present in the license.[180] These prohibited clauses may lead a cautious licensor to include a provision that makes it clear that it will not use its patent to take steps to try to prevent import by third parties of goods manufactured by licensees in other EEC member states and to deny the licensee the right to use the licensed patent for such a purpose if national law permits licensees to enforce patents.

Know-How Group Exemption.[181]   The Know-How Group Exemption came into effect in April 1989. To qualify for the Group Exemption, the license must relate to unpatented technical know-how that is "secret, substantial and identified", as defined in the regulation.[182]

"Secret" is given a broad meaning and covers a know-how package as a body that is not generally known as easily accessible, so that part of its value consists of the lead-time the licensee gains when it is communicated to him. It is specifically stated that the term should not be construed narrowly so as to require every element to be totally unknown or unobtainable outside the licensor's business.

---

[180] Article 3 prohibits, among others, clauses that:
   a. prohibit challenges to the validity of any industrial or commercial property right;
   b. prolong the agreement beyond the expiration of any licensed patent existing at the time of the agreement, unless the agreement provides each party with a right to terminate the agreement at least annually after the expiration of the licensed patents existing at the date of the agreement. It is, however, made clear that royalty payments can be extended for use during the life of the patent beyond the expiration date of the last patent;
   c. restrict competition in research, development, manufacture, use or sales;
   d. base royalty rates on products not entirely or partially covered by patents or produced by use of secret know-how;
   e. limit the maximum amount of use the licensee may make of the patented invention;
   f. restrict either party determining prices;
   g. restrict customers;
   h. require the licensee to assign improvements to the licensor;
   i. require the licensee to take licenses under patents or to agree to use patents, goods or services he/she does not want unless necessary for a technically satisfactory exploitation of the licensed invention;
   j. attempt in any way to require the licensee to refrain from selling in the Common Market outside the licensed territory for more than five years after first sale in the Common Market; and
   k. require in any way that either party refuse, without any objectively justified reason, to meet demand from users or re-sellers who might sell in other areas of the Common Market or make it difficult for such users or re-sellers to sell in such areas.
[181] Know-How Group Exemption (Regulation 556/89).
[182] Know-How Group Exemption Article 1(7).

"Substantial" essentially means that the know-how being licensed must be of a technical nature that is not trivial and is useful in improving the competitive position of the licensee.

"Identified" means that the know-how is described or recorded in such a way as to enable one to determine whether the criteria of secrecy and substantivity have been met. It is not necessary that the licensed know-how be set out in detail in the license agreement itself.

The exemption applies both to pure know-how licenses and to mixed patent and know-how licenses in which part of the technology licensed is covered by patents in one or more countries of the licensed territory. However, the license cannot be covered by the patent license group exemption because the patented element is "not necessary for the achievements of the objects of the technology."[183]

The group exemption specifically does not extend to licensing of non-technical know-how such as marketing know-how.[184] Nor does it extend to licensing of designs, trademarks or software except when the licensing of such rights is clearly ancillary to the main purpose of the agreement.[185]

The exemption granted is similar to that granted under the patent license group exemption. Article 1 exempts from Article 85 of the Treaty the anti-competitive effects of the grant of exclusivity to a licensee for up to ten years and of any obligation on the licensee not to exploit the know-how in a territory reserved by the licensor or to other licensees for up to ten years. It also grants an exemption for terms in the license agreement restricting the licensee from engaging in an active sales policy in the territories of other licensees within the Common Market for ten years and from putting the product on the market in the territories of other licensees for five years. Where patents exist in the relevant territories, the ten-year terms noted are extended to the end of the life of the patents. As with the patent license group exemption, the exemption on limitations on the licensor to exploit the property in the territory and the exemptions for limitations on the licensee's sales policies are permitted only if the licensee will manufacture the licensed products itself or will have them manufactured by a sub-contractor.

The Know-How Group Exemption further contains an exemption similar to that in the patent license group exemption, namely, for clauses requiring the licensee to use a licensor's trademark as long as the licensee is not precluded from identifying himself as the manufacturer of the licensed products.

The group exemption also covers clauses limiting the licensee's use of the know-how to quantities required in manufacturing its own products and to selling licensed products only as an integral part of, or a replacement part for, the licensee's own products.

The presence of certain types of clauses will, however, take an agreement outside the exemption. These "black list" clauses are set out in Article 3.[186]

---

[183] Patent License Group Exemption (Regulation 2349/84) recital 9.

[184] Know-How Group Exemption Recital 5.

[185] Know-How License Group Exemption Article 5(4).

[186] The "black listed" clauses in Article 3 are as follows:

    a. obligations on the licensee not to use the licensed know-how after the agreement has expired if the know-how has meanwhile become publicly known, unless due to the fault of the licensee;

    b. assignments back to the licensor of rights in improvements made by the licensee;

    c. imposition of unnecessary quality standards or an unwanted obligation to obtain goods or services from the licensor or a designated source unless necessary for a technically satisfactory exploitation of the licensed technology;

(ii) Japan.   Japan's Anti-Monopoly Law of 1947[187] outlaws unreasonable restraints of trade and unfair business practices. Enforcement is entrusted to the Japanese Fair Trade Commission, which in 1989 issued new guidelines[188] on technology licensing.

According to the revised guidelines, clauses are divided into three groups: a) those that, in principle, will not be regarded as unfair trade practices, b) those that may constitute unfair trade practices and c) those that are highly likely to be regarded as unfair trade practices. This tripartite classification differs from the preceding set of guidelines that simply split clauses between those that presumptively were not likely to cause a problem and those that the Commission regarded as unfair business practices.

Under the new guidelines, certain types of clauses are likely to be deemed unfair trade practice, although it should be noted that in many cases there is an official comment indicating circumstances that might permit exceptions to this general rule.[189] Neverthe-

---

    d. non-challenge clauses;

    e. customer allocations (however, field of use restrictions including restrictions to one or more product markets are permitted);

    f. quantity limitations except where these are appropriate because of a need to provide for second sourcing; and

    g. price fixing.

[187] Act No. 54 of April, 14 1947 as amended.

[188] Guidelines for Regulation of Unfair Trade Practices with Respect to Patent and Know-How Licensing Agreements issued February 15, 1989 by the Executive Bureau of the Japanese Fair Trade Commission.

[189] Clauses strongly suggesting unfair trade practices are those that:

    a. restrict the price or re-sale price in Japan of goods covered by the licensed patent or produced in accordance with the licensed know-how;

    b. deny the licensee the right to handle competing goods or employ competing technology after the expiration of the licensing agreement;

    c. restrict the use of the licensed technology after any relevant patents have expired or, in the case of a know-how license, the technology has become publicly known without fault of the licensee or impose royalties for continued use after these events have occurred;

    d. impose limitations on the research and development programs of the licensee or its ability to enter into joint research and development with a third party;

    e. impose exclusive grant-back of rights for improvements made by the licensee (a comment on this, however, indicates that in the case of reciprocal obligations in connection with improvements in cases where the licensor is not dominant in the market, such a provision could conceivably be justified).

Potentially unfair clauses include those that:

    a. prohibit competition throughout the life of the agreement;

    b. restrict the right of the licensee to sell products of the licensed technology to persons other than those designated by the licensor;

    c. oblige the licensee to keep the licensor advised about the market conditions relating to the product of the licensed technology without an equal obligation on the licensor;

    d. grant-back rights in improvements made by the licensee unless the licensor has similar obligations imposed upon it;

    e. impose a trademark use requirement on the licensee since this could restrict the licensee's freedom to select a trademark "which is one of the means of competition;"

    f. impose quality controls on the licensed product beyond those necessary "for guaranteeing the effectiveness of the licensed patent or for maintaining the goodwill of a trademark, etc.;"

    g. tie the grant of the license to the supply of raw materials, components, etc. from the licensor or some person designated by the licensor unless such requirements are necessary

less, the provisions under the new guidelines are fairly similar to those in the EEC's group exemptions on patent and know-how licensing.

10.8 REGISTRATION REQUIREMENTS

At present, most countries in the world recognize some form of trademark and patent licensing, and many require the recording of license agreements. As to jurisprudence in regard to trademark and patent licensing, most countries are divided into two categories. The first group, British law (or common law) countries, are those that follow the development of British trademark law and the enactment of the registered user procedure defined in the United Kingdom Trade-Marks Act of 1938. India, Israel, Australia, Hong Kong, and South Africa are among a significant number of British law countries that provide for registered user entries as in § 28 of the British Trade-Marks Act. If two parties are financially or otherwise related, there is generally no requirement that a trademark license agreement be filed, but a simple registered user application can be filed, setting forth the terms and conditions of the licensing arrangement. Furthermore, countries whose laws are modeled on the British Trade-Marks Act of 1938 contain provisions for the simultaneous filing of trademark and registered user applications.[190]

Furthermore, should the proprietor of a trademark be financially related to the user so as to own a controlling interest in the company, a trademark license generally need not be submitted in support of the registered user application. Instead, in most circumstances, a

---

to ensure the effectiveness of the licensed technology or to maintain the goodwill of the trademark, etc. in cases where quality restrictions on the raw materials and components used would be an insufficient guarantee;

h. restrict exports except to the extent that these prevent the licensee from exporting to countries in which the licensor has patent rights;

i. "conducting continuous marketing" of the licensed goods or assigning an exclusive sales territory to a third party;

j. impose volume limitations on the export of products of the licensed technology except to the extent permitted in accordance with paragraph 8;

k. oblige the licensor to pay a royalty based on something other than the licensed products (unless it is to facilitate calculation where the licensed product is a component it is more convenient to base the royalty calculation on the finished product). In other cases where it is inconvenient to do otherwise, royalties may also be based on consumption of raw materials;

l. package license additional patents or know-how not necessary to guarantee the effectiveness of the basic licensed subject matter;

m. impose arbitrary termination provisions in favor of the licensor;

n. oblige the licensee not to contest the validity of a licensed patent or the secrecy of any licensed know-how.

Clauses likely to be acceptable include those that:

a. restrict the grant of a license for a limited period within terms of the patent rights;

b. restrict the field of use;

c. require minimum production or sales;

d. require royalty payments to continue after the agreement expires as long as this payment is for activities that occurred while the agreement was valid;

e. permit terminating the agreement if there is a challenge to validity of a patent or the secrecy of the know-how license and oblige the licensee to use its best efforts to exploit the licensed technology.

[190] U.K. Trade-Marks Act (T.M.A.) 1938, § 29 (1) (b).

declaration attesting to the relationship between the parties is sufficient to allow the registered user to be approved and entered.

Although a registered user entry can be independently obtained in most British law jurisdictions, the laws in some countries permit only entry of a registered user that has been extended from a registered user entry obtained in the United Kingdom. Such jurisdictions include Antigua, Belize, Gibraltar, Grenada, and Montserrat.

In the second category, civil law countries, the law can vary widely as to the requirements and procedures of recording trademark, patent, and copyright license agreements. Generally, a certified copy of the license agreement and, in some cases, an originally executed agreement need to be submitted, whether or not the parties are related.

In some civil law jurisdictions, such as Mexico, a trademark license may be recorded against a pending trademark application; however, many civil law countries require a trademark registration or granted patent to be obtained prior to the recording of the license agreement. Submission of an original or certified copy of the license agreement is generally required in civil law countries whether or not the parties are financially related. In certain civil law jurisdictions, recordal is mandatory. In other civil law jurisdictions, recordation of license agreements is highly advisable in order for the agreement to be enforceable between the parties or against third parties.

(a) Approval of License Agreements. A substantial number of foreign jurisdictions require governmental approval of the license agreement to record the agreement at their respective patent or trademark offices. This requirement frequently exists where the licensor is a foreign company, the licensee is a national company, and there are provisions in the agreement for the remittance of royalties outside the jurisdiction. Government agencies also examine the agreement for restrictive clauses or provisions that violate local antitrust laws.

In Brazil,[191] companies have encountered difficulties in the past when attempting to transfer technology because of strict registration requirements for licensing agreements, coupled with severe limits on remittance of royalty payments abroad. To encourage new foreign investment, a presidential decree in 1991 partially reduced such restrictions. Nevertheless, royalty remittances still require approval from the National Institute of Industrial Property (INPI) and registration with the Central Bank of Brazil.

In Venezuela,[192] most technology contracts and patent and trademark license agreements no longer require prior approval, as a result of Decree 2095. Nevertheless, these agreements must be registered with the Superintendency of Foreign Investments (SIEX) within 60 days after execution. Decree 2095 also specifies that licensing agreements may not include certain tying-in or restrictive clauses as outlined in Article 14 of Andean Pact Decision 291 of 1991. There is no requirement of approval or restrictions regarding limitations on royalty payments.

The Indian government's[193] industrial policy, as of July 1991, provides for the automatic approval by the Reserve Bank of India (RBI) of foreign technology agreements if lump-sum payments and royalties fall within prescribed limits. Applications must be filed

---

[191] International Licensing & Trading Conditions Abroad, Business International Corp. Brazil, January 1993 (London, The Economist Intelligence Unit of the Economist Group).

[192] International Licensing & Trading Conditions Abroad, Business International Corp., Venezuela, October 1992 (London, The Economist Intelligence Unit of the Economist Group).

[193] International Licensing & Trading Conditions Abroad, Business International Corp., India, November 1992 (London, The Economist Intelligence Unit of the Economist Group).

with the RBI's Foreign Investment and Technology Transfer Section. Following approval, the licensee may obtain the necessary foreign exchange at market rates for remittances.

In Taiwan,[194] all agreements involving foreign-exchange payments previously required prior approval from the Investment Commission of the Ministry of Economic Affairs (MOEA), even though limits were no longer set for the amount of foreign exchange involved. The MOEA, pursuant to a Directive dated July 30, 1993, abolished the prescribed criteria for approving the licensing of intellectual property by foreign enterprises. The criteria had required that certain conditions (such as approved foreign investment or technical cooperation) be met to secure the approval for such licensing by the National Bureau of Standards (NBS). Although the NBS is no longer authorized to examine and verify the payment of royalties, the relevant regulations governing payment and tax exemption of such royalties remain in force.

(b) Maintenance of License Agreements. Specific additional steps may be required in many jurisdictions, even after recordation and approval of a license agreement has been completed at the appropriate governmental authority, to preserve the registration of the license. For example, Brazilian trademark practice requires that each time a trademark is renewed, the corresponding license must be re-recorded as well. In Turkey, the certificate of registration must be endorsed with registration of the license each time a trademark is renewed. Accordingly, proper record-keeping procedures and practices should be instituted to ensure that license registrations remain valid and subsisting.

Many foreign patent laws also require payment of annuities during the life of the patent, as well as working obligations. The requirement that a patent invention must be used within the country is usually satisfied by the licensee commencing working of a patent; however, certification of such working may have to be submitted to the respective patent office. In the case of annuities, if the required payment is not made in a timely fashion, a significant and profitable intellectual property right could lapse.

10.9 SUBLICENSING

A sublicense results when a licensor grants a license to one party, and that party grants a license to a second party. The first party is a licensee, and the second party is a sublicensee. A patent or trademark licensee may authorize the issuance of sublicenses, provided that it is authorized by the terms of the original license from the property owner.[195] As in the case of a "pure" license, an authorized sublicense may be either written or oral, and the rights granted are determined by the terms and conditions of the sublicense agreement.[196] The sublicense agreement need not expressly use the word *sublicense* in order to be construed as one.[197]

It is, nevertheless, important to be aware of the dangers of reliance on oral contracts, such as their possible unenforceability under the Statute of Frauds. New York's Statute of Frauds,[198] for instance, provides that:

---

[194] International Licensing & Trading Conditions Abroad, Business International Corp., Taiwan, September 1992 (London, The Economist Intelligence Unit of the Economist Group).

[195] See, e.g., *Raufast S.A. v. Kicker's Pizzazz Ltd.*, 208 USPQ 699 (EDNY, 1980).

[196] *National Pigments & Chemical Co. v. C.K. Williams & Co.*, 94 F.2d 792 (8th Cir. 1938).

[197] Courts have held that a sublicense may exist where the license agreement was silent as to licensing. See, e.g., *Westinghouse Electric and Manufacturing Company v. Tri-City Radio Electric Supply Company*, 23 F.2d 628 (8th Cir. 1927).

[198] N.Y. Gen. Obl. Law § 5–701(a) (1).

Every agreement . . . is void, unless it or some note or memorandum thereof be in writing and subscribed by the party to be charged therewith . . . if such agreement, promise or undertaking: (1) By its terms is not to be performed within one year from the making thereof or the performance of which is not to be completed before the end of a lifetime . . .

Accordingly, oral licenses should be for a relatively short term and made in recognition of statutory and case law in the appropriate forum.

Until fairly recently, the sublicensing of intellectual property was not accepted because of the perception that quality control would be adversely affected inasmuch as the intellectual property's owner would be one step further removed from the user of the property. However, courts have held that proper quality control standards may resolve this problem.

(a) **Quality-Control Provisions.**   All too often, vague or careless drafting of license provisions results in litigation. The relationships between licensor and licensee, licensee and sublicensee, and licensor and sublicensee, therefore, should always be clear and explicit.

A licensee may act as a licensor's agent or representative in the maintenance of quality control over the production of goods bearing the trademark or the performance of services associated with the service marks. If exercised properly, quality-control provisions ensure that a consumer will receive the same value in the product or service as provided by the licensor. This is the legal fiction whereby the public is assured that goods or services originate from the same source. The U.S. District Court in California held in *Yamamoto & Co. (America) Inc. v. Victor United, Inc.*[199] that the same dangers inherent in a pure licensing arrangement exist in a sublicensing arrangement: "Trademark licensing without quality control is naked licensing and is fraud on the public; naked licensing is unlawful, voids the licensed trademark, and constitutes unclean hands."[200]

Specific quality-control requirements for a trademark license or sublicense are not clearly defined in the Lanham Act. However, case law indicates that a trademark proprietor must exercise actual control over the licensee, and that a mere contractual or passive right to control will be deemed a "naked" license, which will result in the trademark ceasing to function as a symbol of quality and controlled source, which will, in turn, lead to the abandonment of the mark.

With respect to patents, the sublicense agreement should identify the agreement under which the sublicensor has authority to grant sublicenses. The agreement may also provide for termination of the sublicense upon termination of the primary license. If the sublicensee would like a self-sustaining term for the sublicense, the sublicensee should get an express agreement on that point from the primary licensor.[201] The necessity for protecting the quality level of the primary licensor's product by express agreement was forcefully shown by the court in *Good Humor Corp. v. Bluebird Ice Cream & C.R.*,[202] which held that a primary licensor who is not a party to the sublicense agreement cannot enforce any provision of the sublicense directly against the sublicensee.

Although the courts appear to have established a duty to exercise control in such sublicensing situations, they have not clearly addressed how this duty may be fulfilled.

---

[199] 219 U.S.P.Q. 968 (1982).

[200] See also *Hurricane Fence Co. v. A-1 Hurricane Fence Co.*, 468 F. Supp. 975 (S.D. Ala. 1978: "The most crucial issue going to the abandonment question is the lack of supervision over the defendant's use of the mark by the plaintiffs.")

[201] Nordhaus, *Patent-Antitrust Law*, § 54–1.

[202] 1 F. Supp. 850 (EDNY, 1932), *affirmed per curiam*, 66 F.2d 1013 (1933).

Whether the quality control to be exercised by the licensor over the sublicensee may be achieved by delegating this duty to an authorized agent or a third party, as it is in pure licensing situations, has not been settled. It can be argued that an owner's delegation of the duty to supervise quality control creates "privity of contract" between the owner and the end user of the intellectual property right through the concept of agency. Case law is not well settled on just how often inspections and reviews of samples must take place to show that the level of quality control exercised is adequate.

In general, parties to sublicensing arrangements should be aware that the courts will focus on their activities in addition to the rights and obligations set forth in license or sublicense arrangements when deciding issues arising from a contractual relationship. The parties' actions can lead to implicit extensions or terminations of rights under the agreement.[203]

(b) Contract Interpretations and the Courts.   On issues that arise from sublicensing intellectual property rights, many courts base their resolution on contract rather than trademark or patent law.[204] Although it appears that no reported sublicensing case has yet discussed the issue of whether contract law is controlling, the value of a trademark right may be jeopardized and a court of law may refuse to enforce a sublicense agreement that lacks sufficient "privity of contract" between parties. For example, A, a licensor, enters into an agreement with B, a licensee, to use a trademark and sublicense another, C, without the requirement for approval by A. Thereafter, B enters into an agreement with C without obtaining the consent or approval of A. Accordingly, C is now using A's trademark or patent without an express grant or the consent of A. Furthermore, A may not even be aware that C exists. It is possible that a court may interpret the sublicense agreement as appointing B as A's agent to bind A to C. However, failure to execute a written agreement may lead to ambiguities with respect to obligations and undertakings of A, B, and C and might prevent recoveries by A against C should claims be filed.

A prudent owner of intellectual property should be contractually bound to the end user of the sublicensed right. Otherwise, the property right could be further jeopardized by making the source of the right even more remote from the property owner.

---

[203] See, e.g., *Yamamoto & Co. (America) Inc. v. Victor United, Inc.*, 219 U.S.P.Q. 968 (1982).
[204] See *Silver-Star Enterprises, Inc. v. Aday et al.*, 218 USPQ 142.

CHAPTER 11

AVAILABLE REMEDIES FOR DISPUTE RESOLUTION IN INTERNATIONAL AND U.S. TRADEMARK LICENSES

David Bressman, Esq.

The Donna Karan Company
New York, New York

Theodore C. Max, Esq.

Nancy M. Hirsch, Esq.

Phillips, Nizer, Benjamin, Krim & Ballon
New York, New York

A trademark license agreement should be drafted to anticipate and forestall potential disputes between licensor and licensee. This chapter discusses areas of likely dispute between licensor and licensee, basic drafting suggestions to avoid them and remedies available for their resolution.

11.1 FOCAL POINTS IN DRAFTING A TRADEMARK LICENSE: ANTICIPATING DISPUTES

(a) Quality Control of Licensed Products. A trademark owner has "an affirmative duty . . . to take reasonable measures to detect and prevent misleading uses of [its] trademark."[1] As a result, a trademark license must specifically provide a licensor with approval rights over the licensed product. The trademark owner is in the position to ensure that quality standards are maintained and that the best interests of the public are protected.[2] If the licensor fails to maintain requisite quality control, the trademark may be construc-

---

[1] *Dawn Donut Co. v. Hart's Food Stores, Inc.*, 267 F.2d 358, 366 (2d Cir. 1959). *See also Gorenstein Enters., Inc. v. Quality Care–USA, Inc.*, 874 F.2d 431 (7th Cir. 1989); *Bon Mathusalem & Matusa, Inc. v. Ron Matusalem, Inc.*, 872 F.2d 1547 (11th Cir 1989); *Shiela's Shine Prods., Inc. v. Sheila Shine, Inc.*, 486 F.2d 114 (5th Cir. 1973); *Franchised Stores of New York, Inc. v. Winter*, 394 F.2d 664 (2d Cir. 1968); *Denison Mattress Factory v. Spring-Air Co.*, 308 F.2d 403 (5th Cir. 1962).

[2] *Susser v. Carvel Corp.*, 332 F.2d 505 (2d Cir.), *cert. granted*, 379 U.S. 885 (1964), *cert. dismissed*, 381 U.S. 125 (1965).

tively abandoned and subject to cancellation.[3] The reason is that such failure may cause a trademark to lose its significance as an indication of origin.[4] It also is the trademark owner's prerogative to determine what grade or quality of product may be sold under the trademark[5] but it is not necessary that the trademark owner manufacture the product.[6] The trademark owner need only be responsible for the approval of samples of the licensed product.[7] If a licensee could freely decide what goods may be marketed under a given trademark, the trademark's very identity would be undermined severely and its value likewise would be diminished.[8]

(b) Specification of Licensed Goods, Services, Technology, and Rights.   A key clause in any trademark license is the "grant clause," which specifies the scope of the license, including the nature of the goods or services licensed under the trademark. The grant not only defines the goods or services for which the licensor will be paid a royalty (and which accordingly will be included in the computation of gross sales in computing royalties), but also determines what is not licensed. Any rights that are not specifically licensed are, by implication, reserved by the trademark owner. Moreover, any use of a mark for a purpose not granted in the license constitutes an infringement.[9] It is for this reason that the grant clause should be drafted with great care to define the rights granted and retain the rights reserved.

Frequently, licensors specify by classification the trademark rights that have been licensed and define what is meant by "goods" or "services" in the license.[10] The grant

[3] *Gorenstein*, supra at 1. *Power Test Petroleum Distribs., Inc. v. Calc. Gas, Inc.*, 754 F.2d 91 (2d Cir. 1985); *Stock Pot Rest., Inc. v. Stockpot, Inc.*, 737 F.2d 1576 (Fed Cir. 1984); *Franchised Stores v. Winter*, 394 F.2d 664 (2d Cir. 1968); *Denison Mattress Factory v. Spring-Air Co.*, 308 F.2d 403 (5th Cir. 1962); 15 U.S.C. § 1064. *Amoco Oil Co. v. D.Z. Enters. Inc.*, 607 F. Supp. 595 (E.D.N.Y. 1985).

[4] *Franchised Stores v. Winter*, 394 F.2d 664 (2d Cir. 1968).

[5] *Edward J. Sweeney & Sons, Inc. v. Texaco, Inc.*, 478 F. Supp. 243 (E.D. Pa. 1979), *aff'd*, 637 F.2d 105 (3d Cir. 1980), *cert. denied*, 451 U.S. 911 (1981); see also *Power Test Petroleum Distributors v. Calcu Gas*, 754 F.2d 91 (2d Cir. 1985) (trademark owner alone has the right to place its trademark on gasoline; franchisee could not decide independently that other gas was equivalent); *Redd v. Shell Oil Co.*, 524 F.2d 1054 (10th Cir. 1975), *cert. denied*, 425 U.S. 912 (1976); *Blue Bell Co. v. Frontier Refining Co.*, 213 F.2d 354 (10th Cir. 1954); *Smith v. Mobil Oil Corp.*, 667 F. Supp. 1314 (W.D. Mo. 1987) (although trademark holder may only specify requirements that product must meet, holder is not required to allow anyone who can obtain or produce a passable substitute to market it under the trademark); *Amoco Oil Co. v. D.Z. Enters. Inc.*, 607 F. Supp. 595 (E.D.N.Y. 1985).

[6] *Amoco Oil Co.*, *supra*, n. 3.

[7] *Amoco Oil Co. v. D.Z. Enters. Inc.*, 607 F. Supp. 595 (E.D.N.Y. 1985) (citing *Mendez v. Holt*, 128 U.S. 514 (1888); *Smith v. Mobil Oil Corp.*, 667 F. Supp. 1314 (W.D. Mo. 1987); *Edward J. Sweeney & Sons, Inc.v. Texaco, Inc.*, 478 F. Supp. 243 (E.D. Pa. 1979), *aff'd*, 637 F.2d 105 (3d Cir. 1980), *cert. denied*, 451 U.S. 911 (1981).

[8] *Edward J. Sweeney & Sons, Inc. v. Mission Gas Oil Co., Inc.*, 478 F. Supp. 243 (E.D. Pa. 1979).

[9] *Gilliam v. American Broadcasting Cos., Inc.*, 538 F.2d 14, 21 (2d Cir. 1976); *SAS Inst., Inc. v. S&H Computer Sys., Inc.*, 605 F. Supp. 816 (M.D. Tenn. 1985); *Edward J. Sweeney & Sons, Inc. v. Texaco, Inc.*, 478 F. Supp. 243 (E.D. Pa. 1979), *aff'd*, 637 F.2d 105 (3d Cir. 1980), *cert. denied*, 451 U.S. 911 (1981).

[10] For example, if the license agreement provides for product advertising or promotions by the licensee in association with the sale of the licensed goods or services, care must be taken to extend the grant of license for the trademark to such activities. The license agreement should specify whether sales or distribution of complementary items (for which a nominal fee is often charged) are to be included in the license and, if so, whether they also are to be included within "gross sales" of the licensed product under the license agreement.

clause should specify the nature of the rights conveyed, as well as the name and place of any approved and/or required manufacturing facilities. If possible, the license also should specify any quality standards or procedures that are to govern quality control. The more care given to the grant clause, the less chance there will be of disputes over the scope of rights granted in the license.

(c) Territory of the License.   Another crucial specification in the grant clause is the scope of the licensed territory. A licensor may choose to restrict the area in which the licensee may manufacture and sell the licensed goods. Practically, this may be accomplished in one of three ways: (1) by designating an area or territory of primary responsibility, (2) by inserting a location clause, and (3) by utilizing a pass-over clause.[11]

By designating an area of primary responsibility, a licensor assigns to a licensee a geographic area in which he or she is primarily responsible for exploiting the trademark by selling licensed products.[12] The limitation of a trademark license to a particular country often effectively limits the territory of the license if separate registrations (and licenses) are required in other jurisdictions. Where a license has been granted for a designated territory within a country, the licensee is not necessarily precluded from selling outside the designated territory, but is required to focus sales efforts in the specified area.[13] Such designations of areas of primary responsibility do not offend antitrust laws where the basis for the territorial limitation is motivated by business considerations.[14] In designating areas of primary responsibility, a trademark licensor must base its decision on the need to provide appropriate sales and services to consumers in those territories.

Pass-over clauses require one licensee to pay a fee to another licensee for sales made in the other's territory. In *Response of Carolina, Inc., v. Leasco Response, Inc.,*[15] 15% and 70% pass-over fee royalties payable to the licensor and franchisor, respectively, were held to violate the antitrust laws, because the disparity between the royalties and the actual cost to the competing franchisee was too great and, therefore, anticompetitive intent could be inferred.[16] The lesson for drafters is that pass-over clauses should not work a penalty upon a licensee who wishes to sell in a fellow licensee's area of primary responsibility.

Pass-over payments that are designed to prevent free riding by an out-of-area licensee are permissible when justified.[17] In drafting license agreements, however, the licensor

---

[11] It should be noted that a discussion of territorial clauses necessarily invokes a consideration of antitrust issues. 1 Jerome Gilson, Trademark Protection and Practice § 6.03 [4] (1993). For purposes of this chapter they are referred to summarily and are not discussed in detail.

[12] Gilson, § 6.03[4].

[13] Gilson, § 6.04[4].

[14] *Kaiser v. General Motors Corp.*, 396 F. Supp. 33 (E.D. Pa. 1975), *aff'd*, 530 F.2d 964 (3d Cir. 1976); see also *New York v. Anheuser-Busch, Inc.*, 673 F. Supp. 664 (E.D.N.Y. 1987) (exclusive territory agreement not illegal per se where restraint increased distributor's efficiency within his territory). *Continental T.V., Inc. v. GTE Sylvania, Inc.*, 461 F. Supp. 1046 (N.D. Cal. 1978), *aff'd*, 694 F.2d 1132 (9th Cir. 1982) (location restriction clause that restricted retailer from selling to other locations was a reasonable restraint of trade because its overall effect fostered competition and was one of the less restrictive means by which the manufacturer could strengthen its market position by limiting competition among its retailers).

[15] 537 F.2d 1307 (5th Cir. 1976).

[16] In addition, an internal memo stating that the purpose of the 70% royalty was to discourage franchisees from selling out of their areas bolstered the court's conclusion.

[17] *Ohio-Sealy Mattress Mfg. Co. v. Sealy, Inc.*, 585 F.2d 821 (7th Cir. 1978), *cert. denied*, 440 U.S. 930 (1979); *Superior Bedding Co. v. Serta Assocs., Inc.*, 353 F. Supp. 1143 (N.D. Ill. 1972) (no courts have held pass-over fees per se illegal).

should avoid imposing charges that do more than compensate the invaded licensee for its advertising and promotion of the mark, because excessive charges have been deemed anticompetitive and a barrier to intrabrand competition.[18] A pass-over clause, therefore, should be designed to compensate the invaded licensee for actual increased costs attributable to another licensee's exploitation of its territory. If the fee exacted is equivalent to the invaded licensee's advertising and promotion costs, it will not be deemed punitive and likely will be upheld even where the amount of the pass-over fee imposed makes it impossible for a licensee to profit from sales outside its designated territory.[19]

(d) Best Efforts Clauses. License agreements often contain clauses that require the licensee to use its best efforts to promote and sell the licensed product. As one court has noted, "'Best efforts' is a term 'which necessarily takes its meaning from the circumstances.'"[20] A determination of whether a licensee has applied its best efforts usually takes into account the licensee's abilities and the opportunities it created or faced.[21] The analysis is not restricted to a licensee's financial ability but may also include the marketing expertise and experience of the average, prudent licensee in that field.[22] For example, in *Bloor v. Falstaff Brewing Corp.*,[23] it was held that the licensee did not use reasonable efforts to promote and maintain a high volume of sales of Ballantine brand products in light of the distributor's capabilities and its prior merchandising of like products. Similarly, in *Perma Research & Development Co. v. Singer Co.*,[24] best efforts under a patent assignment were judged according to the assignee's financial and business capabilities.

Consequently, care should be taken in drafting the best efforts clause to reflect the extent of the licensee's expertise with the licensed product or service. A best efforts clause should set forth, in definite and certain terms, every material element of the bargain with a clear set of guidelines against which the parties' best efforts can be measured.[25]

A best efforts clause may be subject to an attack on grounds of vagueness where the license is silent on performance. Performance required by the best efforts clause may be either expressly set forth in the contract or implied from the circumstances. Where, however, a license contains a "best efforts" clause, but no objective criteria from which best efforts may be discerned, the clause may be held to be void because of vagueness.[26]

The marketing of competing brands by an exclusive distributor does not constitute a breach of a best efforts clause in and of itself.[27] Where the licensee's distribution of a

[18] *Ohio-Sealy Mattress Mfg. Co. v. Sealy, Inc.*, 585 F.2d 821 (7th Cir. 1978).

[19] See, e.g., *Superior Bedding Co. v. Serta Assocs., Inc.*, 353 F. Supp. 1143 (N.D. Ill. 1972)

[20] *Bloor v. Falstaff Brewing Corp.*, 454 F. Supp. 258, 266 (S.D.N.Y. 1978), *aff'd*, 601 F.2d 609 (2d Cir. 1979) (quoting *Perma Research & Development Co. v. Singer Co.*, 308 F. Supp. 743, 748 [S.D.N.Y. 1970]); see also *Polyglycoat Corp. v. C.P.C. Distributors, Inc.*, 534 F. Supp. 200 (S.D.N.Y. 1982).

[21] In re Gulf Cities Svce. Tender Offer Litig., 725 F. Supp. 712 (S.D.N.Y. 1989); *Triple-A Baseball Club Assocs. v. Northeastern Baseball*, 655 F. Supp. 513 (D. Me 1987), *rev'd on other grounds*, 832 F2d 214 (1st Cir. 1987), *cert. denied*, 485 U.S. 935 (1988). *Bloor*, at n.19.

[22] *Bloor*, at n.19.

[23] 454 F. Supp. 258 (S.D.N.Y. 1978), *aff'd*, 601 F.2d 609 (2d Cir. 1979).

[24] 308 F. Supp. 743 (S.D.N.Y. 1970).

[25] *Pinnacle Books, Inc. v. Harlequin Enterps. Ltd.*, 519 F. Supp. 118 (S.D.N.Y. 1981); *Cross Properties, Inc. v. Brook Realty Co.*, 430 N.Y.S.2d 820 (2d Dep't 1980).

[26] *Pinnacle Books, Inc. v. Harlequin Enterps. Ltd.*, 519 F. Supp. 118 (S.D.N.Y. 1981).

[27] *Joyce Beverages of New York, Inc. v. Royal Crown Cola Co.*, 555 F. Supp. 271 (S.D.N.Y. 1983). *Polyglycoat Corp. v. C.P.C. Distributors, Inc.*, 534 F. Supp. 200 (S.D.N.Y. 1982) (citing *Parev Prods. Co. v. I. Rokeach & Sons, Inc.*, 124 F.2d 147 (2d Cir. 1941)).

competitive line of products results in giving preference to a competing brand with regard to shelf space, however, a breach of the best efforts clause has been found.[28]

(e) Restrictions upon Assignment.   Trademark licenses customarily contain prohibitions against assignment by the licensee.[29] Consent of a licensor usually is required prior to an assignment, because the licensor has the right and obligation to evaluate the character, reputation, business acumen, and dependability of those to whom it lends its name.[30] In fact, where a trademark licensor fails to exercise such control, it is in peril of forfeiting its trademark rights.[31] Drafters should be careful, however, not to condition the grant of a license upon the licensee's agreement not to deal with the licensor's competitors. Such a restriction may be construed as an illegal exclusive dealing arrangement.[32]

Another type of clause that is often featured in a license in lieu of a prohibition on assignments is the right of first refusal to take an assignment of the license.[33] Where a legitimate right of first refusal is exercised in a discriminatory fashion, however, this clause, too, may be deemed anticompetitive.[34]

(f) Royalty Clauses, Guaranteed Minimum Royalties, and Quotas.   The royalty clause is crucial in that it sets forth the means by which the parties agree to compensation for the use of the licensed trademark. As this clause may often become a subject of controversy once the license has been granted, it is important that the parties clearly set forth the royalty scheme, including any guaranteed minimum royalties or quotas.

A license agreement may confer upon the licensor the right to cancel the license if the licensee fails to maintain particular sales levels or pay guaranteed minimum royalties over a finite period of time.[35] Both parties should make sure that the license carefully sets forth the conditions and circumstances under which royalties will be computed and paid and ensures that they are not excessive in light of projected sales.[36] In addition, the terms of guaranteed minimum royalties must be clearly set forth.[37]

---

[28] Polyglycoat Corp., *supra*. (Other factors considered in the court's decision were the licensee's attempt to sell other competing products to established customers of the licensor's products, and its plan to use advertising methods developed by the licensor for the competing product.)

[29] *Superior Bedding Co. v. Serta Assocs., Inc.*, 353 F. Supp. 1143 (N.D. Ill. 1972).

[30] *Seligson v. Plum Tree, Inc.*, 361 F. Supp. 748 (E.D. Pa. 1973).

[31] *Dawn Donut Co. v. Hart's Food Stores, Inc.*, 267 F.2d 358 (2d Cir. 1959); *R.C.W. Supervisor*, 220 F. Supp. 453; *Superior Bedding Co. v. Serta Assocs., Inc.*, 353 F. Supp. 1143 (N.D. Ill. 1972); 15 U.S.C. § 1055 *et seq.*

[32] *Satellite Financial Planning Corp. v. First Nat'l Bank of Wilmington*, 633 F. Supp. 386 (D. Del. 1986).

[33] *Ohio-Sealy Mattress Mfg. Co. v. Sealy, Inc.*, 585 F.2d 821 (7th Cir. 1978), *cert. denied*, 440 U.S. 930 (1979); *Satellite Financial Planning Corp. v. First Nat'l Bank*, 633 F. Supp. 386 (D. Del.), *modified in part*, 643 F. Supp. 449 (D. Del. 1986).

[34] *Ohio-Sealy Mattress Mfg. Co. v. Sealy, Inc.*, 585 F.2d 821 (7th Cir. 1978).

[35] *Heaton Distributing Co. v. Union Tank Car Co.*, 387 F.2d 477 (8th Cir. 1967).

[36] The license should specify the accounting procedures to be followed and the method by which sales, returns, and shipments are to be calculated. If this is not done, issues may arise in the context of a dispute concerning the amount of royalties or whether minimum sales necessary for renewal have been reached. Consequently, the parties should agree in advance as to the method and procedure for the accounting of sales.

[37] In licensing disputes, licensees may claim that a licensor's failure with regard to trademark enforcement and policing of infringing or counterfeit goods has led to an inability to meet minimum sales or quotas for renewal of the license. To avoid such disputes the terms and conditions with regard to such assistance by the licensor should be set forth explicitly.

A trademark license may require the payment of royalties by the licensee in a variety of forms.[38] A royalty may be paid in a lump sum upon execution of the license agreement, as a percentage of sales, or as a fixed amount for each licensed product sold. A percentage royalty that decreases as sales increase is useful in creating a sales incentive for the licensee. In addition, a license may provide for the payment of a guaranteed minimum royalty annually to ensure that the licensor is compensated adequately for the use of the trademark. Further, a licensor may require royalties to be paid for products sold by the licensee, which do not bear the trademark. Moreover, as in a franchise situation, where the licensor provides organizational or management services in addition to licensing its trademark, the licensor may require royalties on total sales as a measure of the value of the relationship.[39]

Another royalty-related clause gives the licensor the right to an accounting or audit. Such a clause provides the licensor with the means to ensure that royalty payments are correct. Because an audit or accounting may lead to disputes, the audit provision should be drafted carefully so as to anticipate and avoid them. One way in which this may be done is to create a threshold discrepancy figure, up to which the costs of the audit are borne by the licensor. This discourages frequent unnecessary audits or audits that may be a way of harassing an unfavored licensee. Another way to desensitize the audit process is to name a neutral auditor in whom both parties have confidence. This can lessen the otherwise confrontational nature of license audits when conducted by the licensor's chosen auditors. A further means of avoiding difficulty lies in the prudent exercise of the audit provision. If a licensor audits a licensee early or frequently in a relationship, this may undermine trust in the licensor-licensee relationship and precipitate other disputes. If the audit provision is fixed as to frequency and its operation is exercised with care, unnecessary disputes may be avoided.

(g) Term of License Agreements and Conditions for Renewal. The license term and the conditions for renewal should be stated unambiguously. If an agreement does not specify an expiration date, the contract is likely terminable at will.[40] License agreements may last for a certain number of years, after which they may be renewed on a yearly basis, subject to termination by either the licensor or licensee as a result of default or on other enumerated grounds.[41] Agreements commonly provide the licensee with an option to renew the agreement conditioned on the licensee's sales figures.[42] Licensors should be cautioned that any granting of trademark rights in perpetuity may be interpreted as equivalent to an assignment of those rights, in which case the licensor will lose ownership of its trademark.[43]

The conditions for renewal should be set forth with precision. If renewal is conditioned upon sales figures, the exact means by which such figures will be calculated (and whether any discounts or adjustments should apply) should be agreed to between the parties and

---

[38] *Ohio-Sealy v. Sealy*, 686 F.2d 821 (7th Cir. 1978).

[39] See, e.g., *Ohio-Sealy v. Sealy*, 585 F.2d 821 (7th Cir. 1978) (Sealy provided uniform product specifications, national advertising, product development services, engineering assistance, sales training, etc. to its licensees); see also *Zenith Radio Corp. v. Hazeltine Research, Inc.*, 395 U.S. 100 (1969).

[40] Gilson, § 6.03 (15) (citing Corbin, *Contracts*, § 96).

[41] Gilson, § 6.03 (15).

[42] Gilson, § 6.03 (15).

[43] Gilson, § 6.03 (15) (citing *Ex parte Teca Corp.*, 117 U.S.P.Q. 367 (Comm'r 1958)).

set forth in the license. In addition, there should be provisions stipulating what would occur if the licensee were to fail to meet the necessary conditions for renewal.[44] Such terms often include a sell-off period and rules governing reduction of the price of the licensed goods (for example, a close-out sale), which could affect the reputation and value of the mark.

(h) A Licensee is Estopped from Challenging the Licensed Trademark.   Under the licensee-estoppel doctrine, the existence of a contractual relationship between a licensor and licensee constitutes a bar to a licensee's challenge of the validity or ownership of a licensed trademark.[45] American courts are split, however, as to whether this estoppel survives termination of the license agreement.[46] Some courts have held the view, which is prevalent internationally, that the former licensee may challenge the validity of the licensor's trademark, based on facts arising after the termination or expiration of the license.[47] Other courts have held that a license agreement works a complete estoppel against all subsequent challenges to the licensor's trademark.[48]

(i) Non-Compete Clauses.   License agreements often contain restrictive covenants proscribing the licensee's working for a competitor or acting as a licensee for a competing trademark within a designated geographic area and time. Despite the fact that non-compete covenants, by their very nature, restrain trade to some extent,[49] such clauses are generally beyond cavil if they are ancillary to the main business purpose of a lawful license

---

[44] Such provisions often are drafted also to operate in case of a termination of the license as the result of a default on the license.

[45] *Chrysler Motors Corp. v. Alloy Automotive Co., Inc.*, 661 F. Supp. 191 (N.D.Ill. 1987); *Heaton Distri. Co. v. Union Tank Car Co.*, 387 F.2d 477 (8th Cir. 1967); *Smith v. Dental Prods. Co.*, 140 F.2d 140 (7th Cir.), *cert. denied*, 322 U.S. 743 (1944) (where defendant was granted the right to use trademarks on a royalty basis and used them for many years without contesting plaintiff's right, title or ownership, defendant was estopped from claiming title to or ownership in the trademarks); *Seven-Up Bottling Co. v. Seven-Up Co.*, 420 F. Supp. 1246 (E.D. Mo. 1976), *aff'd*, 561 F.2d 1275 (8th Cir. 1977) (plaintiff was estopped from seeking cancellation of trademark registrations and applications on the ground that they were void for being fraudulently retained).

[46] *Professional Golfers Ass'n of America v. Bankers Life & Casualty Co.*, 514 F.2d 665 (5th Cir. 1975).

[47] See, e.g., *Professional Golfers Ass'n of America v. Bankers Life & Casualty Co.*, 514 F.2d 665 (5th Cir. 1975); *Bucky v. Sebo*, 208 F.2d 304 (2d Cir. 1953); *Eskimo Pie Corp. v. National Ice Cream Co.*, 26 F.2d 901 (6th Cir. 1928); *Chrysler Motors Corp. v. Alloy Automotive Co.*, 661 F. Supp. 191 (N.D. Ill. 1987); *Medd v. Boyd Wagner, Inc.*, 132 F. Supp. 399 (N.D. Ohio 1955).

[48] See, e.g., *Heaton Distributing*; *E.F. Pritchard Co. v. Consumers Brewing Co.*, 137 F.2d 512 (6th Cir. 1943), *cert. denied*, 321 U.S. 763 (1944). It is also well accepted that the use of the trademark by a licensee builds up no right in the licensee as against the licensor. *Church of Scientology Int'l v. Elmira Mission Church of Scientology*, 794 F.2d 38 (2d Cir. 1986); *Pike v. Ruby Foo's Den, Inc.*, 232 F.2d 683 (D.C. Cir. 1956). In addition, where a mark is used legitimately by licensees, use of the trademark by the related company will inure to the benefit of the trademark owner. *Franchised Stores v. Winter*, 394 F.2d 664 (2d Cir. 1968).

[49] The antitrust implications are beyond the scope of this chapter and are not discussed in detail. For these purposes it is adequate to note that the federal antitrust laws, with few exceptions, have not been applied to these types of restrictive covenants. See e.g., *Capital Temporaries, Inc. v. Olsten Corp.*, 506 F.2d 658 (2d Cir. 1974); *Bradford v. New York Times Co.*, 501 F.2d 51 (2d Cir. 1974); *Ungar v. Dunkin Donuts*, 68 F.R.D. 65 (E.D. Pa. 1975) (citing Blake, *Employee Agreements Not to Compete*, 73 Harv. L. Rev. 625 (1960); Goldschmid, *Antitrust's Neglected Stepchild: A Proposal for Dealing with Restrictive Covenants Under Federal Law*, 73 Colum. L. Rev 1193 (1973)).

agreement and are necessary to protect the parties' legitimate property interests.[50] Any limitations with respect to the time, geographic area, and product scope of such covenants must be reasonable.[51] A noncompete covenant will be judged not only according to its terms, but also by the parties' course of dealing and the licensor's enforcement of the covenant.[52]

(j) Choice of Forum. License agreements may indicate a choice of forum, that is, the particular court or tribunal before which a dispute shall be litigated. Such clauses, when subject to dispute, are generally enforced.[53] Before a venue provision can be disregarded, it must be established that enforcement would significantly inconvenience and prejudice the complaining party.[54]

(k) Genuine Goods and Gray-Market Goods. Gray-market goods are products legitimately made by a foreign manufacturer in a foreign country under a license, which are then imported into the United States and sold in competition with goods manufactured in the United States under a license for the identical trademark.[55] A number of courts have concluded that the mere importation of foreign gray-market goods that compete with the goods of an exclusive domestic licensee does not constitute trademark infringement, because "trademark law generally does not reach the sale of genuine goods bearing a true mark even though such sale is without the mark owner's consent."[56] It is reasoned that so long as the competing goods are genuine and bear the actual mark, there can be no confusion as to the origin of the goods.[57]

Confusion in this instance, however, is not strictly limited to confusion of origin but includes any kind of confusion.[58] Of particular relevance to gray-market goods is the likelihood of confusion as to sponsorship, that is, the identity of the company that stands behind the quality of the licensed goods.[59] Therefore, even though there may be no actual confusion as to the source or origin of genuine goods, there may still be confusion as to

---

[50] *Lektro-Vend Corp. v. Vendo Co.*, 660 F.2d 255 (7th Cir. 1981) *cert. denied*, 455 U.S. 921 (1982); *United States v. Addyston Pipe & Steel*, 85 F. 271 (6th Cir. 1898), *aff'd as modified*, 175 U.S. 211 (1899).

[51] *Snap-On Tools Corp. v. Federal Trade Commission*, 321 F.2d 825 (7th Cir. 1963).

[52] *Lektro-Vend Corp. v. Vendo Co.*, 660 F.2d 255 (7th Cir. 1981) (a non-compete clause enforceable despite the fact that the clause was overly broad where the defendant sought to enforce only reasonable time, space, and product limits).

[53] *Scherk v. Alberto-Culver Co.*, 417 U.S. 506 (1974); *Brown v. Gingiss Int'l, Inc.*, 360 F. Supp. 1042 (E.D. Wis. 1973).

[54] *Brown v. Gingiss Int'l, Inc.*, 360 F. Supp. 1042 (E.D. Wisc. 1973).

[55] *Vivitar Corp. v. United States*, 761 F.2d 1552, 1555 (Fed. Cir. 1985), *cert. denied*, 474 U.S. 1055 (1986); *Dial Corp. v. Encina Corp.*, 643 F. Supp. 951 (S.D. Fla. 1986).

[56] *K Mart Corp. v. Cartier, Inc.*, 486 U.S. 281 (1988); *Weil Ceramics & Glass, Inc. v. Dash*, 878 F.2d 659 (3d Cir.), *cert. denied*, 493 U.S. 853 (1989); *NEC Electronics v. CAL Circuit Abco*, 810 F.2d 1506, 1509 (9th Cir.), *cert. denied*, 484 U.S. 851 (1987); *Olympus Corp. v. United States*, 792 F.2d 315 (2d Cir. 1986), *cert. denied*, 486 U.S. 1042 (1988); *Monte Carlo Shirt, Inc. v. Daewoo Int'l Corp.*, 707 F.2d 1054 (9th Cir. 1983); *Parfums Stern, Inc. v. U.S. Customs Svce.*, 575 F. Supp. 416 (S.D. Fla 1983).

[57] *NEC Electronics, Supra*; *Monte Carlo Shirt, Supra*.

[58] *Dallas Cowboys Cheerleaders, Inc. v. Pussycat Cinema, Ltd.*, 604 F.2d 200 (2d Cir. 1979); *Syntex Labs, Inc. v. Norwich Pharmacal Co.*, 437 F.2d 566 (2d Cir. 1971); *Disenos Artisticos e Industriales, S.A. v. Work*, 676 F. Supp. 1254 (E.D.N.Y. 1987).

[59] *Disenos Artisticos*; *Weil Ceramics*, 618 F. Supp. at 705; *Bell & Howell*, 548 F. Supp. at 1063.

their sponsorship.[60] Furthermore, a trademark owner has the right to control the quality of the goods manufactured and sold under its mark. Thus, the courts have held that confusion may arise if the unauthorized sale of licensed goods threatens quality control and genuineness.[61] Such is often the case when the goods manufactured and licensed abroad differ from the goods sold under the United States license.[62] This is sometimes the case where the licensed product is created from indigenous ingredients,[63] locally grown or manufactured.

A foreign trademark license does not necessarily immunize such goods from trademark liability. In *Original Appalachian Artworks*, the Second Circuit held that foreign gray-market "Cabbage Patch" dolls did not constitute "genuine goods," because they differed from U.S. Cabbage Patch dolls and were not authorized for sale here even though the goods carried the authorized trademark and were manufactured under a license.[64] Similarly, shoes made by a Brazilian company under contract with El Greco and sold to Shoe World without El Greco's prior quality inspection as required by contract, constituted trademark infringement.[65] The court reasoned that customers would be deceived into thinking that the trademark owner had approved the shoes for sale: "The actual quality of the goods is irrelevant; it is the control of quality that a trademark owner is entitled to maintain."[66]

However, where the goods are identical and both the foreign and United States trademarks are owned and licensed by the same entity, or the foreign and domestic trademark owners are parent and subsidiary companies (or otherwise are subject to common control), the importation of competing gray-market goods will be permitted.[67] A

---

[60] *Disenos Artisticos, Supra.*

[61] *El Greco Leather Prods. Co. v. Shoe World, Inc.*, 806 F.2d 392, 395 (2d Cir. 1986), *cert. denied*, 484 U.S. 817 (1987); *Matrix Essential, Inc. v. Emporium Drug Mart, Inc.*, 756 F. Supp. 280, 282 (W.D. La. 1991), *aff'd*, 988 F.2d 587 (5th Cir. 1993); *Adolph Coors Co. v. A. Genderson & Sons, Inc.*, 486 F. Supp. 131, 135 (D. Colo. 1980).

[62] *Ferrero U.S.A., Inc. v. Ozak Trading, Inc.*, 753 F. Supp. 1240, 1241 n.1 (D.N.J. 1991), *aff'd*, 935 F.2d 1280 (3d Cir. 1991); *Original Appalachian Artworks, Inc v. Granada Electronics, Inc.*, 816 F.2d 68 (2d Cir.), *cert. denied*, 484 U.S. 847 (1987) (the U.S. trademark owner for Cabbage Patch dolls enjoined the importation of gray-market goods bearing the trademark manufactured abroad under license where it was likely that consumers would be confused and the owner would suffer a loss of goodwill); see also *Dial Corp. v. Encina Corp.*, 643 F. Supp. 951 (S.D. Fla. 1986) (the United States trademark holder sued the importer of Dial soap manufactured in Greece by a company under a Dial license for infringement. The foreign manufactured soap was not identical to the soap manufactured in the United States: it had a different fragrance, was not a deodorant soap, and was not labeled according to FDA requirements. The court held that the plaintiff had stated a cause of action); *Osawa & Co. v. B & H Photo*, 589 F. Supp. 1163 (S.D.N.Y. 1984).

[63] *Societe Des Produits Nestle, S.A. v. Casa Helvetia, Inc.*, 982 F.2d 633, 636 (1st Cir. 1992); *Lever Bros. Co. v. U.S.*, 796 F. Supp. 1 (D. D.C. 1992), *aff'd*, 981 F.2d 1330 (D.C. Cir. 1993).

[64] 816 F.2d at 73; see also *Lever Bros., Co. v. United States*, 877 F.2d 101 (D.C. Cir. 1989) (where a third party acquired cleaning products produced in United Kingdom and imported them to the United States over the objections of the United States affiliate and domestic trademark proprietor, importation constituted infringement because goods differed materially from goods produced in the United States); *Ferrero, U.S.A., Inc. v. Ozak Wodng., Inc.*, 19 U.S. P.Q. 2d 1463 (3d Cir 1991) (designated unpublished), (importation of "tic tacs®" manufactured in the United Kingdom differed materially from domestic tic tacs®); *Pepsico, Inc. v. Nostalgia Prods. Corp.*, 18 U.S.P.Q.2d 1404 (N.D. Ill. 1991) (importation of Pepsi products bottled in Mexico which differed materially from domestic Pepsi products constituted trademark infringement and unfair competition).

[65] *El Greco Leather Prods. Co. v. Shoe World*, 806 F.2d 392 (2d Cir. 1986).

[66] *El Greco Leather Prods. Co.* at 395.

[67] *K Mart Corp. v. Cartier, Inc.*, 486 U.S. 281 (1988).

trademark infringement action will not succeed, because there is no loss of any bargained-for benefits when there is common control of the trademark, inasmuch as the trademark licensor still benefits from profits received from a subsidiary as part of the overall corporate entity.[68] Moreover, where the goods are identical, there is no consumer confusion and goodwill remains unscathed because consumers receive what they expect to receive.[69]

(l) Termination of Trademark License Agreements.   A trademark licensor may terminate a license for breach of contract where the licensee sells, under a trademark owner's mark, a product that is not made or approved by the trademark owner.[70] Thus, in a case where a franchisee sold nonfranchisor gasoline under a franchisor trademark, the franchisor was justified in terminating the agreement.[71]

Furthermore, a franchise relationship may impose a duty upon the franchisor not to act arbitrarily in terminating a franchise.[72] The franchisor-franchisee relationship requires the parties to deal with each other in good faith, in a commercially reasonable manner.[73]

Termination may also be conditioned upon a variety of events, including a default in the terms of the agreement, that is, upon failure to pay royalties, failure to meet a delivery schedule, failure to meet quality standards, or upon an event unrelated to the license but bearing on the licensee's ability to perform under the agreement, such as insolvency or bankruptcy or a failure to secure necessary licenses or governmental authorization.[74] As mentioned earlier, other causes of termination may be the expiration of a term of years or the failure of a licensee to meet certain sales figures or quotas. Whatever the conditions of termination, they should be defined with great precision inasmuch as wrongful termination is one of the more common claims asserted against the licensor by the licensee.

Unauthorized use of a trademark by a formerly authorized dealer generates an especially strong risk of consumer confusion.[75] When a licensor terminates a trademark license agreement, any subsequent use of the trademark by the licensee constitutes

---

[68] *Weil Ceramics & Glass, Inc. v. Dash*, 878 F.2d 659 (3d Cir.), *cert. denied*, 493 U.S. 853 (1989); *NEC Electronics v. Cal Circuit Abco*, 810 F.2d 1506 (9th Cir. 1987).

[69] *Weil Ceramics & Glass, Inc. v. Dash*, 878 F.2d 659 (3d Cir. 1989).

[70] *Ron Matusalem & Matusa, Inc. v. Ron Matusalem, Inc.*, 872 F.2d 1547 (11th Cir. 1989); *Amoco Oil v. D.Z. Enterprises*, 607 F. Supp. 595 (E.D.N.Y. 1985).

[71] *Haynes v. Exxon Co., U.S.A.*, 512 F. Supp. 543 (E.D. Tenn. 1981).

[72] *Ray v. Lafferty*, 99 F.2d 1379 (1st Cir. 1993), *cert. denied*, 114 S.Ct. 94 (1993); *Arnott v. American Oil Co.*, 609 F.2d 873 (8th Cir. 1979), *cert. denied*, 446 U.S. 918 (1980) (action by a service station dealer alleging that the oil company breached its fiduciary duty to the dealer by terminating the lease without good cause); *Marinielo v. Shell Oil Co.*, 511 F.2d 853 (3d Cir. 1975) (New Jersey law protects franchisees from termination without good cause); *Culligan Int'l Co. v. Culligan Water Conditioning*, 563 F. Supp. 1265 (D. Minn. 1983) (The Minnesota Franchise Act requires a franchisor to give the franchisee specific notice of its delinquencies so the franchisee can have a meaningful opportunity to cure them); *Atlantic Richfield Co. v. Razumic*, 480 Pa. 366, 390 A.2d 736 (1978).

[73] *Larese v. Creamland Dairies, Inc.*, 767 F.2d 716 (10th Cir. 1985); see also *Arnott v. American Oil Co.*, 609 F.2d 873 (8th Cir. 1979) (fiduciary duty inherent in franchise relationship); *Atlantic Richfield v. Razumic*, 390 A.2d 736 (1978) (a franchisor cannot arbitrarily terminate the relationship because it has an obligation to deal in good faith and in a commercially reasonable manner).

[74] *See, e.g., S&R Corp. v. Jiffy Lube International, Inc.*, 968 F.2d 371 (9th Cir 1992).

[75] *Downtowner/Passport Int'l Hotel Corp. v. Norlew, Inc.*, 841 F.2d 214 (8th Cir. 1988); *Burger King Corp. v. Mason*, 710 F.2d 1480 (11th Cir. 1983), *cert. denied*, 465 U.S. 1102 (1984).

infringement.[76] For example, when a hotel operator whose hotel had its franchise revoked nevertheless continued to use licensed items, such as credit card applications, ash trays, key rings, and billing receipts, and continued to display a sign outside the hotel bearing the franchisor's trademark, a case of infringement was established.[77]

11.2 NONJUDICIAL DISPUTE RESOLUTION

(a) Audit Provisions and Procedures. Although audit provisions and procedures are but one means by which disputes as to the proper royalty may be resolved short of judicial intervention, they can serve as a safety valve for the licensor and licensee on a material licensing issue. Drafted properly, they can establish a quick, inexpensive, efficient, and noncontroversial means of addressing a potentially inflammatory problem.

Audit provisions and procedures should be drafted with this goal in mind. The terms and conditions under which an audit is conducted should be set forth clearly in advance of the actual audit. Consequently, it is generally a good idea to require a written notice and demand for an audit, including provisions for reasonable notice, so that a licensee's business and operations will not be disturbed unnecessarily. In addition, to the extent the parties can agree on a time period in which the audit is to be completed (including the preparation and issuance of an audit report and a response by the licensee), the procedure can be streamlined and protracted disputes over royalty reporting avoided.

(b) Arbitration: Advantages and Disadvantages. Every year, as the costs of litigation throughout the world mushroom, business persons are turning to arbitration, mediation, and other nonjudicial methods of dispute resolution, rather than the courts. Trademark licensing disputes are no exception, and, every day, parties execute licenses containing provisions for arbitration or alternate means of dispute resolution.

The increase of arbitration and alternate means of dispute resolution in trademark licenses is a direct response to the cost of litigation and the delay in obtaining timely determination of the parties' rights. Commercial arbitration generally takes much less time than civil litigation. In fact, most commercial arbitrations involving claims of $1 million or more take less than 18 months from inception to award; smaller claims generally

---

[76] *Original Great American Chocolate Chip Cookie Co., Inc., v. River Valley Cookies, Ltd.*, 970 F.2d 273 (7th Cir. 1992). *Century 21 Real Estate Corp. v. Sandlin*, 846 F.2d 1175 (9th Cir. 1988) (a former franchisee's use of the word "Century" for a real estate business after the termination of a Century 21 franchise constituted trademark infringement and unfair competition); *Ramada Inns, Inc. v. Gadsden Motel Co.*, 804 F.2d 1562 (11th Cir. 1986) (a licensee infringed a trademark in disregarding that part of the termination notice that required the licensee to remove any materials identifying the motel as a Ramada Inn); *Church of Scientology Int'l v. Elmira Mission Church of Scientology*, 794 F.2d 38 (2d Cir. 1986); *Bill Blass Ltd. v. SAZ Corp.*, 751 F.2d 152 (3d Cir. 1984); *United States Jaycees v. Philadelphia Jaycees*, 639 F.2d 134 (3d Cir. 1981) (Continued use of the designation "Jaycees" after the expiration of the license constiututed infringement); *Smith v. Dental Prods. Co.*, 140 F.2d 140 (7th Cir.), *cert. denied*, 322 U.S. 743 (1944) (where under a licensing agreement a plaintiff retained ownership of the trademark, the defendant who used the mark after cancellation of the agreement was liable for infringement); *Oleg Cassini, Inc. v. Couture Coordinates, Inc.*, 297 F. Supp. 821 (S.D.N.Y. 1969) (any use of a trademark after expiration of the license constitutes infringement). *Tanning Research Laboratories, Inc. v. Worldwide Import & Export Corp.*, 803 F. Supp. 606 (E.D.N.Y. 1992) (Manufacturer's importation of inferior products constituted counterfeiting where license had been terminated ten years earlier).

[77] *Downtowner/Passport Int'l Hotel Corp v. Norlew, Inc.*, 841 F.2d 214 (8th Cir 1988).

take less time.[78] One reason that arbitrations tend to be less time-consuming is the limitation of discovery to an exchange of documents and the avoidance of prearbitration depositions and motion practice.

The advantages of arbitration are the lower costs, expedited by a resolution, and the fact that the arbitrators tend to be persons familiar with the business issues at hand. This last factor often can save time as the parties will not have to educate the arbitrator and can focus directly on the issues. In trademark licensing disputes, time is often at a premium; any time during in which the ability to use a trademark is in question is time in which the licensor's ability to exploit the trademark is diminished and the licensee's ability to promote sales of the licensed goods is undermined.[79]

Yet there are also disadvantages to arbitration, the most commonly voiced of which are as follows:

1. The success of an arbitration depends on the experience and knowledge of the arbitrators,
2. Arbitration offers virtually no appeal,
3. There is no discovery in arbitration, and
4. Arbitrators tend to reach compromise results.

Although every participant's experience with arbitration may be different, there is validity to each of these concerns. This does not mean, however, that arbitration, generally, does not provide a less expensive and more efficient alternative to civil litigation.

The knowledge and experience of the arbitrator is key to the efficient and fair resolution of the issues. Thus, if an inexperienced, ineffective, or prejudiced arbitrator is engaged, the process may not operate efficiently at all. A number of organizations offer experienced, trained arbitrators or mediators and, in some cases, former judges who bring to the process their wealth of knowledge and experience. Selection of an arbitrator or mediator can be crucial. Every effort should be made to learn about the arbitrator's background and prior experience with arbitration.

It generally is the case that a decision of an arbitration tribunal may not be appealed unless a party can demonstrate that the result was patently irrational, the outcome of egregious misconduct, or that the arbitration panel lacked subject matter jurisdiction over the claim. However, the absence of appeal has the positive effect of limiting costs and imposing finality on the process. In the courts, a great deal of time and money can be consumed in heated motion practice and on appeals, which can result in a judgment being vacated and remanded for a new trial. Especially where licensing is concerned, the expedited nature of arbitration can avoid the scenario in which a licensor gains a Pyrric court victory confirming the termination of a license after the term of the license has expired.

Discovery generally is not provided for in an arbitration clause, but this does not preclude the parties' agreeing in advance to limited, streamlined discovery. The reason discovery parameters are not ordinarily set forth in an arbitration clause is that one of the positive aspects of arbitration is the minimization of costs and delays caused by full-scale,

---

[78] B. Hoeniger, *Commercial Arbitration Handbook* 1–2 (1992).

[79] In addition, if a licensee is terminated prior to the expiration of the license, this may have an adverse impact on the licensee's ability to secure other licenses in the future.

adversarial discovery. The absence of discovery can be a disadvantage for some parties; however, if careful records are kept during the course of the license, such records will not only assist with the prosecution of defense of a claim, but can give that party a distinct advantage over its adversary where discovery is limited.

Arbitration is different from litigation both procedurally and substantively. Arbitration results tend to be based less on legal precedent and more on equity, justice, and commercial reasonableness. Consequently, the result is usually not so one-sided and may take into consideration the strengths and weaknesses of each party's case in arriving at a decision.

The perceived drawbacks of arbitration may be reduced by using certain modified arbitration or nonadjudicative alternate dispute resolution devices. For example, there is the last-offer or "baseball" arbitration, wherein the parties agree in advance to the extent of the award which (1) the claimant is willing to accept under the circumstances and (2) the respondent is willing to pay. At the conclusion of the arbitration, the arbitrator must award the relief that most closely approximates the award that the arbitrator would have awarded independently. The key attribute of this form of arbitration is that it forces the parties to evaluate critically the strengths and weaknesses of their cases. This type of arbitration generally is most advantageous where the major issues concern the extent of damages, as opposed to liability. Where liability is hotly disputed, baseball arbitration may render widely disparate potential awards, thereby defeating an attempt to circumscribe the extent of awards. Another means of limiting the extent of an award is for the parties to agree in advance as to the ceiling and floor of the amount of an award. This has the effect of limiting the potential exposure of the parties and avoiding unduly excessive awards.

Mediation, mini-trials, and other similar practices afford the parties a means of settling a dispute, short of litigation. Recently, the International Trademark Association (INTA) and the CPR Legal Program launched a program to give companies access to a roster of United States trademark panelists to serve as third party neutrals to resolve trademark, trade dress and often unfair competition disputes through nonbinding alternative dispute resolution.[80] In mediation, the mediator acts as a facilitator of settlement. The mediator does this first by earning the confidence of the parties and then using his or her skills to bring the parties to an agreement.[81] To make mediation effective, the parties must be willing to settle their dispute amicably and the mediator must have the knowledge, training, experience, and ability to convince each party that a proposed settlement is in its best interest. An arbitrator cannot usually serve as a mediator, unless both parties waive an objection to the arbitrator taking part in settlement negotiations.

Mini-trials generally are an abbreviated form of litigation before an adjudicative body. The process typically consists of an adversarial exchange by counsel (which includes critical documents, testimony, and/or evidence) in the presence of representatives of the

---

[80] The INTA-CPR program seeks to build alternative dispute resolution into contracts and hopes that this process will be utilized to resolve a wide range of disputes, including trademarks, source marks and trade names, false advertising claims, trade dress, unfair trade practices, and the licensing and franchising of trademarks. A key feature of this program is the selection and training of distinguished trademark attorneys nominated by INTA. A reference book, *ADR in Trademark and Unfair Competition Disputes*, is available from INTA.

[81] For an insightful text on the role of a mediator, see R. Carlson, *Business Mediation: What You Need to Know* (American Arbitration Assoc. 1987); see also *Alternate Dispute Resolution: An APR Primer* (ASA—).

parties who are authorized to settle. Following presentations and rebuttal, the representatives meet and confer in an attempt to settle. If they are unable to do so, the administrator generally will meet with each of the representatives to discuss an evaluation of the issues raised at the mini-trial and the likely outcome of the case. If a settlement is not forthcoming, the administrator will render a settlement recommendation. A judicial variation of the mini-trial, the summary jury trial, has been used in federal and state courts. In a summary jury trial, the parties give a summary presentation of their cases to a jury and the jury renders a nonbinding verdict. This approach is a less expensive alternative to a trial, which provides the parties with a realistic snapshot of the potential outcome of the case before a typical jury in that district. In a summary jury trial, the process tends to be more formal and at the behest of the judge. As a result, the Federal Rules of Evidence are usually followed. In a mini-trial, the parties generally may set the procedures and the rules to be followed. Of course, as is the case with any alternative dispute resolution forum agreed to between the parties, the procedures and applicable rules of evidence may be controlled by the arbitration clause or otherwise set by the parties in advance of the litigation.

11.3 JUDICIAL DISPUTE RESOLUTION

Where there is no arbitration clause in a license agreement or the subject matter of the dispute is not within the scope of the arbitration clause, the parties may avail themselves of judicial dispute resolution. In some instances, this avenue may prove to be more direct and expedient than arbitration. In addition, in cases where equitable relief is necessary, the courts may be utilized in conjunction with arbitration to obtain injunctive relief before the arbitration is heard or even before arbitrators are appointed.[82] Although an entire book could be devoted to this topic, the discussion in this chapter will serve to identify the salient issues regarding judicial dispute resolution and the types of relief that courts afford to licensors.

(a) **Jurisdiction and Venue Selection.**   In contemplating the commencement of a lawsuit, care should be given to selecting the court and jurisdiction in which the action is commenced. Principles of *forum non conveniens* (see the following subsection[c]) as well as practical concerns such as legal cost, substantive law, and the availability of evidence and witnesses should all be considered before filing an action for trademark infringement or unfair competition. Indeed, the commencement of an action in one state or federal jurisdiction versus another (or one nation versus another) can impact critically on the pace of the litigation and the law of the case and, therefore, the result.

Where a licensor has commenced an action to terminate a license, attention must be given to the local state contract and licensing law. For example, under certain circumstances a licensing relationship that may not fall within the ambit of a franchise under the Federal Trade Commission's franchising trade regulations may fall within the scope of

---

[82] For example, where a licensee is selling licensed trademarked goods following termination of the license, a dispute may require the commencement of an action in federal or state court seeking injunctive relief in anticipation of an arbitration of the issues concerning the termination of the license. This is necessary because arbitration panels are often reluctant to grant injunctive relief.

related state franchise statutes.[83] In addition, differences in case law between jurisdictions may have a significant impact on the possible counterclaims that may be asserted against a licensor seeking termination.[84]

(b) Venue in United States Federal Court.   Section 1391 of Title 28 provides the basis for venue in federal court. Unlike federal actions for copyright and patent infringement, which are governed by a special venue statute,[85] trademark and unfair competition cases governed by the federal venue rules are generally applicable to civil cases. Consequently, the options available to a plaintiff in a trademark or unfair competition action are more restricted.

If the claim for federal jurisdiction is based on diversity of citizenship, venue is proper under § 1391(a) in the federal district court located in the following locations:

1. In the location where any defendant resides, if all defendants reside in the same state, or
2. Where a substantial part of the events or omissions giving rise to the claim occurred, or a substantial part of the property that is subject to the action is located, or
3. Where defendants are subject to personal jurisdiction.

In 1990, § 1391(b) was amended so that venue in any district "in which the claim arises" now includes a district "in which a substantial part of the events or omissions giving rise to the claim occurred." This raises an issue as to whether the United States Supreme Court

---

[83] Twelve of the 15 states with franchise registration/disclosure laws have adopted regulations impacting relationships that constitute "franchises" within the "marketing plan or system" definition where there is an express or implied contract (written or oral) by which:

   a. A franchisee is granted the right to engage in the business of offering, selling, or distributing goods or services under a marketing plan or system prescribed or suggested in substantial part by a franchisor,
   b. The operation of the business by the franchisee pursuant to any such plan is associated with the franchisor's marks, and
   c. The franchisee is required to pay a fee, directly or indirectly, for the franchise.

See, e.g., West's A.I.C. 23–2–2.5–1(a) (1,2); 23.2–2.7–1(7) (Indiana); West's Ann. Cal. Bus. & Prof. Code §§ 20000 *et seq.* (California); West's RCWA 19.100.010(4) (Washington). Thus, there may be occasions where state reporting requirements may apply even though there was no formal franchise agreement and the parties did not even consider or treat the arrangement a franchise.

[84] Eighteen states in the United States have laws that govern the substantive aspect of the relationship between franchisor and franchisee and the franchisor's ability to terminate or refuse to renew the franchise agreements:

Arkansas	Minnesota
California	Mississippi
Connecticut	Missouri
Delaware	Nebraska
Hawaii	New Jersey
Illinois	South Dakota
Indiana	Virginia
Iowa	Washington
Michigan	Wisconsin

These state laws govern general contractual relationships, which satisfy the state definition of a "franchise" or, in some instances a dealership. There are also state laws that deal with specific industries, such as motor vehicles or petroleum products.

[85] See 28 U.S.C. § 1400.

decision in *Leroy v. Great Western United Corp.*,[86] which held that where a claim arises in several districts, contacts with a particular venue such as availability of witnesses, accessibility of evidence and convenience of the defendant should be balanced. The new statute focuses on "a substantial part of the events or omissions giving rise to the claim" and implies that the underlying events of a lawsuit may occur in more than one district and that the plaintiff may choose one of the several possible districts in which "a substantial part" of the events occurred.[87]

In trademark infringement cases, the courts have held that the location where the wrong takes place includes any district where the infringing goods are produced or where consumer confusion occurs.[88] Thus, a plaintiff may choose between the district where infringing goods are sold or advertised and the district where the infringing goods are produced.[89]

Where there is no diversity of jurisdiction and there is no district in which "substantial events" took place, § 1391(b)(3) may provide a proper venue in "a judicial district in which any defendant may be found, if there is no district in which the action may otherwise be brought." This option generally is not of much use in trademark or unfair competition cases, because a "substantial part of the events" will usually have occurred in more than one district if the goods are widely distributed.

If the defendant is a corporation, it is deemed to reside in any judicial district where it is subject to personal jurisdiction at the time the action is commenced.[90] In other words, § 1391(c) provides that a corporation is deemed to reside in any district in which it can be sued, based on the law of personal jurisdiction.

(c) *Forum Non Conveniens* and 28 U.S.C. § 1404.   *Forum non conveniens* is a legal doctrine whereby an action is transferred to another district "for the convenience of parties and witnesses."[91] An application for transfer based on *forum non conveniens* may be made even where a federal district court has proper venue and personal jurisdiction, but such an application should be made promptly.[92]

A court may *not* make a transfer pursuant to § 1404(a) unless the district to which the court is transferring the case would have had personal jurisdiction and venue in the first instance. A number of factors, including the location of witnesses and condition of the court's docket, are considered in determining whether a transfer should be made pur-

---

[86] 443 U.S. 173, 61 L. Ed. 2d 464, 99 S. Ct. 2710 (1979), *on remand*, 602 F.2d 1246 (5th Cir. 1979).

[87] Siegel, Wright, Miller, and Cooper have suggested that *Leroy* is no longer good law in light of the 1990 revision of § 1391. See Siegel, "Changes in Federal Jurisdiction and Practice Under the New Judicial Improvements Act," 133 F.R.D. 61, 71 (1991) (The *Leroy* case is "now made largely academic by the 1990 amendment of § 1391"); 15 Wright, Miller & Cooper, *Federal Practice and Procedure* § 3806 (Supp. 1992). But see 1A Moore's *Federal Practice* ¶0.342[5.3], p. 4158 (1992 Rev.).

[88] *Vanity Fair Mills, Inc. v. T. Eaton Co.*, 234 F.2d 633, 109 U.S.P.Q. 438 (2d Cir. 1956), *cert. denied*, 352 U.S. 871, 1 L. Ed. 2d 76, 77 S. Ct. 96, 111 U.S.P.Q. 468 (1956), *reh'g. denied*, 352 U.S. 913,
1 L. Ed. 2d 120, 77 S. Ct. 144 (1956).

[89] See, e.g., *Sidco Industries Inc. v. Winar Tahoe Corp.*, 768 F. Supp. 1343, 19 U.S.P.Q.2d 1850 (D. Or. 1991) (Oregon Horizon Motor Inn sued Nevada Horizon Casino/Resort for trademark infringement in Oregon, where confusion is likely to occur, *not* in Nevada).

[90] 28 U.S.C. § 1391(c).

[91] 28 U.S.C. § 1404(a).

[92] *Spence v. Norfolk & W.R. Co.*, 89 F. Supp. 823 (D. Ohio 1950).

suant to § 1404(a).[93] If the transfer of venue merely shifts the inconvenience from defendant to plaintiff, the courts will usually deny the request for transfer.[94]

If several alternate jurisdictions are available, a motion for dismissal on the grounds of *forum non conveniens* may be entertained where the location of the parties and witnesses as well as the situs of the contract militate toward litigation in another forum.[95] This is especially true where the court is required to interpret the laws of a foreign state or where the admission of documents or testimony of witnesses in a foreign language would require an interpreter.[96] Although advantages may be garnered if an adversary has difficulty litigating on foreign soil, care should be taken to avoid a circumstance in which a motion to dismiss for *forum non conveniens* may delay the prosecution of an action while the motion is before the court (sub judice). Thus, if the licensor seeks to resolve the dispute swiftly, without substantial expense, care should be taken to avoid unnecessary or extensive motion practice on the issue of venue.

Federal courts retain the authority to dismiss cases for *forum non conveniens* where the more convenient forum is located outside the United States.[97] Under certain circumstances, the court may grant leave to the plaintiff to avail itself of the court's jurisdiction where the foreign court does not offer comparable relief.[98]

Challenges to improper venue are made in federal court by a motion to dismiss pursuant to Federal Rule of Civil Procedure 12(b)(3).[99] An objection to venue is waived if not made in a motion to dismiss or in the defendant's answer.[100]

Where a case has been filed in an improper venue, a court may dismiss or transfer the action to any district in which the action could have been brought pursuant to 28 U.S.C. § 1406(a).[101] A transfer may be granted to a district of proper venue, even where the court transferring venue lacks personal jurisdiction over the defendants.[102]

(d) Equitable Relief.   Section 34 of the Lanham Act invests in federal courts the traditional remedies of equitable relief:

---

[93] Location of witnesses: *Findley Adhesives, Inc. v. Williams*, 751 F. Supp. 184 (D. Or. 1990); *Williams v. Kerr Glass Mfg. Corp.*, 630 F. Supp. 266 (E.D.N.Y. 1986); *Kaiser Industries Corp. v. Wheeling Pittsburg-Steel Corp.*, 328 F. Supp. 365 (D.C. Del. 1971); calendar: *Hernandez v. Graebel Van Lines*, 761 F. Supp. 983 (E.D.N.Y. 1991); *United Cos. Life Ins. Co. v. Butler-Phillips Mgmt. Svcs., Inc.*, 741 F. Supp. 1244 (M.D. La. 1990).

[94] *Ford Motor Co. v. Rally Accessories, Inc.*, 5 U.S.P.Q.2d 1767 (E.D. Mich. 1987); *Scheiffelin & Co. v. Jack Co. of Boca, Inc.*, 725 F. Supp. 1314, 13 U.S.P.Q.2d 1704 (S.D.N.Y. 1989); *Valmedix, Inc. v. Instromedix*, 230 U.S.P.Q. 558 (E.D. Mich. 1986); *Holder Corp. v. Meyer Sheet Distributing, Inc.*, 2 U.S.P.Q.2d 1507 (9th Cir. 1987).

[95] *Sinko v. St. Louis Music Supply Co.*, 603 F. Supp. 649 (D.C. Tex. 1984); *Pepsi-Cola Co. v. Dr. Pepper Co.*, 214 F. Supp. 377 (D.C. Pa. 1963).

[96] *Mercier v. Sheraton Int'l Inc.*, 935 F.2d 419 (1st Cir. 1991); *Pain v. United Technologies Corp.*, 637 F.2d 775 (D.C. Cir.), *cert. denied*, 454 U.S. 1128 (1980).

[97] *Piper Aircraft Co. v. Reyno*, 454 U.S. 235, 70 L. Ed. 2d 419, 102 S. Ct. 252 (1981), *reh'g. denied*, 455 U.S. 913, 1 L. Ed. 2d 120, 77 S. Ct. 144 (1956); *Yerostathis v. A. Luisi, Ltd.*, 380 F.2d 377 (9th Cir. 1967); *Vanity Fair Mills, Inc. v. T. Eaton Co.*, 234 F.2d 633, 109 U.S.P.Q. 438 (2d Cir. 1956), *cert. denied*, 352 U.S. 871, 1 L. Ed. 2d 76, 77 S. Ct. 96, 111 U.S.P.Q. 468 (1956), *reh'g. denied*, 354 U.S. 913, 1 L. Ed. 2d 120, 77 S. Ct. 144 (1956).

[98] *Chemical Carriers, Inc. v. L. Smit & Co.'s Internationale Sleepdienst*, 154 F. Supp. 886 (S.D.N.Y.), *aff'd*, 265 F.2d 418 (2d Cir. 1957).

[99] 28 U.S.C. § 1404 (1948).

[100] 28 U.S.C. § 1406 (1948) (Federal Rule of Civil Procedure 12 [h] [1]).

[101] 28 U.S.C. § 1406(a).

[102] *Goldlawr, Inc. v. Heiman*, 369 U.S. 463, 8 L. Ed. 2d 39, 82 S. Ct. 193 (1962).

The several courts vested with jurisdiction of civil actions arising under this Act shall have power to grant injunctions, according to the principles of equity and upon such terms as the court may deem reasonable, to prevent the violation of any right of the registrant of a mark registered in the Patent and Trademark Office or to prevent a violation under section 43(a) (15 U.S.C. § 1116[a]).

Ordinarily, injunctive relief is granted in cases of deceptive or false advertising, trademark infringement, or trademark dilution to protect the plaintiff and the public from the likelihood of future harm.[103]

The standard in federal courts for preliminary injunctive relief varies from circuit to circuit. For example, the United States Court of Appeals for the Second Circuit requires a showing of:

(a) irreparable harm and (b) either (1) likelihood of success on the merits or (2) sufficiently serious questions going to the merits to make them a fair ground for litigation and a balance of hardships tipping decidedly toward the party requesting the preliminary relief.[104]

The First Circuit requires that the following standards be met: (1) there is likelihood of success on the merits, (2) there is the potential for irreparable injury, (3) the balance of the equities and hardship tips in favor of the plaintiff, and (4) the imposition of injunctive relief furthers the public interest.[105] The Sixth Circuit has followed the tests outlined by the Second Circuit and the Fifth Circuit.[106] The Seventh,[107] Eighth,[108] and Eleventh circuits[109] employ tests similar to the First Circuit's test. The test in the Ninth Circuit requires that the party seeking the injunction show both probable success on the merits and the possibility of irreparable injury without injunctive relief or, alternatively, that serious questions are raised about the merits of the case and that the balance of the equities and hardships tip decidedly in the favor of the movant.[110]

It is axiomatic that monetary relief alone cannot constitute an adequate remedy: "For it has always been that irreparable injury means injury for which a monetary award cannot be adequate compensation and that where money damages is adequate compensation a preliminary injunction will not issue."[111] In this regard, the Ninth Circuit observed. "Injunctive relief is the remedy of choice for trademark and unfair competition cases,

---

[103] See Restatement (Third) of Unfair Competition 35, comment b (Tentative Draft No. 3, 1991).

[104] *Power Test Petroleum Distributors v. Calcu Gas*, 754 F.2d 91, 95 (2d Cir. 1985); *Jackson Dairy, Inc. v. H.P. Hood & Sons, Inc.*, 596 F.2d 70, 72 (2d Cir. 1979).

[105] *Keds Corp. v. Renee International Trading Corp.*, 888 F.2d 215 (1st Cir. 1989); *Hypertherm, Inc. v. Precision Products, Inc.*, 832 F.2d 697 n.2 (1st Cir. 1987).

[106] See, e.g., *Frisch's Restaurants, Inc. v. Elby's Big Boy, Inc.*, 670 F.2d 642 (6th Cir. 1982), *cert. denied*, 459 U.S. 916, 74 L. Ed. 2d 182, 103 S. Ct. 231 (1982).

[107] *Schwinn Bicycle Co. v. Ross Bicycles, Inc.*, 870 F.2d 1176 (7th Cir. 1989); *A. J. Canfield Co. v. Vass Beverages, Inc.*, 796 F.2d 903, 230 U.S.P.Q. 441 (7th Cir. 1986).

[108] See, e.g., *Calvin Klein Cosmetics Corp. v. Lenox Laboratories, Inc.*, 815 F.2d 500 (8th Cir. 1987) ("the extraordinary remedy of a preliminary injunction should not be granted unless the movant has demonstrated: (1) the threat of irreparable harm to it; (2) the state of the balance between this harm and the injury that granting the injunction will inflict on other parties; (3) the probability that it will succeed on the merits; and (4) the public interest").

[109] *Tally-Ho, Inc. v. Coast Community College Dist.*, 889 F.2d 1018 (11th Cir. 1989); *Shatel Corp. v. Mao Ta Lumber & Yacht Corp.*, 697 F.2d 1352 (11th Cir. 1983).

[110] *California Cedar Products Co. v. Pine Mountain Corp.*, 724 F.2d 827 (9th Cir. 1994); *First Brands Corp. v. Fred Meyer, Inc.*, 809 F.2d 1378 (9th Cir. 1987); *California Cooler, Inc. v. Loretto Winery, Ltd.*, 774 F.2d 1451 (9th Cir. 1985).

[111] Id., 72 (citations omitted).

since there is no adequate remedy at law for the injury caused by a defendant's continuing infringement."[112]

Where a licensor sues a former licensee for trademark infringement, the standard of irreparable harm requires that a licensor demonstrate only infringing use and consumer confusion: "The unauthorized use of a mark by a former licensee invariably threatens injury to the economic value of the goodwill and reputation associated with a licensor's mark."[113] Consequently, "a licensor who establishes a likelihood of confusion as to product source in a trademark infringement suit simultaneously demonstrates the requisite irreparable harm essential to obtaining a preliminary injunction."[114] Moreover, where a licensee who is authorized to use the licensor's trademarks becomes associated in the public's mind with those trademarks and continues to use the mark following the termination or expiration of the license, "the potential for consumer confusion is greater than in the case of a random infringer:"[115]

> Consumers have already associated some significant source identification with the licensor. In this way the use of a mark by a former licensee confuses and defrauds the public.[116]

The quantity of proof required to prove a likelihood of confusion is less when a terminated licensee continues to use the mark of the licensor.[117] Some courts impose a greater duty upon former licensees to distinguish themselves from the licensor and its trademark so as to avoid any misperception or misrepresentation of association with the licensor.[118] Other courts have declined to go so far and have held a former licensee to the mere standard of avoiding a likelihood of confusion.[119]

Where there is proof of intentional infringement, the trademark holder is generally entitled to an injunction, because the defendant has no equitable basis for objection.[120]

---

[112] *Century 21 Real Estate Corp. v. Sandlin*, 846 F.2d 1175, 6 U.S.P.Q.2d 2034 (9th Cir. 1988).

[113] *Gorenstein Enterprises, Inc. v. Quality Care-USA, Inc.*, 874 F.2d 431 (7th Cir. 1989); *Church of Scientology Int'l. v. Elmira Mission of the Church of Scientology*, 794 F.2d 38, 43–44 (2d Cir. 1986).

[114] Id., 43–44.

[115] Id., 44.

[116] Id., 44 (citing *Burger King Corp. v. Mason*, 710 F.2d 1480, 1493 (11th Cir. 1983), *cert. denied*, 465 U.S. 1102, 104 S. Ct. 1599, 8 L. Ed. 2d 130 (1985); *United States Jaycees v. Philadelphia Jaycees*, 639 F.2d 134 (3d Cir. 1981); *Professional Golfers Ass'n v. Bankers Life & Casualty Co.*, 514 F.2d 665 (5th Cir. 1975), 2 *J. Thomas McCarthy, McCarthy on Trademarks and Unfair Competition* § 257 (2d Ed. 1984)).

[117] *Downtowner/Passport International Hotel Corp. v. Norlew, Inc.*, 841 F.2d 214 (8th Cir. 1988); *Ramada Inns, Inc. v. Gadseden Motel Co.*, 804 F.2d 1562 (11th Cir. 1987), *reh'g denied* 811 F.2d 612 (11th Cir. 1987) (en banc); *Burger King Corp. v. Mason*, 710 F.2d 1480 (11th Cir. 1983), *reh'g denied*, 718 F.2d 1115 (11th Cir. 1983), *cert. denied*, 465 U.S. 1102, 80 L. Ed. 2d 130, 104 S. Ct. 1599 (1984); *Mobil Oil Corp. v. Auto-Brite Car Wash, Inc.*, 223 U.S.P.Q. 269 (D. Mass. 1984).

[118] *Holiday Inns, Inc. v. Alberding*, 493 F. Supp. 1025 (N.D. Tex. 1980), *aff'd*, 683 F.2d 931 (5th Cir. 1982); *Kampgrounds of America, Inc. v. North Delaware A-OK Campground, Inc.*, 415 F. Supp. 1288 (D. Del. 1976), *aff'd without opinion*, 556 F.2d 566 (3d Cir. 1977); *Louisiana-Pacific Corp., Weather-Seal Div. v. Nu-Sash of Pittsburgh, Inc.* 184 U.S.P.Q. 593 (W.D. Pa. 1974).

[119] *Blue Bell Bio-Medical v. CitiBad, Inc.*, 864 F.2d 1253 (5th Cir. 1989); *Shakey's, Inc. v. Covalt*, F.2d 416 (9th Cir. 1983).

[120] *Safeway Stores, Inc. v. Dunnell*, 172 F.2d 649 (9th Cir.), *cert. denied*, 337 U.S. 907, 6 S. Ct. 1049, 93 L.Ed. 1719 (1949); *Aunt Jemima Mills Co. v. Rigney & Co.*, 247 F. 407 (2d. Cir. 1917), *cert. denied*, 245 U.S. 672, 30, S. Ct. 222, 62 L.Ed. 540 (1917); *Quality Inns Intern., Inc. v. McDonald's Corp.*, 695 F. Supp. 198, 221 (D. Md. 1988); *Travelodge Corp. v. Siragusa*, 228 F. Supp. 238 (N.D. Ala. 1964), *aff'd*, 352 F.2d 516 (5th Cir. 1965).

Thus, in licensing disputes where the license has been terminated, it is not unusual to obtain injunctive relief, because the licensee's post-termination acts often can only constitute intentional infringement.

District courts have a wide range of discretion in devising an injunction that is tailored to prevent wrongful conduct.[121] Generally, the injunctive relief will be limited in scope to those areas where a likelihood of confusion among consumers is possible.[122] As a result, an injunction will issue only if market penetration is sufficiently significant to pose a real likelihood of confusion among consumers in that area[123] or if the trademark holder can demonstrate that expansion into the defendant's market is likely in the normal course of its business.[124]

A court may order the licensee to take affirmative steps to distinguish its products so as to avoid confusion in the marketplace and indicate the true source of the product to the public.[125] Such affirmative action may include destruction of the infringing goods,[126] corrective advertising,[127] deleting telephone listings under an infringing mark, enjoining the telephone company from accepting advertising using an infringing mark,[128] product recall,[129] and customer refunds and returns of infringing goods.[130]

(e) Seizure Remedies Under the Trademark Counterfeiting Act of 1984.   In 1984, § 34(d) of the Lanham Act was amended to provide that where a defendant uses a counterfeit trademark in connection with "the sale, offering for sale, or distribution of goods or

[121] *Springs Mills, Inc. v. Ultracashmere House, Ltd.*, 724 F.2d 352, 255 (2d Cir. 1985).

[122] See, e.g., *George Basch Co., Inc. v. Blue Coral, Inc.*, 968 F.2d 1532 (2d Cir. 1992), *cert. denied*, — U.S. — 113 S.Ct. 510 (1992).

[123] *Charles Jacquin et Cie., Inc. v. Destilesia Seralles, Inc.*, 784 F. Supp. 231 (E.D. Pa. 1992) (to determine the extent of market penetration of an allegedly infringed upon product for purposes of granting an injunction, the court considered the volume of sales of the trademarked product, growth trends in area, number of persons actually purchasing product, and the amount of product advertising in the area; the fact that a party has more than a minimal (*de minimis*) presence in a market does not automatically entitle it to injunctive relief).

[124] *Dawn Donut Co. v. Hart's Food Stores, Inc.*, 267 F.2d 358, 364 n.4 (2d Cir. 1959); *Davidoff Extension S.A. v. Davidoff Comercio E Industria Ltda.*, 747 F. Supp. 122, 129 (D. P.R. 1990).

[125] *Kellogg Co. v. National Biscuit Co.*, 305 U.S. 111, 83 L. Ed. 73, 59 S. Ct. 109, *reh'g denied*, 305 U.S. 674, 83 L. Ed. 437, 59 S. Ct. 246 (1938); *B. H. Bunn Co. v. AAA Replacement Parts Co.*, 451 F.2d 1254 (5th Cir. 1971).

[126] *Veryfine Products, Inc. v. Colon Brothers*, 799 F. Supp. 240 (D. P.R. 1992), *Nike, Inc. v. "Just Did It" Enterprises*, 799 F. Supp. 894 (N.D. Ill. 1992); *Lon Tai Shing Co., Ltd. v. Koch & Lowy*, 21 U.S.P.Q.2d 1853 (S.D.N.Y. 1992), *Gale Group, Inc. v. Diane Corp.*, 20 U.S.P.Q.2d 1550 (N.D. Fla. 1991).

[127] *Alpo Petfoods, Inc. v. Ralston Purina Co.*, 720 F. Supp. 194 (D. D.C. 1989), *aff'd in part, reversed in part*, 913 F.2d 958 (D.C. Cir. 1990); *Big O Tire Dealers, Inc. v. Goodyear Tire & Rubber Co.*, 408 F. Supp. 1219 (D. Col. 1976), *rev'd*, 561 F.2d 1365 (10th Cir.), *cert. denied*, 434 U.S. 1052, 54 L. Ed. 2d 805, 48 S. Ct. 905 (1976).

[128] *South Cent. Bell Tel. Co. v. Constant, Inc.*, 304 F. Supp. 732 (E.D. La. 1969); *Union Tank Car Co. v. Lindsay Soft Water Corp.*, 257 F. Supp. 510 (D. Neb. 1966), *aff'd*, 387 F.2d 477 (8th Cir. 1967).

[129] *Nikon, Inc. v. Ikon Corp.*, 987 F.2d 91 (2d Cir. 1993); *Bausche & Lomb, Inc., v. Nevitt Sales Corp.*, 810 F. Supp. 466 (W.D.N.Y. 1993) Recall has been improved extraterritorially under certain circumstances, *See Baldwin Harlwape Corp. v. Fransky Goterprice Corp.*, 24 U.S.P.Q. 2d 1700 (CD Calif. 1992). *Perfect Fit Industries, Inc. v. Acme Quilting Co.*, 646 F.2d 800 (2d Cir. 1981), *later appeal*, 673 F.2d 53 (2d Cir. 1982), *cert. denied*, 459 U.S. 832, 74 L. Ed. 2d 71, 103 S. Ct. 73 (1982).

[130] *Ebeling & Russo Co. v. International Collectors Guild, Ltd.*, 462 F. Supp. 716 (E.D. Pa. 1978); *Sensory Research Corp. v. Pasht, Inc.*, 192 U.S.P.Q. 168 (S.D.N.Y. 1976); *Matsushita Electric Corp. v. Solar Sound Systems, Inc.*, 381 F. Supp. 64 (S.D.N.Y. 1974).

services," a district court, upon ex parte (one party's) application, may grant an order providing for "the seizure of goods and counterfeit marks involved in such violation and the means of making such marks, and records documenting the manufacture, sale, or receipt of things involved in such violation."[131] Where the court found there was danger, defendant would dissipate its assets; the Ninth Circuit has held that its inherent equitable power authorizes it to freeze the defendant's assets provisionally.[132] The statute specifically provides that the term *counterfeit mark* does not include any mark or designation used on or in connection with goods or services that were manufactured or produced under authority of the trademark holder.[133] Prior to making an application for ex parte seizure, the plaintiff must give reasonable notice to the United States Attorney for the district in which the order is sought. The United States Attorney may participate in the proceedings if it is determined that such proceedings may impact evidence of an offense against the United States.[134]

The application for seizure is based on an affidavit or verified complaint establishing sufficient facts to support the findings of fact and conclusions of law required for such an order.[135] Under § 34(d), an order pursuant to § 1116(d)(5) must set forth the following:

1. The findings of fact and conclusions of law required for the order,
2. A particular description of the objects to be seized with a description of the location of the object to be seized,
3. The time period during which the seizure shall be made, which shall be not later than seven days after the date on which such order is issued,
4. The amount of the security required to be provided under the law, and
5. The date for the hearing following seizure.[136]

The Second Circuit has held that a seizure order is not appealable when it is granted, but only at the end of the case, because such orders do not have the requisite finality for reviewability.[137] On the other hand, the Third Circuit has held that such orders are immediately appealable pursuant to 28 U.S.C. § 1292(a)(1), because they are a form of injunctive relief.[138]

A seizure order will not be granted unless (1) the plaintiff provides adequate security to pay any damages that may result from a wrongful seizure or attempted seizure, (2) the court finds that such an order is the only means to achieve the purposes of § 32 of the Act, (3) the plaintiff has not published the requested seizure, and (4) the plaintiff has demon-

---

[131] 15 U.S.C. § 1116(d)

[132] *Reebok International, Ltd. v. Marnatech Enterprise, Inc.*, 970 F.2d 552 (9th Cir. 1992).

[133] Consequently, the ex parte seizure provisions of the statute do not, by definition, apply to parallel imports, gray-market goods, and production overruns. 15 U.S.C. § 1116(d) (1) (B) ("a counterfeit of a mark . . . does not include any mark or designation used on or in connection with goods or services of which the manufacturer or producer was, at the time of the manufacture or production in question, authorized to use the mark or designation for the type of goods or services so manufactured or produced by the holder of the right to use such mark or designation"). See also Senate-House Joint Explanatory Statement on Trademark Counterfeiting Legislation, 130 Cong. Rec. H12076 at 12079 (October 10, 1984).

[134] 15 U.S.C. § 1116(d) (2).

[135] 15 U.S.C. § 1116(d) (5).

[136] 15 U.S.C. § 1116(d) (5).

[137] *General Motors Corp. v. Gibson Chemical & Oil Corp.*, 786 F.2d 105 (2d Cir. 1986).

[138] *Louis Vuitton v. White*, 445 F.2d 569 (3d Cir. 1991).

strated (a) the likelihood of success of showing that the person against whom the seizure would be ordered used a counterfeit mark in connection with the sale, offering for sale, or distribution of goods or services, (b) an immediate and irreparable injury would occur if such seizure is not ordered, (c) the harm to the plaintiff in denying a seizure order outweighs the harm to the person against whom the seizure would be ordered, (d) the goods to be seized are located at the place identified in the application, and (e) if the plaintiff were to proceed on giving advance notice to defendants, the counterfeit goods in question likely would be destroyed, moved, or otherwise rendered inaccessible to the court.[139]

Usually, a showing must be made that the defendant is not a reputable merchant but one who trades in counterfeit goods.[140] In a licensing context, the Counterfeiting Act of 1984 is of limited application or value unless the goods in question were manufactured, designed, and sold outside the scope of the trademark license and without the licensor's approval.

(f) Legal Relief.   In an action at law, a licensor or licensee may seek various forms of relief. A licensor may, in the first instance, seek a declaratory judgment terminating the license because of a material uncured default by the licensee. The licensor may also seek monetary damages. In a trademark or unfair competition case, a trademark owner may seek a monetary award measured in a number of ways:

1. An award measured by the defendant's profits
2. An award measured by the plaintiff's actual business losses and the harm caused by the wrong in question
3. An award measured by the plaintiff's loss of profits attributable to the infringement in question
4. An award of punitive damages in addition to actual damages for the purpose of punishing the defendant and deterring others
5. An award of reasonable attorneys' fees incurred in the prosecution of the claim

In addition, a licensor may seek an award of royalties and liquidated damages in a licensing dispute, pursuant to the terms of the license agreement, or an accounting of accrued royalties.

(g) Termination of License.   A licensor may terminate a license agreement where there is "good cause" for termination. Although the determination of what constitutes "good cause" varies from state to state, it is well accepted that where the licensee has failed to cure a material default under the license agreement after receiving a prior notice, there exists "good cause." Preferably, the license agreement specifies those circumstances that would constitute a material default. On other occasions, the determination of whether termination is justified by "good cause" must be supported by the totality of the circumstances. As a general rule, a valid termination requires a proper notice of termination.

---

[139] 15 U.S.C. § 1116(d) (4).

[140] See Senate-House Joint Explanatory Statement on Trademark Counterfeiting Legislation, 130 Cong. Rec. H12076 at 12081 (Oct. 10, 1984). ("This provision is the key to obtaining an ex parte seizure order under this act. . . . The most compelling proof on this point would be evidence that the defendant acted in bad faith towards the judicial process in the past. A court, however, may consider any other evidence relevant to this determination.")

Proper notice is required to ensure that the licensee is afforded ample time to cure any deficiencies in its performance prior to termination. The failure to provide proper notice of default and an opportunity to cure may preclude termination and result in reinstatement of the licensee and claims of damage against the licensor.[141]

11.4 MONETARY AWARD

(a) An Accounting of Profits.   Courts generally require that a plaintiff demonstrate the defendant's knowing intent to infringe or to gain from another's mark or advertising in order to obtain an accounting of profits.[142] Awards of punitive damages also have been based on acts committed deliberately, intentionally,[143] fraudulently,[144] or in bad faith.[145] Generally, an accounting of profits will not be granted unless the defendant's knowledge and conduct shows egregious conduct or intentional infringement.[146] Where the defendant has acted in good faith, based on a bona fide belief of its rights in its trademark, a plaintiff will not be entitled to a monetary award.[147] This is true even if the defendant is held to be an infringer, so long as the court determines that injunctive relief alone will suffice.[148] In this regard, one court held that "an accounting for profits is not appropriate where the infringer, while in a judge's eyes having violated the statute, nonetheless acted in good faith."[149] Such a determination generally depends on the particular facts of each case.[150]

Some courts also require proof of actual confusion as a condition for recovery of damages or an accounting of profits. The rationale for this requirement is that without actual confusion, there can be no damage to a plaintiff or unjust enrichment of the defendant. However, some courts have endorsed monetary recovery as a general rule in cases of willful infringement.[151]

(b) Recovery of Plaintiff's Actual Monetary Damages.   Trademark damages are measured by the actual damages caused by the acts of trademark infringement or unfair competi-

---

[141] See *Maude v. General Motors Corp.*, 626 F. Supp. 1081 (W.D. Mo. 1986).

[142] *L.P. Larson, Jr. Co. v. Wm. Wrigley, Jr., Co.*, 277 U.S. 97, 72 L. Ed. 800, 48 S. Ct. 449 (1928).

[143] *National Lead Co. v. Wolfe*, 223 F.2d 195 (9th Cir. 1955), *cert. denied*, 350 U.S. 883, 100 L. Ed. 778, 76 S. Ct. 135 (1955).

[144] *W.E. Bassett Co. v. Revlon, Inc.*, 435 F.2d 656 (2d Cir. 1990).

[145] *Foxtrap, Inc. v. Foxtrap, Inc.*, 617 F.2d 636 (D.C. Cir. 1982).

[146] *Champion Spark Plug Co. v. Sanders*, 331 U.S. 125, 91 L. Ed. 1386, 67 S. Ct. 1136 (1947).

[147] *Carl Zeiss Stiftung v. Veb Carl Zeiss Jena*, 433 F.2d 686, 706–07 (2d Cir. 1970), *cert. denied*, 403 U.S. 905, 29 L. Ed. 2d 680, 91 S. Ct. 2205 (1971); *Consumers Petroleum v. Consumers Co. of Illinois*, 169 F.2d 153 (7th Cir. 1948), *cert. denied*, 335 U.S. 902, 93 L. Ed. 437, 69 S. Ct. 406 (1949).

[148] Id., 433 F.2d 686.

[149] *Cuisinarts, Inc. v. Robot-Coupe International Corp.*, 580 F. Supp. 634 (S.D.N.Y. 1984); see also *Robert Bruce, Inc. v. Sears, Roebuck & Co.*, 343 F. Supp. 1333 (E.D. Pa. 1972).

[150] Cf. *Wolfe v. National Lead Co.*, 272 F.2d 867, 871 (9th Cir. 1959), *cert. denied*, 362 U.S. 950, 4 L. Ed. 2d 868, 80 S. Ct. 860 (1960).

[151] *Louis Vuitton S. A. v. Lee*, 875 F.2d 584, 588–89 (7th Cir. 1989) ("The principles of equity . . . do not in our view justify withholding all monetary relief from the victim of a trademark infringement merely because the infringement was innocent. As between the innocent infringer who seeks to get off . . . and the innocent infringed who has neither engaged in any inequitable conduct nor sought treble damages or treble profits . . . the stronger equity is with the innocent infringed. . . . 'Equity' is not a roving commission to redistribute wealth from large companies to small ones. The Lanham Act was not written by Robin Hood"); *Burger King Corp. v. Mason*, 855 F.2d 779 (11th Cir. 1988).

tion, whether or not such damages were anticipated by the infringer. Where the plaintiff and defendant do not compete directly, the plaintiff may be awarded both defendant's profits as well as plaintiff's damages.[152] Damages and profits may not be awarded, however, if the result would be to overcompensate the plaintiff.[153] This is especially so where the plaintiff seeks *both* the profits of the infringer as well as the lost profits on sales diverted by the defendants' infringement. The Act specifically forbids the award of a penalty.[154]

To recover damages from lost sales owing to trademark infringement, the plaintiff must prove actual consumer deception or confusion.[155] The Second Circuit has held that a presumption of confusion necessary to prove damages is demonstrated by proof of intentionally deceptive conduct: "Once it is shown that a defendant deliberately engaged in a deceptive commercial practice, we agree that a powerful inference may be drawn that the defendant has succeeded in confusing the public. Therefore, upon a proper showing of deliberate conduct, the burden shifts to the defendant to demonstrate the absence of consumer confusion."[156] Such a showing generally can be made by introducing evidence of actual consumer confusion or consumer surveys.[157] Where the trademark is strong, however, such proof is not necessarily required and a jury may arrive at a commonsense determination of consumer confusion.[158] This is especially true where a licensee who had previously been authorized to use the trademarks of the licensor continues to use the mark following the termination or expiration of the license, inasmuch as the licensee has become associated in the public's mind with the trademark.[159] The quantity of proof required to establish consumer confusion in the case of a terminated licensee may be less than that necessary under ordinary circumstances. Indeed, some courts impose a duty upon former licensees to take care to avoid any misperception or misrepresentation.[160]

(c) Willful Infringement. No wrongful or deliberate infringement by a defendant is required for a plaintiff's recovery of actual damages. "Even the victim of an innocent infringer is entitled to simple damages, as distinct from the infringer's profits."[161] Nevertheless, the absence or presence of wrongful intent to cause confusion or deception is significant in the assessment and recovery of damages.[162]

---

[152] *Hamilton-Brown Shoe Co. v. Wolf Bros. & Co.*, 240 U.S. 251, 60 L. Ed. 629, 36 S. Ct. 269 (1969); *Aladdin Mfg. Co. v. Mantle Lamp Co.*, 116 F.2d 708 (7th Cir. 1941).

[153] *Polo Fashions, Inc. v. Extra Special Products, Inc.*, 208 U.S.P.Q. 421 (S.D.N.Y. 1980); *Big O Tire Dealers, Inc. v. Goodyear Tire & Rubber Co.*, 408 F. Supp. 1219 (D. Colo. 1976), *modified*, 561 F.2d 1365 (10th Cir. 1977), *cert. dismissed*, 434 U.S. 1052 (1978).

[154] *Foxtrap, Inc. v. Foxtrap, Inc.*, 671 F.2d 636 (D.C. Cir. 1982).

[155] *Resource Developers, Inc. v. Statue of Liberty-Ellis Island Foundation, Inc.*, 926 F.2d 134 (2d Cir. 1991); *Web Printing Controls Co. v. Oxy-Dry Corp.*, 906 F.2d 1202 (7th Cir. 1990); *Shen Mfg. Co. v. Suncrest Mills, Inc.*, 673 F. Supp. 1199 (S.D.N.Y. 1987).

[156] *Resource Developers, Inc. v. Statue of Liberty-Ellis Island Foundation, Inc.*, 926 F.2d 134 (2d Cir. 1991).

[157] Restatement (Third) of Unfair Competition § 36, Comment h (Tentative Draft No. 3, 1991); *Brunswick Corp. v. Spirit Reel Co.*, 832 F.2d 513 (10th Cir. 1987); *Schutt Mfg. Co. v. Kiddell, Inc.*, 673 F.2d 202, 216 (7th Cir. 1982).

[158] *Getty Petroleum Corp. v. Island Transp. Corp.*, 878 F.2d 650 (2d Cir. 1989).

[159] See notes 36 through 42.

[160] See note 45.

[161] *General Electric Co. v. Speicher*, 877 F.2d 531 (7th Cir. 1988), *reh. denied, en banc*, 1989 U.S. App. LEXIS 16046 (7th Cir. 1989).

[162] *W. E. Bassette Co. v. Revlon, Inc.*, 435 F.2d 656 (2d Cir. 1970); *Cuisinarts, Inc. v. Robot-Coupe Int'l Corp.*, 580 F. Supp. 634 (S.D.N.Y. 1984).

(d) Reasonable Royalty as a Measure of Damages.   Where a claim of damages involves a franchisee or licensee which continues after termination to use the licensed mark, courts have awarded reasonable royalty-based recoveries when the trademark proprietor has lost the royalty stream that could have been generated from the use of the trademark, or its use of the trademark in a particular market.[163] Thus, when a former licensee of the Howard Johnson trademark and trade dress failed to take proper steps to avoid any consumer confusion following the termination of its franchise, royalties that the franchisor would have received from the use of the trademark were held to be a sufficient basis to support an award of sanctions for contempt.[164]

This measure of damages has been criticized, because it fails to deprive the trademark infringer of an economic incentive for infringement.[165] Moreover, an award of a reasonable royalty was held to be an inappropriate measure of damages where an independent dealer used advertising to create the false impression that it was a franchisee, because the award did not bear a "rational relationship to the rights appropriated."[166] Where a license was requested and a fee was quoted, however, the license fee that the defendant offered to pay and which plaintiff would have received was held a proper measure of damages.[167]

(e) Trademark Infringement and Counterfeiting Damages Pursuant to § 35(a) of the Lanham Act.   A successful plaintiff is not automatically entitled to a monetary award in all cases.[168] Such an award is "subject to the principles of equity." Consequently, where injunctive relief satisfies the equities of the case and there has been no showing of fraud or palming off, no monetary relief will be granted.[169] Likewise, an accounting will not be permitted where a defendant's actions were based on a good-faith belief that its use of a trademark was not an infringement.[170] Innocent infringement does not preclude damages for a demonstrable loss to a plaintiff owing to the infringement, however (as opposed to a recovery of the defendant's profits), because under such circumstances the stronger equities rest with the plaintiff.[171]

Section 35 of the Lanham Act invests the court with discretion to enter judgment "according to the circumstances of the case, for any fair sum above the amount found as actual damages, not exceeding three times such amount" or "for such a sum as the court may in its discretion find to be just" if the amount of recovery based on profits is "either inadequate or excessive."[172] As a result, trial judges have wide latitude to adjust mone-

---

[163] *Howard Johnson Co. v. Khimani*, 892 F.2d 1512 (11th Cir. 1990); *Ramada Inns, Inc. v. Gadsden Motel Co.*, 804 F.2d 1562 (11th Cir. 1986), *reh. denied, en banc*, 811 F.2d 612 (11th Cir. 1987); *KFC Corp. v. Lilleoren*, 821 F. Supp. 1191 (W.D. Ky. 1993); *Holiday Inns, Inc. v. Airport Hotel Corp.*, 493 F. Supp. 1025 (N.D. Tex. 1980), *aff'd*, 683 F.2d 931 (5th Cir. 1982).

[164] *Howard Johnson Co. v. Khimani*, 892 F.2d 1572.

[165] *Playboy Enterprises, Inc. v. Baccarat Clothing Co.*, 692 F.2d 1272, 1274–75 (9th Cir. 1982).

[166] *Bandag, Inc. v. Al Bolser's Tire Stores, Inc.*, 750 F.2d 930 (Fed. Cir. 1984).

[167] *Boston Professional Hockey Assoc. v. Dallas Cap & Emblem Mfg., Inc.*, 597 F.2d 71 (5th Cir. 1979); see also *Deering, Milliken & Co. v. Gilbert*, 269 F.2d 191 (2d Cir. 1959); *National Bank of Commerce v. Shaklee Corp.*, 207 U.S.P.Q. 1005 (W.D. Tex. 1980).

[168] *Maier Brewing Co. v. Fleischmann Distilling Corp.*, 390 F.2d 117, 120 (9th Cir. 1968).

[169] *Champion Spark Plug Co. v. Sanders*, 331 U.S. 125, 91 L. Ed. 1386, 67 S. Ct. 1136 (1947).

[170] *Faberge, Inc. v. Saxony Products, Inc.*, 605 F.2d 426 (9th Cir. 1979); *Bandag, Inc. v. Al Boser's Tire Stores, Inc.*, 750 F.2d 903 (Fed. Cir. 1984); *Carl Zeiss Stiftung v. Veb Carl Zeiss Jena*, 433 F.2d 686 (2d Cir. 1970), *cert. denied*, 403 U.S. 905, 29 L. Ed. 2d 680, 91 S. Ct. 2205 (1971).

[171] *Louis Vuitton S. A. v. Lee*, 874 F.2d 584 (7th Cir. 1989).

[172] 15 U.S.C. § 1117 (a).

tary awards according to the facts of the case.[173] Although the statute specifically provides that such an adjustment "shall constitute compensation and not a penalty," courts generally have no problem in increasing an award of damages if such an adjustment is seen as having a remedial effect.

Section 35(b) was amended by Congress in 1984 to give courts in civil cases the authority to grant ex parte seizure orders and to award certain monetary remedies, including prejudgment interest. In addition, § 35(b) provides that "unless the court finds extenuating circumstances" it will "enter judgment for three times such profits or damages, whichever is greater, together with a reasonable attorney's fee" where the infringement "consists of intentionally using a mark or designation, knowing such mark or designation is a counterfeit mark."[174] Under such circumstances, the plaintiff need only demonstrate intent by showing that the defendant knew the goods were counterfeit and intended to sell them.[175]

(f) Punitive Damages.   Section 35 of the Lanham Act does not authorize punitive damages in actions for infringement of trademarks registered in the United States Patent and Trademark Office.[176] Indeed, the proscription of § 35, that an increase of damages shall not constitute a penalty by implication, precludes any such inference. Nevertheless, the trebling of damages pursuant to § 35, for the most part, obviates any need for punitive damages.[177]

State courts often permit punitive damages in cases of common-law trademark infringement and unfair competition. One often-considered factor in determining whether punitive damages should be awarded is the size and financial status of the defendant. Where a defendant is large and has the capability to retain counsel, punitive damages may be awarded. Also, punitive damages will not be awarded where no actual damages are demonstrated. In addition, the conduct of the defendant must have been egregious. There must have been a willful, malicious, or reckless disregard of the plaintiff's trademark rights.[178]

(g) Attorney's Fees.   Attorney's fees are awarded to prevailing plaintiffs in trademark actions where a plaintiff can establish an "exceptional case," meaning willful, intentional,

---

[173] *Playboy Enterprises, Inc. v. Baccarat Clothing Co.*, 692 F.2d 1272 (9th Cir. 1982); *Holiday Inns, Inc. v. Alberding*, 682 F.2d 931 (5th Cir. 1982).

[174] 15 U.S.C. § 1117 (b).

[175] Senate-House Joint Explanatory Statements on Trademark Counterfeiting Legislation, 130 Cong. Rec. H12076 at 12083 (Oct. 10, 1984).

[176] *Getty Petroleum Corp. v. Bartzo Petroleum Corp.*, 858 F.2d 103 (2d Cir. 1988), *cert. denied*, 490 U.S. 1006, 104 L. Ed. 2d 158, 109 S. Ct. 1642 (1989); *Ceasars World, Inc. v. Venus Lounge, Inc.*, 520 F.2d 269 (3d Cir. 1975); *Electronics Corp. of America v. Honeywell, Inc.*, 358 F. Supp. 1230 (D.C. Mass. 1973), *aff'd*, 487 F.2d 513 (1st Cir. 1973), *cert. denied*, 415 U.S. 960, 39 L. Ed. 2d 575, 94 S. Ct. 1491 (1974).

[177] In *American Society of Mechanical Engineers v. Hydrolevel Corp.*, 456 U.S. 556, 576, 102 S. Ct. 1935, 1947, 50 L.Ed.2d 701 (1977), the Supreme Court noted that although antitrust treble damages are designed to punish past violations of antitrust laws, they do not constitute punitive damages.

[178] See, generally, *Triangle Sheet Metal Works, Inc. v. Silver*, 154 Conn. 116, 222 A.2d 220 (1966); *Transgo, Inc. v. Ajac Transmission Parts Corp.*, 768 F.2d 1001 (9th Cir. 1985); *Zazu Designs v. L'Oreal S.A.*, 979 F.2d 499 (7th Cir. 1992); *Murphy Door Bed Co. v. Interior Sleep Systems, Inc.*, 874 F.2d 95 (2d Cir. 1989).

or deliberate infringement.[179] Consequently, where a former licensee infringes upon a trademark that it had licensed previously, attorney's fees will usually be available to the plaintiff. In a licensing dispute, attorney's fees may be provided by contract, but courts, as a general rule, do not always honor such agreements. Indeed, such clauses may be deemed contrary to public policy.

11.5 MAINTAINING AN ACTION FOR TRADEMARK INFRINGEMENT

Traditionally, by statute[180] and at common law for unfair competition, the remedy for trademark infringement lies solely in hands of the trademark registrant or owner.[181] However, the courts also have given trademark licensees the right to maintain actions for trademark infringement and unfair competition in certain instances. It has been held that an exclusive licensee has an interest in a trademark sufficient to entitle the licensee to maintain such actions.[182] In addition, a user of a mark may bring an action when a mark has acquired a secondary meaning as to that user.[183]

There appear to be no cases, however, in which a nonexclusive licensee has been able to maintain an action for trademark infringement, acting apart from the trademark owner, assignee, or exclusive licensee.[184] Thus, in *Quabaug Rubber Co. v. Fabiano Shoe Co.*,[185] although the plaintiff was a licensee and sole manufacturer of the licensed goods in the United States, it did not have the full powers of an exclusive licensee because it could not exclude imports and sales by the owner of the United States trademark in the United States. The court concluded, therefore, that the United States trademark owner was an indispensable party to the action. In contrast, in *Browne-Vintners Co. v. National Distillers & Chemical Corp.*,[186] Browne-Vintners, as the exclusive distributor of a brand of champagne in the United States, had a monopoly over its sale in this country and was

---

[179] *Texas Pig Stands Inc. v. Hard Rock Cafe Int'l, Inc.*, 951 F.2d 684, 696 (5th Cir. 1992); *CJC Holdings, Inc. v. Wright & Lato, Inc.* 979 F.2d 60 (5th Cir. 1992); *Wynn Oil Co. v. American Way Service Corp.*, 943 F.2d 595 (6th Cir. 1991). *Polo Fashions, Inc. v. Extra Special Products, Inc.*, 208 U.S.P.Q. 421 (S.D.N.Y. 1980); *Quaker State Oil Refining Corp. v. Kooltone, Inc.*, 649 F.2d 94 (2d Cir. 1981); *Vuitton et Fils, S.A. v. Crown Hudbags*, 492 F. Supp. 1071 (S.D.N.Y. 1979), *aff'd without op.*, 622 F.2d 577 (2d Cir. 1980).

[180] 15 U.S.C.A. § 1114 (1) and (2).

[181] See, e.g., *House of Westmore, Inc. v. Denney*, 151 F.2d 261 (3d Cir. 1945); *Cine-Pak Corp. v. Pathecolor, Inc.*, 187 F. Supp 498 (D.N.J. 1960). A buyer does not have standing to sue. *See Shonac Corp. v. AMKO International, Inc.*, 763 F. Supp. 918 (S.D. Oh. 1991).

[182] *Quabaug Rubber Co. v. Fabiano Shoe Co.*, 567 F.2d 154 (1st Cir. 1977); *See also National Football League Properties, Inc. v. Playoff Corp.*, 808 F. Supp. 1288 (N.D. Tex. 1992); *National Rural Electric Cooperative Ass'n v. National Agricultural Chemical Ass'n*, 26 U.S.P.Q. 2d 1294 (D.D.C. 1992); *National Cooperatives, Inc. v. Petroleum Co-op System*, 168 F. Supp 259 (S. D. Ind. 1958); *Browne-Vintners Co. v. National Distillers & Chemical Corp.*, 151 F. Supp. 595 (S.D.N.Y. 1957).

[183] *Cine-Pak Corp. v. Pathecolor, Inc.*, 187 F. Supp. 498 (D.N.J. 1960) (citing *Armstrong Paint & Varnish Works v. Nu-Enamel Corp.*, 305 U.S. 315 [1935]); *Perry v. American Hecolite Denture Corp.*, 78 F.2d 556 (8th Cir. 1935); *Alfred Dunhill of London, Inc. v. Kasser Distillers Prods. Corp.*, 350 F. Supp. 1341 (E.D. Pa. 1972), *aff'd*, 480 F.2d 917 (3d Cir. 1973) (a plaintiff who was the exclusive user of the mark in the United States on some goods and the concurrent user on other good had a right to bring action).

[184] *Quabaug Rubber Co. v. Fabiano Shoe Co.*, 567 F.2d 154 (1st Cir. 1977); *Acme Valve & Fittings Co. v. Wayne*, 386 F. Supp 1162 (S.D. Tex. 1974).

[185] 567 F.2d 154 (1st Cir. 1977).

[186] 151 F. Supp. 595 (S.D.N.Y. 1957).

therefore deemed to have a sufficient interest of its own in the marks to entitle it to register the marks in its own name. Consequently, the related companies that owned the marks and Browne, as their exclusive distributor, were "united in a common enterprise" and had interests in the trademarks sufficient to enable any one of them to maintain an action.[187]

It should be noted, however, that although a licensee may have standing to bring an infringement action against an unrelated entity, it does not have the right to maintain such an action against the trademark licensor.[188] A licensee's interest in a trademark arises solely out of the contractual relationship with the licensor and therefore is derivative of, and secondary to, the rights of the licensor.[189]

11.6 TORT LIABILITY OF THE LICENSOR

There exists a degree of control in a licensor-licensee relationship which, under certain circumstances, can impose vicarious liability upon the licensor for the licensee's misconduct.[190] The relationship does not necessarily render the licensor liable[191] unless the control retained by the licensor is sufficient to equate it to a master-servant relationship. This depends on the nature and extent of control as defined in the franchise or license agreement or by the actual practice of the parties.[192] The fact that an agreement expressly denies any such relationship is not controlling.[193] In determining whether a franchisor is vicariously liable for a franchisee's acts under a theory of apparent agency, the crucial focus is not on what agreements were entered into between the parties but, rather, what representations were actually made to the franchisee's customers. That is, vicarious liability will be imposed if the franchisor held itself out to the public as the owner or operator of the franchise.[194]

Because a licensor may be subject to liability, it may want to include in the agreement a provision whereby the licensee agrees to indemnify and hold the licensor harmless for vicarious tort liability. Indemnification should extend beyond the term of the license agreement in order to protect against claims arising or asserted subsequent to termination.[195]

---

[187] See also *G.H. Mumm Champagne v. Eastern Wine Corp.*, 142 F.2d (2d Cir. 1944) (A Delaware company that had the sole right to import and sell wines in the eastern United States could maintain an infringement action where the company had a monopoly on the sale of Mumm's and the defendant's sales would directly impact the plaintiff imposter's rights. The Delaware company had sufficient interest to register the trademark as its own).

[188] *Silverstar Enterprises, Inc. v. Aday*, 537 F. Supp. 236 (S.D.N.Y. 1982); *Shoney's, Inc. v. Schoenbaum*, 686 F. Supp. 554 (E.D. Va. 1988), aff'd, 894 F.2d 92 (4th Cir. 1990).

[189] *Silverstar Enterprises, Inc. v. Aday*, 537 F. Supp. 236 (S.D.N.Y. 1982).

[190] *Spencer, supra.*

[191] *Drexel v. Union Prescription Centers, Inc.*, 582 F.2d 781 (3d Cir. 1978); *Drummond v. Hilton Hotel Corp.*, 501 F. Supp. 29 (E.D. Pa. 1980).

[192] *Drexel v. Union Prescription Centers, Inc.*, 582 F.2d 781 (3d Cir. 1978); *Drummond v. Hilton Hotel Corp.*, 501 F. Supp. 29 (E.D. Pa. 1980).

[193] *Drexel*; *Drummond.*

[194] *Drexel.*

[195] Gilson, § 6.03 (19).

CHAPTER 12

BANKRUPTCY AND INTANGIBLE HOLDINGS: REDEEMING YOUR INVESTMENT WHEN DISASTER STRIKES

William M. Goldman
Charles G. Klink

Brown & Wood
New York, New York

The commencement of a bankruptcy case under Title 11 of the United States Code (the Bankruptcy Code),[1] can have dramatic consequences on the disposition of intellectual property. This chapter explains the effects of the bankruptcy of a licensor of intellectual property, as well as the effects of the bankruptcy of a licensee of intellectual property. However, in order to understand bankruptcy cases involving intellectual property specifically, it is necessary to be familiar with some basic bankruptcy concepts, which are discussed in the following section of this chapter.

12.1 THE BANKRUPTCY CODE

(a) **Introduction.** Many states have insolvency laws,[2] but because the United States Constitution prevents a state from passing a law that impairs the obligations of contract,[3] these laws cannot grant a debtor a discharge (i.e., relief from its obligation to repay its debts).[4] However, the United States Constitution specifically grants Congress the power to enact laws governing bankruptcy,[5] which necessarily includes the ability to impair the obligations of a contract.[6] In addition, under the Supremacy Clause of the United States

---

[1] 11 U.S.C. § 101 *et seq.*

[2] E.g., Idaho Code § 68–201 (1989); Md. Com. Law Ann. Code §§ 15–101–103 (Michie 1992); Mass. Gen. Laws Ann. Ch. 203 §§ 40–42 (West 1992); N.J. Stat. Ann. § 2A: 19–6 (West 1987); N.Y. Debt. and Cred. Law, art. 2 & 2A (McKinney 1992); see generally Benjamin Weintraub and Alan N. Resnick, *Bankruptcy Law Manual*, 3d ed. (1992), Chap 11.

[3] U.S. Const. art. I, § 10, cl. 1.

[4] See *Boese v. King*, 108 U.S. 379 (1882).

[5] U.S. Const. art. I, § 8, cl. 4. This specific grant is interesting, considering the relatively few specific powers granted to the federal government in the United States Constitution.

[6] See *In re Weber*, 674 F.2d 796 (9th Cir.), *cert. denied*, 459 U.S. 1086 (1982).

Constitution,[7] any state laws regulating insolvency must yield to conflicting provisions contained in the federal bankruptcy laws.[8] Consequently, state insolvency laws are of limited usefulness to debtors.

Thus, bankruptcy cases in the United States are governed by federal law. The Bankruptcy Code was enacted into law by the Bankruptcy Reform Act of 1978[9] and became effective on October 1, 1979. Since that time there have been several important amendments to the Bankruptcy Code. These address specific problems that have arisen and have shaped the Bankruptcy Code so that it better serves its primary goals.[10]

Among the primary goals embodied in the Bankruptcy Code are (1) the equitable distribution of a debtor's assets through the equal sharing of losses by creditors who are of equal rank, (2) the maximization of the value of the debtor's assets available to creditors, and (3) in Chapter 11 reorganization cases, the restructuring of the debtor's business in order to preserve jobs and the going concern value of the business entity.[11]

Before discussing substantive bankruptcy issues related to intellectual property, a few clarifications must be made with respect to terminology. First, although many people frequently use the word *bankrupt* to mean that a person or entity has insufficient assets to fully satisfy the claims of creditors against such assets, the term properly refers to an entity that has voluntarily sought protection under, or has been involuntarily forced to seek relief under, the Bankruptcy Code.

However, neither the word *bankrupt* nor *bankruptcy* appears in the Bankruptcy Code itself. This omission is the result of a conscious decision of the drafters of the Bankruptcy Code to remove the stigma associated with these words. The Bankruptcy Code substitutes the word *debtor* for *bankrupt*. Thus, technically, and as used in this chapter, *debtor* means an individual or entity subject to a case under the Bankruptcy Code. Similarly, a case under the Bankruptcy Code is technically referred to as a "case under Title 11 of the United States Code." However, this phrase has not been widely accepted, even by bankruptcy practitioners. Therefore, although it is technically incorrect, this chapter uses the phrase "bankruptcy case" to refer to a case under Title 11 of the United States Code.

There are two general forms of relief available to a debtor under the Bankruptcy Code. The alternatives are reorganization, which usually takes place under Chapter 11 of the Bankruptcy Code,[12] or liquidation, which can take place under either Chapter 11 or Chapter 7 of the Bankruptcy Code. Although the contemplated end result of a typical Chapter 11 case is the reorganization of the debtor's business through the confirmation of

---

[7] U.S. Const. art. 6, cl. 2.

[8] See, e.g., *In re Goerg*, 844 F.2d 1562 (11th Cir. 1988); *National Collection Agency, Inc., v. Trahan*, 624 F.2d 906 (9th Cir. 1980).

[9] Pub. L. No. 95–598, 92 Stat. 2549.

[10] For example, in 1984, the president signed the Bankruptcy Amendments and Federal Judgeship Act of 1984, Pub. L. No. 98–353, 98 Stat. 333, and, in 1986, signed the Bankruptcy Judges, United States Trustees, and Family Farmer Bankruptcy Act of 1986, Pub. L. No. 99–554, 100 Stat. 3097, 3103, 3104–3114, 3116.

[11] See H.R. Rep. No. 95–595, 95th Cong., 1st Sess. 220 (1977); *United States v. Whiting Pools, Inc.*, 462 U.S. 198, 203 (1983).

[12] Chapter 11 is not the only debtor rehabilitation Chapter in the Bankruptcy Code. However, the other debtor rehabilitation chapters are designed for particular types of debtors that are unlikely to have substantial involvement with intellectual property and are, therefore, beyond the scope of this book. The specialized debtor relief chapters are Chapter 9, designed for readjusting the debts of municipalities; Chapter 12, designed to provide relief for family farmers; and Chapter 13, which permits individual debtors to repay their debts from a portion of their future earnings.

a plan of reorganization, a Chapter 11 plan may provide for the liquidation of the debtor's assets and a distribution of the proceeds to the claimants against such assets.[13]

(b) Commencement of the Case. A bankruptcy case is commenced by the filing of a petition for relief under one of the Bankruptcy Code's substantive Chapters (e.g., Chapter 7 or Chapter 11). The petition is usually filed by the debtor, in which instance the case is referred to as a "voluntary case."[14] However, in certain circumstances the debtor's creditors may file a petition in order to force the debtor into bankruptcy. This type of case is referred to as an "involuntary case."[15]

The vast majority of large business cases are commenced as Chapter 11 cases and remain as Chapter 11 cases regardless of whether the debtor is ultimately reorganized or liquidated. Nonetheless, Chapter 11 cases do not necessarily have to end with the confirmation of a plan of reorganization. The bankruptcy court may dismiss a Chapter 11 case or convert the case into a case under Chapter 7.[16] Chapter 7 cases can also be dismissed.[17] A case can be converted or dismissed only for cause, which, among other things, includes the inability of the debtor to propose or carry out a feasible plan of reorganization, an unreasonable delay that causes harm to creditors, or failure of the debtor to pay required fees and expenses.[18]

Dismissals are uncommon, however, and generally do not occur unless the debtor has no unencumbered assets. The reason for this is that dismissals terminate the automatic stay,[19] which protects the debtor from collection actions by creditors, as discussed more fully in the following subsection f. Thus, when a case is dismissed there is often a race to the courthouse by creditors seeking to initiate or continue actions to collect on the debts that are owed to them.

(c) The Chapter 11 Debtor-in-Possession. Upon the entry of an order for relief under Chapter 11,[20] the debtor is automatically authorized to continue to operate its business and manage its property as a Chapter 11 "debtor-in-possession," commonly referred to as a DIP.

The DIP continues to operate its business throughout the Chapter 11 case,[21] unless a Chapter 11 trustee is appointed by the Bankruptcy Court.[22] While the DIP is in control of the business, it is granted a variety of powers, similar to the powers that a trustee would receive if a trustee were appointed. These powers include the right to use, sell, or lease all

---

[13] Bankruptcy Code §§ 1123(b) (4), 1129(a) (11). See, e.g., *In re Coastal Equities*, 33 B.R. 898, 904 (Bankr. S.D. Cal. 1983).

[14] Bankruptcy Code § 301.

[15] Bankruptcy Code § 303. Involuntary petitions are not allowed in Chapters 9, 12, or 13. Bankruptcy Code, § 303(a).

[16] Bankruptcy Code § 1112.

[17] Bankruptcy Code § 707(a).

[18] Bankruptcy Code §§ 707(a), 1112(b).

[19] For a discussion of the automatic stay, see the following subsection f in this chapter.

[20] An order for relief is entered automatically upon the filing of a voluntary petition (Bankruptcy Code, § 301). In an involuntary case, the order for relief is entered only if the court determines that the grounds for involuntary bankruptcy have been satisfied or if the debtor fails to controvert, in a timely manner, the allegations set forth in the involuntary petition. Bankruptcy Code § 303(h).

[21] Bankruptcy Code §§ 1107(a), 1108.

[22] Bankruptcy Code § 1104(a). A Chapter 11 trustee is appointed only "for cause, including fraud, dishonesty, incompetence or gross mismanagement of the affairs of the debtor, either before or after the commencement of the case."

property of the estate, except cash collateral,[23] in the ordinary course of the debtor's business;[24] the right to obtain postpetition credit, known as DIP financing;[25] the right to assume or reject certain executory contracts;[26] and the right to exercise the Bankruptcy Code's "avoiding powers," which include the power to recover preferences[27] and fraudulent conveyances[28] and to avoid unperfected security interests.[29]

(d) The United States Trustee and the Chapter 7 Trustee.   In addition to the trustee who may be appointed in Chapter 11 cases, there are several other types of trustees in bankruptcy cases who serve quite different purposes and, accordingly, have distinct powers. One is the United States Trustee, whose duties include the administration and supervision of all bankruptcy cases that are filed within a designated geographic area.[30] In addition, in all Chapter 7 cases, a bankruptcy trustee must be appointed or elected to manage the assets of the business and to dispose of the debtor's assets through an orderly liquidation sale or sales.[31]

Initially, an interim trustee is appointed by the United States Trustee[32] substantially contemporaneously with the entry of the order for relief.[33] The interim trustee becomes the permanent trustee unless the requisite majority of creditors[34] elects a different trustee at the meeting of creditors held pursuant to § 341(a) of the Bankruptcy Code.[35] The Chapter 7 trustee's primary responsibility is to gather together all of the debtor's nonexempt assets and to convert these assets to cash "as expeditiously as is compatible with the

---

[23] Cash collateral is defined by Section 363(a) of the Bankruptcy Code to include any cash, negotiable instruments, documents of title, securities, deposit accounts, or other cash equivalents in which both the debtor and another entity have some interest. Before cash collateral can be sold, used, or leased, either there must be notice and a court hearing to authorize such action or each entity that has an interest in the cash collateral must consent to such use, sale, or lease. Bankruptcy Code § 363(c) (2).

[24] Bankruptcy Code § 363(c) (1). If the use, sale, or lease is not in the ordinary course of the debtor's business, the trustee or DIP must request a court hearing to authorize such action and must give notice to the other interested party or parties. Bankruptcy Code § 363(b) (1).

[25] Bankruptcy Code § 364.

[26] Bankruptcy Code § 365. This power is very important in the context of intellectual property and is discussed more fully in section 12.2(b) of this chapter.

[27] Bankruptcy Code § 547.

[28] Bankruptcy Code §§ 544(b), 548.

[29] Bankruptcy Code § 544(a); see also U.C.C. 9–301 (1) (b).

[30] The United States Trustee is responsible for supervising various administrative aspects of bankruptcy cases that were previously the responsibility of bankruptcy judges under the predecessor statute to the Bankruptcy Code. See generally, George M. Treister, J. Ronald Trost, Leon S. Forman, Kenneth N. Klee, Richard B. Levin, *Fundamentals of Bankruptcy Law*, at 85 (2d ed. 1991). The Office of the United States Trustee is part of the Justice Department, and a United States Trustee is appointed by the United States Attorney General to serve for five years in each of 21 regions of the country. 28 U.S.C. §§ 581, 586.

[31] Bankruptcy Code § 704(1).

[32] The United States Trustee is required to select the interim trustee from the panel of trustees that the United States Trustee is required to establish in the region of the country for which that United States Trustee is responsible. 28 U.S.C. § 581 (a) (1); Bankruptcy Code § 701(a) (1).

[33] Bankruptcy Code § 701(a) (1).

[34] The trustee can be elected only if creditors holding at least 20% of unsecured debt request an election and if one candidate receives a majority of the dollar amount of the unsecured claims that vote for candidates. Bankruptcy Code § 703(c).

[35] Bankruptcy Code §§ 701(b), 702(d).

best interest of parties in interest."[36] The bankruptcy trustee is also charged with the responsibility of distributing the resulting proceeds to creditors in the strict ordering of priority set forth in § 507(a) of the Bankruptcy Code.[37]

(e) The Bankruptcy Estate and Classification of Claims. The commencement of a bankruptcy case creates an "estate" that is expansively defined to include all legal and equitable interests of a debtor in property as of the commencement of the case, wherever located and by whomever held.[38] Property that is acquired after the commencement of the case (except for earnings from services performed by an individual debtor) and the proceeds, products, rents, and profits derived from property of the estate are also deemed property of the estate. In addition, defenses of the debtor to claims and lawsuits become defenses assertable by the estate.[39]

Claims against the estate are divided into different categories, depending on whether the underlying debts are secured by collateral (secured claims) or whether they merely represent debts for which no specific collateral has been taken (unsecured claims). Claims are also distinguished according to whether they relate to debts created before the bankruptcy case was commenced (prepetition claims) or after the commencement of the case (administrative claims.)[40] Furthermore, as described in a later paragraph, claims are also distinguished according to their priority, as established by applicable law.

Secured claimants are entitled to receive the collateral that secures their claim or the value of that collateral before any unsecured creditors share in any value associated with that collateral.[41] Unsecured creditors are entitled to receive payment from the assets remaining after payment in full of the secured creditors' claims against these assets, together with any assets that are not subject to the claims of secured creditors. In a liquidation case, the proceeds of these assets, which are typically referred to as a debtor's "free assets," must be distributed in accordance with the priorities established by § 507 of the Bankruptcy Code.

Section 507 establishes eight levels of priority claims, listed in descending order of priority. In all cases, all senior priority claims must be paid in full before any money is distributed for claims of a lower priority. The first level of priority claims contains administrative expense claims,[42] that is, the actual, necessary costs and expenses of

---

[36] Bankruptcy Code § 704(1).

[37] Bankruptcy Code § 726.

[38] Bankruptcy Code § 541.

[39] Bankruptcy Code § 558.

[40] For a discussion of administrative claims, see pages 409–410.

[41] The interests of secured creditors in their collateral are property rights protected under the Due Process Clause of the Fifth Amendment to the United States Constitution, and these property interests cannot be "taken" from secured creditors by the United States government without providing "just compensation" for that property. U.S. Const. Amend. 5. See *In re Gifford*, 669 F.2d 468, 471, *on reh'g*, 688 F.2d 447 (7th Cir. 1982); *Rodrock v. Security Indus. Bank*, 642 F.2d 1193, 1197–98 (10th Cir. 1981), *aff'd*, 459 U.S. 70 (1982). However, holders of secured claims can be forced to pay for administrative expenses that have been deemed to be "reasonable, necessary costs and expenses of preserving, or disposing of, such property to the extent of any benefit to the holder of such claim," if the secured creditor is directly benefited by the expense. Bankruptcy Code § 507 (c). See *In re Senior - G & A Oper. Co.*, 957 F.2d 1290, 1298–1302 (5th Cir. 1992); *In re Flagstaff Foodserv. Corp.*, 739 F.2d 73 (Part I) (2d Cir. 1984), 762 F.2d 10 (Part II) (2d Cir. 1985), but see *In re McKeesport Steel Castings Co.*, 799 F.2d 91, 94 (3d Cir. 1986) (broader benefit to bankruptcy estate suffices).

[42] Bankruptcy Code § 507(a) (1).

preserving the estate, including associated professional fees and expenses.[43] The second level of priority claims[44] exists only in involuntary cases and consists of claims that arose in the ordinary course of the debtor's business or financial affairs during the "gap period" between commencement of the case and the appointment of a trustee or the entry of the order for relief in the case.[45] The third level of priority claims includes certain claims for wages, salaries, or commissions, including certain claims for vacation, severance, and sick leave pay.[46] The fourth level of priority contains certain claims for contributions to an employee benefit plan.[47] The fifth level contains certain special claims held by parties employed in the grain and fishing industries.[48] The sixth level includes certain claims of individuals for deposits paid for the purchase, lease, or rental of property or services.[49] The seventh level contains certain tax claims of governmental units.[50] The eighth level contains certain claims of governmental agencies based on commitments to maintain the capital of an insured depository institution.[51]

After all priority claims have been paid in full, the nonpriority claims, that is, general unsecured claims, are paid. These claims are generally paid pro rata, unless an applicable statutory or contractual subordination provision or some inequitable conduct compels different treatment.[52] Finally, at the lowest level are any interests in a debtor corporation that are held by shareholders.

Although all creditors can, in theory, receive the full dollar value of their claims against the estate, in the vast majority of bankruptcy cases there are insufficient funds to pay all claims in full. In the typical business case, general unsecured creditors receive fairly small distributions, which are often as low as 10 cents on the dollar.[53]

(f) The Automatic Stay.   The commencement of a bankruptcy case invokes an "automatic stay."[54] Specifically, the commencement of the case operates generally as a stay against the commencement or continuation of most actions or judicial proceedings to collect a debt and acts to create, perfect, or enforce liens or to collect on or take a setoff against a prepetition claim.[55] In short, the automatic stay stops virtually all collection efforts on account of prepetition obligations of the debtor, including any foreclosure proceedings.

The Bankruptcy Code provides specific exceptions to the automatic stay to allow certain governmental or regulatory acts and other specified activities to continue.[56] However, these exceptions are narrowly construed by the courts, because one of the

---

[43] Bankruptcy Code § 503(b).

[44] Bankruptcy Code § 507(a) (2).

[45] Bankruptcy Code § 502(f).

[46] Bankruptcy Code § 507(a) (3).

[47] Bankruptcy Code § 507(a) (4).

[48] Bankruptcy Code § 507(a) (5).

[49] Bankruptcy Code § 507(a) (6).

[50] Bankruptcy Code § 507(a) (7).

[51] Bankruptcy Code § 507(a) (8).

[52] Bankruptcy Code § 510. See generally, Daniel C. Cohn, "Subordinated Claims: Their Classification and Voting Under Chapter 11 of the Bankruptcy Code," 56 *Am. Bankr. L.J.* 293 (1982).

[53] See Michael J. Herbert and Domenic E. Pacitti, "Down and Out in Richmond, Virginia: The Distribution of Assets in Chapter 7 Proceedings Closed During 1984–87," 22 U. Rich. L. Rev. 303, 315, 316 (1988); see also Teresa Sullivan, Elizabeth Warren, and Jay L. Westbrook, "As We Forgive Our Debtors: Bankruptcy and Consumer Credit in America," 203–05 (1989).

[54] Bankruptcy Code § 362(a).

[55] Bankruptcy Code § 362(a).

[56] Bankruptcy Code § 362(b).

purposes of the automatic stay is to provide the trustee and the debtor a "breathing spell" and, in a Chapter 11 case, with an opportunity to attempt to reorganize.[57] If a creditor feels compelled to take action or to continue a proceeding against the debtor, the creditor can seek relief from the automatic stay by formally requesting that the court lift or modify the stay.[58]

There are two grounds upon which a creditor can base a request for relief from an automatic stay. First, a creditor can seek to prove that the debtor is not providing "adequate protection" to the creditor's interest in property of the estate.[59] Second, with respect to actions against property, a creditor can claim that the debtor has no equity in the property and that the property is not necessary for a successful reorganization of the debtor.[60]

However, unless a creditor is granted relief from the automatic stay under § 362(d) of the Bankruptcy Code or proves that the contemplated action falls within one of the exceptions to the automatic stay found in § 362(b) of the Bankruptcy Code, no actions should be taken outside the Bankruptcy Court to collect a debt or pursue a legal action against the debtor. Violation of the automatic stay is, at best, futile, inasmuch as actions taken in violation of the automatic stay are null and void.[61] At worst, such actions can be very costly to overeager creditors, because any deliberate or willful violation of the automatic stay is punishable by holding the responsible party in civil contempt and awards of compensatory damages caused by the violation,[62] including attorney's fees.[63] Furthermore, under certain circumstances involving particularly egregious violations of the automatic stay, punitive damages may be assessed.[64]

12.2 TREATMENT OF INTELLECTUAL PROPERTY IN BANKRUPTCY

(a) Intellectual Property as Executory Contract.   Although intellectual property[65] rights are generally deemed to be "property of the estate" under § 541(a) of the Bankruptcy Code,[66] the value of intellectual property is frequently maximized through the use of

---

[57] *In re Computer Communic, Inc.*, 824 F.2d 725, 729 (9th Cir. 1987).

[58] Bankruptcy Code § 362(d).

[59] Bankruptcy Code § 362(d) (1). *Adequate protection* is defined in § 361 of the Bankruptcy Code.

[60] Bankruptcy Code § 362(d) (2). See *United Savings Ass'n v. Timbers of Inwood Forest*, 484 U.S. 365, 369–376 (1988).

[61] See *Ellis v. Consolidated Diesel Elec. Corp.*, 894 F.2d 371, 372 (10th Cir. 1990); *Borg-Warner Acceptance Corp. v. Hall*, 685 F.2d 1306, 1308 (11th Cir. 1982); see generally Martin J. Bienenstock, *Bankruptcy Reorganization*, 127–130 (1987).

[62] Bankruptcy Code § 362(h). See, e.g., *In re Crysen/Montenay Energy Co.*, 902 F.2d 1098 (2d Cir. 1990).

[63] *In re Computer Communic., Inc.*, 824 F.2d at 731; *In re Carter*, 691 F.2d 390 (8th Cir. 1982).

[64] See, e.g., *Budget Serv. Co. v. Better Homes of Va., Inc.*, 804 F.2d 289 (4th Cir. 1986); *In re Brockington*, 129 B.R. 68, 71 (Bankr. D.S.C. 1991).

[65] The term *intellectual property* is used here as defined in Section 101(56) of the Bankruptcy Code to mean (1) patents, (2) trademarks, trade names, and service marks, (3) copyrights, (4) trade secrets, (5) inventions, process, designs, or plants protected under Title 35 of the United States Code, (6) patent applications, (7) plant varieties, (8) works of authorship protected under Title 17 of the United States Code, (9) and masks work protected under Chapter 9 of Title 17 of the United States Code.

[66] See, e.g., *In re Taylor*, 91 B.R. 302, 311 (Bankr. D.N.J. 1988) (recording contract); *In re Nettie Lee Shops of Bristol, Inc.*, 49 B.R. 946, 947 (Bankr. D. Va. 1985) (trademark); *In re Varisco*, 16 B.R. 634, 637 (Bankr. M.D. Fla. 1981) (franchise rights); *In re R.S. Pinellas Motel P'shp*, 2 B.R. 113, 116–17 (Bankr. M.D. Fla. 1979) (motel license); but see *Harris v. Emus Records Corp.*, 734 F.2d 1329, 1334 (9th Cir. 1984) (copyright license not property of estate).

agreements that impose continuous obligations on the agreeing parties. These agreements are typically deemed to be executory contracts under the Bankruptcy Code.[67]

It is not always clear, however, whether a particular agreement is an executory contract for bankruptcy purposes. This uncertainty occurs, in part, because the term *executory contract* is not specifically defined by the Bankruptcy Code and no universally accepted definition has been developed by the courts.

The majority of courts[68] have used the definition of executory contracts developed by Vern Countryman in his seminal article on the subject[69] that was published in the early 1970s.[70] Countryman defines an executory contract as "a contract in which the obligation of both the bankrupt and the other party to the contract are so far unperformed that the failure of either to complete performance would constitute a material breach excusing the performance of the other."[71]

Clearly, most intellectual property agreements can be considered executory contracts under this definition, because there are normally significant remaining obligations to be performed by the parties to such agreements. For example, courts have found that computer software and trademark licenses,[72] franchise agreements,[73] distributor agreements,[74] patent licenses,[75] and recording contracts[76] are executory contracts. It has been held, however, that a recording contract was not executory where the debtor-record company's only remaining obligation was to pay royalties to the recording artist-licensor.[77] Furthermore, in cases involving book publishing contracts where the publisher-

---

[67] See the discussion of executory contracts on page 413.

[68] See, e.g., *Gloria Mfg. Corp. v. Int'l Ladies' Garment Workers' Union*, 734 F.2d 1020, 1022 (4th Cir. 1984); *In re Select-A-Seat Corp.*, 625 F.2d 290 (9th Cir. 1980); *In re Holland Enterp., Inc.*, 25 B.R. 301, 303 (E.D.N.C. 1982); *In re A.J. Lane & Co., Inc.*, 107 B.R. 435, 436 (Bankr. D. Mass. 1989); see also *NLRB v. Bildisco & Bildisco*, 465 U.S. 513, 522 n.6 (1984); H.R. Rep. No. 95–595, at 347 (1987).

[69] Vern Countryman, "Executory Contracts in Bankruptcy," 57 *Minn. L. Rev.* 439 (1973) (Part I) and 58 *Minn. L. Rev.* 479 (1974) (Part II).

[70] Some courts have applied another definition, under which a contract is executory for bankruptcy purposes when only one of the parties has remaining affirmative obligations other than the mere payment of money. See, e.g., *In re Tonry*, 724 F.2d 467, 468 (5th Cir. 1984); *In re Jackson Brewing Co.*, 567 F.2d 618, 623 (5th Cir. 1978). Other courts treat a contract as executory if such treatment yields a result that is consistent with the underlying policies of the Bankruptcy Code. This is often called the "balancing of the equities" approach. See, e.g., *In re Martin Bros. Toolmakers, Inc.*, 796 F.2d 1435, 1439 (11th Cir. 1986); *In re Becknell & Crace Coal Co.*, 761 F.2d 319, 322 (6th Cir. 1985); *In re Fox*, 83 B.R. 290, 299 (Bankr. E.D. Pa. 1988). These other definitions are not discussed in detail because they are beyond the scope of this chapter and because Countryman's definition is the majority view.

[71] Countryman, "Executory Contracts" Part I, 460. This definition, which is referred to as the "material breach" test, has as one of its key elements the requirement that there must be a mutuality of obligations that remain to be performed by the parties to the contract. See *In re Dolphin Titan Int'l, Inc.*, 93 B.R. 508, 510 (Bankr. S.D. Tex. 1988); 2 *Collier on Bankruptcy* ¶ 365.02, at 365–15 (15th ed. 1992).

[72] See, e.g., *In re Select-A-Seat*, 625 F.2d 290, 292 (9th Cir. 1980); *In re Rooster, Inc.*, 100 B.R. 228, 231 (Bankr. E.D. Pa. 1989); *In re Specialty Foods, Inc.*, 91 B.R. 364, 374 (Bankr. W.D. Pa. 1988); *In re Luce Indus., Inc.*, 14 B.R. 529, 530 (S.D.N.Y. 1981).

[73] See, e.g., *In re Silk Plants, Etc. Franchise Sys., Inc.*, 100 B.R. 360, 362 (M.D. Tenn. 1989); *In re ERA Central Reg. Serv., Inc.*, 39 B.R. 738, 739 (Bankr. C.D. Ill. 1984).

[74] See, e.g., *In re Auto Dealers Serv., Inc.*, 110 B.R. 68, 70 (Bankr. M.D. Fla. 1990); *In re Logical Software, Inc.*, 66 B.R. 683, 686 (Bankr. D. Mass. 1986).

[75] See, e.g., *In re Alltech Plastics, Inc.*, 71 B.R. 686 (Bankr. W.D. Tenn. 1987).

[76] See, e.g., *In re Taylor*, 91 B.R. at 310.

[77] See *In re Monument Record Corp.*, 61 B.R. 866 (Bankr. M.D. Tenn. 1986).

licensee has filed for bankruptcy, several courts have held that the contract was not executory because the author-licensor did not owe any remaining duties to the debtor-licensee.[78]

Although these cases all involved debtor-licensees, this does not mean that a license agreement is an executory contract only when the debtor is the licensee.[79] The decision as to whether a license agreement is an executory contract depends on the extent and type of obligations that remain to be performed under the contract—facts that do not necessarily depend on which party is in bankruptcy. Accordingly, several courts have held that license agreements can be executory contracts even when the debtor is the licensor.[80]

(b) The Options: Assumption, Assumption and Assignment, or Rejection of the Contract. Once it is determined that an intellectual property agreement is an executory contract, the trustee[81] has three options pursuant to § 365 of the Bankruptcy Code. Specifically, the trustee can (1) assume the contract, (2) assume and assign the contract, or (3) reject the contract.

(i) Assumption of the Contract. The trustee should decide to assume an executory contract when the sum of the benefits received from continued performance of the agreement outweigh the obligations that are imposed. However, not all executory contracts can be assumed by the trustee. The three major types of executory contracts that cannot be assumed are (1) contracts that are of a type which, by their very nature, are nonassumable under applicable nonbankruptcy law,[82] (2) executory contracts to make loans or extend financial accommodations to, or issue securities of, the debtor,[83] and (3) leases of nonresidential real property that have been terminated under applicable nonbankruptcy law prior to the order for relief in the bankruptcy case.[84]

If a particular executory contract is of the type that can be assumed, three things must occur before a trustee may assume the contract. First, the trustee must cure any defaults under the contract or provide "adequate assurance" that there will be a prompt cure of such defaults.[85] Second, the trustee must compensate the other party to the contract "for

---

[78] See *In re Learning Publications, Inc.*, B.R. 763, 765 (Bankr. M.D. Fla. 1988); *In re Stein & Day, Inc.*, 81 B.R. 263, 267 (Bankr. S.D.N.Y. 1988).

[79] See *In re Quintex Entertainment, Inc.*, 950 F.2d 1492, 1496 (9th Cir. 1991).

[80] See *In re Three-Star Telecast, Inc.*, 93 B.R. 310, 312 (D.P.R. 1988) (television programming license); *In re New York Shoes, Inc.*, 84 B.R. 947, 960 (Bankr. E.D. Pa. 1988) (trademark contract); *In re Best Film & Video Corp.*, 46 B.R. 861, 869 (Bankr. E.D.N.Y. 1985) (movie distribution contract).

[81] As set forth in section 12.1 (c) of this chapter, in a Chapter 11 case, the DIP exercises most of the powers that are granted to the trustee. Therefore, the term *trustee* is used here to refer to either the actual trustee or the DIP performing the role of a trustee.

[82] Bankruptcy Code § 365 (c) (1). The prime example of such nonassumable contracts are so-called personal service contracts, which involve the unique skills or talents of a party thereto and cannot be assumed without the consent of the other party because the other party is relying on those skills or talents. See, e.g., *In re Alltech Plastics, Inc.*, 71 B.R. 68 at 689 (patent license not assumable). However, other types of contracts, such as dealership agreements, are also covered by § 365 (c) (1). See *In re Pioneer Ford Sales*, 729 F.2d 27 (1st Cir. 1984). Such nonassumable contracts are discussed more fully below in Section 12.2 (d) (v) of this chapter, on page 415.

[83] Bankruptcy Code § 365 (c) (2); see, e.g., *In re Cardinal Indus. Inc.*, 146 B.R. 720 (Bankr. S.D. Ohio 1992).

[84] Bankruptcy Code § 365 (c) (3).

[85] Bankruptcy Code § 365 (b) (1) (A).

any actual pecuniary loss to such party resulting from such default."[86] Finally, the trustee must provide "adequate assurance of future performance" under the contract.[87]

When the trustee assumes an executory contract, the contract must be assumed in its entirety, including all of the contract's burdens and benefits.[88] Thus, the trustee cannot selectively assume provisions of an executory contract that are beneficial and simultaneously attempt to reject burdensome provisions.[89] Exceptions to this rule are that the trustee can essentially ignore most anti-assignment clauses (clauses that restrict the trustee's ability to assign the contract to a third party[90]) or so-called ipso facto clauses (clauses that terminate the contract or create a default upon the insolvency or commencement of the bankruptcy case[91]).

(ii) Assumption and Assignment of the Contract.   Although a trustee or DIP presumably will not assume an executory contract unless there is some value that can be realized from doing so, the decision to assume may be based on the fact that a third party will be able to use these benefits better than, or instead of, the bankruptcy estate. Pursuant to the Bankruptcy Code, once an executory contract is assumed, the trustee or DIP may assign (i.e., sell) the contract to an entity that will pay for the ability to receive the benefits under the contract.[92] Thus, assumption and assignment of an executory contract can be very beneficial to the estate, because the funds received upon the sale can be used to repay creditors or provide operating capital to facilitate the process of reorganization.

Another major advantage of assumption and assignment of an executory contract is that once the contract has been assigned, the trustee and the debtor's bankruptcy estate are relieved from any liability for breaches of the contract that occur after the date of the assignment.[93] This allows the trustee to free the debtor's bankruptcy estate from burdensome obligations and risks once a third party has been located who is willing to step into the role that the debtor previously occupied.

---

[86] Bankruptcy Code § 365 (b) (1) (B).

[87] Bankruptcy Code § 365 (b) (1) (C).

[88] *NLRB v. Bildisco & Bildisco*, 465 U.S. at 531–32; *In re Chicago Rock Island and Pac. R. Co.*, 860 F.2d 267, 272 (7th Cir. 1988); *In re Office Prod. of America, Inc.*, 140 B.R. 407, 410 (Bankr. W.D. Tex. 1992).

[89] *In re Auto Dealer Serv., Inc.*, 110 B.R. at 70 (Bankr. M.D. Fla. 1990); *In re Executive Tech. Data Sys.*, 79 B.R. 276 (Bankr. E.D. Mich. 1987).

[90] Bankruptcy Code §365 (f) (1). See, e.g., *In re Office Prod. of America*, 140 B.R. at 410; *In re Cafe Partners/Washington 1983*, 90 B.R. 1, 6 (Bankr. D.D.C. 1988). However, it must be remembered that the Bankruptcy Code prohibits a debtor from assigning an executory contract, regardless of whether the contract itself prohibits or restricts assignment, if "applicable law" excuses the nondebtor party "from accepting performance from or rendering performance to an entity other than the debtor or the debtor in possession." Bankruptcy Code § 365 (c) (1) (A); (see section 12.2(b) of this chapter.)

[91] Bankruptcy Code §365 (e) (1). See, e.g., *In re Compass Van & Storage Corp.*, 65 B.R. 1007 (Bankr. E.D.N.Y. 1986). However, Bankruptcy Code §365 (e) (2) provides that such ipso facto clauses *can* be enforced if "applicable law" excuses the nondebtor party to the contract "from accepting performance from or rendering performance to the trustee or to an assignee of such contract or lease, whether or not such contract or lease prohibits or restricts assignment of rights or delegation of duties" and "such party does not consent to such assumption or assignment."

[92] Bankruptcy Code § 365 (f) (2). See, e.g., *In re Bronx-Westchester Mack Corp.*, 20 B.R. 139, 141–43 (Bankr. S.D.N.Y. 1982).

[93] Bankruptcy Code §365(k); See, e.g., *In re Sapolin Paints, Inc.*, 20 B.R. 497, 500 (Bankr. E.D.N.Y. 1982).

(iii) Rejection of the Contract.   Conversely, if the trustee determines that the contract is overburdensome or otherwise undesirable to the estate, the trustee can reject the contract. There are a variety of consequences of the decision to reject an executory contract. For example, if the trustee rejects a contract that has not been previously assumed,[94] rejection constitutes a breach of the contract[95] that entitles the nondebtor party to a prepetition claim for damages against the debtor's bankruptcy estate.[96] However, this claim is of limited value, because it will entitle the nondebtor party to a pro rata share in the typically small distribution that is made at the end of the Chapter 11 case to satisfy the claims of general unsecured creditors.[97]

(iv) Effect of Rejection.   Prior to 1988 many courts held that a debtor-licensor's rejection of an intellectual property license simply freed the debtor-licensor from its obligations under the license (including permitting the debtor to license its product to other parties) while permitting the licensee to continue to use the property that was the subject of the license.[98] Although this approach to rejection of license agreements created problems for the intellectual property licensees whose licenses were rejected in bankruptcy, it did not lead to an organized effort by licensees to have the law changed. Accordingly, licensees suffered through the problems that resulted from rejection of their license agreements when the licensor entered bankruptcy.

However, this approach to rejection of license agreements changed dramatically when, in *Lubrizol Enterprises, Inc. v. Richmond Metal Finishers, Inc.*,[99] the Court of Appeals for the Fourth Circuit held that a licensee could not use previously licensed technology after the debtor-licensor rejected the license agreement. The result in *Lubrizol* caused severe hardship to many nondebtor intellectual property licensees, who would no longer be allowed to use the debtor-licensor's property after rejection, even though such property may have been critical to their business, and were left with a mere prepetition claim for damages caused by the rejection.

(v) The Intellectual Property Protection Act.   In an effort to remedy the hardship for licensees that was caused by the *Lubrizol* decision, in 1988 Congress passed and the President signed into law the Intellectual Property Bankruptcy Protection Act (IPBPA).[100] Congress intended to "clarif[y] the rights of parties if a licensor or licensee declares bankruptcy."[101] It added § 365(n) to the Bankruptcy Code, which allows a licensee to elect to continue using previously licensed property even after a debtor-licensor rejects a license agreement.[102]

---

[94] If an executory contract is rejected after it has already been assumed by the trustee or DIP, the creditor's claim will be elevated to the level of an administrative expense claim under Bankruptcy Code § 365(g)(2) and will be entitled to priority of payment. See the discussion of priority of claims in section 12.1(e) of this chapter.

[95] See Bankruptcy Code § 365(g)(1).

[96] Bankruptcy Code § 502(g); see, e.g., *In re Executive Tech. Data Sys.*, 79 B.R. at 282.

[97] See section 12.1(e) of this chapter.

[98] See *In re Select-A-Seat Corp.*, 625 F.2d 290.

[99] *In re Richmond Metal Finishers*, 756 F.2d 1043 (4th Cir. 1985), *cert. denied*, 475 U.S. 1057 (1986).

[100] Pub. L. No. 100–506, 102 Stat. 2538 (1988); S. Rep. No. 100–505, 100th Cong. 2d Sess. (1988), reprinted in 1988 U.S.C.C.A.N. 3200.

[101] 133 Cong. Rec. 133, 100th Cong., 1st Sess. (1987) (statement of Sen. DeConcini).

[102] Section 365(n) also amended certain subsections of section 101, the definitional section of the Bankruptcy Code.

(vi) The Scope and Limitations of § 365(n).   Section 365(n) does not apply to all situations involving a license of intellectual property. Specifically, § 365(n) does not cover situations where the debtor-licensor assumes the license or where the licensee files for bankruptcy. Furthermore, § 101(56) of the Bankruptcy Code limits the definition of intellectual property to: "(A) trade secret; (B) invention, process, design, or plant protected under title 35; (C) patent application; (D) plant variety; (E) work of authorship protected under title 17; or (F) mask work protected under chapter 9 of title 17; to the extent protected by applicable non-bankruptcy law." Therefore, certain types of intellectual property, most notably trademarks, trade names, and service marks (hereafter in this chapter collectively referred to as trademarks) are not covered by § 365(n).[103]

The exclusion of trademarks from the protections of § 365(n) leaves trademark licensees facing the risk that a licensor will be allowed to use the *Lubrizol* approach to reject the license and deny the trademark licensee access to the licensed property. This distinction between trademark licenses and other types of intellectual property licenses creates further complications, because a license is often granted to cover not only a patent or copyright, but also the corresponding trademark associated with the goods produced. A licensor thus may be able to reject a license of a trademark even though the underlying license of a patent or copyright is subject to § 365(n). The licensee would thereby have the ability to create the products under the patent or copyright of the license but might not be able to market them under the trademark. This would remove the licensee's major incentive for entering into a license agreement in the first place, by denying the licensee the name recognition and added value associated with the trademark.

Despite the complications and problems created by such treatment of trademarks, Congress intentionally excluded trademarks from § 365(n), thereby deferring the issue to the equitable powers of bankruptcy courts.[104] In so doing, Congress determined that rejection of executory trademark licenses raised issues that cannot be simply resolved under the IPBA, because trademark licensing relationships depend to a large extent on control of the quality of the products or services sold.[105]

Although this issue has not been authoritatively decided by the courts, another important limitation is that § 365(n) apparently does not apply to licenses of intellectual property that are created under foreign law. Section 365(n) protects a licensee of intellectual property from rejection by a debtor-licensor, and the definition of intellectual property found in § 101(56)(E) of the Bankruptcy Code refers only to works protected under Title 17 of the United States Code (the Copyright Act).[106]

Because other nations have their own methods of protecting intellectual property rights, intellectual property created outside the United States does not automatically receive the protection of the Copyright Act, which protects only against unauthorized publication or reproduction of copyrighted material for "original works of authorship"

---

[103] *In re Blackstone Potato Chip Co.*, 109 B.R. 557 (Bankr. D.R.I. 1990). Apparently, franchises are also excluded from the protection of section 365(n) because they are essentially contractual relationships in which the franchisee receives a special right or privilege to market certain goods under a trademark. Franchises are thus equivalent to licenses to use the name or logo associated with the franchisor, i.e, its trademark, and, because trademarks are not protected by section 365(n), franchises should similarly remain unprotected by section 365(n).

[104] See S. Rep. No. 100–505, 100th Cong. 2d Sess. (1988), reprinted in 1988 U.S.C.C.A.N. 3200, 3204.

[105] See S. Rep. No. 100–505, 100th Cong. 2d Sess., Supra, n.105.

[106] 17 U.S.C. §§ 101–914.

created by citizens and domiciliaries of the United States.[107] Thus, foreign-created intellectual property appears to fall outside the Bankruptcy Code definition of the term *intellectual property.*

However, various treaties have been enacted to grant protection to foreign works of intellectual property within the signatory nations, the most important of which is the Berne Convention. It is possible that, pursuant to the Berne Convention, a party granted rights under a license of foreign-created intellectual property might gain protection under the Copyright Act and, thereby, also receive protection under § 365(n) of the Bankruptcy Code. Nonetheless, although the parties to a license may be able to obtain *some* protection for foreign-created intellectual property in the United States by registering a foreign copyright, it is unclear whether this results in the type of protection under the Copyright Act that is required for protection under the Bankruptcy Code. In addition, the operation of the Berne Convention is limited by language in the Copyright Act, which states that the Berne Convention cannot be used to expand or create rights in foreign intellectual property.[108]

(vii) The Effect of § 365(n) on the Rights and Obligations of the Parties. Under § 365(n), the debtor-licensor's rejection of a license agreement leaves the licensee with two options: the licensee may elect to treat the rejection as a termination of the agreement[109] or may elect to retain its rights under the rejected agreement,[110] including exclusivity rights.[111] However, if the licensee elects to retain its rights under the license agreement, it cannot force the debtor-licensor to perform its obligations under the agreement.[112]

If the licensee elects to retain its rights under the agreement, it must continue to make all royalty payments to the debtor-licensor,[113] and the debtor-licensor must continue to provide the property to the licensee[114] and must not interfere with the licensee's rights to such property.[115] An election by the licensee to retain its rights has the effect of waiving any setoff rights and administrative claims that are related to the rejection.[116] However, the licensee is still allowed to file a prepetition claim for damages caused by the debtor-licensor's rejection.[117]

Inasmuch as the debtor-licensor will be relieved of all of its obligations under the license agreement (except for exclusivity obligations), the licensee may not want to elect to retain its rights, because the debtor-licensor will no longer have to provide the continued maintenance, support, and training that may be crucial to the licensee's effective use of the property. Prior to the debtor-licensor's decision to assume or reject, the licensor must continue to provide the licensee with the property and to comply with the license agreement in all respects.

---

[107] 17 U.S.C. § 102.

[108] 17 U.S.C. § 104(c).

[109] Bankruptcy Code § 365(n) (1) (A).

[110] Bankruptcy Code § 365(n) (1) (B).

[111] Exclusivity rights are simply the rights of the licensee to remain as the sole distributor of the licensor's relevant intellectual property within an agreed-upon geographic area.

[112] Bankruptcy Code § 365(n) (1) (B). The only exception to this general prohibition against specific enforcement of a licensee's rights is that a licensee is granted the power to enforce any exclusivity provision against the licensor.

[113] Bankruptcy Code § 365(n) (2) (B).

[114] Bankruptcy Code § 365(n) (3) (A).

[115] Bankruptcy Code § 365(n) (3) (B).

[116] Bankruptcy Code § 365(n) (2) (C) (i).

[117] Bankruptcy Code § 365(g).

If the licensee elects to treat rejection as a termination of the license agreement, it may file a general unsecured claim for damages caused by the debtor-licensor's termination of the agreement and an administrative claim for postpetition damages, if any.[118]

(viii) Prebankruptcy Planning.   Pursuant to § 365(n), the rights that are retained by a licensee whose license has been rejected are the rights that existed immediately prior to the commencement of the case.[119] Such rights continue for the duration of the agreement, and any extensions of the agreement that are exercisable by the licensee.[120] Licensees should therefore structure their license agreements carefully so that the agreements will protect their rights to use and control distribution of any and all of the property covered.

Specifically, a license agreement should clearly set forth the rights that are available to the licensee if the licensor breaches the agreement. The agreement should further provide for the licensee's absolute right to obtain any existing intellectual property upon the licensor's breach of the agreement.

The legislative history of § 365(n) states that the licensee is able to obtain only *existing* intellectual property, however, and not any intellectual property that is produced or completed after the licensor enters bankruptcy.[121] This approach makes sense, but because § 365(n) allows the licensee to retain only the rights that existed immediately prior to the moment when the debtor-licensor filed for bankruptcy, the results can be disastrous for a licensee when there is partially completed intellectual property at the time the debtor-licensor enters bankruptcy.

For example, the licensor might have been creating a film, book, or computer software program that was to be distributed by the licensee, but ran out of funds in the middle of the project or met some other unforeseen difficulties. If there was intellectual property that had not yet been completed at the time of the licensor's bankruptcy filing, the licensee would not be authorized to obtain that property from the debtor-licensor and would not be able to force the licensor to complete the intellectual property at issue.

This situation can create significant problems, because the licensee would almost certainly need to use the intellectual property but would have no effective means of access to that property. Of course, the licensee may be able to negotiate with the debtor-licensor in order to obtain access to the intellectual property, but the licensee has little or no leverage over the licensor in such circumstances. Although the licensor may need cash to assist in its reorganization efforts, there is no reason that the licensor will feel bound to maintain its license with the licensee if it appears that a third party might be willing to pay more for the right to use the intellectual property.

(ix) Planning Suggestions for Trademark Licensees.   As stated earlier in this chapter,[122] the protections afforded to licensees of intellectual property under § 365(n) do not apply to licensees of trademarks. Thus, if the *Lubrizol* theory (rejection as destruction of the contract) is applied, trademark licensees are still confronted with the pre-§ 365(n) hardships associated with having the debtor-licensor reject their trademark license agreements. Rejection of a license is particularly damaging to the trademark licensee when a

---

[118] Bankruptcy Code § 503(b).
[119] Bankruptcy Code § 365(n) (1).
[120] Bankruptcy Code § 365(n) (1) (B).
[121] Sen. Rep. No. 100–505, 100 Cong., 2d. Sess. 8–11 (1988).
[122] See section 12.2(b)(vi) of this chapter.

licensor is the licensee's only source for the property, which thereby threatens to put the licensee out of business.

However, the result of rejection may not be so drastic for a licensee whose trademark licenses have been rejected. Several recent cases have interpreted § 365 of the Bankruptcy Code so that rejection creates a much less dramatic readjustment of the rights and obligations of the parties to an agreement. For example, in *In re Walnut Assoc.*,[123] the Bankruptcy Court for the Eastern District of Pennsylvania held that rejection does not effect a complete destruction or elimination of the contract.

The court explained that a debtor's decision to reject an executory contract simply represents a decision not to assume the contract, so that the nondebtor party does not receive an administrative priority claim against the debtor's bankruptcy estate if the debtor fails to complete its obligations under the contract.[124] Thus, the debtor was not permitted to use § 365 of the Bankruptcy Code as a justification for automatically escaping from all of its obligations through rejection of the contract. The court explained that the question of whether the agreement was still enforceable depended on an interpretation of state law governing contract rights.[125]

The *In re Walnut Assoc.* case also followed the reasoning of *In re Drexel Burnham Lambert Group, Inc.*,[126] in which it was held that rejection of an executory contract merely created a breach of the agreement pursuant to § 365(g) of the Bankruptcy Code. The court in *In re Drexel Burnham Lambert* stated that rejection does not alter the property rights or other interests that the nondebtor party has acquired pursuant to the executory contract.[127]

Although these two cases provide a stark contrast to the line of cases that culminated in the *Lubrizol* decision, many prior decisions have clearly supported this interpretation of the effect of rejection. Courts have repeatedly held that rejection cannot be equated with rescission or complete cancellation of an executory contract[128] and that only future obligations under the contract are affected by rejection.[129] According to this view, any fully performed portion of an executory contract remains undisturbed by rejection, regardless of whether the performance occurred prepetition or postpetition.[130]

For example, in *In re A.J. Lane & Co.*, a real estate developer, as a Chapter 11 DIP, moved to reject a repurchase option agreement that had been negotiated as part of the debtor's purchase of a tract of land from a railroad company. The debtor was allowed to reject the repurchase option without disturbing the underlying real estate sale that had already been performed. The court explained that although executory contracts must be assumed or rejected in their entirety, the debtor could only "reject the entire *remaining*

---

[123] 145 B.R. 489, 494 (Bankr. E.D. Pa. 1992).

[124] 145 B.R. at 494. The court in *In re Walnut Assoc.* explicitly adopted the reasoning of several commentators regarding the proper manner of interpreting the effect of rejection of executory contracts. See Michael T. Andrew, "Executory Contracts in Bankruptcy: Understanding 'Rejection'" 59 *U. Colo. L. Rev.* 845 (1988); see also Jay L. Westbrook, "A Functional Analysis of Executory Contracts," 74 *Minn. L. Rev.* 227 (1989).

[125] 145 B.R. at 495.

[126] 138 B.R. 687 (Bankr. S.D.N.Y. 1992).

[127] 138 B.R. at 711.

[128] See, e.g., *In re A.J. Lane & Co., Inc.*, 107 B.R. at 437; *In re Metro Transp. Co.*, 87 B.R. 338, 343 (Bankr. E.D. Pa. 1988); *In re Rudaw/Empirical Software Prod., Ltd.*, 83 B.R. 241, 246, (Bankr. S.D.N.Y. 1988); *In re Exec. Tech. Data Sys., Inc.*, 79 B.R. at 282.

[129] *In re Exec. Tech. Data Sys.*, 79 B.R. at 282.

[130] See *In re A.J. Lane & Co., Inc.*, 107 B.R. at 437; *In re Metro Transp. Co.*, 87 B.R. at 343.

portion of the contract."[131] The court stated that rejection does not disturb the "property which has become part of the bankruptcy estate under § 541 [of the Bankruptcy Code]."[132]

In addition, in *In re Metro Transp. Co.* a Chapter 11 DIP was allowed to reject two agreements with cabdrivers, without the need to reject previously completed aspects of this agreement, because "performances completed by the Debtor or by the other parties pursuant to the Agreements in issue are not affected by the Debtor's instant motions [to reject the Agreement]."[133] The court reasoned that rejection was not equal to rescission of the contract and, therefore, partial performance of an executory contract is not thereby "undone."

Accordingly, under this line of cases, a debtor-licensor should not be able to use rejection to cut off all of the trademark licensee's rights under an executory contract. Rather, the debtor-licensor should be able to use § 365 of the Bankruptcy Code to protect itself from burdensome obligations only by choosing not to assume the contract.

Regardless of whether the trustee can actually avoid or destroy all of the rights and obligations of a trademark license, there are a variety of tools that a trademark licensee can employ to attempt to avoid this dilemma. The following paragraphs describe several useful means of protecting rights in a trademark license, but this list is by no means intended to be exhaustive; other solutions may be appropriate in certain situations.

The first option is for the licensee to draft the license agreement so that it is not executory. There are two ways to accomplish this goal. One approach is to have either or both parties fully perform their contractual obligations so that the entire agreement falls outside the scope of § 365. A drawback to this approach is that drafting a license agreement so that it is not executory is difficult, and perhaps impossible, in many situations. The problem is that in order to draft an agreement that is not executory, there must be no significant obligations that remain to be performed by the parties. Another approach is to "bifurcate" the agreement by placing all ongoing obligations in a separate contract from the licensing agreement itself. Here the problem is that even if the parties completely bifurcate the license agreement in this manner, a bankruptcy court may ignore the form of the transaction and focus on its substance, thereby deeming the entire contract executory and subject to § 365.

A second option is to plan for the possibility of bankruptcy by specifically describing the intellectual property that would be transferred to the licensee upon the debtor-licensor's rejection of the license agreement (and the licensee's subsequent election to retain its rights under the agreement) pursuant to § 365. The parties could also specify the damages to be paid to the licensee upon the debtor-licensor's rejection. One risk in using this tactic is that such a provision in a license agreement might be construed as an ipso facto clause, triggered by the debtor's bankruptcy.[134] In addition, a liquidated damages clause would also have to be enforceable under applicable nonbankruptcy law, or it would be unenforceable in bankruptcy as a nonallowable penalty.

A third option is for the licensee to purchase the trademark outright instead of obtaining a license. One obvious difficulty is that trademark owners are understandably reluctant to part with their trademarks and the revenue streams they provide. Therefore,

---

[131] 107 B.R., at 437 (emphasis in original).

[132] Id., at 437–38.

[133] 87 B.R., at 343.

[134] The trustee's power to ignore ipso facto clauses is discussed in section 12.2 (b)(i) of this chapter, on page 414.

even if the licensor was willing to sell the trademark, the licensee would probably end up having to pay a premium for the trademark, which it might not be able to afford.

As a fourth alternative, the licensee could structure the license agreement as a secured transaction by obtaining a security interest in the intellectual property and underlying goodwill. This would elevate the licensee's claim against the licensor's bankruptcy estate to a secured claim instead of merely a prepetition unsecured claim. Because a security interest grants the secured creditor a property right in the collateral, the licensee could end up owning the trademark postpetition. However, it is doubtful that many licensors would grant a security interest in their trademarks because of their reluctance to relinquish control over such property.

A fifth alternative is to structure the transaction so that the ownership of the trademark transferred to a special-purpose subsidiary such that the trademark would not be included as part of the licensor's bankruptcy estate upon the licensor's filing. If successful, this strategy would completely prevent the bankruptcy dilemma faced by trademark licensees. However, this approach raises a number of other problems under the Bankruptcy Code, which, although not insurmountable, could make it difficult to implement this solution.

These problems include the need to make certain that the transaction would not be deemed a fraudulent conveyance. Thus, the licensor must be solvent at the time of, and as a result of, the transaction, and the licensee must give a "reasonably equivalent value" for the trademark.[135] Furthermore, the parties to the agreement would have to be certain that the deal resulted in a "true sale" rather than the creation of a security interest in the trademark. Finally, the separate identity of the two corporations must be sufficiently clear that a court could not "substantively consolidate"[136] the debtor and the subsidiary, thereby effectively treating the two corporations as a single entity.

A sixth option is that, in the event the trademark license agreement is onerous to the licensee, the licensee could attempt to terminate it prior to the licensor's bankruptcy filing. Prompt termination of licenses is desirable, because if an intellectual property license has not been terminated prior to commencement of a bankruptcy case,[137] the automatic stay will protect the rights created under such an agreement against termination during the bankruptcy case.[138]

One option is to draft the trademark license so as to provide for its automatic termination upon the expiration of the period in which defaults may be cured under the license. Although there is some debate on this issue, many courts have held that if a licensor files for bankruptcy after this period elapses[139] without having cured such

---

[135] See Bankruptcy Code § 548.

[136] See generally, *Augie/Restivo*, 860 F.2d 515, 518 (2d Cir. 1988); *In re Flora Mir Candy Corp.*, 432 F.2d 1060, 1062 (2d Cir. 1970).

[137] See, e.g., *In re Tudor Motor Lodge Assoc., Ltd. P'shp*, 102 B.R. 936 (Bankr. D.N.J. 1989); *In re ERA Central Reg. Serv., Inc.*, 39 B.R. at 740; *In re Moody*, 31 B.R. 216 (Bankr. W.D. Mich. 1982); *In re McLouth Steel Corp.*, 20 B.R. 688, 691 (Bankr. E.D. Mich. 1982).

[138] Bankruptcy Code § 362(a) (3). See, e.g., *In re Wills Motors, Inc.*, 133 B.R. 297, 300 (Bankr. S.D.N.Y. 1991); *In re Varisco*, 16 B.R. at 637; *In re R.S. Pinellas Motel*, supra 2 B.R. at 118.

[139] This issue is somewhat complicated by the fact that § 108(b) of the Bankruptcy Code permits debtors to cure defaults at any time before the later of the end of the contractually agreed upon time period or 60 days after the order for relief in the bankruptcy case. Although there is some disagreement regarding the effect of Bankruptcy Code § 108(b) on the actual period of time that a debtor has to cure defaults, this makes little practical difference because the debtor has, at most, an additional 60 days to cure defaults after the time period specified in the agreement has expired.

defaults, the license will automatically terminate and will be neither property of the estate nor an executory contract.[140]

Licensees must be careful to draft the notice of termination so that the license automatically terminates upon expiration of the period to cure defaults. If the licensee mistakenly drafts a notice of termination that is conditional, that is, if the notice states that termination will occur unless certain action is taken, the license will not terminate automatically.[141] The notice may then be interpreted as a mere statement of intent to terminate in the future, and the licensor will have the power to cure any defaults through a plan of reorganization.[142]

Automatic termination provisions should also be drafted so that it is clear that termination occurs because of failure to cure defaults after the lapse of a specified time period, rather than upon the bankruptcy or insolvency of the licensor. This is necessary to avoid the risk that the provision will be a voidable ipso facto clause triggered by the insolvency or commencement of a bankruptcy proceeding of the debtor.[143]

(c) Other Effects of Licensor's Bankruptcy.   In addition to the § 365(n) issues discussed previously, a variety of other issues arise concerning the treatment of intellectual property in bankruptcy. These issues will directly affect the strategies used by intellectual property licensors and licensees when drafting agreements.

(i) Multiple Obligations: Single Contract or Series of Separate Contracts?   Because executory contracts must be assumed or rejected in their entirety, a common concern for both parties to a contract is whether agreements containing multiple obligations will be treated as a single contract or deemed to be a series of contracts, of which each may be separately assumed or rejected. There is no clear answer to this question, because several documents may, in reality, represent only one executory contract whereas a single document may contain several separate executory contracts.

For example, a bankruptcy court in the Southern District of Texas[144] has held that even if certain obligations within a transaction are contained in separate documents, the underlying agreement itself has to be assumed or rejected as a single executory contract.[145] The court refused to allow the DIP to reject a burdensome equity participation provision of a real estate option while at the same time obtaining the benefits of the rest of the agreement. In holding that the DIP could not selectively reject certain elements of the agreement simply because they happened to be embodied in separate writings, the bankruptcy court reasoned by analogy that a debtor could not reject a deed of trust as separate from the underlying obligation to pay principal and interest on the debt secured by the deed of trust.

---

[140] Bankruptcy Code, §365; *In re B-K of Kansas, Inc.*, 69 B.R. 812 (Bankr. D. Kan. 1987); *In re Enrique M. Lopez*, M.D.S.C., 93 B.R. 155 (Bankr. N.D. Ill. 1988). The status of agreements as property of the estate and executory contracts is discussed in section 12.2(a) of this chapter.

[141] See *In re Independent Mgmt. Assoc.*, 108 B.R., at 462.

[142] See Id., at 462.

[143] The trustee's ability to ignore ipso facto clauses is discussed in section 12.2(b)(i) of this chapter.

[144] See *In re Texstone Venture, Ltd.*, 54 B.R. 54 (Bankr. S.D. Tex. 1985).

[145] Id. at 56.

In contrast, many courts have held that a single document containing several independent and severable agreements can be assumed or rejected separately.[146] Deciding whether there are severable contracts within a single agreement is primarily a matter of state law regarding the obligations of contract.[147] The court will attempt to determine whether the parties intended to create several contracts, notwithstanding that the agreements were contained in a single document.[148] Some courts have focused on three factors to help determine whether a document contains more than one contract. Multiple contracts within a single document have been found to exist, for example, when (1) the various subagreements have a different nature and purpose, (2) there is a separate and distinct consideration for the subagreements, and (3) the obligations of the parties under the subagreements are not closely interrelated.[149]

This issue frequently arises in the context of covenants not to compete, which are often included in franchise agreements. For example, in a case involving the bankruptcy of a franchisee, one court held that a covenant not to compete was not an executory contract separate from a franchise agreement because the parties intended the covenant to be an integral part of the franchise. The covenant not to compete was therefore held to be indivisible from the underlying agreement and had to be rejected along with the franchise.[150]

The same result was reached in *In re Register*,[151] which involved a franchisee that wished to reject a covenant not to compete along with its rejection of a franchise. The franchisor argued that the covenant not to compete could not be rejected because it was not executory. According to the franchisor, the covenant not to compete was a severable agreement based on separate consideration by the franchisor that had already been provided to the franchisee, that is, providing certain training and information when the franchise began. The court rejected this argument and held that the covenant not to compete was not severable from the franchise.[152]

However, if one of the severable agreements within a single document has already been performed, that particular agreement cannot be assumed or rejected inasmuch as it is no longer an executory contract.[153] Accordingly, in a case involving a computer equipment lease, the Court of Appeals for the Ninth Circuit held that a maintenance agreement and a software license were separate executory contracts even though they constituted part of the same equipment lease.[154] Because the equipment lease was a fully performed installment sale and security agreement, unlike the maintenance agreement and software license contained therein, the lease could not be assumed or rejected by the trustee.[155]

---

[146] See *In re Gardinier, Inc.*, 831 F.2d 974, 975–76 (11th Cir. 1987), *cert. denied*, 488 U.S. 853 (1988); *In re Holly's, Inc.*, 140 B.R. 643, 681 (Bankr. W.D. Mich. 1992); *In re McLean Indus. Inc.*, 132 B.R. 247, 265 (Bankr. S.D.N.Y. 1991); *In re Cutters, Inc.*, 104 B.R. 886, 889 (Bankr. M.D. Tenn. 1989).

[147] *In re Pollock*, 139 B.R. 938, 940 (B.A.P. 9th Cir. 1992); *In re Royster Co.*, 137 B.R. 530, 532 (Bankr. M.D. Fla. 1992).

[148] *In re Gardinier*, 831 F.2d at 976; *In re Royster Co.*, 137 B.R. at 532.

[149] See, e.g., *In re Gardinier, Inc.*, 831 F.2d at 975–76; *In re Holly's, Inc.*, 140 B.R. at 681; *In re Pollock*, 139 B.R. at 940–41; *In re Royster Co.*, 137 B.R. at 532.

[150] *In re JRT, Inc.*, 121 B.R. 314, 323 (Bankr. W.D. Mich. 1990).

[151] 95 B.R. 73, 74 (Bankr. M.D. Tenn. 1989).

[152] 95 B.R. at 75.

[153] *In re JRT, Inc.*, 121 B.R. at 323.

[154] *In re Pacific Express, Inc.*, 780 F.2d 1482, 1486 (9th Cir. 1986).

[155] Id. at 1488.

(ii) Timing of Assumption or Rejection.   Another problem area concerns the timing of the decision to assume or reject an executory contract. For the purpose of determining whether a contract is executory, it normally makes little difference whether the case is proceeding under Chapter 7 or under Chapter 11. However, with regard to the time period within which executory contracts can be assumed or rejected, there is a fundamental difference between cases under Chapter 7 and cases under Chapter 11.

In Chapter 7 cases the trustee must assume or reject executory contracts within 60 days after the order for relief, or such contracts are automatically deemed to be rejected.[156] However, the 60-day period may be extended by the bankruptcy court upon the timely filing of a motion by the trustee with notice to creditors.[157]

In contrast, in Chapter 11 cases the trustee can assume or reject most executory contracts and unexpired leases at any time prior to confirmation of a Chapter 11 plan of reorganization or as part of the plan of reorganization itself.[158] Nonetheless, the other party to the contract is not necessarily helpless as it awaits the decision to assume or reject. The nondebtor party can file a motion with the bankruptcy court to compel the trustee to assume or reject the contract within a specified time period.[159] However, bankruptcy courts have broad discretion to decide such motions, which are frequently denied because courts are reluctant to place the interests of a single creditor above the interests of the bankruptcy estate unless the nondebtor party provides sufficient reason for so doing.[160]

(iii) When Is the Contract Property of the Estate?   Many courts have held that executory contracts, unlike other property of a debtor, do not become property of the estate until they are assumed.[161] This treatment of executory contracts has been defended as necessary so that the bankruptcy estate is neither burdened with the obligations of the contracts nor loses its rights under any executory contracts until the trustee makes a conscious decision to shoulder such obligations or forfeit such rights *and then evidences this decision through affirmative action.*[162]

There is some disagreement, however, concerning the steps that must be taken by the trustee in order to assume or reject. Generally, courts require the trustee to obtain court

---

[156] Bankruptcy Code § 365(d)(1); see, e.g., *In re Feyline Presents, Inc.*, 81 B.R. 623 (Bankr. D. Colo. 1988).

[157] Bankruptcy Code § 365 (d) (1); see, generally, *In re Bon Ton Rest. and Pastry Shop, Inc.*, 52 B.R. 850 (Bankr. N.D. Ill. 1985).

[158] Bankruptcy Code § 365(d)(2). The major exception to this rule is that in a case under any chapter of the Bankruptcy Code, if the debtor is a lessee under a lease of nonresidential real property, the lease must be assumed or rejected within 60 days after the order for relief is granted. If no decision is made by the trustee within that time, the lease is deemed rejected and the trustee must immediately surrender the property to the lessor. Bankruptcy Code § 365(d)(4).

[159] Bankruptcy Code § 365(d) (2).

[160] See *In re Public Serv. Co.*, 884 F.2d 11, 15 (1st Cir. 1989); *In re Monroe Well Serv., Inc.*, 83 B.R. 317, 323 (Bankr. E.D. Pa. 1988).

[161] See, *In re Quintex Entertainment*, 950 F.2d at 1496; *In re Tleel*, 876 F.2d 769, 770 (9th Cir. 1989); *In re Tonry*, 724 F.2d 467, 469 (5th Cir. 1984). However, as discussed in section 12.2 (b) (ix) of this chapter, unless the agreement has previously been terminated, the debtor's rights under an executory contract are deemed to be property of the estate and are therefore protected from most collection or enforcement actions, pursuant to the automatic stay imposed by section 362 of the Bankruptcy Code.

[162] *In re Lovitt*, 757 F.2d 1035, 1041 (9th Cir. 1985).

approval of a decision to assume or reject an executory contract, as is specifically required by § 365(a) of the Bankruptcy Code.[163] Yet in some circumstances, a court will allow executory contracts to be assumed through the acceptance of the benefits of a contract or through other actions that unequivocally evidence an intent to assume the contract without requiring prior court approval of the assumption of the contract.[164]

One major flaw of the latter approach of implied assumption is that it ignores the specific requirement of the Federal Rules of Bankruptcy Procedure (the Bankruptcy Rules) that the trustee file a formal motion with the court and provide notice to creditors of a hearing on the issue before a contract can be assumed or rejected.[165] This requirement clearly contradicts the notion that a debtor can assume or reject an executory contract without obtaining a ruling from a court on the propriety of such action.

Furthermore, even if one accepts the proposition that court approval is not necessary before a debtor assumes or rejects an executory contract, the debtor still must perform unequivocal acts to "manifest an unconditional and unambiguous decision."[166] This requirement leads to serious disputes between parties to executory contracts regarding whether the decision to assume or reject was, in fact, evidenced in an "unequivocal" manner. An even greater drawback to this approach is that the trustee's decision may be reversed by a court if no prior court approval has been obtained.[167] Accordingly, even if it is permissible, it is unwise for a debtor-licensor not to obtain court approval for its decision to assume or reject an executory contract. Considering the uncertainty in this area and the risks involved, there is no point in attempting to avoid the minor inconvenience of requesting court approval of the decision to assume or reject.

(iv) Assumption of the Contract by the Debtor-Licensor and the Lanham Act's Duty to Control Quality. Because the benefits to the estate that accrue through the collection of royalties often outweigh the corresponding costs that are imposed on the debtor-licensor, licensors frequently decide to assume a license agreement. One cost associated with this decision stems from the fact that the Lanham Act[168] imposes a duty on the licensor to control "the

---

[163] See, e.g., *In re Whitcomb & Keller Mortg. Co.*, 715 F.2d 375, 380 (7th Cir. 1983); *In re Four Star Pizza, Inc.*, 135 B.R. 498, 501 (Bankr. W.D. Pa. 1992); *In re Uly-Pak, Inc.*, 128 B.R. 763, 765 (Bankr. S.D. Ill. 1991); *In re Urbanco, Inc.*, 122 B.R. 513, 515 (Bankr. W.D. Mich. 1991); *In re Del Grosso*, 115 B.R. 136 (Bankr. N.D. Ill. 1987).

[164] See, e.g., *In re Miami Int'l Gen. Hosp., Inc.*, 89 B.R. 980, 987–88 (Bankr. S.D. Fla. 1988); *In re Re-Trac Corp.*, 59 B.R. 251, 255 (Bankr. D. Minn. 1986); *In re 1 Potato 2, Inc.*, 58 B.R. 752, 755 (Bankr. D. Minn. 1986).

[165] Bankruptcy Rules 6006(a), 9014. See *Sea Harvest Corp. v. Riviera Land Co.*, 868 F.2d 1077, 1079 (9th Cir. 1989); *In re Treat Fitness Center, Inc.*, 60 B.R. 878, 879 (9th Cir. B.A.P. 1986).

[166] *In re 1 Potato 2*, 58 B.R. at 755 (citing *In re Bon Ton Rest.*, 52 B.R. at 854.

[167] Id. at 755.

[168] The Lanham Act, 15 U.S.C. §§ 1051–1127, was enacted in 1945 in order to clarify and strengthen the rules for registering and protecting trademarks. Congress intended to protect consumers from being deceived about the quality of goods that they were purchasing. Congress also sought to ensure that only the trademark owners received the benefits of reputation and goodwill derived from investing in new products, by preventing the diversion of these benefits to other parties. 1946 U.S.C.C.S. 1274, 1275; see *Weil Ceramics & Glass, Inc. v. Dash*, 878 F.2d 659 (3d Cir. 1989), *cert. denied*, 493 U.S. 853; *Keebler Co. v. Rovira Biscuit Corp.*, 624 F.2d 366 (1st Cir. 1980).

nature and quality of the goods or services" sold by its licensees.[169] This duty can result in added expenses that the trustee either cannot, or does not want to, incur.

In fact, in a Chapter 7 case, because the trustee is not authorized to operate the debtor's business without obtaining specific court approval for doing so,[170] it may be impossible for the trustee to fulfill the Lanham Act obligation to control licensees. In Chapter 11 cases, it may simply be too expensive for the trustee to maintain the quality of goods produced under the license in light of the benefits that will accrue from assumption.

(v) Sale and Assignment of Intellectual Property. Although courts have upheld a trustee's right to "sell" a debtor's trademark and accompanying licenses, this can only be done if the trustee first assumes and then assigns the trademark and licenses.[171] Furthermore, although a licensor has property rights in its trademarks, this does not necessarily mean that the licensor is always able to freely assign a trademark after filing for bankruptcy. Notwithstanding the broad authority to sell, lease, or otherwise transfer property of the estate conferred by § 363 of the Bankruptcy Code,[172] there are limits to the trustee's power to assign a trademark.

One obstacle to assignment of a trademark is that the Lanham Act provides that a registered trademark may be assigned only together with "the good will of the business in which the mark is used."[173] An assignment of a trademark without a concurrent assignment of the goodwill to which it is attached results in an assignment "in gross" and is therefore invalid.[174] The transfer of the goodwill together with the trademark is required because a trademark is not a property right itself, but only a right that is appurtenant to an established business with which the trademark is used.[175] Requiring the transfer of goodwill upon assignment is also designed to assure that trademarks remain associated with the same or closely similar products, thereby protecting the expectations of consumers.[176]

Although the Lanham Act requires that a trademark be assigned together with the goodwill associated with its use,[177] the trustee does not need to sell any tangible assets of the trademark owner along with the trademark.[178] The trustee needs only transfer some part of the trademark owner's business along with the trademark. Merely relinquishing to the assignee the right to do business under the trademark has been deemed to be a

---

[169] 15 U.S.C. §§ 1055, 1127. See, e.g., *Taco Cabana Int'l, Inc. v. Two Pesos, Inc.*, 932 F.2d 1113 (5th Cir. 1991), *aff'd*, 112 S.Ct. 2753, *reh'g denied*, 113 S. Ct. 20 (1992) (licensor exercised adequate control to ensure quality of licensee's product); *Oberlin v. Marlin American Corp.*, 596 F.2d 1322 (7th Cir. 1979) (licensor must control operators of licensee to ensure that the public is not deceived about the quality of trademarked goods).

[170] Bankruptcy Code § 721. See, e.g., *California State Bd. of Equalization v. Goggin*, 191 F.2d 726 (9th Cir. 1951), *cert. denied*, 342 U.S. 909 (1952) (continued operation of debtor's business within sound discretion and trustee not empowered to do so merely by virtue of appointment); *In re Richter*, 40 F. Supp. 758 (S.D.N.Y. 1941) (*trustee has no authority to conduct* business without specific authorization by bankruptcy court).

[171] Bankruptcy Code § 365(f) (2) (A). See, e.g., *In re Dartmouth Audio, Inc.*, 42 B.R. 871, 877 (Bankr. D.N.H. 1984).

[172] See section 12.1(c) of this chapter.

[173] 15 U.S.C. § 1060. See, e.g., *Greenlon, Inc. v. Greenlawn, Inc.*, 542 F.Supp. 890, 893 (S.D. Ohio 1982).

[174] *Marshak v. Green*, 746 F.2d 927 (1984).

[175] *Greenlon*, 542 F.Supp. at 893.

[176] *Syntex Laboratories, Inc. v. Norwich Pharmacal Co.*, 315 F.Supp. 45, 55 (S.D.N.Y. 1970).

[177] 15 U.S.C. § 1060.

[178] *Glamorene Prod. Corp. v. Proctor & Gamble Co.*, 538 F.2d 894 (C.C.P.A. 1976).

sufficient transfer of a portion of the trademark owner's business to satisfy this requirement.[179]

(vi) Security Interests in Intellectual Property. The validity of a party's security interest in intellectual property is extremely important in the bankruptcy context because the existence of a properly perfected security interest places its holder in a better position than that of an unsecured creditor. As described earlier in this chapter,[180] a secured party must receive the value of its interest in the collateral that has been pledged by the debtor, thereby greatly increasing the extent to which its claim will be repaid in the bankruptcy.

Generally, the creation and perfection of security interests in personal property is governed by Article 9 of the Uniform Commercial Code (Article 9), which applies to all transactions that are designed to create a security interest in personal property.[181] There is some question, however, of whether security interests in certain types of intellectual property are perfected by following the procedures set forth in Article 9 or whether separate federal statutes must be adhered to by the secured party.[182] Some courts have held that certain types of intellectual property come within the definition of "general intangibles" provided by Article 9,[183] and any security interests sought to be perfected therein are thus governed by Article 9.[184] A major complication in regard to security interests in intellectual property is that Article 9 specifically provides that it does not apply if a statute of the United States has been enacted to govern the rights of "parties to and third parties affected by transactions in particular types of property."[185]

Although intellectual property rights are often affected by separate federal statutes that are applicable to copyrights, patents, and trademarks, courts have reached different conclusions about the degree to which these statutes preempt the provisions of Article 9 concerning the proper method of perfecting a security interest in these properties. The case law is fairly limited in this area, thereby leaving the issue of how to perfect a security interest in many types of intellectual property somewhat unsettled.

In the case of copyrights, several courts have held that the Copyright Act[186] preempts Article 9 regarding the creation and perfection of security interests, because the Copyright Act provides comprehensive rules governing the recordation of transfers and assignments of copyrights.[187] Therefore, a creditor can perfect a security interest in a copyright only by recording it with the United States Copyright Office.[188]

---

[179] See, e.g., *Greenlon*, 542 F. Supp. at 895; see also *H & J Foods, Inc. v. Reeder*, 477 F.2d 1053, 1055 (9th Cir. 1973).

[180] See section 12.1 (e).

[181] U.C.C. § 9–102 (1) (a).

[182] See, e.g., G. Larry Engel and Mark F. Radcliffe, "Intellectual Property Financing for High-Technology Companies," 19 *U.C.C.L.J. 3* (1986) (hereinafter referred to as Engel and Radcliffe); Note, "Security Interests in Intellectual Property: Recent Developments," 22 *Golden Gate U.L. Rev.* 413 (1992).

[183] According to U.C.C. § 9–106, general intangibles are defined as "any personal property (including things in action) other than goods, accounts, chattel paper, documents, instruments and money."

[184] See, e.g., *In re Topsy's Shoppes, Inc.*, 131 B.R. 886, 888 (D. Kan. 1991) (general intangibles include intellectual property); *In re Lady Madonna Indus., Inc.*, 99 B.R. 536, 539 (S.D.N.Y. 1989) (trademarks are general intangibles).

[185] U.C.C. § 9–104 (a).

[186] 17 U.S.C. §§ 101–810.

[187] See, e.g., *In re AEG Acquisition Corp.*, 127 B.R. 34 (Bankr. C.D. Cal. 1991), *aff'd*, 161 B.R. 50 (9th Cir. B.A.P. 1993); *In re Peregrine Ent., Ltd.*, 116 B.R. 194 (Bankr. C.D. Cal. 1990).

[188] See *In re AEG*, 127 B.R. at 41; *In re Peregrine*, 116 B.R. at 199.

The same issue arises in the context of perfecting security interests in trademarks. Several courts have held that a security interest in a trademark may be perfected by following the procedures required by Article 9, that is, filing a financing statement pursuant to the filing procedures established by state law.[189] The reasoning underlying this conclusion was that the Lanham Act[190] requires only that *assignments* of trademark rights be recorded at the United States Patent and Trademark Office (PTO), and the grant of a security interest is not an assignment of rights.[191]

Still, it is possible that a secured party's rights in a trademark will not be protected against the claims of any "bona fida purchasers"[192] of the trademark unless the secured party files the security interest with the PTO.[193] However, in light of the holding in *In re Peregrine*[194] that the Copyright Act clearly preempts Article 9 with regard to the perfection of security interests in copyrights, courts may adopt a similar rule—that the Lanham Act preempts Article 9 for trademarks.[195]

The Patent Act[196] provides that all conveyances of patents must be recorded with the PTO.[197] Basing its rationale on this language, one court has suggested that the patent recordation system of the Patent Act fully preempts Article 9.[198] However, several courts[199] have held that a state law filing under Article 9 may be sufficient to perfect a party's security interest in a patent, at least as against a creditor that has been granted a judicial lien against the debtor. These courts explained that a federal filing with the PTO is not required because, unlike an assignment of a patent, the grant of a security interest does not convey title to the patent. As is true for trademarks, a secured party must record its security interest in a patent with the PTO in order to be protected against claims of bona fida purchasers of the patent. Thus, the safest course for perfecting a security interest in a patent is to record under both Article 9 and the Patent Act.

(vii) Abandonment of Intellectual Property.   If the owner of intellectual property has filed a bankruptcy petition, there may be a brief period during which the owner does not use the property in question. Such nonuse can provide an opportunity for a claim by the other party to an agreement that the intellectual property has been abandoned. The fact that a licensor

---

[189] *In re 199Z, Inc.*, 137 B.R. 778 (Bankr. C.D. Cal. 1992); *Roman Cleanser Co. v. National Acceptance Co.*, 43 B.R. 940 (Bankr. E.D. Mich 1984), *aff'd sub nom*, *In re Roman Cleanser Co.*, 802 F.2d 207 (1986); *In re TR-3 Indus.*, 41 B.R. 128 (Bankr. C.D. Cal. 1984).

[190] 15 U.S.C. §§ 1051–1127.

[191] *Roman Cleanser*, 43 B.R. at 946; see also *Red Barn, Inc. v. Red Barn Systems, Inc.*, 322 F.Supp. 98 (N.D. Ind. 1970).

[192] The U.C.C. defines a bona fida purchaser as one who buys property or receives a document of title in good faith and without notice of any defense or claim to the property. U.C.C. 7–501.

[193] Several commentators have recommended that a secured party file under both the state law of Article 9 and the Lanham Act because of the uncertainty regarding how to perfect a security interest in a trademark. See Engel and Radcliffe, supra n. 182; Melvin Simensky, "Enforcing Creditors' Rights Against Trademarks," 79 *Trademark Rptr.* 569, 577 (1989).

[194] 116 B.R. at 194.

[195] See Note, "Perfection of Security Interests in Intellectual Property: Federal Statutes Preempt Article 9," 57 *Geo. Wash. L. Rev.* 135, 138–39 (1988); but see *In re 199Z*, 137 B.R. at 782 (same court that decided the *Peregrine* decision found no preemption for trademarks from Lanham Act).

[196] 35 U.S.C. § 101–307.

[197] 35. U.S.C. § 261.

[198] *In re Peregrine*, 116 B.R. at 203.

[199] *City Bank and Trust Co. v. Otto Fabric, Inc.*, 83 B.R. 780, 782 (D. Kan. 1988); *In re Transp. Design & Tech., Inc.*, 48 B.R. 635, 639 (Bankr. S.D. Ca. 1985).

has filed for bankruptcy, however, does not necessarily mean that the debtor-licensor's rights in its trademark or other types of intellectual property are abandoned.[200]

In regard to trademarks, abandonment occurs when the owner of a trademark demonstrates that it will not continue using the trademark.[201] The consequences of abandonment are that the trademark returns to the public domain, which means that anyone may then freely use it.[202] A new holder may thus adopt the trademark and seek to establish exclusive usage and ownership rights over the trademark.[203]

In deciding whether a trademark has been abandoned, the key question is whether the owner intended to abandon it.[204] To answer this question, courts focus on whether the trademark owner's business continues to operate and generate sufficient goodwill to protect the trademark,[205] inasmuch as the lack of an operating business is evidence of an owner's intent to abandon a trademark.

A relatively brief cessation of business after a filing for bankruptcy will most likely not amount to abandonment of a trademark.[206] Courts are reluctant to find an abandonment of trademark rights in such circumstances, because goodwill does not normally disappear overnight.[207] However, if the goodwill of a trademark owner's business is terminated because of the cessation of business, the termination will, at some point, lead to an abandonment of any trademarks.[208] Thus, where the intention to use the goodwill associated with the mark is not demonstrated within a reasonable time, courts have deemed the trademark to be abandoned.[209] In addition, a court may find that a trademark has been abandoned if the owner does not maintain sufficient control over a licensee's use of the trademark.[210]

In the context of franchise agreements, courts have also refused to find abandonment where there has been only a brief cessation of the debtor's business. For example, although a debtor holding a franchise agreement for a car dealership ceased operation of the dealership for more than 10 days, a court held that the debtor-franchisee had not abandoned the franchise and had not forfeited its rights under the franchise.[211]

Similar rules apply to the abandonment of patents and copyrights. Abandonment of an invention occurs if the creator of the invention takes no steps to publicize it within a reasonable time after its completion.[212] Under the Patent Act, a person who abandons an

---

[200] *Miller Brewing Co. v. Oland's Breweries Ltd.*, 548 F.2d 349 (C.C.P.A. 1976); *In re Merry Hull & Co. v. Hi-Line Co.*, 243 F.Supp. 45, 50 (S.D.N.Y. 1965).

[201] 15 U.S.C. § 1127 (1988).

[202] See, generally, J. Thomas McCarthy, 1 *McCarthy on Trademarks and Unfair Competition* § 17.01 (3d ed. 1992).

[203] See *P. Daussa Corp. v. Sutton Cosmetics, Inc.*, 462 F.2d 134 (2d Cir. 1972).

[204] See *General Bus. Serv., Inc. v. Rouse*, 495 F.Supp. 526, 539 (E.D. Pa. 1980).

[205] See *Hot Shoppes, Inc. v. Hot Shoppe, Inc.*, 203 F.Supp 777, 781 (M.D.N.C. 1962); *Person's Co. v. Christman*, 900 F.2d 1565 (Fed. Cir. 1990).

[206] *Hot Shoppes*, 203 F.Supp. at 781.

[207] *Defiance Button Machine Co. v. C&C Metal Products Corp.*, 759 F.2d 1053, 1060 (2d Cir.), *cert. denied*, 474 U.S. 844 (1985).

[208] Under the Lanham Act, a federally registered trademark is presumed to be abandoned if it is not used for a period of two or more consecutive years. 15 U.S.C. § 1127.

[209] See *Silverman v. CBS, Inc.*, 870 F.2d 40 (2d Cir.), *cert. denied*, 492 U.S. 907 (1989) (intent to resume commercial use required to rebut presumption of abandonment); *Reconstruction Finance Corp. v. J.G. Menihan Corp.*, 28 F.Supp. 920 (Bankr. W.D.N.Y. 1939).

[210] See, e.g., *Defiance Button*, 759 F.2d at 1059; *Sheila's Shine Prod., Inc., v. Sheila Shine, Inc.*, 486 F.2d 114, 125 (5th Cir. 1973).

[211] *In re Tom Stimus Chrysler-Plymouth, Inc.*, 134 B.R. 676, 679 (S.D. Fla. 1991).

[212] *International Glass Co. v. United States*, 408 F.2d 395 (Ct. Cl. 1969); *Oak Indus., Inc. v. Zenith Electronics Corp.*, 726 F.Supp. 1525 (N.D. Ill. 1989).

invention is not entitled to a patent for that invention.[213] Furthermore, once filed, a patent application must be prosecuted within six months or the application will be deemed to have been abandoned.[214] However, once a patent has actually been issued, it remains in force regardless of whether it is used.[215] A copyright is abandoned when the proprietor of the copyright intends to surrender its interest in the copyright[216] and manifests this intent by an affirmative act.[217]

(d) Effects of Licensee's Bankruptcy on Licensor.   Just as the bankruptcy of a licensor can have a dramatic effect on the rights and obligations of a licensee, the licensee's bankruptcy can have substantial consequences for the fortunes of a licensor. The following paragraphs explain the status of intellectual property and a license agreement, and the associated rights and obligations, as they exist during a licensee's bankruptcy.

(i) Rejection of License by Debtor-Licensee.   Pursuant to § 365 of the Bankruptcy Code, subject to court approval, a licensee can reject an executory license agreement. Although a licensee's decision to assume or reject is primarily one of business judgment, as is the case with a licensor, some courts also look to whether the license is burdensome to the estate and attempt to balance the respective rights of the parties, including other creditors.[218] However, unlike rejection by a licensor, rejection of an executory contract by a licensee is not governed by § 365(n) of the Bankruptcy Code.[219]

If the trustee does not have a legitimate business purpose for rejecting the contract, or if rejection would cause disproportionate harm to the other party as compared with the benefits that would accrue to the bankruptcy estate, rejection may not be approved. Therefore, a bankruptcy court may not allow a trustee to reject an agreement near expiration of the license when the debtor's sole purpose for rejection is avoidance of covenant not to compete.[220] In the absence of such equitable considerations, however, a noncompetition clause is subject to rejection[221] along with the rest of the contract.[222]

As is true for licensees that are facing the bankruptcy of a licensor,[223] the automatic stay similarly hampers the licensor's exercise of its duty to control the licensee's use of its property. For example, although quality-control provisions may generally be enforced through termination clauses, the automatic stay prevents the licensor from issuing a notice of termination once the licensee's bankruptcy case has commenced.[224]

Nonetheless, if a notice of termination has been issued before the commencement of the bankruptcy case, the automatic stay does not toll or otherwise stop the running of any time

---

[213] 35 U.S.C. § 102.
[214] 35 U.S.C. § 133.
[215] *Kling v. Haring*, 11 F.2d 202, 203 (D.C. Cir.), *cert. denied*, 271 U.S. 671 (1926).
[216] *Hadady Corp. v. Dean Witter Reynolds, Inc.*, 739 F.Supp. 1392, 1398 (C.D. Cal. 1990).
[217] *Transgo, Inc. v. Ajax Transmission Parts Corp.*, 768 F.2d 1001, 1019 (9th Cir. 1985), *cert. denied*, 474 U.S. 1059 (1986).
[218] *Group of Institutional Investors v. Milwaukee R. Co.*, 318 U.S. 523 (1943); *King v. Baer*, 482 F.2d 552 (1973), *cert. denied*, 414 U.S. 1068 (1973).
[219] See section 12.2 (b)(vi) of this chapter.
[220] *In re Noco, Inc.*, 76 B.R. 839 (Bankr. N.D. Fla. 1987).
[221] See section 12.2 (c)(i) of this chapter.
[222] *In re Golconda, Inc.*, 56 B.R. 136 (Bankr. M.D. Fla. 1985).
[223] See section 12.2 (b)(ix) of this chapter.
[224] See *In re Wills Motors*, 133 B.R. at 300–01; *In re R.S. Pinellas Motel*, 2 B.R. at 118.

period for the licensee to cure defaults.[225] Obviously, this does not mean that the licensor should immediately terminate the agreement at the slightest default by the licensee. The licensor should promptly issue a notice of termination once sufficient defaults have remained uncured long enough to lead the licensor to decide that termination of the license or franchise is appropriate under the circumstances. The danger is that if the licensor waits too long before issuing a notice of termination, the licensee may file for bankruptcy, thereby triggering the automatic stay and blocking the licensor's ability to proceed with termination.[226]

The licensor may attempt to have the automatic stay modified so that it can terminate the license.[227] However, modification of the stay requires court approval, and obtaining court approval is much more complicated than the process that can be followed if the notice of termination is issued before the licensee files for bankruptcy. In addition, although § 362(d) (1) of the Bankruptcy Code allows a court to grant relief from the stay for "cause," courts may be reluctant to grant relief from the stay early in a case, particularly when loss of an important contract may effectively terminate the debtor's business. Many courts prefer to allow a trustee significant time to assume or reject a contract.[228] Therefore, because of the significant risk that a court will not grant a request to lift the stay, licensors must remain vigilant when dealing with financially troubled licensees.

Alternatively, under appropriate circumstances a licensor could move the court to order the licensee to assume or reject the contract within a specified time period.[229] However, the licensor would need to convince the court that there is a compelling reason for the decision to assume or reject to be expedited. In doing so, the licensor would have to overcome the reluctance of courts to force a trustee to decide quickly.[230]

Once the licensee rejects the contract, the automatic stay is terminated with respect to that contract. As discussed earlier in this chapter,[231] some courts have held that rejection of an executory contract relieves each party of its duties and obligations under the contract, including a licensor's duty to control the quality of the licensed goods, and terminates all rights under the contract, including the licensee's right to use the property. Thus, under this line of cases, if a licensee attempts to continue using the licensed property after rejection, a court may issue an injunction to prevent infringement of the trademark.[232]

(ii) Damages upon Rejection.   After rejection of its license, the licensor has a general unsecured claim for damages, including unpaid royalties.[233] However, the licensor must continue to perform its duties under the agreement until the trustee assumes or rejects the license. Thus, the licensor may file an administrative expense claim for, among other things, uncollected royalties that accrue while it is waiting for the trustee to assume or reject the license.[234]

---

[225] See *In re Wills Motors*, 133 B.R. at 301; *In re Tudor Motor Lodge*, 102 B.R. at 948. It must be remembered, however, that section 108(b) of the Bankruptcy Code may serve to extend the time period for curing defaults until 60 days after the order for relief has been entered in the bankruptcy case. See section 12.2 (b)(ix) of this chapter.

[226] See section 12.2 (b)(ix) of this chapter.

[227] See, e.g., *In re Tudor Motor Lodge*, 102 B.R. 955.

[228] *In re Gunter Hotel Assoc.*, 96 B.R. 696 (Bankr. W.D. Tex. 1988).

[229] Bankruptcy Code § 365(d) (2).

[230] *In re Gunter Hotel*, 96 B.R. 696.

[231] See section 12.2(b)(4).

[232] *In re Volpe Enterprises, Inc.*, 23 B.R. 818 (Bankr. S.D. Fla. 1982).

[233] Bankruptcy Code § 502.

[234] Bankruptcy Code §§ 503, 507; *NLRB v. Bildisco & Bildisco*, 465 U.S. at 528–31.

(iii) Assumption of License by Debtor-Licensee.   If there are defaults under a license agreement, a debtor-licensee must first satisfy the conditions for assumption that are required for any trustee.[235] However, because licensees are often financially unable to cure defaults immediately, a court may simply require the licensee to provide adequate assurance of a "prompt" cure[236] rather than requiring an immediate cure. Furthermore, although the Bankruptcy Code does not define what constitutes a prompt cure of defaults, several courts have stated that a cure is prompt if it occurs within a year of confirmation of a plan.[237] Nonetheless, even if the licensee can provide adequate assurance of a prompt cure, the licensee must also provide adequate assurance of future performance under the agreement.[238]

The problem for licensors is that requiring a licensee to provide adequate assurance of future performance does not really guarantee the licensor that the license will be performed in the future; it merely assures the licensor that there is a reasonable probability that such performance will occur. Thus, if the licensee has defaulted in the payment of royalties, it may be wise for the licensor to require that adequate assurance be in the form of cash or nonspeculative collateral.[239]

(iv) Time to Assume or Reject.   Because achieving reorganization is paramount in Chapter 11 cases, courts will often grant a trustee additional time in which to formulate a plan of reorganization through which a licensee's executory contracts are assumed, or assumed and assigned, by the trustee. Courts will grant such additional time when there is a "reasonable prospect of a successful reorganization,"[240] which means that it is likely that a reorganization will occur at some point in the not-too-distant future. This practice of the courts creates significant delays and uncertainty for licensors whose license agreements the trustee proposes to assume or reject through the plan.

The risk is that while the licensor is waiting for the trustee to formulate an effective plan, the licensor has no ability to effectively control the intellectual property held by the licensee, because of the operation of the automatic stay imposed by § 362(d) of the Bankruptcy Code. Therefore, a licensee may repeatedly violate the license agreement and the licensor could be powerless to stop it. To prevent this result, a licensor should move to modify the automatic stay by emphasizing to the court that (1) the value of the licensor's intellectual property is directly tied to the debtor-licensee's use of such property, (2) the licensor has both the right and the obligation to control the use of its trademark by the licensee, (3) the loss of control amounts to irreparable injury to the licensor, and (4) the loss of goodwill resulting from the debtor-licensee's misuse is similarly irreparable.

A licensor may claim that such incurable violations of the license agreement render the license nonassumable because the trustee cannot cure these defaults,[241] as is required by

---

[235] See the discussion of Bankruptcy Code Section 365(b)(1) in section 12.2(b)(i) of this chapter, page 413.

[236] As described in section 12.2(b)(i) of this chapter, page 413, merely providing adequate assurance of a prompt cure of defaults is specifically authorized by section 365(b)(1)(A) of the Bankruptcy Code. See, e.g., *In re French*, 131 B.R. 138, 140 (Bankr. E.D. Mo. 1991); *In re Rachels Indus., Inc.*, 109 B.R. 797, 802 (Bankr. W.D. Tenn. 1990).

[237] *In re French*, 131 B.R. at 141; *GMAC v. Lawrence*, 11 B.R. 44, 45 (Bankr. N.D. Ga. 1981).

[238] *In re Rachels Indus.*, 109 B.R. at 812.

[239] *In re Bronx-Westchester Mack Corp.*, 4 B.R. 730 (Bankr. S.D.N.Y. 1980).

[240] See, e.g., *In re Independent Mgmt. Assoc., Inc.*, 108 B.R. 456, 464 (Bankr. D.N.J. 1989).

[241] See also *In re Toyota of Yonkers, Inc.*, 135 B.R. 471, 477 (Bankr. S.D.N.Y. 1992) (failure to operate auto dealership for seven consecutive days would create an incurable default and result in termination of the franchise).

§ 365(b)(1)(A) of the Bankruptcy Code.[242] In such situations the licensor will often claim that the existence of such incurable defaults warrants lifting of the automatic stay to allow a termination of the license agreement.[243]

In ruling on such claims by licensors, however, some courts have held that a licensor's claim for money damages under the Bankruptcy Code will cure a licensee's breach of "incurable" defaults, such as violations of quality control standards.[244] The courts in these cases therefore prohibited the licensor from terminating the agreement. To prevent this result, a licensor should argue that such an approach overlooks the harm to the public caused by infringement of the license and request that the court enjoin ongoing infringement or unfair competition by the licensee, including breaches of quality control provisions, notwithstanding the fact that the licensor already has a claim for damages from such violations.[245]

(v) Sale or Assignment.   Once assumed, a trustee may attempt to assign a license in order to realize the value of the rights embodied therein. In reaction to such attempts to assume and assign, licensors often raise several objections to defeat the trustee's ability to assign the licensee's rights under the license. One objection that licensors often use is a claim that the trustee cannot provide adequate assurance of future performance[246] inasmuch as the license will be assigned to a third party that is beyond the control of the trustee.[247] This attack rests on the fact that inability to control the assignee would be inconsistent with the licensor's Lanham Act obligations.

The financial status of an assignee and the similarity of an assignee's business to the debtor's business (and management skills) may be relevant to a determination of whether the licensee can provide adequate assurance of future performance, as these factors bear on the ability of the assignee to perform the contract successfully.[248] However, in the absence of a strong showing that an assignee is unlikely to perform, lack of adequate assurance of future performance rarely forms the basis for denying a licensee's attempt to assume and assign.[249]

Another objection that is often used by licensors in an attempt to block assumption and assignment is based on the fact that § 365 of the Bankruptcy Code[250] prohibits assignment when applicable law excuses a party from accepting performance from or rendering service to a party other than the debtor.[251] The most widely recognized examples of this situation are personal service contracts. Licenses that are personal service contracts cannot be assigned

---

[242] See section 12.2(b)(i) of this chapter.

[243] See, e.g., *In re Quinones Ruiz*, 98 B.R. 636 (Bankr. D. P.R. 1988); *In re R.S. Pinellas Motel*, 2 B.R. at 115.

[244] See, e.g., *In re ERA Central Regional Services, Inc.*, supra 39 B.R. 738; *In re R.S. Pinellas Motel*, 2 B.R. at 119.

[245] See *In re New York City Shoes, Inc.*, 84 B.R. at 959 (Bankr. E.D. Pa. 1988).

[246] Bankruptcy Code, § 365(b)(1). For a discussion of the three requirements for assumption see section 12.2(b)(i) of this chapter.

[247] See, e.g., *In re Sunrise Rest., Inc.*, 135 B.R. 149, 153 (Bankr. M.D. Fla. 1991).

[248] *In re Bronx-Westchester Mack Corp.*, 20 B.R. at 142.

[249] See *In re Wills Motors, Inc.*, 133 B.R. at 302; *In re Bronx-Westchester Mack Corp.*, 20 B.R. at 143.

[250] See the discussion of Section 365(c)(1) of the Bankruptcy Code in section 12.2(b)(i) of this chapter, page 413, note 83.

[251] It is important to note that, although the trustee and DIP are considered separate entities from the debtor for many purposes, this distinction is not applicable in the context of section 365 of the Bankruptcy Code. *In re Fastrax, Inc.*, 129 B.R. 274, 277 (Bankr. M.D. Fla. 1991).

unless the licensor consents, because these contracts involve the special skills or unique talents of the licensee.[252]

In many cases, the licensor will point to a provision in the license that prohibits a licensee from assigning the license without obtaining the licensor's permission as evidence that the license is a personal service contract.[253] Such efforts to defeat assignment often fail because, in the absence of a sufficient showing that the license is truly akin to a personal service contract that is based on the licensee's special knowledge, unique skill, or talent, courts generally permit assumption and assignment.[254]

Section 365 of the Bankruptcy Code states that unless assignment is prohibited by applicable law,[255] the trustee can assign a contract, notwithstanding any provision requiring the licensor's consent to assignment.[256] Thus, the licensor's claim that the license is not assignable will be successful only if the licensor can convince the court that the proposed assignee lacks certain unique skills required under the contract and is therefore unable to perform adequately under the license.

(vi) Planning Suggestions.   There are a variety of steps that licensors can and should take, if at all practicable, to protect themselves from the bankruptcy of a licensee. In many cases these precautions and planning strategies for licensors involve adopting virtually the opposite approach that a licensee would take when guarding against the bankruptcy of a licensor.[257] However, in some instances, the prebankruptcy strategies that should be followed by a licensee and a licensor are nearly identical.

For example, the licensor should expressly include a clause that automatically terminates the license upon the occurrence of certain defaults by the licensee. To avoid the danger that such a clause will be a void "ipso facto" clause,[258] the licensor should be careful to draft the termination provision so that it is not triggered by the insolvency or bankruptcy of the licensee.

There are several ways of drafting such a clause. For example, the licensor may wish to include a "key-man" clause that will terminate the license if a particular person or persons are no longer employed by the licensee. Such clauses are especially helpful because, although such vital employees of the licensee may, and often do, leave the licensee at about the time that the licensee files for bankruptcy, the clause is in no way triggered by the bankruptcy filing of the licensee.

The licensor may also want to structure the transaction so that it grants a license for only a limited time rather than a license in perpetuity. This measure will help to demonstrate that the licensor did not intend to sell or otherwise relinquish all of its rights in the intellectual property.

---

[252] *In re Fastrax, Inc.*, 129 B.R. at 278; *In re Sentry Data, Inc.*, 87 B.R. 943, 950 (Bankr. N.D. Ill. 1988).

[253] See, e.g., *In re Sunrise Rest., Inc.*, 135 B.R. at 152.

[254] See, e.g., *In re Sunrise Rest., Inc.*, 135 B.R. at 153; *In re Rooster, Inc.*, 100 B.R. 228, 233 (Bankr. E.D. Pa. 1989); *In re Sentry Data, Inc.*, 87 B.R. at 949–50, *In re Bronx-Westchester Mack Corp.*, 20 B.R. at 143.

[255] See the discussion of Section 365 (c) of the Bankruptcy Code in section 12.2 (b)(i) of this chapter.

[256] Bankruptcy Code, § 365 (f) (1). See, e.g., *In re Compass Van & Storage Corp.*, 65 B.R. at 1013. Compare *In re Varisco*, 16 B.R. 634 (Bankr. M.D. Fla. 1981).

[257] For a discussion of these suggested planning techniques for licensee's, see section 12.2 (b)(ix) of this chapter.

[258] See section 12.2 (b)(i) of this chapter.

Another step that a licensor may wish to take, for two related reasons, is to obtain a properly perfected security interest in any royalties provided for by the license agreement. A licensor may improve the status of a future claim against the bankruptcy estate of the licensee by obtaining a security interest in the royalties earned through the licensee's use of the property.[259] Another advantage of obtaining a security interest in royalties is that secured royalties from the sale of licensed goods are entitled to additional protection as "cash collateral" under § 363 of the Bankruptcy Code.[260]

The security interest should be granted in a document that is clearly separate from the underlying license agreement, because rejection of the license could result in rejection of all of the covenants in the security agreement, including the security interest itself.[261] The agreement containing the security interest must therefore be carefully drafted to avoid a court's determination that it is part of (and can thus be rejected with) the license agreement.

---

[259] See, e.g., *In re Navigation Tech. Corp.*, 880 F.2d 1491 (1st Cir. 1989).

[260] See the discussion of cash collateral in section 12.1 (c) of this chapter.

[261] *In re Rovine Corp.*, 5 B.R. 402 (Bankr. W.D. Tenn. 1980); *In re Executive Tech. Data Sys.*, 79 B.R. 276.

CHAPTER 13

SOME PRACTICAL APPLICATIONS OF BRAND VALUATION TO CORPORATE TRADEMARK MANAGEMENT

Steven M. Getzoff

American Express
New York, New York

For corporate brand/trademark managers, brand valuation has a number of practical applications. The internal workings of the process itself are not necessary to discuss, or even to know, in such cases. Neither are they the focus of this chapter. Rather, its departure point is that you, the reader, are the corporate brand/trademark manager at an imaginary corporation.

Various situations (scenarios) are presented in which you might find yourself. Their purpose is to illustrate when and how applications of brand valuation may prove useful. The hypothetical format includes imaginary dialogues with imaginary clients.

Suppose, for instance, that you are the trademark manager at the XYZ Corporation. Your company is the world's foremost producer of top quality Wompoms. The "XYZ" trademark is internationally famous. Your responsibility, as corporate trademark manager, is to maintain the equity, the value, of the XYZ trademark. This means, of course, fulfilling all the requirements of the trademark registrations for the XYZ trademark in the category of Wompoms in each country around the world.

One day, one of the most famous financial journals in the world publishes an article on "brand valuation." It refers to a study published by a firm that specializes in this process. That study cites the XYZ trademark as one of the 10 most powerful trademarks in the world irrespective of product category.

What does that mean for the XYZ Corporation's bottom line? You might ask the corporate attorneys. They would review the current U.S. and foreign trademark statutes and say that trademarks legally are held to have no intrinsic value under the various statutes around the world, including the U.S. statute, the Lanham Act. Strictly speaking, the legal definition and perception of a trademark is merely as a product quality and source indicator, conferring enforceable rights to protect the consumer, not the mark owner. Such rights are distinct from those of a patent or copyright owners. The latter are constitutional *exceptions* to the First Amendment for reasons of public policy and the public good. They recognize the *intrinsic* worth of copyrights and patents as valuable and defensible property rights. Brand names and trademarks are not so perceived.

In fact, the phenomenon of brand valuation is the most recent step in a long historical process of recognizing the intrinsic value of trademarks. The franchising industry, the nostalgia craze that started in the 1970s, the massive wave of corporate acquisitions in the

1980s, the emergence in the late 1980s of a phenomenon called "spokesbrands," the third-party licensing boom of the last 20 years or so, and the inexorable growth in international trademark law of the Dilution Doctrine, together illustrate the value of trademarks. In each of these instances someone paid to use someone else's trademark. Plainly stated, one does not pay money for something that has no value.

These same processes collectively have altered forever the sociohistorical role of trademarks. They are the latest stages of an overarching process that began with the Industrial Revolution of the nineteenth century. An individual trademark is no longer merely an indicator of source and quality. An individual trademark is both that and more. The individual trademark is a "wave-particle" to the trademark "continuum" beginning a century ago in the Industrial Revolution and culminating with the conscious recognition of trademarks' value as a social process, called brand valuation.

Brand valuation establishes the value of a trademark by enabling the trademark owner to measure trademark value over time in a way that is generally accepted. The worth of brand valuation to the corporate trademark management process may be noted in the following areas:

1. Intracompany use
2. Extracompany use
3. Financial statements
4. Collateral for loans
5. Corporate acquisitions
6. Third-party licensing

The effect of brand valuation in each of these areas will, in turn affect your customers. Those customers are your colleagues in the legal and marketing departments and other XYZ corporate personnel at all levels throughout the corporation, as well as the corporation's shareholders and the worldwide customer group that purchases Wompoms.

All of these groups, which in many cases overlap, are better served if you as corporate trademark manager conduct a brand valuation of the XYZ trademark. A good way to start such an evaluation is to explore the intracompany use of the XYZ trademark.

13.1 INTRACOMPANY USE

Scenario One: Intracompany Brand Extension

In this scenario, the XYZ trademark is used currently in connection with the Wompom product:

XYZ® Wompoms

A business decision has been made to go into another area of commercial activity, the warranty and repair of Wompoms.

The current wisdom in the trademark, advertising, and marketing industries tends to argue against trying to develop new brands and trademarks. The overwhelming majority of such new products and marks are never able to overcome the success of preexisting products in the marketplace and build a distinctive reputation of their own, especially in the Wompom business, an "aging business" with many competitors offering Wompoms of various qualities.

Based on this argument, all other factors being constant, the best decision would be to use the house brand, XYZ, thus:

XYZ® Wompom Warranty and Repair Services

or

XYZ® Wompom Repair

thereby enabling the well-known distinctive house mark to obtain recognition and a distinctive position in the marketplace for the new product. This occurs because of the historically vindicated commitment to provide Wompoms of consistent quality by XYZ Corporation's management *and* the public's perception of such quality embodied in the goodwill of the XYZ brand and trademark.

There are a number of arguments to support or condemn a decision of this type. The first and most obvious argument goes both ways. If this new product is successful, it will enhance the value of the trademark. If it is unsuccessful, it will do the reverse.

Second, it is possible, by moving the brand into another product category, to effect what is called "self-dilution." A pattern of brand extension can, in theory, have the net result of removing the distinctive role of the trademark for a particular product and render it meaningless.

Third, as a result over time of intracompany brand extension uses by other product groups within the XYZ Corporation, you lose your ability to turn people down on the grounds that "we just don't do this type of thing" except for your primary product, namely, Wompoms. You are hard pressed to tell another person who offers a new product called "Squeedunks" that he or she cannot use the house mark to create a better probability of success in the marketplace for their new product, as you have done in the case of the Wompom repair service.

Fourth, it is likely that there are uses of a corporate client's house marks for which no one in the company can figure out the reason they were ever granted. You probably are, in fact, well acquainted with "grandfathered" uses of house marks that continue to be allowed for no other reason but that they are grandfathered. They have always been there; they have always been allowed. Now, the argument goes, they are "grandfathered" and sacrosanct. After brand valuation, the question may be raised as to whether such uses should be allowed, by determining whether they add value to the brand at least commensurate to the value they receive from it.

Without brand valuation, how do you get a commitment from the would-be intracompany licensee that ensures that a particular use does not hurt but will in fact appreciate the value of the brand?

It is easy for Joe or Josephine Manager to say, "Our product is wonderful. According to all our projections we should be making a million dollars for the company next year. This will generally appreciate the overall value of our stock and, therefore, the overall value of the brand." With all due respect to Joe or Josephine Manager, who have all the best intentions in the world, this response is anecdotal, imprecise, and insufficient.

A rigorous brand valuation program is required so that you can determine whether a particular use of a brand is appreciating or depreciating its value. If you monitor such developments each year, and individually, you will be able, upon review of the next year's valuation process, to determine whether brand value has been lost. You are then able to go over each of the particular areas to which the brand has been licensed intracompany and review those uses to determine where depreciation, if any, has occurred. It is then possible to terminate that intracompany use of the brand, to place more restrictions on it, or to maintain watchdog observation for the purpose of subsequent revocation of the intracompany license should that depreciation continue.

Scenario Two: Intracompany Brand Premiums

Using a trademark on unrelated third-party goods or commemorative items (such as coffee mugs) is sometimes an effective tool to create goodwill for a brand.

To promote the sale of the XYZ Corporation's Wompoms, Ms. Jones in the marketing department has come up with such a program. You have been asked, as trademark manager, to review it. This program will offer a commemorative XYZ Wompom logo-bearing coffee mug to every purchaser of 10 or more XYZ Wompoms over the next several months.

The role of brand valuation in instances of third-party unrelated goods bearing your trademark offered for sale is discussed at length in section 13.2 of this chapter. However, for a premium that is not purchased by the customer but given away as a commemorative or goodwill ambassador item bearing your trademark, there is a basic question that must be asked. Does this premium (1) enhance, (2) not change, or (3) erode the goodwill, that is, the value, of the trademark?

If the premium, in this case the coffee mug, can demonstrably be proven to increase the goodwill of the trademark, this provides useful and important market information. It may be a premium that you may want to consider offering again—or not. If the value of the trademark is not enhanced but is left the same, there are several possibilities to consider. Was this premium offering inherently flawed? Is the Wompom not a product which, when paired with a premium offering, does not evoke a positive market response? Or was this simply a matter of the wrong premium in the wrong situation, perhaps at the wrong time to the wrong target market?

Brand valuation can help in gauging more accurately the value of a premium offering to a brand. If a significant premium offering is made, it may be worth considering a full in-depth review of whether the trademark's value was enhanced as projected by its proposer. Suppose the value of the brand went down directly after the period of the premium coffee mug offering. Was the problem the very offering of a premium in connection with Wompoms? Or was the problem the particular premium offered with Wompoms and, if so, what other premium might possibly have enhanced the value of the brand? How can the relative merits of a subsequent premium be measured?

Brand valuation as just described, measures whether there was an enhanced value (or not, as the case may be) to the brand chronologically subsequent to the offering of the premium. This, given further research, can clarify the situation.

Measuring the success of a premium through instinct, hunch, or anecdotal information rather than a process of scientific review of customers' response to the offering can tend to place XYZ Corporation in situations where such premiums either accomplish nothing or actually hurt the brand. However, if those premiums are politically popular in the XYZ bureaucracy, they may continue to be offered, without brand valuation to provide concrete evidence that they hurt the brand or, at best, did nothing. However, should there be, for whatever reason, bureaucratic intracorporate opposition to a premium offering that was successful, brand valuation provides the supporters of that premium with useful information to overcome such opposition.

The benefit of brand valuation in such a scenario is clear.

Scenarios Three (a) and (b): Intracompany Use as Corporate or Division or Brand Identifier

(a) XYZ Corporation has just acquired the QXR Corporation, which produces another particular product called "Wompom-Prime." The QXR Corporation is now the QXR Wompom-Prime Production Company, Inc. It is a third-tier, indirect, wholly-owned subsidiary of XYZ Corporation. The new president of this new subsidiary, Ms. Dorsey, has asked that QXR Wompom-Prime Production Company, Inc. be allowed to use the house mark of the XYZ parent company standing alone with the Wompom-Prime product. Corporate policy disallows third-tier subsidiary use of a stand-alone version of the house mark. This is a prerogative reserved only for the parent company.

Ought policy to be set aside or at least reconsidered in this case? If so, why?

The question is addressed to you as trademark manager of XYZ Corporation, the parent company: How can it be ensured that this particular use of the house mark by the company's subsidiary will increase the house mark's value? In addition how can it be ensured that this use does not merely accomplish nothing, or that it does not depreciate the value of the trademark?

The burden should be, as a matter of company policy, on the new subsidiary. Corporate parent policy should dictate that use of the corporate parent's house mark, standing alone, is expressly a right reserved to the corporate parent unless the subsidiary can demonstrate how and to what extent the value of the brand will be enhanced if this right is given to it.

If there is a brand valuation program in effect, the trademark manager will know the value of the house brand at any given point. This provides an absolute measurement by which to calculate, over time, whether the house brand's equity has grown, has been maintained, or has been lost. Thus, brand valuation allows a flexibility in applying the company's policy that is otherwise unavailable.

To Ms. Dorsey's request to use a stand-alone house mark, the correct response should be obvious if brand valuation has been performed.

As trademark administrator, you might say, "That use of a stand-alone house mark as a clean, concise image of goodwill, that is, of years of the parent company's maintenance of its commercial standards and promise to provide quality in the marketplace to its consumers, will benefit the new product. It is not so clear to us that this is a 'two way street.' If we were to do this every time someone asked for such permission without question, we would see brand equity slowly eaten away. The proposed user must be able to ensure there is a two-way street. That two-way street means the user must show us how its use of the house mark standing alone will not only benefit the user, but will benefit the corporate parent, that is, will enhance the value of the brand.

"Currently, the value of the brand is estimated at $140 million. By what time, and by what amount, do you expect the value of the brand to be increased? On what basis do you make these projections, and what penalties are you willing to offer should these projections not be reached? Are you willing to offer out of your reserves, a recompense, say, to the amount the value of the brand is demonstrably diminished? If we determine that the value of the brand has gone down, subsequent to our allowing you over time to use the stand-alone brand, and if we are able to determine that all other factors are constant, we would have to reach the conclusion it was your use of the stand-alone brand that caused the value of the brand to go down for a reason integral to your operation. You would then be responsible to make that value good. The amount would be the difference between $140 million and the subsequent value of the brand. Are you prepared to make that kind of commitment to the XYZ family of companies?"

Of course, as manager of the XYZ trademark unit, you are perfectly empowered to enforce that policy even if you do not have a current and complete brand valuation. Yet consider the relative likelihood of success in making this argument if you do not have an exact valuation of the brand, but a purely speculative one based on a hunch or on anecdotal information.

You are now in the position of having to argue something like this: "We have here something called a trademark, which we assert has a value. We do not know what that value is. We have no concrete measurement of that value. We do not want to let you use the trademark, which you can currently prove would help you sell your products, because we are concerned that this might erode the value of the brand (which we cannot quantify)."

You owe it to your shareholders, whose property the brand is, to maximize your ability to manage such situations. Brand valuation can be an invaluable tool in doing so, allowing you a new flexibility in applying your branding policy so as not to lose business opportunities because of rigidity and constructive underutilization of the brand. Without brand valuation, you could never determine scientifically when an exception ought to be made to your policy prohibition.

(b) Mr. Smith is general manager of the XYZ Corporation Widget Division, which developed and now produces a new product, the Widget. Mr. Smith approaches you, the trademark manager, and requests that you allow him to use the XYZ trademark as a corporate identifier for his division and as a brand identifier for his division's new Widget product. Keep in mind that XYZ has been declared one of the 10 most powerful and (thus valuable) brands in the world. Its brand valuation has been estimated at $140 million U.S. By what criteria do you determine whether to grant Mr. Smith's request?

Had brand valuation not taken place, there would be no criteria to apply. Mr. Smith no doubt would argue that such proposed uses of the XYZ house mark are, of course, directly in accord with current marketing wisdom—that developing a new brand identifier and/or corporation identifier trademark is not as effective in cutting through the "noise" in the marketplace to reach the consumer and distinguish a company's products from those of others, as using a powerful existing trademark. And Mr. Smith would be right.

Yet does such a use give anything back to the trademark? The question is not metaphysical. In a situation where brand valuation has not taken place, the question remains and is still in need of answer. It is, however, impossible to raise the question without brand valuation and not appear to be dealing in useless metaphysics. Consider the following reply given in the absence of brand valuation.

"I appreciate the fact that your use of the XYZ house mark would be valuable to your division and to your division's bottom line. However, as a matter of company policy I have to consider the value of our own house mark. Can you tell us whether there would be any return of brand equity to the house mark? Is the value of the house mark going to be maintained and/or augmented by our allowing you and your division to do what you ask?"

Again in the absence of brand valuation, the answer from Mr. Smith might be, "We project that using the brand will increase our sales X%, as compared with a decrease of Y% if we do not use the brand and instead used a new brand identifier. And new products coming out of your division would also suffer the same fate; that is, being less viable in the marketplace, as far as sales are concerned, than they would be if the house mark is used as a corporate identifier for the division as well."

In fact, what Mr. Smith is asking is not only to use the house mark in connection with this individual product, but to use it with the entire line of products that he is projecting will come out of the new Widget division. Mr. Smith argues that it is an undisputed fact that using the house mark in this fashion will increase his division's sales. Does that not increase the value of the brand equity of the house mark? The answer is, maybe—and maybe not.

If Widgets are a hit and take their position after Wompoms as the second most important product of the XYZ Corporation, based on their meeting consumer's expectations, then Mr. Smith is right. But suppose Widgets bomb in the marketplace. The fact that the house brand has been used in connection with this product is obviously to the house brand's detriment in terms of the goodwill on which its value rests. This means that the value of the house mark in connection with its Wompoms, the original company product, will be diminished.

Having been associated with the disaster of the Widget product, the XYZ trademark will no longer carry the same assurance of quality as it once did. Thus, when a consumer sees the brand, it will not be as certain as it was in XYZ's halcyon days, when it was one of the world's most powerful trademarks, that the consumer will choose an XYZ brand Wompom. Thus, XYZ Corporation's ability to market its original products will be more difficult in the face of competition.

If in this scenario brand valuation *has* been effected, your response as trademark manager might be something like this:

"Mr. Smith, as you know, XYZ is the house mark of the corporate parent and is associated in the marketplace with the successful Wompom product. I appreciate and acknowledge what you are saying about using a powerful existing brand and corporate identifier trademark in lieu of trying to grow a new brand and corporate identifier from scratch. However, you must realize that the value of the brand XYZ is, as an intangible asset of the company belonging to its shareholders, 140 million U.S. dollars. Without further information from you and a commitment from you to protect the brand's value, and thus the shareholders' interests, I am loathe to proceed. It is possible that you will be successful, and I certainly wish you well. But if you are not, and we have concurred with your request, what we would be doing, in effect, is asset stripping. We would be taking corporate assets and using them in such a way as to lose them.

"So I must ask, what assurances can you make against that possibility? Are you willing to guarantee us X number of sales in the first six months of production? Are you willing to submit to a decision when we revalue the brand, if it is shown that the brand's value has gone down and there is a causal relationship between your efforts and that diminishment of the brand's value, that you will have to stop using the brand no matter what the effect on your bottom line?"

Because the brand valuation is now a solid fact, Mr. Smith is compelled to reply to these issues. He may appeal over your head to the powers that-be, saying that you, as trademark/brand manager, are hurting his bottom line by not letting him compete effectively.

With brand valuation as an accomplished fact, *you* can go to the powers that be and make the point about asset stripping. Should they decide asset stripping is their desire, at least the decision will be made with adequate information. Without brand valuation, that decision will be made on a "gut feeling" or hunch about Mr. Smith's projected sales figures or may depend on how well connected Mr. Smith is—or how well connected you are.

In the best outcomes of these scenarios, Ms. Dorsey's or Mr. Smith's efforts will result in benefits for the shareholders that they will not even be able to see. In the worst outcomes, Ms. Dorsey's or Mr. Smith's efforts will cause the company's equity in trademark XYZ to erode. The shareholders will not see this result directly. They will simply be aware that their return on investment is not what it should be and that management does not know why.

Scenario Four: Brand Valuation and Proper Use

As manager of trademarks at the XYZ Corporation, you have in place an education program for your clients concerning the proper means of using and maintaining the integrity of the trademark. Integral to this program are the Rules of Proper Trademark Use:

1. Use a trademark distinctively; that is, so that it stands out from the surrounding text in some way.
2. Use a trademark with proper notice, including either TM for a trademark under common law, SM for a service mark under common law, or one of the three statutorily recognized forms of

registered federal notice, ®, "Registered in U.S. Patent and Trademark Office," or "Reg. U.S. Pat. & Tm. Off."

3. Always use a trademark as a proper adjective modifying a generic noun; for example, XYZ® Wompoms.

4. Never use a trademark as a noun or verb.

5. Never change a trademark's form.

A proper-use awareness program can comprise a number of media: educational brochures, periodic bulletins, posters in the workplace, audio and visual monitor miniseries bulletins, trademark education seminars, and others.

Of course, adherence to the Rules of Proper Trademark Use is the means to the end of developing or maintaining a trademark's distinctiveness as an indicator of source and guarantor of quality. Such adherence alone used to be but is no longer seen as proof of that status in itself. Their application is a creative, demanding process. Failure to apply any one of these rules may not in and of itself cause serious harm, but ignoring them as a group may. Each of the rules is important, and all must be adhered to.

Brand valuation can play a pivotal role in enforcing the Rules of Proper Trademark Use on a commonsense basis among clients when they question the need. Without brand valuation, you lack an important tool to help in motivating clients to adhere to the rules in the interest of developing or maintaining the equity of valuable brands.

Consider this situation: Ms. Brown comes to you with a proposal to use the XYZ logo, which is a blue square, on a sign that will appear on a fence surrounding the staging area for a rodeo. Because of sizing, she wishes you to given her permission to cut the square logo down into a rectangle so that it fits inside the available space and to use it in connection with another color—green—which is the official color of the rodeo.

Arguing against Ms. Brown without brand valuation having been effected, you will appear to be an obstructionist at best. She will say, "This will help my bottom line and thus be good for our shareholders." You will say, "It is possible that this particular application will offend any number of our customers, who will then cease buying our products. We are not certain that this will be the case. Moreover, we cannot risk misapplication of the Rules of Proper Trademark Use to our house-brand trademark."

As brand manager, you know that this intangible—the trademark—has value. But Ms. Brown is not focused on the intrinsic value of a trademark. She sees it as something that will help her group's bottom line. From her own perspective, she is right.

With brand valuation, you can make an argument something like this: "Ms. Brown, I appreciate your position. However, the value of the XYZ logo is $140 million. That value is based on its distinctive goodwill among consumers. Violation of the Rules of Proper Trademark Use puts that value at risk. I am obligated to protect the trademark's equity in the interest of our shareholders. Your obligation is to bring me sufficient information and evidence to prove that your use will not be to the detriment of that equity. Without that, and without a commitment to adhere to the Rules of Proper Trademark Use when you use the trademark, I cannot allow you to proceed."

Ms. Brown will no doubt try to protest this decision to higher authorities. You then can go to the higher authorities with your own argument, bolstered with protection of a $140 million concrete asset as part of your arsenal.

Should the decision of the senior management of the XYZ Corporation be to support Ms. Brown's project, it will be based on the knowledge that some of the equity of the trademark will, in effect, be stripped off and that it will be used in a risky situation with the hope of an augmented bottom line. Yet at least it will be a decision based on concrete information, not on how well connected Ms. Brown is, not on how well or poorly connected you are, and not on anecdote or instinct. It will be an informed, rigorous decision.

Scenario Five: Brand Valuation as A Basis for Intracompany Trademark Use Royalty Payments

At the XYZ Company there is currently a set formula for payments of royalties for intangible assets, including trademarks, between a subsidiary of XYZ and the parent company. Such formulas are generally arithmetic ones, based in part on a perception by the subsidiary of what it thinks it ought to pay. The formula may be a percentage of total sales, for instance, without correlating in any direct way to actual value of the trademark or brand, because there is no brand valuation. For example, in the case of one internationally famous mark, brand valuation was affixed at more than double its international annual sales. Therefore, any such royalty formula based on a percentage of sales figures would be lacking.

Because brand valuation is absent, the ultimate royalty formula is in no way connected to the actual value of the asset being used. Accordingly, it can be argued that to fix a royalty in this fashion is ultimately to the detriment of the brand's equity, as well as to the asset's value. The shareholders, therefore, are the customer group that suffers.

Had the XYZ Corporation effected a brand valuation of the house mark, this information could be included in the deliberations of senior management as to how to fix royalty payments.

In addition, as discussed earlier in regard to using the house mark XYZ as a corporate or brand identifier, indemnification could also now be quantified. This means, given that the XYZ house mark is valued today at $140 million, that the valuation can be measured again after a certain amount of time. Should the value go down and subsequent research show that this decline is connected to the permission given to the division to use the house brand as a corporate or brand identifier, the user can be required to pay a penalty out of its profits.

Without brand valuation there is no way that a brand manager can assert such a position without seeming ridiculously metaphysical. In this case you, as trademark administrator, would simply be asserting that the value of the brand has declined, based on anecdote and gut feeling, a position easily refutable in the absence of an actual brand valuation. After all, how can you argue that something is losing its value when you cannot even state what that value is? Thus, the significance of brand valuation is to ensure that divisions that use the brand/trademark are aware that there are consequences for its misuse and, should their products fail, loss of its equity in the marketplace. This also holds true for divisions that do not consistently follow the Rules of Proper Trademark Use.

13.2   EXTRACOMPANY USE

As discussed in the preceding paragraphs, brand valuation enables the brand/trademark manager to price royalty payments for the use of a brand by company divisions or subsidiaries. Brand valuation also enables a manager to assess possible penalties against users, should that brand's value be diminished through their fault, either by the nature of their use or their lack of adherence to the Rules of Proper Trademark Use.

Scenario One: Brand Valuation and Damages to the Brand by Unauthorized Third Parties—Litigation

Brand valuation provides a useful gauge of harm done to a brand through unauthorized use by third parties, which is recoverable in money damages in litigation.

Consider this situation: You, as XYZ Corporation's trademark manager, learn that the ABC Corporation is offering to the consuming public a competing product to your company's Wompom. The XYZ trademark is one of the world's most powerful, so the ABC Corporation decides to "piggyback" on the goodwill of the XYZ trademark. It offers its own brand of Wompoms under the brand/trademark "WXYZ" Wompoms.

You have received and confirmed reports of your company's Wompoms and those of ABC Corporation being sold in stores that provide both corporations' products, side by side in general displays for Wompoms, without differentiation.

XYZ and ABC target the same customers. They sell to the same customers and reach them through the same retail networks.

Because XYZ is one of the world's most powerful brands, the decision to offer Wompoms competing with XYZ's Wompoms under the rubric "WXYZ" can mean only one thing, namely, a decision by ABC Corporation to piggyback on your brand's goodwill. Letters from XYZ customers are received through your corporation's networks, as well as letters and phone calls from suppliers, indicating that both the ultimate consumers and suppliers have actually been confused into purchasing ABC's Wompoms, thinking that they were XYZ Corporation's product because of the similarity of the XYZ mark and the WXYZ mark. XYZ Corporation initiates litigation, wins its lawsuit, and is awarded damages. How, in its initial complaint, is XYZ Corporation to arrive at a specific figure for damages? How is the court to quantify damages?

Without brand valuation, formulas might be used involving differences in price between the junior and the senior user. For example, XYZ Wompoms sell at $10 each; ABC's at $3 per Wompom. One million ABC Wompoms were sold under the WXYZ brand. Therefore, the damage might be assessed using a total "infringing" income of ABC Corporation of $3 billion.

Damages might also be assessed by using the difference consumers would have paid for the real brand in potential sales for XYZ Corporation, which were lost to ABC, the infringer. One million ABC units bought means one million XYZ units not bought: lost XYZ income equals $10 billion.

Fortunately, however, brand valuation is not absent. The XYZ brand has been valued at $140 million. As a case in point, the "Marlboro" brand has been valued at $31 billion, more than twice its 1992 annual sales of $14 billion. Therefore, instead of the formulas used in the preceding example (or perhaps in addition to them), the court needs to include absolute damage to the brand. If brand valuation after ABC Corporation's little caper shows, all other things being constant, a diminution of the XYZ brand value of $30 million, that too may be included.

The logic of brand valuation also works in reverse. Should XYZ Corporation's damages claim be based on perceptually excessive numbers, brand valuation by ABC may provide the court an alternative basis on which to determine damages. Indeed, if faced with conflicting bases for damages by the results of conflicting brands valuations, the court might even consider retaining (at both parties' expense) its own independent brand valuation firm from which to secure an independent result.

Scenario Two: Brand Valuation and Damages to the Brand by Unauthorized Third Parties—Arbitration

Suppose, given the circumstances of the preceding scenario, that the XYZ Corporation initiated legal proceedings only to have the ABC Corporation agree to binding arbitration. In the absence of brand valuation, XYZ Corporation can bring to an arbitration process a claim for damages based only on various formulas of sale, as discussed earlier in the instance of an actual lawsuit.

As already discussed, sales figures do not necessary lay the basis for actually providing recompense for the damages done to a brand. The XYZ trademark and brand are valued at $140 million. When XYZ Corporation's position is given to the arbitrator, the claim for damages must include not only the arithmetic formulas based on sales, but also an estimate of the actual damage done to the brand based on its prior valuation, its current valuation, and the difference between these figures. Otherwise, XYZ may in fact be settling for a damages figure which significantly unvalues the damage done and the penalty that ABC Corporation ought to pay.

However, because, brand valuation has been effected previously, you, the trademark manager, are now able to effect a subsequent brand valuation and to determine the difference between those two figures. You are able to add onto a lost-sales figure or wrongful-profits figure another quantification of damage. Thus, you arrive at an absolute damage figure that comes closer to the real damage done to the brand by ABC's activities.

The plaintiff is not the sole party to whom brand valuation is useful in a situation such as the lawsuit described earlier. An independent brand valuation performed by the defendant in a lawsuit or in an arbitration proceeding may be valuable in ensuring that the plaintiff's claims for damages correspond to objective reality.

In an arbitration proceeding, not only do both plaintiff and defendant have a vested interest in effecting brand valuations to bolster their respective positions and raise questions about the opposing side's position, but the arbitrator as well has a vested interest in the brand valuation process.

In a situation where either plaintiff or defendant (or both) have effected brand valuations for affixing the basis of damages in a case, the arbitrator may feel the need to effect a brand valuation process of his or her own. This will allow the arbitrator to determine, independent of information coming from either party, a basis on which to calculate damages.

Therefore, in an arbitration proceeding, not only does the brand valuation process provide value for the plaintiff, and for the defendant, it also provides value for an independent arbitrator in establishing a basis for damages that both sides can accept.

**Scenario Three: Brand Valuation and Damages to the Brand
by Unauthorized Third Parties—Amicable Settlement**

In a less formal setting than actual litigation or formal arbitration proceedings, in an instance where both sides have resolved to settle their differences amicably, the role of brand valuation is similar to that discussed earlier. The XYZ Corporation (the injured party) and the ABC Corporation (the injuring party) may find brand valuation an excellent way to resolve the matter between them. That is, they could agree in advance to settle their differences based on a totality of the arithmetic formula *lost profit plus whatever an independent brand valuation firm might assess the lost value of the brand to be, if any.* Both sides could agree to retain the brand valuation firm at their joint expense as a mutual gesture of good faith. In this way, brand valuation can be the basis of an amicable resolution in this even less formal setting.

13.3 FINANCIAL STATEMENTS

As of this writing, the Generally Accepted Accounting Principles (GAAP) in the United Kingdom allow the use of brand valuation as part of a corporation's financial statement. Also as of this writing, brand valuation is not considered proper in a corporation's financial statement in the United States, except as a footnote to the statement. This procedure is being considered by U.S. accountants and may be the basis of significant changes in the U.S. GAAP in the future.

Thus a footnote to the financial statement of the XYZ Corporation (a U.S. Company) would cite the $140 million brand valuation of its house mark XYZ.

Consider this scenario: XYZ Corporation is the parent company that owns, worldwide, the XYZ trademark and brand. It has a direct, wholly-owned subsidiary, XYZ-UK, in the United Kingdom. Currently, XYZ-UK pays a royalty to its parent company, XYZ Corporation, based on a formula of percentage of sales for use of the parent's intangible assets, which include the house mark XYZ. In the absence of brand valuation, all XYZ can expect the U.K. subsidiary to do is to pay a percentage of sales based on what the subsidiary perceives is a fair price for the use of the trademark.

However, brand valuation has established the value of the XYZ trademark at $140 million. Given that this is reflected in the U.K. subsidiary's financial statement and recognized as an asset in the United Kingdom for tax purposes, it might be interesting to consider and explore whether the royalty formula for the U.K. subsidiary to pay its U.S.-based parent company for use of the house mark should more closely reflect the actual book value of the trademark itself, as determined in the U.K., and the fact that the U.K. subsidiary can cite such payments for tax purposes. It would also be interesting to consider and explore how this might work with royalty formulas to U.K. parent companies by non-U.K. subsidiaries.

13.4 COLLATERAL FOR LOANS

Although brand valuation is a subject of some controversy in regard to financial statements and other financial reporting, it can prove an invaluable tool in related areas, such as in providing collateral for loans.

Consider this scenario: XYZ Corporation wishes to acquire QXR Corporation. It goes to the bank to obtain the necessary loans to make the purchase. In evaluating whether XYZ Corporation has adequate collateral to make granting a loan request a reasonable business risk, brand valuation can help. It can help the bank, the would-be lender, and the would-be borrower corporation.

It has been stated in section 13.2 of this chapter that the book value of a brand is at any point in time quite distinguishable from the level of its annual sales. As mentioned earlier, the Marlboro trademark was valued at $31 billion, whereas annual sales under that brand approximated less than half of that amount. If, therefore, the Bank of Whatever, in examining XYZ Corporation's request for a loan of $100 million does not take into account the $140 million asset value that brand valuation has established for the house mark XYZ it might be leaving out of its deliberations on whether to grant a loan, significant market information that ought to be considered.

The bank may wish to perform its own brand valuation to ensure the accuracy of the data it uses to make this determination. It is also worthwhile for the would-be borrower, in this case the XYZ Corporation, to provide such information to the bank, for fear the bank might not even consider this area of intangible assets in its decision. Accordingly, brand valuation can work as part of an argument in support of a loan to the would-be borrower. It could also be used by the lender, in this case the Bank of Whatever, to confirm the information provided by the would-be borrower. Thus, brand valuation is capable of helping both sides in the instance of a loan request to determine mutually whether the loan should take place.

The Bank of Whatever ought to consider the following questions: If the bank needs to foreclose on XYZ Corporation and take its trademark as forfeited collateral against an unpaid loan, how can the trademark, a symbol of the corporation's goodwill, commitment to quality, and guarantee of the source of product, be transferred to the bank? Does this mean XYZ Corporation's actual business of providing Wompoms is also automatically forfeited to the bank? After all, assignments of trademarks rest on whether the underlying goodwill, that is, the business activities, were sold. How can the trademark's goodwill, the basis of its value, be transferred to the bank in such a case without transferring the business too? If such an assignment is made between two corporations in the course of a usual sale of a trademark, it is considered an "assignment in gross." A registered mark so assigned might be targeted for cancellation on such grounds. This decision may ultimately be one of relative business risk made by senior bank management.

13.5 ACQUISITIONS

The acquisition craze of the 1980s underscored the importance of the brand valuation process. Corporations were bought and sold not for their projected sales nor for any other asset, except for the estimated brand value of their trademark portfolio. With the greater scrutiny of corporate boards of directors by shareholders, and the greater scrutiny of executive management by boards of directors themselves, brand valuation today has an important contributing role to play.

Consider the following scenario: The XYZ Corporation has announced an intention to acquire the QXR Corporation at a given price. Brand valuation of the QXR portfolio of trademarks can provide important information as to the quality of the decision to make the purchase at all, and as to the agreed-upon price. The chairman of XYZ Corporation, if he is astute, would guarantee independent brand valuation of the house brand of the QXR Corporation, to ensure that QXR management's asking price for the company reflects its actual value inclusive of the brand.

The XYZ board of directors itself may wish to commission an independent brand valuation of the QXR Corporation trademark portfolio in order to ensure that the reported negotiations and brand valuations taken into account by the chairman of XYZ are in fact accurate, and to maintain the board's own responsibility to look after the interests of the corporation's shareholders.

Independent shareholder groups themselves may wish to initiate brand valuation processes of the QXR trademark portfolio for similar reasons. Shareholder groups are becoming much more vigilant to ensure that shareholders' own interests are being looked after, not only by chairmen of corporations, but also by boards of directors. Boards of directors have been much criticized lately for undue compliance with their chairpersons. The XYZ shareholders may feel the need to ensure that not only has the board initiated its own independent brand valuation to ascertain that the asking and purchase prices of the QXR Corporation are not overvalued but, as well, that the board of directors' own independent brand audit, if it has made one, is not unduly compliant with the chairman's own audit.

The target company may engage in this process as well. The chairman of the QXR Corporation might well initiate brand valuation, if it has not been done before, to ensure that this factor is taken into account in the asking price for his company. As noted earlier, brand valuation can significantly affect the market value of a corporation. In the case of Marlboro, its trademark has been cited at a book value of more than twice its company's annual sales. Therefore, the chairman of the QXR Corporation may very well feel the need to ensure that the numbers used are not only those provided by brand valuation firms commissioned by the XYZ Corporation.

The board of directors of QXR may feel the same need to initiate independent brand valuation of their own trademark portfolio to ensure that the QXR chairman's deliberations are not based on erroneous information.

Furthermore, the shareholders of QXR may wish to ensure that their interests are being looked after as rigorously as they ought to be. By initiating a brand valuation independent of the QXR board of directors' and the QXR chairman's brand valuations, the shareholders of QXR themselves can ascertain that the asking price for their corporation will not be to the detriment of their own interests.

For both XYZ Corporation (the would-be acquirer) and QXR Corporation (the would-be acquired), brand valuation can play an important role in ensuring that dealings are above board and reflect the true value of the purchased stock. It allows the respective chairpersons of both corporations to make informed decisions as to price. It also allows the respective boards of directors to maintain proper supervision of their chairpersons to make certain that the asking price, as well as the negotiating price and the final price, all reflect the proper value of the brand in the purchased stock—no more, no less. The shareholders of both companies are able to ensure that their interests are being looked after by their respective chairpersons and boards of directors.

Such brand valuation processes on both sides can be, in the end, the basis of intervention by the boards in changing the negotiating positions of their chairpersons, or of challenging the position of the respective companies' leadership by shareholder groups.

Brand valuation thus contributes to the democratization of corporations, a process recently characterized by social and business commentators as intrinsically good.

13.6 THIRD-PARTY LICENSING

Use of the XYZ house mark by third parties unrelated to the XYZ Corporation, is permitted (as, indeed, is any corporation's or entity's licensing of its trademarks for use by unrelated third parties) as long as the "quality control" provision is met. This means that the XYZ Corporation can benefit from others' use of its trademark as long as it makes sure that their use of the XYZ trademark is equal in quality to the services and products that XYZ has promised to consumers throughout its history in the marketplace.

In other words, because a trademark exists to assure the consumer that the product or service on which it appears comes from the same source and is guaranteed to have the same level of quality as did those other products and services that historically bore this trademark, the same holds true for products and services that are sourced elsewhere but whose source companies are under the quality control of the trademark's owner company.

Third-party licensing allows you, as trademark manager of XYZ Corporation, to increase the value of the brand to the corporation and its shareholders, as well as to increase the potential for profits. Through brand extension, spokesbrands, or franchising, the equity of the trademark as the indicator of source and quality may be enhanced and XYZ Corporation's profits increased.

The disadvantage of third-party licensing arises with the omission of proper oversight of the quality of products or services offered under your brand by that third party.

Scenario One:Brand Valuation as a Monitor of Third-Party Licensees

Consider this situation: Mr. Cooper, executive vice president of marketing of XYZ Corporation has come to you, trademark manager of the corporation, with a request for some guidance.

Marketing has determined that it is a natural fit for XYZ Corporation to go into the "Whosis" business. XYZ Corporation has never made Whosis products, nor is it in a position to acquire a company that does make them. What XYZ has decided to do in marketing is to pursue a third-party licensing arrangement with the LMN Corporation, which has been in the Whosis business for a number of years and has a good reputation for producing a quality-level Whosis. You have been asked to provide input into this process.

Your advice on the matter, directed to Mr. Cooper, might be something like this: "Whether to extend this brand in this fashion is a business decision beyond the scope of my office. However, although there are opportunities and profits to be made in such a venture, there are also losses that can be incurred. I am remiss in my duties if I do not warn management that with the potential for opportunities and profits come specific types of risks to the equity of the brand.

"Our brand has a current market value of $140 million. The primary objectives of this exercise are to increase the equity of the brand along with the profits of the company in connection with this product offering, and thus enhance the return to our shareholders.

"The XYZ Trademark Management Unit is responsible for preparing this license agreement. In addition to the requisite quality-control provisions and other provisions to the license agreement that ensure that the quality control will in fact—not just nominally—be adhered to, I strongly insist on something else to protect our trademark's equity.

"That is, we have the right, at our sole discretion, should we find our brand's equity diminished as a result of this licensing agreement, to terminate the license and immediately revoke the licensing permission.

"I think we should make certain that in the license agreement language is included to the effect that our brand is valued at $140 million. In addition, we reserve the right at any time for any reason, with no notice, to effect a subsequent evaluation for the explicit purpose of ensuring at any point that we have not lost equity through this license arrangement.

"We need also to state that should our subsequent brand valuation show that equity has been lost, we reserve the right without further explanation to revoke the license, terminate the relationship, and ensure that all branded inventory is destroyed at the expense of licensee."

Scenario Two: Brand Valuation as a Monitor of Trademark Licensors

Brand valuation can play a role in the process of monitoring trademark licensors, as well.

Consider this situation: XYZ Corporation wishes to license the use of the Whoosis trademark belonging to the LMN Corporation in connection with a new line of Wompoms; namely, Whoosis brand Wompoms. As trademark manager of XYZ Corporation, you wish to ensure there is language in the licensing agreement that takes brand valuation into account—but this time from a different perspective.

In Scenario one, you were the trademark owner trying to protect yourself. Now you are the trademark user or licensee, and, as such, you also want to use brand valuation as a tool to protect yourself. Your position might be articulated to the LMN Corporation something like this:

We acknowledge the ownership and rights and title held by LMN Corporation to the Whoosis trademark. We also acknowledge your right to terminate the contract pursuant to the terms of the licensing agreement. This includes the right to terminate should you effect brand valuation and are able to determine that equity has been lost to your brand because of the activities governed by this agreement. However, we reserve the right to effect, simultaneously upon your doing so, a brand valuation of our own by an independent contractor. Should both our brand valuation firms come to the same conclusion, either in your corporation's favor or in our favor, we should both agree to abide by those conclusions. Suppose your position is that the brand has lost value, but my position is that it has not. Subsequently, our brand valuations prove that you are right. We will then, of course, abide by the termination provisions of the contract.

"However, the reverse is also true. If we both determine that, in fact, brand valuation shows that brand devaluation has not occurred, we then would reserve the right to keep the contract open and you would agree in writing to do so."

Thus we see, from the perspective of both the licensor and the licensee, brand valuation can provide the basis for ensuring that actual, rather than anecdotal or unsupported, information is the basis of the decision to effect a license agreement or to terminate or continue a license agreement that is in place.

There are a number of practical applications of brand valuation for the corporate trademark manager to be aware of. As this process becomes increasingly well recognized and more widely accepted, especially in the accounting field, many new practical applications will arise.

PART IV

OTHER COMMERCIAL EXPLOITATION: TAKING A SECURITY INTEREST IN INTELLECTUAL PROPERTY

LIBERATING UNTAPPED MILLIONS FOR INVESTMENT COLLATERAL: THE ARRIVAL OF SECURITY INTERESTS IN INTANGIBLE ASSETS

Melvin Simensky, Esq.

Hall, Dickler, Kent, Friedman & Wood
New York, New York

Howard A. Gootkin, Esq.

Sanus Corp. Health Systems
Fort Lee, New Jersey

In American jurisprudence, intellectual property has always occupied a position of great prominence. Its doctrines and principles have been expounded and clarified over the decades by leading jurists.[1] Indeed, patents and copyrights, two of the most important forms of intellectual property, are expressly mentioned in the Constitution as areas over which Congress was granted power to legislate.[2]

In sharp contrast to its prestige in legal circles, intellectual property and its potential value have until recently evoked relatively little interest in or appreciation within the financial markets. This attitude shifted radically in the 1980s as bankers and business persons came to acknowledge the significant value represented by intellectual property.

Despite these developments, the full financial potential of intellectual property cannot be realized unless it can readily be used as a source of funding to facilitate other commercial transactions. It is the purpose of this chapter to explain how that can be accomplished.

14.1 DEFINITIONS

Intellectual property is an umbrella term that encompasses four main types of such property: patents, copyrights, trademarks, and trade secrets.

---

[1] For example, Learned Hand, one of the great judges of this century, wrote numerous influential decisions in the area of intellectual property, a number of which remain governing law. E.g., *Nichols v. Universal Pictures Corp.*, 45 F.2d 119 (2d Cir. 1930).

[2] U.S. Const., art. I, §8, cl. 8 ("The Congress shall have power . . . To promote the progress of science and useful arts, by securing for limited time to authors and inventors the exclusive right to their respective writings and discoveries.")

Copyright protects original works of authorship from reproduction, public distribution, public performance, public display, or the creation of derivative works based on such works without the authorization of the copyright holder.[3] Although the Constitution envisions copyright as protecting authors' "writings," in fact, the term *writings* has been construed very broadly to include, among other things, such disparate forms of creativity as choreography, maps, sculpture, pictures, and computer software. All that is necessary for copyright protection is that the work exhibit a modicum of creativity and be fixed in a tangible form.[4]

Because this standard can be so easily met, copyright provides only limited protection to the copyright holder. The only prohibition is the copying of a copyrighted work. If another person independently creates the same work without reference to a copyrighted work, that person may fully exploit his or her own creation even if it is identical to the copyrighted work. As compensation for the limited protection accorded a copyrighted work, the term of a copyright is relatively lengthy. Currently, it is the life of the author plus 50 years.[5]

A patent, conversely, provides much greater protection to the patent holder but is much more difficult to obtain. Patents are granted to processes or machines that meet the following criteria: (1) *novelty*, in that the invention was not previously known or used by others, (2) *unobviousness* to a person having ordinary skill in the relevant art, and (3) *utility*, in that the invention has a useful purpose, actually works, and is not frivolous or immoral.[6] Patents do not protect only against copying a patented work. Even if a second person independently invents a process or procedure without knowledge of the patented work but duplicates it, the patent holder may bar this person from selling, using, or making the independently generated invention. Because it grants the patentee a virtual monopoly on a patented work, the term of a patent is limited to 17 years.[7]

Although copyrights and patents are the exclusive domain of the federal government,[8] trademarks implicate both state and federal law. A trademark is a word, design, or symbol used by a person to identify his or her goods and to distinguish them from those of another. If the goods are used exclusively in intrastate commerce, the marks used in connection with them are governed by state law. If the goods are used in interstate commerce, the trademarks used may be registered under federal law.[9]

Trade secrets are protected, if at all, only under state law. Trade secrets are usually defined as "any formula, pattern, device or compilation of information which is used in one's business and which gives him an opportunity to obtain an advantage over competitors who do not know or use it."[10] In determining whether information qualifies as a trade

---

[3] 17 U.S.C. §106.

[4] *Feist Publications, Inc. v. Rural Telephone Service Company, Inc.*, 111 S.Ct. 1282 (1991); 17 U.S.C. §101.

[5] 17 U.S.C. §302(a).

[6] 35 U.S.C. §§102–103.

[7] 35 U.S.C. §154.

[8] Under the 1909 Copyright Act, federal copyright protection arose when a work was published. Prior to publication the work could be protected under state common-law copyright. This opening for state law was to a large degree closed by the Copyright Act of 1976, under which federal copyright protection attaches as soon as a work is fixed in a tangible form of expression, even if it has not yet been published. It is possible that the states may still protect works that have not yet been fixed in a tangible medium of expression, although that is not clear inasmuch as the full extent of federal preemption in the copyright area is murky. See 17 U.S.C. §301.

[9] The Lanham Act, 15 U.S.C. §1051 *et seq.*

[10] Restatement (First) of Torts §757, cmt. b at 5 (1939).

secret, the courts will consider, among other things, the extent to which others already know the information or the ease with which they could learn it, the means taken by the party claiming a trade secret to keep the information confidential, and the value of the information.[11]

14.2 THE NEW RESPECT FOR INTELLECTUAL PROPERTY

Commercial transactions involving intellectual property are not an invention of the 1980s. They are, in fact, quite old. What the 1980s witnessed was a shift in the priority assigned to intellectual property in such transactions. From its status as merely one among other assets bought and sold, intellectual property in certain instances came to dominate transactions as the financial markets began to appreciate the significant value intellectual property represents. Thus, when the Saks chain was sold in a $1.5 billion transaction, the real estate value of the stores was estimated to be only $500,000,000. The Saks trademarks were themselves valued at $1 billion. The trademarks associated with Marlboro cigarettes have been valued at more than $30 billion, dwarfing the value of the tangible assets involved in the cigarette's production.[12]

Undoubtedly, this recognition, albeit belated, of the enormous value of intellectual property was heavily influenced by the mergers and acquisitions trend of the 1980s. The assets of potential targets were closely scrutinized to determine whether a company was undervalued by the market (or, a skeptic might add, to determine which assets might be spun off when the acquired company was cannibalized by its acquirers). Inevitably and increasingly, closer attention was paid to the value of a company's intellectual property as well.[13]

However, the mergers and acquisitions trend of the 1980s is only part of the reason that greater attention is being paid to intellectual property. To a large degree, this growing interest reflects broader shifts in the U.S. economy.

Introducing a new brand in the marketplace, especially when it must compete against well-established brands enjoying widespread consumer awareness, has become prohibitively expensive. It has been estimated to cost $100 million to launch a new soap brand and $300 million for a new cigarette brand.[14] Even with these huge expenditures, the odds against success are enormous. With such formidable barriers to entry, it is not surprising that well-entrenched, existing marks should be perceived as so valuable.[15]

More fundamentally, in the past two decades, there has been a dramatic shift from a manufacturing-based to an information-based economy in the United States. So profound has been this shift, that it has been hailed in certain quarters as the Second Industrial Revolution.[16]

---

[11] Because it is often difficult to keep important information secret, trade secret protection is oftentimes limited in effect.

[12] Simensky, "The New Role of Intellectual Property in Commercial Transactions," N.Y.L.J., May 8, 1992 p. 1.

[13] A cynic might comment that if the takeover had been financed by high-yield junk bonds, the acquirer would find it useful to assign an enhanced value to the intellectual property it had acquired in order to offset on its books the huge interest obligations it assumed in order to finance the takeover.

[14] Simensky, "The New Role of Intellectual Property in Commercial Transactions," N.Y.L.J., May 8, 1992 p. 4.

[15] Ibid.

[16] The central role, envisioned by President Clinton, of high-technology industries in the emerging American economy, reflects this shift.

Intellectual property is well suited to this new information-based economy. At its most abstract, intellectual property in each of its forms represents ownership of or control over particular combinations of information. Because information is the basis of the new economy, it was almost inevitable that intellectual property would enjoy enhanced prestige as this new economic paradigm became dominant.

Changes in the Law.   The law affecting intellectual property also underwent several changes in the 1980s, which both reflected and contributed to the increased importance and value of intellectual property.

One of the most far-reaching legal changes was the establishment of the Federal Circuit in the 1980s to hear, among other things, appeals in patent cases from the federal district courts and from the Patent and Trademark Office.[17] Previously, an appeal from a district court decision was brought in the Federal Circuit located where the district court that issued the decision sat. The result was an extensive body of patent decisions, reflecting widely divergent attitudes among the Circuits toward patents and the 17-year monopoly they award.[18] That diversity was lost with the establishment of the Federal Circuit. As many of its critics feared, the Federal Circuit has shown a distinctly propatent bias.[19]

In response to this propatent shift, companies began aggressively to assert claims of patent infringement, no longer inhibited by the fear that a court would invalidate either their patents or the broad scope of their patent claims. Other companies began to pay steep licensing fees to patent holders rather than incur the risk of an adverse judgment for patent infringement. Patentees, such as Texas Instruments, earned far more in licensing revenues under their old patents than they did from new inventions.[20]

Arguably, when it set up the Federal Circuit, Congress had not intended that more patents be upheld as valid or that they appreciate in value as a result.[21] In its 1984 amendments to the Food and Drug Act, in contrast, Congress expressly sought to provide pharmaceutical companies with additional patentlike monopolies even if their products did not meet the criteria for patents.

Under these amendments, any drug approved as a "new drug"[22] by the Food and Drug Administration (FDA) between 1982 and 1984 became entitled to 10 years of market exclusivity, regardless of whether the drug had been patented. Any drug approved as a new drug after 1984 is entitled to 5 years of market exclusivity, regardless of whether it is patentable. Any drug previously approved by the FDA, but for which a new use has been found, is entitled to 3 years of market exclusivity for that new use of the drug.[23] Finally,

---

[17] 28 U.S.C. §§ 1295(a)(1), 1338.

[18] See Engel and Radcliffe, "Intellectual Property Financing for High-Technology Companies," 19 U.C.C. L.J. 3, 10 (1986).

[19] See Dreyfuss, "Federal Circuit: A Case Study in Specialized Courts," 64 N.Y.U. L. Rev. 1, 26–27 (1989); Engel and Radcliffe, "Intellectual Property Financing for High-Technology Companies."

[20] Fisher, "Aggressive Defender Branches Out," *The New York Times*, 25 January 1992, p. 38.

[21] But see Dreyfuss, "Federal Circuit: A Case Study in Specialized Courts," 64 N.Y.U. L. Rev. 1 p. 27.

[22] A drug is approved as a "new drug" if the FDA passes favorably on the New Drug Application submitted by the manufacturer. To win such approval, the manufacturer must prove, on the basis of clinical tests, that the drug is both safe and effective. Virtually all new drug products are considered "new drugs" in the statutory sense and thus require FDA approval before they can be marketed. See generally 21 U.S.C. §355 *et. seq*.

[23] 21 U.S.C. §355(c)(3)(C)(ii)-(iii); (j)(4)(D)(ii)-(iv).

any drug approved as a new drug for the treatment of diseases affecting fewer than 200,000 people is entitled to 7 years of market exclusivity.[24]

As can be expected whenever monopolies are awarded, the result of these changes has been a marked increase in pharmaceutical companies' revenues. Whatever the wisdom of these amendments,[25] they could only lead financial analysts to appreciate the significant revenue-generating potential of intellectual property.

Indeed, it is precisely because of this potential that the United States has pressed for respect for intellectual property rights in its trade negotiations with foreign countries. Reflecting this concern, the North American Free Trade Agreement (NAFTA) obligates the signatories to accord the same protection to the intellectual property of the others' nationals that each gives to its own nationals' intellectual property. At a minimum, the parties must abide by the provisions of the leading international treaties governing intellectual property.[26] It is estimated that because of these provisions, Canada will pay an additional $5 billion for drugs because it will have to revise its law to accord enhanced patent protection to pharmaceuticals.[27]

14.3 SECURITY INTERESTS UNDER ARTICLE 9 OF THE UNIFORM COMMERCIAL CODE

Although the capital markets have come to recognize the significant value associated with intellectual property, its full potential to facilitate commercial transactions has not been exploited. Creditors will not provide substantial funding to those using intellectual property as the primary collateral, unless they are confident they will have easy recourse against the collateral—the intellectual property—in the event the debtor does not repay the borrowed funds. In light of the substantial amounts at which certain types of intellectual property have been valued, large amounts of capital could be made available to companies if it were easy to collateralize intellectual property. This is especially critical for start-up high-technology companies, which frequently have no assets other than their patents or copyrights. Unless these assets can be used as collateral, there is less chance these firms will receive the necessary infusion of capital.[28]

Historically, the law has created a number of devices to enable the creditor to go against specific property to satisfy a debt owed him or her. Chattel mortgages, conditional sales, equipment trusts, and trust receipts were developed in order to reassure a lender that a loan would be repaid from specific, identifiable assets in the event that the debtor defaulted on the loan.[29] Each of these devices was governed by a separate set of rules and was limited in its application to only particular types of transactions.

---

[24] 21 U.S.C. §360cc(a).

[25] The amendments were passed to induce the drug companies to withdraw their opposition to legislation making it easier for generic drug manufacturers to obtain FDA approval for their generic equivalent drugs.

[26] North American Free Trade Agreement, Part 6, Articles 1703, 1701, ¶2, 44 *BNA's Patent, Trademark & Copyright Journal* 511 (September 17, 1992).

[27] Freudenheim, "Canadians See Rise in Drug Costs," *The New York Times*, 16 November 1992, D1.

[28] Although start-up companies are frequently used as the model for the debtor relying on intellectual property to secure loans, they may not be the best example. Because they are start-up companies and are therefore without a track record, the value assigned their intellectual property would probably be heavily discounted. It is more likely that these companies will be funded by venture capitalists, who take equity in the corporation in exchange for funding, rather than by banks, which use intellectual property as collateral for the loans they make.

[29] U.C.C. §9–102(2) and *Official Comment*.

In the case of the chattel mortgage, for example, title to the collateral was assigned to the creditor, reverting back to the debtor when the debt was repaid.[30] The obvious disadvantage to relying on this device is that it forces the creditor to become involved in the substantive business of the debtor when all the creditor is interested in doing is providing funding in the hope of earning a return.

To remove these impediments to complex commercial transactions, Article 9 of the Uniform Commercial Code (UCC)[31] was drafted. Its goal was to simplify the process of securing a loan by subsuming these various security mechanisms under a single umbrella term, the "security interest."

As defined by the UCC, a security interest is "an interest in personal property or fixtures which secures payment or performance of an obligation."[32] It does not transfer title to the creditor, nor does it give the creditor a present right of possession. Whatever rights it gives the creditor vest only upon default by the debtor of the underlying obligation. It is the non-real estate equivalent of the mortgage that a bank takes in a house. So long as the mortgage payments are made, the bank has no present possessory interest in the house. Only if the mortgage is not repaid can the bank take possession of the house to satisfy the debt owed it.

Grant Gilmore, one of the chief architects of Article 9, stated that its goal was to make taking a security interest as easy as rolling off a log.[33] Although that may be an exaggeration, Article 9 unquestionably simplified the law of secured transactions.

To create a security interest, the debtor must grant the creditor a security interest in the designated collateral pursuant to a signed, written agreement that describes the collateral. The debtor must have rights in the collateral in which he or she grants a security interest, and the debtor must receive value in exchange for the security interest granted.[34] When these conditions are met, the security interest is said to "attach."[35]

The security interest alone is not enough to protect the creditor fully in the event of default. If others also hold security interests in the same collateral, the collateral may be insufficient to satisfy all the debts it secures. It is therefore imperative that the creditor's security interest have priority over other security interests so that the debt it secures is satisfied first, before other creditors have recourse against the collateral.

To achieve priority under Article 9, the creditor must "perfect" his security interest. This is done by filing or recording it in the appropriate state office.[36] The creditor need not file the security agreement creating the security interest. It is sufficient that he or she file a financing statement which identifies the debtor's address, the creditor's name, and the collateral in which a security interest has been taken.[37]

---

[30] E.g., *Waterman v. Mackenzie*, 138 U.S. 252 (1890).

[31] Unless otherwise indicated, all references to the Uniform Commercial Code are to the official text and commentary of the 1972 version of the Code.

[32] U.C.C. §1–201(37).

[33] See *Official Comment*, §9–101 ("The aim of this Article is to provide a simple and unified structure within which the immense variety of presentday secured financing transactions can go forward with less cost and with greater certainty.")

[34] §9–203(1)(a)-(c).

[35] §9–203(2).

[36] §9–302. Perfection may also be accomplished by taking possession of the collateral. However, by its nature, intellectual property cannot be physically possessed. Hence, the discussion of perfection and its implications will ignore possession as a means of perfection. See Weinberg & Woodward, "Easing Transfer and Security Interest Transactions in Intellectual Property: An Agenda for Reform," 79 Ky. L. J. 61, 74 n.65 (1990–91).

[37] §§9–302; 9–402.

Once the security interest is perfected, it will have priority over any subsequently filed security interest, even if that later-filed security interest was created first. By not filing the earlier-created security interest, the creditor fails to give notice to third parties of his or her security interest and, therefore, cannot in fairness assert priority over their interests. Priority is determined solely according to who first perfected an interest by recording it.[38]

14.4 THE PROBLEM OF PREEMPTION

Article 9 governs security interests in, among other things, general intangibles, which are defined as "any personal property (including things in action) other than goods, accounts, chattel paper, documents, instruments and money."[39] Intellectual property appears to meet this definition. Indeed, the *Official Comment* lists "copyrights, trademarks and patents" as examples of general intangibles.[40] Taking a security interest in intellectual property would, therefore, appear to be a simple matter of following the provisions of Article 9.

For trade secrets and trademarks used in intrastate commerce only, that is indeed the case. Because these forms of intellectual property are governed exclusively by state law, taking a security interest in them is simply a straightforward application of Article 9.

The issue is more complicated in connection with copyrights, patents, and trademarks used in interstate commerce. Since these forms of intellectual property are governed to a greater or lesser extent by federal law, it is unclear whether security interests in them should be governed by Article 9 or by federal law. Unfortunately, Article 9 itself provides no clear resolution of the issue.[41]

(a) The Official Comments. As the examples of general intangibles given in the *Official Comment* make clear, the drafters of Article 9 apparently were of the view that security interests in copyrights, patents, and trademarks fell within the purview of Article 9 at least to some degree. Unfortunately, the drafters never resolved the extent to which Article 9 governs security interests taken in these forms of intellectual property.

Article 9 incorporates the doctrine of federal preemption of state law in two of its provisions: §9–104(a) and §9–302(3)(a). Section 9–104(a) states:

> This Article does not apply (a) to a security interest subject to any statute of the United States, to the extent that such statute governs the rights of parties to and third parties affected by transactions in particular types of property.

Under §9–302(3)(a),

> (3) The filing of a financing statement otherwise required by this Article is not necessary or effective to perfect a security interest in property subject to
>
> (a) a statute or treaty of the United States which provides for a national or international registration or a national or international certificate of title or which specifies a place of filing different from that specified in this Article for filing of the security interests.

---

[38] §9–312(b) and *Official Comment* thereto.

[39] §9–106.

[40] *Official Comment*, §9–106.

[41] As discussed, federal law, at least with regard to patents and trademarks, is totally silent on the issue of security interests. This is not surprising inasmuch as both the Patent Act and the Trademark Act (Lanham) antedate the creation of the modern secured transaction under Article 9. It is more surprising that Article 9 itself handles the issue in such a confused manner.

Both provisions recognize the preemption of federal law by state law. However, the interplay between federal and state law is different under each of them.

Under §104, Article 9 seems to have no role to play. Federal law preempts it totally ("This Article does not apply"). Under §302, in contrast, state law continues to play an important role. Preemption is limited to those provisions of Article 9 dealing with recording a security interest in order to perfect it ("The filing of a financing statement otherwise required by this Article is not necessary or effective to perfect a security interest . . ."). The other provisions of Article 9, however, continue to govern the transaction.[42]

Whether Article 9 governs security interests in patents, trademarks, or copyrights depends on whether the federal statute governing each of them triggers these preemption provisions. Unfortunately, the *Official Comment* seems to take inconsistent positions on that question.

The *Official Comment* to §104 states:

> Although the Federal Copyright Act contains provisions permitting the mortgage of a copyright and for the recording of an assignment of a copyright (17 USC §§28, 30) such a statute would not seem to contain sufficient provisions regulating the rights of the parties and third parties to exclude security interests in copyrights from the provisions of this Article. . . . Compare also with respect to patents, 35 USC §47. The filing provisions under these Acts . . . are recognized as the equivalent to filing under this Article. § 9–302(3) and (4).

The position of the *Comment* appears to be that neither the Patent Act nor the Copyright Act is sufficiently comprehensive to totally preempt Article 9, pursuant to §104. The recording provisions of each statute are, however, sufficient under §302(3) to preempt Article 9's provisions for perfecting the security interest by recording it.

This *Comment* creates several difficulties. First, it appears flatly inconsistent with the *Official Comment* to the definition of "general intangibles." The *Official Comment* there suggests that the patent, copyright, and trademark statutes are outside the purview of Article 9, pursuant to the preemption provision of §104(a).[43] That position is expressly denied in the *Comment* to §104(a) quoted earlier.

More important, the *Comment* to §104(a) totally ignores the Trademark (Lanham) Act. Because that statute also contains a recording provision, the *Comment*'s silence might be an indication that in contrast to the recording schemes of the Copyright and Patent Acts, that of the Trademark Act does not supplant the recording provisions of Article 9. Or the *Comment*'s silence may simply be an oversight.

Even worse, the positions that the *Official Comment* does take with regard to the Copyright and Patent Acts appear inconsistent with opinions expressed in the *Official Comments* to other provisions of Article 9. The *Official Comment* to §302(3) lists several statutes whose recording provisions are adequate to trigger that section's preemption rule. Although the Copyright Act is mentioned, the Patent Act is not, even though it was so listed in the *Comment* to §104(a).[44]

---

[42] §9–302 (4); see Note, "Perfection of Security Interests in Intellectual Property: Federal Statutes Preempt Article 9," 57 Geo. Wash. L. Rev. 135 (1988).

[43] *Official Comment*, §9–106 ("Other examples of [general intangibles] are copyrights, trademarks and patents, except to the extent that they may be excluded by Section 9–104 [a].")

[44] *Official Comment*, §9–302 ("Examples of the type of federal statute referred to in paragraph [3][a] are the provisions of 17 U.S.C. §§28, 30 [copyrights], 49 U.S.C. §1403 [aircraft], 49 USC §20[c] [railroads].")

Finally, the *Official Comments* are based on an outdated version of the Copyright Statute no longer in force. From their references to the Copyright Statute, it is clear that the *Official Comments* worked with the 1909 version of that statute. However, in 1976, Congress passed a new Copyright Statute which differs significantly from the 1909 statute. Given the profound differences between the two, it is highly questionable whether any of the views expressed in the *Comments* regarding the Copyright Statute remain relevant.

As this analysis of the *Comments* demonstrates, far from resolving the question of preemption, the *Official Comments* create additional confusion. Only a careful review of each of the federal statutes in question can determine whether those statutes meet the criteria set forth in either §104 or §302 so as to preempt Article 9 in its totality (§104) or only partially (§302).

(b) Copyright Act

(i) Preemption of Recording Provisions.   Under §302(3), a federal statute that provides for a "national or international registration . . . or which specifies a place of filing different from that specified in this Article for filing of the security interest" preempts the filing provisions of Article 9. The recording provisions of the Copyright Act almost certainly satisfy that test.

Section 205 of the Copyright Act provides, in relevant part, as follows:

> (a) Condition for Recordation—Any transfer of copyright ownership or other documents pertaining to a copyright may be recorded in the Copyright Office.
> . . . .
> (c) Recordation as Constructive Notice—Recordation of a document in the Copyright Office gives all persons constructive notice of the facts stated in the recorded document, but only if—
>
> > (1) the document . . . specifically identifies the work to which it pertains . . .
> >
> > (2) registration has been made for the work.
> . . . .
> (d) Priority Between Conflicting Transfers—As between two conflicting transfers, the one executed first prevails if it is recorded, in the manner required to give constructive notice under subsection (c), within one month after its execution in the United States or within two months after its execution outside the United States, or at any time before recordation in such manner of the later transfer. Otherwise the later transfer prevails if recorded first in such manner, and if taken in good faith, for valuable consideration or on the basis of a binding promise to pay royalties, and without notice of the earlier transfer.

These provisions set up a comprehensive procedure for recording documents that transfer copyright ownership or that otherwise touch on copyright. Compliance with those procedures, although not mandatory, constitutes constructive notice to third parties of the contents of the recorded document. Chief among the procedural requirements for constructive notice is registration of the underlying copyright in the Copyright Office.

In accordance with these provisions, grants of security interests in a copyright may be recorded in the Copyright Office. Such documents meet the criteria for filing set forth in §205(a), quoted earlier. Not only do these documents pertain to a copyright, but they are "transfers of copyright ownership" as that term is defined in the Copyright Statute.

As set forth in §101 of the Copyright Act, a " 'transfer of copyright ownership' is an assignment, mortgage, exclusive license, or any other conveyance, alienation, or hypothecation of a copyright." Inasmuch as a security interest is a form of hypothecation or pledge, granting a security interest in a copyright is a transfer of copyright ownership under the Copyright Statute. As such, under §205(a), the security agreement (or financing statement) granting the security interests may be recorded in the Copyright Office. Filing the document will be deemed constructive notice to third parties of its content, provided the copyright in which the security interest is granted is registered with the Copyright Office.[45]

Under UCC 9-§§302 (3)(a) and (4), a federal statute that specifies a place of filing different from that specified by Article 9 for filing security interests supersedes Article 9's recording provisions. Security interests can be perfected only by filing in the place designated by the federal statute. As such, under §9–302(3)(a) and (4), a security interest in a copyright can be perfected only by recording it in the Copyright Office. *In re Peregrine Entertainment, Ltd.*, 116 BR 194, 203 (C.D. Cal. 1990) (Kozinski, J.) ("The Copyright Act provides for national registration and 'specifies a place of filing different from that specified in [Article Nine] for filing of the security interest.' UCC §9–302(3)(a). Recording in the U.S. Copyright Office, rather than filing a financing statement under Article Nine is the proper method for perfecting a security interest in a copyright.")[46]; *In Re AEG Acquisition Corp.*, 127 B.R. 34, 40 (Bkrtcy. C.D.Cal. 1991.) ("A security interest in a film is perfected under the United States Copyright Act, and not under the Uniform Commercial Code. The Copyright Act preempts the UCC for security interests in films.") (citations omitted.)

(ii) Preemption of Priority Provisions.   Indeed, in *Peregrine*, the court went even further. It ruled that §205 of the Copyright Act preempted not only the recording provisions of Article 9 but also its provisions regarding priority among competing security interests.[47] According to the court, those provisions were preempted under §9–104(a).

Section 205(d) of the Copyright Act establishes the priority among competing transfers of copyright ownership as follows:

> (d) Priority Between Conflicting Transfers—As between two conflicting transfers, the one executed first prevails if it is recorded, in the manner required to give constructive notice under subsection (c), within one month after its execution in the United States or within two months after its execution outside the United States, or at any time before recordation in such manner of the later transfer. Otherwise the later transfer prevails if recorded first in such manner, and if taken in good faith, for valuable consideration or on the basis of a binding promise to pay royalties, and without notice of the earlier transfer.

Security interests are a form of transfer of copyright ownership (see the preceding subsection [i]). Hence, the rules of priority set forth in §205 (d) are applicable to conflicts between competing security interests or between a security interest and another form of transfer of an interest in copyright.

---

[45] 17 U.S.C. §205(c). In *In re AEG Acquisition Corp.*, 127 B.R. 34, 41 n. 8 (Bkrtcy. C.D. Cal. 1991), the court was of the opinion that registration of the copyright must precede recording the security interest.

[46] In *Peregrine*, the court based its conclusion, that the Copyright Act preempted the recording provisions of Article 9, on federal as well as state law. As a matter of state law, the court found that the Copyright Act satisfied the criteria for preemption set forth in §§9–302(3)(a) and (4). See text, *supra*. In addition, the court found that as a matter of federal law, the recording provisions of the Copyright Act are so comprehensive that Congress must have intended to preclude any state role in the area of recording transfers of copyrights. 116 B.R. at 199–201.

[47] 116 BR at 204.

Section 9–104 excludes from Article 9's purview "a security interest subject to any statute of the United States, to the extent that such statute governs the rights of parties to and third parties affected by transactions in particular types of property." Section 205(d) of the Copyright Act is such a statute, inasmuch as it governs the rights of parties to, and third parties affected by, the transfer of copyright ownership.[48] Hence, to that extent, it preempts any competing rules of priority set forth in Article 9.[49]

Although the reasoning of the court in *Peregrine* appears correct, its expansive view of federal preemption creates pitfalls for a creditor trying to take a security interest in a copyright. The most serious problem is establishing priority of the creditor's security interest. Under Article 9, priority is established by filing first. Under §205(d), that may not be sufficient. This section creates a "look-back" period during which a security interest filed first may lose its priority to a subsequently filed interest, so long as that second security interest is filed within 30 days after it attached. An example will clarify this point.

Assume that Secured Creditor A (SCA) is granted a security interest in a registered copyright on September 15. Before entering into the agreement with the debtor, he has his attorney check the files at the Copyright Office. The lawyer reports back that no prior security interest is recorded there. Satisfied that he is the first to file, SCA makes the loan to the debtor on September 15 and files his security agreement the same day.

What SCA does not know is that on September 1, the debtor granted a security interest in the same copyright to Secured Creditor B (SCB), who delayed filing the security agreement until September 28. Under Article 9, SCA would have priority over SCB because SCA was the first to file even though SCA's security interest was created after that of SCB. Filing first is what determines priority under Article 9 (see pages 458–459).

Under 205(d) of the Copyright Act, in contrast, SCB would have priority over SCA since she filed within a month after the debtor granted her a security interest. That result seems unfair. Not only did SCB file after SCA, but SCA was induced to enter into his agreement with the debtor because there was no prior security interest recorded with the Copyright Office. Nevertheless, under *Peregrine*, SCB's security interest would enjoy priority over that of SCA.

To guard against that result, SCA should include in his security agreement a warranty from the debtor that the debtor has not entered into any prior security agreements. More important, the transaction should be structured so that SCA's obligation to provide financing is triggered only two months after execution of the security agreement and terminates in the event that a prior security agreement is recorded in the Copyright Office during that two-month period.[50] Of course, such a delay impedes the transaction, which security interests are supposed to facilitate. However, so long as the look-back period threatens SCA's security interest in the collateral, it is the prudent course of action.[51]

(iii) Works in Progress.   *Peregrine* raises even more serious problems for those seeking to finance works that are in the process of being completed. Under *Peregrine*, federal law

---

[48] Section 205(d) speaks of "conflicting transfers," not merely transfers of copyright ownership. It is unclear from the opinion in *Peregrine* whether the court regarded the terms as equivalent.

[49] *Peregrine*, 116 BR at 205.

[50] Mesrobian and Schaefer, "Secured Transactions Based on Intellectual Property," 72 J. Pat & Tm. Off. Soc. 827, 837 (1990).

[51] The ABA has proposed eliminating or, at the very least, substantially reducing this look-back period in order to eliminate the risk to the secured creditor that his or her priority will be forfeited. See page 479 of this chapter.

preempts the perfection of a security interest in a copyright. Therefore, the security interest may be perfected only by following the procedures set forth in §205 of the Copyright Act. Those procedures appear to assume that the copyrighted work has been completed. They are, as a practical matter, virtually impossible to follow in the case of works in progress.

The difficulty arises because under the Copyright Act, copyright attaches as soon as the work becomes fixed in a tangible medium of expression, not when the work is ultimately completed. Hence, in shooting a movie, each portion of the movie that is fixed on film is under copyright at the moment it is so fixed even if the final version of the movie is completed months later.

Because each portion of the film is protected by federal copyright, under *Peregrine* a security interest in that copyright is perfected pursuant to §205 exclusively. Under that section, the security interest can be perfected only if the copyright is registered (see page 461). The copyright in the film would therefore have to be registered on an ongoing basis as each segment is completed, in order to minimize the period during which the security interest is unperfected. Ultimately, the most prudent course for a creditor would be to insist on daily registration of each day's production.[52] That, however, is absurdly impractical. Not only would it be expensive, but it would paralyze the Copyright Office with an avalanche of requests to register copyrights and record security interests in them.[53]

---

[52] An example may help illustrate the difficulty:

A young film producer named Sike Mee (SM) needs financing for his first feature film. A movie that he produced as a student, entitled *She Must Get It*, was a surprise hit, and he is now ready for the big leagues.

Film Mogul (FM) speaks with SM and likes his idea for his new movie, *What Is the Right Thing to Do?* which focuses on conflicts on the Lower East Side of New York City between the expanding Chinese community and the dwindling Hassidic community. Unfortunately, other than the critical reviews his first movie received, SM does not have any assets to use as collateral for a loan from FM. Smelling a success, FM agrees instead to take a security interest in the copyright of *What Is the Right Thing to Do?*

FM's lawyer, Vapid Formalism (VP), is faced with a dilemma. When should he file the security agreement at the Copyright Office? Filing immediately, even before SM begins shooting, seems to accomplish little. Prior to filming there is no copyrighted work. Because there is no copyright, there can be no copyright transfer to record. Similarly, there can be no registration of the copyright as required under §205, because there is no copyright to register.

VP can choose to wait until the movie is completed and SM registers the copyright in the movie. However, if he waits until then, FM's security interest will be unperfected throughout the period in which the movie is being made. This would become particularly problematic should SM go bankrupt.

VP could file after the first day's shooting. However, under §205(c)(2), third parties will be deemed to have constructive notice of the security interest granted under the security agreement only if the copyright is registered. Hence, the copyright in the first day's shooting would have to be registered if the security interest in the copyright is to be perfected.

More important, the film shot on the subsequent days are also works of authorship. If the copyrights in them are not registered, the security interest in those copyrights will not be perfected. They could be registered on a weekly basis but, to the extent that registration on any day's shoot is delayed, FM's security interest is, to that extent, unperfected.

Nor would the requirement of daily registration end once the shooting ends. Editing the film is also copyrightable as a derivative work. (See 17 U.S.C. §103.) Hence, each day's worth of editing would also have to be separately registered so as not to create a gap in perfection.

Unfortunately for VP, FM is legendary for his fiery temper. If he informs FM that his investment is at risk unless he registers SM's work on a daily basis, VP might lose his most profitable client.

What should VP do?

[53] Since *Peregrine*, requests to record copyright transfers have increased 50%. 139 Cong. Rec. S1618 (daily ed. Feb. 16, 1993) (statement of Sen. DeConcini.)

Because piecemeal registration is not feasible, several commentators have concluded that it is impossible to perfect a security interest in a copyright in an ongoing work.[54] If that is true, then it could have unfortunate consequences for the film industry. Creditors would almost certainly become more reluctant to provide financing if certain of their security interests remain vulnerable to attack because they must remain unperfected until the film is completed. Creditors would be especially reluctant to fund up-and-coming talent who may have no assets for collateral other than the copyrights in the films they seek to make.

The problem created by works in progress does not exist under the UCC. The UCC allows security agreements to cover "after-acquired property." Under this rule, a perfected security interest in particular collateral automatically extends to after-acquired property of the same sort if the parties have so agreed.[55] Hence, under the UCC, a perfected security interest in the copyright of a film in progress would extend to the copyright in each portion of the film as it is produced if the security agreement so provides. At no time would the interest be unperfected.

The problem is that under *Peregrine*, the Copyright Act preempts the UCC in regard to the perfection of a security interest in a copyright, and the Act makes no allowance for after-acquired copyrights. If it were possible to read *Peregrine* narrowly so that the UCC was not preempted in connection with works in progress, then the problem of perfecting the security interest could be easily resolved. *Peregrine* can indeed be so read.

In *Peregrine*, the court found that the registration system set up by §205(a):

> . . . clearly does establish a national system for recording transfers of copyright interests, and it specifies a place of filing different from that provided in Article Nine. Recording in the Copyright Office gives nationwide constructive notice to third parties of the recorded encumbrance.
>
> . . . .
>
> The court therefore concludes that . . . recording in the U.S. Copyright Office, rather than filing a financing statement under Article Nine, is the proper method for perfecting a security interest in a copyright.[56]

In the case of works in progress, however, Congress did not provide for a national system for recording security interests or nationwide constructive notice to third parties. Although §205(a) appears to create such a system, it was obviously never intended to include works in progress. The criteria set down are completely unworkable in that context. Because the Copyright Act effectively provides for no equivalent form of registration for security interests in copyrightable works in progress, the preemption provisions of §9–302(3)(a) are not implicated, and Article 9 remains the governing law for recording such security interests.

Admittedly, this argument is less than compelling and hard to reconcile with *Peregrine*'s sweeping language regarding federal preemption. Nevertheless, in light of the potential havoc that *Peregrine* could wreak in financing movies, a court might be sympathetic to this attempt to limit *Peregrine*'s holding.[57] However, given the *current* state of the

---

[54] E.g., "Transfers of Copyrights for Security under the New Copyright Act," 88 Yale L. J. 125, 131 (1978).

[55] E.g., §9–204(1).

[56] 116 BR, 202, 203.

[57] In the future, it may not be necessary to make such arguments in order to circumvent *Peregrine*'s broad holding. In its final report, the ABA Task Force on Security Interests in Intellectual Property has recommended that security interests in intellectual property would apply to after acquired property and that security interests could be filed even prior to federal registration. *Report of the ABA Task Force on Security Interests in Intellectual Property*, June 18, 1993, at 14. If these recommendations are enacted into law, then perfecting a security interest in the copyright of a work in progress would no longer raise any special concerns.

law, a creditor who takes a security interest in the copyright in a work in progress runs the risk that his or her security interest cannot be perfected until the work is completed.

(iv) Conclusions. Although the law in this area is far from settled, certain tentative conclusions can be made. The reader should keep in mind that this area of the law is, to a great extent, in flux[58] and that a lawyer should be consulted about the state of the law at the time of the proposed transaction.

In taking a security interest in a copyright:

- If the copyright is registered, then the security agreement should be recorded in the Copyright Office.
- If the copyright is not yet registered but can be, then the security agreement should require the debtor to register the copyright, and the security agreement should then be filed in the Copyright Office.[59] The dicta in *AEG Acquisition Corp.*, that the copyright must be registered before the security agreement is filed, should be kept in mind (see note 45 in this chapter).
- If the copyright cannot be registered because the work is in progress, then the security agreement should require the debtor to register the copyright as soon as the work is completed, at which point the security agreement should be recorded in the Copyright Office.[60] In the interim, the security agreement should be filed under the provisions of the UCC in the appropriate state office. However, it is very uncertain whether this state filing has any legal effect whatsoever.

Finally, there is an important precaution to be noted. Because it cannot be absolutely certain that *Peregrine* and the reasoning behind it will be followed in any particular jurisdiction, so as to influence the jurisdiction's requiring the filing of security interests in the Copyright Office, it is recommended that the security interest be filed in both the Copyright Office as well as in the appropriate state depository.

(c) Patent Act

(i) The UCC and Preemption. The comparable recording provisions of the Patent Act are set forth in 35 U.S.C. §261. They provide, in relevant part, as follows:

> Applications for patent, patents, or any interest therein, shall be assignable in law by an instrument in writing.
>
> . . . .
>
> An assignment, grant or conveyance shall be void as against any subsequent purchaser or mortgagee for a valuable consideration, without notice, unless it is recorded in the Patent and Trademark Office within three months from its date or prior to the date of such subsequent purchase or mortgage.

---

[58] See page 00 of this chapter.

[59] See, e.g., Mesrobian and Schaefer, "Secured Transactions Based on Intellectual Property," 72 J. Pat & Tm. Off. Soc. 827, 844 (1990); Langlois and Wall, "Security Interests in Intellectual Property," p. 47–48 (1988).

[60] See, e.g., Mesrobian and Schaefer, "Secured Transactions Based on Intellectual Property," 72 J. Pat. & Tm. Off. Soc. pp. 827, 852 (1990.)

To what extent, if at all, these provisions preempt Article 9 is quite problematic. As discussed earlier, the *Official Comment* to the UCC provides little guidance in resolving the issue, because it appears to take inconsistent positions on the question. The *Comment* to §104 takes the position that the Patent Act, like the Copyright Act, "would not seem to contain sufficient provisions regulating the rights of the parties and third parties to exclude security interests in [patents] from the provisions of this Article." However, in regard to the recording provisions of the Patent Act, the *Comment* is of the view that those filing provisions "are recognized as the equivalent to filing under this Article. Section 9–302(3) and (4)." Yet, the *Comment* to §9–302(3) does not include the Patent Act among the examples given of federal statutes that establish a filing system that supersedes that of Article 9 (see page 460).

(ii) The Courts and Preemption.   This division within the *Comment* is mirrored in the conflicting positions taken by the courts on the issue of patent preemption. The court in *Peregrine* seems to have adopted the position of the *Official Comment* to §104, that the recording provisions of the Patent Act do preempt the filing provisions of Article 9.[61] In contrast, the courts in *In re Transportation Design & Technology Inc.*, 48 B.R. 635 (Bankr. S.D.Cal. 1985) and in *City Bank & Trust Co. v. Otto Fabrics, Inc.*, 83 B.R. 780 (D. Kan. 1988) adhere to what seems to be the position of the *Official Comment* to §302, that the recording provisions of the Patent Act do not supersede those of Article 9, which remain applicable.

In both *Transportation Design* and *Otto Fabric*, the courts ruled that a security interest in a patent was properly perfected when the filing statement was recorded in the appropriate state office but not in the Patent and Trademark Office. The courts viewed the recording provisions of the Patent Act as intended to protect only a bona fide purchaser or mortgagee of a patent. If either records his or her purchase or mortgage in the Patent and Trademark office, it will have priority over an earlier "assignment, grant or conveyance" of the patent that was not recorded within three months of the transfer. Because a security interest is a "grant or conveyance," it must be recorded in the Patent and Trademark Office if a subsequent purchaser or mortgagee is to take title to the patent subject to it.

However, a creditor granted a security interest in a patent is not a "purchaser" of the patent. Nor is that creditor a "mortgagee" of the patent. As used in the Patent Act, the term *mortgage* refers to a chattel mortgage, under which title to the patent is assigned to the creditor until the underlying debt is repaid, at which point title is reassigned back to the debtor. A security interest, in contrast, leaves title unaffected. Indeed, it was created precisely to obviate the need to shift title back and forth between the creditor and the debtor. Inasmuch as a creditor holding a security interest in a patent is neither a "purchaser" nor a "mortgagee," the creditor need not record his or her security interest in the Patent and Trademark Office in order to preserve its priority over a subsequent security interest or lien creditor. The Patent Act imposes no federal recording requirements in such a situation. Because there is no federal law, there is nothing to preempt the recording provisions of Article 9, which remain in effect.[62]

---

[61] *Peregrine*, 116 BR, 203–204.

[62] *Otto Fabrics*, 83 BR at 782; *Transportation Design*, 48 BR at 638. The court in *Otto Fabrics* seems to hold that although recording in the Patent and Trademark Office is not *required* in order to perfect the security interest, a security interest that is recorded there will have priority over subsequent lien creditors. 83 BR, 782.

The court in *Peregrine* disagreed with this reasoning. It claimed that the opinions in *Transportation Design* and *Otto Fabric* confused two distinct issues: perfection through recording and priority in the case of competing security interests. The issue under §9–302(3)(a) is simply whether the

> ... federal statute provides for a national system of recordation or specifies a place of filing different from that in Article Nine. [If it does, then] the methods of perfection specified in Article Nine are supplanted by that national system; compliance with a national system of recordation is equivalent to the filing of a financing statement under Article Nine. UCC §9–302(4). Whether the federal statute also provides a priority scheme different from that in Article Nine is a separate issue. . . . Compliance with a national registration system is necessary for perfection regardless of whether federal law governs priorities.[63]

The *Peregrine* court did not decide whether the Patent Act set up a system of national registration that supersedes the methods of perfection of Article 9. However, there seems little doubt that it would so find. In addition to the Patent Act, the court also discussed the recording provisions of the Trademark (Lanham) Act. Two courts had reached the same conclusion about perfecting a security interest in trademarks that *Otto Fabric* and *Transportation Design* reached about patents, that is, that recording the security interest in the Patent and Trademark Office was not required in order to perfect it. *Peregrine* distinguished those cases on the ground that "the Lanham Act's recordation provision refers only to 'assignments' and contains no provision for the registration, recordation or filing of instruments establishing security instruments in trademarks."[64] Because the court did not distinguish the comparable patent cases on the same ground, it must believe that the Patent Act, in contrast to the Lanham Act, does provide for the national registration of security interests. If so, then that system preempts the comparable recording provisions of Article 9.

(iii) Conclusions.   As the preceding analysis of the case law suggests, the courts appear to be divided over whether recording in the Patent and Trademark Office is the exclusive means of perfecting a security interest in a patent. Until this disagreement is resolved, the prudent course would be to record a security interest in both the Patent and Trademark Office, pursuant to the Patent Act, and the appropriate state office, pursuant to Article 9. In that way, the views of *Peregrine*, *Transportation Design*, and *Otto Fabric* can all be accommodated.

All three courts agree that a federal filing is required. The point on which they disagree is why. *Peregrine* appears to take the position that the system of national registration established by the Patent Act preempts the methods of perfection of Article 9, so that recording the security interest at the Patent and Trademark Office is the exclusive means of perfecting the security interest. Filing in the state office accomplishes nothing.

According to *Transportation Design*, in contrast, a security interest must be recorded in the Patent and Trademark Office, but only for a limited purpose. If the patent is not recorded, then a subsequent purchaser or mortgagee takes title to the patent unencumbered by the security interest. To interpose the security interest against such a transfer, it must be recorded in the Patent and Trademark Office.

The creditor does not merely want to impede the debtor in transferring title to the patent. The creditor also wants to assert priority over a competing or subsequent security

---

[63] 116 BR, 204.

[64] Id., n. 14.

interest. According to *Transportation Design*, the creditor cannot do that by a federal filing. The Patent Act does not require a filing in those circumstances and therefore does not preempt the recording provisions of Article 9. To assert priority over a competing or subsequent security interest, the creditor must record his or her interest pursuant to Article 9 as well.[65]

Of course, the creditor can circumvent the complexities of Article 9 altogether by designing the transaction as a collateral assignment or chattel mortgage, in which he or she is presently assigned title to the patent until such time as the debt is repaid.[66] Because the transaction is a *present* assignment of the title, it falls squarely within the parameters of the recording provisions of the Patent Act and, therefore, outside the purview of Article 9.

This approach, however, may create more problems than it is intended to solve. Because the creditor becomes the owner of the patent, the legal obligations concomitant with ownership devolve upon him or her. The creditor must police the patent by initiating infringement actions against third parties encroaching on the patent and by defending the patent in infringement actions brought by the owners of closely related patents.[67] Performing these functions may prove difficult and costly, because it is unlikely that the creditor will have a sophisticated knowledge of the technology at issue in the patent dispute.

Worse, as owner of the patent, the creditor will subject to product liability for any injuries caused by the invention incorporating the patent.[68] The potential exposure could be significant, depending on the nature of the injuries that could be caused by the patented invention and the number of people who might be injured by it.

In summary:

- A security interest in a patent should be recorded both in the Patent and Trademark Office, pursuant to the Patent Act, and in the appropriate state office, under Article 9.[69]
- Alternatively, the transaction might be structured as a chattel mortgage or a collateral assignment in which legal title is vested in the creditor. However, by so fashioning the transaction, the creditor assumes extensive legal obligations and potential liabilities that he or she may have difficulty discharging.

(d) Trademark

(i) The Courts. In contrast to the recording provisions of the Copyright and Patent Acts, those of the Trademark (Lanham) Act are the most limited in scope. Only assignments of a trademark must be recorded.

---

[65] 48 BR, 639–640. As mentioned earlier, the court in *Otto Fabrics* appears to suggest that recording a security interest in the Patent and Trademark Office will protect it against a subsequent lien creditor and arguably, by extension, a subsequent secured creditor (see note 62 in this chapter).

[66] Weinberg and Woodward, "Easing Transfer and Security Interest Transactions in Intellectual Property: An Agenda for Reform" 79 Ky. L.J. pp. 61, 63 n. 3, 72 1990. One commentator suggests that "a collateral assignment is the preferred form of security agreement for use in patents." Bramson, "Intellectual Property as Collateral—Patents, Trade Secrets, Trademarks and Copyrights," 36 Bus. Law. 1567, 1587 (1981); *Otto Fabrics*, 83 BR at 783.

[67] *Otto Fabric*, 83 BR, 783.

[68] Id.

[69] According to the ABA Task Force on Security Interests in Intellectual Property, the Patent and Trademark Office will not accept a UCC financing statement for filing. The security agreement is filed instead (*Report of the ABA Task Force on Security Interests in Intellectual Property*, p. 5).

As set forth in 15 U.S.C. §1060, the relevant provisions of the Lanham Act are as follows:

> A registered mark . . . shall be assignable along with the goodwill of the business in which the mark is used. . . . An assignment shall be void as against any subsequent purchaser for a valuable consideration without notice, unless it is recorded in the Patent and Trademark Office within three months after the date thereof or prior to such purchase.

Because recording under the Lanham Act is limited to assignments of the trademark, the Act does not preempt Article 9 at all. As the court explained in *In the Matter of Roman Cleanser Co.*, 43 B.R. 940, 944 (Bkrtcy. E.D.Mich. 1984), "Since a security interest in a trademark is not equivalent to an assignment, the filing of a security interest is not covered by the Lanham Act. Accordingly, the manner of perfecting a security interest in trademarks is governed by Article 9 and not by the Lanham Act." *Accord In re Tr-3 Industries*, 41 B.R. 128, 131 (Bkrcty. C.D. Cal. 1984) ("1. Neither Section 10 of the Lanham Act (15 U.S.C. §1060) nor the Lanham Act as a whole (15 U.S.C. §§1051 through 1127) contains any statutory provision for the registration, recording or filing of any instrument or document asserting a security interest in any trademark, tradename or application for the registration of a trademark. The omission of such provision was intentional when the Lanham Act was enacted. 2. It was not the purpose or intent of Congress in enacting the Lanham Act to provide a method for the perfection of security interests in trademarks, tradenames or applications for the registration of the same, or as a method for giving notice of the existence of a claim of a security interest therein.")

Indeed, even the court in *Peregrine*, which took a broad view of federal preemption in connection with copyright and, to a lesser extent, with patent, seems to have acknowledged that the Lanham Act does not preempt the recording provisions of Article 9.[70]

The clear holding of the preceding line of cases is that a security interest in a trademark must be recorded, pursuant to Article 9, in the appropriate state office. Must it nevertheless also be recorded in the Patent and Trademark Office to defeat a subsequent assignment of the mark by a debtor?

Recall that in connection with a security interest in a patent, the court in *Transportation Design* stated that although a security interest recorded in the appropriate state office was perfected, it must nevertheless also be recorded in the Patent and Trademark Office in order to give notice of the security interest to any subsequent purchaser or mortgagee of the patent. Does *Transportation Design*'s logic hold true in the context of trademark filing so that dual filings are also required? Or is the state filing itself constructive notice to the subsequent assignee of the trademark so that he or she cannot claim the status of a bona fide purchaser without notice of the prior security interest?[71]

Although the answer is far from certain, it appears from the previously cited cases that a federal filing should not be necessary. It is very difficult to reconcile such a requirement with the courts' clear holding that the Lanham Act's recording provisions are expressly limited to assignments and do not include security interests.

For example, in *Tr-3 Industries*, the court ruled that "it was not the purpose or intent of Congress in enacting the Lanham Act to provide . . . a method for giving notice of the existence of a claim of a security interest [in a trademark]."[72]

---

[70] *Peregrine*, 116 BR, 204, n. 14.

[71] See Engel and Radcliffe, "Intellectual Property Financing for High-Technology Companies," 19 U.C.C. L.J.3, p. 21. (1986)

[72] 41 B.R., 131.

In a similar vein the court in *Roman Cleanser* stated that a regulation of the Patent and Trademark Office that permitted the Commissioner of Patents to record "other instruments which may relate to such marks" would be invalid if that regulation "intended to suggest that a security interest is embraced within the term 'assignment' and therefore subject to filing under the Lanham Act."[73] There obviously cannot be a filing requirement when the Patent and Trademark Office cannot accept the document for filing.

The inescapable conclusion drawn from these cases is that for trademarks, recording a security interest in accordance with Article 9 gives constructive notice to both subsequent creditors and subsequent assignees of the interest. Nevertheless, until the matter is resolved definitively, a federal filing should be made as a matter of prudence.[74]

(ii) Conclusion   To perfect a security interest in a trademark, the security interest must be recorded in the applicable state office, pursuant to the provisions of Article 9. Although that should be sufficient, a federal filing should also be made, to exercise appropriate caution.

14.5 ARTICLE 9 AND INTELLECTUAL PROPERTY: ADDITIONAL CONSIDERATIONS

The focus of section 14.4 in this chapter has been the complicated question of the extent to which the provisions of Article 9 are preempted by the federal statutes governing intellectual property. Preemption, however, is not the only difficulty created in taking a security interest in intellectual property. A number of other problems—some common to all forms of intellectual property and some unique to each form—must also be resolved if the creditor's goal of limiting risk is to be accomplished.

(a) Issues Common to All Intellectual Property.   One of the obvious prerequisites under Article 9 for granting a security interest is that the debtor has rights in the collateral. Clearly, a debtor cannot grant rights in property in which the debtor holds no interest.

In the context of intellectual property, this requirement has a dual meaning. First, as with all collateral, the creditor must be certain that the debtor has not assigned his or her interest in the collateral to another party prior to granting the security interest.[75]

The recording provisions of the Copyright, Patent, and Lanham Acts make this "due diligence" both easier and more difficult than with other collateral. Each of the Acts makes provisions for recording assignments. Thus, the creditor can easily check public records for the chain of title of the proposed collateral. Unfortunately, the creditor cannot be certain that those records, in fact, accurately reflect the locus of title.

Each of the recording provisions contains a look-back period of varying length. Any assignment recorded during that period will be treated as if it had been filed at the beginning of the period and, therefore, has priority over transactions that took place afterward, even if it was prior to the recording of the assignment.

For example, the look-back period for a domestic transfer of a copyright interest is one month. If on April 1, 1993, Debtor assigns his copyright to Assignee but Assignee does

---

[73] 43 B.R., 944.

[74] Id.; Mesrobian and Schaefer, "Secured Transactions Based on Intellectual Property," 72 J. Pat. & Tm. Off. Soc. pp. 827, 852 (1990).

[75] The creditor should also examine the extent to which the debtor has licensed others to use the intellectual property even if the debtor retains title to it. Extensive licensing can diminish the value of the intellectual property as security. Byrne, "Licenses as Assets in Secured Transactions: The United States Experience," p. 2 (1992).

not record the assignment until April 28, 1993, Assignee will take title clear of any security interest that Debtor might have granted between April 1 and April 28, even though any creditor who checked the records in the Copyright Office would have found nothing that indicated that Debtor no longer owned the copyright (see page 463).

To protect against the look-back period, a creditor should include within the security agreement a representation from the debtor that that debtor has not assigned the intellectual property to another party.[76] In addition, the creditor's obligation to provide financing should become binding only after the look-back period ends. If during that period a prior assignment is recorded, the creditor's obligations under the security agreement would end.[77]

Of course, if the collateral itself is valueless, it matters little that the debtor is its owner. Hence, the creditor must assure him- or herself that the claim to intellectual property is in fact valid.[78] That the patent, trademark, or copyright is registered does not establish that fact. Registration is only prima facie evidence of validity, which can be rebutted by contrary evidence.[79]

A review of what might invalidate a claim to each form of intellectual property is beyond the scope of this chapter. The question of validity requires a thorough knowledge of the legal principles applicable to each type of intellectual property. Those principles are highly technical and at times abstruse. It is therefore *essential* that counsel be retained to review the intellectual property proposed as collateral to determine whether it is legally defective in any respect.

In the security agreement itself, the creditor should insist on a warranty from the debtor that his or her claim to intellectual property is valid.[80] In addition, the debtor should be required to do whatever is necessary to maintain the validity of the claim.[81] This is particularly crucial in the area of trademark. Not only must federal registration of the mark be renewed periodically, but failure to use the mark in commerce or to supervise its use by licensees of the mark can result in the loss of the mark's registration on the ground of abandonment.[82]

In addition to these general problems common to all forms of intellectual property, there are problems created specific to each type of intellectual property in taking a security interest. Although a sampling of those issues are examined in the following paragraphs, it is neither intended to be nor can it be exhaustive. It cannot be sufficiently

---

[76] For the reasons set forth in the preceding footnote, the agreement should contain a similar representation regarding licenses granted to third persons.

[77] Mesrobian and Schaefer, "Secured Transactions Based on Intellectual Property," 72 J. Pat. & Tm. Off. Soc. pp. 827, 837 (1990). Because the look-back period applies to prior, unrecorded security interests as well, the security agreement should incorporate comparable provisions protecting the creditor against prior, unrecorded security agreements.

[78] E.g., Engel and Radcliffe, "Intellectual Property Financing for High-Technology Companies," 19 U.C.C. L.J. pp. 3, 21 (1986); Mesrobian and Schaefer, "Secured Transactions Based on Intellectual Property," pp. 827, 839 (1990); Byrne, "Licenses as Assets in Secured Transactions" The United States Experience p. 14 (1992).

[79] 17 U.S.C. §410(c) (copyright); 35 U.S.C. §282 (patent). In the case of a trademark, after five years' registration, the trademark becomes incontestable and may be invalidated only under limited circumstances. 15 U.S.C. §1064.

[80] E.g., Engel and Radcliffe, "Intellectual Property Financing for High-Technology Companies," pp. 3, 21.; Langlois and Wall, "Security Interests in Intellectual Property," 19 U.C.C. L.J. pp. 48–49 (1986).

[81] Langlois and Wall, "Security Interests in Intellectual Property," pp. 48–49 (1988).

[82] 15 U.S.C.§§ 1059, 1115(b), 1127.

emphasized that counsel should always be consulted in order to avoid the pitfalls into which the unwary can easily fall.

(b) Problems Specific to Copyright.   Copyright law distinguishes between the work of authorship and the medium that embodies the work.[83]

Copyright protection attaches to the author's work. His or her work, however, is distinct from the medium in which it is embodied. Hence, it is possible for the author to retain ownership of the copyright in the work while transferring ownership of the material object in which the work is embodied. Thus, if J.D. Salinger donates his letters to Harvard University, Salinger retains the copyright in his letters even though Harvard owns the actual letters themselves.[84]

This distinction between owning the copyright and owning the medium in which the copyrighted work is embodied could create problems for a secured creditor whose security interest is limited to the copyright. Taking a security interest in only the copyright does not give the secured party any rights in the medium in which the copyrighted work is fixed. A security interest in the movie *Dancing with Wolves*, for example, does not give the creditor any rights to the frames of film on which the movie is recorded. Yet, without the actual film, the creditor cannot exploit his or her rights under the copyright to distribute the work to movie theaters or to produce videocassettes for home viewing.[85] It is therefore imperative that the creditor take security interests in both the copyright and the medium in which the copyrighted work is fixed.[86]

The need to take dual security interests is a problem common to all copyrighted works.[87] Works that were registered under the predecessor Copyright Act raise additional problems exclusive to such works.

Under the 1909 Copyright Act, the term of a copyright was 28 years with a right to renew the copyright for an additional 28 years. The 1976 Copyright Act preserved the

---

[83] E.g., 17 U.S.C. §202 ("Ownership of a copyright, or of any of the exclusive rights under a copyright is distinct from ownership of any material object in which the work is embodied").

[84] Id.

[85] Taking a security interest in the frames of films without also taking a security interest in the copyright leads to equally disastrous results. If the creditor does not also have a right to the copyright, then he or she cannot distribute copies of the movie to theaters for public viewing or make additional copies for videocassettes. Those are rights reserved to the copyright holder. 17 U.S.C. §106(1), (3) and (4). To fully exploit the financial potential of the copyrighted work, the secured creditor must acquire title to both the copyright and the object in which the work is embodied. See, generally, Byrne, "Licenses as Assets in Secured Transactions: The United States Experience," p. 14 (1992); Engel and Radcliffe, "Intellectual Property Financing for High-Technology Companies," 19 U.C.C. L.J. pp. 3, 21 (1986); Bramson, "Intellectual Property as Collateral—Patents Trade Secrets Trademarks and Copyrights " pp. 1567, 1595–96 (1981).

[86] The court in *AEG* suggested that the security interest in the copyright extends to the medium in which the work is embodied as well because it is "integral to the copyright" itself. 127 B.R. at 40, n. 4. That dicta seems flatly inconsistent with the Copyright Act, which distinguishes between ownership of the copyright and ownership of the "material object in which the work is embodied." 17 U.S.C. §202. See id., §109. A separate security interest in the medium of fixation is therefore required. Because the object of fixation is ordinary property, distinct from the copyright, the security interest taken in it is governed exclusively by Article 9 (Bramson, "Intellectual Property as Collateral—Patents Trade Secrets Trademarks and Copyrights," 36 Bus. Law., pp. 1567, 1595–96.

[87] Similarly, with patents, it may be necessary to take a security interest in both the patent and the "tangible embodiment of the patented invention" (Engel and Radcliffe, "Intellectual Property Financing for High-Technology Companies," 19 U.C.C. L.J. pp. 3, 21 (1986).

renewal term for copyrights that had been registered under the old Act, but it extended the duration of the renewal term from 28 to 56 years.

The purpose of the renewal term is to enable the author to renegotiate licenses or grants that he or she made during the first term of the copyright. These grants automatically end when the author renews the copyright at the end of the first term. Of course, the author can enter into licenses or grants for both the initial term and the renewal term of the copyright, but the author's intent to do so must be unambiguous.

More important, for the grant to continue into the renewal term, the author must be alive at the end of the first term. If he or she is not, then the grants that the author made for the renewal term automatically terminate at the end of the first term, even if the author expressly agreed that the term of the grant extended into the renewal term. The author's rights to the renewal term terminate at the time of his or her death.[88]

The reason that the author's clear intentions are ignored lies in the protection the Copyright Act accords an author's statutory heirs. The right to renew the term of the copyright in the first instance belongs to the author. If, however, he or she should die within the first term, the right devolves by statute upon the author's spouse and children (17 U.S.C. §304). The author cannot strip these statutory heirs of the renewal right by bequeathing it to others.[89] He or she has no posthumous rights to the renewal term. The right to the renewal term ends at the time of the author's death.

Similarly, licenses or other grants that the author makes in the first term cannot extend beyond the first term if the author should die before the term ends. Because he or she has no posthumous rights to the renewal term, the author cannot make grants of rights that he or she does not possess. Hence, even if the author expressly agreed that the license should extend into the renewal term, the license is of no legal effect if the author dies during the first term.[90]

Although no court has ever ruled on the matter, it would follow that if the author should die within the first term, security interests granted by him or her would terminate at the end of the first term, even if the author granted a security interest for the entire life of the copyright. The author, having no posthumous rights to the renewal term, cannot grant a security interest in something in which he or she has no possessory interest.

To circumvent *this* problem, a creditor might try to secure the agreement of both the author and the author's statutory heirs. In that way, the security interest will have been consented to by whoever will end up as the owner of the renewal term. Although this proposal might work legally, it is probably not feasible as a practical matter. Of course, it must be remembered that this entire problem is limited to works in their first term under the 1909 Copyright Act.

(c) Problems Unique to Trademarks. The most serious obstacle to taking a security interest in a trademark is the prohibition against assignments in gross. Trademarks function to identify and distinguish the owner's goods from those of others and to indicate the source of those goods. As such, they can exist only as part of the ongoing business with which they have become associated. If a mark were separated from that business, it could no longer function to identify the source of the goods to which it was attached. It would therefore cease to be a trademark.[91]

---

[88] *Stewart v. Abend*, 495 U.S. 207, 217–18 (1990).

[89] *Saroyan v. William Saroyan Foundation*, 675 F.Supp. 843 (S.D.N.Y. 1987).

[90] *Stewart v. Abend*, 495 U.S. 207, 217–18 (1990).

[91] Simensky, "Enforcing Creditors' Rights Against Trademarks," 79 Trademark Rep. 569, 571–572, 579–580 (1989); see, generally, 1 J. T. McCarthy, *Trademarks and Unfair Competition*, §18.01 [2] at 18–5 (1992).

Because a trademark cannot exist apart from the business to which it is associated, it cannot be assigned in gross, that is, by itself. To avoid this prohibition, the assignee need not purchase all of the assets of the underlying business. The assignee need acquire only those assets necessary to ensure that the mark will continue to be connected with substantially the same products with which it has become associated.[92] "The situation sought to be avoided is customer deception resulting from abrupt and radical changes in the nature and quality of the goods or services, after assignment of the mark."[93]

Merely taking a security interest in a trademark does not itself violate the rule against assignments in gross, inasmuch as a security interest is not an assignment. If, however, the debtor defaults and the creditor tries to take title to the mark pursuant to the security agreement, the prohibition against assignments in gross will be triggered.[94]

To circumvent that prohibition, the creditor must also take a security interest in those assets of the debtor that will enable the creditor to reproduce the same goods that the public has been accustomed to purchasing under the mark.[95] By taking this additional security interest, the creditor ensures that the consumer goodwill that has been built up in the mark will be assigned along with the mark itself in the event of default. Under those circumstances, the assignment cannot be voided as an assignment in gross.[96]

This precautionary measure, however, will no longer be necessary once NAFTA goes into effect. Among its numerous provisions affecting intellectual property, this treaty eliminates the prohibition against assignments in gross.[97] Although that change will fundamentally alter American trademark law, for the secured creditor it will obviate the need to take additional security interests in other assets of the debtor merely to avoid the prohibition against assignments in gross.

In deciding whether to use a particular mark as collateral, the creditor should bear in mind two additional considerations. First, the Lanham Act was amended several years ago to modify slightly the requirement that to be valid, a trademark must be used in connection with an ongoing business. The Act permits registration of marks that the registrant intends to use in commerce, although he has not yet done so.[98] Because of various extensions that may be granted, the registrant has three years in which to begin using the mark. However, the registrant may not assign it unless he or she is in fact using it.[99] Pursuant to that rule, a secured creditor could be barred from taking title to such a trademark in the event that the debtor defaults. This may be of little practical concern inasmuch as it seems unlikely that a creditor would accept as collateral a mark that had never been used in the marketplace.

Similarly, the secured creditor must verify that others do not have the right to use the mark in other areas of the country or for different products. Under the Lanham Act, someone using the mark prior to the registrant's using it and without knowledge of the

---

[92] Simensky, "Enforcing Creditors' Rights Against Trademarks," pp. 569, 571–573, 579–580 (1989).

[93] 1 J. T. McCarthy, *Trademarks and Unfair Competition* §18.02, 18–16 (1992).

[94] E.g., *Haymaker Sports, Inc. v. Turian*, 581 F.2d. 257 (C.C.P.A. 1978).

[95] Because these assets are ordinary property, the security interest taken in them is governed exclusively by Article 9.

[96] See, generally, Simensky, "Enforcing Creditors' Rights Against Trademarks," 79 Trademark Rep. p. 569; McCarthy, *Trademarks and Unfair Competition*, §§18.01–18.07 (1992).

[97] North American Free Trade Agreement, Part 6, Articles 1708, ¶11, 44 *BNA's Patent, Trademark & Copyright Journal* 513 (September 17, 1992).

[98] 15 U.S.C. §1051(b), (d)(2)

[99] 15 U.S.C. §1060.

registrant's use may be granted the right to use the trademark concurrently with the registrant.[100] Depending on the nature of the concurrent use, the value of the mark could be affected. Counsel should be engaged to conduct a thorough search of the trademark register to determine whether others have the right to make use of the mark or of marks similar to it.

(d) Problems Unique to Patents and Trade Secrets. Although they are governed by different bodies of law, patents and trade secrets should be considered together because of the way they can interact with each other. A particular procedure that a company uses may, over time, become eligible for patent protection. Once it does, the procedure can no longer be considered a trade secret. The hallmark of a trade secret is that the information is not known to others in the industry but is kept confidential by the trade secret holder. Patents, in contrast, provide protection for procedures in exchange for making those procedures or inventions public. Hence, anything that enjoys patent protection cannot simultaneously enjoy legal protection as a trade secret.[101]

The maturation process from trade secret to patent can create problems for the secured creditor if the security agreement is drafted too narrowly. If the creditor limits the security interest taken to trade secrets and makes no mention of patents, then the security interest will terminate at the time the trade secret becomes patented. Because it would no longer be a trade secret, the security interest would have nothing to which it could attach.[102]

To guard against that development, the security agreement should include a clause obligating the debtor to notify the creditor of all applications for patents and the results of those applications, which the debtor must pursue. If a patent is granted, then an additional filing of the security interest will have to made at the Patent and Trademark Office.[103]

More important, the agreement should also include a clause granting the creditor a security interest in all future patents.[104]

Trade secrets, even when they do not mature into patents, can still create problems for the secured creditor. Only information that a company treats as confidential can be

---

[100] 15 U.S.C. §1115(b)(5).

[101] See Weinberg and Woodward, "Easing Transfer and Security Interest Transactions in Intellectual Property," p. 121 ("The trade secret is necessarily extinguished when the patent issues").

[102] Byrne, "Licenses as Assets in Secured Transactions," p. 14. The U.C.C. does state that a security interest in an asset can continue in the "proceeds" of the asset. However, for technical reasons, the patent probably cannot be considered the "proceeds" of the trade secret. See Weinberg and Woodward, "Easing Transfer and Security Interest Transactions in Intellectual Property," pp. 179–118.

[103] Byrne, "Licenses as Assets in Secured Transactions," p. 10.

[104] Currently, even if the security agreement contains such an "after acquired" patents clause, the secured creditor's priority cannot date earlier than the date the patent is registered. Until the patent is registered, the creditor cannot file with the Patent and Trademark Office so as to give constructive notice to third parties. The ABA Task Force on Security Interests in Intellectual Property has recommended changing the law so that a federal filing can be made prior to federal registration of an intellectual property and prior to the imposition of the security interest. See *Report of the ABA Task Force on Security Interests in Intellectual Property*, p. 14. If those changes are adopted, a security agreement containing a "future patents" clause would enjoy the same priority as any security agreement with an after acquired property clause. Priority would be determined from the date of the initial filing of the agreement rather than the date the debtor actually gained rights in the after acquired property. See Weinberg and Woodward, "Easing Transfer and Security Interest Transactions in Intellectual Property: An Agenda for Reform," 79 Ky. L.J. 61 pp. 109–110 (1990).

protected as a trade secret. If the information becomes generally known in the industry, it can no longer be regarded as a trade secret.

A secured creditor who takes a security interest in a trade secret would lose his or her collateral if the trade secret were disclosed. It is therefore imperative that the secured creditor, or the creditor's counsel, satisfy him- or herself that the debtor has taken the necessary precautions to ensure that the trade secret will remain confidential.[105]

14.6 FORECLOSURE

The reader, particularly if he or she is not a lawyer, may have formed the impression that much of this analysis appears to be intellectual hairsplitting, reflecting more the way of thinking of the medieval Scholastic than of the harried business person of the 1990s. Such an impression is totally erroneous. The concern of this chapter is fundamentally pragmatic—how can a creditor take a valid security interest in intellectual property—even if the problems that stand in the way of that goal may appear esoteric.

The reason it is so critical that the security interest be valid becomes obvious in the event the debtor defaults in repaying the underlying debt to the creditor. If the debtor has not filed for bankruptcy, then the creditor can proceed under §§9–503 and 504 of the UCC to foreclose on the collateral without judicial intervention.[106] By allowing the creditor to proceed via "self-help," the UCC greatly expedites the process of taking possession of collateral in the event of default.

Although a comprehensive treatment of foreclosure under the UCC is not feasible within the scope of this chapter, the basic procedure can be outlined. Under §§9–503 and 504, the creditor may take possession of the collateral without judicial process if this can be done without "breach of the peace."[107] If he or she can,[108] the creditor may either resell the collateral in a commercially reasonable manner or keep it him- or herself.[109] If the latter course is chosen, the creditor cannot recover from the debtor the difference between the value of the collateral and the amount the debtor owes.[110] However, if he or she sells the collateral, the debtor remains liable to the creditor for the difference between the amount owed and the amount the collateral fetches at sale.[111] If the creditor intends to keep the collateral, he or she must so notify the debtor. If the debtor objects, the creditor must arrange for the sale of the collateral.[112]

The collateral may be sold in either a public or private sale. If the sale is private, then the creditor will be barred from bidding for the collateral unless it "is of a type customarily sold in a recognized market or is of a type which is the subject of widely distributed standard price quotations."[113] Unlike shares on the New York Stock Exchange, most

---

[105] Byrne, "Licenses as Assets in Secured Transactions," p. 10 (1992).

[106] The ABA Task Force Report recommends that Article 9 be amended to clarify that its foreclosure provisions apply to intellectual property.

[107] §9–503. Numerous cases have construed what constitutes "breach of the peace." Although the courts have mentioned a number of elements in deciding whether the creditor can repossess without breaching the peace, a critical factor is the extent of the opposition by the debtor to the creditor's attempt at self-help. See, e.g., *Deavers v. Strandridge*, 242 S.E.2d 331 (Ga. App. 1978).

[108] If he or she cannot, then the creditor must seek judicial intervention to take possession of the collateral.

[109] §§9–504, 505.

[110] §9–503(2).

[111] §9–504(1)(c).

[112] §9–505(2).

[113] §9–504(3).

intellectual property is not "of a type which is the subject of widely distributed standard price quotations." Therefore, the creditor, if wanting to bid on the collateral, will opt for a public sale. Whatever type of sale the creditor chooses, it must be conducted in a commercially reasonable manner if it is to survive judicial scrutiny.[114]

In the case of intellectual property, there is no tangible object of which the creditor may take physical possession. Repossession in this context can only mean transferring title in the collateral to the creditor. The security agreement must therefore provide for the automatic transfer of title in the collateral to the creditor in the event of default.[115] In addition, the agreement must grant the creditor an irrevocable power of attorney to effect assignment of the collateral by executing the appropriate documents.[116]

After executing those documents, the creditor should file the assignments to him or her of the intellectual property in the relevant federal office, an assignment of copyright in the Copyright Office, and an assignment of trademark or patent in the Patent and Trademark Office.

14.7 THE FUTURE OF INTELLECTUAL PROPERTY LAW

Because the current state of the law is so unsettled, the financial potential of intellectual property cannot be fully tapped. In recognition of this fact, a number of proposals have been made to reform the law in this area in order to facilitate secured transactions using intellectual property as collateral.

The most comprehensive analysis of the problem of security interests in intellectual property has been done by the American Bar Association (ABA) Task Force, which was appointed to study the issue and to propose necessary reforms. The final report of the Task Force calls for a mixed system, drawing upon both federal and state law.

This mixed system would operate much like the current procedure for taking a security interest in a patent. Security interests in copyrights, trademarks, and patents would be recorded in the appropriate state office under Article 9, whereas assignments of title to such properties would be recorded in the Copyright Office and in the Patent and Trademark Office, respectively.[117]

Under this system, a creditor would have to make two searches before entering into a secured transaction. It would be necessary to search the state UCC filing office for any prior security interests recorded in the collateral, and to search the appropriate federal register to confirm that the debtor retains title to the intellectual property. The creditor would also have to make two filings of his or her security interest, one in the state office to establish priority over any subsequent security interests and one in the federal office to give notice of the creditor's security interest in any subsequent sale of the collateral.[118]

Currently, a secured creditor cannot be certain even after checking the appropriate federal register that the debtor has not assigned the proposed collateral to another,

---

[114] §9–504(1).

[115] This provision in the security agreement will no longer be necessary if the recommendations of the ABA Task Force Report are adopted. The Task Force suggested that federal law be changed so that the secured party can automatically file to transfer record title to the intellectual property to him once the second creditor initiates default proceedings. *Report of the ABA Task Force on Security Interests in Intellectual Property*, p.11.

[116] See Simensky, "Enforcing Creditors' Rights Against Trademarks," p. 583; Byrne, "Licenses as Assets in Secured Transactions: States Experience," p. 14.

[117] "*Report of the ABA Task Force on Security Interests in Intellectual Property*," p.13.

[118] Ibid.

because of the look-back period provided by the Copyright, Patent, and Trademark Acts. Under each of these statutes, an assignee has one to three months to record his or her assignment. If the assignment is recorded within that period, the assignee takes priority over any interest granted after his or her assignment even if that second interest was recorded first. The ABA committee proposes eliminating or substantially shortening this look-back period to minimize the risk to a secured creditor that he or she has taken a secured interest in property owned by someone other than the debtor.[119]

Finally, searches of the federal registers would be made easier by converting the recording system to match that used by state UCC filing offices. Assignments would be recorded by name of the assignor/debtor—not by the registration number assigned or by the title of the work, as is the system currently in use.[120]

In contrast to the systematic reform proposed by the ABA Task Force, Senator Dennis DeConcini has proposed a more limited reform. He has introduced a bill that would merely overrule the *Peregrine* decision by expressly excluding the perfection of security interests in copyrights from federal preemption under the Copyright Act.[121]

It is too early to know which, if any, of the current proposals will be adopted. There is, however, little doubt that the law will be changed in some way to facilitate secured transactions in intellectual property.

---

[119] Ibid., p. 14.
[120] Ibid.
[121] 139 Cong. Rec. S1619 (daily ed. Feb. 16, 1993).

CHAPTER **15**

INTERNATIONAL LAWS AND DEVELOPMENTS ON SECURITY INTERESTS IN INTANGIBLE ASSETS

15.1 AUSTRALIA

Simon D. Williams
Kate Johnston

Williams Niblett
Sydney, Australia

(a) **Introduction.** The granting of security interests in intellectual property rights in Australia is unusual but not exceptional. As discussed in this section, the lack of any common practice in this regard is perhaps more the result of the limitations of relevant legislation rather than the lack of interest in intellectual property as security.[1]

Although incorporeal monopoly rights such as patent, copyright, trademark, and design rights may not accurately be described as "choses in action", they are generally treated as such in Australia. Like choses in action, they may be mortgaged or charged as security.[2]

Other than the system of registration of company charges (charges over the assets of Australian corporations) under the Corporations Law 1989, there is, however, no specific legislative framework dealing with mortgages or charges over intellectual property (c.f. securities over real property and chattels).

There are several categories of security relevant to intellectual property rights that determine their operation. For example, a distinction is made between legal and equitable mortgages, the former taking effect as an assignment of the legal interest to the mortgagee (the mortgagor retaining the equity of redemption) and the latter providing the mortgagee with only a future right to the assignment upon exercise of some power of sale or pursuant to a court order. Alternatively, a security may take the form of a charge by which

---

[1] See, generally, E. I. Sykes; *The Law of Securities*, 4th ed., (Sydney; The Law Book Company Limited, 1986) pp.728–732.

[2] A mortgage involves the transfer of a legal title or equitable interest in property to a mortgagee, usually as security for a debt and on condition that the mortgaged interest reverts to the mortgagor upon repayment of the debt. A charge is a form of security, usually for a debt, by which the property is charged with the debt, the chargor retaining ownership but the chargee having the right to have the property sold if the debt is not discharged within time.

the chargee has neither legal nor equitable title to the asset charged (as in the case of a mortgage) or possession to it (in the case of a pledge or possessory lien over chattels), but merely has certain rights, once default has occurred, to enforce against the asset charged. Further, a security may be fixed or floating. Both legal and equitable mortgages provide fixed security, whereas a charge may be either fixed or floating. A fixed security prevents the mortgagor/chargor from dealing in the title to the asset secured. In the case of a floating charge, the security is over the chargor's assets existing from time to time. The chargor is free to deal with those assets until such time as default or other event crystallizes the floating charge so as to create a fixed security over the chargor's assets.

The most secure protection would be provided by way of legal mortgage; however, the assignment of legal title in intellectual property to a mortgagee may raise considerable questions as to, for example, who is to conduct/defend infringement proceedings, who is responsible for renewal fees, and who has an obligation to exploit the property. It may be possible to address some, but perhaps not all, of these problems in the security document.

Of paramount importance is the protection of the mortgagee/chargee against bona fide purchasers for value without notice. Such purchasers, although unable to take title with priority over legal mortgagees, may defeat equitable mortgagees unless the purchaser has notice of the mortgagee's prior equitable rights. In the case of Australian corporations, this notice can be provided by the registration of a fixed or floating charge against the company's assets under the Corporations Law. However, where this is not possible (for example, in relation to assets belonging to an individual or a foreign corporation), there may be difficulty for a mortgagee/chargee in bringing notice of its prior interest to the attention of later purchasers.

Not all Australian legislation concerning intellectual property provides for the registration of security interests. Even when registration provisions do exist, it is not at all certain whether such registration will necessarily constitute notice to protect the priority of the mortgagee/chargee against later competing interests.

It should also be noted that the Certificate of Registration of a patent, trademark, or design is not, of itself, an instrument of title. Unlike, for example, share script (the certificate evidencing title to shares in a company), its delivery to a mortgagee or its endorsement with the mortgagee's interest may not provide notice to a subsequent competing interest.

Independent of specific requirements under intellectual property legislation, the creation of a legal mortgage by an assignment of a legal interest in the intellectual property should be in writing and signed by the mortgagor.[3] Similarly, an assignment of an equitable interest in intellectual property to an equitable mortgagee should be in writing and signed by the mortgagor.[4]

However, these requirements are subject to equity "regarding as done that which ought to have been done," especially in the case of an oral agreement to assign for valuable consideration and capable of specific performance,[5] or, in the case of fraud or dishonesty or where there have been sufficient acts of part performance.[6]

Security documents are written contracts that normally recite the terms and conditions of the security, including payments, interest, restrictions on dealing with the secured

---

[3] Conveyancing Act of 1919 (NSW), § 12 (corresponding legislation exists in other states).
[4] Section 23C(I)(c) Conveyancing Act of 1919 (NSW) § 23C (I)(c) (corresponding legislation exists in other states).
[5] *Oughtred v. IRC*, AC 206 (1960).
[6] *Maddison v. Alderson*, 8 App Cas 467 (1883).

property, powers of sale and appointment, and powers of receivers. Security documents usually take the form of a deed. A deed is a written document signed, sealed, and delivered by the maker. A document is usually construed as a deed if it is described as such and attested to by at least one witness who is not a party to the deed. The advantages of a deed over a normal contract include the following:

- No consideration is necessary.
- The doctrine of estoppel will usually prevent a person from disputing his or her own deed.
- More generous limitation periods apply under relevant statutes of limitation.
- Statutory powers of sale and powers of appointment of receivers are implied by relevant state legislation.[7]

It appears, however, that a mortgagee will not have the power to institute proceedings in his or her own name for infringement of a statutory intellectual property right unless that person is a legal mortgagee to whom the legal and registered title has been transferred.[8]

Depending on the nature of the transaction and the parties concerned, the transaction may be subject to relevant commonwealth and state legislation dealing with credit and, especially, consumer credit transactions. The transaction may also be subject to relevant provisions of the Trade Practices Act of 1974 (and corresponding state legislation) dealing with "misleading and deceptive conduct."

Security documents may be subject to ad valorem stamp duty payable under applicable state and territory legislation.[9] Until recently, it had been (perhaps erroneously) considered that as intellectual property rights in the nature of patents, trademarks, designs, and copyright were subject to commonwealth legislation, the states were prevented from imposing stamp duty on transactions concerning this type of property. The better view[10] is that for the purposes of the various Stamp Acts, these forms of property are property located in the state concerned and that, in certain circumstances, dealings in those properties may be subject to payment of ad valorem stamp duty. For example, if the instrument were limited to an industrial property right in a particular state or territory, duty would probably be payable.[11] Section 14(2) of the Patents Act of 1990 provides:

> A patent may be assigned for a place in, or part of, the patent area [defined as, inter alia, Australia and the Australian continental shelf].

The possibility of an assignment of copyright limited to a place in or part of Australia is contemplated by § 196(2)(b) of the Copyright Act of 1968.

A legal mortgage over a patent or copyright work limited to a particular state or territory may, therefore, be liable to ad valorem stamp duty in that state or territory.

---

[7] Conveyancing Act 1919 (NSW), Part IV, Div. 3 (corresponding legislation exists in other states).

[8] *Van Gelder, Apsimon & Co v. Sowerby Bridge United District Flour Society*, 44 ChD 374 (C.A.) (1890).

[9] Stamp Duties Act of 1920 (NSW) (corresponding legislation exists in other states).

[10] *JV Crows Nest v. Commissioner of Stamp Duties*, (NSW) 16 ATR 373, 2Day FM (1985); *Australia Pty. Limited v. Commissioner of Stamp Duties*, (NSW) 16 I.P.R. 451. (1989).

[11] Tolhurst, Wallace & Zipfinger, Australian Revenue Duties [2.51].

Similarly, a legal or equitable mortgage over an intellectual property license limited to a particular state or territory may be dutiable.

Even if not subject to ad valorem stamp duty, a security document in the form of a deed will be subject to nominal stamp duty as a deed.

(b) Security Registration Provisions Under the Corporations Law of 1989.   A system of registration of fixed or floating charges over the property of Australian corporations is provided by the Corporations Law of 1989. No method of recording interests against the property of foreign corporations is provided. Section 262(1) identifies the charges requiring registration as including:

> . . . a charge on goodwill, on a patent or license under a patent, on a trademark or service mark or a license to use a trademark or service mark, on a copyright or a license under a copyright or on a registered design or a license to use a registered design.

If such a charge is not registered, the charge is not invalid although it may be void as a security enforceable against the liquidator or official manager.[12] Registration of a charge will ensure priority over competing interests including subsequent registered charges and prior unregistered charges (in the absence of notice).[13]

Notice of a charge, in a specified form, must be lodged for registration with the Australian Securities Commission within 45 days of the creation of the charge together with a copy of the instrument or deed creating or evidencing the charge.[14]

(c) The Patents Act of 1990.   On April 30, 1991, the Patents Act of 1990 came into force, repealing and replacing the Patents Act of 1952.

Legal mortgages over patents by way of assignment are unusual in Australia, primarily because of the problems referred to earlier, concerning whether the mortgagee or the mortgagor will be responsible for enforcing and maintaining the patent. However, despite these problems, a legal mortgage is possible under the Patents Act. Section 13(2) provides that the patentee's exclusive rights "are personal property and are capable of assignment." Section 14(1) of the 1990 Act provides that "an assignment of a patent must be in writing signed by or on behalf of the assignor and assignee."

The recordal of an equitable mortgagee's interest over a patent is contemplated by the Patents Act.

Although Section 188 provides that:

> Notice of any kind of trust relating to a patent or license is not receivable by the Commissioner and must not be registered,

§ 187 states that "prescribed particulars relating to patents (if any) *must* be registered" (emphasis added).[15] Regulation 19.1 of the Patent Regulations to the 1990 Act provides that:

> For the purposes of Section 187 of the Act . . . the following particulars are prescribed, that is, particulars of:

---

[12] (1) Corporations Law, §266 (1).
[13] Corporations Law, §280.
[14] Corporations Law, §263.
[15] See also *Stuart v. Casey*, 8 RPC 259 (1891).

(a) an entitlement as mortgagee, licensee or otherwise to an interest in a patent;

(b) a transfer of an entitlement to a patent or license or to a share in a patent or license.

However, the recording in the Register of Patents of an equitable mortgagee's interest may not necessarily provide priority against competing interests in the patent. If the mortgagor is an Australian corporation, the best form of protection would be by way of an equitable mortgage over the patent, registered as a fixed charge under the Corporations Law, as well as recording that interest in the Register of Patents.

(d) The Trade Marks Act of 1955.   Section 82(2) of the Trade Marks Act provides that:

> Subject to this section, a registered trademark may be assigned . . . with or without the goodwill of the business concerned in the goods or services in respect of which the trademark is registered or of some of those goods or services.

Unlike the Patents Act, the Trade Marks Act stipulates no requirement for an assignment of a registered trademark to be in writing or signed by the assignor or assignees.[16]

In the case of a legal mortgage over a registered trademark, the assignment of the legal title to the mortgagee could and in fact should be recorded under the Trade Marks Act. Section 20(1) of that Act provides that:

> Where a person becomes entitled by assignment . . . to a registered trademark, he *shall* make application to the Registrar to register his title (emphasis added).

Furthermore, § 82(7) of the Trade Marks Act suggests that an assignment does not have effect until it is registered. However, if a legal mortgagee is so registered as the proprietor of a registered trademark, then there is a significant risk that the trademark would not be distinctive of the registered proprietor as required by the Trade Marks Act and would thus be in danger of expungement—the continued use of the trademark by the mortgagor/assignor being deceptive or confusing.[17]

Perhaps the only solution to this problem is to record the mortgagor/assignor as a registered user of the mark, in conformity with Part IX of the Trade Marks Act, pursuant to a bona fide license with appropriate quality-control provisions. Even in these circumstances, the assignment may still be invalid under § 82(2)(b) of the Trade Marks Act, which provides that an assignment of a registered trademark without the goodwill of the business concerned will be invalid if:

> . . . a substantially identical or deceptively similar trademark continues to be used by the assignor, after the assignment, in relation to other goods or services, where there exists a connection in the course of trade between those goods or services and the assignor and where those goods or services are of the same description as those in respect of which the trademark has been assigned, or of such a description that the public is likely to be deceived by the use of the trademark by the assignor and assignee upon their respective goods or services.

An assignment of a registered trademark to the mortgagee "with goodwill" would be unusual, as it would be unlikely to be attractive either to the mortgagor or mortgagee. Furthermore, a legal mortgage by way of a recording of assignment of the legal interest in a registered trademark also raises similar problems to those discussed in regard to

---

[16] See Trade Marks Act, § 6(1).

[17] See *R. J. Reuter Co. Ltd. v. Mulhens*, 70 R.P.C. 235 at 251 (C.A.) (1953).

the Patents Act; that is, who is responsible for the protection and enforcement of the registered trademark?

Unlike the Patents Act, the Trade Marks Act offers no specific provision for an equitable mortgagee to register his or her interest against a registered trademark. Although the Registrar of Trade Marks does have discretion under § 19(1)(v) of the Trade Marks Act to enter "a disclaimer or memorandum relating to the trademark," it is not the current practice of the Trade Marks Office to permit the registration of security interests.[18]

This practice appears to be followed notwithstanding the fact that § 57 of the Trade Marks Act provides:

1. Subject to this Act, the registered proprietor of a trademark has, subject to any rights appearing from the Register to be vested in some other person, power to assign the trademark and to give good discharges for any consideration for the assignment.
2. Equities in respect of a trademark may be enforced in like manner as in respect of other personal property.

If one were to be successful in convincing the Registrar of Trade Marks to record on the Register a mortgagee's interest, § 57(1) may arguably protect the mortgagee against competing interests.

Thus, the most suitable form of recording a security interest over a registered trademark would appear to be by way of an equitable charge over the registered trademark *together with* the goodwill of the business producing the goods or services for which the mark is registered. However, the only apparent method of recording that equitable interest would appear to be as a charge under the Corporations Law which, as indicated earlier, is possible only if the chargor is an Australian corporation.

The aforementioned limitations under the Trade Marks Act have now been recognized by the Working Party to Review the Trade Mark Legislation. In its report to the Minister for Science and Technology published in 1992, this body recommended, among other things, that provisions should be made for the entry, on a voluntary basis, of any person claiming an interest in, or rights with respect to, a registered trademark and not required by any other provision of the Act to be entered on the register.[19] The Working Party, however, also recommended that any amendment should make clear that "the mere fact of recordal of these interests will not give rise to any rights in the registration.[20] These recommendations of the Working Party have been incorporated in Sections 122 and 125 of the draft Trade Marks Bill.

(e) Common-Law Trademarks. A legal mortgage by way of assignment of a common-law trademark raises a significant problem as to whether the trademark continues to indicate a connection in the course of trade with the mortgagor/assignor, and as to whether the continuing use of the mark by the mortgagor/assignor is deceptive. Furthermore, it is probably true that a common-law trademark cannot be assigned in any event without the relevant goodwill in the business concerned (which, as previously indicated, would not be attractive to the mortgagor or mortgagee).[21]

As no form of registration of such marks exists, the only solution to the problem appears to be to provide for an equitable mortgage of the trademark together with the

---

[18] Cf. The United Kingdom - Svenska A/B Gasaccumulator's Trade Marks 4 RPC 106 [1962].
[19] Recommendation 27A at p. 83
[20] Ibid., par. 2.4E.
[21] *Pinto v. Bordman*, 8 R.P.C. 181 (1891).

goodwill of the business concerned and, if the mortgagor were an Australian corporation, to register that equitable interest against the mortgagor as a charge under the Corporations Law.

(f) Designs Act of 1906.   Section 38A of the Designs Act, like the Patents Act, allows for and indeed requires an equitable mortgagee to register his or her title, together with the particulars of the instrument creating the interest. That section provides:

> 'Where a person becomes entitled as mortgagee . . . to an interest in a registered design, he *shall* apply to the Registrar to register his title, and the Registrar shall, on receipt of the application, and on proof to the satisfaction of the Registrar of the title of the applicant, cause notice of the interest to be entered in the register, together with the particulars of the instrument creating the interest (emphasis added).

Again, however, the registration of such an interest under the Designs Act may not necessarily protect the mortgagee's priority over competing interests. The best form of protection would, therefore, appear to be by way of a legal mortgage and the recording of the assignment of the mortgagee's interest under the Designs Act. Section 38 of the Act provides:

> Where a person becomes entitled to a registered design by assignment . . . [or] agreement . . . he shall apply to the Registrar to register his title, and the Registrar shall, on receipt of the application, and on proof to the satisfaction of the Registrar of the title of the applicant, cause the name of the applicant to be entered in the register as the owner of the design.

Protection of an equitable mortgagee's interest in a registered design recorded in the name of an Australian corporation could, of course, be provided by registration of that interest as a fixed charge against that mortgagor pursuant to the Corporations Law.

(h) Copyright Act of 1968.   The Copyright Act (which has no system of registration or deposit) does not recognize the ability of a mortgagee to record his or her interest over works and other subject matter protected by the Copyright Act. However, unlike the Trade Marks Act, the Copyright Act permits a legal mortgagee's interest to be protected by way of an assignment of the copyright concerned, without endangering that copyright. Section 196(1) of the Copyright Act provides that:

> Copyright is personal property and, subject to this section, is transmissable by assignment.

Such assignment presumably could be by way of legal mortgage.[22] It should, however, be borne in mind that there is no system of registration of copyright under the Copyright Act by which a mortgage (by way of assignment or otherwise) over copyright material may be recorded. Again, therefore, the most appropriate protection would be, if applicable, to record the mortgagee's interest as a charge under the Corporations Law.

---

[22] E. I. Sykes; *The Law of Securities*, 4th ed. (The Law Book Company Limited, 1986), p. 730.

15.2 BRAZIL

Luiz Henrique O. do Amaral

Peter D. Siemsen

Dannemann, Siemsen, Bigler & Ipanema Moreira
Rio de Janeiro, Brazil

In Brazil, trademarks, patents, and copyrights are not commonly used as collateral to guarantee a debtor's obligation for repayment of a loan, although some 30 years ago the National Bank for Economic Development (BNDE) financed the establishment of an industry to process zinc ore in accordance with a patented method. As collateral for the debt, the bank accepted the debtor's Brazilian and foreign patents.[1]

Neither the Industrial Property Code[2] nor the Copyright Act[3] addresses the pledge of vested intellectual property rights as security for the satisfaction of a debt. Thus, the possible existence of a "security interest" in intellectual property in Brazil must be examined in the light of the provisions of the Civil and Commercial Codes affecting the supplementary security for performance of the obligations undertaken by a borrower.

Under the Civil Code,[4] a loan may be secured by a pledge of chattels, which may consist of personal and movable property. The pledge of such property is secondary to the main loan agreement. A pledge of chattels normally occurs upon the effective transfer of assets to the creditor's possession. The creditor then has a temporary interest in the property until the loan is repaid.

Such a system would be clearly inadequate, with respect to intellectual property, where the trademarks, patents, and copyrights are still used by the debtor to carry out its commercial activities which, in turn, would generate the income needed to settle the debt and eventually remove the "security interest."

The Commercial Code[5] deals with commercial collateral security by means of a fictitious transfer of possession of the collateral to the debtor, although it is necessary to have an express contractual clause whereby the debtor concedes having transferred legal possession to the creditor. In this type of transaction, the borrower remains as a mere trustee of the collateral property.

The Federal Supreme Court, Brazil's highest court, has upheld the enforcement of a collateral security whenever the transfer of possession was explicitly set forth in the agreement.[6]

---

[1] Cia. Mercantil Ingá

[2] Law no. 5.772/71.

[3] Law no. 5.988/73.

[4] Brazilian Civil Code (Law no. 3071, January 1, 1916, Title III, Chapter IX).

[5] Brazilian Commercial Code (Law no. 556, June 25, 1850, Section 13, Chapter II).

[6] "Revista does Tribunais," no. 476, page 235—Extraordinary Appeal no. 72500/SP, 1st Senate, *In re Intervest S/A Crédito Financiamento e Investimentos vs. Leonardo Campana and others.* Decision: These dockets having been seen, reported and discussed, the Ministers of the 1st Senate of the Federal Supreme Court unanimously agree not to acknowledge the appeal, in accordance with the tachygraphic notes of the judgment. Brasília, April 30, 1974; Luiz Galloti, president; Rodrigues de Alckmin, reporter.

More recently, the Superior Court of Justice,[7] in a very clear decision, reaffirmed that in the case of a commercial collateral security in accordance with the Commercial Code,[8] the transfer of the asset may be symbolic; that is, although title to the asset is transferred to the creditor, possession remains with the debtor.

There is, therefore, an increasing recognition of the debtor's need to retain commercially useful property so as to be able to repay the debt.

Copyrighted works are defined and considered as chattels or movable property according to the provisions of the Civil Code,[9] and are thus subject to the "security interest" regime. Though the Code makes no reference to patents or trademarks, all intellectual property rights share the same basic concept and characteristics and, accordingly, deserve the same legal treatment under the Civil Code.

Under the Equivalence Doctrine, patents and trademarks, do legally receive the same treatment as copyrights, being regarded as movable property. As a result, patents and trademarks should also be subject to the "security interest" regime set forth in the Civil and Commercial Codes.

The commercial collateral security is perfected by execution of a security agreement or a security clause within a loan agreement, which must contain, among other things, the amount borrowed, the purpose of the loan, type of security interest, date by which the loan must be paid, and the value of the secured property.

Under Brazilian law, lenders obtain a lien on the debtor's intellectual property by operation of the contract so that, in the event of default, the creditor is able to exclude such property for satisfaction of the debt, putting it beyond the reach of other creditors.

The Civil Code,[10] however, contains certain peculiarities that severely affect a security interest in intellectual property, specifically, clauses that provide that ownership of the property is immediately transferred to the lender in the event of loan default, are null and void. In case of default, the creditor is given the right to apply for an executory order with

---

[7] *Judicial Gazette*, June 8, 1992, p. 8620, Special appeal no. 7187-0—São Paulo. Reporter: Minister Sálvio de Figueiredo: Appellant: Banco Safra de Investimentos S/A; Lawyers: Dr. Rubens Ferraz de Oliveira Lima and others; Appellees: Cofarma Comercial Farmacêutica Ltda. and other; Lawyers: Dr. Pedro Alcides Barense and other; Summary: Commercial Law. Mercantile pledge. Symbolic Delivery. Admissibility. Commercial Code, art. 274. Period of validity. Action of detinue. Good faith. Appeal accepted. I. As far as mercantile pledge is concerned, the symbolic delivery of the objects is admissible, the rule of article 274 of the Commercial Code being in force. II. The acceptance of the task by the depositary, in the mercantile pledge, entails the presumption of delivery of the goods given as a guarantee so that the lack of delivery of the objects characterizes the depositary's infidelity. III. The reality of the relations in trade nowadays repudiates the unjustifiable formalities, thus the "consecration of the moral obligation of not deceiving another person" dwells upon good faith. Decision: These dockets having been seen, reported and discussed, the Ministers of the Fourth Senate of the Upper Court of Appeals, in accordance with the following votes and tachygraphic notes, unanimously decide to acknowledge the appeal and accept it. The Ministers Barros Monteiro, Bueno de Souza, Athos Carneiro and Fontes de Alencar gave the same vote as the Reporter. Brasília, May 12, 1992 (date of the judgment).

[8] Brazilian Commercial Code, article 274: "The delivery of the pledge may be real or symbolic and by the same means through which delivery of the asset which has been sold can be made (art. 199)."

[9] Brazilian Civil Code, article 48: The following are considered chattels for legal purposes:

1. The real rights over movable things and the corresponding actions.

2. The rights of obligation and the respective actions.

3. The copyrights.

[10] Civil Code, § 765, states that any provision that may authorize that the lender may keep the secured property for the amount of the loan or, in case of noncompliance by debtor, is null.

a view to selling out the rights during a judicial auction. The creditor cannot automatically seize ownership of the secured property if the loan becomes overdue.

The attachment of secured property would be important in order to perfect and enforce the security interest against third parties. In the absence of specific provisions in intellectual property legislation for the recordation of security interest agreements, the Public Registries Law applies and hence such agreements can be registered with the Registry of Titles and Deeds to be enforceable against third parties.[11]

In addition, as the recordation of an assignment before the Patent and Trademark Office is essential for the effective transfer of title and considering, furthermore, that the Copyright Act[12] provides that an assignment has to be recorded against the certificate of registration, security interest agreements should also be submitted to those government agencies for attachment purposes. Such attachment would avoid fraudulent assignments by dishonest debtors and would permit actual control over ownership in case of the registrants' bankruptcy.

Although there are no rules established for attachment of security interests in intellectual property, the Patent and Trademark Office has been reacting positively to judicial executory orders for transfer of title. This may encourage the submission of such agreements with those agencies, which may record the agreements against the subject intellectual property so as to curb breach of contracts.

However, as the Industrial Property Code permits the recordation of any limitation rights only upon judicial or administrative orders, governmental bodies may be reluctant to attach the security interest. In this case, judicial steps would be available to bind both the Patent and Trademark Office and the Copyright Office. The creditor may enter a judicial notice with the Federal Courts which would, in turn, issue a notice to warn such governmental bodies that the intellectual property has been given as security for a loan and should be attached so as to prevent subsequent assignment.

The obvious reason for the limited use of intellectual property rights as collateral is based on the difficulty in accurately evaluating such rights. Most of the proposed methods of evaluation have severe shortcomings, and usually a measurable value can be ascertained only when there has been an acquisition or, possibly, in the case of an onerous license agreement.

Some years ago, the Brazilian fiscal authorities proposed requiring intellectual property rights to be included in the books of their owners as assets of financial value, but then relinguished this idea because of the aforementioned difficulties.

Despite the lack of precedents in Brazil, the enforceability of security interest in an intellectual property is legally feasible, provided that certain formalities are observed. As the use of intellectual property as collateral becomes more common, further instruments to guarantee the execution of the security interest should become available.

---

[11] The Industrial Property Code of 1945 (Law no. 7903, amended by Law no. 8481 of 1945) provided in its articles 46, sole paragraph, and 145, sole paragraph, that any limitations to patents or trademark registrations should be recorded with the Patent Office. This could be interpreted as covering inclusively limitations deriving from the use of patents or trademarks as collateral securities to guarantee debts. However, under the present Code of Industrial Property (Law no. 5772 of 1971) the corresponding articles 27, paragraph 3, and 88, paragraph 3, were changed, stating that solely limitations resulting from decisions of an administrative or judicial nature will be recorded, therefore changing the meaning in relation to the previous law. This does not mean, however, that the possibility of recording has been excluded.

[12] Law no. 5988/73.

It is noteworthy that the bill for a new patent and trademark law, which was approved by the House of Representatives on June 2, 1993, and will proceed now to the Senate, takes such need into account. In fact, the bill provides that the Patent and Trademark Office will record any limitation or encumbrance on the rights. This provision will permit the parties to record a security agreement with the Patent and Trademark Office, which will automatically attach the title.

Such improvements will certainly assure an easier and far more effective use of intellectual property rights as collateral for loans.

15.3 CANADA

Gervas W. Wall, Esq.

Deeth Williams Wall
Toronto, Ontario, Canada

(a) Introduction

(i) Common-Law and Civil-Law Jurisdictions. The legal system of nine of the provinces and the territories of Canada is based on English common law. The legal system in Quebec is based on the Civil Code. Most of this chapter addresses the common law of Ontario in particular. There are references to civil law, but the reader is encouraged to review more specialized works for civil-law attributes and for the laws of each province.

(ii) Federal and Provincial Jurisdictions. Under the system of federalism in Canada, governmental powers are distributed between the federal and provincial governments. There are a number of federal statutes that relate to intellectual property, governing patents,[1] trademarks,[2] copyright,[3] industrial designs,[4] mask works,[5] and plant breeders' rights. Common law passing off trade secrets and personality rights[6] as discussed in subsection b(i) fall within provincial jurisdiction.

In general, a transfer of, or dealing with, property rights falls within provincial jurisdiction.[7] Thus, security interests (provincial jurisdiction) in intellectual property (federal jurisdiction, except for personality rights and trade secrets) raise the following constitutional problems:

1. Can the provincial laws addressing security and priority govern security interests in federally regulated intellectual property? and
2. Can federal intellectual property legislation provide a mechanism for taking security in, or conveyance of, property?

In Canadian constitutional law, conflicts between inconsistent federal and provincial laws are resolved in favor of the federal law, under the Doctrine of Paramountcy.[8] However, the Paramountcy doctrine is applicable only where there are conflicting federal and provincial laws, each of which is valid.[9]

The Author would like to thank Terrence Langlois for his contribution to this chapter.
[1] *Patent Act*, R.S.C. 1985, c. P-4.
[2] *Trade-marks Act*, R.S.C. 1985, c. T-13.
[3] Copyright Act, R.S.C. 1985 c. C-42.
[4] *Industrial Design Act*, R.S.C. 1985, c. I-9.
[5] *Integrated Circuit Topography Act*, S.C. 1990, c.37.
[6] *Plant Breeders' Rights Act*, S.C. 1990, c.20.
[7] *Constitution Act*, 1867, § 92(13).
[8] P.W. Hogg, *Constitutional Law in Canada*, 2d ed. (Toronto: The Carswell Company Limited, 1985) p. 354.
[9] Ibid.

Laws made by either level of government may incidentally affect a matter falling within the class of subjects allocated to the other level of government. Thus, the answers to the preceding questions 1 and 2 are both likely to be yes.

(b) Relevant Legislation. The following legislation is relevant to security interests in intellectual property in Canada:

- *Provincial Security Legislation.* Each province has enacted legislation governing security interests within that province. In Ontario, the Personal Property Security Act[10] (PPSA) governs most consensual transactions in which personal property is used as security for the fulfillment of obligations. For the purposes of this discussion, the Ontario PPSA is used as an example. At present Ontario, Manitoba, Saskatchewan, Alberta, British Columbia, and the Yukon Territories have PPSA-type legislation; the other common law provinces are considering implementing such legislation, and Quebec has its own version in its civil code. PPSA-type legislation is based on the Uniform Commercial Code (UCC) and conforms in most respects to this code.
- *Bank Act.* This federal act applies to secured creditors which are Canadian chartered banks taking security in inventory and receivables. As intellectual property is usually not inventory, the Bank Act[11] has little application to intellectual property.
- *Federal Intellectual Property Legislation.* The creation, transfer and regulation of rights in most types of intellectual property are governed by federal intellectual property legislation (i.e., the Patent Act, the Trade-marks Act, the Copyright Act, the Industrial Design Act, the Plant Breeders' Rights Act, and mask work legislation). Intellectual property legislation is not really security legislation, but some of these statutes make reference to the creation, assignment, and registration of various interests in the intellectual property governed by the statute.
- *Provincial Intellectual Property Legislation.* Certain types of intellectual property, such as trade secrets and certain personality rights, may be regulated by provincial governments. The Privacy Acts passed by British Columbia, Manitoba, Saskatchewan, and Newfoundland contain special provisions relating to commercial appropriation of personality.
- *Bankruptcy and Insolvency Act.* The administration and distribution of a bankrupt entity's estate is dealt with under the Bankruptcy and Insolvency Act.[12]

(i) Provincial Legislation: The PPSA and Its Relation to Intellectual Property. The PPSA applies to every transaction that in substance creates a security interest, as indicated in § 2:

Subject to subsection 4(1), this Act applies,

(a) to every transaction without regard to its form and without regard to the person who has title to the collateral that in substance creates a security interest, including, without limiting the foregoing,

---

[10] *Personal Property Security Act*, R.S.O. 1990, c. P-10.

[11] *Bank Act*, S.C. 1991, c. 46.

[12] D. Mendes da Costa and R.J. Balfour, *Property Law* (Toronto: Emond-Montgomery Limited, 1982) pp. 42–43.

(i) a chattel mortgage, conditional sale, equipment trust, debenture, floating charge, pledge, trust indenture, or trust receipt, and

(ii) an assignment, lease, or consignment that secures payment or performance of an obligation; . . .

Accordingly, the PPSA applies to a transaction involving intellectual property as collateral or security, provided the transaction in substance creates a security interest. The term *security interest* is defined in § 1 of the PPSA as follows:

"Security interest" means an interest in personal property that secures payment or performance of an obligation . . .

Section 1 of the PPSA defines *personal property* as including intangibles, and *intangible* as "all personal property, including choses in action, that is not goods, chattel paper, documents of title, instruments or securities." As in the following paragraphs, intellectual property falls within the ambit of personal property (chattels personal), as a chose in action. Consequently, the PPSA, which classifies intellectual property as an intangible, applies to security interests in intellectual property.

In common law, all property is divided into real property and personal property.[13] Personal property, or "personalty," consists of chattels real and chattels personal, a category that is further subdivided into choses in possession (tangible property that is capable of being possessed) and choses in action (incorporate property, in respect to which one has no actual possession, but a mere right enforceable only through legal action).[14]

As early as 1848, English authors have classified patents, trademarks, copyrights, and similar rights among choses in action.[15] In § 9–106 of the UCC, general intangibles are defined as "any personal property . . . other than goods." The comments following this provision in the UCC state that copyrights, trademarks, and patents are included within this definition.[16]

There is support, in Canadian law in general and Ontario law in particular, for the proposition that intellectual property is personal property and thus falls within the ambit of choses in action. For example, in a discussion of the meaning of intangible property under the PPSA, the author of a leading text in sales financing in Canada states that intangibles include accounts receivable and such exotic forms of collateral as goodwill and intellectual property.[17] Fox also notes that "trade-marks, being property of an incorporeal nature, are classed with patents and copyright, and are usually considered as choses in action."[18]

It is uncertain whether trade secrets should be classified as property. If trade secrets are indeed property, they would be classified as choses in action. *R. v. Stewart*[19] held that

---

[13] Ibid.

[14] W.R. Warren, *Choses in Action* (London: Sweet and Maxwell, 1899) at 2.

[15] See also R.S. Bramson in *Bender's Uniform Commercial Code Service* (New York: Mathew Bender & Co., 1982) vol 1C at 25A-15.

[16] M.H. Bridge and F.H. Buckley, *Sales and Sales Financing in Canada* (Toronto: The Carswell Company Limited, 1981) at 464.

[17] H.G. Fox, *The Canadian Law of Trade Marks and Unfair Competition* (Toronto: The Carswell Company Limited, 1972) at 19; and H.G. Fox, *The Canadian Law and Practice Relating to Letters Patent for Interventions* (Toronto: The Carswell Company Limited, 1969) at 280.

[18] *R. v. Stewart* (1988), 21 C.P.R. 289 (S.C.C.).

[19] *Patent Act*, § 42.

confidential information does not qualify as property for the purposes of § 283 of the Criminal Code. It is important to note, however, that this ruling determines that confidential information is not property only for the purposes of criminal, and not civil law.

(ii) Perfection of Security Interests in Intellectual Property Under the PPSA. A creditor who relies on the provisions of the PPSA to protect its security interest against third parties must comply with certain formal requirements. To begin with, § 11 provides that a security interest is not enforceable against a third party unless the collateral is in the possession of the secured party or the debtor has signed a security agreement containing a description of the collateral. The requirement of a description of the collateral is somewhat vague; thus, as a precaution a security interest in less than all the assets of a borrower should have a sufficient description to identify the collateral fully.

In addition to this writing requirement for nonpossessory interests, a secured party who seeks priority over collateral must perfect its security interest. Perfection is a term used in the PPSA to indicate that the best statutory position under the Act, or the greatest bundle of rights with respect to the collateral secured, has been attained. This does not mean that a secured party who perfects its interest will always have priority, as several parties may have perfected security interests in the same collateral. In such circumstances, the PPSA priority rules govern disputes. Unperfected security interests, although valid, are often of little or no value, because they are subordinated to various other interests listed in § 20(1), including the debtor's trustee in bankruptcy and bona fide purchasers for value without notice.

Perfection occurs under § 19 when a security interest has "attached" and all steps required for perfection under any provision of the Act have been completed. *Attachment* is a term indicating that all steps necessary for the creation of a security interest have occurred. A security interest attaches when (1) the parties intend it to attach, (2) value is given, and (3) the debtor has rights in the collateral. At this point, the secured party has rights in the collateral vis-à-vis the debtor.

The term *perfection* refers to the status achieved when the secured party has rights in the collateral vis-à-vis other interests in the same collateral. Security interests in intangibles, including intellectual property, may be perfected only by registration.

Because the PPSA is a "notice filing" system, only a financing statement, and not the security agreement itself, is registered.

(c) Canadian Federal Intellectual Property Statutes and Their Relation to Security Interests. As previously indicated, there is no constitutional objection to federal intellectual property statutes incidentally affecting security interests. However, these statutes must be closely examined to determine whether in fact they do create, perfect, regulate, or otherwise affect security interests in intellectual property. Provisions for recording assignments and other documents affecting title on federal registers are found in the federal patent, trademark, copyright, and industrial design statutes, but none of these statutes contain any other provisions regarding the rights, obligations, or priorities of secured parties or lenders. This raises the question of the purpose of registering documents under the federal intellectual property statutes. Does such registration serve to perfect security interests in intellectual property, or are the registers simply intended to record assignments of intellectual property rights to avoid fraud against subsequent third-party purchasers of intellectual property rights? This issue has not yet been completely settled, as discussed in the following paragraphs.

(i) Patent Act. The grant of a patent under the Patent Act confers upon the patentee the exclusive right to make, use, and sell the patented invention.[20] By virtue of § 53(1) of the Patent Act, every issued patent is assignable in law, either as to the whole interest, or as to any part thereof, by an instrument in writing. Such assignment and "every grant and conveyance of any exclusive right to make and use and to grant to others the right to make and use the invention patented" must be registered in the Patent Office in the prescribed manner.

It is not only registered patents that may be assigned. The right to obtain a patent may also be assigned by an instrument in writing; however, registration of such an assignment is stated to be permissible rather than mandatory.[21]

Although registration of an assignment of a right to obtain a patent is optional, failure to register any assignment may have serious consequences. It is provided that every assignment affecting a patent is void against any subsequent assignee, unless such assignment is registered as prescribed, before registration by a subsequent assignee.[22]

Whether security interests fall within the aforementioned registration provisions of the Patent Act remains unclear. The Patent Act provides only for the registration of "assignments" and "every grant and conveyance of any exclusive right to make and use and to grant to others the right to make and use the invention patented." One authority has suggested that this latter phrase refers to exclusive licenses;[23] however, it is also arguable that security interests are included within the scope of this phrase, as the grant of a security interest in a patent confers upon the secured party the right to make or use the patented invention, conditional upon default under the security agreement.

What, then, is the effect of a registration of a security interest? Does such registration perfect the security interest or grant it some degree of priority? The term *perfection* is peculiar to the PPSA and does not appear in the Patent Act. However, in a discussion of federal chattel security law in *Secured Transactions in Personal Property in Canada*, McLaren includes the Patent Act and the Trademarks Act in the category of "laws establishing their own schemes for the perfection of security interests but leaving by implication all other questions to be decided by provincial law."

Rule 90 of the Patent Rules complicates matters further:

> An assignment or other document affecting the rights in an invention described in a pending application may be presented for registration by the applicant or any other person.

This rule provides for the presentation for registration of "other documents affecting the rights in an invention"; however, its application is limited to pending applications (i.e., applications for which a patent has not yet issued). It is unclear why the drafters of this

---

[20] id. § 49(2).

[21] id. § 51. The section does not refer to the state of knowledge of the protected subsequent purchaser who is a prior registrant, but Canadian courts have refused to apply the section to benefit a subsequent purchaser with actual notice of an earlier disposition. Thus, the prior encumbrancer will have priority over the subsequent purchaser if the subsequent purchaser had actual notice of the encumbrance even if the subsequent purchaser registers his assignment first. The question remains whether registration under the PPSA without more will constitute sufficient notice to protect the prior encumbrancer. See, for example, *Colpitts v. Sherwood*, [1927] 3 D.L.R. 7 (Alta C.A. and *Saskatchawan Economic Development Corp. v. Westfalia DME, Inc. et al.* (1993), 46 C.P.R. (3d) 322 (F.C.T.D.). See also note 29.

[22] H.G. Fox *The Canadian Law and Practice Relating to Letters Patent for Inventions* (Toronto: The Carswell Company Limited, 1969) p. 286.

[23] R.H./ McLaren, *Secured Transactions in Personal Property in Canada*, Part 1 (Toronto: The Carswell Company Limited, 1985) pp. 1-9, 1-10.

regulation would provide for the registration of "other documents" only where they affect rights in an invention described in a pending application. Despite this anomaly in the legislation, the practice of the Patent Office is to record all documents affecting rights in granted patents, provided the applicable fee is paid and the requesting party complies with the formalities associated with the registration of assignments.

(ii) Trade-marks Act.   A trademark, whether registered or unregistered, is transferable, either in connection with or separately from the goodwill of the business and in respect of either all or some of the wares or services in association with which it has been used. Prior to 1953, a trademark was assignable only with the goodwill of the business in which it was used and could not be assigned in gross. By virtue of § 47(1) of the 1953 Act,[24] trademarks may now be assigned without any assignment of the business or goodwill of the assignor.

With respect to the registration of transfers, § 48(3) provides as follows:

> The Registrar shall register the transfer of any registered mark upon being furnished with evidence satisfactory to him of the transfer and the information that would be required by paragraph 29(9) in an application by the transferee to register such trade-mark.

The *Trade-marks Act* does not make registration of a transfer mandatory; rather, it requires the Registrar to recognize and register the transfer of a trademark upon receipt of a written request for such recognition and receipt of satisfactory evidence of the transfer. (In practice, this means:

- the original instrument of transfer or a certified copy thereof, or
- other evidence of the transfer satisfactory to the Registrar if he or she is satisfied that the original or a certified copy is not available).

In addition, the Registrar must be supplied with the information that would be required by § 30(g) of the Act in an application to register a trademark, that is, the address of the assignee's principal office or place of business in Canada, if any, and otherwise the name and address of a representative for service in Canada.

Unlike the Patent Act and the Copyright Act, the Trade-marks Act has no provision to render an unregistered transfer void against subsequent registered assignments. Where a trademark owner assigns a trademark and that assignment is not registered, a subsequent registered assignee cannot acquire title from the assignor, which has already divested itself of all title capable of being assigned.[25]

In contrast to the Patent Act and the Copyright Act, the Trade-marks Act makes reference to "transfers" rather than "assignments." Judicial interpretation of the term *transfer* in Canada is anything but homogenous and varies with the particular statute under consideration. However, for the purposes of the Trade-marks Act, the Trial Division of the Federal Court of Canada held that the term *transfer* is synonymous with *assignment* and does not include "liens, caveats, mortgages, conditional sale agreements, etc." In *Long v. Pacific Northwest Enterprises Inc.*[26], the plaintiff, a barrister and solicitor, obtained a judgment in the Supreme Court of British Columbia for recovery of legal fees

---

[24] Now Trade-marks Act, R.S.C. 1985, c. T-13, § 48(1).

[25] H.G. Fox, *The Canadian Law of Trade Marks and Unfair Competetion* (Toronto: The Carswell Company Limited, 1972) pp. 269–270.

[26] *Long v. Pacific Northwest Enterprises, Inc,.* (1985), 7 C.P.R. (3d) 410 at 413–414.

from one of the defendants. Shortly thereafter, the same defendant assigned its trade-mark to a second corporate defendant. This assignment was submitted to the Trade-marks Office and the mark was subsequently registered in the name of the second defendant. As the trademark appeared to be the major asset of the first defendant, the plaintiff sought and obtained an interim injunction enjoining the defendants from trans-ferring or otherwise dealing with the trademark. The plaintiff then brought an action in the Federal Court seeking the following relief: an interlocutory injunction restraining the defendants from dealing with the trademark, an order directing the entry of the interlocu-tory injunction obtained in the provincial court in the Trade-marks Register, and an order striking out the entry of the assignee as the owner of the trademark.

The application for interlocutory injunction was dismissed on the basis that it would be vexatious and an abuse of the court process to grant such an injunction when essentially the same relief was granted by a superior court of a province. The orders were also refused because they would not be proper amendments pursuant to § 58(1) of the Trade-marks Act, which provides as follows:

> The Federal Court of Canada has exclusive original jurisdiction, on the application of the Registrar or of any person interested, to order that any entry in the register be struck out or amended on the ground that at the date of such application the entry as it appears on the register does not accurately express or define the existing rights of the person appearing to be the registered owner of the mark.

In this regard, the court stated:

> Amendments can be ordered in respect of an inaccuracy in the register with respect to the description of the trade-mark, or the words or services in connection with which it is used by the registered owner, etc. They may also provide a means for correcting the record where the registered owner should not have been registered as such because the assignment was, e.g., void for fraud or lack of authority in the assignor, although no jurisprudence was brought to my attention on this latter point. But [we] do not understand the purpose of the register to be to demonstrate or authenticate otherwise the beneficial ownership of the trade-mark. Instead, the purpose of the register is to record the name of the registered owner, the precise trade-mark claimed, and the nature of the goods or services in respect of which it is to be used.

> Any other conclusion would mean that the Registrar should accept for inclusion with the registra-tion of a trade-mark a variety of documents indicating the beneficial interests of non-registered owners in respect of the trade-mark: for example, holders of liens, caveats, mortgages, conditional sale agreements, etc. [We] do not understand that to be the purpose of the register and [we] can find no indication in the Trade-marks Act that the registrar is obliged to record such instruments on the title of the registered owner. If he is not so obliged, it would not be appropriate for the court under [§ 58(1)] to direct "amendments" to the register of this nature.

The court also indicated that it may be possible for the plaintiff to seek a correction of the Trade-marks Register after there has been a determination in the action in the Supreme Court of British Columbia that the assignment between the defendants was void. Finally, the court emphasized that the Trade-marks Act does not purport to, nor could it, regulate the matter of conveyance of assets to defeat creditors.

This decision does not affect the right of a secured party to register an assignment of a trademark intended as security. In fact, neither is the registration of other documents affecting title precluded; the judgment merely states that the Registrar is not *obliged* to register certain instruments. In practice, the Trade-marks Office will record security interests against trademark applications and registrations.[27] The Trade-marks Office will

---

[27] Trade Marks Journal, vol. 35 no. 1693, April 8, 1987 p. 72.

not only place a copy of the security agreement in the file, but may also record a notation about the security interest on the record of the registration itself.

(iii) Copyright Act. As in the case of patents, the copyright in any work may be assigned by its owner, either wholly or partially, through an instrument in writing signed by the owner or the owner's agent.[28] Registration of such assignment in the Registers of Copyrights at the Copyright Office is optional. Nonetheless, registration of an assignment appears to be more important than registration of the copyright itself; any assignment of an interest in a copyright is void against any subsequent assignee for valuable consideration without notice, unless such prior assignment is registered in the prescribed manner before registration by the subsequent assignee.[29]

Section 57(1) of the Copyright Act provides that[30] "any grant of an interest in a copyright, either by assignment or license, may be registered. . . ." Without the limiting phrase "either by assignment or license," this provision would clearly allow for the registration of all security interests in copyrights. However, the effect of this limiting phrase is that it is unclear whether registration of security interests in copyright is provided for under the Copyright Act. Accordingly, the previous discussion related to patents applies equally to copyrights. Again, it is the practice of the Copyright Office to register all security interests in copyright, regardless of the form in which they are drafted. In fact, the Copyright Office will even register security interests in unregistered copyrights. Such registrations, however, must identify each work individually, as the Copyright Office will not record a blanket interest in "all copyright of a particular debtor."

(iv) Industrial Design Act. Section 13(1) of the Industrial Design Act provides as follows:

> Every design is assignable in law, either as to the whole interest or any undivided part thereof, by an instrument in writing, which shall be recorded in the office of the Minister on payment of the fees prescribed by this Act in that behalf.

As can be seen from this provision, the Industrial Design Act makes specific reference only to assignments, and therefore the effect of registering a security interest in an industrial design under the Industrial Design Act is also unclear. Despite an absence of statutory authority, security interests in industrial designs, like those in patents, trademarks, and copyrights, are accepted for registration upon payment of the prescribed fee and compliance with the formalities required for the registration of assignments.

(d) Conclusions. From the preceding discussion, there are a number of practical conclusions that can be drawn:

1. Registration of security interests under the federal intellectual property statutes is likely unnecessary but may be a prudent step in exercising caution,

2. Registration of security interests under provincial PPSA legislation is important,

---

[28] *Copyright Act*, R.S.C. 1985 c. C-42, § 13(4).

[29] *Copyright Act*, R.S.C. 1985 c. C-42, § 57. Nevertheless, the validity of the assignment may be determined under provincial law: *Pollman* v. *Eiffel Productions S.A. et al.* (1991), 35 C.P.R. (3d) 384 (F.C.T.D.). Thus, in the Poolman case, a subsequent purchaser, who registered after the previous purchaser, was considered to be the true owner as that was the result under the relevant provisions of the Québec Civil Code. This case was an interlocutory, and not final, decision.

[30] Supra, note 19.

3. Unless registration is accomplished under both the applicable federal statute and the applicable provincial statute, the security may be open to attack from a bona fide purchaser for value without notice,

4. Purchasers should, therefore, search under the provincial statute that relates to security interests and the federal statute that applies to the intellectual property, and

5. In the case of long-term credit arrangements, the registration in the federal intellectual property offices in particular should be updated to reflect newly acquired property.

15.4 GERMANY

Wilhelm J.H. Stahlberg, Esq.
Andreas Ebert-Weidenfeller, Esq.

Boehmert & Boehmert, Nordemann & Partner
Breman, Germany

Unlike its position in common-law countries, the financing of corporate acquisitions and of companies' current credit requirements by special security interests in intangibles has not progressed very far in Germany. This is due in part to certain statutory provisions that make using this kind of security difficult, as well as problems in regard to the proper valuation of the intangibles concerned.

(a) Economically Disposable Corporeal Rights

(i) Protection of Absolute Rights.   Registered trademarks, trademarks that have acquired secondary meaning, and intellectual property rights in the technical and cultural fields create absolute rights in German law, which guarantee exclusive use to their owners and prevent unauthorized use by third parties. These rights also often have economic benefits, which are constitutionally protected under Article 14 of the Basic (Constitutional) Act (*Grundgesetz*).[1]

The following types of intellectual property may, under special statute law, give rise to such rights in Germany:

Commercial Sector
- Technical inventions: patents, utility models (patents of a lesser degree)[2]
- Aesthetic configurations: registered designs (design patents)[3]
- Registered trademarks and trademarks that have acquired secondary meaning in respect to certain goods and/or services within the relevant public circles[4]

Cultural Sector
- Works of literature, science, and art: copyright[5]
- Achievements that do not constitute copyrightable creations (works of photographers, performing artists, producers of sound recording media, broadcasting companies, and compilers of scientific publications): protected performing rights[6]

The difficulty in relying on these "absolute rights" is that they are often considered as not having been "made real", being a prerequisite for making them disposable, and therefore cannot always form a full-fledged basis for lending.

---

[1] Compare, e.g., with respect to trademarks: Federal Constitutional Court (BVerfG), *Gewerblicher Rechtsschutz und Urheberrecht* (GRUR) 773, 778 (1979)—Weinbergsrolle.

[2] Patents Act 1 (PatG), §§ 1 *et seq.*; Utility Models Act (GebrMG) 1 §§ 1 *et seq.*

[3] Registered Designs Act (GeschmMG), §§ 1 *et seq.*

[4] Trademarks Act (WZG), §§ 1 *et seq.*; § 25.

[5] Copyright Act (UrhG), §§ 1 *et seq.*

[6] UrhG §§ 70 *et seq.*

(ii) Significance of Personal Rights.   There is no way of disposing of an absolute right if the basis for lending is purely personal in nature. Only if the substance of the right in question can be regarded exclusively as an intangible is it also suitable as security.

The legal approach as to protected industrial property rights is, therefore, largely unambiguous. Rights acquired in these areas, although of intellectual origin, are considered subjective rights within the control of the proprietor. As the underlying intellectual property has been realized, they largely constitute an incorporeal right. These rights are therefore marketable and are essentially available to be disposed of commercially. The economic function of intellectual property becomes secondary to the personal interests of the owner of the intellectual property whenever the right is used to safeguard the justified personal interests of the intellectual property inventor/author. A personal element enters into protected intellectual property rights in the following cases:

Patents/Utility Models

- The inventor's right[7] protects the personal interests of the inventor to a considerable extent and therefore has strong personal characteristics that cannot be easily separated from the property aspects. The personal rights of the inventor cannot be abandoned or waived and remain with the inventor even after the "pecuniary" part of the invention has been transferred.[8]

- The prospect of the protected right,[9] the patent right,[10] and the utility patent right[11] acquired through application/registration of the invention at the Patent Office are pure incorporeal rights or expectancy (inchoate) rights therein, simply with added personal characteristics, such as acknowledgement of the inventor's repute and inventorship.[12]

Trademarks

Trademark rights were originally regarded as personal rights. As a mark points less to a person than to its origin in a particular business operation,[13] it is considered to be purely an incorporeal right. However, marks may include a personal component insofar as they contain the name of the trader or the trader's reputation is tied sufficiently closely to the mark to be worthy of protection.[14]

Registered Designs

- Before registration, there is, under certain conditions, an expectancy (inchoate) right to registration that still has strong personal characteristics, but does not extend to the right of recognition of the author.

- The protected right acquired through registration is purely an incorporeal one. Personal aspects are reduced to a minimum.

---

[7] Inventor's rights are created by the Inventive Act, PatG, § 6; GebrMG § 13 (3).

[8] Federal Court of Justice (BGH), *GRUR* 583, 585 (1978)—Motorkettensäge; Federal Patent Court (PatG) *GRUR* 234 (1987)—Miterfinder.

[9] Compare PatG § 7; GebrMG § 13 (3).

[10] Creation with publication of grant, PatG § 58.

[11] Creation with entry on the utility patent roll at the Patent Office, GebrMG § 11.

[12] Compare PatG §§ 63 (2) and 37. Abandonment of the inventor's repute is legally ineffective; BGH, *GRUR* 583, 585 (1978)—Motorkettensäge. This is less pronounced in registered designs law.

[13] Compare WZG § 1 (1).

[14] Baumbach/Hefermehl, *Warenzeichenrecht*, Einl. WZG note 27 (12th ed. 1985).

Copyrights

As compared with other rights, the personal component in copyrights is disproportionately greater. This may be attributed to the special position of the author, who has intellectual title to his or her work or achievement, based on the author's creative act. No registration or other type of formality is required to substantiate this type of intellectual property.

German copyright offers strong protection for the personal relationship of the author with his or her work or achievement. Personal rights of particular importance include publication rights, claim to recognition of authorship, right to prevent corruption of the work, prevention of changes, indication of source, and the requirement for the author's consent to the transfer of user rights.[15] Copyright as such is nontransferable, except by inheritance.[16]

However, copyright creates various individual powers that take into account the author's interest in disposal. These include, in particular, reproduction rights, distribution rights, exhibition rights, and publication rights.[17] These rights support the notion that copyright is marketable, so that the author's legal entitlements may to that extent be regarded as incorporeal rights.

(iii) Association with Business Establishment.   Incorporeal rights may be used as a basis for security only if they are not inseparably linked with the business establishment as such.

Under German law, a business establishment (as a whole or as part of a business) cannot form the basis of security, as it is neither a thing nor a right but an embodiment of property. Consequently, only individual chattels and rights that belong to business can form the basis of security.[18]

The result is that, in German law, rights in marks, if tied to a business establishment, cannot be used as a security interest on their own (for such rights based on the Trademarks Act, see the following subsection [c]). Commercial designations protected by competition law[19] and the "firm" (i.e., the trader's name) protected under commercial law[20] are inseparably linked with the business establishment, so that no isolated disposal of these rights is possible. The intention underlying this principle[21] is to prevent the business and its designation from being separated, so that the function of the designation as an indication of origin is maintained.[22]

(b) Relevant Security Interest.   Under German law, suitable means of security in the case of incorporeal rights include the following:

1. The establishment of a contractual pledge (*Pfandrecht*), and
2. The grant of a collateral security in rights by transfer of title (*Sicherungsübereignung*)

In neither case is there any need or opportunity for registration of the security provisions.

---

[15] UrhG §§ 12–14, 34, 39, 62, 63.
[16] UrhG § 25 (2).
[17] UrhG §§ 15 *et seq.*
[18] BGH, *GRUR* 329, 331 (1968)—Der kleine Tierfreund.
[19] Act Against Unfair Competition (UWG), § 16.
[20] Commercial Code (HGB), §§ 17 *et seq.*
[21] Compare HGB § 23.
[22] Baumbach/Duden/Hopt, *Handelsgesetzbuch*, HGB §. 23 note 1 (28th ed. 1989).

(i) Contractual Pledge.   Under German civil law, a contractual pledge may be established, not only on chattels but also on a right. It is created by a legal transaction to which the provisions of the Civil Code apply.[23] The pledge is at all times dependent on the concrete claim that is to be secured and expires simultaneously with it. Any property right can be pledged, provided it is transferable; therefore, corporeal rights can also be pledged.[24] A pledge is secured by the same rules that apply to transfer of the right. The agreement between the creditor and the pledger must include the establishment of the conventional lien, the pledge, and the secured claim. The same form applies to transfers; this means that, for example, a trademark can in principle be pledged without adhering to any particular form. In principle, an older lien has priority over subsequent liens of any kind.

A lien does not automatically extend to income accruing from the pledged right (especially royalties). A separate contractual lien on the claim would be necessary.

(ii) Security Interest by Sicherungsübereignung.   Under German law, the *Sicherungsübereignung*, which corresponds to some extent to the American concept of a chattel mortgage, is a viable instrument to secure receivables through a security interest on chattels. The agreement has, in contract practice, largely superseded the statutory model of security in the form of pledging chattels. This type of agreement can in principle also be applied to incorporeal rights.

The *Sicherungsübereignung* and its underlying safeguard grant of security are not governed by statute. This agreement is dealt with in civil law largely like any other form of ownership. As there is no statutory model contract for this agreement, it is left to the parties concerned to establish the rights and obligations in each case by individual contract.

The absence of any statutory basis, therefore, enables the parties to reconcile their interests appropriately. However, it must be clear to the parties that excessive limitation of the legal position of the debtor may result in avoidance of the relevant clauses and, possibly, even in the nullity of the entire contract through breach of *bonos mores* (public policy).[25]

In general, limits are placed on the parties on the basis of good faith,[26] so that whether a *Sicherungsübereignung* is legally permissible and enforceable must be decided on the merits of each case.

A *Sicherungsübereignung* is structured within the same framework as a transfer of ownership. This means that the same rules apply, especially those relating to form.

The essence of the security is the security agreement on which the transfer is based. This is an agreement under ordinary contract law, which may be freely drafted to suit a particular case. The parties, therefore, have an opportunity to decide on the proposed duration of the transfer of ownership, the underlying security interests, and the secured liabilities. In addition, it is possible for the legal position of the creditor to be fixed in relation to the underlying incorporeal rights.

It is also advisable for the contract to include a contractual obligation to assign receivables resulting from the transfer of the rights (especially royalties) to the proprietor of the security in advance.

---

[23] Civil Code (BGB), §§ 1273 *et seq.*; §§ 1204 *et seq.*
[24] BGB § 1274 (2).
[25] BGB § 138.
[26] BGB § 242.

On termination of the security relationship, the debtor is entitled to retransfer of the collateral.

(c) Security Rights in Intangibles. The following discussion applies in particular to security rights under the contractual pledge and the *Sicherungsübereignung* with regard to individual incorporeal rights.

(i) Patents and Utility Models. Because patents and utility models are especially marketable, the security interests in such properties can be used extensively. The subject of the security may be the inventor's right to the patent, the expectant right to the granting of a patent for an invention already filed at the Patent Office, the rights under a patent,[27] or the rights to a utility model.

In case of doubt between the parties, however, the pledgee is not entitled to use the patented invention or to issue a license.[28]

It is not established practice for a pledge to be entered on the Patent Register at the Patent Office.[29] Transfer in favor of the creditor of a *Sicherungsübereignung* is "a change in the person of the patent proprietor," so that the Patent Office must record the transfer on the Register upon receipt of proof of such a transfer.[30]

(ii) Registered Designs. Because property rights are a strong component of the Registered Designs Act, pledging and *Sicherungsübereignung* for registered designs are possible. These transfers of legal rights are independent of the ownership of possession of the design or model, so that these need not be handed over.[31]

(iii) Trademarks. Until 1992, German trademark law required that a mark be tied to the business establishment. The business had to be indicated on an application to register a trademark, and trademark rights could "pass to another person only with the business or the part of the business to which the trademark belong[ed]." The consequence was that a security interest could only be a part of the associated business that served as the basis for the security together with the mark.[32] Parliament's aim was to prevent trading in trademark rights. Against this background, however, attempts had already been made to take into account the needs of commercial dealing. For example, it was considered that a mark provided adequate, lawful protection if it was registered before the business commenced, provided that the setting up of the business was seriously intended within a reasonable period. The underlying principle was that obtaining a trademark may, in fact, be a condition to raising borrowed capital, so that the mark itself constitutes the essential basis for the formation of the business that requires the borrowed capital.[33]

---

[27] Meurer, "Nießbrauch, Nutznießung und Pfandrecht an Patenten unter Berücksichtigung des internationalen Privatrechts", *Markenschutz und Wettbewerb* 397, 398 (1936); Benkard/Ullmann, *Patentgesetz*, PatG § 15 note 28 (8th ed. 1988).

[28] BGB § 1213 (2); § 1273 (2).

[29] For a different view, see Stöber, *Forderungspfändung*, 859 note 1724 (9th ed. 1990).

[30] Reimer, 1 *Patentgesetz*, PatG § 9, note 20 (1949).

[31] Von Gamm, *Geschmacksmustergesetz*, GeschmMG § 3 note 5 (2d ed. 1989); Nirk/Kurtze, *Geschmacksmustergesetz*, GeschmMG § 3c note 49 (1989).

[32] Higher Regional Court (OLG) Hamm, *GRUR* 697, 698 (1988)—Wz.-Sicherungsübereignung; Busse/Starck, *Warenzeichengesetz*, WZG § 8, note 9 (6th ed. 1990).

[33] Imperial Court (RG), *GRUR* 632, 638 (1939).

The statutory basis for German trademark law changed on May 1, 1992, when the Extension Act became effective,[34] so that greater account might be taken of the trademark proprietor's property interests. The Extension Act for the "new" Federal Republic of Germany not only regulates the reciprocal extension of trademark rights from West Germany (the "old" Federal Republic) and from East Germany (the former German Democratic Republic) and cases of conflict arising between them, but also makes substantial changes intended to remove the tie between a mark and a business.[35] According to § 47 of the Act, the precondition of designating the business when filing the mark no longer applies. Under § 47 (3) 1. of the Act, a mark may pass or be transferred to another person independently of the transfer or passage of the business operation (or, where applicable, the part of the business to which the mark belongs). In case of doubt, however, § 47(3) 1. of the Act provides for the mark to be transferred with the business (or the appropriate part of the business). In the authors' opinion, this change does not mean that the tie between the mark and the business has been entirely abandoned. A particular indication to the contrary is that § 1(1) of the Trademark Act, which lays down the function of a trademark as a distinguishing feature of goods in a *business establishment*, has not been changed. Moreover, according to the explanatory memorandum of Parliament, the present Act is only a halfway house on the road to a comprehensive reshaping of German trademark law in the course of European harmonization.[36]

With regard to the security aspect, the loosening of the tie between the mark and the business does mean that the free transferability of the mark now permits security interests to be established. The mark may therefore be freely pledged without simultaneously specifying an arrangement regarding the business operation. The trademark alone may also be transferred as a basis for a security interest. Consequently, a greater opportunity has recently been created for further security interests in the substance of the business.

In bankruptcy, this may mean that the receiver has even fewer opportunities for disposal, as compared with the situation before the change of law. In many cases, it will no longer be possible to dispose adequately of the remaining property—not curtailed by security interests elsewhere—which frequently comprises only the know-how and the trademarks, if trademarks are charged with independent security interests and can no longer be disposed of.[37]

(iv) Copyright and Ancillary Copyright.   Security interests are not possible in copyrights which are not transferable. However, the user rights of the author, both individually and in their entirety, may be charged with a pledge or transferred as collateral.[38] It should be noted, however, that a user right can be transferred only with the author's consent. One exception to this provision is a transfer as part of a general sale of a business or the sale of parts of a business.[39]

---

[34] Act Concerning the Extension of Protected Industrial Rights (ErstrG) of April 23, 1992 (*BGBl* I, 938).

[35] Memorandum on a Parliamentary Bill for the Extension of Protected Industrial Rights, *GRUR* 760, 765 (1992).

[36] Id., 293/4.

[37] Albrecht calls this an "economically questionable trend": "§ 47 Erstreckungsgesetz—der Beginn des warenzeichenrechtlichen Paradieses?" *GRUR* 660, 663 (1992).

[38] Ulmer, *Urheber- und Verlagsrecht*, 295/6 (2d ed. 1960); Schricker, *Urheberrecht*, Einl. UrhG §§ 28 *et seq.* note 42 (1987).

[39] UrhG § 34.

(d) Disposal of Security Interests

(i) Contractual Pledge. A creditor with a contractual pledge is secure to the extent that the pledged right cannot be affected by a transaction with a third party without the creditor's consent.[40]

Only in the case of a debt transfer,—that is, a change of debtors (with the participation of the same creditor), with the new debtor assuming the identical debt—will the pledge expire simultaneously, even if the new debtor also becomes the legal proprietor of the security interest.[41]

A pledge under a contractual lien may be disposed of if the secured receivable has wholly or partly matured.[42] The statutory framework provides for disposal by forced sale in the absence of an agreement to the contrary.[43] This means that, despite an existing contractual lien, a further enforcement is necessary which gives rise to an "execution lien." Steps toward compulsory disposal are taken by the appropriate court.[44] Disposal of the pledge may result in the sale of the pledge or the appointment of an administrator by the court so that capital can be created, for instance, by issuing licenses in order to avoid a disposal detrimental to the debtor's interest. However, the lender may choose the less cumbersome options of disposal through public auction.[45] It should be noted that any means of disposal other than public sale can be agreed upon only after the secured receivable is due.[46] Furthermore, until the secured receivable matures, there can be no expiry clause providing for title to the lien to pass automatically to the creditor who enforces the lien by means of execution.

(ii) Sicherungsübereignung. With a *Sicherungsübereignung*, it is generally held that the creditor's powers of disposal depend on the underlying agreement, so that the statutory provisions concerning contractual liens are not necessary applicable.[47] Remaining to be finally clarified is the extent to which rules concerning a contractual pledge will apply if the parties have not arrived at an express agreement.

Provided there is no agreement to the contrary, maturity of the security receivable may be assumed if the security is called in. In fact, it does not seem proper to tie the *Sicherungsübereignung* to the rules concerning public auction of a contractual lien; rather, it would be right to permit a so-called private sale by the creditor when a call is made on the security, so that the creditor can obtain satisfaction from the proceeds. Whether it is legally possible under a *Sicherungsübereignung* for forfeiture to be agreed to, so that title would automatically pass to the creditor upon nonpayment of the receivable, is highly debatable. It may be assumed that a forfeiture clause is of very doubtful effect and, consequently, inadvisable.[48]

---

[40] BGB § 1276 (1).

[41] BGB § 418 (1).

[42] BGB § 1273 (2), 1228 (2).

[43] BGB § 1277 (1).

[44] Code of Civil Procedure (ZPO), §§ 828 *et seq.*, 857.

[45] BGB §§ 1233–1239.

[46] BGB §§ 1277 (2), 1245 (2).

[47] Compare Soergel/Mühl, *Bürgerliches Gesetzbuch*, 6 Sachenrecht, BGB § 930 note 59 (12th ed. 1990).

[48] Compare Soergel/Mühl, BGB, § 930 notes 60–62.

A creditor is obliged to undertake disposal with due care and with the least possible damage to the debtor. If the creditor breaches this duty of care and the obligation to safeguard the interests of the debtor, the creditor may be liable for damages to the debtor.

(e) General Assessment and Prospects.   As mentioned at the outset, none of the security interests discussed in this article have been particularly significant in the past, because of practical problems of implementation. Therefore, it is often difficult to establish criteria for valuing the relevant interests. Often they have not been acquired free of charge, nor has the proprietor made any evident valuation of them.[49] It is submitted, however, that the value of the protected right should not be fixed too high, as this would not be in the interests of the capital provider, the other corporate creditors, or the economy as a whole. Although a healthy scepticism appears warranted, this does not mean that a "lending value" cannot be ascribed to intellectual property on market terms in the company's interest, provided the value can be adequately proven.

The uncertainties and difficulties inherent in establishing and disposing of security interests are especially apparent in the case of the pledge, which seems very much forced into the statutory framework. Complexities of pledge disposal, as previously described, and especially the dubiousness of the forfeiture clause, render the pledging of incorporeal rights relatively unsuitable for securing a loan.

However, the theoretical possibilities offered by the *Sicherungsübereignung* give cause for hope. True, there are difficulties here as well, such as the problem of the forfeiture clause. Of note, also, is the copyright principle,[50] whereby the author must participate in disposal of the rights concerned, thereby obliging the disposing company to disclose its situation to the author as well. However, in this case, as there is no statutory straightjacket into which the *Sicherungsübereignung* must be forced, it seems conceivable that imaginative lawyers and business persons might be able to create new forms of disposal.

What is important here, however, is that the contract must take into account the reciprocal positions, including rights of inspection, information, and due diligence. In this connection, virgin territory may therefore be trod, and practice will show to what extent the courts will approve of the contractual and disposal arrangements.

The fact that it will be worth establishing a security interest only if full disposal of the rights (should that become necessary) by the lender is possible, is also an important aspect. It may therefore be necessary, in regard to incorporeal rights, for the lender to sell the rights or dispose of them in some other way. The personal rights of the author, inventor, or bearer of the name may then become a problem, as illustrated earlier.

Competition law could also form a barrier in this connection, namely that under § 3 of the Unfair Competition Act. With a view to ensuring competition, this "small general-purpose clause" in competition law prohibits the publication of misleading information in commercial matters. This aspect could become decisive where protected industrial rights and copyright are to be sold by a creditor. For example, disposal of a trademark could conflict with § 3 of the Unfair Competition Act if certain presumptions as to origin from a quite specific business were associated with a known mark. These assumptions by the public would be deceptive, however, if a completely different company were to apply the mark to its own goods or services. Unlawful deception would occur if the relevant public were to erroneously attach certain quality assumptions to the mark as an indication

---

[49] With regard to trademarks, compare Rohnke, "Bewertung von Warenzeichen beim Unternehmenskauf", 45 *Der Betrieb* 1941 (1992).

[50] UrhG § 34.

of origin. Similar risks are possible in the case of other protected industrial rights as well as copyright, so that consideration must be given in each case to whether disposal may contribute to confusing to the public.

The debate on the disposal of intangible assets that is taking place in the common-law countries is being heard in Germany, and it is not unlikely, therefore, that similar concepts will be adopted in Germany as well, thereby ensuring greater flexibility in raising capital. The changes recently made in the German Trademarks Act through the Extension Act and the changes to come with the new German Trademark Act, which is being discussed presently, are a suitable starting point for an increase in the creation of security interests, facilitating a reorientation conducive to growth of the national economy.

15.5 HUNGARY

Eva Szigeti

Danubia Patent & Trademark Attorneys, Limited
Budapest, Hungary

There is no legislation in Hungary on the subject of security interests in intangible assets. Therefore, this section is based solely on theoretical considerations through interpretation of analogous statutory law.

(a) Creating and Obtaining Security Interest in Intellectual Property.   Section 263(1) of the Civil Code[1] provides that a mortgage can be obtained on rights that are transferable. Thus, because intellectual property rights are transferable, it can be concluded that, in principle, they can be mortgaged. However, a security interest cannot be obtained in the *personality rights* of an author (this is excluded by § 12(2) of the Copyright Act) or an inventor (§ 75(3) of the Civil Code on the prohibition of restricting personality rights).

However, the *pecuniary rights* of an author or inventor can be charged by pledge, although the effects of such a mortgage differ between a mortgage on patents and trademarks on the one hand, and copyrights on the other hand. With respect to a mortgage on patents or trademarks, the interpreting rules of the Patent Act[2] (§ 16 [n]) and of the Trademark Act[3] (§ 7 [k]) provide, with literally identical wording, that "on written request of the entitled, based on a notarial document or deed having the force of evidence . . . all facts or circumstances, having signification to the patent (resp. trademark protection) have to be recorded in the Registry."

The Patent Act provides in § 37(2) that as against a buyer in good faith, rights relating to a patent can be invoked only if these rights are recorded in the Registry. The Trademark Act contains an identical provision in § 23(2). Obviously, if a mortgage relating to a patent or a trademark is recorded in the Registry, a security interest has been obtained.

However, the Copyright Act[4] does not provide for the recording of a copyright. This does not mean that a security interest cannot be obtained in a copyright, but that the owner of security interest must be more cautious. Because copyrights are not registered, he or she could, for example, request the State Copyright Office to take notice of the security interest.

(b) Perfecting a Security Interest.   A useful measure to perfect a security interest is to obtain a notarial document on the mortgage agreement, as provided by § 260(1) of the Civil Code. Such a document would ensure enforcement of the security interest without a court order. Of course, the notarial document would not survive cancellation of the patent or the trademark, or a court decision denying the existence of copyright.

The only reliable "perfecting" measure would, therefore, seem to be a combination of a mortgage and another legal instrument—for example, a bank guarantee, as provided by § 249 of the Civil Code. The author has no doubt that such a double security interest would be considered valid, as both kinds of security are provided by statutory law.

---

[1] Civil Code of 1959, revised (Magyar Törvénytár, 1992).
[2] Trademark Act of 1969 with Rules on implementation (Magyar Törvénytár, 1990).
[3] Copyright Act of 1969, revised (Magyar Törvénytár, 1992).
[4] V. Sziglizsti.

(c) Enforcing Security Interest. As mentioned earlier, if the mortgage agreement is contained in a notarial document, it can be enforced directly, that is, without a court order. However, if the mortgage agreement is contained in an ordinary deed, the holder of the deed must bring an action requesting condemnation of the debtor. As to the nature of the enforcement, the Act on Execution does not provide for judicial action relating to such rights.

Because the Act (§ 79) provides for seizure of accounts receivable, there is no doubt that royalties due to the debtor can also be seized.

The leading commentary[5] on the subject of enforcement, says that all kinds of assets can be seized, including "movables, accounts, titles, rights, e.g., 'copyright.'" However, the commentary does not address the question of whether a right (patent, trademark, or copyright) can be the subject of a judicial action.

Inasmuch as no judicial auction relating to intellectual property has taken place in Hungary in the last 50 years, it is still very much an open question whether, in a given case, enforcement really would be ordered by the Court.

---

[5] V. Szigligeti, Vògrohajtási Lörveny, Budapest, 1969.

15.6 ISRAEL

Neil J. Wilkof, Adv.

Drs. Friedman, Wilkof & Co., Tel Aviv, Israel

Aaron S. Lewin, Adv.

Sanford T. Colb & Co., Jerusalem, Israel

(a) Introduction. Under Israeli law, each of the principal intellectual property rights—patent, trademark, copyright, and design—is governed by a different statute. Each statute defines the conditions under which the particular intellectual property right exists and the means for protecting that right against unauthorized use by third persons.[1]

A review of these statutes reveals that only the Patents Law[2] explicitly refers to a security interest, addressing both the creation and the realization of a security interest in a patent. In the laws governing the other intellectual property rights, no explicit reference to a security interest is made. However, Israel does have a general law pertaining to charges on "property,"[3] and it is presumed that the provisions of this general law apply not only to real and personal property but also to the various forms of intellectual property recognized under Israeli law.

(b) The Pledges Law. The Pledges Law, 5727–1967,[4] is the general statutory basis under Israeli law for the creation of charges on all forms of property. Section 1 of the Pledges Law defines *pledge* as a "charge on property as security for an obligation; it entitles the creditor to recoup himself out of the pledged property if the obligation has not been discharged." "Pledge" in this context is the (unfortunate) official English translation of the Hebrew term *mashkon* and should not be confused with the much narrower American or English usage of the term connoting a charge created by the transfer of movable property to the safekeeping of a creditor or a third party.

The provisions of the Pledges Law apply "where no other law contains special provisions applicable to the matter[5] . . . [and] to every transaction, however designated, the intention of which is to charge property as security for an obligation."[6]

(i) Creation of a Pledge. A pledge is created by agreement between the debtor and the creditor.[7] The Pledges Law does not stipulate that the agreement must be in writing, but a written notice signed by the creator of the pledge is required in order to effect recording of the pledge.[8]

---

[1] See the following subsections for a discussion of each of these rights.

[2] See the discussion of the Patents Law in subsection (c)(i).

[3] The Pledges Law, 5727–1967. See the discussion of this law in the following subsection (b).

[4] *Sefer Chukim*, No. 496, of 11th Nissan 5727 (21 April 1967), p. 48 (hereinafter: The Pledges Law).

[5] The Pledges Law, § 2(a).

[6] Id., § 2(b).

[7] Id., § S. 3(a).

[8] Section 3(a) of the Pledges Regulations (Rules of Procedure and Inspection), 5727–1967, *Kovets Takkanot*, No. 2105 of 13 September 1967, p. 3245 (hereinafter: the Pledges Regulations). Cf. the discussion in subsection (c)(i) concerning § 89 of the Patents Law, which specifically requires a written document for effecting a security interest in a patent.

(ii) Restrictions Applicable to a Pledge. Any restriction applying by law or by agreement to the transfer of ownership of a property will also apply to the pledge of the property.[9]

(iii) Effect of a Pledge. According to § 4(2) of the Pledges Law, a pledge of movable property provides effective security to the creditor against other creditors of the debtor with respect to the pledged property only if the pledged property is deposited with the creditor or with a bailee on behalf of the creditor. According to § 4(1), if there exists a specific law with respect to a form of property, then a pledge of that property will be effective against other creditors upon the fulfilling of the special provisions applicable to the matter contained in the specific law.[10] According to §4(3), in all other cases a pledge of property will be effective against other creditors only upon the registration of the pledge in accordance with regulations promulgated under the Pledges Law.[11]

(iv) The Pledges Register. The Pledges Regulations set up a decentralized registration system with separate registers—Jerusalem, Tel Aviv, Beer Sheva, Haifa, and Nazareth.[12] The recording of a pledge of property belonging to an individual is effected at the register in whose jurisdiction the individual resides, based on the individual's address as recorded on the Population Register of the Ministry of the Interior.[13] If the individual is not listed in the Population Register, recording of the pledge is effected at the Jerusalem District Register.[14] If the debtor is a company, a partnership, or other form of legal entity, its address for purposes of the recording of a pledge is its registered address or its principal place of doing business.[15]

Each register consists of a chronological listing of the recorded pledges, a brief summary of the nature of each pledge, and an alphabetical index of the names of the debtors.[16] There is no central data base of recorded pledges. In view of this fact, a complete search for recorded pledges of a given debtor requires a search of each of the five registers.

The pledge of a registered company or a cooperative society need not be recorded at one of the Registers of Pledges in order to be effective against third parties, pursuant to the Pledges Law.[17] If the pledge of a registered company or a cooperative society is recorded on the registers set up under the Companies Ordinance or the Cooperative Society Ordinance, such recording is deemed to be recording for purposes of § 4(3) of the Pledges Law.[18]

(v) Realizing a Pledge. In principle, a pledge may be realized only by order of the court.[19] This means that the creditor must first lodge an appropriate complaint with the court of

---

[9] The Pledges Law, § 3(b).

[10] One example is the Land Law, 5729–1969, which contains special provisions concerning the creation of a mortgage on real property and the recording of the mortgage on the Land Register.

[11] The Pledges Regulations.

[12] The Pledges Regulations, § 1.

[13] Id., § 3(a) and 4(a).

[14] Id., § 4(b).

[15] Id., § 4(c).

[16] Id., §§ 5 and 6.

[17] Id., § 17A.

[18] Id.

[19] The Pledges Law, § 17, first sentence.

jurisdiction, and only after a judgment has issued on the complaint will the creditor be authorized to realize the pledge by execution of the judgment. However, a pledge that has been registered pursuant to § 4(3) of the Pledges Law may be realized by order of the Chief Execution Officer.[20] This means that the creditor may apply directly to the Chief Execution Officer for realization of the registered pledge, without the need for a court judgment.

(c) Security Interests Under the Specific IP Statutory Schemes. In the following discussion, a brief outline of the various statutory schemes governing each of the principal intellectual property rights is presented, with a focus on three issues particularly pertinent to the subject matter of security interests:

1. Does the specific law governing the intellectual property right provide for the recording of a security interest?
2. What is the effect of such a recording, particularly in view of the provisions of the Pledges Law?
3. In view of the fact that realization of a security interest involves transfer of ownership, does the law in any way restrict the transfer of ownership of the intellectual property right?

(i) Patents. In Israel, patents are governed by the Patents Law, 5727–1967.[21] A patent will be granted for an invention if it is a product or a process, if it is novel and useful, and if it involves an inventive step.[22]

A patent may be singularly or jointly owned.[23] Presumably, each of the joint owners may individually encumber its interest in the patent. Each of the joint owners may transfer its ownership interest in the patent to a third party, without need for the approval of the other owner(s), unless the joint owners otherwise agree and the limitation is recorded on the Patents Register.[24] By analogy, the same requirement would appear to apply as well to the granting of a security interest.

The Patents Law provides explicitly that the owner of a patent may charge its interest in the patent or in the income derived from the patent, in accordance with the provisions of the Pledges Law.[25] However, the Patents Law also contains several special provisions with regard to the creation and realization of a charge on a patent that do not correspond to the provisions of the Pledges Law. This seeming contradiction is resolved by § 2(a) of the Pledges Law, which stipulates that its provisions will apply "where no other law contains special provisions applicable to the matter."[26] Thus, the special provisions of the Patents Law take precedence over the general provisions of the Pledges Law, and to the extent that the Patents Law is silent, the general provisions of the Pledges Law prevail.

The special provisions of the Patents Law include the following:

---

[20] Id., § 17(2).
[21] *Sefer Chukim*, No. 510, of August 17, 1967, p. 48 (hereinafter: the Patents Law).
[22] The Patents Law, § 2.
[23] *Id.*, § 77.
[24] *Id.*, § 80.
[25] *Id.*, § 89.
[26] The Pledges Law, § 2(a).

1. The grant of a security interest must be embodied in a written document.[27]
2. To be effective against a third party, a security interest in a patent must be recorded on the Patents Register within 21 days after the security interest is granted, the security interest being subject to any other right in the patent that was granted and duly recorded before the security interest was created.[28]
3. Realization of a security interest in a patent requires permission of the court.[29]

A grant of a license to exploit a patent that is subject to a charge, other than a floating charge (created by a company on its assets) requires agreement in writing of the secured party.[30]

(ii) Designs. Registered designs are governed by the Patents and Designs Ordinance.[31] This Ordinance was enacted during the period of the British Mandate over Palestine, and at one time governed patents as well as designs. However, with the enactment of the Patents Law in 1967, only those provisions of the Designs Ordinance that refer to the regulation of registered designs remain in effect.[32]

The Designs Ordinance governs the registration of a novel or original industrial design that satisfies the requirement of eye appeal.[33] No explicit reference is made to the creation of a security interest in a registered design.

Recordal of a Security Interest in a Design. Section 3(2) of the Designs Ordinance provides that the Designs Register will contain various information concerning the ownership of the registered design, including assignments, licenses, and "other matters." Section 43(1) further provides that the beneficiary of any interest or benefit in a registered design must register its right on the Designs Register. The recording will be deemed evidence of the interest or beneficiary (although, even in the absence of a recording, a court may apparently, in its discretion, take cognizance of a written document evidencing the grant of the interest or benefit).[34]

It is arguable that a secured party might be deemed to be a beneficiary within the meaning of § 43(1) of the Ordinance. If so, recording of the benefit on the Register would be required. There is no reported court decision on this issue. In the absence of any decision, it is advisable that a party seeking to establish a security interest in a registered design apply for recording of the interest on the Designs Register as well as on the Pledges Register under the provisions of the Pledges Law.

Protection of a Security Interest in a Design. The owner of a registered design is permitted to assign its interest to a third party.[35] As indicated earlier, the Designs

[27] The Patents Law, § 89.
[28] The Patents Law, § 90. However, no recording of the security interest on the Patents Register is required if the security interest has been granted by a company or a cooperative society as part of a floating charge (§ 91). This corresponds with the provisions of § 17A of the Pledges Regulations.
[29] Thus, the abbreviated procedure allowed in connection with charges recorded pursuant to the Pledges Law (realization by order of the Chief Execution Officer) is apparently not available for recorded charges on patents. Section 92 of the Patents Law further provides that the court may grant all relief that is appropriate under the circumstances, including the appointment of a receiver or the issue of an order for the sale of the patent.
[30] The Patents Law, § 91.
[31] Laws of Palestine, vol. 2, p. 1053 (hereinafter: the Designs Ordinance).
[32] There currently is a draft bill that would radically change the design law in Israel.
[33] The Designs Ordinance, § 2.
[34] *Id., § 43(3)*.
[35] *Id.,* § 43(2).

Ordinance provides that a party that has been granted a right in a registered design by way of transfer must record the transfer on the Designs Register.[36] In view of this provision, perfection of a security interest in a design in accordance with the provisions of the Pledges Law will be effected by recording on the Designs Register the transfer of ownership in favor of the secured party.

(iii) Registered Trademarks. The registration of trademarks in Israel is governed by the Trade Marks Ordinance (New Version), 5732–1972.[37] The Trademarks Ordinance, like the Designs Ordinance, is derived from legislation enacted by the British government during the period of the Mandate over Palestine.[38]

The Trademarks Ordinance provides for the registration of trademarks and service marks on the Trademarks Register, after examination and the satisfaction of various requirements regarding registrability. Only registered trademarks are protected under the Trademarks Ordinance.[39]

Memorandum on the Trademarks Register. There is no explicit reference in the Trademarks Ordinance to the recording on the Trademarks Register of a security interest in a registered trademark. However, two sections of the Trademarks Ordinance suggest that some notation or memorandum on the Register in respect to a security interest may be possible.

Subsection 36(a)(4) of the Trademarks Ordinance provides that:

> The Registrar may, on request made in the prescribed manner by the registered proprietor . . . enter in respect of the trade mark any disclaimer or memorandum which does not in any way extend the rights given by the existing registration.[40]

It is arguable that a memorandum indicating that the registered trademark is subject to a security interest may, at the discretion of the Registrar, be entered on the Register. However, there is no reported decision regarding the possibility of entering such a memorandum.

More important, the effect of the recording is uncertain. In view of the provisions of the Pledges Law, it is difficult to imagine that such a memorandum alone would be deemed to put third parties on notice of the fact that a security interest has been granted in the trademark. Moreover, the memorandum would not give the secured party any right to realize its security interest in the trademark. Thus, even if entering a memorandum in respect of a security interest is possible under this section, the practical value of going to the expense and effort of obtaining the recording is questionable.

Limitation as a Condition to Registration. § 18 of the Trademarks Ordinance provides that the Registrar has the power, in accepting an application for registration, to make the registration subject "to such limitations as to mode or place of use or *otherwise* as he may think right to impose" (emphasis added). It is conceivable that a registration could be made subject to the fact of a security interest in the trademark, and that such a limitation

---

[36] *Id.*, § 43(1).

[37] Published in *Dinei Medinat Yisrael (Nusach Chadash,)* No. 26 of the 19th Sivan, 5732 (1 June 1972), p. 511 (hereinafter: the Trademarks Ordinance).

[38] *Palestine Gazette*, No. 843, 1938. Interestingly, the 1938 legislation was enacted the same year that the U.K. Trade-Marks Act of 1938 was passed (1 & 2 Geo. 6, c. 22). The Israeli and the English trademark statutes are, however, quite different in many places in their language and structure.

[39] See, however, the discussion on unregistered trademarks in the following subsection (iv).

[40] This provision is identical to § 34(1)(e) of the U.K. Trade-Marks Act.

could be entered on the Register. Here, as well, however, the question concerning the practical value of the recording on the Trademarks Register of such a limitation can be raised.

Realization of a Security Interest in a Trademark. In the absence of any specific reference in the Trademarks Ordinance to a security interest in a trademark, realization of a security interest in a trademark must be carried out subject to the provisions of the Pledges Law and in accordance with § § 48 and 49 of the Trademarks Ordinance. These sections set out the conditions under which ownership of a trademark may be transferred.

Under the Trademarks Ordinance, a trademark may be assigned by its owner to a third party with or without the transfer of goodwill related to the underlying business.[41] However, the Registrar may refuse to register an assignment if he or she finds that the assignment is likely to deceive the public, or that the assignment would be contrary to the public order.[42] Thus, the assignment of a trademark is not automatic, and the interest of the public must be taken into account.[43]

A pending trademark application may also be assigned as well, subject to the same restrictions that apply to the assignment of a registered trademark.[44]

There is no reported case that defines the standard for rejection of an assignment on the ground of deception or harm to the public order. It is suggested that unless the assignment is a blatant transfer of the trademark right in gross,[45] the assignment will pass muster under the Trademarks Ordinance. It is also suggested that these standards will apply to the realization of a security interest in a trademark.

(iv) Unregistered Trademarks. The Trademarks Ordinance regulates registered trademarks only. However, there also exists a class of marks that are unregistered, either because their proprietors have elected not to seek registration, or because registration under the Trademarks Ordinance has been refused.[46] Such unregistered marks and other trade symbols have been recognized as actionable based upon the tort of passing off under § 59 of the Civil Wrongs Ordinance.[47] Moreover, the right to such unregistered marks has been deemed to be a form of a property right under case law.

A creditor that seeks to create and realize a security interest in an unregistered trademark stands on much more uncertain ground than does a creditor that takes a security interest in a registered trademark. There are two reasons for this: (1) the precise legal status of an unregistered trademark as a property right has not been resolved under Israeli law and; (2) even if an unregistered trademark is recognized as an intellectual property right, the conditions under which it may be transferred are not settled.

Goodwill has been recognized by the Israeli Supreme Court as a protectible property interest.[48] Assuming that an unregistered trademark, as a species of goodwill, is protectible, the question is then raised as to what constitutes a valid assignment of such an unregistered trademark.

---

[41] The Trademarks Ordinance, § 48.

[42] *Id.*

[43] Cf. the provisions of § § 48 and 49, where the public interest looms large, with the right to assign a patent by operation of law under § 82 of the Patents Law.

[44] The Trademarks Ordinance, § 49.

[45] For example, the assignment provides that the assignor will continue to use the mark.

[46] See also the references to unregistered trademarks in § §1 and 58 of the Trademarks Ordinance.

[47] *Dinei Medinat Yisrael (Nusach Chadash)*, No. 10, p. 266.

[48] *Ilan Leibovitch vs. A. and I. Eliyahu Ltd.* R.C.A. 371/89, 44(2) PD 1990, 309.

The assignment of an unregistered trademark (in contrast to a registered trademark) requires the transfer of goodwill. However, it would be risky to rely upon the transfer of goodwill as symbolized by an unregistered trademark alone. Rather, a security interest should also be granted in a portion of the underlying assets related to the mark, to ensure that the secured party can legitimately claim that the goodwill in the mark has also been passed to that party.

(v) Copyright. Copyright in Israel is principally governed by the English Copyright Law of 1911, which was made binding on the Mandate over Palestine in 1924 and still remains in effect.[49] The Copyright Law has been supplemented by the provisions of the so-called Copyright Ordinance, also enacted during the Mandate and amended from time to time thereafter.

Under the Copyright Law, there is no recording system nor any required formalities to establish ownership in the copyright of a work. Copyright exists in any original literary, dramatic, musical, or artistic work, as defined by the Copyright Law.[50]

In most instances, the author of the work is also the first owner of the copyright. The primary exceptions are works created by an employee in the course of his or her employment, a limited class of commissioned works that belong to the commissioning party, and a narrow exception for a journalist's work.[51]

Copyright comprises a bundle of divisible rights, each of which may be separately transferred or otherwise disposed of by the owner of the copyright. It is possible that various rights of the copyright may belong to different persons, with the result that no single person will own all of the copyright in a given work.

Neither the Copyright Act nor the Copyright Ordinance contains any provision regarding the creation and recording of a security interest in a copyright. In the absence of any such provision, it is suggested that the general provisions of the Pledges Law will apply to the creation and recording of a security interest in a copyright.

Realization of a Security Interest in a Copyright. Realization of a security interest in a Copyright will be effected in accordance with the general provisions of the Pledges Law and with reference to the assignment provisions of the Copyright Law.[52]

Because there is no copyright register, the principal requirement of an assignment of copyright is that the assignment be contained in a written document. The assignment document must clearly set forth the copyright that is being transferred. The critical part of a copyright assignment is, therefore, the description of the rights being transferred. It is on the basis of this description that the transfer will be carried out.

It should be carefully noted that copyright in a work differs from any rights in the tangible property in which the copyrighted material is embodied. The assignment of copyright is separate and distinct from any assignment of the tangible property, such as a book or record.

(d) Conditional Assignment. Sometimes a security interest in property is fashioned in the form of a conditional assignment. Such an arrangement provides that the owner of the property right assigns ownership of the right to a third party, typically a lender, upon the condition that ownership will be reassigned to the original owner following the satisfaction

---

[49] Herinafter: the Copyright Law.
[50] The Copyright Law. § 1.
[51] *Id.,* § 5.
[52] *Id.*

of certain financial or other obligations. Until the satisfaction of such an obligation, the assignor continues to use the property right as a licensee.

There is no reported case law in Israel that has ruled on the validity of a conditional assignment of this type in connection with any form of intellectual property. Should a conditional assignment be stated for the purpose of stating a security interest, the following concerns are noted:

1. A conditional assignment, although not labeled a charge, may still be deemed a charge on the property, pursuant to §2(b) of the Pledges Law.[53] If so, recording in accordance with the provisions of the Pledges Law would still be necessary for the assignment to be effective against third parties.

2. An assignment and reassignment must satisfy the general requirements for a valid assignment under the particular law involved.

3. As a precaution, all of the necessary documents to carry out a reassignment should be executed at the outset, including an appropriate power of attorney.

4. A licensing back to the assignor during the pendency of the conditional assignment may have to be recorded on the appropriate register. This is especially likely under the Trade Marks Ordinance, which requires that a licensee be recorded as a registered user and that the terms of the recordal be complied with in order to maintain the validity of the license.[54]

(e) Conclusion.   Israeli law provides for the creation, perfection, and valuation of security interests in intellectual property rights. A greater awareness of the legal mechanisms available should make it easier for parties to make better use of intellectual property rights as a valuable form of security.

---

[53] See the preceding subsection (b)

[54] The Trademarks Ordinance, § 50–52. It should be noted that the Israeli Supreme Court has suggested that quality control may not be the sine qua non of a valid trademark license, provided that use of the mark by the licensee (registered user) is otherwise in accordance with the terms of the registered user registration: *Ampisal Ltd. vs. Ampisal (Israel) Ltd.*, C.A 808/82, 39(4) PD (1985), p. 21.

15.7 ITALY

Domenico de Simone, Esq.
Giovanni Guglielmetti, Esq.

Ing. Barzano & Zanardo S.P.A.
Rome, Italy

(a) **Introduction.** Italian law does not provide special security rights in goods considered to be intellectual property, but treats it no differently from material goods in respect of security rights. Drawing on the several laws governing patents, trademarks, and copyright, it is possible to establish some security rights in intellectual property, the effects of which are governed by the general discipline for material goods. Consequently, the security rights that can be established in intellectual property have substantially the same content and the same discipline as those rights in material goods.

The civil code provides two different security rights in material goods: the right of pledge (Civil Code, Article 2784 *et seq.*,) and the right of mortgage (Civil Code, Article 2808 *et seq.*). The common features of pledge and mortgage rights are that they both vest the creditor with the right to:

1. A preferential claim to the creditor's credit in the charged property over other creditors of the same debtor,[1] and

2. "Follow" the charged property even if the ownership has been assigned to third parties, with the possibility to oppose the security right to the third-party assignee of the property.[2]

Because of this latter feature, the rights of pledge and of mortgage are considered "real rights," that is, rights which persist on the property and can be enforced against all other parties ("absolute rights"), and which, as a consequence, are established only through proper formalities that permit third parties to be aware of the existence of a security right in the property itself.

The right of pledge[3] can be established in the ownership or in other real rights of use, in personal estate, credits, or other rights (Civil Code, Article 2784). For the creditor to be able to act with preferential right in respect to other creditors, it is essential for the pledge to be in writing (Civil Code, Articles 2787, 2800, 2807).

A pledge in a property is established by delivering to the creditor the property or the document conferring the exclusive availability of the property (Civil Code, Article 2786).

---

[1] In the absence of a security right a general rule applies, according to which all unsatisfied creditors have an even right to seek satisfaction through the debtor's property (*par condicio creditorium*). Therefore, the several creditors who are party to the compulsory sale have the right to satisfy themselves through the proceeds of the sale in proportion to their credits, if the proceeds of the sale are not able to satisfy all credits entirely.

[2] In absence of real rights the creditors can ask only for seizure of the goods that belong to the debtor at the moment when the action is filed.

[3] For a discussion of pledges in general, see Rubino-"La responsabilità patrimoniale-Il pegno" in Trattato diritto civile Italiano, Vassalli, Torino, 1956; Gorla - "Del Regno—Delle ipoteche", in Commento al codice civile, Cicu e Messineo, III edition, Bologna - Roma, 1968; Realmonte, "Il pegno" in Trattato diritto privato, Rescigno, vol. 19, Torino 1985.

The debtor may request the restitution of the property only if the debtor has fully discharged its debt (Civil Code, Article 2794). In the event of a default in timely payment, the creditor can—even if the debtor has meanwhile assigned ownership of the property to others—sell the property at public auction, or (depending on the case) in other ways, and satisfy the creditor with preferential right over the proceeds of its sale (Civil Code, Article 2796) or can otherwise ask the court for the pledged property in payment (Civil Code, Article 2798). A pledge is extinguished by the restitution of the property to the debtor, by compulsory sale, by an assignment as payment, or by the destruction of the pledged property.

A pledge in credits is established by delivering to the creditor the document(s) proving the credit; furthermore, in order to acquire a preferential right in respect to other creditors, it is necessary to serve the debtor with an authentic copy of the document (Civil Code, Article 2808). At the due date the creditor must cash the debtor's credit received in pledge and keep the amount owed to the creditor (Civil Code, Articles 2802, 2803). If not fully satisfied, the creditor can request the pledged credit to be assigned to it in payment or that the credit be sold at public auction, or by other ways if necessary, and then satisfy its credit from the proceeds of the sale (Civil Code, Article 2804).

The pledge in rights other than credits is established by following the same formalities provided for their assignment (Civil Code, Article 2806); the written form is essential for the exercise of the creditor's right with preference in respect to other creditors (Civil Code, Articles 2806, 2807). For the redemption of a pledge in credits or in other rights, the charged obligation must be removed, an act must be performed contrary to the establishment of the pledge, a compulsory sale must take place, the pledged property must be assigned to the creditor, or—for whatever cause—the right must be extinguished.

A mortgage right[4] concerns the property and other real rights of use of real estate and other registered personal property (such as motor vehicles, ships, and aircraft) which, like real estate, are registered on public registers (Civil Code, Article 2810).[5] A pledge differs from a mortgage in that the latter is not established by delivering the property, but by entering the charge on public registers. As in the case of a pledge, a mortgagee who is not satisfied has the right to ask for the compulsory sale and to satisfy its credit with preference, in respect to other creditors, over the proceeds of the sale, or by assignment to the mortgagee of the property secured by the mortgage, even if the debtor has meanwhile assigned ownership of the property to third parties (Civil Code, Article 2808). A debtor can cancel the mortgage only after full payment of its debt.

The law provides three different forms of justifying the registration of a mortgage. The first is through the law itself (lien): in the case of sale or division of real estate, a mortgage can be registered on the property as a guarantee for the obligations that originate from these operations on the parties to them. Furthermore, in case of a criminal conviction, a mortgage can be registered on all of the defendant's real estate as a guarantee for the state's credits (Civil Code, Article 2187).

The second way that a mortgage registration can be justified is through a domestic court decision, orders of the domestic courts; an arbitrator's award, enforceable in Italy;

---

[4] For a discussion of mortgage rights in general, see Rubino, "L'ipoteca immobiliare e mobiliare", Milano 1956; Gorla, "Del Regno"; Ravazzoni, "Le ipoteche", in Trattato diritto privato, Rescigno, vol. 20, Torino 1985.

[5] For a discussion of mortgages on personal property, see Ferrara, Jr. "L'ipoteca mobiliare", Roma 1932.

or the decisions of foreign courts made enforceable in Italy, requiring the debtor to pay an amount of money or to comply with other obligations, or which give judgment against the debtor for damages still to be liquidated (judicial mortgage), (Civil Code, Articles 2818–2820).

The third instrument consists of a voluntary written agreement or of a written unilateral statement by the debtor (conventional mortgage).

Liens are registered as a matter of course, whereas judicial and contractually agreed mortgages can be registered at the request of the interested parties (Civil Code, Article 2821).

(b) Patents of Inventions.   The Patent Act (text of the legislation's provisions concerning patents for industrial inventions)[6] provides the possibility to establish security rights in patents only for monetary credits (Article 69). These rights can be regarded as rights of mortgage of registered personal property.[7] According to the general principles discussed in Section(a), the holder of the security in a patent has the right to:

1. Have the charged patent compulsorily sold, even if the debtor has assigned it to third parties, and
2. Be given preference over other creditors to the proceeds of the compulsory sale.

The securities concern only the patrimonial rights vested in the patent, whereas the inventorship right is a moral right and as such cannot be disposed of, even to establish rights of guarantee.

Securities in a patent are established by entering them in the Patents Register held by the Italian Patent and Trade Mark Office.[8] To register a security, the creditor must file an application, enclosing a certified copy (legalized, if foreign) of the instrument empowering it to register the charge. The patent law does not specify which instrument, so it should

---

[6] Royal Decree n. 1127, June 29, 1939, as amended particularly by Presidential Decree n. 338, June 22, 1979.

[7] For a discussion in agreement, see Ferrara, "L'ipoteca mobiliare," p. 315 *et seq.*; Rubino, "L'ipoteca," p. 221; Rubino, "La responsabilità," p. 217; Ascarelli, "Teoria della concorrenza e dei beni immateriali, III edition Milano 1960, p. 665.

Substantially in agreement also are Greco, "I diritti sui beni immateriali", Torino 1948, p. 481 and Greco-Vercellone, "Le invenzioni e i modelli industriali", in "Trattato diritto civile italiano", Vassalli, Torino 1968, p. 279.

Views to the contrary are presented in Gorla, "Del Regno–Delle ipoteche," pp. 24, 138 (considers the guarantee in patents equal to the pledge), and in Corrado, "Opere dell'ingegno-Privative Industriali" in Trattato diritto civile, Grosso e Santoro-Passarelli, Torino 1961, p. 130 (considers it as a privilege right different from pledge and mortgage rights).

Only two published court precedents are known: Supreme Court June 6, 1929, in *Rivista diritto commerciale*, 1929, II p. 449, and Court of Appeal of Bologna, April 4, 1912, in *Rivista diritto commerciale* 1912, II p. 672. Both qualify the guarantee in a patent as a pledge. However, both were rendered under the former laws.

[8] The Italian Patent and Trade Mark Office is the former Central Patent Office, whose appellation has been amended by Law n. 480 of December 4, 1992. The Patents Register has been replaced—according to Presidential Decree n. 540/June 30, 1972—with the collection of the originals of the Letters Patent. Therefore, recordings are materially entered into the Letters Patent held by that office.

be either judicial or contractual.[9] The instrument may therefore be a written agreement between the debtor and the creditor, a debtor's unilateral written statement, a court judgment or equivalent orders, an arbitrator's award, or a foreign court decision enforceable in Italy, ordering the debtor to pay a monetary amount.

The patent law restricts mortgages to guarantees for monetary credits only.[10] If the credit is not expressed in domestic currency, it must be converted into the equivalent domestic amount before the entry application is filed (Article 69). Upon receipt of the entry, the Italian Patent and Trade Mark Office examines the formal regularity of the application and enclosures and proceeds to record the mortgage. The entry date is the date of the application (Article 67).

A security may be recorded on the same patent charged with a security already recorded by other creditors; in that case mortgages are ranked in precedence according to the entry dates. The proceeds of the sale go the creditors in order of entry.

A creditor who has recorded a security in a patent can ask the court to order the assignment or the compulsory sale of the patent if the creditor has obtained an enforceable judgment or other enforceable instruments[11] ordering the debtor to pay, and has served the debtor with such judgment or instrument together with a warning to pay, and 10 days thereafter payment has still not been made (Procedure Code, Article 502). If a different creditor has already instituted proceedings for the same patent, the patent law provides that before the compulsory sale of the patent the acting creditor must notify the other recorded creditors of the attachment order and the decree fixing the date of the sale (Article 73 of the Regulation on patents for industrial invention). This safeguards the right of the recorded creditors to take part in the enforcement procedure and to have preference in the distribution of the proceeds of the compulsory sale of the patent.

The recorded creditor is not authorized to work the invention. Therefore, its use belongs to the debtor and to the debtor's licensees if not otherwise expressly agreed. However, the creditor can have an interest in ensuring that the patent is actually worked, in order to avoid subjecting it to compulsory licensing or to prevent it from lapsing because of failure to work it (according to Article 54 of the Patent Act)[12]; in this case the creditor can institute legal proceedings for an order to the debtor to work out the patent or

---

[9] According to Rubino, "L'ipoteca," p. 222, the title can be based on provisions of the law. Yet, at least for the deeds assigning patent rights and for those dividing patent rights, the law does not provide that the Office must record the mortgage as a matter of course. The possibility remains for the state to record security rights in patents of criminally convicted persons. For those who favor the opinion that a security in a patent is a pledge, this security right can only be established on a voluntary basis.

[10] According to Rubino, "L'ipoteca," p. 223, it is arguable that a security can also be charged for other types of credits.

[11] Article 473 of the Civil Procedure Code states that enforceable titles are (1) sentences and other deeds expressly considered equal thereto, (2) bills of exchange and other titles of credit and other deeds expressly considered equal thereto, (3) deeds received by a notary public or by other public officers, limited to the pecuniary obligations contained therein.

[12] The obligation to work an invention is due within three years after grant or four years after filing, whichever is later. Should the patentee or the patentee's assignee directly, or through licensees, have failed to exploit the invention within the territory of the state, or to have accomplished it to an extent that is severely disproportional with the needs of the country, compulsory nonexclusive licenses may be granted in favor of interested parties having made such a request. However, the European Community (EC) Court Judgment of February 18, 1992, stated that importation into Italy of patented goods from other EC countries should be regarded as tantamount to local working of the patent.

for authorization to the creditor to work it out personally,[13] or, alternatively, for substitution of the guarantee or the immediate payment of the debt.[14] These provisions also apply to the payment of the annual maintenance fees, which are a charge of the debtor or the patent owner (if different from the debtor), but are certainly of direct interest to the creditor as well.

A security is discharged when the entry of the security is canceled from the Patents Register. This is possible if:

1. The creditor agrees by a written and authenticated deed,
2. The cancellation is ordered by a final and binding court decision, or
3. The secured credit has been satisfied.

The expiration or the lapse of the charged patent extinguishes the security.

The advantage of recording securities in pending patent applications is also worthy of note, considering that several years may elapse before a patent is granted.

Patent law does not provide expressly for the possibility of recording securities on pending patent applications. However, the rules state that creditors may obtain the seizure of patents pending so that, mutatis mutandis, the possibility of recording securities on pending applications may be may be inferred.[15] More debatable is the possibility of establishing securities in an invention before a patent application is filed.[16] It might be argued that it is admissible to establish a security in the right to file a patent application, in which case the guarantee should be regarded as a pledge in other rights and must therefore be instituted by a written instrument according to Articles 2806 and 2807 of the Civil Code.[17]

A securities can be established in the consideration owed to the patentee by a licensee. In that case it will be an ordinary security in credits.[18]

(c) Utility Model, Design, and Plant Varieties Patents.   The principles discussed earlier, in respect to patents of inventions, also apply to utility model and design patents,[19] as well as plant varieties patents.[20]

(d) Registered Trade/Service Marks (Trademarks).   Before the recent amendment[21] of the Trademark Law,[22] there was no provision for the possibility of establishing securities in a

---

[13] See Greco, "I diritti sui beni immateriali," p. 481; Rubino, "L'ipoteca," p. 223; Greco-Vercellone, "Le invenzioni," p. 280.

[14] See Gorla, "Del Regno," p. 140.

[15] See Greco-Vercellone, "Le invenzioni," p. 312; also Rubino, "L'ipoteca," p. 221 *et seq.*

[16] Greco-Vercellone, "Le invenzioni," p. 312, excludes it on the ground that it is not possible to hand over a right in such a way as to dispossess the debtor.

[17] See subsection (a).

[18] Rubino, "L'ipoteca," p. 222. See subsection (a). The possibility to establish a security in the proceeds of the exploitation of a creation is expressly provided in the Copyright Law. See section (f).

[19] Presidential Decree n. 1411/August 25, 1940, as amended particularly by Presidential Decree n. 338/June 22, 1979.

[20] Presidential Decree n. 974/August 12, 1975, as amended by Presidential Decree n. 338/June 22, 1979, and Law n. 620/October 14, 1985.

[21] Law Decree n. 480/December 4, 1992, in force as of December 31, 1992.

[22] Royal Decree n. 929/June 21, 1942—EC Directive n. 104/89 of December 21, 1988.

trademark as such. The reason for this was that Italian law did not allow the free assignment of trademarks, but made it compulsory to transfer them together with the business or branch of business connected to them (Trademark Law, § 15, and Civil Code, Article 2573). Securities could, therefore, be established only in the material goods of an enterprise, and the purchase of all the assets of the business implied the transfer of the trademarks to the purchaser, with the exception of trademarks consisting of the seller's name (Civil Code, Article 2573). Since that amendment, used trademarks can now be freely assigned in respect to a part or to the whole of the products for which they are registered (Trademark Law, Article 15) and nonused trademarks can be freely assigned without any attachment at all. Consequently, it is now also possible to record deeds that establish, modify, or extinguish securities in trademarks (Trademark Law, Article 49[1]). The law does not restrict securities in trademarks to monetary credits only (as it does in regard to patents).

Securities in registered trademarks are established by recording them with the Italian Patent and Trade Mark Office, and the procedure is the same as described for patents of inventions. The instruments required to obtain the entry are written agreements between creditors and debtors, unilateral written statements by the debtors, court decisions, or other binding decisions against the debtors.[23] The rights deriving from securities in registered trademarks are the same as acknowledged to the favor of an owner of securities in patents. The creditor, therefore, has no right to use a secured trademark. However, the creditor does have a direct interest to see that the trademark owner or the owner's licensees use the trademark so that it does not lapse for lack of use.[24] Then the creditor may seek the remedies detailed in Section(b), as safeguards for those who have recorded their titles.[25]

The reasons for discharging securities and according to which securities recorded in trademarks can be canceled are those described earlier in respect to patents.[26]

The law does not provide for the entry of securities in filed but not-yet registered trademarks, but, as stated earlier, it may be possible to obtain records of securities before the registrations are granted.[27] In some instances where the law admits a party's right to register a certain trademark,[28] it may be argued that a security can be charged in that right, as described earlier in regard to patents.[29] An ordinary security in credits may be established by using the proceeds to which the trademark owner is entitled from the owner's licensees.[30]

(e) Nonregistered Trademarks and Other Distinctive Signs. The law provides that exclusive rights can be obtained in nonregistered trademarks that are well known nationwide

---

[23] See section (a).

[24] Article 47 of the Law provides a lapse if the trademark is not used for five consecutive years after grant.

[25] See subsection (b).

[26] See subsection (b).

[27] See subsection (b).

[28] For instance, when a sign consists of the portrait of an individual or the name of an individual or of a legal entity that is well known, or consists of a work protected under Copyright Law, or under design or patent laws.

[29] See subsection (b).

[30] See subsection (a) and (b).

(Articles 9 and 17) but does not address the issue as to whether securities can be established in them. Yet because they are not in the Trademark Register, the Trade Mark Office is not authorized to record these securities, and the only available possibility is that of establishing a pledge in them by means of a written agreement[31] registered at the Registry Office and not entered on the Trade Mark Register.

However, it does not appear possible to establish securities in other distinctive signs, such as company names or styles (Civil Code, Article 2563) for individual businesses and commercial names for corporations (Civil Code, Article 2567); this is because these names are inherently additional and connected to the concerns and are not capable of freely circulating separately from them. According to these general principles, real rights to security in the form of a pledge can be established in credits enjoyed by the owners of any distinctive signs against third parties using same with their consent.

(f) Copyright.   Article 111 of the Copyright Law[32] states that the publication rights in an author's work cannot be charged with a pledge, restraint, or attachment where such rights belong personally to the author. This provision aims at protecting the author's personal interests, preventing persons who have not been selected or authorized by the author from deciding on the first publication of a work or from using it in any way.[33] However, securities can be established in an author's patrimonial rights in the publication of a work under copyright. Moreover, securities can be instituted after the patrimonial rights in the work have been assigned to third parties, even if the work has not yet been published by the author.[34] These rights may be transferred either by an assignment of the author's rights, by succession upon the author's death, or by the effect of a legal provision—if any exists—stipulating the direct transfer of the copyright from the author to another person.[35]

The Italian Copyright Law includes the principle of the "independence" of the several exclusive rights to use a work (Article 19), so that the transfer of rights may be partial, in respect to some rights only (e.g., the reproduction right but not the translation or performance rights). In this case securities may be established only in those exclusive rights that have been transferred.[36]

No securities can be established in works whose exploitation rights still vest in the author, even if they have been temporarily given to third parties.[37] Thus, for instance, in

---

[31] See subsection (a).

[32] Law n. 633/April 22, 1941.

[33] Fabiani, "Esecuzione forzata e sequestro delle opere dell'ingegno", Milan, 1958; Greco-Vercellone, "I diritti sulle opere dell'ingegno", Torino 1974, p. 334; Ubertazzi-Ammendola, "Diritto d'autore", in "Digesto" IV ed. Sezione Commerciale vol. IV, Torino 1989, 428.

[34] Fabiani, "Esecuzione," p. 46, and Greco-Vercellone, "Le invenzioni," p. 335. For a view to the contrary, see Piola Caselli, "Codice del diritto d'autore", Torino 1943, p. 537 (until a work is published, the publication right cannot be assigned, and therefore the condition in Article 111 of the Copyright Law would not exist).

[35] See the Copyright Law, Articles 28, 45, 12. Generally speaking, rights in works on commission or created within employment do pertain to the client and 1 employer, respectively.

[36] See Greco-Vercellone, "Le invenzioni," p. 336; Ubertazzi-Ammendola, "Diritto d'autore," p. 428.

[37] Greco-Vercellone, "Le invenzioni," p. 336.

the case of a contract to publish or perform a work, the publisher or the company that organizes the performance does not acquire ownership of the copyright, but only temporary enjoyment. In such cases it is possible to establish securities only in the author's credits originating from the exploitation of the work, according to the general principles of securities in credits.[38] No security is possible in the moral rights of the author.

Pledges in an intellectual work are established by means of a written and authenticated agreement, as provided in general for securities in other rights.[39] Accordingly, a security is also enforceable against third parties who have purchased the rights in a work, which requires proof that purchase was prior to the date of the security.

A charge holder is not authorized to exploit the copyright, and in contrast to the creditor's position as to patents and registered trademarks,[40] the creditor has no interest in the prompt exploitation of the copyright by the owner or by the owner's licensees, because copyright does not lapse for lack of use. A security interest is extinguished when the debt is fully discharged or—if the debtor has not paid—when the copyright has been sold at auction or assigned in payment to the creditor, or when the copyright expires.

(g) Copyright Related Rights. A pledge can be established according to the same terms and formalities as for a copyright and in respect to the rights related to it.[41] This is particularly true for the related right of the producers of gramophone recordings (Article 72 of the Copyright Law) and of the broadcasting radio and television stations (Article 79); for the related rights of artists, performers, and players (Article 80); for the related rights in scripts of scenarists (Article 86); For related rights in photography; (Article 87); and for the related rights in so-called engineering projects (Article 99). It is debatable whether the limit provided in Article 111 of the Copyright Law[42] is also applicable to these related rights. That limit can be excluded for the related rights that the law ascribes directly to subjects other than the authors, such as producers and broadcasting stations.[43] Again, in this instance, moral rights cannot be pledged.[44]

Titles of works such as newspapers, magazines, and the like are protected under Article 110 of the Copyright Law. It is debatable whether a pledge can be established in the rights to such titles. The correct interpretation probably depends on whether the works are single works or periodical publications. In respect to single works, the title is an additional and purely accessory element as opposed to the whole work and so is not capable of being charged by a guarantee right separately from the work itself. For

---

[38] See subsection (a).

[39] See subsection (a).

[40] See subsection (b).

[41] See Fabiani, "Esecuzione,", p. 75 *et seq*.

[42] See subsection (f).

[43] Fabiani, "Esecuzione," p. 92, applies the limit stated in Article 111 only to the related rights of photographers, scenarists, and authors of "engineering projects."

[44] Article 81 of the Copyright Law acknowledges to artists, performers, and players the moral right to oppose forms of use of their representations that may be prejudicial to their honor or reputation.

periodicals, however, the title has a function very similar to that of trademarks, so that the title can be admitted separately from the publication; and consequently there is also the possibility to establish the pledge in the titles per se.

A creditor is not entitled to exploit a work protected by copyright, even in a case of nonworking by the owner of the right. For redemption of the guarantee, the principles of copyright apply.

15.8 JAPAN

Eiichiro Kubota, Esq.

Nakamura & Partners
Tokyo, Japan

(a) Introduction.   Japanese law regarding security interests in intellectual property is not well developed. In Japan, intellectual property has not generally been looked upon as an "asset" valuable for security interests, and even when such intellectual property rights have been viewed as valuable, it has been very difficult to evaluate the worth of such rights. However, with the expansion in Japan of the general concept that intellectual property is an important asset, the use of intellectual property as security will most likely begin to grow. Moreover, because the only assets of some venture business companies are their technology, there is a need for the establishment of security interests in intellectual property in order for such companies to be financed.[1]

Under current Japanese law, a pledge is the only instrument expressly provided for in taking security interests in intellectual property. However, because the official registration fee for a pledge in intellectual property is, as described later, rather expensive, other means of security interests are used more frequently.[2]

This section examines what the law provides and what other possible means exist to obtain a security interest in intellectual property in Japan.

(b) Patents, Utility Models, Designs, and Trademarks

(i) The Pledge[3]

Obtaining a Pledge.   In deciding to make a loan collateralized by intellectual property and to enter into a loan agreement, questions of how to evaluate the intellectual property arise. If the owner has licensed the right and is earning royalty income, the value of such a right may be calculated based on such royalty and the value of the relevant market. However, if the owner has not licensed the right and is the sole user of the right, the creditors will have to judge the value of the right themselves. In the case of patents and other industrial property rights, it is also very difficult to find an expert who is able to evaluate a right. The reason is that in evaluating such a right, many aspects—the validity of the registered right, whether further development is needed to use the right, and whether the right may add value to the product—must be judged at the same time. A total

---

[1] For an overall study on security interests in intellectual property in Japan, see *Chiteki zaisan no kinyu shouhinka ni kansuru chousa kenkyu"* (The research and study on financial marketability of intellectual properties), published by Sangyo Kenkyu-sho (Japan Industrial Policy Research Institute) 1992 (hereafter referred to as JIPRI's report).

[2] The number of pledges (both new and assignment of) registered before the Japanese Patent Office in 1992 was 19 for patents, 2 for utility models, 0 for designs, and 22 for trademarks. Pledges of copyright registered before the Agency for Cultural Affairs is said to be about 1 or 2 each year, and the number is the same for pledged of copyrights on computer programs.

[3] For a study on pledges of patents, see Takashi Hashiba, *Tokkyohou-jou no shichiken ni tsuite* (Pledge under the Patent Law), (1) to (3); Tokkyo-Kanri Vol.20, No. 12, p. 1211, Vol.21, No.6, p. 649, Vol.22, No.10, p. 985, registered before SOFTIC. For a study of pledges made before the Patent Office from 1986 to 1991, see Koichiro Suda, *Chiteki zaisan no kaihatsusha no tachiba kara no jitsurei*, JIPRI's report II.

evaluation cannot be done by a single person. Unfortunately, at present, there are no adequate entities in Japan capable of making such evaluations; however, in some cases lawyers specialized in intellectual property law have been making such evaluations with the information provided by owners, creditors and/or other experts who are more familiar with the relevant market and technology.[4]

In entering into a loan agreement, which usually defines the scope of a pledge, certain matters must be decided: the amount of credit, the intellectual property or properties to be pledged, the term of the loan agreement, and the term of pledge.

Under Japanese law, there are two different types of pledges. One is called *Shichi-ken*, and the other is *Ne-Shichi-ken*.

Although the *Shichi-ken* covers only a specific credit, the *Ne-Shichi-ken* covers credits under a certain category. If the creditor and debtor have an ongoing business relationship, they may decide to make a *Ne-Shichi-ken* that will cover all credits that arise in the course of their transactions. In the *Ne-Shichi-ken*, the limit of the total amount of credits covered must be decided. It is said that the number of registrations of *Ne-Shichi-ken* on industrial properties in Japan is about the same as the number of registrations of *Shichi-ken*.

The debtor and the pledger do not have to be the same person. The credit may be secured by an industrial property held by a person other than the debtor. In such cases, the pledger will not directly owe any debts to the creditor, and its liabilities will be limited to the value of the industrial property that is taken as a pledge.

In many cases, it seems that not just one but many properties are pledged simultaneously under one pledge agreement. This is because industrial property rights may be invalidated under certain circumstances and because the value of such rights may decrease instantaneously when a new invention is made. Therefore, the value of a specific industrial property right pledged is not necessarily stable.

The term of a *Shichi-ken* is limited to 10 years from the date of registration. Thus, even if a term greater than 10 years is agreed upon, the term is deemed to be 10 years (Civil Code, Articles 362 and 360). The date on which the credits of a *Ne-Shichi-ken* become "fixed" may be decided by an agreement between the pledger and the pledgee. Under the Japanese Civil Code, the date that the *Ne-Shichi-ken* becomes fixed must be within five years from the date of registration of the pledge (Civil Code, Articles 362, 361, and 398-6). On such a date, the credits that are outstanding at the time will be the only credits covered by the pledge, and even if there remain other credits payable after the fixed date, such credits will not be covered by the pledge. If the date to "fix" a *Ne-Shichi-ken* is not decided upon by the parties, the pledger may request the pledgee to have the credits fixed after three years from the date of the pledge. Upon the pledger's request, the *Ne-Shichi-ken* will come to an end, and it will cover only the outstanding credits existing after two weeks from the pledger's request (Civil Code, Articles 362, 361, and 398-19). When the date to fix the credits of the *Ne-Shichi-ken* arrives, the *Ne-Shichi-ken* will turn into a right similar to the *Shichi-ken*. Naturally, both in the case of a *Shichi-ken* and of a *Ne-Shichi-ken*, the total term cannot exceed the term of the intellectual property right itself.

Article 95 of the Japanese Patent Law stipulates that "where a patent right or an exclusive or non-exclusive license is the object of a pledge, the pledgee may not work the patented invention except as otherwise provided by contract." Similar stipulations are provided in the Utility Model Law, Article 25 (1), the Design Law, Article 35 (1), and the Trademark Law, Article 34 (1). The purpose of a pledge of industrial property is to let the

---

[4] For arguments on evaluation of intellectual properties, see Yasuyuki Ishii, *Kachi-hyouka no kijun to sono apurouchi* (The standards of evaluation and approach to it). JIPRI's report 144.

pledger benefit from the use of the rights while paying its debts to the creditor. As such, although it is called a "pledge" under Japanese law, this security interest is more like a mortgage.

Registering the Pledge. The grant of a pledge will not become effective unless it is registered with the Japanese Patent Office (Patent Law, Article 98 [1] [iii], Utility Model Law, Article 25 [3], Design Law, Article 35 [3], and Trademark Law 34 [3]). Therefore, the pledgee may not claim any rights to the intellectual property, even if it has a pledge agreement with the pledger, unless the pledge has been registered.

In order to register a pledge, the acknowledgment of the grant of the pledge executed by the pledgee must be submitted to the Japanese Patent Office. The application for registration of the pledge usually must be made in the names of both the pledgee and the pledger, but it may be made in only the pledgee's name with the consent of the pledger. A corporation nationality certificate executed by a notary public will also have to be submitted if the pledgee is a non-Japanese corporation.

The official registration fee for pledges on patents, utility models, designs, and trademarks is 4% of the amount of the credit that is covered by such pledges. In the case of a *Ne-Shichi-ken*, the official registration fee will be 4% of the limit of the total amount of credits (the value of the industrial property that is taken as a pledge). It seems that such expensive registration fees prevent the pledge on intellectual property from being used very often in Japan.

Exercising the Pledge. Article 96 of the Patent Law states as follows:

> A pledge on a patent right or an exclusive or nonexclusive license may be exercised against the remuneration received as consideration for the patent right or the license or against money or goods that the patentee or exclusive licensee would be entitled to receive for the working of the patented invention. However, an attachment order shall be obtained prior to the payment or delivery of the money or property.

To obtain an attachment order, a petition must be filed at a district court. Such attachment orders are seldom applied for under Japanese practice, because it is the purpose of the pledge to let the pledger use the patent and benefit from it. Similar provisions are given in the Utility Model Law, Article 25 (2), the Design Law, Article 35 (2), and the Trademark Law, Article 34 (2).

Compulsory execution of a pledge of patents and other industrial property rights are provided for in Article 167 of the Law of Civil Execution. Pursuant to this Article, the compulsory execution of a pledge of patents will be carried out as in the manner of compulsory execution of credits. The possible methods of compulsory execution are (1) the assignment order, (2) the sale order, (3) the administration order, and (4) "other reasonable means." The district court will decide which order is to be given or what means are to be used. In an assignment order, the court will decide the value of the pledged right and will have the right assigned to the pledgee for that value. Usually, the value of the right will be assessed by lawyers. In a recent case in the Tokyo District Court where a trademark was the subject of a pledge, the procedure to evaluate and assign the trademark right to the pledgee took approximately one year. A sale order is given when the court considers it proper that the pledged right should be sold to a third party. An administration order is given to have the pledged right administered. In this case, the pledgee will continue to receive consideration for the use of such rights while the ownership of the rights remain with the pledgee. Because it is difficult to think of any other "reasonable means, " and because it is also difficult to find a third party who will purchase the pledged rights, the assignment order and the administration order seem most suitable for compulsory execution of pledged industrial property rights.[5]

(ii) Other Security Interests

Johto-Tanpo.　As stated earlier, a pledge is the only security interest that is expressly provided for in law. However, there are other forms of security interests that have developed under Japanese practice, one of them being the *Johto-Tanpo*, which seems to be used more often than the pledge.

A *Johto-Tanpo* is an assignment of the intellectual property that is the subject of the security interest. If intellectual properties, such as patents, are put to a *Johto-Tanpo*, the debtor will assign all of its rights in the patents to the creditor. If the debtor pays all of its debts, the patents will be assigned back to the debtor. However, if the debts cannot be paid in full, the creditor will have the right to hold its rights in the patents. In such *Johto-Tanpo* agreements, it appears that the parties may agree on letting the creditor hold the patent rights whenever the debtor fails to pay its debts, however much remains of the debts.

Under the Japanese Court's precedents,[6] however, the "freedom of contract" is restricted and it is the creditor's obligation to pay the debtor the difference between the amount of the debt remaining and the value of the patent right so that the creditor will not benefit excessively from the *Johto-Tanpo*.

In the case of real estate, a provisional registration of assignment is often used to register a *Johto-Tanpo*. Such provisional registration of assignment can also be used for industrial properties, such as patents to register a *Johto-Tanpo* (Patent Registration Act Article 2 [ii]), but the procedures to convert such provisional registrations into a formal registration of assignment are rather complicated. When the debt is not paid in full by the date agreed upon, the creditor, in order to obtain the rights in the patents, will first have to evaluate the patent rights (such evaluation would be better done by an expert) and then notify the debtor of the amount of difference the creditor has to pay the debtor for the assignment of the patent. Two months after notification, the creditor will have to pay the difference to the debtor. The creditor and debtor will jointly arrange to register the formal assignment after such payment of difference is made.

Considering such complicated procedures, it will be more advantageous for the creditor to have the formal registration of assignment in advance, rather than having a provisional registration of assignment when entering into a *Johto-Tanpo* agreement, if the debtor should agree to such registration.

The official registration fee of assignment is 15,000 yen per right for patents, 9,000 yen per right for utility models and designs, and 30,000 yen per right for trademarks. The official registration fee for provisional registration of assignment is 1,000 yen per right in any of the aforementioned categories.

Assignment with the Right of Redemption.　Another possible means to take security interests in intellectual property is an assignment with the right of redemption. This will also take the form of an assignment of intellectual property, and the debtor will have the option to redeem the rights in the intellectual property before a certain date agreed upon by the parties.

---

[5] See Tadashi Takura, *"Chukai Tokkyohou Joukan,"* p. 818.
[6] The leading case is the ruling of March 25, 1971, of the Supreme Court, *Hanrei Jihou*, No. 625, p. 50.

Although there is little difference between a *Johto-Tanpo* and an assignment with the right of redemption, if the assignment is made for a *Johto-Tanpo* for security interests, the assignor shall pay the assignee the difference between the value of the right assigned and the amount of credit; whereas if the assignment is made simply with the right of redemption, the assignor will not need to pay the assignee any difference.

(c) Copyright

(i) The Pledge

Obtaining the Pledge. In entering into a loan agreement with a copyright as security, the copyright must be evaluated. The creativity and copyrightability of musical works, literary works, art, and cinematographic works may not be so difficult to judge, and the evaluation of copyright on such works may be done by the people in the relevant industries. However, creativity and copyrightability of, for example, a computer program, would be difficult to evaluate and, therefore, would require an expert evaluation.

In entering into a loan agreement and determining the scope of a pledge, certain factors must be decided: the amount of credit, the copyright that will be pledged, the term of the loan agreement, and the term of the pledge.

The creditor and debtor will have to decide whether the pledge should cover only a specific credit or should cover a certain category of credits. If the parties choose to agree on the former, the pledge will be a *Shichi-ken*, and if they choose the latter, the pledge will be a *Ne-Shichi-ken*. The debtor and the pledger (copyright owner) do not have to be the same person. It is also common for the creditor to include more than one copyright in a pledge at one time, in order to increase the stability of the pledge.

There is no limit on the term of a *Shichi-ken* on copyrights, except that the term may not exceed the term of the copyright itself. The date on which the credits of the *Ne-Shichi-ken* become "fixed" can be decided by the parties, but this date must be within five years from the the date of commencement of the pledge. If a date to have the credits fixed is not decided by the parties, then after three years from the date on which the pledge commenced, the pledger may request the pledgee to have the credits fixed. When such a request is made, the credits of the *Ne-Shichi-ken* become fixed and the pledge will cover only the outstanding credits present after two weeks from the date the pledger's request is made.

Article 66 (1) of the Japanese Copyright Law states that "unless otherwise stipulated in the contract establishing the right of pledge, the copyright owner shall exercise the copyright on which the pledge has been established." As in a pledge of industrial property rights, the nature of the pledge of copyright is more like that of a mortgage.

Registering the Pledge. A pledgee cannot claim its rights against third parties if the pledge of a copyright is not registered (Copyright Law, Article 77 [2]). This provision is different from those in regard to the pledges of patents and other industrial rights, because in the case of copyrights the pledge itself will be made effective by an agreement, whereas in the case of other industrial property rights, the pledge will not be effective until it is registered.

An organization called SOFTIC (Software Information Center) is in charge of registration of a pledge of copyrights in the case of computer programs, and the Commissioner of the Agency for Cultural Affairs is in charge of registration of other copyrighted works. In order to register a pledge, the acknowledgment of the grant of pledge executed by the pledgee must be submitted. If a copyright in a work has not been previously registered, a specification of the copyrighted work will also have to be submitted. The specification must include, inter alia, the title, the name and nationality of the creator, the date when and the country where the work was first made public, and the nature and contents of the work. In registering a pledge for computer programs, a copy of the source code or the object code of the program must also be submitted in a microfiche. The application for the registration of the pledge must be made in the names of both the pledgee and the pledger or, if the pledger consents, in the pledgee's name only.

The official registration fee for a pledge on copyright works is 4% of the amount of the credit that is covered by the pledge. In case of a *Ne-Shichi-ken*, the official registration fee will be 4% of the limit of the total amount of credits covered by the pledge.

Exercising the Pledge. Article 66 (2) of the Copyright Law states as follows;

> A pledge on copyright may be exercised against the remuneration received as consideration for the copyright or against money or goods that the copyright owner would be entitled to receive for the use (including the consideration for the establishment of the right of publication) of the copyright. However, an attachment order shall be obtained prior to the payment or delivery of the money or property.

Such an attachment order must be obtained through procedures before the district court, but such procedures are very seldom used.

Compulsory execution of a pledge of copyright is provided under Article 167 of the Law of Civil Execution, and the procedures are the same with other industrial rights (see the preceding subsection [b] [i]). The assignment order and the administration order appear most suitable for compulsory executions of pledges on copyrighted works.

(ii) Other Security Interests

Johto-Tanpo. In copyrights, as well, a *Johto-Tanpo* is used more often than a pledge. A registration of the assignment is not necessary to put into a copyright as *Johto-Tanpo*, but a *Johto-Tanpo* cannot be claimed against a third party if the assignment is not registered. This means that if a third party registers an assignment of the copyright before the assignment for a *Johto-Tanpo* is registered, the *Johto-Tanpo* will have no effect on the copyright. Thus, such registration procedures should be taken in order to secure the Johto-Tanpo. There is no provisional registration of assignment for copyrights.

If the debtor fails to pay its debts, the creditor will be able to hold the rights in the copyright. However, the creditor will have to remit to the debtor the difference between the amount of the debt remaining and the value of the patent right.

Assignment with the Right of Redemption. Assignment under the right of redemption is another means to take a security interest in a copyright. The difference between a *Johto-Tanpo* and an assignment under the right of redemption lies in the fact that in the case of assignment with the right of redemption, the assignor does not have an obligation to pay the difference between the value of the right assigned and the amount of credit.

15.9 KOREA

Soon Yung Cha, Esq.
Yoon Kun Cha, Esq.

S.Y. Cha Patent Office
Seoul, Korea

(a) **Introduction.** The recognition of intellectual property rights, is a recent development in Korea, and the value of such rights has become increasingly important. However,
because the few cases of creating security interests in intellectual property rights have not
been able to prompt active discussion of such interests, there are few theories and
precedents in this regard in Korea.

Korean laws are statute laws, and particular matters of security interests in intellectual
property rights are codified in the respective intellectual property rights laws. Intellectual
property rights are generally treated as property rights in Korea. Accordingly, matters of
security interests in intellectual property rights are interpreted by legislation and practice
in connection with security interests in general property rights, as well as by relevant
legislation in regard to intellectual property rights.

Security interests, which a creditor creates in the property of a debtor or surety on
things (i.e., guarantor for impersonal security) in order to obtain satisfaction of that
creditor's claim in preference to other creditors, are generally provided for in the Korean
Civil Code.

Security interests, classified mainly as pledges and mortgages according to the Civil
Code, include security by assignment of right, which is established by case law.[1] The
objects of a pledge are a movable estate and a property right including a credit and
incorporeal property such as an intellectual property and a copyright, while the objects of
a mortgage are an immovable estate and an immovable real right, namely the property
such as a property which has a means of public notification. This does not assign
possession of an object to a creditor, but gives the creditor the right to obtain preferential
satisfaction. These two security interests are provided for in the Civil Code as to their
creation, effect, enforcement, and other general matters, and they are generally interpreted according to provisions of the Civil Code, as well as some specific provisions of
other laws. A third type of security, assignment of right, which was established earlier
than legal securities, is created in any kind of property, such as movable, immovable,
property rights, and so forth, and delivers ownership of a property from a debtor to a
creditor, on the condition that the object is returned to the debtor when the debtor pays
the debt secured. This type of security interest is interpreted according to the general
practice established by case law.

Korean laws concerned with intellectual property rights are classified within five
categories: Patent Law, Utility Model Law, Design Law, Trademark Law (these four are
called "Industrial Property Rights Law," as a general term), and Copyright Law. Intellectual property rights are protected in the respective relevant laws by classifying them as
patents, utility rights, design rights, trademark rights, and copyrights. The Civil Code
provides that a property right such as intellectual property rights may be the object of a
pledge in Korea in the nature of a security interest.[2] However, because of a distinction

---

[1] Kim Joosoo, *An Introduction to the Civil Code* (Seoul; Samyong Publishing Company, 1986),
p. 339. Kwak Yoonjeek, *Real Right Law* (Seoul; Parkyong Publishing Company, 1993).

[2] See Civil Code, Article 354.

between general property rights and intellectual property rights (i.e., the former is material and the latter is immaterial), the respective intellectual property laws have some particular provisions. Accordingly, specific matters of a pledge as a security interest in an intellectual property right are interpreted according to the relevant provisions in the respective intellectual property right laws. Other general matters are construed according to the Civil Code.

Intellectual property rights form part of a foundation (i.e., the objects of a foundation mortgage which is to include an entire range of business assets, including lands, buildings, intellectual parties, etc.), as assets of enterprise, and may be the object of a mortgage on such a foundation. A mortgage on a foundation is provided by the Factory Foundation Mortgage Law and interpreted according to the general provisions for mortgages in the Civil Code.

In addition, security by assignment of right may be also used for an intellectual property right.

(b) Security Interests Relevant to Intellectual Property Rights.   Although the respective Korean Intellectual Property Rights Laws provide for a pledge as a security interest in each of the various intellectual property rights, there are also provisions concerning general matters of pledges in the Civil Code. This section discusses such general matters, as well as security interests, mortgages, and security by assignment of right, which may be created in intellectual property, as based on the Civil Code, the relevant law, and general practices.

(i) Pledge.   A pledge is a security interest that may indirectly force a debtor (pledger) to pay its debt secured by assigning possession of its object, that is, a right, to a creditor (pledgee), and to let the creditor obtain preferential satisfaction from the property if the debt is not satisfied.[3]

A pledge is created by a contract between parties, a creditor and a pledger, except in some specific cases. Creation of a pledge becomes effective upon delivery of the property pledged to the pledgee.[4] A pledgee may possess the property pledged, which is delivered by the debtor, until the secured debt is satisfied.[5] The retention of a pledge raises the question of whether the pledgee is allowed to use and to take profit from the pledged property. The Civil Code provides that a pledgee may not use and take profit from the pledged property without the pledger's consent.[6] Accordingly, the property right a pledge creates cannot be provided for use, profit taking, or exercise. Therefore, for the property right in which a pledge causes a hindrance to the national economy, the law provides a mortgage system in which the mortgagor holds possession of the property.

It is uncommon to create more than two pledges in a property, because a pledge requires delivery of the property in question. Therefore, it is necessary to limit the scope of the debt secured. A pledge secures a claim for compensation for damages caused by nonperformance of obligation or defect (i.e., product's liability) of the property pledged,

---

[3] See Civil Code, Article 329: "A pledgee of movables is entitled to possess the movables which are furnished as a security of a debt by a debtor or a third party and to obtain satisfaction of his claim in preference to other creditors." See also Civil Code, Article 345: "A property right may be the object of a pledge."

[4] See Civil Code, Article 330.

[5] See Civil Code, Article 335.

[6] See Civil Code, Articles 343, 324, and 355.

as well as the principal obligation, interest, penalty, expenses for execution of the pledge, and maintenance of the pledged property.[7]

A pledge has an effect on the fruits of the pledged property.[8] It may have an effect on the financial or other material benefits that the pledger is entitled to receive by reason of loss, damage, or public requisition of the property.[9] However, such property must be seized before payment or delivery.

If the object of a pledge is a property right, the pledger cannot extinguish the right or change the right in any way that is detrimental to the rights of the pledgee, without the pledgee's consent.[10]

The requirements for execution of a pledge are the existence of a secured claim and a delay in performance. Methods of execution of a pledge are classified according to the property pledged. If the object of the pledge is a material object, official auction is the basic method. If the object is a property right (such as a claim right) other than a material object, the pledge may be executed by direct collection of the claim or by a method provided in the Code of Civil Procedure.[11] This procedure does not require any other final judgment or rights other than the existence of requirements for execution.

A pledgee has not only a right to obtain preferential satisfaction, but also a right to satisfy its claim from the general property of the debtor. If the pledgee's claim is not sufficiently satisfied from the pledged property, it may be satisfied from the other property of the debtor.

(ii) Mortgage. A mortgage is a security interest allowing a creditor to obtain preferential satisfaction from property furnished by a debtor or a third party, that is, surety on property without the delivery of possession of such property.[12]

Like a pledge, a mortgage is created through the formation of contract between parties, except in certain cases. A mortgage is differentiated from a pledge in that possession of the property is retained by the mortgagor. In order to set up a mortgage, registration as a method of public notification is required. A mortgage becomes effective upon its registration.[13]

The significant features of a mortgage include the following:

- A mortgage secures the principal obligation, interest, penalty, and claim for compensation for damages caused by nonperformance of obligation and the expense of execution of the mortgage. These provisions become effective only upon registration.[14]
- A mortgage does not have an effect on the fruits of its subject matter's secured property, inasmuch as the mortgagee has the right to use the mortgaged property.

---

[7] See Civil Code, Article 334: "However, if any special agreement is entered into the contract, such shall govern."

[8] See Civil Code, Article 343: Article 323 shall apply, mutatis mutandis.

[9] See Civil Code, Article 342.

[10] See Civil Code, Article 352.

[11] See Civil Code, Article 354.

[12] See Civil Code, Article 356.

[13] See Civil Code, Article 186.

[14] See Code of Registration of Real Estates, Articles 40 and 143 (obligation provisions for registration of the principal obligation and the interest): It is a popular view that registration is required for the penalty.

- Like a pledge, a mortgage may have an effect on financial or other material returns that the mortgagor is entitled to receive by reason of loss, damage, or public requisition of the mortgaged property.[15]

- Like a pledge, the requirements for execution of a mortgage are the existence of a secured claim and delay of performance. It is not necessary to inform a third person, the purchaser, to obtain the right to own or use the mortgaged property.

- The general method of execution of a mortgage is an official auction. This procedure is provided by virtue of the Auction Law, and the Code of Civil Procedure shall apply, mutatis mutandis. The enforcement of a mortgage requires a document proving the existence of the mortgage.

- By virtue of some Foundation Mortgage Laws,[16] a foundation may become the object of a mortgage.

(iii) Security by Assignment of a Right. As a kind of security interest, security by assignment of a right takes effect upon delivery of ownership of the secured property by a debtor to a creditor, on the condition that ownership of the property is returned to the debtor when the debtor pays the secured debt. There is no provision for such assignment in the Civil Code. However, security by assignment of a right has been established by case law and theory.

According to the popular view and precedents concerning the legal effect of security by assignment of a right, a person entitled to such security obtains ownership of the secured property and has an obligation not to enforce the security interest over the scope of the secured claim.[17] "Scope" means the object execution of a secured claim and the maintenance of the value of a security.

Security by assignment of a right is created through a contract between a creditor and a debtor or a third party. Such a contract becomes effective upon delivery of the secured property to the donor of the security, registration of delivery of the property, or the accomplishment of the requirements for the secured property.

The object of the security may be used by either the creator of the security or by a person entitled to that security. It is usually the creator of the security that uses the secured property.

The requirement for execution is a delay in performance. There are two methods of execution, which are used according to the type of security by assignment of a right. One method is that after sale or evaluation of the subject matter of security, the estimated value is applied to the repayment of an amount with interest added. Also, if there is a difference between the two prices, this difference is returned to a debtor. The other method is to deliver complete ownership of the property to the person entitled to the security. In the latter case, if the value of the property exceeds the total amount of the principal obligation and the interest, the exceeding amount would be considered invalid.[18] If the value is insufficient, it is a general practice not to request the insufficient amount from the debtor.

---

[15] See Civil Code, Article 370: Article 342 shall apply, mutandis mutatis, to Article 370.

[16] See Factory Foundation Mortgage Law, Article 11; Mining Foundation Mortgage Law, Article 5.

[17] Case No. 4287 *Minsang* 124 (May 31, 1955) in the Supreme Court; 66 *DA* 218 (March 6, 1966), the Supreme Court; 74 *DA* 183 (December 10, 1974), the Supreme Court and etc.

[18] Case No. 4294 *Minsang* 112 (May 17, 1962), the Supreme Court.

(c) Security Interests in Intellectual Property Rights. Intellectual property rights, including industrial property rights such as patents, utility rights, design rights, trademarks, and copyrights, are considered as property rights in Korea, and therefore may be the object of a pledge, a kind of security interest, according to the Civil Code. Each of the Intellectual Property Right Laws guarantees creation of a pledge in the respective intellectual property right, provided that there is a distinction in the creation of a pledge between industrial property rights—including patents, utility rights, design rights, and trademarks—and copyrights. A pledge in intellectual property rights is generally interpreted by virtue of the respective Intellectual Property Right Laws. Matters other than those provided for in these laws are interpreted by the relevant laws, such as the Civil Code and the Code of Civil Procedure.

Intellectual property rights may take a part of an enterprise foundation and may be the object of a mortgage created in a foundation. Such a mortgage is operated pursuant to the Civil Code, the Code of Civil Procedure, and the Factory Foundation Mortgage Law. Intellectual property rights may also be the object of a security by assignment of a right.

(i) A Pledge in Industrial Property Rights. Industrial property rights may be the object of a pledge, according to the Civil Code. (Industrial property rights may not be the object of a mortgage alone.) The provisions of a pledge in the respective Industrial Property Right Laws are based on the Civil Code.

A pledge in an industrial property right is created by a contract between the parties, pursuant to the provisions of the respective Industrial Property Right Laws[19] stipulating that a pledge in the industrial property right becomes effective not upon delivery of possession of the secured right, but upon registration of the pledge in the Register of Industrial Property Rights. The reason is that industrial property rights are immaterial rights, such as scientific ideas or goodwill of a business, and their possession cannot be delivered.

To register the creation of a pledge, the pledger and the pledgee must apply for such registration to the Korean Industrial Property Office in a written document. A written application must not only indicate the secured industrial property right and the amount of the secured claim (the value equivalent to the secured claim must be stated in cases other than claims for money) but must also state—if the contract for creating the pledge includes any special requirements, such as whether the pledgee can use the industrial property right pledged, or the scope of the claim secured—those special requirements.[20]

Regarding whether the pledgee is allowed to use the pledged industrial property right, the respective Industrial Property Right Laws (except for the Trademark Law) provide, according to the Civil Code, that the pledgee may not use the industrial property right without the pledger's consent.[21] Even if the pledger consents to the pledgee's use of the pledged industrial property right, the pledgee may not use this right. This is because the possibility exists that the pledgee's use of the right will cause confusion to the consumers regarding the source of the trademark.

In relation to whether the pledger may use the object of a pledge, a pledge in industrial property rights is distinguished from a pledge in movable or general property rights in a

---

[19] See Patent Law, Article 101; Utility Law, Article 29 Design Law, Article 48; Trademark Law, Article 56.

[20] See Patent Law, Article 101; Utility Law, Article 29; Design Law, Article 48; Trademark Law, Article 56.

[21] See Patent Law, Article 121; Utility Law, Article 29; Design Law, Article 56.

claim. In case of a pledge in a movable or a general property right, possession of the object is delivered to the pledgee and the pledger then may not use the object. In the case of a pledge in an industrial property right, the pledger can work or use the object because of the property's character, that is, because it is an immaterial property. Thus, an industrial property right can be used or worked in spite of the creation of a pledge. This characteristic of an industrial property right removes the problem that a pledge in an industrial property right is likely to cause a hindrance to the national economy through nonuse. By the same reasoning, in order to avoid causing a loss in the national economy, if the registrant has worked the industrial property right, such as a patent, utility right, or design right, prior to the creation of a pledge in the right, the registrant is entitled to acquire a legal nonexclusive license even after execution of the pledge.[23] In this case, the registrant will pay a fee equivalent to the nonexclusive license to the pledgee.

A pledge may have an effect on the compensation that the pledger is entitled to receive by reason of public requisition of the right, or money or materials in exchange for a license to work or use the right.[24] But such interests must be attached before payment or delivery, inasmuch as it is difficult to distinguish them from the pledger's general property after payment or delivery.

The pledger cannot abandon the secured right without the pledgee's consent.[25] This is to prevent unexpected damage to the pledgee.

The Industrial Property Laws do not provide for execution of a pledge in the case that a debt is not satisfied. Execution of a pledge is interpreted pursuant to the Civil Code. The popular interpretation, according to the Civil Code, is that a pledge is executed by methods of realization, which are provided for in the Code of Civil Procedure.[26] Realization is affected upon a pledgee's request to the court. The court's realization orders include (1) an order to deliver the secured property right to the pledgee, (2) an order to allow a bailiff to sell the secured right, (3) an order to allow a selected manager to administer the secured right, and (4) other appropriate orders. The court will interrogate the debtor (pledgee) prior to issuing an order.[27]

(ii) A Pledge in a Copyright. A copyright, a kind of intellectual property right, is considered as a property right. Copyright may be the object of a pledge, according to the Civil Code. Copyright comes into existence without registration, and, therefore, a pledge in a copyright becomes effective once a contract between the parties is accomplished. A pledge in a copyright shall not be effective against a third party unless the pledge is registered.[28]

A pledge in a copyright may have an effect on money[29] or materials that the owner of the copyright is entitled to receive in exchange for the use of the object of the copyright or

---

[23] See Patent Law, Article 123; Utility Law, Article 29; Design Law, Article 58.

[24] See Patent Law, Article 123; the Utility Law, Article 29; Design Law, Article 57; Trademark Law, Article 63.

[25] See the Patent Law, Article 119; Utility Law, Article 29; Design Law, Article 54; Trademark Law, Article 60.

[26] Kim Joosoo, *An Introduction to the Civil Code* (Seoul; Samyong Publishing Company, 1986), p.359; Kwak Yoonjeek *Real Right Law* (Seoul; Parkyong Publishing Company, 1993), p.572.

[27] See Code of Civil Procedure, Articles 584 and 574.

[28] See Copyright Law, Article 52, par. 2.

[29] Includes money in exchange for the creation of a publishing right.

the delivery of the copyright.[30] However, these interests must be attached before payment or delivery.

Other matters concerned with pledges in copyright are interpreted pursuant to the Civil Code and the Code of Civil Procedure.

(iii) A Mortgage in Industrial Property Rights. Industrial property rights such as patents, utility rights, design rights, and trademarks may not be the object of a mortgage alone. However, they may be the object of a factory foundation mortgage as a part of factory foundation.[31]

General matters concerning a mortgage are interpreted pursuant to the Civil Code.

(iv) Security by Assignment of a Right in an Intellectual Property Right. Security by assignment of a right may be created in an intellectual property right. Such a security by assignment may be used more easily for an intellectual property right than other security interests, in which it is difficult to value the intellectual property right in creating or executing the pledge. Security by assignment of a right is both an easy procedure and effective.

Security by assignment of a right in an intellectual property right delivers ownership of the right to a creditor on the condition that the right is assigned to the debtor when the debtor pays the secured debt. However, it is general practice that the creator of the security uses the intellectual property secured by assignment.

A security by assignment of the right is created through a contract between a creditor and a debtor or a third party. The contract becomes effective upon registration of delivery of the secured intellectual property right.

Other matters concerning security by assignment of an intellectual property right depend on general practice.

---

[30] See Copyright Law, Article 44.
[31] See Factory Foundation Mortgage Law, Article 11.

15.10 MEXICO

Horacio Rangel-Ortiz, Esq.

Uhthoff, Gomez Vega & Uhthoff
Mexico City, Mexico

In recent years, intellectual property owners in Mexico have shown interest in a subject virtually unexplored in Mexican law, namely, whether companies that intend to borrow money to finance acquisitions are permitted to use trademarks, patents, and copyrights as collateral until the loan is repaid.

The current industrial property law[1] and the copyright law[2] do not expressly address this issue. Nevertheless, the author submits that the absence of express statutory authority allowing a borrower to use its trademarks, patents, and copyrights as collateral for a loan should not be construed as preventing intellectual property owners and banking institutions from engaging in this sort of transaction. This is only one of many subjects not expressly addressed in the industrial property law or in the copyright law. It is therefore appropriate to rely on other codes and on other branches of law for authority for such transactions, rather than simply to assume that they are not viable because the specific code governing copyrights or industrial property rights does not expressly address the issue. If the intellectual property of a borrower is to be used to guarantee a loan, the Mexican civil and commercial law applicable to the transaction should be relied upon.

There is a dearth of literature by Mexican commentators and practitioners on the subject of security interests in intellectual property. The law applicable to guarantees, specifically to loan guarantees, whether in civil or commercial law, was drafted without taking into account the possibility that intellectual property could be used to guarantee an obligation, such as repayment of a loan. Instead, under Mexican law there appear to be two basic forms of guarantees, depending on whether the object given as a guarantee constitutes personal property or real property. The applicable law focuses on tangible property (*bienes muebles,*) akin to "movables" or personal property in U.S. law, and *bienes inmuebles* (real property). Property of an intangible nature, such as intellectual property, is contemplated constructively only in determining the law applicable to the transaction.

(a) Intellectual Property as Personal Property (Bienes Muebles).   As a general proposition, whenever a guarantee is represented by personal property, the appropriate guarantee will be in the form of a pledge (*prenda*). If, however, the guarantee constitutes real property, the guarantee most commonly used is a mortgage (*hipoteca*).

Under Articles 759 and 752 of the Civil Code for the Federal District for state matters and for the Mexican Republic for federal matters—hereafter the Civil Code—when property does not qualify as real estate either by reason of the nature of the subject matter or because the law expressly disqualifies it as real estate, then the subject matter should be regarded as personal property. Because by their nature trademarks and patents may not be regarded as real property and there is no specific provision establishing that they are to

---

[1] *Diario Oficial*, June 27, 1991.

[2] *Diario Oficial*, December 21, 1963. The last amendment was published in *Diario Oficial*, July 17, 1991.

be regarded as real property, it follows that trademarks and patents are to be regarded as personal property.

Unlike the situation with regard to trademarks and patents, the Civil Code expressly provides that copyrights are to be regarded as *bienes muebles*, that is, as movables or personal property (Civil Code), Article 758.

It follows, therefore, that whenever intellectual property is the basis for a guarantee, such intellectual property is to be regarded as a movable, or personal, property, and thereby subject to a pledge.

Under Mexican law, pledges are governed by either civil law (e.g., Civil Code, Article 2859) or commercial law (e.g., General Law on Credit Instruments and Transactions [GLCIT]), depending on a number of issues, which are not discussed here in detail. Suffice it to say that among the criteria used to determine whether civil or commercial law applies, a pledge as a rule will be treated as supplementary to the main transaction, namely, the loan. Loan transactions may be governed by either civil or commercial law. If it appears that the law applicable to the main transaction is civil, then civil law will apply to the pledge as well. A similar proposition is applicable if commercial law applies to the main transaction, in which case commercial law will apply to the transaction whereby the pledge is created.

Among the criteria that have been used to establish whether civil or commercial law applies to the main transaction, are the following:

- The loan will be regarded as having been made for commercial purposes, and thereby as being governed by commercial law, when the transaction takes place among business persons, traders, or merchants (*comerciantes*). In these circumstances, the commercial purpose of the loan will be assumed unless otherwise established by the parties (Code of Commerce, Article 358).[3]
- The loan will also be regarded as having been made for commercial purposes whenever the lender and borrower agree that the loan was made for such purpose and not for other than commercial purposes. Again, in these cases the loan is governed by commercial law.

This discussion focuses on the commercial approach rather than the civil approach.[4] Among the various forms in which a pledge may be created pursuant to commercial law (GLCIT, Article 334), there are two that are worthy of mention here: (1) pledges created through the delivery of the subject matter being pledged and (2) pledges created through the recording of documents supporting the pledge at a Public Registry.

(b) Pledges Created Through Delivery of the Subject Matter Pledged. Questions have been raised as to whether pledges on intellectual property necessarily imply an assignment of the patent, trademark, or copyright involved from the borrower to the lender or, indeed, whether the transaction may take place at all without such an assignment. These questions

---

[3] See Ramón Sanchez Medal, *De Los Contratos Civiles*, (México, 1988) p. 220.

[4] A civil pledge differs from a commercial pledge not only in the formalities inherent in the completion of the transaction, but also in regard to some of the effects that follow the adoption of one approach or the other. See Sanchez Medal, *De Los Contratos Civiles*, p. 470; José María Abascal Zamora, "La Prenda Mercantil," *Diccionario Jurídico Mexicano*, T. VII (Unam, México, 1984), p. 177; Miguel Angel Zamora y Valencia, *Contratos Civiles* (México, 1981), p. 179; Jorge Barrera Graf, *Tradato de Derecho Mercantil* (México, 1957), pp. 11, 137.

have arisen not only as a result of business concerns, but also as a consequence of legal distinctions inherent in the delivery of the subject matter being pledged.

(c) Actual Delivery and Juridical Delivery.   In dealing with pledges, the law distinguishes between the actual delivery of the subject matter being pledged and the juridical delivery thereof. In the first case, the property so pledged is actually placed in the lender's hands or at the disposal of the lender, who is compelled to give it back to the borrower once the borrower's obligation has been met (by payment of the loan).

The delivery of the subject matter being pledged is deemed juridical rather than actual when the borrower keeps the pledged property, but acts as a custodian appointed by the lender. Under the juridical delivery scheme, it is assumed as a matter of law that the subject matter being pledged has been delivered to the lender, even though the pledged property actually remains in the hands of the borrower.

All indications are that when the relevant provisions were drafted, the Mexican legislature did not have in mind intangible property (such as intellectual property) as conceivable subject matter to be pledged, but rather only tangible property. This is perhaps confirmed by a Superior Court decision holding that in commercial pledges the delivery may not be of a juridical nature. Instead, according to the decision, in commercial pledges—as distinguished from civil pledges—the delivery of the property so pledged must be an actual delivery.[5]

Because of the intangible nature of intellectual property, it is difficult to establish its actual delivery. However, actual delivery could take place by assigning to the lender the borrower's intellectual property being pledged so that the lender would become the assignee of the intellectual property, which would be assigned back to the borrower once the borrower's obligations under the agreement are discharged.

The following are some of the features of actual delivery of intellectual property:

1. The lender is allowed to make use of the subject matter being pledged—and assigned—that is, to use the intellectual property so pledged. (The question of whether this permits an agreement to the contrary is not very clear in the law. See GLCIT, Article 338.)

2. Unless otherwise agreed by the borrower and the lender, the profits and benefits deriving from the use of the subject matter being pledged must be applied against the borrower's debt (GLCIT, Article 338).

3. The lender is under an obligation to take all steps to maintain the subject matter being pledged (for example, proof of use, renewal of the trademark registration, annuity payments, etc.).

4. Costs for the maintenance steps referred to in item 3 are borne by the borrower.

5. Agreements establishing that the lender shall not be responsible for the due maintenance of the subject matter being pledged and delivered are null and void (GLCIT, Article 338.)

If under the actual delivery scheme the borrower is to continue using, for example, a trademark supporting the pledge, the borrower should be licensed back and recorded as a

---

[5] See Oscar Torres, SJF, *Quinta Epocha*, T. LXIII, p. 943; see also AD 475/56, Banco Commercial Mexicano, S.A., Tercera Sala, *Boletín de Informacion Judicial* (Mexico, 1956), p. 671; Abascal Zamora, *Prenda Mercantil*, p. 178.

licensee. If royalties are to be paid from the borrower-licensee to the lender-licensor, such royalties would have to be applied to reduce the principal and/or interest payable under the transaction, unless otherwise established by the parties (GLCIT, Article 338). (Conceivably, the parties could enter into a royalty-free license as well.)

Likewise, under the actual delivery approach, if the trademark is not licensed back to the borrower, but rather to a third party, the royalties obtained by the lender in exchange for the license or any other benefits or profits made by the lender from the use (as a trademark or otherwise) of the pledged mark would have to be applied against the borrower's debt, unless the parties agree otherwise (GLCIT, Article 338).

It has been suggested that the actual delivery approach could be challenged in favor of the juridical delivery approach in transactions involving pledged trademarks. Acknowledging that there is precedential authority to the contrary, at least in theory, it is conceivable to challenge this approach on the basis that when the Supreme Court decision was rendered, intangible property was not at issue. Yet, again, in attempting to challenge the Supreme Court decision, the fact that the rules derived from the text of GLCIT, Article 338—to the effect that the lender be responsible for exercising the rights inherent in the subject matter being pledged—are for maintaining the subject matter, as well as the fact that agreements to the contrary are null and void, should also be taken into consideration. How could the lender be responsible for the obligations referred to in GLCIT, Article 338, if the subject matter being pledged is not actually transferred to the lender?

(d) Delivery Requirement Not Regarded as Assignment of Ownership.   The delivery of the subject matter being pledged should not be regarded as an assignment of ownership, but rather as an assignment representing the delivery requirement mandated by GLCIT, Article 334, whenever the parties decide to follow this approach. The nature of this assignment should be clearly set forth in the corresponding papers in completing the transaction, so as to avoid actual or apparent contradictions that may arise as a result of the adoption of this approach.

Because of the absence of statutory authority or commentary on the subject, a good deal of controversy is likely to surround the topic of the *delivery of intangible goods*, particularly in regard to determining the circumstances under which an *actual delivery* vis à vis a *juridical delivery* takes place, so as to conform to some of the criteria that have governed the delivery of the subject matter being pledged in commercial law.

(e) Pledges Created Through the Recording of Documents.   The basis for the alternative to the delivery approach—whether actual or juridical—is found in the provisions governing pledges under commercial law, notably GLCIT, Article 334. There, in addition to the possibility that a pledge can be created through the delivery of the subject matter being pledged (GLCIT, Article 334-I), it is also provided that a pledge can be created upon recording of the documents attesting the corresponding engagement at the Registry issuing the title being pledged (GLCIT, Article 334-III).

As noted earlier, none of the provisions presently governing the creation of pledges was drafted with the idea that intellectual property would be pledged. It thus follows that when the corresponding provision (GLCIT, Article 334) stipulated that a pledge arises upon filing of the corresponding documents at the Registry issuing the title supporting the pledge, such provision did not intend to refer to intellectual property titles, such as a trademark registration, letters patent, or a copyright registration. Instead, it seems that the reference to the "title"[6] in GLCIT, Article 334, contemplated monetary and credit instruments such as those governed by the commercial statute that contains this provision.

In spite of this situation, and given the present state of the law, it is submitted that in the absence of express provisions addressing the question under consideration, the parties may legitimately rely on the aforementioned provisions to create a pledge on a patent, a trademark, or a copyright, by recording the pledge at the Registry issuing the letters patent, the trademark registration, or the copyright registration. To reiterate, it is not necessary to deliver the subject matter being pledged under the two approaches referred to earlier. Instead, it is submitted that Mexican law, in general, and commercial law, specifically, provide sufficient means to support the creation of a valid pledge on intellectual property by the recording of the documents attesting to the engagement in question with the corresponding Registry, even if no delivery takes place, in the same way that pledges that do not involve intellectual property are created.

(f) Title to Collateral.   The discussion thus far has focused on the legal basis for the creation of a pledge in circumstances where the subject matter being pledged is not delivered, and therefore not assigned, to the lender. However, even in cases where the subject matter being pledged is delivered—whether by actual or juridical delivery—to the lender, there is no basis to assert that such delivery implies a transfer of an ownership interest to the lender. That is, title to the collateral does not pass to the lender. Only in the event of the borrower's subsequent failure to repay may the collateral be possessed, owned, and sold by the lender to reimburse the loan.[7]

(g) Procedural Issues Regarding Pledges on Intellectual Property.   In most cases, in order for a pledge to be effective against third parties, it should be recorded at the Commercial Public Registry in the corresponding commercial file. In other cases, the recording of a pledge at the Public Registry is not only a requirement for it to be effective against third parties, but also a condition precedent to the creation of the pledge itself (GLCIT, Article 344). In either case, the problem with this recording is that unless the intellectual property owner is a Mexican company (the borrower), there will generally not be a commercial file where the transaction—the pledge on the borrower's assets—can be recorded.

Furthermore, since in as much as the primary purpose of the recording at the Registry is to provide notice to third parties,[8] this purpose would not be met by recording at the Commercial Public Registry, because, as a rule, no third party would go to the Commercial Public Registry to check on the status of a patent or registered trademark and the questions related to it (concerning, e.g., a pledge), but rather to the public records of the Patent and Trademark Registry, which is administered by the Patent and Trademark Office. This is also true in the case of copyrights.

The idea that pledges on patents, registered trademarks, and copyrights are to be recorded at the Patent and Trademark Registry or at the Copyright Registry, and not at

---

[6] And the recording of the papers related to the pledge at the Registry issuing the title supporting the pledge.

[7] See GLCIT, Article 344. In regard to the situation in other countries, see Melvin Simensky, "The New Role of Intellectual Property in Commercial Transactions," *Trademark World* (July/August 1992): p. 30. See also Ian Jay Kaufman, Melvin Simensky, and Lanning G. Bryer, "The Sequel International Laws on Security Interests in Intellectual Property," *Trademark World*, (July/August 1991): p. 30; and *Trademark World*, (February 1991): p. 35.

[8] See, e.g., José de Jesús Lopez Monroy, "Prenda," *Diccionario Jurídico Mexicano*, T. VII (Unam, México, 1984) p. 175.

the Commercial Public Registry, finds support in GLCIT, Article 334-III, which provides i.a. that a pledge takes place when a recording to that effect is made at the Registry issuing the corresponding title. Acknowledging that GLCIT, Article 334-III, does not refer specifically to patents, trademarks, or copyrights, it is submitted that this authority may still be relied upon for the proposition that the recording of the pledge is to be made at the Patent and Trademark Registry or at the Copyright Registry, because it was the Patent and Trademark Registry (Patent and Trademark Office) and the Copyright Registry (Copyright Office) that issued the corresponding certificate.

Because the Patent and Trademark Office and the Copyright Office have among their normal functions the maintenance of a public Registry regarding patents, registered trademarks, and copyrights, it is also submitted that the requirement of recording the pledge at the Commercial Public Registry should be waived in favor of the recording of the pledge at the Patent and Trademark Registry and at the Copyright Registry.[9]

(h) The Lender as Legal Owner. It should be noted that in attempting to enforce the pledge agreement, the lender may not become the legal owner of the subject matter being pledged, unless the borrower has expressly consented thereto in writing and after the pledge has been created (GLCIT, Article 344). Because a borrower in default is extremely unlikely to execute a document of this nature once the borrower has learned of the lender's intention to enforce the pledge agreement, lender's counsel should take care to secure the corresponding consent immediately after execution of the agreement creating the pledge.

(i) Conclusion. The observations on intellectual property in Mexico presented here should be scrutinized in light of actual facts and circumstances. In actually implementing a pledge, a number of technicalities and formalities inherent to their validity are to be observed and reflected in the contract and related documents (e.g., the transaction must be in writing, the subject matter being pledged must be determined and specified, the transaction and related documents should be reduced to a public deed with a notary public, and so on). Furthermore, in implementing a pledge it is recommended that the matter be handled not only by intellectual property specialists but jointly with corporate law specialists who are often more familiar with the law and practice applicable to pledges of property generally, including the technicalities and formalities relative to the implementation of this type of transaction.

---

[9] In support of this proposition, there is at least one authority who has expressly stated that pledges on industrial property rights may be recorded at the Trademark Office under the provisions governing assignments and transfers in the abrogated Law on Inventions and Marks of 1975 (LIM, Article 142). See Arturo Diaz Bravo, *Contratos Mercantiles*, (México, 1983). See also Abascal Zamora, "La Prenda Mercantil," p. 180.

15.11 TAIWAN

Kwan-Tao Li, Esq.
Daisy Wang, Esq.
C. T. Chang, Esq.
C. W. Ting, Esq.
Julia Ho

Lee and Li
Taipei, Taiwan, Republic of China

(a) Background.   In current practice in Taiwan, the creation of a pledge on intellectual property rights is occasionally used as a security interest. The pledge agreement must set forth the rights and duties of the pledger and the pledgee. However, there are still problems with the recordation of a pledge agreement with the Patent Office.

According to the Copyright Law of the Republic of China (ROC), it is possible to create a pledge on a copyright. In addition, the pledge agreement can be recorded with the Copyright Office so that it may have *locus standi* against a third party.

According to the ROC Patent Law, a pledge can be created on a granted patent, but is silent as to the creation of a pledge on patent applications. Although a pledge agreement concerning the creation of a pledge on patent application(s) is valid as being in accordance with Article 900 of the ROC Civil Code, the Patent Office does not provide for the recordation of such an agreement.

According to Article 30 of the ROC Trademark Law, the right of exclusive use of a trademark can be the subject of a pledge. The creation, change, or extinguishment of a pledge should be recorded with the Trademark Office.

(b) Copyright

(i) Summary of the Copyright Law.   The ROC Copyright Law came into effect on June 12, 1992. ROC nationals are entitled to copyright upon completion[1] of oral and literary works, musical works, dramatic and choreographic works, artistic works, photographic works, pictorial works, audiovisual works, sound recordings, architectural works, and computer programs.[2]

Copyrights are divided into moral rights and economic rights to a work. The moral rights are exclusive to the author of a work, are unassignable and noninheritable,[3] and include rights of the author to (1) release his or her work,[4] (2) indicate his or her real name or alias, or not to indicate his or her name on the original or reproduction of a work or at the time of releasing the work,[5] and (3) maintain the integrity of the contents, form, and title of the work.[6] The economic rights in a work, also exclusive to the author, include

---

[1] ROC Copyright Law, Article 13.
[2] Id., Article 5.
[3] Id., Article 21.
[4] Id., Article 15.
[5] Id., Article 16.
[6] Id., Article 17.

rights to (1) reproduce the work, (2) publicly recite an oral and/or literary work, (3) publicly broadcast a work, (4) publicly present an audiovisual work, (5) publicly perform an oral and/or literary work, musical work, or dramatic and/or choreographic work, (6) publicly exhibit the original of an artistic work or photographic work that has not been published, (7) adapt a work to create a derivative work or to edit a work to create a compilation, and (8) lease a work to others.[7]

Pursuant to the ROC Copyright Law, assignment of economic rights; restriction of disposal and exclusive license of economic rights; and creation, assignment, alteration, extinguishment, or restriction of disposal of a pledge of economic rights should be duly recorded; otherwise, no claim concerning the same can be raised as a defense against third parties.[8]

Works of a foreign national conforming to any of the following conditions are entitled to copyright protection under the ROC Copyright Law, unless otherwise provided in a treaty or agreement that has been approved by a resolution of the Legislative Yuan[9]:

1. Where a work is first published in the territory of the Republic of China or in a place outside the territory of the Republic of China and published simultaneously in the territory of the Republic of China within 30 days thereafter, provided that it has been duly verified, the work of an ROC national is entitled to the same protection under similar conditions in the home country of the said foreign national.

2. Where, according to a treaty, agreement, laws, regulations, or customary practices in his or her home country, a work produced by an ROC national is entitled to copyright protection in that country.

(ii) Pledge of Economic Rights to a Work.   An exclusive property right to a work is a reward and an incentive for an author to create a new work; thus, the modern concept of intellectual property rights is to let an intellectual property right claimant enjoy the broadest economic benefit of the created work.

The ROC Civil Code recognizes that a transferable claim and other rights may be the object of a pledge.[10] Because economic rights to a work may be assigned, in whole or in part, to another person, or owned by co-owners,[11] an economic right to a work can be the object of a pledge. A pledge of economic rights to a work is obtained by execution of a Copyright Security Agreement or a Covenant of Pledge to a Work by the creditor and debtor (the claimant of economic rights to a work).

(c) Trademarks

(i) Summary of the Trademark Law.   Trademark protection in the ROC is obtained by registration. The ROC Trademark Law adopts the "first to file" principle and stipulates that any person who desires to introduce a trademark for exclusive use to distinguish the

---

[7] Id., Articles 22–29.
[8] Id., Article 75.
[9] Id., Article 4.
[10] ROC Civil Code, Article 900: "A transferable claim and other rights may be the object of a pledge."
[11] ROC Copyright Law, Article 36, par. 1.

goods that person deals in within the scope of his or her business, and intends to use that trademark, will apply for registration of the trademark.[12]

In addition to trademarks, the ROC Trademark Law also protects service marks, certification marks, and collective marks. The provisions for trademarks are also applicable, mutatis mutandis, to the registration and protection of these three categories of marks.[13]

Under the ROC Trademark Law, a service mark is one that is used to distinguish services; a certification mark is one that is used to certify the characteristics, quality, precision, or other features of another person's goods or services; and a collective mark is one that is used to distinguish the organization or membership of a business association, club, social organization, or any other group.[14]

After being approved for registration by the Trademark Office, the mark will be published in the official *Trademark Gazette* for opposition by any party. If no opposition is filed within three months following its publication or the opposition is finally dismissed, the mark will mature to registration for a period of ten years,[15] which is renewable for similar periods through filing an application within one year prior to the expiration date of the registration,[16] accompanied with evidence of use dated within the period of three years prior to the filing of the renewal application.

A trademark application or registration is assignable, and before completion of recordation of the assignment with the Trademark Office, no claim in connection with the trademark can be cited as a defense against third parties.[17]

(ii) Pledge on a Trademark Right.   The ROC Trademark Law provides that the right of exclusive use of a trademark is an object of a pledge.[18] Because a trademark right refers to an intangible asset, in order to avoid prejudice to third parties it is stipulated further in the Trademark Law that the creation of a pledge on a trademark and the alteration and/or extinguishment of the pledge will be registered with the Trademark Office for the purpose of giving public notice.[19]

After registration of a pledge with the Trademark Office, the pledgee may not make use of the trademark unless otherwise licensed by the owner of the right of exclusive use of the trademark.[20]

(d) Patents

(i) Summary of the Patent Law.   The ROC Patent Law was last amended on December 28, 1993, and the amended Patent Law took effect on January 23, 1994. There are three categories of patents in the ROC, namely, inventions, new utility models, and new design patents.[21] A patent right takes effect from the publication date and endures for a period of 20, 12, and 10 years, respectively, from the filing date of an invention, a new utility model,

---

[12] ROC Trademark Law, Article 2.

[13] Id., Article 77.

[14] Id., Articles 72–1, 73–1, and 74.

[15] Id., Articles 41 and 24.

[16] Id., Article 25–1.

[17] tId., Article 28.

[18] Id., Article 30–1.

[19] Id., Article 30–1.

[20] Id., Article 30–2.

[21] ROC Patent Law, Article 2.

and a new design patent. It is feasible to obtain a patent term extension for pharmaceutical and agrichemical patents under special circumstances.[22]

The ROC patent system is based on the principles of "first to file"[23] and "absolute novelty.[24] According to the Patent Law, priority can be claimed on reciprocity basis.[25] Because the ROC is not a signatory to any international treaty or convention concerning patent matters, the reciprocal basis required for claiming priority may be formed if a foreign country provides reciprocal treatment to ROC nationals. There is no "laying-open" practice in the ROC, a patent application will be published in the *Patent Gazette* only after it has been approved through substantive examination. A patent application is forwarded to an examiner(s) for review and decision automatically, once the filing procedure is completed. The application will be published in the *Patent Gazette* only after it has been approved by the Patent Office.[26]

A patent application or a granted patent may be assigned to other(s) for use.[27] However, the transfer of ownership must be recorded with the Patent Office in order to have *locus standi* against a third party.

(ii) Pledge on a Granted Patent. According to the ROC Patent Law, a pledge can be created on a granted patent right.[28] In the case of creation, alteration, or extinguishment of a pledge, a recordation application must be filed with the Patent Office concerning such action so that it will have *locus standi* against third parties.[29]

The Patent Law also stipulates that in the case of a pledge on a granted patent, the pledgee is not allowed to work the patent unless this is otherwise provided in a written agreement.[30] Where a patent under pledge is jointly owned by two or more co-owners, none of the co-owners can create a pledge on the patent without the consent of the other co-owner(s).[31]

(iii) Pledge on a Patent Application. The ROC Patent Law is silent on the creation of a pledge on patent applications. However, because a patent application or a granted patent is assignable, creation of a pledge on a patent application is possible as provided for in Article 900 of the Civil Code, which states, "A transferable right may be the object of a pledge."

Although it is legally possible to create a pledge on a patent application, the Patent Office does not accept recordation of such a pledge. As an alternative, however, a pledger and a pledgee may enter into a Patent Assignment Agreement, through which the pledger assigns his or her patent application(s) to the pledgee as collateral for a debt. The pledger and pledgee may then file recordation applications with the Patent Office concerning the assignment of the patent application(s).

---

[22] Id., Articles 50, 51, 100, and 109.
[23] Id., Article 27.
[24] Id., Articles 20, 98, and 107.
[25] Id., Article 24.
[26] Id., Article 39.
[27] Id., Article 15.
[28] ROC Civil Code, Article 6.
[29] ROC Patent Law, Article 64.
[30] Id., Article 6.
[31] Id., Article 62.

(e) Perfection of a Pledge on Intellectual Property Rights

(i) Pledge Agreement.   A pledge agreement, duly executed by the pledger and the pledgee, is an essential document required to perfect a security interest in intellectual property.[32] Such an agreement is also the basis for recordation of the pledge. A pledge agreement, in a normal transaction, must include the following particulars:

1. Contracting parties (description of the pledger and the pledgee),
2. Offer and acceptance of the creation of the pledge on the intellectual property,
3. The content and a detailed description of the intellectual property in question (e.g., the registration and the documents evidencing such a registration),
4. Additional security (upon the pledgee's discretion),
5. Expenses (burden of the expenses incurred in establishing the agreement),
6. Acceleration of maturity (a description of all the events of default),
7. Liability for unpaid balance (the pledger will remain liable for the unpaid balance even after foreclosure),
8. No waiver (the pledgee will not be liable for failure to exercise any power, right, or remedy),
9. Amendment (the method of amending the agreement, or no amendment allowed),
10. Notices (the means that constitute valid notice),
11. Assignments (whether the agreement is assignable or not),
12. Tax reimbursement (the pledger may be required to reimburse the additional tax payment to be paid by pledgee, other than income tax), and
13. The governing law and jurisdiction.

Such transactions may, depending on the needs of the parties, vary as to the terms and conditions to be included in the pledge agreement.

(ii) Recordation

Copyright.   Recordation of a pledge agreement serves as notice to the public, and therefore a pledge will have *locus standi* against third parties. As mentioned earlier in subsection (a), a pledge on a copyright can be recorded with the Copyright Office. In addition, the Copyright Law expressly recognizes the effect of the recordation of a pledge under Article 75, which provides as follows:

> *None of the following arrangements, unless duly recorded, shall be set up as a defense against a third party*:
> 2. The creation, assignment, alteration, extinguishment or restrictions on disposal of a pledge on the economic rights to a work, except in the case where the pledge is extinguished due to merger of the economic rights or extinguishment of the economic rights or secured claim.

In addition, the ROC Copyright Law also provides that where the economic right is used as the subject matter of a pledge, unless otherwise provided by contract at the time of

---

[32] Id., Article 153.

the pledge, the owner of the economic right may exercise his or her rights therein.[33] Therefore, recordation with the Copyright Committee of the Ministry of Interior (Copyright Office), the authority in charge of copyright matters,[34] of the creation, assignment, alternation, extinguishment, or restrictions on disposal of a pledge on the economic rights to a work is necessary to secure the pledgee's right.

An application filed with the Copyright Committee for recording a pledge of economic rights to a work will indicate the scope of the object of the pledge in the case of a recordation of a pledge creation or a pledge assignment, or alterations in the case of a pledge alteration, or the contents of restrictions in the case of restrictions on disposal of the pledge.[35]

Evidential documents pertaining to creation, assignment, alteration, extinguishment, or restrictions on disposal of a pledge will be submitted to the Copyright Committee for its recordation and reference.[36]

Where a pledge involved in the application filed for recordation of assignment, alteration, restrictions on disposal, or extinguishment of a pledge was registered prior to the effective date of the Law, the certificate of creation of a pledge on copyright originally obtained will be recalled.[37]

For recordation with the Copyright Committee, the following information and documents must be submitted in regard to a pledge of economic rights to a work:[38]

1. The name or title, nationality, date of birth or date of incorporation, and domicile or address of the pledgee and the pledger, or the assignor and the assignee of the pledge,
2. The name or title, date of birth or date of incorporation, and domicile or address of the debtor,
3. The amount of the claim of the pledge, and
4. The covenants, if any, in respect to duration, date of discharge, interest rate, amount of default penalty, or indemnity involved in the recordation.

Items 2 through 4 may be omitted in an application for recordation of pledge alteration or extinguishment.[39]

Patents. The Patent Office does not accept the recordation of a pledge over patent applications. However, as mentioned earlier in subsection (d) (iii), a pledgee and a pledger may enter into a patent assignment arrangement and use the assigned patent(s) as collateral for a debt. Under such circumstances, the patent assignment may be recorded by submitting the following documents:

- A Deed of Assignment executed by both the assignor and the assignee,
- A Power of Attorney from the assignee,
- A Certificate of Corporate Nationality for the assignee, and
- The original Patent Certificate issued to the patent under assignment.

---

[33] ROC Copyright Law, Article 34.
[34] Id., Article 2.
[35] Enforcement Rules of the ROC Copyright Law, Article 13, par. 3.
[36] Id., par. 4.
[37] Id., par. 5.
[38] Id., par. 1.
[39] Id., par. 2.

The Patent Office accepts the recordation of a pledge over a granted patent. According to the draft Enforcement Rules amendment, the following documents must be submitted to the Patent Office for recordation of the creation, alteration, or extinguishment of a pledge:

1. A written application, listing information regarding the pledgee(s) and the patent owner(s), patent number, information regarding the debtor, amount of monetary debt guaranteed, reason(s) for recordation, and scope of subject matter under the pledge creation, as well as other essential details related to the recordation,
2. Documents in support of the recordation, such as a pledge agreement or other related agreement(s) and document(s), and
3. The original Patent Certificate issued to the patent(s) under the pledge creation.

Trademark.   According to Article 30–1 of the ROC Trademark Law, the creation of a pledge on the right of exclusive use of a trademark, or any change or extinguishment of a pledge, will be recorded with the Trademark Office. Without prior registration, the pledge or the change or extinguishment of the pledge will not serve as defense against third parties.

The following information and documents are required for recordation of a pledge of trademark rights:

1. An Application Form,
2. Qualification certificates, qualifying the owner of the right of exclusive use of the trademark, and the pledgee,
3. A pledge agreement, stating the name and registration number of the trademark, amount of liability, and term of the pledge, and
4. The original Trademark Registration Certificate.

Upon registration of the pledge, the creation and the particulars thereof will be endorsed on the Trademark Registration Certificate.

(f) Enforcing a Pledge on Intellectual Property Rights.   Under current laws and regulations, there are no specific provisions for the enforcement of a pledge on a patent, a trademark, or a copyright. Therefore, the Compulsory Execution Law and other relevant laws govern the procedures concerning these rights.

In enforcing rights based on a patent, trademark, or copyright, the execution court usually prohibits, *ex officio*, the debtor,[40] (the pledger) from making any disposition of such rights and prohibits a third party from paying money, if any, to the debtor.[41] At the same time, the execution court will also request the competent authority to register such an event in the registry.[42] Moreover, according to the same law, the execution court should notify any interested third party of such an event.[43] However, if there is no specific third party concerned in a patent, trademark, or copyright foreclosure case, some scholars

---

[40] ROC Compulsory Execution Law, Article 117.
[41] Id., Articles 115 and 116.
[42] Attention Rules for Compulsory Execution Matters, Article 62.
[43] ROC Compulsory Execution Law, Article 118.

have suggested that a public announcement in a newspaper would serve the same purpose as that prescribed by the afore-mentioned Article.[44] Such publication would also protect the bona fide third party from conducting any business transaction with the debtor in question.

Thereafter, the execution court may conduct the execution (sale) procedure of the patent, trademark, or copyright by the following means:

1. The execution court may issue an order allowing the pledgee to collect the royalty which may be received from a third party or transfer that right to the pledgee,[45] or

2. The execution court may, when it deems appropriate, order an assignment of the right and effect payment to the pledgee with the proceeds derived from the sale.[46] Such an assignment may be effected by the court or by the pledgee through an auction or, when the execution court deems the price appropriate, through a private sale.[47]

(g) Conclusion. In view of the amendments to the Patent Law and the Trademark Law, which allow creation of a pledge on patent rights and trademark rights, the creation of pledges on intellectual property rights may become more frequent in the ROC. Proprietors of intellectual properties should pay attention to this trend and formulate their future strategies for creating further profits based on creation of a pledge on their intellectual properties.

---

[44] Yang Yu-Lin, *Compulsory Execution Law*, 7th ed. (Taipei:, June 1984) p. 617. Distributed by San Min Book Co. Ltd.

[45] Compulsory Execution Law, Article 115.

[46] Id., Article 117.

[47] Id., Article 45.

15.12 UNITED KINGDOM

Mark Lewis, Esq.
Morag Macdonald, Esq.

Bird & Bird
London, England

(a) **Introduction.**   In England, as in other jurisdictions, there are various ways of creating security interests or rights analogous to security interests in intellectual property rights. There are also different categories of intellectual property rights, each of which is more or less suited to being secured in particular ways. Certain rights may be equally valuable in the hands of the borrower or the lender, whereas others may be valuable in the hands of the borrower but less valuable if the lender has to enforce the security. The extent to which different methods of taking security in intellectual property rights are explored and analyzed in practice is likely to depend on the perceived value and strength of the particular intellectual property right in question.

As intellectual property rights are intangible assets, it is important in taking security in them to understand what they are and exactly what comfort the asset might give to a lender. The following paragraphs discuss the various types of intellectual property rights.

(i) *Patents.*   In exchange for publishing details of an invention and how to put it into effect, the inventor will obtain from the state a limited monopoly over his or her invention for a period of 20 years, subject to payment of renewal fees. Thereafter, the invention will be available for the public to use freely.

The first step in obtaining patent protection is an application for a patent, which describes the invention and details in the "claims" the extent of the monopoly sought. This gives very little protection other than in terms of priority. It is possible to take security in an application, although the value of such security might be difficult to determine. Once a patent has been granted, however, its full monopolistic rights take effect and its value for the purposes of taking a security increases.

(ii) *Trademarks and Service Marks.*   The economic value of trademarks and service marks arises because of the monopolistic rights that may exist for an indefinite period. In fact, their "indefinite" character makes it possible for trademarks or service marks effectively to provide partial protection for other intellectual property rights that would otherwise expire with time.

A trademark can exist independently of registration, but registration does provide considerable advantages in the case of infringement and is virtually essential for the purposes of taking enforceable security, except in certain specific circumstances.

In return for the protection provided by the law, a proprietor of a mark is required to observe a number of rules as to its management. The proprietor is required, when licensing its rights, to ensure that the licensee observes certain undertakings as to quality[1] and, if there are a number of licensees (or if infringers enter the market), to ensure that the mark does not lose its distinctiveness. If a mark is not used for five or more years, the

---

[1] Trade-Marks Act of 1938, § 28.

Registrar may strike the mark from the Register.[2] If renewal fees are not paid, similarly, the mark will not remain on the Register.[3] It is also prohibited to "deal" in trademarks, although whether this applies to the taking of security is debatable[4] and will no longer be the case changed with the imminent new trademark legislation (United Kingdom Trade Marks Bill—presently expected to come into force in 1995).

(iii) Copyright. Like patents, copyright is effectively a creature of statute. Here the basic similarity ends, however, as there is no registration requirement for copyright. The boundaries of copyright protection in the jurisdiction have been extended beyond artistic, literary, and musical works to prevent the reproduction of such properties as computer software, film and broadcasts, and, until recently, functional designs.

Copyright is usually described as a "negative" right, as it provides a period of exclusivity for 50 years after the death of the author (or often shorter periods for certain protected works) by permitting the creator to prevent unauthorized copying and reproduction of the work. Copyright is treated as a "chose in action" in this jurisdiction and can, therefore, be treated as a property right for the purposes of taking a security.

Because no registration is required in England and the right arises upon creation of the work, copyright is one area in which ascertaining ownership can be problematic.

Copyright exists independently of the material upon which it is printed, and it is possible for licenses to be granted of the copyright for various purposes—for example, a license to broadcast over a public network, but not to produce and sell or hire videos of the work, or a license to use but not copy (except in a limited fashion) a purchased software package.

(iv) Designs. Protection of designs may be in the form of either registered design rights (for industrially applicable designs with "eye appeal") or unregistered design rights (for purely functional designs). The position of each of these changed following the introduction of the Copyright, Designs and Patents Act of 1988 (CDPA 1988). Functional designs are not now intended to be dealt with under copyright law.

The regime protecting registered designs is, in many respects, similar to that protecting patents. The designer permits his or her design to be published in return for securing limited monopoly rights. Protection is granted for the eye appeal of new designs and lasts for 25 years (15 years for registrations prior to CDPA 1988). The design must be capable of industrial application, although the functional aspects of designs cannot be protected under this Act. Renewal fees are payable every 5 years, and it is possible for a registered design to be invalidated.

Unregistered design rights arise automatically under English law, in much the same way as copyright. The owner of a design has the exclusive right to reproduce the design for commercial purposes by making articles with that design or through a design document recording the design enabling such articles to be made. This right operates to prevent unauthorized commercial copying of the design of the articles. An unregistered design right lasts for 10 years from the end of the year when the article is first marketed or 15 years after it is first designed—whichever period expires first. It is important to note that for the last 5 years of its life, anyone will be able to obtain a license as of right (a form of

---

[2] Id., § 26.
[3] Id., § 20.
[4] See "Holly Hobbie" (1984) 1WLR 189.

compulsory license) at a royalty to be determined by the Patent Office in the absence of an agreement.

(v) Know-How and Confidential Information.   The significant disadvantage to know-how and confidential information is that their value is likely to diminish in the event of either authorized or unauthorized disclosures. Neither has been recognized as a kind of property under English law, although it has been acknowledged that there is a commercial value attached to them that can be the subject of valuable agreements.[5] These intellectual properties can be licensed, and a form of information transfer coupled with a nonuse/secrecy agreement can act in similar fashion to an assignment.

In a sense, therefore, neither can be said to be "owned," but it is clear that some right exists, which is retained by someone. Although it is conceivable in some situations that security could be taken in these "rights," it would be fair to say that it would be of particularly high risk. Much would depend on the nature of the information, the ability to actually identify the confidential information, to effectively prevent disclosure, and to perfect the security in the event of default.

Frequently, however, to benefit from security in, for example, a patent or portfolio of patents, there can be merit in including the related know-how, for example, as to production or manufacture.

(vi) Licenses.   This section does not address the possibility of taking security in licensees' interests in licenses of intellectual property rights, because in most cases those interests will be rendered valueless by the licensee's becoming terminable at the very time when the lender would wish to enforce its security.

(b) Types of Security Interests.   There are only a limited number of rights recognized by English law as security interests, although there has been some pressure that may yet result in the recognition of further categories.[6] The security interests in assets currently recognized under English law are described briefly in the following paragraphs.

(i) Legal Mortgage.   Usually viewed as the safest form of security, as it involves an assignment of the legal title (and therefore ownership) to the lender, is the legal mortgage. The borrower has a right to have the legal title transferred back to it once it has fulfilled its repayment and other obligations. The lender has the right of foreclosure and sale.

(ii) Charge.   Usually viewed as a lesser form of security (although probably the most frequently used by companies in financing transactions), a charge does not involve an initial assignment of legal title. It is a right to look to an asset (or assets) upon the occurrence of a particular event or events for the purposes of discharging a debt. A charge is an encumbrance that attaches to an asset (or assets) and travels with the asset into the hands of third parties. It is a right to appropriate an asset in satisfaction of a debt upon the occurence of an event of default.

---

[5] As has been recognized by the European Community of the Know-How Licensing Block Exemption OJ No.L 61/1 4.3.89.

[6] See the report entitled "A Review of Security Interests in Property" by A.L. Diamond (1988) in which the author proposed sweeping changes, including the recognition as security interests of other interests such as leases.

A charge may be a fixed charge, which means it is taken over a definable and identifiable asset. Where it is not possible to identify precisely a particular asset and possible only to identify a class of asset, and it is necessary that the person giving the charge has a right to deal with the individual assets in the class (each of which may change over time), then a floating charge may be taken. The person giving the charge is able to deal with the assets with third parties until such time as the charge "crystallizes" upon the occurrence of a particular event. When that happens, the charge is enforceable over the identifiable assets in that class of assets in existence at the time of crystallization.

Intellectual property rights may fall into either category of asset for this purpose, and it is common in security documents creating charges over assets generally (including intellectual property rights) to express them as fixed over those intellectual property rights on which they can be fixed, and floating on all other intellectual property rights.

(iii) Equitable Mortgage. It is possible to take a mortgage on the basis that something less than a legal mortgage arises. For example, an agreement to give a mortgage is considered to effect an equitable mortgage. In this situation, there exists a right to have the legal title (ownership) assigned to the lender on the occurrence of an event of default for the purposes of appropriating the asset to satisfy the debt. Most equitable mortgages therefore also constitute a charge.

(iv) Delivery of Possession—Liens and Pledges. A pledge involves delivery of an asset by way of security, and although ownership does not change, the person taking the pledge has the right to sell it in the event of nonrepayment. Intellectual property rights do not lend themselves well to this type of security, given that possession of the intellectual property right, an intangible asset, is not possible, and that possession of a particular document evidencing title is not conclusive evidence of ownership.

A lien is similarly reliant on possession, but because a lien is a right vested in the lender to *detain* something until payment, it is not transferable.

Most other "security rights" do not give genuine security rights *in* an asset; rather, they provide rights of prohibition on acts performed by a creditor (e.g., negative pledge), or there may be no transfer of any interest to the borrower (e.g., lease, hire-purchase, etc.). None of these rights is generally considered to create an interest in assets under English law.

The security interests described will confer differing degrees of priority in the event of the insolvency of the borrower. A first legal mortgage or a fixer charge will entitle the lender to rank in priority to all other creditors. The holder of a floating charge will rank after the holder of a fixed charge and will also rank behind preferential creditors.[7] In most cases the security documentation permits the lender to follow the proceeds of sale of any assets in the event of a default and provides a power of sale to the person taking the security.

As a general rule, a purchaser of the legal interest in an asset who purchases in good faith and without notice of any other interest (whether such notice is imputed or not) will acquire the asset free of other interests existing in it. Thus, the importance of registering any security interest held is emphasized (discussed further in the following subsection [d]).

---

[7] Insolvency Act of 1986, § 386 and Schedule 6.

(c) Creation.   Creating and perfecting security interests in intellectual property rights gives rise to a number of issues, depending on the security interest that is to be created and the intellectual property right in which it is to be created. The following paragraphs consider some of the major issues in this regard.

(i) Patents.   The Patents Act of 1977 refers in clear terms to the possibility of taking a security interest in patents (unlike trademarks and copyright).[8] It confirms that any patent, application for a patent, or any right in a patent may be assigned or mortgaged, and it provides that a mortgage (as defined in Section 130 of that Act) will include a charge securing money or money's worth.[9] To the extent that a license of a patent or patent application so provides, any license or sublicense may itself be mortgaged. However, unless the mortgage is in writing and signed by both parties, it will be void.[10]

An assignment of a patent under a legal mortgage is the strongest form of security. An exclusive license back to the borrower to enable the borrower to use the patent will be essential in that case, and the license will have to be registered at the Patents Registry so as to obtain priority over any subsequent licensees. The lender will need to ensure that the license terms dealt adequately with a number of issues important to the continuing value of the patent, such as policing and responding to infringements and payment of renewal fees to the Patents Registry.

Charges and equitable mortgages are clearly contemplated by the legislation.[11] These will need to include a negative pledge preventing the creation of other security interests and clauses preventing the sublicense and assignment of the patent. The usual mechanisms for ensuring that legal title is transferred in the event of default (discussed further in relation to trademarks) will also have to be included.

There is no reason in principle why security should not be taken in the same ways over an application for a patent as they may be over a patent. However, until it is granted, an application's value as security is limited, as there is no guarantee that it will be granted. Expert advice would be required in each individual case as to the likelihood of this event.

(ii) Trademarks and Service Marks.   A legal mortgage can be taken on a trademark or a service mark. In either case, this must be by way of assignment and licensing back. Given the special nature of trademarks and service marks, some care is required in taking security.

The position in relation to unregistered trademarks is governed by the common law. In fact, an unregistered mark cannot be considered as a property right as such. A certain degree of exclusivity of use of an unregistered trademark can be maintained by use of the "law of passing-off," which operates to prevent one trader passing off its services or goods as those of another and, consequently, damaging that other party, usually by using that party's unregistered trademarks. However, this means that an unregistered trademark is inextricably linked to a particular business and to the goodwill in that business and, therefore, cannot be assigned without these assets. Thus, a form of security could be taken in an unregistered trademark by means, for example, of a fixed equitable charge

---

[8] Patents Act of 1977, § 30(2).

[9] Id., §§ 30(2) and 130.

[10] Id., § 30(6)(a).

[11] Id., §§ 30 and 130.

over the borrower's business, goodwill in the business, and the unregistered trademark; a floating charge over the goods will be more appropriate for unregistered marks.

Legislation has changed the position of registered trademarks and service marks.[12] An assignment may take place without the associated goodwill in a business, but it will not take effect unless within a six-month period the assignment is advertised in accordance with directions given by the Trade-Marks Registrar. The second provision in this procedure is (as with patents) that to preserve the trademark and to preserve the borrower's right to use the trademark, the borrower will require an exclusive license back. In the case of registered trademarks and service marks this stipulation has the following implications:

1. *Registered-User Agreements.* It is necessary to register a registered-user agreement at the U.K. Trade-Marks Registry. This has the effect of deeming use by the borrower (licensee) as use by the lender (licensor) and thereby helping to prevent the mark from being struck off the Trade-Marks Register for nonuse.

2. *Control.* It is essential that in the registered-user agreement there are details of how the lender (licensor) will exercise control over use of the trademark by the borrower (licensee), as registration will be allowed only if the lender can properly control such use, for example, in respect to the quality of the products to which it is applied. The lender (licensor) must also exercise that control, and it may be that in practice the lender will have to appoint an agent whose function is to ensure that the borrower fulfills its obligations and does not diminish the value of the security by its conduct.

3. *Deceptiveness and Trafficking.* Any arrangement for a legal mortgage will have to be reviewed with care to ensure that it does not leave the mark vulnerable to claims for invalidity by reason of deceptiveness or trafficking, and that proper provision is made for policing the mark against counterfeits and other infringements.

4. *Sublicensing.* Rights to sublicense should be controlled.

5. *Value Protection.* Safeguards should be considered for protecting the value of the mark in the marketplace, especially in the face of certain disasters such as occurred with the Perrier mark when benzine was found in the French mineral water product.

It should be noted that the same and similar marks on the Register in the name of the same proprietor (that is, associated marks) can normally only be assigned together and, therefore, a security interest would have to be taken in them together. Moreover, if there are any unregistered marks associated with the registered marks in which an interest is to be taken, provision should be made for controlling their use as well, so as not to affect detrimentally the value of the registered marks.

The mechanism for creating a fixed charge or equitable mortgage is simpler. As there is no transfer of ownership at the time a security is taken, most of the problems of assignment do not apply. However, some of the problems will arise if the security must be enforced. Consideration should be given, in any event, where valuable trademarks or service marks are involved, to including in the security documents specific restrictions and covenants designed to protect the value of the marks, such as policing and prosecuting infringements.

It is extremely unlikely that trademarks and service marks in themselves would ever be appropriate subjects of a floating charge, as they are not assets lending themselves readily to belonging to a shifting pool. However, with brand extensions new registered rights can

---

[12] Trade-Marks Act of 1938, § 22.

be created for the same mark but for different goods or services. Yet anyone following this route might run the outside risk of having marks struck off the Register on the basis of trafficking.

An application for a trademark is unlikely to be a good security on its own account, as there is no certainty of registration. It may be possible to take security in the associated goodwill and business for a mark as unregistered, as discussed earlier, with an option to extend or transfer the security to the mark if it becomes registered. However, the value of such a security would have to be assessed carefully against the facts of each individual case.

It should be noted that new trademark legislation presently proposed in the United Kingdom allows for a procedure for registering a security interest in a trademark application, and this legislation is expected to come into force at the beginning of 1995.

(iii) Copyright.   The safest form of security in a copyright is a legal mortgage from the owner of the legal title. Ownership will then be vested in the lender. To enable the borrower to use the copyright, an exclusive license back to the borrower will be required. In this way it will be possible to obtain security in an "after acquired" or future copyright, given that an assignment is part of the transaction. If either an exclusive license or full assignment of the legal title is taken, then it must be in writing. If the assignment is not in writing, then all that may be obtained by the lender is an equitable interest.[13]

There is no reason that copyright should not be the subject of a fixed charge or an equitable mortgage. The ownership of the copyright is left with the borrower. In the usual way, the security documents must provide for the protection of the lender's position and (so far as possible) the value of the copyright concerned during the life of the security. A warranty as to the ownership of the copyright is also usually appropriate.

In most cases, the lender will need copies of, or at least access to, the relevant copyright materials evidencing ownership of the copyright and the date it came into being, together with any other title documents, such as assignments from third-party contractors.

A lender with either form of security in respect to computer software may well require an escrow arrangement to be put in place in relation to the source code, which the borrower is not normally willing to release.

(iv) Designs.   There are some particular problems arising from the nature of design rights. In general, however, registered design rights, in respect to the requirements of registration and the problems arising on the taking of security, are almost identical with patents. Equally, in general, most of the issues relevant to copyright and taking security in copyright will arise for unregistered design rights. However, for the purpose of valuing the security in unregistered design rights, particular note should be taken of the last five-year period of a license.

(d) Perfection.   In addition to those dealt with in the preceding subsection, "Creation," there are a number of issues to be kept in mind. These are discussed in the following paragraphs.

(i) Companies Act Registration.   If the borrower is a company registered in, or having a branch or place of business in, England or Wales, any charge (as defined in the Companies Act of 1985), which includes mortgages and most of the other types of charge described in

---

[13] Copyright, Designs and Patents Act of 1988, §§ 90 and 92.

this section must be registered with the Registrar of Companies within 21 days of its creation. The effect of nonregistration is that the charge will be void against a liquidator or administrator or any creditor of the company.[14]

(ii) Patents.   Any assignment or exclusive license for a patent must be filed at the Patents Registry within six months of the date of the transaction. Failure to do so will prevent the relevant proprietor or licensee from claiming any damages upon infringement of the patent prior to the date of filing of any such transaction.

(iii) Registered Trademarks and Service Marks.   There is no time limit within which the assignment of a registered mark must be filed with the Trade-Marks Registry, but such registration is required, of course, before any title can be asserted against a third party, such as an infringer. The registered-user agreement for a licensee should be filed prior to the licensee's using the mark, so that any use of the mark by the licensee is deemed use by the licensor. Any other security interest in a registered mark may be notified on the Trade-Marks Register by way of a memorandum under § 34(1)(e) of the Trade-Marks Act of 1938. Such notification is not mandatory, but it acts as notice against third parties. With the new trademarks legislation expected to come into force at the beginning of 1995, registration of a security interest at the Trade-Marks Registry will be required within six months of its creation.

(iv) Security Documents.   If any security less than a full legal mortgage is taken, the security documents should include appropriate provisions relating to the perfection of the security once it becomes enforceable.

(e) Enforcement.   Any lender taking security in intellectual property rights in England and Wales, needs to consider issues of enforcement, many of which are peculiar to this jurisdiction and are addressed in the previous subsection (c), "Creation." Other points of particular note include the following:

1. *Specific Performance.* This is an equitable remedy in this jurisdiction and as such will not be available where damages constitute an adequate remedy, nor in a number of other circumstances.
2. *Control.* In drafting any security documents, care should be taken not to provide the lender with positive control over the business of the borrower. This could lead to problems in the event of the insolvency of the borrower, such as responsibility for fraudulent trading.[15]
3. *Value of the Intellectual Property Right.* The value of an intellectual property right in the hands of the lender may not be as great as in the hands of the borrower. The lender, often not being in the same line of business, may find difficulty in exploiting the intellectual property right should the borrower default on the loan. The lender should, therefore, consider carefully at the outset how it would exploit the intellectual property rights that are to be the subject of the security interest and, where necessary, make appropriate future plans for this.

---

[14] Companies Act of 1985, § 395.
[15] Insolvency Act of 1986, § 213.

(f) Conclusion.   Although taking security interests in intellectual property rights is not at present widespread in the United Kingdom, there is, in most cases, as can be seen from preceding discussion, no particular legal reason for this. Provided that lenders take some care in the selection of the intellectual property rights involved, the value in each case that they can reasonably attribute to them, and the provisions in the documentation, they will often be able to establish perfectly adequate security interests in intellectual property rights.

15.13 VENEZUELA

Gabriel Bentata, Esq.

Bentata Hoet & Asociados
Caracas, Venezuela

Although Venezuelan legislation does not have an exact conceptual equivalent for the term *security interest*, this section discusses the traditional *guarantees* existing in the legislation relating to the special area of "security interests." It also analyzes other legal forms, such as sales agreements with repurchase clauses and usufructuary rights. These are all forms of securing a credit; however, according to this country's legislation, they are not guarantees per se.

(a) Creation and Obtaining of Security Interests in Intellectual Property.   Certain forms of security interests in intangible rights, that is, principally copyrights, trademarks, and patents, are discussed in the following paragraphs.

(i) Sales Agreements with Repurchase Clauses.   Although sales agreements with repurchase clauses are not frequently used in the Venezuelan system, and when utilized refer to real property, this method of sale may have practical use when intellectual rights are transferred.

The pure sale or transfer of an intellectual right is carried out like the sale or transfer of any other good, and once consensual agreement exists on the essential terms of the contract, such as determination of price and object of sale, it is likewise consummated. It should be noted, however, that in matters relating to industrial property rights, such sales are subject to a special registration in the Industrial Property Registry Office. In the case of copyrights, this registration is not required; nevertheless, the sale must be registered in the Federal District Subalternate Registry Office. A sales agreement with the right of revocation is a form of general sales agreement, which, as defined in Article 1534 of the Venezuelan Civil Code, is an agreement in which the seller reserves the right to recover that which is sold by means of restitution of the sales price and the reimbursement of the expenses indicated in Article 1544. These include not only the price received, but also the expenses and costs of sale, and all necessary repairs and improvements that increased the value of the property sold to the greatest value it obtained. However, it is difficult to imagine what maintenance expenses and repairs would be incurred in the case of intellectual property rights.

Note that all recovery obligations imposed on the seller are null. There is another limitation on the right of revocation, which is that a term greater than five years may not be stipulated, and if exceeded, the term shall be limited to this duration.

If no period has been established to exercise the right of revocation, the right to do so will lapse within five years after the date of the agreement. The law advises that these provisions do not prevent the granting of extensions to exercise the right of revocation, even though the term established and the extensions granted exceed five years. If the seller does not exercise its right of revocation during the agreed-upon term, the buyer irrevocably acquires the property (Article 1536).

To further guarantee this operation and the seller's rights, Article 1538 establishes that a seller who has stipulated the right of revocation may file an action against third-party buyers, even though in their respective agreements no mention has been made of the agreed-upon revocation.

Article 1539 of the Civil Code states that the buyer in a revocation agreement acquires all the seller's rights. A statute of limitation would be in the buyer's favor against both the legitimate owner and those who claim to have mortgages or other rights against the goods sold.

The other provisions of the Civil Code relating to this form of sale are more applicable to real property, although in any situation not foreseen or described in this discussion, by analogy any of the rights established in the Civil Code could possibly be exercised.

(ii) Usufruct.   Usufruct is the temporary right to use, enjoy, and receive the profits of property belonging to another, in the same way that the owner would. In Latin the term is defined as *jus in aliena rebus, utendi, fruendi salva rerum substantia.*

The features of usufruct are similar to those of a lease, or as expressed in regard to intellectual property, of license agreements for the use of intellectual rights; but unlike a lease arrangement, it creates an in rem right. In Venezuelan law, the difference between an in rem and personal right is a *summa divisio* (a major division, which includes all types of assets). The rights acquired are either real or personal (rights correlative to obligations).

Basically, an in rem right is incorporated in the thing that is the object of the right, as compared with personal rights which, *grosso modo* (roughly), are the correlative rights of obligations of a contractual nature.

Article 584 of the Civil Code states that this right may not be for an unlimited duration, and may be established conditionally, or in favor of one or more persons, either simultaneously or successively. In the case of successive enjoyment, the only persons who may take advantage of the usufruct are those who were alive when the first usufructuary attained its rights. If, during the formation of the usufruct, no term is established for its duration, it is understood as being for the life of the usufructuary.

A usufruct is a division of a property right into two of its main attributes: the ability (1) to dispose of, (2) to enjoy, and (3) to use the property, within the corresponding limitations imposed by law. Usufruct occurs when property rights are divided and a right is created to use and enjoy the property without having the right to dispose of it.

In rem rights have certain qualities, which are that they are transmitted with the thing and allow for the right of replevin, that is, recovery of the thing transferred from one who has wrongfully distrained, taken, or wrongfully retains it. The usufruct of these rights, with the exception of copyrights, is not common. Nevertheless, on one occasion the author used this mechanism, the right was registered in the Industrial Property Registry Office, and it continues for the length of time established.

A usufruct may be established conventionally by setting the characteristics of same, without being able to derogate norms of public order, which are few in this subject matter.

(iii) Specific Guarantees.   Venezuelan legislation has a *summa divisio* of goods in real and personal property. Because of their characteristics, copyrights are assimilated into personal property. Traditionally, in Venezuela, matters concerning security interests in personal property, are referred to as a pledge. Up until 1973 only one form of pledge existed in Venezuela, currently known as "common, traditional or classic," which, to be valid, had to be accompanied by delivery of the thing given in guarantee to the creditor. This did not make the guarantee very practical, and so it continued until 1973, when the

Law on Pledge Without Dispossession and Chattel Mortgage (*Ley de Prenda sin Desplazamiento de Posesion e Hipoteca Mobiliaria*) came into effect. In accordance with this law, it is possible to create pledges and mortgages without transferring possession, which remains with the pledger.

In connection with intellectual rights, this special law creates the unique form known in Venezuelan legislation as the "chattel mortgage." This does not mean that the common pledge is no longer used. However, in matters relating to intellectual or intangible rights, it is very difficult to establish possession, unless it refers to a physical element such as the corresponding registration certificate, which is given to the creditor. This problem is what makes this type of security interest difficult in the Venezuelan legal system. However, the problem does not exist in the case of a chattel mortgage.

A chattel mortgage in intellectual rights is subject to a series of requirements established in the corresponding law and, in particular, its registration before the corresponding Subalternate Registry Office and prior authorization from the competent authorities, which in this case is the Ministry of Development.

To the contrary, a common pledge requires only a private document that establishes the pledge and can be notarized for greater security. The Industrial Property Office maintains records of all these liens or encumbrances.

The special law referred to earlier contains provisions that are common to the chattel mortgage and the pledge without transfer of possession (*prenda sin desplazamiento de posesión,*) other provisions governing only the chattel mortgage, and, finally, some that specifically relate to the chattel mortgage in intellectual rights.

The principal regulations governing intellectual rights establish that these may not be constituted until their purchase price has been totally paid, unless a mortgage guaranteeing the total or partial payment has been granted. These liens cannot be made on goods already encumbered. The debtor giving the guarantee may not transfer ownership or pledge the intellectual rights without the prior consent of the creditor. Nevertheless, the debtor may use these rights, sui juris, and is under the obligation to cover all expenses required for its conservation and conditioning.

A chattel mortgage may be executed in guarantee of an open line of credit, letters of exchange, or other endorsable credit instruments, with the document indicating a series of conditions for its execution. In addition, the chattel mortgage may be made to guarantee periodic debts or payments, or future obligations or those obligations subject to precedent or resolutory conditions. The guaranteed credit may be alienated, transferred, or assigned in whole or in part by means of a public document and subject to certain requirements. Failure to obtain the creditor's prior approval to transfer or pledge the mortgaged property carries a penalty of imprisonment, as it is a criminal act. Moreover, if it involves a legal entity, the penalty will be imposed on those persons who carried out the act on behalf of their principals. The law establishes that a mortgage creates a privilege to be collected in preference of the property given in guarantee, (Civil Code, Article 1871), which privilege is superseded only by litigation costs incurred in conservatory or executory action taken against the personal property for the benefit of the creditors (Civil Code, Article 1870, Ord. 1).

The possibility of foreclosing the guarantee lapses after two years from the date on which it was possible to bring the action. Only certain public and private persons may obtain this type of guarantee. When foreign banks and international financial institutions are involved, they should obtain the prior authorization of the Superintendency of Banks. National and foreign companies may obtain this guarantee on intellectual rights through authorization by the Ministry of Development.

The document in which the mortgage is granted should contain a complete and total identification of the parties, amount of credit to be guaranteed in Venezuelan currency, type of interest stipulated, term, location and form of payment, and the amount reasonably calculated for all costs and expenses to execute the mortgage. In addition, a complete description of the assets, legal purpose, and title being mortgaged should be given, and the document should contain a sworn statement by the mortgagor that these assets are not subject to a mortgage and that the purchase price has been totally paid, with the exception of any liens created in guarantee of the purchase price owed. If the property is insured or there is an obligation to insure it, this information must be provided. An address must be given for forwarding notices or citations. In the event of various guarantees, the percentage of guarantee for each intellectual right should be indicated.

Article 46 of the Law on Chattel Mortgage and Pledge without dispossession establishes that unless there is an express agreement to the contrary, the mortgage on the principal right shall extend to the adaptation, translation, transformation, arrangement, merger, reprinting, new edition, enlargement of, or addition to the work that is the object of the copyright. It further extends to the addition, modification, or improvement of an invention, model or industrial design, trademark, or other industrial property item. This provision is applicable to inventions and states, moreover, that the mortgaging of a trademark will include, unless agreed to the contrary, all complimentary commercial slogans.

Article 47 specifically states that the information to be contained in the document should include the nature, form, and other characteristics of the property; its name and a brief description of the invention, its discovery, improvement, design or industrial models, or the name or description of the trademark, with an indication of the articles to which it applies. In addition to the registration date and other pertinent data, included should be all authorizations, permits, or concessions granted to third parties by the owner of the right, a declaration of being current on all annual patent fees, and a declaration that the patent or trademark registration has not lapsed for any circumstance foreseen in the Law.

The Law establishes that the mortgagor may not renounce a right nor transfer its use or exploitation, either wholly or partially, without the express consent of the mortgagee. The mortgagee is empowered to request the renewals or extensions necessary for the conservation of rights of encumbrance, as well as for paying the amount of the annual patent fees. In accordance with the Industrial Property Law, the mortgagee will enjoy the same rights as the owner of the patent.

This section of the special law under comment concludes by indicating that the mortgagee may cause the mortgage to become due and payable if and when the patent is not exploited or the trademark is not used during a period of more than one year, unless otherwise established in the mortgage document.

(b) Perfection of Security Interest.   Security credits have been discussed, but not in a strict sense as credit guarantees, as well as sales agreements with repurchase clauses, usufruct, and chattel mortgage. Because these rights that create the aforementioned securities constitute in rem rights in favor of the guaranteed creditors (see the concept of in rem in subsection [a][ii]), they should be recorded in a public office of registry. If it deals with usufruct or a sales agreement with a repurchase clause, it should be registered in the Industrial Property Registry Office. However, the chattel mortgages on copyrights should be registered in the corresponding or competent Subalternate Registry Office, in addition to the Industrial Property Registry Office.

The author does not fully understand this last requirement, inasmuch as copyrights are normally registered in the designated Subalternate Registry Office (Federal District Second Circuit) and have no relation to industrial property. A draft reform to the Copyright Law, presently before the National Congress, creates an intellectual production registry in which copyrights and all liens made against them will be registered. It is worth remembering that in spite of the fact that protection of copyrights in Venezuela is automatic from their creation, and does not require complimentary registration for their perfection, in accordance with international treaties entered into by Venezuela (the Berne and Geneva Conventions) and internal law, it is convenient to register these rights in Venezuela, even though these rights have been registered abroad, to be used as documentary evidence that permits certification of the liens made against them.

As of October 1, 1993, chattel mortgages dealing with copyrights have to be registered in the Special Registry of the intellectual property when they are created, although the draft reform has not eliminated the need to obtain prior approval from the Ministry of Development.

In regard to industrial property rights, in its Resolution No. 1832 of July 1, 1988, the Ministry of Development attributes the authorizations corresponding to the Ministry of Development to the Industrial Property Registrar, which is attached to that ministry. However, Resolution No. 15 of May 31, 1974, issued by the Ministry of Justice, makes reference to the Registration Books and attributes registration of all these chattel mortgages to the Federal District Second Circuit Registry.

Resolution No. 4328, of June 25, 1974, issued by the Ministry of Development, establishes the procedure for processing authorization requests from physical persons or legal entities who want to create copyright and industrial property mortgages in their favor. Among the most relevant documents required are a certified copy of the by-laws of the beneficiary of the guarantee, as well as the balance sheet and profit-and-loss statement, guarantee document, and Power of Attorney, if it relates to a legal representative or administrator for a legal entity.

(c) Foreclosure of a Security Interest. As a general rule, in the case of sales with repurchase clauses and usufruct, if no knowledge of these contracts exists, it is possible to request compliance from the corresponding court. In this event, documents that evidence the type of security chosen must also be included with the written complaint and processed in the normal manner; this claim is subject to appeal and eventual abeyance if the law has been violated.

The Chattel Mortgage Law deals extensively with the procedures to be followed in a foreclosure of a chattel mortgage, providing a quick and functional system in addition to being brief and expeditious, in order to make effective the guaranteed rights (intellectual rights) on the mortgaged property.

The classic procedure is followed in foreclosing a guarantee, in that after the written request is made, the auction notice and public sale follow, ending with payment of the debt. The Law would facilitate and hasten the process considerably with the following procedures:

1. The complaint is presented before a competent court in the debtor's domicile, previously chosen by the parties to the foreclosure, in accordance with the provisions of the Civil Procedure Code, and attached to which is the legal representative's Power of Attorney, the title or titles of which evidence the creditor's right, and

the mortgage document. Justification of the mortgage should be made 15 days prior to filing the complaint.

2. Once the complaint has been filed, the court admits it and rules on immediate payment by the debtor, a nondebtor mortgagor, or any third party; payment must be made within eight days following notification. This notice will be made by publication in a local court and published in the newspapers and by other means of circulation.

In the aforementioned admission process, the court will order attachment of the mortgaged property and its delivery and deposit with the creditor or the creditor's designee.

If the defendant in the mortgage foreclosure is the third holder of the mortgaged property, the defendant's notice of the amount to be paid will be understood as having been made on the date on which attachment of the property has taken place.

(i) Auction Notice.   After eight days have elapsed since the last notice, the judge, upon the request of the creditor, the debtor, the mortgagor, or any third-party holder, will order the auction of the mortgaged property. Notice of the auction shall be made eight days prior to the auction by means of one notice given at the domicile of each of the parties involved and in a public location in the town or municipality where the property is located. Notice will also be published to the complete satisfaction of the court in a newspaper widely circulated within the court's jurisdiction.

In addition to all identification details, the publication of notice will contain the sales price to be used as a basis for the auction, which will be the exact price indicated in the mortgage document, as well as the location, day, and hour on which the auction will take place.

If any of the parties is not in agreement with the agreed value of the mortgaged property, an appraisal may be requested to be made by an expert designated by the court, as long as it is carried out before the posting and publication of the auction notice.

The auction will take place at the location, and on the day and hour, indicated and posted. The creditor may intervene as a bidder without the need of giving a guarantee. To take part in the auction, all other bidders must deposit 10% of the base price with the court.

Other auctions may take place, or at least a second, if the base price of the auction is not reached or if the creditor does not exercise the faculty granted to him by law to acquire the auctioned property.

If the base price is not reached during a second auction, other auctions may be carried out, as many times as requested by the interested parties.

(ii) Consignment of Price.   Once an auction has been verified, the auctioneer will deposit, within three days following the date of the award, the difference between the price and amount deposited in order to participate in the auction. If the auctioneer is the mortgagee, the auctioneer will deposit only that price which exceeds his or her credit, interests insured with the mortgage, and a reasonable amount established for all court costs and expenses.

If no deposit has been made, the interested parties may ask that a new auction be carried out. In such case, in order to bid, a deposit shall be made to cover all expenses incurred and those that may arise in subsequent auctions, and any remainder will be applied to payment of the credit, interest, and court costs.

(iii) Cancellation of the Guarantee.   Once the auction or the award has taken place or the price has been established and deposited, the judge will order, by means of a writ issued by the court, payment of the chattel mortgage and, if necessary, all subsequent registrations. The auction price will be applied immediately to the payment of the credit, interest, expenses, and court costs, and any excess will be given to the party entitled to it.

The Law contains a special caution, common in all guarantees, that if the auction price obtained is not sufficient to cover the amount of the credit, interest, court costs, and expenses, the creditor will maintain its rights against the debtor for the balance.

The Law also foresees that there may be events during the court process, such as death, insolvency, bankruptcy, or incapacity of the debtor, or of the guarantors, that will not cause suspension of the process, except in the following cases:

- When certification of the registration evidencing payment of the mortgage has been filed
- When third-party intervention is proposed
- When evidence is presented that penal action has commenced, prior to admission of the mortgage claim, for misrepresentation of the title upon which the process was initiated.
- When at any moment prior to the award, it is demonstrated that a chattel mortgage with priority to the chattel mortgage of reference exists.

In any of these events, the opposing party must so declare within the eight-day period given to the debtor for payment. The judge will briefly decide upon the request for suspension of the process in any such events. The judge may also order that the process continue with regard to the property not affected by the opposition. In this event, the other party has the right to object to the suspension and to show evidence in its own favor through a brief process established in the Law.

It should be noted that the decisions handed down in the special foreclosure process will not be final (res judicata) and the debtor, mortgagee, and any third-party holder will have recourse to ordinary judicial process to reclaim the rights corresponding to them. However, the motion to have the right to discuss the consequences arising from foreclosure of the chattel mortgage in the ordinary judicial trial must be done within three months after the conclusion of the special process. This ordinary judicial process will not prevent either the commencement or the suspension of the chattel mortgage foreclosure process.

All appeals made in this process will be heard to produce a single effect, that of sending a lower court decision to an appellate court, and not for adjournment.

Mortgage registrations will expire and be canceled by official notice and at the request of a party when six years have elapsed after termination of the guaranteed obligation.

(d) Conclusion.   Except for chattel mortgages, no extensive or general treatment exists for the execution of security interests and guarantees covering intellectual rights.

The chattel mortgage obligation is subject to many formalities. In respect to copyrights, as yet no agency exists similar to that proposed in the Law reform mentioned previously, where titles may be registered and consulted chronologically. However, the requirements of approval by competent authorities or by the Superintendent of Banks seems excessive and not justified and, in the author's opinion, serve only statistical purposes. Although accelerated foreclosure of chattel mortgage guarantees is also foreseen, the there is still a possibility that decisions can be appealed in an ordinary recourse process, which could make the process of defending the foreclosure of the guarantee time-consuming and costly. Of course, this recourse is not always available for this type of principal or ordinary process.

The other forms of security interest discussed earlier are not common, although they may be used for purposes other than to guarantee the granting of credits.

INDEX